MKTG
Are you in?

an innovative concept in teaching and learning solutions designed to best reach today's students

"MKTG is so much more readable and modern. It is much easier to sit down and read multiple chapters at a time and stay interested. If all my textbooks were designed this way I would be more apt to bring them to every class, read more often, and stay interested in the material."
– Stephanie, *University of Massachusetts, Dartmouth*

"This was my first time using 4LTR Press. I enjoyed the material. I attribute my good grades to it. It was quite valuable to me for studying."
– Doreen, *Delgado Community College*

"As a student, I really like the fact that the text does not look like a typical textbook. Overall, it's a good textbook. I would be interested in using a text from 4LTR Press for another class."
– Emily, *George Fox University*

SOUTH-WESTERN
CENGAGE Learning

MKTG4 2010–2011 Edition
Charles W. Lamb
Texas Christian University

Joseph F. Hair, Jr.
Kennesaw State University

Carl McDaniel
University of Texas–Arlington

EVP/Publisher: Jonathan Hulbert

VP/Editorial Director: Jack W. Calhoun

VP/Director of Marketing: Bill Hendee

Editor-in-Chief: Melissa Acuña

Sr. Acquisitions Editor: Michael Roche

Developmental Editor: Laura Rush,
    B-books, Ltd.

Editorial Assistant: Kayti Purkiss

Product Development Manager,
    4LTR Press: Steven E. Joos

Executive Brand Marketing Manager,
    4LTR Press: Robin Lucas

Marketing Communications Manager:
    Sarah Greber

Production Director: Amy McGuire,
    B-books, Ltd.

Sr. Content Project Manager:
    Tamborah Moore

Managing Media Editor: Pam Wallace

Media Editor: John Rich

Manufacturing Coordinator:
    Miranda Klapper

Production Service: B-books, Ltd.

Sr. Art Director: Stacy Jenkins Shirley

Internal Designer: KeDesign, Mason, OH

Cover Designer: KeDesign, Mason, OH

Cover Image: © Ron Bouwhuis/Canopy
    Photographer/Veer

Photography Manager: Deanna Ettinger

Photo Research: Dana Freeman, Laura Rush,
    B-books, Ltd., & Terri Miller

For product information and technology assistance, contact us at
Cengage Learning Academic Resource Center, 1-800-423-0563

For permission to use material from this text or product,
submit all requests online at **www.cengage.com/permissions**
Further permissions questions can be emailed to
permissionrequest@cengage.com

Library of Congress Control Number: 2009943807

SE ISBN-13: 978-0-538-46824-4
SE ISBN-10: 0-538-46824-6

South-Western
5191 Natorp Boulevard
Mason, OH 45040
USA

Cengage Learning products are represented in Canada by Nelson Education, Ltd.

For your course and learning solutions, visit **www.cengage.com**
Purchase any of our products at your local college store or at our preferred online store **www.CengageBrain.com**

Printed in the United States of America
1 2 3 4 5 6 7 13 12 11 10

Brief Contents

Contents

PART 1
THE WORLD OF MARKETING

PART 2
ANALYZING MARKETING OPPORTUNITIES

6 Consumer Decision Making 72

7 Business Marketing 98

8 Segmenting and Targeting Markets 116

9 Decision Support Systems and Marketing Research 134

PART 3 PRODUCT DECISIONS

10 Product Concepts 152

11 Developing and Managing Products 166

PART 4
DISTRIBUTION DECISIONS

15 Retailing 226

PART 6
PRICING DECISIONS

PART 7 TECHNOLOGY-DRIVEN MARKETING

21 Customer Relationship Management (CRM) 328

CHAPTER 1 An Overview of Marketing

"Marketing is too important to be left only to the marketing department."

—David Packard

LO 1 What Is Marketing?

AFTER YOU FINISH THIS CHAPTER GO TO **PAGE 13** FOR **STUDY TOOLS**

What does the term *marketing* **mean to you?** Many people think it means the same as personal selling. Others think marketing is the same as advertising. Still others believe marketing has something to do with making products available in stores, arranging displays, and maintaining inventories of products for future sales. Actually, marketing includes all of these activities and more.

Marketing has two facets. First, it is a philosophy, an attitude, a perspective, or a management orientation that stresses customer satisfaction. Second, marketing is an organization function and a set of processes used to implement this philosophy. The American Marketing Association's definition of marketing focuses on the second facet. **Marketing** is the activity, set of institutions, and processes for creating, communicating, delivering, and exchanging offerings that have value for customers, clients, partners, and society at large. [1]

Marketing involves more than just activities performed by a group of people in a defined area or department. In the often-quoted words of David Packard, co-founder of Hewlett-Packard, "Marketing is too important to be left only to the marketing department." Marketing entails processes that focus on delivering value and benefits to customers, not just selling goods, services, and/or ideas. It uses communication, distribution, and pricing strategies to provide customers and other stakeholders with the goods, services, ideas, values, and benefits they desire when and where they want them. It involves building long-term, mutually rewarding relationships when these benefit all parties concerned. Marketing also entails an understanding that organizations have many connected stakeholder "partners,"

marketing the activity, set of institutions, and processes for creating, communicating, delivering, and exchanging offerings that have value for customers, clients, partners, and society at large

What do you think?

Marketing is selling.

1   2   3   4   5   6   7
STRONGLY DISAGREE   STRONGLY AGREE

Find out what others think at 4ltrpress.cengage.com/mktg

© ISTOCKPHOTO.COM/CHRIS SCHMIDT

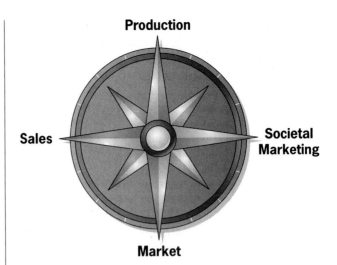

Production

Sales

Societal Marketing

Market

exchange people giving up something to receive something they would rather have

production orientation a philosophy that focuses on the internal capabilities of the firm rather than on the desires and needs of the marketplace

including employees, suppliers, stockholders, distributors, and others.

Research shows that companies that reward employees with incentives and recognition on a consistent basis are those that perform best.[2] Home Depot CEO Frank Blake rejects the notion that you should pay employees as little as you can and get as much work out of them as possible.[3] The motto of Wegmans Food Markets, the Rochester-based grocery chain that has been ranked by *Fortune* magazine as one of the best companies to work for in America, states, "Employees first, customers second." The rationale is that if employees are happy, customers will be too.[4]

One desired outcome of marketing is an **exchange**; people giving up something to receive something they would rather have. Normally, we think of money as the medium of exchange. We "give up" money to "get" the goods and services we want. Exchange does not require money, however. Two people may barter or trade such items as baseball cards or oil paintings. An exchange can take place only if the following five conditions exist:

CONDITIONS OF EXCHANGE

1 There must be at least two parties.

2 Each party has something that might be of value to the other party.

3 Each party is capable of communication and delivery.

4 Each party is free to accept or reject the exchange offer.

5 Each party believes it is appropriate or desirable to deal with the other party.[5]

Exchange will not necessarily take place even if all these conditions exist. They are, however, necessary for exchange to be possible. For example, you may place an advertisement in your local newspaper stating that your used automobile is for sale at a certain price. Several people may call you to ask about the car, some may test-drive it, and one or more may even make you an offer. All five conditions are necessary for an

exchange to exist. But unless you reach an agreement with a buyer and actually sell the car, an exchange will not take place. Notice that marketing can occur even if an exchange does not occur. In the example just discussed, you would have engaged in marketing even if no one bought your used automobile.

LO 2 Marketing Management Philosophies

Four competing philosophies strongly influence an organization's marketing processes. These philosophies are commonly referred to as production, sales, market, and societal marketing orientations.

Production Orientation

A **production orientation** is a philosophy that focuses on the internal capabilities of the firm rather than on the desires and needs of the marketplace. A production orientation means that management assesses its resources and asks these questions: "What can we do best?" "What can our engineers design?" "What is easy to produce, given our equipment?" In the case of a service organization, managers ask, "What services are most convenient for the firm to offer?" and "Where do our talents lie?" Some have referred to this

MARKETING CAN OCCUR EVEN IF AN EXCHANGE DOES **NOT** OCCUR.

orientation as a *Field of Dreams* orientation, from the well-known movie line, "If we build it, they will come." The furniture industry is infamous for its disregard of customers and for its slow cycle times. This has always been a production-oriented industry.

There is nothing wrong with assessing a firm's capabilities; in fact, such assessments are major considerations in strategic marketing planning (see Chapter 2). A production orientation falls short because it does not consider whether the goods and services that the firm produces most efficiently also meet the needs of the marketplace. Sometimes what a firm can best produce is exactly what the market wants. For example, the research and development department of 3M's commercial tape division developed and patented the adhesive component of Post-It Notes a year before a commercial application was identified. In other situations, as when competition is weak or demand exceeds supply, a production-oriented firm can survive and even prosper. More often, however, firms that succeed in competitive markets have a clear understanding that they must first determine what customers want and then produce it, rather than focusing on what company management thinks should be produced.

Sales Orientation

A **sales orientation** is based on the ideas that people will buy more goods and services if aggressive sales techniques are used and that high sales result in high profits. Not only are sales to the final buyer emphasized but intermediaries are also encouraged to push manufacturers' products more aggressively. To sales-oriented firms, marketing means selling things and collecting money.

The fundamental problem with a sales orientation, as with a production orientation, is a lack of understanding of the needs and wants of the marketplace. Sales-oriented companies often find that, despite the quality of their sales force, they cannot convince people to buy goods or services that are neither wanted nor needed.

Some sales-oriented firms fail to understand what is important to their customers. Many so-called dot-com businesses that came into existence in the late 1990s are no longer around because they focused on the technology rather than the customer.

Market Orientation

The **marketing concept** is a simple and intuitively appealing philosophy that articulates a market orientation. It states that the social and economic justifica-tion for an organization's existence is the satisfaction of customer wants and needs while meeting organizational objectives. It is based on an understanding that a sale does not depend on an aggressive sales force, but rather on a customer's decision to purchase a product. What a business thinks it produces is not of primary importance to its success. Instead, what customers think they are buying—the perceived value—defines a business. The marketing concept includes the following:

▸▸ Focusing on customer wants and needs so that the organization can distinguish its product(s) from competitors' offerings

▸▸ Integrating all the organization's activities, including production, to satisfy these wants

▸▸ Achieving long-term goals for the organization by satisfying customer wants and needs legally and responsibly

The recipe for success is to consistently deliver a unique experience that your competitors cannot match and that satisfies the intentions and preferences of your target buyers.[6] This requires a thorough understanding of your customers and distinctive capabilities that enable your company to execute plans on the basis of this customer understanding, and delivering the desired experience using and integrating all of the resources of the firm.[7]

Firms that adopt and implement the marketing concept are said to be **market oriented**, meaning they assume that a sale does not depend on an aggressive sales force but rather on a customer's decision to purchase product. Achieving a market orientation involves obtaining information about customers, competitors, and markets; examining the information from a total business perspective; determining how to deliver superior customer value; and implementing actions to provide value to customers.

What are the names of some firms known for delivering superior customer value and satisfaction? The third annual National Retail Federation/American Express Customer Service Survey listed L.L. Bean, Zappos.com, Amazon.com, Overstock.com and Blair as the top five U.S. retailers for customer service.[8] *Business Week* listed USAA, L.L. Bean, Fairmont Hotels, Lexus, and Trader Joe's as its best-in-class Customer Service Champs.[9]

Understanding your competitive arena and competitors' strengths and weaknesses is a critical component

sales orientation the ideas that people will buy more goods and services if aggressive sales techniques are used and that high sales result in high profits

marketing concept the idea that the social and economic justification for an organization's existence is the satisfaction of customer wants and needs while meeting organizational objectives

market orientation a philosophy that assumes that a sale does not depend on an aggressive sales force but rather on a customer's decision to purchase product; it is synonymous with the marketing concept of a market orientation. This includes assessing what existing or potential competitors might be intending to do tomorrow as well as what they are doing today. Western Union failed to define its competitive arena as telecommunications, concentrating instead on telegraph services, and was eventually outflanked by fax technology. Had Western Union been a market-oriented company, its management might have better understood the changes taking place, seen the competitive threat, and developed strategies to counter the threat.

Societal Marketing Orientation

The **societal marketing orientation** extends the marketing concept by acknowledging that some products that customers want may not really be in their best interests or the best interests of society as a whole. This philosophy states that an organization exists not only to satisfy customer wants and needs and to meet organizational objectives, but also to preserve or enhance individuals' and society's long-term best interests. Marketing products and containers that are less toxic than normal are more durable, contain reusable materials, or are made of recyclable materials is consistent with a societal marketing orientation. The American Marketing Association's definition of marketing recognizes the importance of a societal marketing orientation by including "society at large" as one of the constituencies for which marketing seeks to provide value.

Although the societal marketing concept has been discussed over 30 years, it did not receive widespread support until the early 2000s. Concerns such as climate change, the depleting ozone layer, fuel shortages, pollution, and raised health concerns have caused consumers and legislators to be more aware of the need for companies and consumers to adopt measures that conserve resources and cause less damage to the environment. Studies reporting consumers' attitudes toward, and intentions to buy, more environmentally friendly products show widely varying results. One study that helps explain some of this contradiction found that 44 percent of consumers were "theoretically" interested in buying environmentally friendly products, but the proportion doing so was much less.[10] The three top reasons customers gave for not following through by purchasing and using these more environmentally friendly products were: doubts about effectiveness, expense, and lack of availability at convenient outlets.[11] In another study, 50 to 75 percent of consumers reported that environmental issues are important, but they are not willing to make tradeoffs for higher costs or lower performance. Only 5 to 10 percent are willing to accept tradeoffs to buy environmentally friendly products.[12] Some believe that many consumers want to "go green" but don't know where to start.[13] One study found that while half of its respondents thought a company's environmental record was important, only 7 percent could name an environmentally friendly product they had purchased.[14]

Many marketers have made substantial commitments to either producing products using more environmentally friendly processes or making more environmentally friendly products. Coca-Cola has committed to spending $44 million to build the world's largest plastic-bottle-to-bottle recycling plant.[15] The company has also set a goal of returning to communities and nature an equivalent amount of water as used in its beverages and their production.[16] Home Depot, UPS, and Wal-Mart are also among the business leaders in the so-called "eco-friendly" movement.[17]

What will the future bring? The current trends are that more customers are becoming concerned about the environment each year, more customers are trying to buy environmentally friendly products and support more environmentally friendly companies, and more companies are joining the movement by developing processes and products that do less damage to the environment than in the past. The number of "green" products released in the United States more than doubled from 2005 to 2007, and even more were introduced in 2008.[18] Adopting a societal marketing orientation and clearly communicating this decision and the actions that support it helps firms differentiate themselves from competitors and strengthens their positioning.

LO 3 Differences between Sales and Market Orientations

The differences between sales and market orientations are substantial. The two orientations can be compared in terms of five characteristics: the organization's focus, the firm's business, those to whom the product is directed, the firm's primary goal, and the tools used to achieve those goals.

The Organization's Focus

Personnel in sales-oriented firms tend to be "inward looking," focusing on selling what the organization makes rather than making what the market wants. Many of the historic sources of competitive advantage—technology, innovation, economies of scale—allowed companies to focus their efforts internally and prosper. Today, many successful firms derive their competitive advantage from an external, market-oriented focus. A market orientation has helped companies such as the Royal Bank of Canada and Southwest Airlines outperform their competitors. These companies put customers at the center of their business in ways most companies do poorly or not at all.

A sales orientation has led to the demise of many firms including Streamline.com, the Digital Entertainment Network, and Urban Box Office. As one technology industry analyst put it, "No one has ever gone to a Web site because they heard there was great Java running."[19]

Customer Value **Customer value** is the relationship between benefits and the sacrifice necessary to obtain those benefits. Customer value is not simply a matter of high quality. A high-quality product that is available only at a high price will not be perceived as a good value, nor will bare-bones service or low-quality goods selling for a low price. Instead, customers value goods and services that are of the quality they expect and that are sold at prices they are willing to pay. Value can be used to sell a Mercedes Benz as well as a $3 Tyson frozen chicken dinner.

Lower income consumers are price sensitive, but they will pay for products if they deliver a benefit that is worth the money.[20]

The automobile industry provides another illustration of the importance of creating customer value. To penetrate the fiercely competitive luxury automobile market, Lexus adopted a customer-driven approach, with particular emphasis on service. Lexus stresses product quality with a standard of zero defects in manufacturing. The service quality goal is to treat each customer as one would treat a guest in one's home, to pursue the perfect person-to-person relationship, and to strive to improve continually. This pursuit has enabled Lexus to establish a clear, high-quality image and capture a significant share of the luxury car market. Marketers interested in customer value:

> **customer value** the relationship between benefits and the sacrifice necessary to obtain those benefits

- ▸▸ *Offer products that perform*: This is the bare minimum requirement. The Downy fabric softener example featured below illustrates the importance of listening to customers to determine the performance characteristics that are most important to them.

- ▸▸ *Earn trust*: A stable base of loyal customers can help a firm grow and prosper. About 80 percent of Starbucks'

SOFTENING UP MEXICO

In the early 2000s, Mexican market share for Downy fabric softener was low and stagnant. Not wanting to compromise the Downy brand by dropping the price too much, Procter & Gamble decided to try to come up with something specific to the needs of the lower-income consumer.

After spending time with low-income Mexican women, P&G found that 90 percent liked to use softener and they had high standards for performance. However, doing the laundry (often by hand) was arduous and time consuming, and required large amounts of water.

Having identified a problem (making laundry easier and less water-intensive), P&G turned to its labs for an answer. Their solution: Downy Single Rinse. In Mexico, a typical load of laundry goes through the following six-step process: wash; rinse; rinse; add softener; rinse; rinse. Instead of a six-step process, DSR reduced it to three—wash, add softener, rinse—saving enormous time, effort, and water. The product was launched in 2004 and became an immediate hit.[21]

customer satisfaction
customers' evaluation of a good or service in terms of whether it has met their needs and expectations

revenues come from customers who visit the store an average of 18 times per month.[22]

▸▸ *Avoid unrealistic pricing*: E-marketers are leveraging Internet technology to redefine how prices are set and negotiated. With lower costs, e-marketers can often offer lower prices than their brick-and-mortar counterparts. The enormous popularity of auction sites such as eBay and Amazon.com and the customer-bid model used by Priceline and uBid illustrates that online customers are interested in bargain prices. Many are not willing to pay a premium for the convenience of examining the merchandise and taking it home with them. Others will gladly pay a premium for an experience that is not only functionally rewarding, but emotionally rewarding as well. Executives at Starwood Hotels and Resorts'"W" chain believe that they are able to make an emotional connection when customers walk through the door of their hotel room and see the bed with clean-looking, sumptuous linens and other amenities.[23]

▸▸ *Give the buyer facts:* Today's sophisticated consumer wants informative advertising and knowledgeable salespeople. It is becoming very difficult for business marketers to differentiate themselves from competitors. Rather than trying to sell products, salespeople need to find out what the customer needs, which is usually a combination of products, services, and thought leadership.[24] In other words, salespeople need to start with the needs of the customer and work toward the solution.

▸▸ *Offer organization-wide commitment in service and after-sales support:* According to Gartner Research vice president Michael Maoz, organizations should incorporate customer service as a wide-ranging business strategy in order to keep up with customer expectations. "In the past, customer service was a department, the place that you called for specific redress of a grievance or information about your bill. Right now, rather than a function in that department, it is an enterprise strategy. That transition has profound implications on how we design all our processes across all our different communications channels."[25]

▸▸ *Co-Creation*: Some companies and products allow customers to help create their own experience. For example, TiVo makes it possible for people to record and watch chosen TV shows on their own schedules.

Customer Satisfaction **Customer satisfaction** is the customer's evaluation of a good or service in terms of whether that good or service has met their needs and expectations. Failure to meet needs and expectations results in dissatisfaction with the good or service.

Some companies, in their passion to drive down costs, have damaged their relationships with customers. Dell Computers, Home Depot, and Northwest Airlines are examples of companies where executives lost track of the delicate balance between efficiency and service.[26] Each has realized change is needed and have implemented improvements. Firms that have a reputation for delivering high levels of customer satisfaction do things differently from their competitors. Top management is obsessed with customer satisfaction, and employees throughout the organization understand the link between their job and satisfied customers. The culture of the organization is to focus on delighting customers rather than on selling products.

Nordstrom's impeccable reputation for customer service comes not from its executives or its marketing team, but from the customers themselves. The retail giant is willing to take risks, do unusual and often expensive favors for shoppers, and reportedly even accept returns on items not purchased there. Still, they keep improving. The company recently installed a new database enabling salespeople to assist customers in locating items in inventory somewhere in the chain, but not in a particular store. Customers can then purchase these items online.[27]

Building Relationships Attracting new customers to a business is only the beginning. The best companies view new-customer attraction as the launching point for developing and enhancing a long-term relationship. Companies can expand market share in three ways: attracting new customers, increasing business with existing customers, and retaining current customers. Building relationships with existing customers directly addresses two of the three possibilities and indirectly addresses the other.

Relationship marketing is a strategy that focuses on keeping and improving relationships with current customers. It assumes that many consumers and business customers prefer to have an ongoing relationship with one organization rather than switch continually among providers in their search for value. USAA is a good example of a company focused on building long-term relationships with customers. In 2007, a *Business Week*/J.D. Powers & Associates survey ranked USAA as the top provider of customer service among U.S. firms.[28] Customer retention was a core value of the company long before customer loyalty became a popular business concept. USAA believes so strongly in the importance of customer retention that managers' and executives' bonuses are based, in part, on this dimension.

Most successful relationship marketing strategies depend on customer-oriented personnel, effective training programs, employees with authority to make decisions and solve problems, and teamwork.

Customer-Oriented Personnel For an organization to be focused on building relationships with customers, employees' attitudes and actions must be customer oriented. An employee may be the only contact a particular customer has with the firm. In that customer's eyes, the employee is the firm. Any person, department, or division that is not customer oriented weakens the positive image of the entire organization. For example, a potential customer who is greeted discourteously may well assume that the employee's attitude represents the whole firm.

Isadore Sharp, founder, chair, and CEO of the Four Seasons hotel chain says that "personal service is not something you can dictate as a policy. It comes from the culture. How you treat your employees is how you expect them to treat the customer."[29]

Some companies, such as Coca-Cola, Delta Air Lines, Hershey Company, Kellogg, Nautilus, and Sears, have appointed chief customer officers (CCOs). These customer advocates provide an executive voice for customers and report directly to the CEO. Their responsibilities include ensuring that the company maintains a customer-centric culture and that all company employees remain focused on delivering customer value.

The Role of Training Leading marketers recognize the role of employee training in customer service and relationship building. Sales staff at The Container Store receive over 240 hours of training and generous benefits compared to an industry average of 8 hours of training and modest benefits.

Empowerment In addition to training, many market-oriented firms are giving employees more authority to solve customer problems on the spot. The term used to describe this delegation of authority is **empowerment**. Employees develop ownership attitudes when they are treated like part-owners of the business and are expected to act the part. These employees manage themselves, are more likely to work hard, account for their own performance and

THE essence OF MARKETING

A theme that you will find running throughout this text is the critical importance of providing a good customer experience. When one strips away all of the functions, plans, and strategies of marketing and asks the simple question, "What is this all about?" the answer is the customer experience. Think about it—whether you buy something a second or third time or become loyal to a brand depends on the experience that you had while purchasing and consuming the product or service. Most products need to be sold to a customer more than once in order for the company to start making money. Pepsico, for example, would have real problems if people bought just one can of Pepsi and then never purchased a Pepsi again.

the company's, and take prudent risks to build a stronger business and sustain the company's success. Employees at Ritz-Carlton hotels are encouraged to take whatever steps they feel are necessary to ensure that guests enjoy their visits. Any employee can spend up to $2,000—without seeking permission from management—to solve a problem for guests. One Ritz-Carlton chef in Bali had special eggs and milk imported from Singapore and personally delivered by plane so that he could cook for a young guest with food allergies.[30]

Empowerment gives customers the feeling that their concerns are being addressed and gives employees the feeling that their expertise matters. The result is greater satisfaction for both customers and employees.

Teamwork Many organizations that are frequently noted for delivering superior customer value and providing high levels of customer satisfaction, such as Southwest Airlines and Walt Disney World, assign employees to teams and teach them team-building skills. **Teamwork** entails collaborative efforts of people to accomplish common objectives. Job performance, company performance, product value, and customer satisfaction all improve when people in the same department or work group begin supporting and assisting each other and emphasize cooperation instead of competition. Performance is also enhanced when cross-functional teams align their jobs with customer needs. For example, if a team of telecommunications service representatives is working to improve interaction with customers, back-office people such as computer technicians or training personnel can become part of the team with the ultimate goal of delivering superior customer value and satisfaction.

The Firm's Business

A sales-oriented firm defines its business (or mission) in terms of goods and services. A market-oriented firm defines its business in terms of the benefits its customers seek. People who spend their money, time, and energy expect to receive benefits, not just goods and services. This distinction has enormous implications. As a senior executive of the Coca-Cola Co. noted, Coke is in the hydration business.[31]

"A MARKET-ORIENTED FIRM DEFINES ITS BUSINESS IN TERMS OF THE BENEFITS ITS CUSTOMERS SEEK."

Because of the limited way it defines its business, a sales-oriented firm often misses opportunities to serve customers whose wants can be met through a wide range of product offerings instead of specific products. For example, in 1989, 220-year-old Britannica had estimated revenues of $650 million and a worldwide sales force of 7,500. Just five years later, after three consecutive years of losses, the sales force had collapsed to as few as 280 representatives. How did this respected company sink so low? Britannica managers saw that competitors were beginning to use CD-ROMs to store huge masses of information, but chose to ignore the new computer technology, as well as an offer to team up with Microsoft.

WHAT IS THIS FIRM'S BUSINESS?

Answering the question "What is this firm's business?" in terms of the benefits customers seek, instead of goods and services, offers at least three important advantages:

▸▸ It ensures that the firm keeps focusing on customers and avoids becoming preoccupied with goods, services, or the organization's internal needs.

▸▸ It encourages innovation and creativity by reminding people that there are many ways to satisfy customer wants.

▸▸ It stimulates an awareness of changes in customer desires and preferences so that product offerings are more likely to remain relevant.

Having a market orientation and a focus on customer wants does not mean offering customers everything they want. It is not possible, for example, to profitably manufacture and market automobile tires that will last for 100,000 miles for $25. Furthermore, customers' preferences must be mediated by sound professional judgment as to how to deliver the benefits they seek. As Henry Ford once said, "If I had listened to the marketplace, I would have built a faster, cheaper horse."[32] Consumers have a limited set of experiences. They are unlikely to request anything beyond those experiences because they are not aware of benefits they may gain from other potential offerings. For example, before the Internet, many people thought that shopping for some products was boring and time consuming but could not express their need for electronic shopping.

> "If I had listened to the marketplace, I would have built a faster, cheaper horse."
>
> —Henry Ford

Those to Whom the Product Is Directed

A sales-oriented organization targets its products at "everybody" or "the average customer." A market-oriented organization aims at specific groups of people. The fallacy of developing products directed at the average user is that relatively few average users actually exist. Typically, populations are characterized by diversity. An average is simply a midpoint in some set of characteristics. Because most potential customers are not "average," they are not likely to be attracted to an average product marketed to the average customer. Consider the market for shampoo as one simple example. There are shampoos for oily hair, dry hair, and dandruff. Some shampoos remove the gray or color hair. Special shampoos are marketed for infants and elderly people. There are even shampoos for people with average or normal hair (whatever that is), but this is fairly small portion of the total market for shampoo.

A market-oriented organization recognizes that different customer groups want different features or benefits. It may therefore need to develop different goods, services, and promotional appeals. A market-oriented organization carefully analyzes the market and divides it into groups of people who are fairly similar in terms of selected characteristics. Then the organization develops marketing programs that will bring about mutually satisfying exchanges with one or more of those groups. Chapter 8 thoroughly explores the topic of analyzing markets and selecting those that appear to be most promising to the firm.

The Firm's Primary Goal

A sales-oriented organization seeks to achieve profitability through sales volume and tries to convince potential customers to buy, even if the seller knows that the customer and product are mismatched. Sales-oriented organizations place a higher premium on making a sale than on developing a long-term relationship with a customer. In contrast, the ultimate goal of most market-oriented organizations is to make a profit by creating customer value, providing customer satisfaction, and building long-term relationships with customers. The exception is so-called nonprofit organizations that exist to achieve goals other than profits.

YOU'LL WANT THAT IN BLACK, RIGHT?

Paying attention to the customer isn't exactly a new concept. Back in the 1920s, **General Motors** began designing cars for every lifestyle and pocketbook. This was a breakthrough for an industry that had been largely driven by production needs ever since Henry Ford promised any color as long as it was black.

Nonprofit organizations can and should adopt a market orientation. Nonprofit organization marketing is explored further in Chapter 12.

Tools the Organization Uses to Achieve Its Goals

Sales-oriented organizations seek to generate sales volume through intensive promotional activities, mainly personal selling and advertising. In contrast, market-oriented organizations recognize that promotion decisions are only one of four basic marketing mix decisions that have to be made: product decisions, place (or distribution) decisions, promotion decisions, and pricing decisions. A market-oriented organization recognizes that each of these four components is important. Furthermore, market-oriented organizations recognize that marketing is not just a responsibility of the marketing department. Interfunctional coordination means that skills and resources throughout the organization are needed to create, communicate, and deliver superior customer service and value.

4 Marketing management philosophies or orientations

3 Basic ways companies can expand market share

$44 MILLION amount spent on Coca-Cola's recycling plant

5 Conditions required for exchange; key characteristics that differentiate the marketing orientation from the sales orientation

7% customers who could name an environmentally friendly product they had purchased

2.5 Tons of food consumed by the average U.S. household in a year

Word of Caution

This comparison of sales and market orientations is not meant to belittle the role of promotion, especially personal selling, in the marketing mix. Promotion is the means by which organizations communicate with present and prospective customers about the merits and characteristics of their organization and products. Effective promotion is an essential part of effective marketing. Salespeople who work for market-oriented organizations are generally perceived by their customers to be problem solvers and important links to supply sources and new products. Chapter 18 examines the nature of personal selling in more detail.

LO4 Why Study Marketing

Now that you understand the meaning of the term *marketing,* why it is important to adopt a marketing orientation, how organizations implement this philosophy, and how one-to-one marketing is evolving, you may be asking, "What's in it for me?" or "Why should I study marketing?" These are important questions whether you are majoring in a business field other than marketing (such as accounting, finance, or management information systems) or a nonbusiness field (such as journalism, education, or agriculture). There are several important reasons to study marketing: Marketing plays an important role in society, marketing is important to businesses, marketing offers outstanding career opportunities, and marketing affects your life every day.

Marketing Plays an Important Role in Society

The total population of the United States exceeds 300 million people.[33] Think about how many transactions are needed each day to feed, clothe, and shelter a population of this size. The number is huge. And yet it all works quite well, partly because the well-developed U.S. economic system efficiently distributes the output of farms and factories. A typical U.S. family, for example, consumes 2.5 tons of food a year. Marketing makes food available when we want it, in desired quantities, at accessible locations, and in sanitary and convenient packages and forms (such as instant and frozen foods).

Marketing Is Important to Businesses

The fundamental objectives of most businesses are survival, profits, and growth. Marketing contributes directly to achieving these objectives. Marketing includes the following activities, which are vital to business organizations: assessing the wants and satisfactions of present and potential customers, designing and managing product offerings, determining prices and pricing policies, developing distribution strategies, and communicating with present and potential customers.

All businesspeople, regardless of specialization or area of responsibility, need to be familiar with the terminology and fundamentals of accounting, finance, management, and marketing. People in all business areas need to be able to communicate with specialists in other areas. Furthermore, marketing is not just a job done by people in a marketing department. Marketing is a part of the job of everyone in the organization. Therefore, a basic understanding of marketing is important to all businesspeople.

Marketing Offers Outstanding Career Opportunities

Between a fourth and a third of the entire civilian workforce in the United States performs marketing activities. Marketing offers great career opportunities in such areas as professional selling, marketing research, advertising, retail buying, distribution management, product management, product development, and wholesaling. Marketing career opportunities also exist in a variety of nonbusiness organizations, including hospitals, museums, universities, the armed forces, and various government and social service agencies.

Marketing Affects Your Life Every Day

Marketing plays a major role in your everyday life. You participate in the marketing process as a consumer of goods and services. About half of every dollar you spend pays for marketing costs, such as marketing research, product development, packaging, transportation, storage, advertising, and sales expenses. By developing a better understanding of marketing, you will become a better-informed consumer. You will better understand the buying process and be able to negotiate more effectively with sellers. Moreover, you will be better prepared to demand satisfaction when the goods and services you buy do not meet the standards promised by the manufacturer or the marketer.

ABOUT HALF
OF EVERY DOLLAR YOU
SPEND PAYS FOR MARKETING COSTS.

STUDY TOOLS
CHAPTER 1

Located at back of the textbook

❏ **Rip out Chapter Review Card**

Located at 4ltrpress.cengage.com/mktg

❏ **Review Key Terms Flash Cards (Print or Online)**

❏ **Download Audio and Visual Summaries for on-the-go review**

❏ **Complete both Practice Quizzes to prepare for tests**

❏ **Play "Beat the Clock" and "Quizbowl" to master concepts**

❏ **Complete "Crossword Puzzle" to review key terms**

❏ **Watch the video on "Method" for a real company example**

Strategic Planning for Competitive Advantage

"A good strategic plan can help protect and grow the firm's resources."

AFTER YOU FINISH THIS CHAPTER GO TO PAGE 28 FOR STUDY TOOLS

LO 1 The Nature of Strategic Planning

Strategic planning is the managerial process of creating and maintaining a fit between the organization's objectives and resources and the evolving market opportunities. The goal of strategic planning is long-run profitability and growth. Thus, strategic decisions require long-term commitments of resources.

A strategic error can threaten a firm's survival. On the other hand, a good strategic plan can help protect and grow the firm's resources. For instance, if the March of Dimes had decided to focus on fighting polio, the organization would no longer exist. Most of us view polio as a conquered disease. The March of Dimes survived by making the strategic decision to switch to fighting birth defects.

Strategic marketing management addresses two questions: What is the organization's main activity at a particular time? How will it reach its goals? Here are some examples of strategic decisions:

▸▸ General Electric Company has initiated an effort called "Ecomagination," which will shift its focus to being an environmentally conscious company that is working to solve some of the planet's most critical environmental issues. This effort represents a complete

strategic planning the managerial process of creating and maintaining a fit between the organization's objectives and resources and the evolving market opportunities

What do you think?

Nothing gets accomplished without planning.

| 1 | 2 | 3 | 4 | 5 | 6 | 7 |

STRONGLY DISAGREE   STRONGLY AGREE

© MICHAEL THOMAS/GETTY IMAGES

planning the process of anticipating future events and determining strategies to achieve organizational objectives in the future

marketing planning designing activities relating to marketing objectives and the changing marketing environment

marketing plan a written document that acts as a guidebook of marketing activities for the marketing manager

transformation in strategy for GE that is changing the way it develops products, sells to customers, and enters emerging markets.[1]

- Toys "R" Us has suffered as younger and younger children abandon traditional toys for electronic entertainment and because parents tend to buy toys during weekly trips to one-stop shops like Wal-Mart. The company responded by expanding its infant line, Babies "R" Us, and is using it to lure parents of older children into their toy selections.[2]
- Amid the health trend and pressure for fast-food restaurants to offer healthy alternatives, McDonald's made the decision to offer healthier foods by focusing on fresh fruits and vegetables with its new line of premium salads.[3]
- SC Johnson introduced Shout Color Catchers, a laundry sheet for the washer that collects loose dyes and prevents clothes from bleeding color onto other laundry items.

EXHIBIT 2.1
Elements of a Marketing Plan

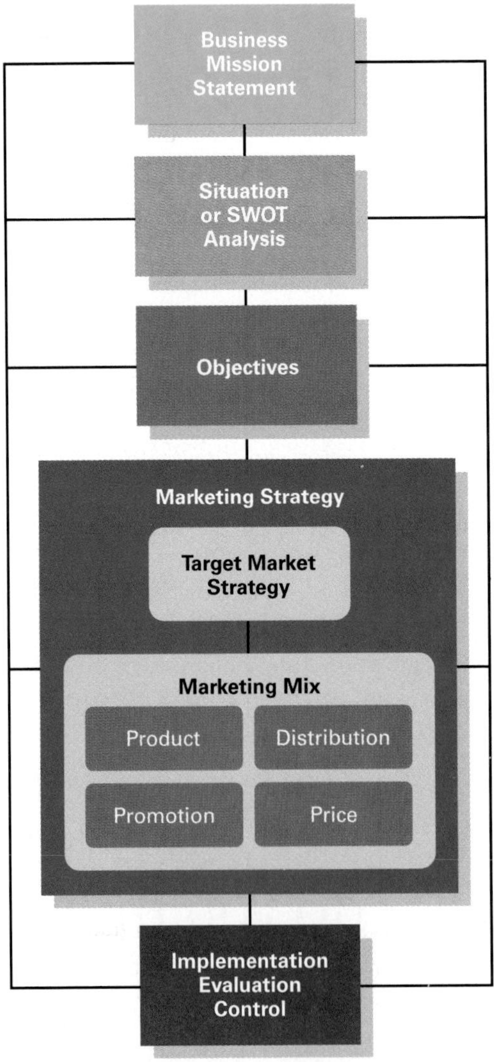

All these decisions have affected or will affect each organization's long-run course, its allocation of resources, and ultimately its financial success. In contrast, an operating decision, such as changing the package design for Post's cornflakes or altering the sweetness of a Kraft salad dressing, probably won't have a big impact on the long-run profitability of the company.

How do companies go about strategic marketing planning? How do employees know how to implement the long-term goals of the firm? The answer is a marketing plan.

What Is a Marketing Plan?

Planning is the process of anticipating future events and determining strategies to achieve organizational objectives in the future. **Marketing planning** involves designing activities relating to marketing objectives and the changing marketing environment. Marketing planning is the basis for all marketing strategies and decisions. Issues such as product lines, distribution channels, marketing communications, and pricing are all delineated in the **marketing plan**. The marketing plan is a written document that acts as a guidebook of marketing activities for the marketing manager. In this chapter, you will learn the importance of writing a marketing plan and the types of information contained in a marketing plan.

Why Write a Marketing Plan?

By specifying objectives and defining the actions required to attain them, you can provide in a marketing plan the basis by which actual and expected performance can be compared. Marketing can be one of the most expensive and complicated business activities, but it is also one of the most important. The written marketing plan provides clearly stated activities that help employees and managers understand and work toward common goals.

Writing a marketing plan allows you to examine the marketing environment in conjunction with the inner workings of the business. Once the marketing plan is written, it serves as a reference point for the success of future activities. Finally, the marketing plan allows the marketing manager to enter the marketplace with an awareness of possibilities and problems.

Marketing Plan Elements

Marketing plans can be presented in many different ways. Most businesses need a written marketing plan because a marketing plan is large and can be complex. Details about tasks and activity assignments may be lost if communicated orally. Regardless of the way a marketing plan is presented, some elements are common to all marketing plans. Exhibit 2.1 shows these elements, which include defining the business mission, performing a situation analysis, defining objectives, delineating a target

market, and establishing components of the marketing mix. Other elements that may be included in a plan are budgets, implementation timetables, required marketing research efforts, or elements of advanced strategic planning. A marketing planning outline and an example of a marketing plan is online at 4ltrpress.cengage.com/mktg.

Selecting which alternative to pursue depends on the overall company philosophy and culture. The choice also depends on the tool used to make the decision. Companies generally have one of two philosophies about when they expect profits. They either pursue profits right away or first seek to increase market share and then pursue profits. In the long run, market share and profitability are compatible goals. Many companies have long followed this credo: Build market share, and profits will surely follow. Michelin, the tire producer, consistently sacrifices short-term profits to achieve market share. On the other hand, IBM stresses profitability and stock valuation over market share, quality, and customer service. As you can see, the same strategic alternative may be viewed entirely differently by different firms.

A number of tools exist to help managers select a strategic alternative. The most common of these tools are in matrix form. The portfolio matrix is described here in more detail.

Writing the Marketing Plan

The creation and implementation of a complete marketing plan will allow the organization to achieve marketing objectives and succeed. However, the marketing plan is only as good as the information it contains and the effort, creativity, and thought that went into its creation. Having a good marketing information system and a wealth of competitive intelligence (covered in Chapter 9) is critical to a thorough and accurate situation analysis. The role of managerial intuition is also important in the creation and selection of marketing strategies. Managers must weigh any information against its accuracy and their own judgment when making a marketing decision.

Note that the overall structure of the marketing plan (Exhibit 2.1) should not be viewed as a series of sequential planning steps. Many of the marketing plan elements are decided on simultaneously and in conjunction with one another. Further, every marketing plan has different content, depending on the organization, its mission, objectives, targets, and marketing mix components. There is not one single correct format for a marketing plan. Many organizations have their own distinctive format or terminology for creating a marketing plan. Every marketing plan should be unique to the firm for which it was created. Remember, however, that although the format and order of presentation should be flexible, the same types of questions and topic areas should be covered in any marketing plan.

LO 2 Defining the Business Mission

The foundation of any marketing plan is the firm's **mission statement**, which answers the question, "What business are we in?" The way a firm defines its business mission profoundly affects the firm's long-run resource allocation, profitability, and survival. The mission statement is based on a careful analysis of benefits sought by present and potential customers and an analysis of existing and anticipated environmental conditions. The firm's mission statement establishes boundaries for all subsequent decisions, objectives, and strategies.

A mission statement should focus on the market or markets the organization is attempting to serve rather than on the good or service offered. Otherwise, a new technology may quickly make the good or service obsolete and the mission statement irrelevant to company functions. Business mission statements that are stated too narrowly suffer from **marketing myopia**—defining a business in terms of goods and services rather than in terms of the benefits customers seek. In this context, *myopia* means narrow, short-term thinking. For example, Frito-Lay defines its mission as being in the snack-food business rather than in the corn chip business. The mission of sports teams is not just to play games but to serve the interests of the fans.

Alternatively, business missions may be stated too broadly. "To provide products of superior quality and value that improve the lives of the world's consumers" is probably too broad a mission statement for any firm except Procter & Gamble. Care must be taken when stating what business a firm is in. For example, the mission of Ben & Jerry's centers on three important aspects of its ice cream business: (1) Product: "To make, distribute and sell the finest quality all natural ice cream and related products in a wide variety of innovative flavors made from Vermont Dairy products;" (2) Economic: "To operate the company on a sound financial basis of profitable growth, increasing value for our shareholders, and creating career opportunities and financial rewards for our employees;" and (3) Social: "To operate the company in a way that actively recognizes the central role that business plays in the structure of society by initiating innovative ways to improve the quality of life of a broad community—local, national, and international."[4] By correctly stating the business mission in terms of the benefits that customers seek, the foundation for the marketing plan is set. Many companies are focusing on designing more appropriate mission statements because these statements are frequently displayed on the company's Web sites.

The organization may need to define a mission statement and objectives for a **strategic business unit (SBU)**, which is a subgroup of a single business or collection of related businesses within the larger organization. A properly defined SBU should have a distinct mission and specific target market, control over its resources, its own competitors, and plans independent of the other SBUs in the organization. Thus, a large firm such as Kraft Foods may have marketing plans for each of its SBUs, which include breakfast foods, desserts, pet foods, and beverages.

LO 3 Conducting a Situation Analysis

Marketers must understand the current and potential environment that the product or service will be marketed in. A situation analysis is sometimes referred to as a **SWOT analysis**; that is, the firm should identify its internal strengths (**S**) and weaknesses (**W**) and also examine external opportunities (**O**) and threats (**T**).

When examining internal strengths and weaknesses, the marketing manager should focus on organizational resources such as production costs, marketing skills, financial resources, company or brand image, employee capabilities, and available technology. For example, a potential weakness for AirTran Airways (formerly ValuJet) is the age of its airplane fleet, which could project an image of danger or low quality. Other weaknesses include high labor turnover rates and limited flights. A potential strength is the airline's low operating costs, which translate into lower prices for consumers. Another issue to consider in this section of the marketing plan is the historical background of the firm—its sales and profit history.

When examining external opportunities and threats, marketing managers must analyze aspects of the marketing environment. This process is called **environmental scanning**—the collection and interpretation of information about forces, events, and relationships in the external environment that may affect the future of the organization or the implementation of the marketing plan. Environmental scanning helps identify market opportunities and threats and provides guidelines for the design of marketing strategy. The six most often studied macroenvironmental forces are social, demographic, economic, technological, political and legal, and competitive. These forces are examined in detail in Chapter 4. Rising gas prices and a weakening dollar have created a complex, but possibly advantageous, environment for McDonald's. While increased gas costs may discourage some consumers from visiting its drive-through windows, the fast food giant hopes that its widespread availability, inexpensive prices, and new gourmet-style coffee offerings will attract consumers trying to save money by downgrading from Starbucks and other pricey venues. McDonald's marketers are even taking advantage of gas price increases by running commercials in which teenagers decide not to fill their empty gas tank and buy $1 double cheeseburgers to fill their stomachs instead.[5]

LO 4 Setting Marketing Plan Objectives

Before the details of a marketing plan can be developed, objectives for the plan must be stated. Without objectives, there is no basis for measuring the success of marketing plan activities.

A **marketing objective** is a statement of what is to be accomplished through marketing activities. To be useful, stated objectives should meet several criteria:

▶▶ *Realistic:* Managers should develop objectives that have a chance of being met. For example, it may be unrealistic for start-up firms or new products to command dominant market share, given other competitors in the marketplace.

- ▸▸ *Measurable:* Managers need to be able to quantitatively measure whether or not an objective has been met. For example, it would be difficult to determine success for an objective that states, "To increase sales of cat food." If the company sells 1 percent more cat food, does that mean the objective was met? Instead, a specific number should be stated, "To increase sales of Purina brand cat food from $300 million to $345 million."

- ▸▸ *Time specific:* By what time should the objective be met? "To increase sales of Purina brand cat food between January 1, 2011 and December 31, 2011."

- ▸▸ *Compared to a benchmark:* If the objective is to increase sales by 15 percent, it is important to know the base line against which the objective will be measured. Will it be current sales? Last year's sales? For example, "To increase sales of Purina brand cat food by 15 percent over 2010 sales of $300 million."

Objectives must also be consistent with and indicate the priorities of the organization. Specifically, objectives flow from the business mission statement to the rest of the marketing plan.

Carefully specified objectives serve several functions. First, they communicate marketing management philosophies and provide direction for lower-level marketing managers so that marketing efforts are integrated and pointed in a consistent direction. Objectives also serve as motivators by creating something for employees to strive for. When objectives are attainable and challenging, they motivate those charged with achieving the objectives. Additionally, the process of writing specific objectives forces executives to clarify their thinking. Finally, objectives form a basis for control; the effectiveness of a plan can be gauged in light of the stated objectives.

© ISTOCKPHOTO.COM/JASMINE AWAD

LO 5 Competitive Advantage

Performing a SWOT analysis allows firms to identify their **competitive advantage**. A competitive advantage is a set of unique features of a company and its products that are perceived by the target market as significant and superior to the competition. It is the factor or factors that cause customers to patronize a firm and not the competition. There are three types of competitive advantages: cost, product/service differentiation, and niche strategies.

Cost Competitive Advantage

Cost leadership can result from obtaining inexpensive raw materials, creating an efficient scale of plant operations, designing products for ease of manufacture, controlling overhead costs, and avoiding marginal customers. DuPont, for example, has an exceptional cost competitive advantage in the production of titanium dioxide. Technicians created a production process using low-cost feedstock, giving DuPont a 20 percent cost advantage over its competitors. The cheaper feedstock technology is complex and can be duplicated only by investing about $100 million and several years of testing time. Having a **cost competitive advantage** means being the low-cost competitor in an industry while maintaining satisfactory profit margins.

A cost competitive advantage enables a firm to deliver superior customer value. Wal-Mart, the world's leading low-cost general merchandise store, offers good value to customers because it focuses on providing a large selection of merchandise at low prices and good customer service. Wal-Mart is able to keep its prices down because it has strong buying power in its relationships with suppliers. Costs can be reduced in a variety of ways:

- ▸▸ *Experience curves:* **Experience curves** tell us that costs decline at a predictable rate as experience with a product increases. The experience curve effect encompasses a broad range of manufacturing, marketing, and administrative costs. Experience curves reflect learning by doing, technological advances, and economies of scale. Firms like Boeing use historical experience curves

competitive advantage a set of unique features of a company and its products that are perceived by the target market as significant and superior to the competition

cost competitive advantage being the low-cost competitor in an industry while maintaining satisfactory profit margins

experience curves curves that show costs declining at a predictable rate as experience with a product increases

as a basis for predicting and setting prices. Experience curves allow management to forecast costs and set prices based on anticipated costs as opposed to current costs.

▸▸ *Efficient labor:* Labor costs can be an important component of total costs in low-skill, labor-intensive industries such as product assembly and apparel manufacturing. Many U.S. manufacturers such as Nike, Levi Strauss, and Liz Claiborne have gone offshore to achieve cheaper manufacturing costs. Many American companies are also outsourcing activities such as data entry and other labor-intensive jobs.

▸▸ *No-frills goods and services:* Marketers can lower costs by removing frills and options from a product or service. Southwest Airlines, for example, offers low fares but no seat assignments or meals. Low costs give Southwest a higher load factor and greater economies of scale, which, in turn, mean lower prices.

▸▸ *Government subsidies:* Governments may provide grants and interest-free loans to target industries. Such government assistance enabled Japanese semiconductor manufacturers to become global leaders.

▸▸ *Product design:* Cutting-edge design technology can help offset high labor costs. BMW is a world leader in designing cars for ease of manufacture and assembly. Reverse engineering—the process of disassembling a product piece by piece to learn its components and obtain clues as to the manufacturing process—can also mean savings. Reverse engineering a low-cost competitor's product can save research and design costs. Japanese engineers have reversed many products, such as computer chips coming out of Silicon Valley.

▸▸ *Reengineering:* Reengineering entails fundamental rethinking and redesign of business processes to achieve dramatic improvements in critical measures of performance. It often involves reorganizing from functional departments such as sales, engineering, and production to cross-disciplinary teams.

▸▸ *Production innovations:* Production innovations such as new technology and simplified production techniques help lower the average cost of production. Technologies such as computer-aided design (CAD) and computer-aided manufacturing (CAM) and increasingly sophisticated robots help companies such as Boeing, Ford, and General Electric reduce their manufacturing costs.

▸▸ *New methods of service delivery:* Medical expenses have been substantially lowered by the use of outpatient surgery and walk-in clinics. Airlines, such as Delta, are lowering reservation and ticketing costs by encouraging passengers to use the Internet to book flights and by providing self-check-in kiosks at the airport.

Product/Service Differentiation Competitive Advantage

Because cost competitive advantages are subject to continual erosion, product/service differentiation tends to provide a longer lasting competitive advantage. The durability of this strategy tends to make it more attractive to many top managers. A **product/service differentiation competitive advantage** exists when a firm provides something that is unique and valuable to buyers beyond simply offering a lower price than the competition's. Examples include brand names (Lexus), a strong dealer network (Caterpillar for construction work), product reliability (Maytag appliances), image (Neiman Marcus in retailing), or service (FedEx). A great example of a company that has a strong product/service competitive advantage is Nike. Nike's advantage is built around one simple idea—product innovation. The company's goal is to think of something that nobody has thought of before or improve something that already exists. Nike Air, ACG, Nike Swift, and Nike Shox are examples of innovative shoes introduced by Nike.[6]

Niche Competitive Advantage

A **niche competitive advantage** seeks to target and effectively serve a single segment of the market (see Chapter 8). For small companies with limited resources that potentially face giant competitors, niche targeting may be the only viable option. A market segment that has good growth potential but is not crucial to the success of major competitors is a good candidate for developing a niche strategy.

Many companies using a niche strategy serve only a limited geographic market. Buddy Freddy's is a very successful restaurant chain, but is found only in Florida. Migros is the dominant grocery chain in Switzerland. It has no stores outside that small country.

Block Drug Company uses niche targeting by focusing its product line on tooth products. It markets Polident to clean false teeth, Poligrip to hold false teeth, and Sensodyne toothpaste for persons with sensitive teeth. The Orvis Company manufactures and sells everything that anyone might ever need for fly fishing. Orvis is a very successful niche marketer.

Building Sustainable Competitive Advantage

The key to having a competitive advantage is the ability to sustain that advantage. A **sustainable competitive advantage** is one that cannot be copied by the competition. Nike, discussed earlier, is a good example of a company that has a sustainable competitive advantage. Others include Rolex (high-quality watches), Nordstrom department stores (service), and Southwest Airlines (low price). In contrast, when Datril was introduced into the pain-reliever market, it was touted as being exactly like Tylenol, only cheaper. Tylenol responded by lowering its price, thus destroying Datril's competitive advantage and ability to remain on the market. In this case, low price was not a sustainable competitive advantage. Without a competitive advantage, target customers don't perceive any reason to patronize an organization instead of its competitors.

The notion of competitive advantage means that a successful firm will stake out a position unique in some manner from its rivals. Imitation by competitors indicates a lack of competitive advantage and almost ensures mediocre performance. Moreover, competitors rarely stand still, so it is not surprising that imitation causes managers to feel trapped in a seemingly endless game of catch-up. They are regularly surprised by the new accomplishments of their rivals.

Companies need to build their own competitive advantages rather than copy a competitor. The sources of tomorrow's competitive advantages are the skills and assets of the organization. Assets include patents, copyrights, locations, equipment, and technology that are superior to those of the competition. Skills are functions such as customer service and promotion that the firm performs better than its competitors. Netflix, for example, created and remains dominant in the market for renting movies by mail. Marketing managers should continually focus the firm's skills and assets on sustaining and creating competitive advantages.

Remember, a sustainable competitive advantage is a function of the speed with which competitors can imitate a leading company's strategy and plans. Imitation requires a competitor to identify the leader's competitive advantage, determine how it is achieved, and then learn how to duplicate it.

> **sustainable competitive advantage** an advantage that cannot be copied by the competition

LO 6 Strategic Directions

The end result of the SWOT analysis and identification of a competitive advantage is to evaluate the strategic direction of the firm. Selecting a strategic alternative is the next step in marketing planning.

RETAIL ENTERTAINMENT

Bass Pro Shops understands how to offer the customer a quality experience by entertaining them while they shop; this experiential aspect provides a strong competitive advantage. About thirty of the Bass Pro Shops are designed to showcase the characteristics of the area where they are located. For example, a Florida store features the hull of a sunken ship, while a Massachusetts store has a 30-foot long blue whale on display.

Classes are offered at the stores, ranging from fly-casting, Dutch-oven cooking, archery hunting, and GPS navigation. Most stores also offer full-service restaurants on site. The Las Vegas store is connected to a casino and cabin-themed resort.

The Bass Pro Shops "experience" has given the stores the status of a tourist destination; some people spend their vacations driving from store to store.[7]

© ISTOCKPHOTO.COM/RICHARD GOERG

Strategic Alternatives

To discover a marketing opportunity, management must know how to identify the alternatives. One method for developing alternatives is Ansoff's strategic opportunity matrix (see Exhibit 2.2), which matches products with markets. Firms can explore these four options:

▸▸ *Market penetration:* A firm using the **market penetration** alternative would try to increase market share among existing customers. If Kraft Foods started a major campaign for Maxwell House coffee with aggressive advertising and cents-off coupons to existing customers, it would be following a penetration strategy. McDonald's sold the most Happy Meals in history with a promotion that included Ty's Teeny Beanie Babies. Customer databases, discussed in Chapters 9 and 21, would help managers implement this strategy.

▸▸ *Market development:* **Market development** means attracting new customers to existing products. Ideally, new uses for old products stimulate additional sales among existing customers while also bringing in new buyers. McDonald's, for example, has opened restaurants in Russia, China, and Italy and is eagerly expanding into Eastern European countries. Sara Lee is entering the market for meals on the go by introducing Hillshire Farm Salad Entrees, kits that contain meat and other ingredients that the company already makes, to be added to lettuce.[8] In the nonprofit area, the growing emphasis on continuing education and executive development by colleges and universities is a market development strategy.

▸▸ *Product development:* A **product development** strategy entails the creation of new products for present markets. McDonald's introduced yogurt parfaits, entrée salads, and fruit to offer their current customers more healthy options. Managers following the product development strategy can rely on their extensive knowledge of the target audience. They usually have a good feel for what customers like and dislike about current products and what existing needs are not being met. In addition, managers can rely on established distribution channels.

▸▸ *Diversification:* **Diversification** is a strategy of increasing sales by introducing new products into

new markets. For example, Ralph Lauren developed a new brand of clothing called Rugby to appeal to young people age 14 to 29.[9] Sony practiced a diversification strategy when it acquired Columbia Pictures; although motion pictures are not a new product in the marketplace, they were a new product for Sony. Coca-Cola manufactures and markets water-treatment and water-conditioning equipment, which has been a very challenging task for the traditional soft drink company. A diversification strategy can be risky when a firm is entering unfamiliar markets. On the other hand, it can be very profitable when a firm is entering markets with little or no competition.

Selecting a Strategic Alternative

Portfolio Matrix Recall that large organizations engaged in strategic planning may create strategic business units. Each SBU has its own rate of return on investment, growth potential, and associated risk. Management must find a balance among the SBUs that yields the overall organization's desired

EXHIBIT 2.2
Ansoff's Strategic Opportunity Matrix

www.starbucks.com

	Present Product	**New Product**
Present Market	*Market Penetration* Starbucks sells more coffee to customers with reloadable Starbucks cards and Duetto Visa cards.	*Product Development* Starbucks develops ready-to-drink coffee beverages Double Shot and bottled Frappuccino.
New Market	*Market Development* Starbucks opens stores in Brazil and Chile.	*Diversification* Starbucks launches Hear Music and buys Ethos Water.

growth and profits with an acceptable level of risk. Some SBUs generate large amounts of cash, and others need cash to foster growth. The challenge is to balance the organization's "portfolio" of SBUs for the best long-term performance.

To determine the future cash contributions and cash requirements expected for each SBU, managers can use the Boston Consulting Group's portfolio matrix. The **portfolio matrix** classifies each SBU by its present or forecast growth and market share. The underlying assumption is that market share and profitability are strongly linked. The measure of market share used in the portfolio approach is *relative market share*, the ratio between the company's share and the share of the largest competitor. For example, if firm A has a 50 percent share and the competitor has 5 percent, the ratio is 10 to 1. If firm A has a 10 percent market share and the largest competitor has 20 percent, the ratio is 0.5 to 1.

Exhibit 2.3 is a hypothetical portfolio matrix for a computer manufacturer. The size of the circle in each cell of the matrix represents dollar sales of the SBU relative to dollar sales of the company's other SBUs. The following categories are used in the matrix:

▸▸ *Stars:* A **star** is a market leader and growing fast. For example, computer manufacturers have identified notebook and handheld models as stars. Star SBUs usually have large profits but need lots of cash to finance rapid growth. The best marketing tactic is to protect existing market share by reinvesting earnings in product improvement, better distribution, more promotion, and production efficiency. Management must capture new users as they enter the market.

▸▸ *Cash cows:* A **cash cow** is an SBU that generates more cash than it needs to maintain its market share. It is in a low-growth market, but the product has a dominant market share. Personal computers and laptops are categorized as cash cows in Exhibit 2.3. The basic strategy for a cash cow is to maintain market dominance by being the price leader and making technological improvements in the product. Managers should resist pressure to extend the basic line unless they can dramatically increase demand. Instead, they should allocate excess cash to the product categories where growth prospects are the greatest. For instance, the Clorox Company owns Kingsford charcoal, the Glad brand of products, Fresh Step, Scoop Away and other pet litters, Brita water filtration systems, and K. C. Masterpiece barbeque sauce, among others. Traditionally, the company's cash cow has been Clorox bleach, which owns the lion's share of a low-growth market. The Clorox Company has been highly successful in stretching the Clorox line to include

scented chlorine bleach as well as Clorox 2, chlorine-free bleach for colored clothing. Another example is Heinz, which has two cash cows: ketchup and Weight Watchers frozen dinners.

▸▸ *Problem children:* A **problem child**, also called a **question mark**, shows rapid growth but poor profit margins. It has a low market share in a high-growth industry. Problem children need a great deal of cash. Without cash support, they eventually become dogs. The strategy options are to invest heavily to gain better market share, acquire competitors to get the necessary market share, or drop the SBU. Sometimes a firm can reposition the products of the SBU to move them into the star category. Zima brand beer, targeted at Generation X, was a problem child for Adolph Coors Company. The company ultimately withdrew its heavy marketing investment in Zima and positioned it as a niche product.

▸▸ *Dogs:* A **dog** has low growth potential and a small market share. Most dogs eventually leave the marketplace. In the computer manufacturer example, the mainframe computer has become a dog. Other examples include Warner-Lambert's Reef mouthwash, and Campbell's Red Kettle soups. Frito-Lay has produced several dogs, including Stuffers cheese-filled snacks, Rumbles granola nuggets, and Toppels cheese-topped crackers—a trio

portfolio matrix a tool for allocating resources among products or strategic business units on the basis of relative market share and market growth rate

star in the portfolio matrix, a business unit that is a fast-growing market leader

cash cow in the portfolio matrix, a business unit that generates more cash than it needs to maintain its market share

problem child (question mark) in the portfolio matrix, a business unit that shows rapid growth but poor profit margins

dog in the portfolio matrix, a business unit that has low growth potential and a small market share

EXHIBIT 2.3
Portfolio Matrix for a Large Computer Manufacturer

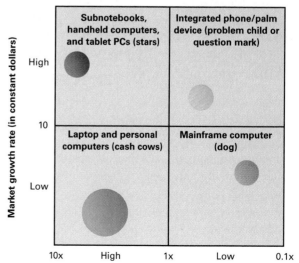

irreverently known as Stumbles, Tumbles, and Twofers. The strategy options for dogs are to harvest or divest.

After classifying the company's SBUs in the matrix, the next step is to allocate future resources for each. The four basic strategies are to:

▸▸ *Build:* If an organization has an SBU that it believes has the potential to be a star (probably a problem child at present) building would be an appropriate goal. The organization may decide to give up short-term profits and use its financial resources to achieve this goal. Procter & Gamble built Pringles from a money loser to a record profit maker.

▸▸ *Hold:* If an SBU is a very successful cash cow, a key goal would surely be to hold or preserve market share so that the organization can take advantage of the very positive cash flow. Bisquick has been a prosperous cash cow for General Mills for over two decades.

▸▸ *Harvest:* This strategy is appropriate for all SBUs except those classified as stars. The basic goal is to increase the short-term cash return without too much concern for the long-run impact. It is especially worthwhile when more cash is needed from a cash cow with long-run prospects that are unfavorable because of low market growth rate. For instance, Lever Brothers has been harvesting Lifebuoy soap for a number of years with little promotional backing.

▸▸ *Divest:* Getting rid of SBUs with low shares of low-growth markets is often appropriate. Problem children and dogs are most suitable for this strategy. Procter & Gamble dropped Cincaprin, a coated aspirin, because of its low growth potential.

LO 7 Describing the Target Market

Marketing strategy involves the activities of selecting and describing one or more target markets and developing and maintaining a marketing mix that will produce mutually satisfying exchanges with target markets.

Target Market Strategy

A market segment is a group of individuals or organizations that share one or more characteristics. They therefore may have relatively similar product needs.

For example, parents of newborn babies need formula, diapers, and special foods.

The target market strategy identifies the market segment or segments on which to focus. This process begins with a **market opportunity analysis (MOA)**—the description and estimation of the size and sales potential of market segments that are of interest to the firm and the assessment of key competitors in these market segments. After the firm describes the market segments, it may target one or more of them. There are three general strategies for selecting target markets.

Target market(s) can be selected by appealing to the entire market with one marketing mix, concentrating on one segment, or appealing to multiple market segments using multiple marketing mixes. The characteristics, advantages, and disadvantages of each strategic option are examined in Chapter 8. Target markets could be smokers who are concerned about white teeth (the target of Topol toothpaste), people concerned about sugar and calories in their soft drinks (Diet Pepsi), or college students needing inexpensive about-town transportation (Yamaha Razz scooter).

Any market segment that is targeted must be fully described. Demographics, psychographics, and buyer behavior should be assessed. Buyer behavior is covered in Chapters 6 and 7. If segments are differentiated by ethnicity, multicultural aspects of the marketing mix should be examined. If the target market is international, it is especially important to describe differences in culture, economic and technological development, and political structure that may affect the marketing plan. Global marketing is covered in more detail in Chapter 5.

LO 8 The Marketing Mix

The term **marketing mix** refers to a unique blend of product, place (distribution), promotion, and pricing strategies (often referred to as the **four Ps**) designed to produce mutually satisfying exchanges with a target market. The marketing manager can control each component of the marketing mix, but the strategies for all four components must be blended to achieve optimal results. Any marketing mix is only as good as its weakest component. For example, the first pump toothpastes were distributed over cosmetic counters and failed. Not until pump toothpastes were distributed the same way as tube toothpastes did the products succeed. The best promotion and the lowest price cannot save a poor product. Similarly, excellent products with poor placing, pricing, or promotion will likely fail.

Successful marketing mixes have been carefully designed to satisfy target markets. At first glance, McDonald's and Wendy's may appear to have roughly identical marketing mixes because they are both in the fast-food hamburger business. However, McDonald's has been most successful at targeting parents with young children for lunchtime meals, whereas Wendy's targets the adult crowd for lunches and dinner. McDonald's has playgrounds, Ronald McDonald the clown, and children's Happy Meals. Wendy's has salad bars, carpeted restaurants, and no playgrounds.

Variations in marketing mixes do not occur by chance. Astute marketing managers devise marketing strategies to gain advantages over competitors and best serve the needs and wants of a particular target market segment. By manipulating elements of the marketing mix, marketing managers can fine-tune the customer offering and achieve competitive success.

Product Strategies

Typically, the marketing mix starts with the product "P." The heart of the marketing mix, the starting point, is the product offering and product strategy. It is hard to design a place strategy, decide on a promotion campaign, or set a price without knowing the product to be marketed.

The product includes not only the physical unit but also its package, warranty, after-sale service, brand name, company image, value, and many other factors. A Godiva chocolate has many product elements: the chocolate itself, a fancy gold wrapper, a customer satisfaction guarantee, and the prestige of the Godiva brand name. We buy things not only for what they do (benefits) but also for what they mean to us (status, quality, or reputation).

Products can be tangible goods such as computers, ideas like those offered by a consultant, or services such as medical care. Products should also offer customer value. Product decisions are covered in Chapters 10 and 11, and services marketing is detailed in Chapter 12.

Place (Distribution) Strategies

Place, or distribution, strategies are concerned with making products available when and where customers want them. Would you rather buy a kiwi fruit at the 24-hour grocery store within walking distance or fly to Australia to pick your own? A part of this place "P"

is physical distribution, which involves all the business activities concerned with storing and transporting raw materials or finished products. The goal is to make sure products arrive in usable condition at designated places when needed. Place strategies are covered in Chapters 14 and 15.

Promotion Strategies

Promotion includes advertising, public relations, sales promotion, and personal selling. Promotion's role in the marketing mix is to bring about mutually satisfying exchanges with target markets by informing, educating, persuading, and reminding them of the benefits of an organization or a product. A good promotion strategy, like using the Dilbert character in a national promotion strategy for Office Depot, can dramatically increase sales. Each element of the promotion "P" is coordinated and managed with the others to create a promotional blend or mix. These integrated

This beef ad informs customers that beef is considered lean by the USDA.

© COURTESY OF THE BEEF CHECKOFF PROGRAM

marketing communications activities are described in Chapters 16, 17, and 18. Technology-driven aspects of promotional marketing are covered in Chapter 21.

Pricing Strategies

Price is what a buyer must give up to obtain a product. It is often the most flexible of the four marketing mix elements—the quickest element to change. Marketers can raise or lower prices more frequently and easily than they can change other marketing mix variables. Price is an important competitive weapon and is very important to the organization because price multiplied by the number of units sold equals total revenue for the firm. Pricing decisions are covered in Chapters 19 and 20.

LO 9 Following Up on the Marketing Plan

Implementation

Implementation is the process that turns a marketing plan into action assignments and ensures that these assignments are executed in a way that accomplishes the plan's objectives. Implementation activities may involve detailed job assignments, activity descriptions, timelines, budgets, and lots of communication. Although implementation is essentially "doing what you said you were going to do," many organizations repeatedly experience failures in strategy implementation. Brilliant marketing plans are doomed to fail if they are not properly implemented. These detailed communications may or may not be part of the written marketing plan. If they are not part of the plan, they should be specified elsewhere as soon as the plan has been communicated.

implementation the process that turns a marketing plan into action assignments and ensures that these assignments are executed in a way that accomplishes the plan's objectives

evaluation gauging the extent to which the marketing objectives have been achieved during the specified time period

control provides the mechanisms for evaluating marketing results in light of the plan's objectives and for correcting actions that do not help the organization reach those objectives within budget guidelines

marketing audit a thorough, systematic, periodic evaluation of the objectives, strategies, structure, and performance of the marketing organization

Evaluation and Control

After a marketing plan is implemented, it should be evaluated. **Evaluation** entails gauging the extent to which marketing objectives have been achieved during the specified time period. Four common reasons for failing to achieve a marketing objective are unrealistic marketing objectives, inappropriate marketing strategies in the plan, poor implementation, and changes in the environment after the objective was specified and the strategy was implemented.

Once a plan is chosen and implemented, its effectiveness must be monitored. **Control** provides the mechanisms for evaluating marketing results in light of the plan's objectives and for correcting actions that do not help the organization reach those objectives within budget guidelines. Firms need to establish formal and informal control programs to make the entire operation more efficient.

Perhaps the broadest control device available to marketing managers is the **marketing audit**—a thorough, systematic, periodic evaluation of the objectives, strategies, structure, and performance of the marketing organization. A marketing audit helps management allocate marketing resources efficiently.

4 CHARACTERISTICS OF A MARKETING AUDIT:

▸▸ *Comprehensive:* The marketing audit covers all the major marketing issues facing an organization and not just trouble spots.

▸▸ *Systematic:* The marketing audit takes place in an orderly sequence and covers the organization's marketing environment, internal marketing system, and specific marketing activities. The diagnosis is followed by an action plan with both short-run and long-run proposals for improving overall marketing effectiveness.

▸▸ *Independent:* The marketing audit is normally conducted by an inside or outside party who is independent enough to have top management's confidence and to be objective.

▸▸ *Periodic:* The marketing audit should be carried out on a regular schedule instead of only in a crisis. Whether it seems successful or is in deep trouble, any organization can benefit greatly from such an audit.

Although the main purpose of the marketing audit is to develop a full profile of the organization's marketing effort and to provide a basis for developing and revising the marketing plan, it is also an excellent way to improve communication and raise the level of marketing consciousness within the organization. It is a useful vehicle for selling the philosophy and techniques of strategic marketing to other members of the organization.

BROUGHT TO YOU BY "DRINKING" AND "SMOKING"

© ISTOCKPHOTO.COM/FABIAN GUIGNARD

Indian law prohibits companies from advertising tobacco and liquor. However, companies that sell these products are among the largest advertisers in the country. They accomplish this by using what are known as "surrogate advertisements," which instead of featuring cigarettes and alcoholic beverages, focus on unrelated products, such as CDs, playing cards, and bottled water that all have the same brand name as the companies' spirits and smokes.

Government actions against surrogate ads are causing the liquor and tobacco companies to use sponsorships of sporting events, concerts, and other entertainment venues as an alternative to promoting their products. For example, the chairman of Royal Challenge whiskey bought a professional cricket team and named it "Royal Challengers." The colors and logos of the team are the same as those of the whiskey brand. Surrogate ads and sponsorships have been blamed for luring more of India's young people (10–14 years old) to take up smoking. One study showed that current use of tobacco was five times lower among students who had not watched surrogate promotions.[10]

What do you think? Is it ethical for India's tobacco and liquor companies to use surrogate advertising to get their brand names in front of customers?

LO10 Effective Strategic Planning

Effective strategic planning requires continual attention, creativity, and management commitment. Strategic planning should not be an annual exercise, in which managers go through the motions and forget about strategic planning until the next year. It should be an ongoing process because the environment is continually changing and the firm's resources and capabilities are continually evolving.

Sound strategic planning is based on creativity. Managers should challenge assumptions about the firm and the environment and establish new strategies. For example, major oil companies developed the concept of the gasoline service station in an age when cars needed frequent and rather elaborate servicing. They held on to the full-service approach, but independents were quick to respond to new realities and moved to lower-cost self-service and convenience-store operations. The majors took several decades to catch up.

Perhaps the most critical element in successful strategic planning is top management's support and participation. For example, Michael Anthony, CEO of Brookstone, Inc., and the Brookstone buying team earn hundreds of thousands of frequent flyer miles searching the world for manufacturers and inventors of unique products that can be carried in its retail stores, catalogs, and Internet site. Anthony has codeveloped some of these products and has also been active in remodeling efforts for Brookstone's 250 permanent and seasonal stores.

4
Quadrants in the portfolio matrix

20%
Dupont's cost advantage

3
Types of competitive advantage

6
Macroenvironmental forces affecting marketing

14–29
Target ages of Ralph Lauren's Rugby line, diversifying the brand

STUDY TOOLS
CHAPTER 2

Located at back of the textbook

❑ **Rip out Chapter Review Card**

Located at 4ltrpress.cengage.com/mktg

❑ **Review Key Terms Flash Cards (Print or Online)**

❑ **Download Audio and Visual Summaries for on-the-go review**

❑ **Complete both Practice Quizzes to prepare for tests**

❑ **Play "Beat the Clock" and "Quizbowl" to master concepts**

❑ **Complete "Crossword Puzzle" to review key terms**

❑ **Watch the video on "Method" for a real company example on Strategic Planning for Competitive Advantage**

CHAPTER **3** **Ethics and Social Responsibility**

"If you have ever resented a line-cutter, then you understand ethics and have applied ethical standards in life."

LO 1 The Concept of Ethical Behavior

AFTER YOU FINISH THIS CHAPTER GO TO PAGE 36 FOR STUDY TOOLS

It has been said that ethics is something everyone likes to talk about but nobody knows exactly what it is. Others have noted that "defining ethics is like trying to nail Jello to the wall. You begin to think that you understand it, but that's when it starts squirting out between your fingers."

ethics the moral principles or values that generally govern the conduct of an individual or a group

Ethics refers to the moral principles or values that generally govern the conduct of an individual or a group. Ethics also can be viewed as the standard of behavior by which conduct is judged. Standards that are legal may not always be ethical, and vice versa. Laws are the values and standards enforceable by the courts. Ethics, then, consists of personal moral principles. For example, there is no legal statute that makes it a crime for someone to "cut in line." Yet, if someone doesn't want to wait in line and cuts to the front, it often makes others very angry.

If you have ever resented a line-cutter, then you understand ethics and have applied ethical standards in life. Waiting your turn in line is a social expectation that exists because lines ensure order and allocate the space and time needed to complete transactions. Waiting your turn is an expected but unwritten behavior that plays a critical role in an orderly society.[1]

So it is with ethics. Ethics consists of those unwritten rules we have developed for our interactions with each other. These unwritten rules govern us when we are sharing resources or honoring contracts. "Waiting your turn" is a higher standard than the laws that are passed to maintain order. Those laws apply when physical

What do you think?

Businesses need to focus on helping people.

1   2   3   4   5   6   7

STRONGLY DISAGREE   STRONGLY AGREE

Find out what others think at 4ltrpress.cengage.com/mktg

force or threats are used to push to the front of the line. Assault, battery, and threats are forms of criminal conduct for which the offender can be prosecuted. But the law does not apply to the stealth line-cutter who simply sneaks to the front, perhaps using a friend and a conversation as a decoy for edging into the front. No laws are broken, but the notions of fairness and justice are offended by one individual putting himself above others and taking advantage of others' time and position.

Ethical questions range from practical, narrowly defined issues, such as a business person's obligation to be honest with his customers, to broader social and philosophical questions, such as a company's responsibility to preserve the environment and protect employee rights. Many ethical conflicts develop from conflicts between the differing interests of company owners and their workers, customers, and surrounding community. Managers must balance the ideal against the practical—the need to produce a reasonable profit for the company's shareholders with honesty in business practices, and larger environmental and social issues.

LO 2 Ethical Behavior in Business

Morals are the rules people develop as a result of cultural values and norms. Culture is a socializing force that dictates what is right and wrong. Moral standards may also reflect the laws and regulations that affect social and economic behavior. Thus, morals can be considered a foundation of ethical behavior.

Morals are usually characterized as good or bad. "Good" and "bad" have different connotations, including "effective" and "ineffective." A good salesperson makes or exceeds the assigned quota. If the salesperson sells a new stereo or television set to a disadvantaged consumer—knowing full well that the person can't keep up the monthly payments—is the

salesperson still a good one? What if the sale enables the salesperson to exceed his or her quota?

"Good" and "bad" can also refer to "conforming" and "deviant" behaviors. A doctor who runs large ads offering discounts on open-heart surgery would be considered bad, or unprofessional, in the sense of not conforming to the norms of the medical profession. "Bad" and "good" are also used to express the distinction between criminal and law-abiding behavior. And finally, different religions define "good" and "bad" in markedly different ways. A Muslim who eats pork would be considered bad, as would a fundamentalist Christian who drinks whiskey.

Morality and Business Ethics

Today's business ethics actually consist of a subset of major life values learned since birth. The values businesspeople use to make decisions have been acquired through family, educational, and religious institutions.

Ethical values are situation specific and time oriented. Nevertheless, everyone must have an ethical base that applies to conduct in the business world and in personal life. One approach to developing a personal set of ethics is to examine the consequences of a particular act. Who is helped or hurt? How long lasting are the consequences? What actions produce the greatest good for the greatest number of people? A second approach stresses the importance of rules. Rules come in the form of customs, laws, professional standards, and common sense. "Always treat others as you would like to be treated" is an example of a rule.

The last approach emphasizes the development of moral character within individuals. Ethical development can be thought of as having three levels:[2]

▸▸ *Preconventional morality*, the most basic level, is childlike. It is calculating, self-centered, and even selfish, based on what will be immediately punished or rewarded.

▸▸ *Conventional morality* moves from an egocentric viewpoint toward the expectations of society. Loyalty and obedience to the organization (or society) become paramount. A marketing decision maker would be concerned only with whether the proposed action is legal and how it will be viewed by others.

▸ *Postconventional morality* represents the morality of the mature adult. At this level, people are less concerned about how others might see them and more concerned about how they see and judge themselves over the long run. A marketing decision maker who has attained a postconventional level of morality might ask, "Even though it is legal and will increase company profits, is it right in the long run?"

ETHICAL DECISION MAKING

There is rarely a cut-and-dried answer to ethical questions. Studies show that the following factors tend to influence ethical decision making and judgments:[3]

▸ *Extent of ethical problems within the organization*: The healthier the ethical environment, the more likely that marketers will take a strong stand against questionable practices.

▸ *Top-management actions on ethics*: Top managers can influence the behavior of marketing professionals by encouraging ethical behavior and discouraging unethical behavior.

▸ *Potential magnitude of the consequences*: The greater the harm done to victims, the more likely that marketing professionals will recognize a problem as unethical.

▸ *Social consensus*: The greater the degree of agreement among managerial peers that an action is harmful, the more likely that marketers will recognize a problem as unethical.

▸ *Probability of a harmful outcome*: The greater the likelihood that an action will result in a harmful outcome, the more likely that marketers will recognize a problem as unethical.

▸ *Length of time between the decision and the onset of consequences*: The shorter the length of time between the action and the onset of negative consequences, the more likely that marketers will perceive a problem as unethical.

▸ *Number of people to be affected*: The greater the number of persons affected by a negative outcome, the more likely that marketers will recognize a problem as unethical.

Ethical Guidelines

Many organizations have become more interested in ethical issues. One sign of this interest is the increase in the number of large companies that appoint ethics officers—from virtually none several years ago to almost 33 percent of large corporations now. In addition, many companies of various sizes have developed a **code of ethics** as a guideline to help marketing managers and other employees make better decisions. Creating ethics guidelines has several advantages:

▸ The guidelines help employees identify what their firm recognizes as acceptable business practices.

▸ A code of ethics can be an effective internal control on behavior, which is more desirable than external controls like government regulation.

▸ A written code helps employees avoid confusion when determining whether their decisions are ethical.

▸ The process of formulating the code of ethics facilitates discussion among employees about what is right and wrong and ultimately leads to better decisions.

Businesses, however, must be careful not to make their code of ethics too vague or too detailed. Codes that are too vague give little or no guidance to employees in their day-to-day activities. Codes that are too detailed encourage employees to substitute rules for judgment. For instance, if employees are involved in questionable behavior, they may use the absence of a written rule as a reason to continue behaving that way, even though their conscience may be saying no. Following a set of ethical guidelines will not guarantee the "rightness" of a decision, but it will improve the chances that the decision will be ethical.

Although many companies have issued policies on ethical behavior, marketing managers must still put the policies into effect. They must address the classic "matter of degree" issue. For example, marketing researchers must often resort to deception to obtain unbiased answers to their research questions. Asking for a few minutes of a respondent's time is

code of ethics a guideline to help marketing managers and other employees make better decisions

It is in business's interest to find ways to attack society's ills and lend a helping hand.

dishonest if the researcher knows the interview will last 45 minutes. Not only must management post a code of ethics, but it must also give examples of what is ethical and unethical for each item in the code. Moreover, top management must stress to all employees the importance of adhering to the company's code of ethics. Without a detailed code of ethics and top management's support, creating ethical guidelines becomes an empty exercise. The American Marketing Association's code of ethics highlights three general norms and six ethical values.

Ethics training is an excellent way to help employees put good ethics into practice. According to the Ethics Resource Center's National Business Ethics Survey, 75 percent of employees across the United States reported in 2007 that they had received training in ethics or compliance. Clients of one ethics training consultancy, LRN, complete approximately 20,000 courses in ethics and compliance *per day*.[4]

LO 3 Corporate Social Responsibility

Corporate social responsibility is a business's concern for society's welfare. This concern is demonstrated by managers who consider both the long-range best interests of the company and the company's relationship to the society within which it operates. The newest theory in social responsibility is called **sustainability**. This refers to the idea that socially responsible companies will outperform their peers by focusing on the world's social problems and viewing them as opportunities to build profits and help the world at the same time. It is also the notion that companies cannot thrive for long (i.e., lack sustainability) in a world where billions of people are suffering and are desperately poor. Thus, it is in business's interest to find ways to attack society's ills.

Another view is that business should focus on making a profit and leave social and environmental problems to nonprofit organizations and government. Economist Milton Friedman believed that the free market, and not companies, should decide what is best for the world.[5] Friedman argued that to the degree that business executives spend more money than they need to—to purchase delivery vehicles with hybrid engines, pay higher wages in developing countries, or even donate company funds to charity—they are spending shareholders' money to further their own agendas. Better to pay dividends and let the shareholders give the money away, if they choose.

Total corporate social responsibility has four components: economic, legal, ethical, and philanthropic.[6] The **pyramid of corporate social responsibility** portrays economic performance as the foundation for the other three responsibilities. At the same time that it pursues profits (economic responsibility), however, a business is expected to obey the law (legal responsibility); to do what is right, just, and fair (ethical responsibilities); and to be a good corporate citizen (philanthropic responsi-

WILL CONSUMERS PAY MORE FOR ETHICAL PRODUCTS?

Researchers conducted

a series of experiments where they showed consumers the same products—coffee and T-shirts—but told one group the items had been made using high ethical standards. They told another group that low standards had been used. A control group got no information. In all of the tests, consumers were willing to pay more for the ethically made goods, but would only buy unethically made products at a steep discount. What's more, consumer attitudes played a big part in shaping those results. People with high standards for corporate behavior rewarded the ethical companies with bigger premiums and punished the unethical ones with bigger discounts.[7]

bility). These four components are distinct but together constitute the whole. Still, if the company doesn't make a profit, then the other three responsibilities are moot.

Growth of Social Responsibility

Social responsibility of businesses is growing around the world. A recent study of social responsibility, in selected countries, asked the following: "Does your company consider social responsibility factors when making business decisions?" The percentage of firms that said "yes" were: Brazil, 62 percent; Canada, 54 percent; Australia, 52 percent; the United States, 47 percent; India, 38 percent; China, 35 percent; Mexico, 26 percent.[8]

Another survey pointed out that 47 percent of American firms was simply not adequate. Seventy-five percent felt that U.S. companies needed to do more in the area of social responsibility.[9]

One way that U.S. firms can do more is by joining the United Nations Global Compact. The United Nations Global Compact, the world's largest global corporate citizenship initiative, has seen its ranks swell over the past few years. In 2001—the first full year after its launch—just sixty-seven companies joined, agreeing to abide by ten principles covering, among other things, human rights, labor practices, and the environment. In 2008, there were more than 5,600 participants in 120 countries around the world.[10]

Firms are realizing that corporate social responsibility isn't easy or quick. It doesn't work without long-term strategy and effort, and coordination throughout the enterprise. It doesn't always come cheap, either. And the payoff, both to society and the business itself, isn't always immediate. Businesses say they want to be responsible citizens, but that's often not their only reason for taking action. In a recent survey, the United Nations Global Compact asked members why they had joined. "Networking opportunities" was the second-most-popular reason; "Addressing humanitarian concerns" was third. The first was to "Increase trust in company."[11]

The Cost of Ignoring Social Responsibilities[12]

In today's environment, a firm that disregards its stakeholders and its social responsibilities does so at its own

peril. In the case of AOL, it didn't treat its customers (key stakeholders) as they should have been treated. A deluge of AOL customers complained that they tried to close their accounts only to be thwarted in their attempts or to discover they were still being billed for services that they thought had been canceled. All cancellation requests had to be made by fax, mail or telephone. Subscribers who phoned AOL to cancel their service sometimes were greeted by aggressive customer service representatives who were paid bonuses of up to $3,000 if they found a way to retain the business. Customers complained that AOL's incentive system created an obstructive culture that made service cancellations difficult. "Consumers who called were put on hold or transferred repeatedly until they hung up in disgust," says Connecticut Attorney General Richard Blumenthal, who described AOL's practices as "outlandish and underhanded."

These customer complaints led to a $3 million settlement with 48 states and the District of Columbia. As part of the resolution, AOL agreed to make it easier for its remaining customers to leave and to maintain an online channel for processing cancellations.

Green Marketing

An outgrowth of the social responsibility movement is green marketing. **Green marketing** is the development and marketing of products designed to minimize negative effects on the physical environment or to improve the environment.[13] Not only can a company aid the environment through green marketing, but it often helps their bottom line as well. Environmentally aware consumers tend to earn more and are willing to pay more for green products.[14] The problem, however, is that only a very small percentage of customers make their buying decisions based primarily on the environmental qualities of the product.[15] Also, it may not be readily apparent how one product is better for the environment than another. Thus, the marketer may have to educate the consumer about the green product. To make the sale, the green marketer may even use a

green marketing
the development and marketing of products designed to minimize negative effects on the physical environment or to improve the environment

© ISTOCKPHOTO.COM/NATASHA JAPP

WHAT GOOD WORKS CAN DO

De Beers has controlled Botswana's GDP for years, but the company has also helped raise the poverty-stricken country into prosperity. De Beers paired with the country's government to begin mining diamonds and sold the government a 15 percent stake in the company. Most of the executives in the government-company venture are black Africans trained by De Beers. In 2008, the company opened the largest, most technologically advanced diamond sorting complex in the world in Gaborone, employing 600 people.

It is a symbiotic relationship: Botswana's citizens need roads, as does De Beers, so De Beers builds roads and infrastructure; De Beers needs a healthy workforce, so it emphasizes HIV awareness and treatment; and a prosperous government gives De Beers a stable environment in which to do business. [16]

traditional non-green benefit. For example, General Electric energy-efficient CFL floodlights are good for the environment. The promotion theme is "Long life for hard to reach places." GE is selling convenience because the floodlight doesn't need replacing as often. [17]

Some green products have practical consumer benefits that are readily apparent to consumers. A few examples are: energy-efficient washing machines and other appliances (cut electric bills), heat-reflective windows (cut air-conditioning costs), and organic foods (no pesticides poisoning the food or planet). Each Dole organic banana has a sticker with a number. If you enter that number at doleorganic.com, a Google Earth application will show you the exact place the fruit was grown. [18]

STUDY TOOLS
CHAPTER 3

Located at back of the textbook

❏ **Rip out Chapter Review Card**

Located at 4lrpress.cengage.com/mktg

❏ **Review Key Terms Flash Cards (Print or Online)**

❏ **Download Audio and Visual Summaries for on-the-go review**

❏ **Complete both Practice Quizzes to prepare for tests**

❏ **Play "Beat the Clock" and "Quizbowl" to master concepts**

❏ **Complete "Crossword Puzzle" to review key terms**

❏ **Watch the video on "Method" for a real company example on Social Responsibility, Ethics, and the Marketing Environment**

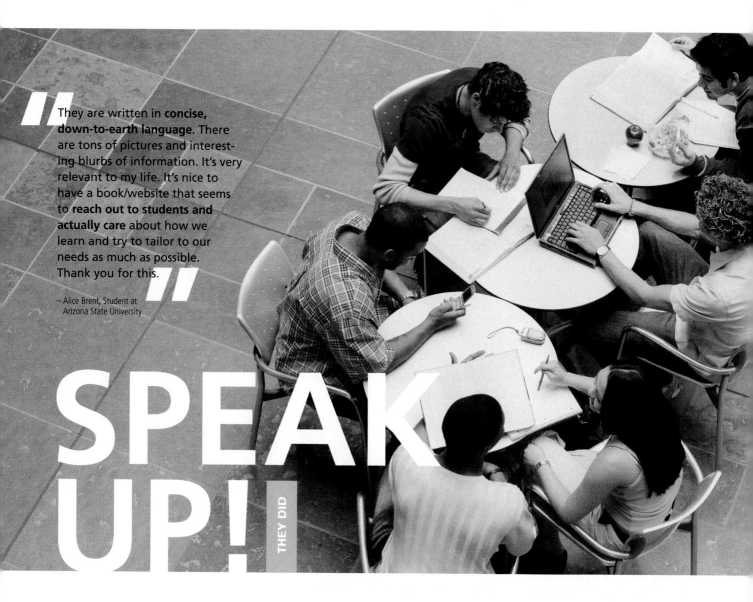

They are written in **concise, down-to-earth language.** There are tons of pictures and interesting blurbs of information. It's very relevant to my life. It's nice to have a book/website that seems to **reach out to students and actually care** about how we learn and try to tailor to our needs as much as possible. Thank you for this.

— Alice Brent, Student at Arizona State University

SPEAK UP! THEY DID

MKTG4 was built on a simple principle: to create a new teaching and learning solution that reflects the way today's faculty teach and the way you learn.

Through conversations, focus groups, surveys, and interviews, we collected data that drove the creation of the current version of MKTG4 that you are using today. But it doesn't stop there – in order to make MKTG4 an even better learning experience, we'd like you to SPEAK UP and tell us how MKTG4 worked for you.

What did you like about it?
What would you change?
Are there additional ideas you have that would help us build a better product for next semester's principles of marketing students?

At **4ltrpress.cengage.com** you'll find all of the resources you need to succeed in principles of marketing – **video podcasts**, **audio downloads**, **flash cards**, **interactive quizzes**, and more!

Speak Up! Go to **4ltrpress.cengage.com**.

The Marketing Environment

"Although managers can control the marketing mix, they cannot control elements in the external environment."

LO 1 The External Marketing Environment

AFTER YOU FINISH THIS CHAPTER GO TO PAGE 51 FOR STUDY TOOLS

Perhaps the most important decisions a marketing manager must make relate to the creation of the marketing mix. Recall from Chapters 1 and 2 that a marketing mix is the unique combination of product, place (distribution), promotion, and price strategies. The marketing mix is, of course, under the firm's control and is designed to appeal to a specific group of potential buyers. A **target market** is a defined group that managers feel is most likely to buy a firm's product.

Over time, managers must alter the marketing mix because of changes in the environment in which consumers live, work, and make purchasing decisions. Also, as markets mature, some new consumers become part of the target market; others drop out. Those who remain may have different tastes, needs, incomes, lifestyles, and buying habits than the original target consumers.

Although managers can control the marketing mix, they cannot control elements in the external environment that continually mold and reshape the target market. Controllable and uncontrollable variables affect the target market, whether it consists of consumers or business purchasers. The uncontrollable elements of the environment continually evolve and create changes in the target market. In

target market a defined group most likely to buy a firm's product

What do you think?

Marketing has to change according to what people care about, or it doesn't work.

1 2 3 4 5 6 7
STRONGLY DISAGREE   STRONGLY AGREE

Find out what others think at 4ltrpress.cengage.com/mktg 39

© ISTOCKPHOTO.COM/MANFRED STEINBACH

environmental management when a company implements strategies that attempt to shape the external environment within which it operates

contrast, managers can shape and reshape the marketing mix to influence the target market. That is, managers react to changes in the external environment and attempt to create a more effective marketing mix.

Understanding the External Environment

Unless marketing managers understand the external environment, the firm cannot intelligently plan for the future. Thus, many organizations assemble a team of specialists to continually collect and evaluate environmental information, a process called *environmental scanning*. The goal in gathering the environmental data is to identify future market opportunities and threats.

Environmental Management

No one business is large or powerful enough to create major change in the external environment. Marketing managers, therefore, are basically adapters rather than agents of change. A firm is not always completely at the mercy of the external environment, however. Sometimes a firm can influence external events, for example, through extensive lobbying. When a company implements strategies that attempt to shape the external environment within which it operates, it is engaging in **environmental management**.

The factors within the external environment that are important to marketing managers can be classi-

fied as social, demographic, economic, technological, political and legal, and competitive.

LO 2 Social Factors

Social change is perhaps the most difficult external variable for marketing managers to forecast, influence, or integrate into marketing plans. Social factors include attitudes, values, and lifestyles. Social factors influence the products people buy, the prices paid for products, the effectiveness of specific promotions, and how, where, and when people expect to purchase products.

American Values

A *value* is a strongly held and enduring belief. During the first 200 years in the United States, four basic values strongly influenced attitudes and lifestyles:

▸▸ *Self-sufficiency*: Every person should stand on his or her own two feet.

▸▸ *Upward mobility*: Success would come to anyone who got an education, worked hard, and played by the rules.

▸▸ *Work ethic*: Hard work, dedication to family, and frugality were moral and right.

▸▸ *Conformity*: No one should expect to be treated differently from everybody else.

These core values still hold for a majority of Americans today. A person's values are key determinants of what is important and not important, what actions

UNDERSTANDING COMPETITION

During the economic downturn of 2007–2009, T.J. Maxx, the off-price retailer, noted that competitors were taking 60–90 days to pay their vendors. T.J. Maxx had the cash and decided to pay within 30 days. This caused the big name fashion brands to flock to the retailer. Now, TJX, which owns T.J. Maxx, Marshall's and Home Goods, has a better assortment of well-known brands to sell in its stores. For the first time, T.J. Maxx is selling items like True Religion jeans for $99 (regularly $160) and Bottega Veneta sweaters for $149 (normally $750). Sales, market share, and profit are up for TJX.[1]

to take or not to take, and how one behaves in social situations.

A person's values are typically formed through interaction with family, friends, and other influencers such as teachers, religious leaders, and politicians. The changing environment can also play a key role in shaping one's values.

Values also influence our buying habits. Today's consumers are demanding, inquisitive, and discriminating. No longer willing to tolerate products that break down, they are insisting on high-quality goods that save time, energy, and often calories. U.S. consumers rank the characteristics of product quality as (1) reliability, (2) durability, (3) easy maintenance, (4) ease of use, (5) a trusted brand name, and (6) a low price. Shoppers are also concerned about nutrition and want to know what's in their food, and many have environmental concerns.

The Growth of Component Lifestyles

People in the United States today are piecing together **component lifestyles**. A lifestyle is a mode of living; it is the way people decide to live their lives. In other words, they are choosing products and services that meet diverse needs and interests rather than conforming to traditional stereotypes.

In the past, a person's profession—for instance, banker—defined his or her lifestyle. Today, a person can be a banker and also a gourmand, fitness enthusiast, dedicated single parent, and Internet guru. Each of these lifestyles is associated with different goods and services and represents a target audience. Component lifestyles increase the complexity of consumers' buying habits. The unique lifestyles of every consumer can require a different marketing mix.

The Changing Role of Families and Working Women

Marriage is a declining institution in America. In the 1950s, the likelihood that someone would marry during his or her lifetime was 95 percent. Today, it's only 85 percent.[2] In the 1950s, 80 percent of all households included a married couple, whereas that figure is just above 50 percent today. The traditional American family of two adults with kids at home represents less than 25 percent of U.S. households for the first time ever and is projected to drop to 20 percent by 2010.[3]

The shift has been to single households, which now outnumber married households with kids.

Already, single people account for 42 percent of the workforce, 40 percent of home buyers, and 35 percent of voters. Single working women are now the second largest group of home buyers after couples. The percentage of children living in mother-only families has increased since 1970 from 11 percent to 24 percent in 1997, and was 23 percent in 2006.[4]

Another significant change in American families is the growth of dual-income families, which has resulted in increased purchasing power. Approximately 60 percent of all females over 16 years old are now in the workforce. Today, nearly 10.4 million women-owned firms in the United States generate $3.6 trillion in sales.[5] The phenomenon of working women has probably had a greater effect on marketing than has any other social change.

As women spend more time in the workplace, they are relying on the Internet to save time gathering information and shopping.[6] Mothers, in particular, have embraced the Internet as a shopping tool. A study by America Online (AOL) shows that 80 percent of mothers in the United States who are online save time every week by using the Internet to do chores, plan trips, research products, find health information, and look for coupons. Overall, mothers who use the Internet spend an average of seven hours per week online, not including at-work usage.[7]

LO 3 Demographic Factors

Another uncontrollable variable in the external environment—also extremely important to marketing managers—is **demography**, the study of people's vital

component lifestyles the practice of choosing goods and services that meet one's diverse needs and interests rather than conforming to a single, traditional lifestyle

demography the study of people's vital statistics, such as their age, race and ethnicity, and location

statistics, such as their age, race and ethnicity, and location. Demographics are significant because the basis for any market is people. Demographic characteristics are strongly related to consumer buyer behavior in the marketplace.

We turn our attention now to a closer look at age groups, their impact, and the opportunities they present for marketers. Why does tailoring the merchandise to particular age groups matter? One reason is that each generation enters a life stage with its own tastes and biases, and tailoring products to what customers value is key to sales. The cohorts have been given the names of tweens, Generation Y, Generation X, and baby boomers. You will find that each cohort group has its own needs, values, and consumption patterns.

Tweens

America's tweens, today's pre- and early-adolescents (ages 8 to 14), are a population 29 million strong. With attitudes, access to information, and sophistication well beyond their years (and purchasing power to match), each of these young consumers will spend an average of $1,500 per year, for an aggregate total of $39 billion annually. Add to this the nearly $150 billion parents will spend on their tweens this year, and one grasps the importance and potential of this market.

Tweens overwhelmingly (92 percent) recognize television commercials for what they are—"just advertising."[8] But even though tweens have a generally positive attitude toward advertising, a majority of the tweens surveyed (52 percent) said they tune out during television commercials, mainly because the commercials are repeats or are "boring."[9]

Generation Y

Those designated by demographics as **Generation Y** were born between 1979 and 1994. They are about 60 million strong, one and a half times as large as Generation X. And though Generation Y is much smaller than the baby boom, which lasted nearly 20 years and produced 78 million children, its members are plentiful enough to put their own footprints on society. Most Gen Yers are the children of baby boomers and sometimes referred to as "echo boomers."

Gen Yers range from college graduates to kids in their teenage years. They already spend nearly $200 billion annually and over their lifetimes will likely spend about $10 trillion.[10] Some have already started their careers and are making major purchasing decisions such as cars and homes; at the very least, they are buying lots of computers, MP3 players, cell phones, DVDs, and sneakers.

Researchers have found Gen Yers to be:

»» *Impatient.* Because they have grown up in a world that has always been automated, it's no surprise that they expect things to be done *now*.

»» *Family-Oriented.* Gen Yers had relatively stable childhoods and grew up in a very family-focused time, so they tend to have a stronger family orientation than the generation that preceded them.

»» *Inquisitive.* Gen Yers tend to be inquisitive, wanting to know the reasons why things happen, how things work, and what they can do next.

»» *Opinionated.* Today's youth have been encouraged by their parents, teachers, and other authority figures to share their opinions. As a result, Gen Yers feel that their opinions are always needed and welcomed.

»» *Diverse.* Gen Y is the most ethnically diverse generation the nation has ever seen, so they're much more accepting overall of people who are different from themselves.

»» *Good time managers.* Their entire lives have been scheduled, from playgroups to soccer camp to Little League, so they've picked up a knack for planning along the way.

»» *Street smart.* Having been exposed to the Internet and 24-hour cable TV news at a young age, Gen Yers are not easily shocked. They're much more aware of the world around them than earlier generations were.[11]

»» *Connected.* Fifty-four percent use social networking sites such as MySpace or Facebook and 44 percent have created profiles featuring photos, hobbies, and interests.[12]

Generation X

Generation X—people born between 1965 and 1978—consists of 40 million consumers. It is the first generation of latchkey children—products of dual-career households or, in roughly half of the cases, of divorced or separated parents. Gen Xers have been bombarded by multiple media since their cradle days; thus, they are savvy and cynical consumers.

With careers launched and families started, Gen Xers are at the stage in life when suddenly a host of demands are competing for their time—and their budgets. As a result, Gen X spending is quite diffuse: food, housing, transportation. Time is at a premium for harried Gen Xers, so they're outsourcing the tasks of daily life, which include everything from domestic help to babysitting. Many Gen Xers work from home.

Over the next 10 years, most Gen Xers will cross over into their 40s, historically individuals' money-making years. Over the past 30 years, people ages 45 to 54 earned 60 percent more on average than any other age group. Although Gen Xers are making and spending money, companies still tend to ignore them, focusing instead on the larger demographic groups—baby boomers and Gen Y.

Baby Boomers— America's Mass Market

Baby boomers make up the largest demographic segment of today's U.S. population. There are 77 million **baby boomers** (people born between 1946 and 1964). The average head of household in the United States is 49.5 years old. For the next five years, one million boomers will join the 65-and-over consumer segment each year.[13] With average life expectancy at an all-time high of 77.4 years, more and more Americans over fifty consider middle age a new start on life. Fewer than 20 percent say they expect to stop work altogether as they age. People now in their fifties may well work longer than any previous generation.[14] Many boomers are postponing retirement because the economic downturn from 2007–2009 resulted in a rapid decline of their savings and housing values. It is estimated that boomers lost more than $2 trillion in the 2008 stock market meltdown.[15]

Still, baby boomers are likely to be vigorous consumers in the future, and even though historically,

consumers lock in brand preferences by age 40, today's over-50 crowd is just as likely—and in some cases more likely—as younger generations to try different brands within a product category.[16] In some categories such as cosmetics and electronics, older consumers are even more willing to brand-hop than younger ones.

Americans on the Move

The average U.S. citizen moves every six years—a trend that has implications for marketing. For this reason, researchers have begun tracking cell phone use to trace national and international migration and communication patterns.[17] A large influx of people into an area creates many new opportunities for all types of businesses. Conversely, significant out-migration from a city or town may force many of its businesses to move or close down and markets to dry up. A new migration trend is stretching from the North to the South and West. A belt stretching from North Carolina south to Florida and then west to California is America's region of net in-migration. Over time, cities that lose population, such as Boston, Cleveland, Detroit, Milwaukee, Minneapolis, Philadelphia, and Toledo, could have problems paying for things like health-care services due to a lower tax base. Migration trends also create age segmentation. For instance, New England has an older population (only 20 percent of households in the region have children) while the West has a younger, and more diverse, population (one that includes 24 percent of the nation's children, 42 percent of its Hispanics, and 46 percent of its Asians).[18]

In addition to migration within its borders, the United States experiences immigration from other countries. In fact, immigration accounts for 40 percent of the total population growth in the United States.[19] The six states with the highest levels of immigration from abroad are California, Illinois, Massachusetts, New Jersey, New York, and Texas. The presence of large numbers of immigrants in an area creates a need for markets that cater to their unique needs and desires.

Generation X people born between 1965 and 1978
baby boomers people born between 1946 and 1964

© ISTOCKPHOTO.COM/KIRBY HAMILTON

LO 4 Growing Ethnic Markets

In 2008, Hispanics wielded more than $1 trillion in spending power, African Americans' spending topped $921 billion, and Asian Americans' spending power soared to $526 billion.[20]

Hispanics are America's largest minority group with 14.4 percent of the population, followed by African Americans, who comprise 13.4 percent of the population, and Asian Americans, who make up 4.9 percent of the population.[21] In California, Hawaii, New Mexico, and Texas, minorities account for more than half of the population. The projected U.S. population by race in 2050 is shown in Exhibit 4.1.

Companies across the United States have recognized that diversity can result in bottom-line benefits. More than ever, diversity is emerging as a priority goal for visionary leaders who embrace the incontestable fact that the United States is becoming a truly multicultural society. Smart marketers increasingly are reaching out and tapping these growing markets. Mio.tv is a new bilingual Internet entertainment network where Latinos watch shows and soccer games or call relatives. It sells advertising to marketers based on the time visitors spend viewing certain pages, offering marketers an efficient way to target the large Latino community in the United States.[22]

Marketing to Hispanic Americans

The term *Hispanic* encompasses people of many different backgrounds. Nearly 60 percent of Hispanic Americans are of Mexican descent. The next largest group, Puerto Ricans, make up just under 10 percent of Hispanics. Other groups, including Central Ameri-

A scene director, right, cues actors from the telenovela "La Fea Mas Bella," or "The Prettiest Ugly Girl" in the Televisa studios in Mexico City, Mexico. Televisa telenovelas are wildly popular. In the United States, popular Spanish-language shows often beat their English-language network competitors.

cans, Dominicans, South Americans, and Cubans, account for less than 5 percent of all Hispanics.[23]

Hispanics, especially recent immigrants, often prefer products from their native country. Therefore, many retailers along the southern U.S. border import goods from Mexico. If the brands found in their homeland are not available, Hispanics will choose brands that reflect their native values and culture. Research shows that Hispanics often are not aware of many mainstream U.S. brands. In general, Hispanics tend to be very brand loyal.[24]

The number of TV, radio, and cable channels aimed at Hispanic Americans continues to expand. There are three Spanish-language television networks: Univision, Telemundo, and Galavision, and Spanish-language programming runs on over 800 radio stations. According to Arbitron, each week radio reaches more than 95 percent of all Hispanic Americans over the age of 12, who listen for an average of 22.25 hours.[25] About 68 percent of U.S. Hispanics have home Internet access. Most use the Web to look for information, rather than to play games or hang out in chat rooms.[26]

Marketing to African Americans

Many firms are creating new and different products for the African American market. Several companies owned by African Americans—such as Soft Sheen,

© AP IMAGES/GREGORY BULL

EXHIBIT 4.1
U.S. Population by Race

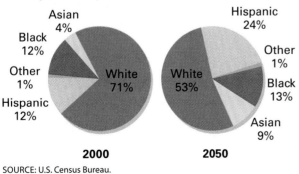

2000: Asian 4%, Black 12%, Other 1%, Hispanic 12%, White 71%

2050: White 53%, Hispanic 24%, Other 1%, Black 13%, Asian 9%

SOURCE: U.S. Census Bureau.

M&M Johnson, and ProLine—target the African American market for health and beauty aids. Huge corporations like Revlon, Gillette, and Alberto-Culver have either divisions or major product lines for this market as well. And never before have there been so many black media choices. ABC Radio Network's Tom Joyner reaches more than 8 million listeners each week in more than 115 markets, and Doug Banks is heard by 1.5 million listeners in 36 markets. BET, the black cable TV network, has more than 76 million subscribers.[27]

Not only are companies designing products and services for the African American market, they are also targeting promotional activities to reach this group of consumers. During Black History Month, Pepsi asked African American students to "Write Your Own History" as part of an essay contest, which awarded ten college tuition scholarships of $10,000 as first prizes, Dell computers as secondary prizes, as well as software and 12-packs of Pepsi.

Marketing to Asian Americans

Asian Americans, who represent only 4.2 percent of the U.S. population, have the highest average family income of all groups. At $66,500, it exceeds the average U.S. household income by more than $10,000. Forty-eight percent of all Asian Americans have at least a bachelor's degree.[28] Because Asian Americans are younger and better educated and have higher incomes than average, they are sometimes called a "marketer's dream." As a group, Asian Americans are more comfortable with technology than the general population is.

A number of products have been developed specifically for the Asian American market. To be successful, marketers must recognize the cultural and linguistic differences that exist among the Chinese American, Filipino, Japanese, Vietnamese, Korean, Indian, and Pakistani markets.[29] Although Asian Americans embrace the values of the larger U.S. population, they also hold on to the cultural values of their particular subgroup. For example, many Asian Americans, particularly Koreans and Chinese, speak their native tongue at home. Filipinos are far less likely to do so. Asian Americans also like to patronize stores owned and managed by other Asian Americans.

Ethnic and Cultural Diversity

Multiculturalism occurs when all major ethnic groups in an area—such as a city, county, or census tract—are roughly equally represented. Because of its cur-rent demographic transition, the trend in the United States is toward greater multiculturalism.

San Francisco County is the most diverse county in the nation. The proportions of major ethnic groups are closer to being equal there than anywhere else. People of many ancestries have long been attracted to the area. Elsewhere, however, a careful examination of the statistics from the latest U.S. Census Bureau reveals that the nation's minority groups, especially Hispanics and Asians, are heavily clustered in selected regions and markets. Rather than witnessing the formation of a homogeneous national melting pot, we are seeing the creation of numerous mini-melting pots, while the rest of America remains much less diverse.

In a broad swath of the country, the minority presence is still quite limited. America's racial and ethnic patterns have taken on distinctly regional dimensions. Hispanics dominate large portions of counties in a span of states stretching from California to Texas. Blacks are strongly represented in counties of the South as well as selected urban areas in the Northeast and Midwest. The Asian presence is relatively small and highly concentrated in a few scattered counties, largely in the West. Native Americans are concentrated in select pockets in Oklahoma, the Southeast, the upper Midwest, and the West. Multiethnic counties are most prominent in California and the Southwest, with mixes of Asians and Hispanics, or Hispanics and Native Americans.

multiculturalism
when all major ethnic groups in an area—such as a city, county, or census tract—are roughly equally represented

LO5 Economic Factors

In addition to social and demographic factors, marketing managers must understand and react to the economic environment. The three economic areas of greatest concern to most marketers are consumers' incomes, inflation, and recession.

Consumers' Incomes and Rising Debt

As disposable (or after-tax) incomes rise, more families and individuals can afford the "good life." After adjustment for inflation, the median household income in the United States in 2008 was approximately $49,000. This means half of all U.S. households earned less and the other half earned more.[30]

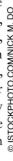

Purchasing Power

Rising incomes don't necessarily mean a higher standard of living. Increased standards of living are a function of purchasing power. **Purchasing power** is measured by comparing income to the relative cost of a set standard of goods and services in different geographic areas, usually referred to as the cost of living. Another way to think of purchasing power is income minus the cost of living (i.e., expenses). In general, a cost-of-living index takes into account housing, food and groceries, transportation, utilities, health care, and miscellaneous expenses such as clothing, services, and entertainment, and so is higher in major urban markets. For example, a worker living in New York must earn nearly $279,500 to have the same standard of living as someone making $90,000 in Youngstown, Ohio.

When income is high relative to the cost of living, people have more discretionary income. That means they have more money to spend on nonessential items (in other words, on wants rather than needs). This information is important to marketers for obvious reasons. Consumers with high purchasing power can afford to spend more money without jeopardizing their budget for necessities, such as food, housing, and utilities. They also have the ability to purchase higher-priced necessities, for example, a more expensive car, a home in a more expensive neighborhood, or a designer handbag versus a purse from a discount store.

Inflation

Inflation is a measure of the decrease in the value of money, generally expressed as the percentage reduction in value since the previous year, which is the rate of inflation. Thus, in simple terms an inflation rate of 5 percent means you will need 5 percent more units of money than you would have needed last year to buy the same basket of products. If inflation is 5 percent, you can expect that, on average, prices have risen about 5 percent over prices in the previous year. Of course if pay raises are matching the rate of inflation, then employees will be no worse off in terms of the immediate purchasing power of their salaries.

Inflation pressures consumers to make more economical purchases and still maintain their standard of living. In creating marketing strategies to cope with inflation, managers must realize that, despite what happens to the seller's cost, the buyer is not going to pay more for a product than the subjective value he or she places on it. No matter how compelling the justification might be for a 10 percent price increase, market-

---

purchasing power
a comparison of income versus the relative cost of a set standard of goods and services in different geographic areas

inflation a measure of the decrease in the value of money, expressed as the percentage reduction in value since the previous year

Education is the primary determinant of a person's earning potential. For example, only 1 percent of those with a high school education earn over $100,000 annually. By comparison, 13 percent of college-educated workers earn six figures or more.[31] Along with "willingness to buy," or "ability to buy," income is a key determinant of target markets. A marketer who knows where the money is knows where the markets are. If you are seeking a new store location for Dollar General, a retail chain that caters to lower-income consumers, you would probably concentrate on the South and Midwest because most households with annual incomes of less than $45,000 are concentrated in these areas.

Twenty-eight percent of Americans say that once they have paid for their essential living expenses, they have no spare cash; by comparison, only 19 percent of Canadian consumers say the same.[32] So, millions of Americans have turned to credit to buy the things they want. Credit gives middle- and lower-income consumers the financial flexibility that only the rich used to enjoy. But credit comes with consequences for individuals and the economy. In 2008, the average household credit card balance reached $8,565 and consumer debt totaled $2.56 trillion.[33] Debt eventually forces consumers to use their income to make interest payments instead of buying more goods and services. Recently, debt has driven many Americans to personal financial ruin, contributing to an overall spending slowdown.

ers must always examine its impact on demand. Many marketers try to hold prices level as long as is practical. (See Chapter 18 for more information on the strategies marketers use during periods of high inflation.)

Recession

A **recession** is a period of economic activity characterized by negative growth. More precisely, a recession is defined as when the gross domestic product falls for two consecutive quarters. *Gross domestic product* is the total market value of all final goods and services produced during a period of time. The National Bureau of Economic Research determined that the most recent recession began in December 2007, and many models predict it will end in late 2009.[34] While the causes of the recession are very complex, it began with the collapse of inflated housing prices. Those high prices led people to take out mortgages they couldn't afford from banks that should have known the money would not be repaid. By 2008, the recession had spread around the globe and financial institutions were forced to rely on government aid to stay afloat.

The declining stock market, growing unemployment, and collapsing home prices have taken a toll on consumer confidence. Many consumers are shifting to store brands which, on average, cost 46 percent less than manufacturers' brands.[35] More consumers are using coupons than ever before.

Some brands that help the consumer save money do very well in a recession. McCormick spices have shown an uptick in sales recently because people are eating out less and cooking more at home. Because people tend to hang on to durable goods longer in a recession, there is a greater demand for repair services, remodeling services, and do-it-yourself products.[36]

LO 6 Technological Factors

Technology is a critical factor in every company's external environment. Our ability, as a nation, to maintain and build wealth depends in large part on the speed and effectiveness with which we invent and adopt machines and technologies that lift productivity. External technology is important to managers for two reasons. First, by acquiring the technology, the firm may be able to operate more efficiently or create a better product. Second, a new technology may render existing products obsolete, as in the case of the traditional film-based camera being replaced by digital camera technology. Staying technologically relevant requires a great deal of research and a willingness to adopt new technologies.

recession a period of economic activity characterized by negative growth, which reduces demand for goods and services

basic research pure research that aims to confirm an existing theory or to learn more about a concept or phenomenon

applied research an attempt to develop new or improved products

Research

The United States excels at both basic and applied research. **Basic research** (or *pure research*) attempts to expand the frontiers of knowledge but is not aimed at a specific, pragmatic problem. Basic research aims to confirm an existing theory or to learn more about a concept or phenomenon. For example, basic research might focus on high-energy physics. **Applied research**, in contrast, attempts to develop new or improved products. The United States has dramatically improved its track record in applied research. For example, the United States leads the world in applying basic research to aircraft design and propulsion systems.

RSS and Blogging

The recent explosion in the popularity of blogs has presented several intriguing opportunities for marketers. RSS (Really Simple Syndication) enables automated, seamless delivery of updated news content or marketing messages to blog sites or mobile phones. For example, if you are interested in extreme sports, opera, and exotic fish (or whatever), you can set up an RSS feed that will pull down articles on those topics every day. Advancing technology also allows today's marketers to scan blogs and learn about consumer opinion as it's being generated. By expanding their searches to include publicly posted blog

content such as photos, user profiles, and hyperlinks, marketers are able to segment markets and profile individuals with newfound speed and accuracy.

LO7 Political and Legal Factors

Every aspect of the marketing mix is subject to laws and restrictions. It is the duty of marketing managers or their legal assistants to understand these laws and conform to them, because failure to comply with regulations can have major consequences for a firm.

Sometimes just sensing trends and taking corrective action before a government agency acts can help avoid regulation.

Marketers must balance caution with risk. It is all too easy for a marketing manager or sometimes a lawyer to say "no" to a marketing innovation that actually entails little risk. For example, an overly cautious lawyer could hold up sales of a desirable new product by warning that the package design could prompt a copyright infringement suit. Thus, it is important to have a thorough understanding of the laws established by the federal government, state governments, and regulatory agencies to govern marketing-related issues.

Federal Legislation

Federal laws that affect marketing fall into several categories of regulatory activity: competitive environment, pricing, advertising and promotion, and the newest, protection of consumer privacy.

These key pieces of legislation are summarized in Exhibit 4.2. The primary federal laws that protect consumers are shown in Exhibit 4.3.

EXHIBIT 4.2

Federal Legislation that Affects Marketers

Legislation	Impact on Marketing
Sherman Act of 1890	Makes trusts and conspiracies in restraint of trade illegal; makes monopolies and attempts to monopolize a misdemeanor.
Clayton Act of 1914	Outlaws discrimination in prices to different buyers; prohibits tying contracts (which require the buyer of one product to also buy another item in the line); makes illegal the combining of two or more competing corporations by pooling ownership of stock.
Federal Trade Commission Act of 1914	Created the Federal Trade Commission to deal with antitrust matters; outlaws unfair methods of competition.
Robinson-Patman Act of 1936	Prohibits charging different prices to different buyers of merchandise of like grade and quantity; requires sellers to make any supplementary services or allowances available to all purchasers on a proportionately equal basis.
Wheeler-Lea Amendments to the FTC Act of 1938	Broadens the Federal Trade Commission's power to prohibit practices that might injure the public without affecting competition; outlaws false and deceptive advertising.
Lanham Act of 1946	Establishes protection for trademarks.
Celler-Kefauver Antimerger Act of 1950	Strengthens the Clayton Act to prevent corporate acquisitions that reduce competition.
Hart-Scott-Rodino Act of 1976	Requires large companies to notify the government of their intent to merge.
Gramm-Leach-Bliley Act (Financial Services Modernization Act)	Requires financial companies to tell their customers how they use their personal information and to have policies that prevent fraudulent access to it.
Health Insurance Portability and Accountability Act	Limits disclosure of individuals' medical information and imposes penalties on organizations that violate privacy rules.

EXHIBIT 4.3
Primary U.S. Laws Protecting Consumers

Legislation	Provisions
Federal Food and Drug Act of 1906	Prohibits adulteration and misbranding of foods and drugs involved in interstate commerce; strengthened by the Food, Drug, and Cosmetic Act (1938) and the Kefauver-Harris Drug Amendment (1962).
Federal Hazardous Substances Act of 1960	Requires warning labels on hazardous household chemicals.
Kefauver-Harris Drug Amendment of 1962	Requires that manufacturers conduct tests to prove drug effectiveness and safety.
Consumer Credit Protection Act of 1968	Requires that lenders fully disclose true interest rates and all other charges to credit customers for loans and installment purchases.
Child Protection and Toy Safety Act of 1969	Prevents marketing of products so dangerous that adequate safety warnings cannot be given.
Public Health Smoking Act of 1970	Prohibits cigarette advertising on TV and radio and revises the health hazard warning on cigarette packages.
Poison Prevention Labeling Act of 1970	Requires safety packaging for products that may be harmful to children.
National Environmental Policy Act of 1970	Established the Environmental Protection Agency to deal with various types of pollution and organizations that create pollution.
Public Health Cigarette Smoking Act of 1971	Prohibits tobacco advertising on radio and television.
Consumer Product Safety Act of 1972	Created the Consumer Product Safety Commission, which has authority to specify safety standards for most products.
Child Protection Act of 1990	Regulates the number of minutes of advertising on children's television.
Children's Online Privacy Protection Act of 1998	Empowers the FTC to set rules regarding how and when marketers must obtain parental permission before asking children marketing research questions.
Aviation Security Act of 2001	Requires airlines to take extra security measures to protect passengers, including the installation of stronger cockpit doors, improved baggage screening, and increased security training for airport personnel.
Homeland Security Act of 2002	Protects consumers against terrorist acts; created the Department of Homeland Security.
Do Not Call Law of 2003	Protects consumers against unwanted telemarketing calls.
CAN-SPAM Act of 2003	Protects consumers against unwanted e-mail, or spam.

State Laws

State legislation that affects marketing varies. Oregon, for example, limits utility advertising to 0.5 percent of the company's net income. California has enacted legislation to lower the energy consumption of refrigerators, freezers, and air conditioners. Several states, including New Mexico and Kansas, are considering levying a tax on all in-state commercial advertising. California has enacted a Notice of Security Breach Law. If any company or agency that has collected the personal information of a California resident discovers that nonencrypted information has been taken by an unauthorized person, the company or agency must tell the resident. (Some 30 other states are considering similar laws.) Marketers must be aware of pending legislation and legal trends in all 50 states.

Regulatory Agencies

Although some state regulatory bodies actively pursue violators of their marketing statutes, federal regulators generally have the greatest clout. The Food and Drug Administration, the Consumer Product Safety Commission, and the Federal Trade Commission are the three federal agencies most directly and actively involved in marketing affairs. These agencies, plus others, are discussed throughout the book, but a brief introduction is in order at this point.

The **Food and Drug Administration (FDA)** is charged with enforcing regulations against selling and distributing adulterated, misbranded, or hazardous food and drug products. In the last decade it took a

Food and Drug Administration (FDA) a federal agency charged with enforcing regulations against selling and distributing adulterated, misbranded, or hazardous food and drug products

Consumer Product Safety Commission (CPSC) a federal agency established to protect the health and safety of consumers in and around their homes

Federal Trade Commission (FTC) a federal agency empowered to prevent persons or corporations from using unfair methods of competition in commerce

very aggressive stance against tobacco products and is now paying attention to the fast-food industry.

The sole purpose of the **Consumer Product Safety Commission (CPSC)** is to protect the health and safety of consumers in and around their homes. The CPSC has the power to set mandatory safety standards for almost all products that consumers use (about 15,000 items). The CPSC consists of a five-member committee and about 1,100 staff members, including technicians, lawyers, and administrative help. The commission can fine offending firms up to $500,000 and sentence their officers to up to a year in prison. It can also ban dangerous products from the marketplace. Recently, Graco Children's Products agreed to pay $4 million to settle charges that it failed to inform the CPSC in a timely matter that more than 12 million of its products were hazardous to young children.[37]

The **Federal Trade Commission (FTC)** also consists of five members, each holding office for seven years. The FTC is empowered to prevent persons or corporations from using unfair methods of competition in commerce. It is authorized to investigate the practices of business combinations and to conduct hearings on antitrust matters and deceptive advertising. The FTC has a vast array of regulatory powers (see Exhibit 4.4), but it is not invincible. After the FTC proposed what businesses considered an overly restrictive ban on advertising to children, companies lobbied to reduce the FTC's power. The two-year effort resulted in passage of the FTC Improvement Act of 1980. The major provisions include congressional oversight hearings on the FTC every six months.

COST OF COMPLIANCE

Small businesses are disproportionately impacted by the burden of federal regulations, including legal, accounting, and consulting costs. Upon passing the Small Business Regulatory Review Act of 2007, Congress has taken a step toward helping to reduce that burden by requiring federal agencies to produce understandable and usable compliance guides.[38]

Cost per employee for a firm to comply with federal regulations:

> < 20 employees = $7,647
> >500 employees = $5,282

Businesses rarely band together to create change in the legal environment as they did to pass the FTC Improvement Act. Generally, marketing managers react only to legislation, regulation, and edicts. It is usually less costly to stay attuned to the regulatory environment than to fight the government. If marketers had toned down their hard-hitting advertisements to children, they might have avoided an FTC inquiry altogether.

Consumer Privacy In addition to its other activities, the FTC also regulates advertising on the Internet, as well as Internet abuses of consumer privacy. The popularity of the Internet for direct marketing, for collec-

EXHIBIT 4.4
Powers of the Federal Trade Commission

Remedy	Procedure
Cease-and-Desist Order	A final order is issued to cease an illegal practice—and is often challenged in the courts.
Consent Decree	A business consents to stop the questionable practice without admitting its illegality.
Affirmative Disclosure	An advertiser is required to provide additional information about products in advertisements.
Corrective Advertising	An advertiser is required to correct the past effects of misleading advertising. (For example, 25 percent of a firm's media budget must be spent on FTC-approved advertisements or FTC-specified advertising.)
Restitution	Refunds are required to be given to consumers misled by deceptive advertising. According to a 1975 court-of-appeals decision, this remedy cannot be used except for practices carried out after the issuance of a cease-and-desist order.
Counteradvertising	The FTC proposed that the Federal Communications Commission permit advertisements in broadcast media to counteract advertising claims (also that free time be provided under certain conditions).

tion of consumer data, and as a repository for sensitive consumer data has alarmed privacy-minded consumers. Most consumers are unaware of how technology is used to collect personal data or how personal information is used and distributed after it is collected. The government actively sells huge amounts of personal information to list compilers. State motor vehicle bureaus sell names and addresses of individuals who get driver's licenses. Hospitals sell the names of women who just gave birth on their premises. Credit card marketers often use consumer credit databases, developed and maintained by large providers such as Equifax Marketing Services and TransUnion, to prescreen targets for solicitations. In response to massive consumer data collection efforts by companies, more than fifty nations have, or are developing, privacy legislation.

LO8 Competitive Factors

The competitive environment encompasses the number of competitors a firm must face, the relative size of the competitors, and the degree of interdependence within the industry. Management has little control over the competitive environment confronting a firm.

Competition for Market Share and Profits

As U.S. population growth slows, costs rise, and available resources tighten, firms find that they must work harder to maintain their profits and market share regardless of the form of the competitive market. For example, while ice cream has long been a favorite American treat, traditional, ready-to-scoop pints and half-gallons are actually losing market share in the frozen dessert market—their sales have decreased nearly 4 percent in the past five years. But Americans aren't actually buying less ice cream; sales of frozen desserts are steadily increasing as shoppers choose frozen novelties like ice-cream bars and sandwiches. Novelty producers such as Nestlé, Wells' Dairy, and Unilever—have increased their market share 2.7 percent by monitoring healthy eating and convenience trends to develop portable, flavorful, and portion-controlled treats that appeal to kids and dieters alike.[39]

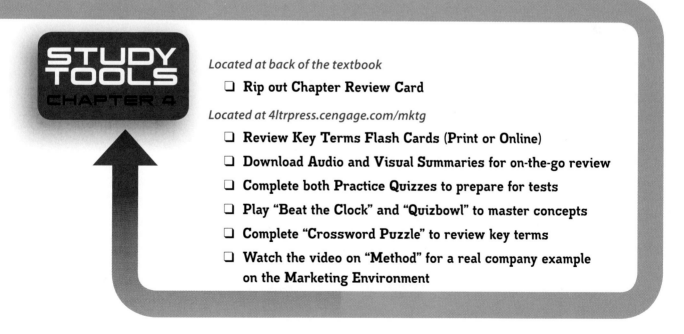

STUDY TOOLS
CHAPTER 4

Located at back of the textbook
❑ **Rip out Chapter Review Card**

Located at 4ltrpress.cengage.com/mktg
❑ **Review Key Terms Flash Cards (Print or Online)**
❑ **Download Audio and Visual Summaries for on-the-go review**
❑ **Complete both Practice Quizzes to prepare for tests**
❑ **Play "Beat the Clock" and "Quizbowl" to master concepts**
❑ **Complete "Crossword Puzzle" to review key terms**
❑ **Watch the video on "Method" for a real company example on the Marketing Environment**

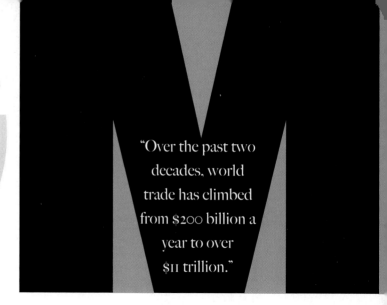

"Over the past two decades, world trade has climbed from $200 billion a year to over $11 trillion."

AFTER YOU FINISH THIS CHAPTER GO TO **PAGE 70** FOR **STUDY TOOLS**

LO 1 Rewards of Global Marketing

Today, global revolutions are under way in many areas of our lives: management, politics, communications, and technology. The word *global* has assumed a new meaning, referring to a boundless mobility and competition in social, business, and intellectual arenas. **Global marketing**—marketing that targets markets throughout the world—has become an imperative for business.

U.S. managers must develop a global vision not only to recognize and react to international marketing opportunities but also to remain competitive at home. Often a U.S. firm's toughest domestic competition comes from foreign companies. Moreover, a global vision enables a manager to understand that customer and distribution networks operate worldwide, blurring geographic and political barriers and making them increasingly irrelevant to business decisions. In summary, having a **global vision** means recognizing and reacting to international marketing opportunities, using effective global marketing strategies, and being aware of threats from foreign competitors in all markets.

Over the past two decades, world trade has climbed from $200 billion a year to over $11 trillion. Countries and companies that were never considered major players in global marketing are now important, some of them showing great skill.

Today's marketers face many challenges to their customary practices. Product development costs are rising, the life of products is getting shorter, and new

global marketing
marketing that targets markets throughout the world

global vision
recognizing and reacting to international marketing opportunities, using effective global marketing strategies, and being aware of threats from foreign competitors in all markets

What do you think?

What a business decides to do overseas doesn't affect me.

| 1 | 2 | 3 | 4 | 5 | 6 | 7 |

STRONGLY DISAGREE   STRONGLY AGREE

Find out what others think at 4ltrpress.cengage.com/mktg

technology is spreading around the world faster than ever. But marketing winners relish the pace of change instead of fearing it.

Adopting a global vision can be very lucrative for a company. Gillette, for example, gets about two-thirds of its annual revenue from its international division. H.J. Heinz, the ketchup company, gets over half of its revenue from international sales. Although Cheetos and Ruffles haven't done very well in Japan, the potato chip has been quite successful. PepsiCo's (owner of Frito-Lay) overseas snack business brings in more than $3.25 billion annually. The William Wrigley Jr. Company, makers of Wrigley's Spearmint, Juicy Fruit, Altoids, Life Savers, and other products, has global annual sales of over $4.7 billion.[1]

Another company with a global vision is Pillsbury. The Pillsbury Doughboy is used in India to sell a product that the company had just about abandoned in America: flour. To reach Indian housewives, the Doughboy has adopted Indian customs, like bowing in the traditional Indian greeting. He speaks six regional languages.

Global marketing is not a one-way street whereby only U.S. companies sell their wares and services throughout the world. Foreign competition in the domestic market was relatively rare but now is found in almost every industry. In fact, in many industries U.S. businesses have lost significant market share to imported products. In electronics, cameras, automobiles, fine china, tractors, leather goods, and a host of other consumer and industrial products, U.S. companies have struggled at home to maintain their market shares against foreign competitors.

© G. PALMER/ALAMY

Importance of Global Marketing to the United States

Many countries depend more on international commerce than the United States does. For example, France, Britain, and Germany all derive more than 19 percent of their gross domestic product (GDP) from world trade, compared to about 12 percent for the United States. Nevertheless, the impact of international business on the U.S. economy is still impressive:

U.S. TRADE STATS

- The United States exports about a fifth of its industrial production.
- One in every five jobs in the United States is directly or indirectly supported by exports.[2]
- Every U.S. state has realized net employment gains directly attributed to foreign trade.[3]
- U.S. businesses export over $800 billion in goods to foreign countries every year, and almost a third of U.S. corporate profits comes from international trade and foreign investment.
- Exports account for 25 percent of U.S. economic growth.
- The United States exports over $1.6 trillion in goods and services each year.[4]

About 85 percent of all U.S. exports of manufactured goods are shipped by 250 companies, and less than 10 percent of all manufacturing businesses, or around 25,000 companies, export their goods on a regular basis. Most small- and medium-sized firms are essentially nonparticipants in global trade and marketing. Only the very large multinational companies have seriously attempted to compete worldwide. Fortunately, more of the smaller companies are now aggressively pursuing international markets.

The Fear of Trade and Globalization The protests during meetings of the World Trade Organization, the World Bank, and the International Monetary Fund (the three organizations are discussed later in the chapter) show that many people fear world trade and globalization. What do they fear? The negatives of global trade are as follows:

- Millions of Americans have lost jobs due to imports, production shifts abroad, or outsourcing of tech jobs. Most find new jobs—that often pay less.

- Millions of others fear losing their jobs, especially at those companies operating under competitive pressure.

- Employers often threaten to outsource jobs if workers do not accept pay cuts.

- Service and white-collar jobs are increasingly vulnerable to operations moving offshore.

Jobs Outsourcing The notion of **jobs outsourcing** (sending U.S. jobs abroad) has been highly controversial for the past several years. Many executives say that it is about corporate growth, efficiency, productivity, and revenue growth. Most companies see cost savings as a key driver in outsourcing. While India, because of its educated, English-speaking population, has always been a popular country for receiving offshoring work, other countries are gaining as well.

Benefits of Globalization Traditional economic theory says that globalization relies on competition to drive down prices and increase product and service quality. Business goes to the countries that operate most efficiently and/or have the technology to produce what is needed. In summary, globalization expands economic freedom, spurs competition, and raises the productivity and living standards of people in countries that open themselves to the global marketplace. For less developed countries, globalization also offers access to foreign capital, global export markets, and advanced technology, while breaking the monopoly of inefficient and protected domestic producers. Faster growth, in turn, reduces poverty, encourages democratization, and promotes higher labor and environmental standards. Though government officials may face more difficult choices as a result of globalization, their citizens enjoy greater individual freedom. In this sense, globalization acts as a check on governmental power by making it more difficult for governments to abuse the freedom and property of their citizens.

Globalization deserves credit for helping lift many millions out of poverty and for improving standards of living of low-wage families. In developing countries around the world, globalization has created a vibrant middle class that has elevated the standards of living for hundreds of millions of people. In many developing countries around the world, life expectancies and health care have improved, as have educational opportunities.[5]

LO2 Multinational Firms

The United States has a number of large companies that are global marketers. Many of them have been very successful. A company that is heavily engaged in international trade, beyond exporting and importing, is called a **multinational corporation**. Multinational corporations move resources, goods, services, and skills across national boundaries without regard to the country in which the headquarters is located.

Many U.S.-based multinationals earn a large percentage of their total revenue abroad, as shown in Exhibit 5.1. ExxonMobil earns a huge 72 percent of its revenue outside the United States. In contrast, America's largest firm, Wal-Mart, has 24 percent of its sales outside the country.

Multinationals often develop their global business in stages. In the first stage, companies operate in one country and sell into others. Second-stage multinationals set up foreign subsidiaries to handle sales in one country. In the third stage, multinationals operate an entire line of business in another country. The fourth stage has evolved primarily due to the Internet and involves mostly high-tech companies. For these firms, the executive suite is virtual. Their top executives and core corporate functions are in different countries, wherever the firms can gain a competitive edge through the availability of talent or capital, low costs, or proximity to their most important customers.

job outsourcing sending U.S. jobs abroad

multinational corporation a company that is heavily engaged in international trade, beyond exporting and importing

EXHIBIT 5.1
America's Largest Firms that Earn at Least 30 Percent of Their Revenue Abroad

Company	Revenue in Billions	Percent Foreign
ExxonMobil	$372.8	72.2
Hewlett-Packard	104.3	66.6
Dow Chemical	53.5	65.9
Chevron	210.8	65.7
International Business Machines	98.8	63.0
Procter & Gamble	76.5	58.2
American Intl. Group	110.1	57.8
Ford Motor	172.5	53.1
United Technologies	54.8	51.0
General Electric	176.7	49.0
Johnson & Johnson	61.1	46.9
General Motors	182.3	44.2
Boeing	66.4	40.7
Dell	61.1	38.9
Microsoft	51.1	38.7
ConocoPhillips	178.6	31.4

SOURCE: "As The World Turns," *Fortune*, May 5, 2008, 225.

A multinational company may have several worldwide headquarters, depending on where certain markets or technologies are. Britain's APV, a maker of food-processing equipment, has a different headquarters for each of its worldwide businesses.

The role of multinational corporations in developing nations is a subject of controversy. The ability of multinationals to tap financial, physical, and human resources from all over the world and combine them economically and profitably can be of benefit to any country. They also often possess and can transfer the most up-to-date technology. Critics, however, claim that often the wrong kind of technology is transferred to developing nations. Usually, it is **capital-intensive** (requiring a greater expenditure for equipment than for labor) and thus does not substantially increase employment. A "modern sector" then emerges in the nation, employing a small proportion of the labor force at relatively high productivity and income levels and with increasingly capital-intensive technologies. In addition, multinationals sometimes support reactionary and oppressive regimes if it is in their best interests to do so. Other critics say that the firms take more wealth out of developing nations than they bring in, thus widening the gap between rich and poor nations. The petroleum industry in particular has been heavily criticized in the past for its actions in some developing countries.

To counter such criticism, more and more multinationals are taking a proactive role in being good global citizens. Sometimes companies are spurred to action by government regulation, and in other cases multinationals are attempting to protect their good brand name.

Blocking Foreign Investment

A new backlash against multinational corporations is that governments from China to Canada are placing restrictions on foreign purchases of factories, land, and companies in their countries. This has a major impact on U.S. multinationals because they serve foreign markets primarily through sales in their foreign affiliates and not through exports from the United States. But the United States could also be seen as erecting barriers to foreign investment. Congress passed legislation to subject foreign investment in the United States, or CFIUS, to review by an interagency council that screens foreign purchases of U.S. assets with national-security implications.[6]

Now China's new regulations let government officials block a local purchase by a multinational if it is a danger to "economic security." Russia has considered blocking foreign ownership in 39 "strategic sectors" of its economy. If more countries begin to block foreign investment by multinationals, it will definitely have a noticeable impact on global trade.

Global Marketing Standardization

Traditionally, marketing-oriented multinational corporations have operated somewhat differently in each country. They use a strategy of providing different product features, packaging, advertising, and so on. However, Ted Levitt, a former Harvard professor, described a trend toward what he referred to as "global marketing," with a slightly different meaning.[7] He contended that communication and technology have made the world smaller so that almost all consumers everywhere want all the things they have heard about, seen, or experienced. Thus, he saw the emergence of global markets for standardized consumer products on a huge

Some governments are blocking foreign investment.

scale, as opposed to segmented foreign markets with different products. In this book, global marketing is defined as individuals and organizations using a global vision to effectively market goods and services across national boundaries. To make the distinction, we can refer to Levitt's notion as **global marketing standardization**.

Global marketing standardization presumes that the markets throughout the world are becoming more alike. Firms practicing global marketing standardization produce "globally standardized products" to be sold the same way all over the world. Uniform production should enable companies to lower production and marketing costs and increase profits. Levitt cited Coca-Cola, Colgate-Palmolive, and McDonald's as successful global marketers. His critics point out, however, that the success of these three companies is really based on variation, not on offering the same product everywhere. McDonald's, for example, changes its salad dressings and provides self-serve espresso for French tastes. It sells bulgogi burgers in South Korea and falafel burgers in Egypt. Further, the fact that Coca-Cola and Colgate-Palmolive sell some of their products in more than 160 countries does not signify that they have adopted a high degree of standardization for all their products globally. Only three Coca-Cola brands are standardized, and one of them, Sprite, has a different formulation in Japan.

Nevertheless, some multinational corporations are moving toward a degree of global marketing standardization. One of the latest attempts at global marketing standardization is Levi's with its button-fly 501 jeans. It has retooled its factories so that the 501 will have the same fit in all 110 countries where it sells jeans. It is also launching its first global marketing campaign in which print and television ads contain the same theme, content and slogan, "Live Unbuttoned." In some cases, the actors will change to resemble the populace in the country where the ad is being presented.[8]

© BETTMANN/CORBIS

A global marketer or a firm considering global marketing must consider the external environment. Many of the same environmental factors that operate in the domestic market also exist internationally. These factors include culture, economic and technological development, political structure and actions, demographic makeup, and natural resources.

Culture

Central to any society is the common set of values shared by its citizens that determines what is socially acceptable. Culture underlies the family, the educational system, religion, and the social class system. The network of social organizations generates overlapping roles and status positions. These values and roles have a tremendous effect on people's preferences and thus on marketers' options. A company that does not understand a country's culture is doomed to failure in that country. Cultural blunders lead to misunderstandings and often perceptions of rudeness or even incompetence. For example, when people in India shake hands, they sometimes do so rather limply. This isn't a sign of weakness or disinterest; instead, a soft handshake conveys respect. Avoiding eye contact is also a sign of deference in India.

Well-developed understanding of a culture can save a failing product by enabling marketers to change their strategy, as P&G discovered with the failure of the Swiffer Wet mop in Italy. Research found that Italian women were using it to polish after mopping rather than as a cleaner, so the firm created a Swiffer with beeswax. "It was a real shift of mindset on how to market

global marketing standardization
production of uniform products that can be sold the same way all over the world

products like these," said Alessandra Bellini, head of marketing for Unilever's home and personal-care products. "If you present a product as quick and easy, [Italian] women may feel like a cheat . . . it took us a while to understand that Italians didn't want that."[9]

Language is another important aspect of culture that can create problems for marketers. Marketers must take care in translating product names, slogans, instructions, and promotional messages so as not to convey the wrong meaning. For example, Mitsubishi Motors had to rename its Pajero model in Spanish-speaking countries because the term describes a sexual activity.

Each country has its own customs and traditions that determine business practices and influence negotiations with foreign customers. In many countries, personal relationships are more important than financial considerations. For instance, skipping social engagements in Mexico may lead to lost sales. Negotiations in Japan often include long evenings of dining, drinking, and entertaining, and only after a close personal relationship has been formed do business negotiations begin.

Making successful sales presentations abroad requires a thorough understanding of the country's culture. The Germans, for example, don't like risk and need strong reassurance. A successful presentation to a German client will emphasize three points: the bottom-line benefits of the product or service, that there will be strong service support, and that the product is guaranteed. In southern Europe, it is an insult to show a price list. Without negotiating, you will not close the sale. The English want plenty of documentation for product claims and are less likely to simply accept the word of the sales representative. Scandinavian and Dutch companies are more likely to approach business transactions as Americans do than are companies in any other country.

Economic and Technological Development

A second major factor in the external environment facing the global marketer is the level of economic development in the countries where it operates. In general, complex and sophisticated industries are found in developed countries, and more basic industries are found in less developed nations. Average family incomes are higher in the more developed countries compared to the less developed countries. Larger incomes mean greater purchasing power and demand not only for consumer goods and services but also for the machinery and workers required to produce consumer goods.

According to the World Bank, the combined gross national income (GNI) of the 210 nations for which data are available is approximately $57.6 trillion. Divide that up among the world's 6.8 billion inhabitants, and you get just $8,470 for every man, woman, and child on Earth. The United States accounts for almost a third of the income earned worldwide, or $14.5 trillion—more than any other single country. If America's GNI were divided equally among its 303 million residents, each American would receive $46,970—5.5 times the world average. Even so, Americans are still not the richest people on the planet. That title goes to the residents of Luxembourg, where the per capita GNI is $64,320.[10]

The most expensive place in the world to live is Moscow (34 percent more expensive than New York, America's most expensive city). Other more expensive places, relative to New York, are: London (26 percent); Seoul (22 percent); Tokyo (22 percent); and Hong Kong (19 percent).[11] A daily newspaper in Moscow costs $6.30. At the other end of the spectrum is Asunción in Paraguay, which is the least

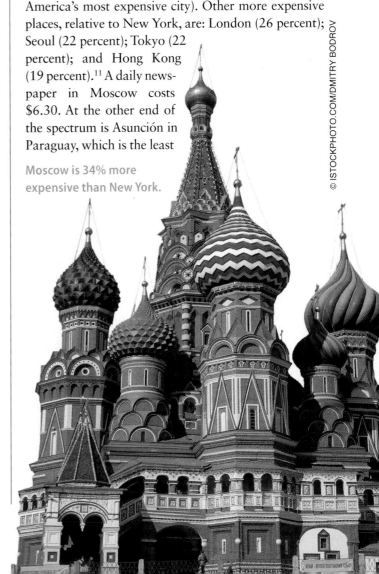

Moscow is 34% more expensive than New York.

expensive city. It costs about half as much as it does to live in New York.

Doing Business in China and India[12]

The two countries of growing interest to many multinationals are India and China because of their huge economic potential. They have some of the highest growth rates in the world and are emerging as megamarkets. Cell phone users in China, for example, exceed 450 million and the estimated figure for India is 150 million—a number that is growing by six million new subscribers each month.

China and India also have the world's two largest populations, two of the world's largest geographical areas, greater linguistic and sociocultural diversity than any other country, and among the highest levels of income disparity in the world—some people are extremely poor whereas others are very rich. Given this scale and variety, there is no "average Chinese customer" or "average Indian customer." Because of this diversity, market success in China and India is rarely possible without finely segmenting the local market in each country and developing a strategy tailored to the needs of the targeted segments.

Haier Group, China's leading appliance maker, has proved to be particularly adept at fine market segmentation. The company's line of washing machines for the Chinese market includes a washing machine for rural peasants that can clean not only clothes but also sweet potatoes and peanuts. Haier also sells a tiny washing machine designed to clean a single change of clothes, which has proved to be a hit with the busy urban customers in Shanghai.

Political Structure and Actions

Political structure is a third important variable facing global marketers. Government policies run the gamut from no private ownership and minimal individual freedom to little central government and maximum personal freedom. As rights of private property increase, government-owned industries and centralized planning tend to decrease. But a political environment is rarely at one extreme or the other. India, for instance, is a republic with elements of socialism, monopoly capitalism, and competitive capitalism in its political ideology.

Some of the world's biggest corporations are facing intense pressure from China to allow state-approved unions to form in their Chinese facilities, though many companies fear that admitting the unions will give their Chinese employees the power to disrupt their operations and increase the cost of doing business.

A recent World Bank study found that the least amount of business regulation fosters the strongest economies.[13] The least regulated and most efficient economies are concentrated among countries with well-established common-law traditions, including Australia, Canada, New Zealand, the United Kingdom, and the United States. On a par with the best performers are Singapore and Hong Kong. Not far behind are Denmark, Norway, and Sweden, social democracies that recently streamlined their business regulation.

Legal Considerations Closely related to and often intertwined with the political environment are legal considerations. In France, nationalistic sentiments led to a law that requires pop music stations to play at least 40 percent of their songs in French (even though French teenagers love American and English rock and roll).

Many legal structures are designed to either encourage or limit trade.

▸▸ *Tariff: a tax levied on the goods entering a country.* Because a tariff is a tax, it will either reduce the profits of the firms paying the tariff or raise prices to buyers, or both. Normally, a tariff raises prices of the imported goods and makes it easier for domestic firms to compete. The United States maintains tariffs as high as 27 percent on Canadian softwood lumber because the Canadian government allegedly subsidizes the industry.

▸▸ *Quota: a limit on the amount of a specific product that can enter a country.* Several U.S. companies have sought quotas as a means of protection from foreign competition. For example, Harley-Davidson convinced the U.S. government to place quotas on large motorcycles imported to the United States, giving them the opportunity to compete with Japanese motorcycles.

▸▸ *Boycott: the exclusion of all products from certain countries or companies.* Governments use boycotts to exclude companies from countries with which they have a political dispute. Several Arab nations boycotted Coca-Cola because it maintained distributors in Israel.

▸▸ *Exchange control: a law compelling a company earning foreign exchange from its exports to sell it to a control agency, usually a central bank.* A company wishing to buy goods abroad must first obtain foreign currency exchange from the control agency. For instance, Avon Products drastically cut back new production lines and products in the Philippines because exchange controls prevented the company from converting pesos to dollars to ship back to the home office. The pesos had to be used in the Philippines.

▸▸ *Market grouping (also known as a common trade alliance): occurs when several countries agree to work together to form a common trade area that enhances trade opportunities.* The best-known market grouping is the European Union (EU).

▶▶ *Trade agreement: an agreement to stimulate international trade.* Not all government efforts are meant to stifle imports or investment by foreign corporations. The largest Latin American trade agreement is **Mercosur**, which includes Argentina, Bolivia, Brazil, Chile, Colombia, Ecuador, Paraguay, Peru, and Uruguay. The elimination of most tariffs among the trading partners has resulted in trade revenues of more than $16 billion annually. The economic boom created by Mercosur will undoubtedly cause other nations to seek trade agreements on their own or to enter Mercosur.

Uruguay Round and the Failed Doha Round, and Bilateral Agreements The **Uruguay Round** is an agreement that has dramatically lowered trade barriers worldwide. Adopted in 1994, the agreement has been signed by 151 nations. It is the most ambitious global trade agreement ever negotiated. The agreement has reduced tariffs by one-third worldwide—a move that has raised global income by $235 billion annually. Perhaps most notable is the recognition of new global realities. For the first time, an agreement covers services, intellectual property rights, and trade-related investment measures such as exchange controls.

The Uruguay Round made several major changes in world trading practices:

▶▶ *Entertainment, pharmaceuticals, integrated circuits, and software:* The rules protect patents, copyrights, and trademarks for 20 years. Computer programs receive 50 years of protection and semiconductor chips receive 10 years of protection. But many developing nations were given a decade to phase in patent protection for drugs. France, which limits the number of U.S. movies and television shows that can be shown, refused to liberalize market access for the U.S. entertainment industry.

▶▶ *Financial, legal, and accounting services:* Services came under international trading rules for the first time, creating a vast opportunity for these competitive U.S. industries. Now it is easier for managers and key personnel to be admitted to a country. Licensing standards for professionals, such as doctors, cannot discriminate against foreign applicants. That is, foreign applicants cannot be held to higher standards than domestic practitioners.

▶▶ *Agriculture:* Europe is gradually reducing farm subsidies, opening new opportunities for such U.S. farm exports as wheat and corn. Japan and Korea are beginning to import rice. But U.S. growers of sugar and citrus fruit have had their subsidies trimmed.

▶▶ *Textiles and apparel:* Strict quotas limiting imports from developing countries are being phased out, causing further job losses in the U.S. clothing trade. But retailers and consumers are the big winners, because past quotas have added $15 billion a year to clothing prices.

▶▶ *A new trade organization:* The **World Trade Organization (WTO)** replaced the old **General Agreement on Tariffs and Trade (GATT)**, which was created in 1948. WTO eliminated the extensive loopholes of which GATT members took advantage. Today, all WTO members must fully comply with all agreements under the Uruguay Round. The WTO also has an effective dispute settlement procedure with strict time limits to resolve disputes.

The latest round of WTO trade talks began in Doha, Qatar, in 2001. For the most part, the periodic meetings of WTO members under the Doha Round have been very contentious. In the summer of 2008, after seven years, the Doha Round collapsed. The demise of the Doha Round was the first multilateral (many nations) free trade act failure since World War II. The cost of the failure is estimated at over $100 billion annually.

The failure of Doha has resulted in many countries seeking bilateral trade agreements. A bilateral agree-

© COURTESY OF THE US GEOLOGICAL SURVEY/CORBIS/IMAGE 100

ment is simply a pact between two nations. America already has bilateral agreements with Australia, Bahrain, Chile, Israel, Jordan, Morocco, and Singapore. The United States has pending bilateral agreements with Colombia, Panama, and South Korea. If all three pending agreements pass, U.S. exports will increase $1.1 billion to Colombia, $5.25 billion to Panama, and $10.3 billion to South Korea.[14]

The trend toward globalization has resulted in the creation of additional agreements and organizations: the North American Free Trade Agreement, the Central America Free Trade Agreement, the European Union, the World Bank, and the International Monetary Fund.

North American Free Trade Agreement At the time it was instituted, the **North American Free Trade Agreement (NAFTA)** created the world's largest free trade zone. Ratified by the U.S. Congress in 1993, the agreement includes Canada, the United States, and Mexico, with a combined population of 360 million and economy of $6 trillion.

The main impact of NAFTA was to open the Mexican market to U.S. companies. When the treaty went into effect, tariffs on about half the items traded across the Rio Grande disappeared. The pact removed a web of Mexican licensing requirements, quotas, and tariffs that limited transactions in U.S. goods and services. For instance, the pact allowed U.S. and Canadian financial-services companies to own subsidiaries in Mexico.

In August 2007, the three member countries met in Canada to tweak NAFTA, but not make substantial changes. For example, the members agreed to further remove trade barriers on hogs, steel, consumer electronics, and chemicals. They also directed the North American Steel Trade Committee, which represents the three governments, to focus on subsidized steel from China. Most Canadians (73 percent) and Americans (77 percent) feel that NAFTA has played a key role in North American prosperity.[15] The survey was not conducted in Mexico.

The real question is whether NAFTA can continue to deliver rising prosperity in all three countries. America has certainly benefited from cheaper imports and more investment opportunities abroad. Exports to Mexico still only account for 1.1 percent of the economy, and imports from Mexico were less than 1.7 percent of the economy. Direct investment in Mexico was just $21 billion in 2007; the United States attracted $190 billion.[16]

President Obama has talked about renegotiating NAFTA because of the number of jobs lost to Mexico since NAFTA took effect. It is true that jobs in textile, auto parts, and electronics production have migrated to Mexico. Yet far more jobs have been lost to China than to Mexico. Investment in automation and information technology has led to massive reductions in factory workers everywhere—including China and Mexico. Moreover, the growth of the Mexican economy under NAFTA has created export opportunities and jobs (different jobs from pre-NAFTA) in America. For example, General Electric recently sold $350 million in turbines built in Houston, more than 100 locomotives made in Erie, Pennsylvania, and numerous aircraft engines to Mexico.[17]

President Obama also wants NAFTA to adopt tougher labor and environmental standards and enforcement. Mexico doesn't guarantee workers' rights to form independent unions or to bargain collectively. In April 2009, President Obama decided not to reopen NAFTA, hoping to explore options without taking that step.

Central America Free Trade Agreement **Central America Free Trade Agreement (CAFTA)** was instituted in 2005. Besides the United States, the agreement includes Costa Rica, the Dominican Republic, El Salvador, Guatemala, Honduras, and Nicaragua.

Between 2005 and 2007, trade between the United States and CAFTA countries grew 18 percent. U.S. exports to CAFTA nations were $23 billion in 2007, up 33 percent since 2005. U.S. imports from CAFTA were $19 billion, up 4 percent since 2005.[18] CAFTA has been an unqualified success. It has created new commercial opportunities for its members, promoted regional stability, and is an impetus for economic development for an important group of U.S. neighbors.

European Union The **European Union (EU)** is one of the world's most important free trade zones and now encompasses most of Europe. More than a free trade zone, it is also a political and economic community. As a free trade zone, it guarantees the freedom of movement of people, goods, services, and capital between member states. It also maintains a common trade policy with outside nations and a regional development policy. The EU represents member nations in the WTO. Recently, the EU also began venturing into foreign policy as well, such as Iran's refining of uranium.

The European Union currently has 27 member states: Austria, Belgium, Bulgaria, Cyprus, the Czech Republic, Denmark, Estonia, Finland, France,

North American Free Trade Agreement (NAFTA) an agreement between Canada, the United States, and Mexico that created the world's largest free trade zone

Central America Free Trade Agreement (CAFTA) a trade agreement, instituted in 2005, that includes Costa Rica, the Dominican Republic, El Salvador, Guatemala, Honduras, Nicaragua, and the United States

European Union (EU) a free trade zone encompassing 27 European countries

Germany, Greece, Hungary, Ireland, Italy, Latvia, Lithuania, Luxembourg, Malta, the Netherlands, Poland, Portugal, Romania, Slovakia, Slovenia, Spain, Sweden, and the United Kingdom. There are currently three official candidate countries: Croatia, the Republic of Macedonia, and Turkey. In addition, the western Balkan countries of Albania, Bosnia and Herzegovina, Montenegro, and Serbia are officially recognized as potential candidates.[19]

The European Union Commission and the courts have not always been kind to U.S. multinationals. First, the EU court blocked a merger between two U.S. companies—General Electric and Honeywell. In late 2007, it concluded that Microsoft used its dominance in desktop computer software to muscle into server software and media players. The EU courts said that Microsoft blocked competition and fined the company $613 million.[20]

The European Union is the largest economy in the world. The EU is also a huge market, with a population of nearly 500 million. The United States and EU have the largest bilateral trade and investment relationship in world history. Together, they account for more than half of the global economy, while bilateral trade accounts for 7 percent of the world total. U.S. and EU companies have invested an estimated $2 trillion in each other's economies, employing directly and indirectly as many as 14 million workers. Nearly every U.S. state is involved with exporting to, importing from, or working for European firms.[21]

The EU is an attractive market, with purchasing power almost equal to that of the United States. But the EU presents marketing challenges because, even with standardized regulations, marketers will not be able to produce a single Europroduct for a generic Euroconsumer. With more than 15 different languages and individual national customs, Europe will always be far more diverse than the United States. Thus, product differences will continue to be necessary.

An entirely different type of problem facing global marketers is the possibility of a protectionist movement by the EU against outsiders. For example, European automakers have proposed holding Japanese imports at roughly their current 10 percent market share. The Irish, Danes, and Dutch don't make cars and have unrestricted home markets; they would be unhappy about limited imports of Toyotas and Nissans. But France has a strict quota on Japanese cars to protect Renault and Peugeot. These local carmakers could be hurt if the quota is raised at all.

© ISTOCKPHOTO.COM/AYZEK

The World Bank and International Monetary Fund Two international financial organizations are instrumental in fostering global trade. The **World Bank** offers low-interest loans to developing nations. Originally, the purpose of the loans was to help these nations build infrastructure such as roads, power plants, schools, drainage projects, and hospitals. Now the World Bank offers loans to help developing nations relieve their debt burdens. To receive the loans, countries must pledge to lower trade barriers and aid private enterprise. In addition to making loans, the World Bank is a major source of advice and information for developing nations. The **International Monetary Fund (IMF)** was founded in 1945, one year after the creation of the World Bank, to promote trade through financial cooperation and eliminate trade barriers in the process. The IMF makes short-term loans to member nations that are unable to meet their budgetary expenses. It operates as a lender of last resort for troubled nations. In exchange for these emergency loans, IMF lenders frequently extract significant commitments from the borrowing nations to address the problems that led to the crises. These steps may include curtailing imports or even devaluing the currency.

Demographic Makeup

The three most densely populated nations in the world are China, India, and Indonesia. But that fact alone is not particularly useful to marketers. They also need to know whether the population is mostly urban or rural because marketers may not have easy access to rural consumers. Belgium, with about 90 percent of the population living in urban settings, is an attractive market.

Another key demographic consideration is age. There is a wide gap between the older populations of the industrialized countries and the vast working-age populations of developing countries. This gap has enormous implications for economies, businesses, and the competitiveness of individual countries. It means that while Europe and Japan struggle with pension schemes and the rising cost of health care, countries like Brazil, China, and Mexico can reap the fruits of a demographic dividend: falling labor costs, a healthier and more educated population, and the entry of millions of women into the workforce. The demographic dividend is a gift of falling birthrates, and it causes a temporary bulge in the number of working-age people. Population experts have estimated that one-third of East Asia's economic miracle can be attributed to a beneficial age structure. But the miracle occurred only because the governments had policies in place to educate their people, create jobs, and improve health.

Natural Resources

A final factor in the external environment that has become more evident in the past decade is the shortage of natural resources. For example, petroleum shortages have created huge amounts of wealth for oil-producing countries such as Norway, Saudi Arabia, and the United Arab Emirates. Both consumer and industrial markets have blossomed in these countries. Other countries—such as Indonesia, Mexico, and Venezuela—were able to borrow heavily against oil reserves in order to develop more rapidly. On the other hand, industrial countries such as Japan, the United States, and much of western Europe, experienced an enormous transfer of wealth to the petroleum-rich nations. The high price of oil has created inflationary pressures in petroleum-importing nations. It also created major problems for airlines and other petroleum-dependent industries. Petroleum is not the only natural resource that affects international marketing. Warm climate and lack of water mean that many of Africa's countries will remain importers of foodstuffs. The United States, on the other hand, must rely on Africa for many precious metals. Vast differences in natural resources create international dependencies, huge shifts of wealth, inflation and recession, export opportunities for countries with abundant resources, and even a stimulus for military intervention.

LO 4 Global Marketing by the Individual Firm

A company should consider entering the global marketplace only after its management has a solid grasp of the global environment.

Companies decide to "go global" for a number of reasons. Perhaps the most important is to earn additional profits. Managers may feel that international sales will result in higher profit margins or more added-on profits. A second stimulus is that a firm may have a unique product or technological advantage not available to other international competitors. Such advantages should result in major business successes abroad. In other situations, management may have exclusive market information about foreign customers, marketplaces, or market situations not known to others. While exclusivity can provide an initial motivation for international marketing, managers must realize that competitors can be expected to catch up with the firm's information advantage. Finally, saturated domestic markets, excess capacity, and potential for economies of scale can also be motivators to "go global." Economies of scale mean that average per-unit production costs fall as output is increased.

Many firms form multinational partnerships—called strategic alliances—to assist them in penetrating global markets; strategic alliances are examined in Chapter 7. Five other methods of entering the global marketplace are, in order of risk, exporting, licensing and franchising, contract manufacturing, joint venture, and direct investment (see Exhibit 5.2).

EXHIBIT 5.2

Risk Levels for Five Methods of Entering the Global Marketplace

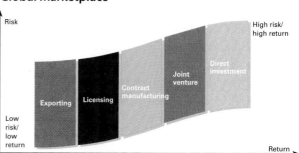

Exporting

When a company decides to enter the global market, exporting is usually the least complicated and least risky alternative. **Exporting** is selling domestically produced products to buyers in another country. A company can sell directly to foreign importers or buyers. Exporting is not limited to huge corporations such as General Motors or 3M. Indeed, small companies account for 96 percent of all U.S. exporters, but only 30 percent of the export volume.[22] The United States is the world's largest exporter.

Instead of selling directly to foreign buyers, a company may decide to sell to intermediaries located in its domestic market. The most common intermediary is the export merchant, also known as a **buyer for export**, which is usually treated like a domestic customer by the domestic manufacturer. The buyer for export assumes all risks and sells internationally for its own account. The domestic firm is involved only to the extent that its products are bought in foreign markets.

A second type of intermediary is the **export broker**, who plays the traditional broker's role by bringing buyer and seller together. The manufacturer still retains title and assumes all the risks. Export brokers operate primarily in agricultural products and raw materials.

Export agents, a third type of intermediary, are foreign sales agents-distributors who live in the foreign country and perform the same functions as domestic manufacturers' agents, helping with international financing, shipping, and so on. The U.S. Department of Commerce has an agent-distributor service that helps about 5,000 U.S. companies each year find an agent or distributor in virtually any country of the world. A second category of agents resides in the manufacturer's country but represents foreign buyers. This type of agent acts as a hired purchasing agent for foreign customers operating in the exporter's home market.

Licensing and Franchising

Another effective way for a firm to move into the global arena with relatively little risk is to sell a license to manufacture its product to someone in a foreign country. **Licensing** is the legal process whereby a licensor allows another firm to use its manufacturing process, trademarks, patents, trade secrets, or other proprietary knowledge. The licensee, in turn, pays the licensor a royalty or fee agreed on by both parties.

Because licensing has many advantages, U.S. companies have eagerly embraced the concept. Caterpillar, the producer of heavy machinery, has licensed Wolverine World Wide to make "CAT" brand shoes and boots. Europeans have latched onto CAT gear as the new symbol of American outdoor culture. CAT is one of Europe's hottest brands, which translates into almost $1 billion in licensing revenues.

A licensor must make sure it can exercise sufficient control over the licensee's activities to ensure proper quality, pricing, distribution, and so on. Licensing may also create a new competitor in the long run, if the licensee decides to void the license agreement. International law is often ineffective in stopping such actions. Two common ways of maintaining effective control over licensees are shipping one or more critical components from the United States or locally registering patents and trademarks to the U.S. firm, not to the licensee. Garment companies maintain control by delivering only so many labels per day; they also supply their own fabric and collect the scraps, and do accurate unit counts.

Franchising is a form of licensing that has grown rapidly in recent years. More than 400 U.S. franchisors operate more than 40,000 outlets in foreign countries, bringing in sales of over $9 billion.[23] Over half of the international franchises are for fast-food restaurants and business services.

Contract Manufacturing Firms that do not want to become involved in licensing or to become heavily involved in global marketing may engage in **contract manufacturing**, which is private-label manufacturing

---

exporting selling domestically produced products to buyers in another country

buyer for export an intermediary in the global market that assumes all ownership risks and sells globally for its own account

export broker an intermediary that plays the traditional broker's role by bringing buyer and seller together

export agent an intermediary that acts like a manufacturer's agent for the exporter; the export agent lives in the foreign market

licensing the legal process whereby a licensor allows another firm to use its manufacturing process, trademarks, patents, trade secrets, or other proprietary knowledge

contract manufacturing private-label manufacturing by a foreign company by a foreign company. The foreign company produces a certain volume of products to specification, with the domestic firm's brand name on the goods. The domestic company usually handles the marketing. Thus, the domestic firm can broaden its global marketing base without investing in overseas plants and equipment. After establishing a solid base, the domestic firm may switch to a joint venture or direct investment.

Joint Venture

Joint ventures are somewhat similar to licensing agreements. In an international **joint venture**, the domestic firm buys part of a foreign company or joins with a foreign company to create a new entity. A joint venture is a quick and relatively inexpensive way to go global and to gain needed expertise.

Joint ventures can be very risky, however. Many fail; others fall victim to a takeover, in which one partner buys out the other. Sometimes joint venture partners simply can't agree on management strategies and policies.

Direct Investment

Active ownership of a foreign company or of overseas manufacturing or marketing facilities is **direct foreign investment**. Direct foreign investment by U.S. firms is currently about $2.1 trillion. Direct investors have either a controlling interest or a large minority interest in the firm. Thus, they have the greatest potential reward and the greatest potential risk. Because of the problems with contract manufacturing and joint ventures in China, multinationals are going it alone. Today, nearly five times as much foreign direct investment comes into China in the form of stand-alone efforts as comes in for joint ventures.

A firm may make a direct foreign investment by acquiring an interest in an existing company, or by building new facilities. It might do so because it has trouble transferring some resource to a foreign operation or getting that resource locally. One important resource is personnel, especially managers. If the local labor market is tight, the firm may buy an entire foreign firm and retain all its employees instead of paying higher salaries than competitors.

The United States is a popular place for direct investment by foreign companies. In 2008, the value of foreign-owned businesses in the United States was more than $650 billion. For example, in 2007 Taiwan-based Aur bought U.S. computer maker Gateway.

LO 5 The Global Marketing Mix

joint venture when a domestic firm buys part of a foreign company or joins with a foreign company to create a new entity

direct foreign investment active ownership of a foreign company or of overseas manufacturing or marketing facilities

To succeed, firms seeking to enter into foreign trade must still adhere to the principles of the marketing mix. Information gathered on foreign markets through research is the basis for the four Ps of global marketing strategy: product, place (distribution), promotion, and price. Marketing managers who understand the advantages and disadvantages of different ways of entering the global market and the effect of the external environment on the firm's marketing mix have a better chance of reaching their goals.

The first step in creating a marketing mix is developing a thorough understanding of the global target market. Often this knowledge can be obtained through the same types of marketing research used in the domestic market (see Chapter 9). However, global marketing research is conducted in vastly different environments. Conducting a survey can be difficult in developing countries, where telephone ownership is growing but is not always common and mail delivery is slow or sporadic. Drawing samples based on known population parameters is often difficult because of the lack of data. In some cities in Africa, Asia, Mexico, and South America, street maps are unavailable, streets are

MARKETING MANAGERS WHO UNDERSTAND HOW TO ENTER THE GLOBAL MARKET HAVE A BETTER CHANCE OF REACHING THEIR GOALS.

unidentified, and houses are unnumbered. Moreover, the questions a marketer can ask may differ in other cultures. In some cultures, people tend to be more private than in the United States and will not respond to personal questions on surveys. For instance, in France, questions about one's age and income are considered especially rude.

Product and Promotion

With the proper information, a good marketing mix can be developed. One important decision is whether to alter the product or the promotion for the global marketplace. Other options are to radically change the product or to adjust either the promotional message or the product to suit local conditions.

One Product, One Message The strategy of global marketing standardization, which was discussed earlier, means developing a single product for all markets and promoting it the same way all over the world. For instance, Procter & Gamble uses the same product and promotional themes for Head & Shoulders in China as it does in the United States. The advertising draws attention to a person's dandruff problem, which stands out in a nation of black-haired people. Head & Shoulders is now the best-selling shampoo in China despite costing over 300 percent more than local brands. In a recent survey, 13,000 consumers in twenty countries were asked about brand preferences across several product categories. In developing countries, local products were often viewed less favorably than global brands. Exhibit 5.3 reveals that Western brands fair quite well in the countries surveyed. The top cola brand in every country was either Pepsi or Coke.[24]

Global media—especially satellite and cable television networks such as CNN International, MTV Networks, and British Sky Broadcasting—make it possible to beam advertising to audiences unreachable a few years ago. Eighteen-year-olds in Paris often have more in common with 18-year-olds in New York than with their own parents. Almost all of MTV's advertisers run unified, English-language campaigns in the twenty-eight nations the firm reaches. The audiences buy the same products, go to the same movies, listen to the same music, and sip the same colas. Global advertising merely works on that premise. Although teens throughout the world prefer movies above all other forms of television programming, they are closely followed by music videos, stand-up comedy, and then sports.

Global marketing standardization can sometimes backfire. Unchanged products may fail simply because of cultural factors. Any type of war game tends to do very poorly in Germany, even though Germany is by far the world's biggest game-playing nation. A successful game in Germany has plenty of details and thick rulebooks.

Sometimes the desire for absolute standardization must give way to practical considerations and local market dynamics. For example, because of the feminine connotations of the word *diet*, the European version of Diet Coke is Coca-Cola Light. Even if the brand name differs by market—as with Lay's potato chips, which are Sabritas in Mexico—a strong visual

BIG MACS TAKE ON A LOCAL FLAVOR

The worldwide operations of **McDonald's** are now far bigger than its U.S. domestic business, and they are growing substantially faster. And as the world has become the principal revenue engine for the company, it has turned this iconic American brand upside down, transforming the way it does business. Overseas managers can choose substantially different décor (think lime green chairs) designed in Paris with the help of an architect named Philippe Avanzi, based in Grenoble, France. The food is also different. McDonald's in Britain in 2008 added freshly ground fair-trade coffee to its menu, along with organic milk. You can even order porridge for breakfast![25]

EXHIBIT 5.3
Emerging Markets Like American Brands

Top Brands in Various Countries

Argentina		Saudi Arabia	
Car:	Ford	Fast food:	McDonald's
Fast food:	McDonald's	Iced tea:	Lipton
Makeup:	Avon	Mobile phone:	Nokia
Mobile phone:	Sony	Packaged cheese:	Kraft
Motorcycle:	Honda	Salty snacks:	Lay's
Television:	Philips	Television:	Sony
Cola:	Coca-Cola	Cola:	Pepsi
China		**South Africa**	
Beer:	Budweiser	Car:	Toyota
Coffee (ready to drink):	Nestea	Designer clothing store:	Levi's
Fast food:	KFC	Fast food:	KFC
Mobile phone:	Panasonic	Lipstick:	Revlon
Soap:	Safeguard	Mobile phone:	Nokia
Television:	Sony	Television:	LG
Cola:	Coca-Cola	Cola:	Coca-Cola
Egypt		**Thailand**	
Designer clothing store:	Nike	Beer:	Heineken
Fuel:	Mobil	Car:	Toyota
Hotel:	Hilton, Sheraton	Convenience store:	7-Eleven
Makeup:	Avon	Moisturizer:	Nivea
Shampoo:	Pert Plus	Whiskey/Scotch:	Johnnie Walker
Television:	Toshiba	Television:	Sony
Cola:	Pepsi	Cola:	Pepsi
India		**Turkey**	
Conditioner:	Garnier	Car:	BMW
Fast food:	McDonald's	Cognac:	Rémy Martin
Motor oil:	Castrol	Designer clothing store:	DKNY, Gucci
MP3 player:	Sony	Fast food:	McDonald's
Coffee (ready to drink):	Nescafé	Hotel:	Hilton
Television:	LG	Iced tea:	Lipton
Cola:	Pepsi	Cola:	Coca-Cola
Romania			
Car:	Mercedes	Shampoo:	Head & Shoulders
Fast food:	McDonald's	Whiskey/Scotch:	Jack Daniels
Lipstick:	Avon	Cola:	Coca-Cola
MP3 player:	Sony		

SOURCE: Synovate, Chicago (2007). Used by permission of Aegis Group, plc.

relationship may be created by uniform application of the brandmark and graphic elements on packaging.

Product Invention In the context of global marketing, product invention can be taken to mean either creating a new product for a market or drastically changing an existing product. Campbell's Soup invented a watercress and duck gizzard soup that is now selling well in China.[26]

McDonald's was once vilified for pushing its American-created fast food on the world. Now it is taking a different approach and selling more than ever in the global marketplace.

Product Adaptation Another alternative for global marketers is to slightly alter a basic product to meet local conditions. Unilever's Rexona brand deodorant sticks sell for 16 cents and up. They are big hits in Bolivia, India, Peru, and the Philippines—where Unilever has grabbed 60 percent of the deodorant market.

One of the world's best at product adaptation is the Korean firm LG Electronics. To meet the needs of Indian consumers, LG rolled out refrigerators with larger vegetable- and water-storage compartments, surge-resistant power supplies, and brightly colored finishes that reflect local preferences (red in the south, green in Kashmir). In Iran, LG offers a microwave oven with a preset button for reheating shish kebabs—a favorite dish. Saudi Arabians like LG's Primian refrigerator, which includes a special compartment for storing dates; the fruit, a Middle Eastern staple, spoils easily.

Promotion Adaptation

Another global marketing strategy is to maintain the same basic product but alter the promotional strategy. Bicycles are mainly pleasure vehicles in the United States. In many parts of the world, however, they are a family's main mode of transportation. Thus, promotion in these countries should stress durability and efficiency. In contrast, U.S. advertising may emphasize escaping and having fun.

Language barriers, translation problems, and cultural differences have generated numerous headaches for international marketing managers. Consider these examples:

- A toothpaste claiming to give users white teeth was especially inappropriate in many areas of Southeast Asia, where the well-to-do chew betel nuts and black teeth are a sign of higher social status.

- In Procter & Gamble's Japanese advertising for Camay soap, a man meeting a woman for the first time immediately compared her skin to that of a fine porcelain doll. The man came across as rude and disrespectful in Japan.

- A teenager careening down a store aisle on a grocery cart in a Coca-Cola ad was perceived as too rebellious in Singapore.

Place (Distribution)

Solving promotional and product problems does not guarantee global marketing success. The product still has to get adequate distribution. For example, Europeans don't play sports as much as Americans do, so they don't visit sporting-goods stores as often. Realizing this, Reebok started selling its shoes in about 800 traditional shoe stores in France. In one year, the company doubled its French sales.

To combat distribution problems, companies are using creative strategies. Colgate-Palmolive has introduced villagers in India to the concept of brushing teeth by rolling into villages with video vans that show half-hour infomercials on the benefits of toothpaste. The company received more than half of its revenue in that nation from rural areas until 2006. The rural market has been virtually invisible, due to a lack of distribution. Unilever's Indian subsidiary, Hindustan Lever, sells its cosmetics, toothpastes, and detergents door-to-door. It now has more than a million direct-sales consultants.

In many developing nations, channels of distribution and the physical infrastructure are inadequate. In China, the main modes of transport are truck and train. But in a fragmented trucking industry with few major companies, multinationals have difficulty determining which companies are reliable. A lack of

SC Johnson's motorcycle distribution project in Nigeria has a twofold goal—to increase sales with smaller retailers, while at the same time developing skills and growing incomes for local entrepreneurs.

refrigerated trucks has meant that poultry giant Tyson Foods can distribute in only a handful of Chinese cities.[27] In the rail system, theft is a major problem.

American companies importing goods to the United States are facing other problems. Logistics has been a growing challenge for U.S. companies seeking to cut costs by shifting more production to countries where manufacturing is cheaper. Now, however, the rising costs for shipping goods are adding to their profit pressures. The surge in global trade in recent years has added to strains and charges for all forms of transport. As a result, some manufacturers are developing costly buffer stocks—which can mean setting up days' or weeks' worth of extra components—to avoid shutting down production lines and failing to make timely deliveries. Others are shifting to more expensive but more reliable modes of transport, such as airfreight, which is faster and less prone to delays than ocean shipping.

Pricing

Once marketing managers have determined a global product and promotion strategy, they can select the remainder of the marketing mix. Pricing presents some unique problems in the global sphere. Exporters must not only cover their production costs but also consider transportation costs, insurance, taxes, and tariffs. When deciding on a final price, marketers must also determine what customers are willing to spend on a particular product. Marketers also need to ensure that their foreign buyers will pay the price. Because developing nations lack mass purchasing power, selling to them often poses special pricing problems. Sometimes a product can be simplified in order to lower the price. The firm must not assume that low-income countries are willing to accept lower quality, however. L'Oréal was unsuccessful selling cheap shampoo in India, so the company targets the rising class. It now sells a $17 Paris face powder and a $25 Vichy sunscreen. Both products are very popular.

Exchange Rates The exchange rate is the price of one country's currency in terms of another country's currency. If a country's currency *appreciates*, less of that country's currency is needed to buy another country's currency. If a country's currency *depreciates*, more of that currency will be needed to buy another country's currency.

How do appreciation and depreciation affect the prices of a country's goods? If, say, the U.S. dollar depreciates relative to the Japanese yen, U.S. residents will have to pay more dollars to buy Japanese goods. To illustrate, suppose the dollar price of a yen is $0.012 and that a Toyota is priced at 2 million yen. At this exchange rate, a U.S. resident pays $24,000 for a Toyota ($0.012 × 2 million yen = $24,000). If the dollar depreciates to $0.018 to one yen, then the U.S. resident will have to pay $36,000 for the same Toyota.

As the dollar depreciates, the prices of Japanese goods rise for U.S. residents, so they buy fewer Japanese goods—thus, U.S. imports may decline. At the same time, as the dollar depreciates relative to the yen, the yen appreciates relative to the dollar. This means prices of U.S. goods fall for the Japanese, so they buy more U.S. goods—and U.S. exports rise.

Currency markets operate under a system of **floating exchange rates**. Prices of different currencies "float" up and down based on the demand for and the supply of each currency. Global currency traders create the supply of and demand for a particular country's currency based on that country's investment, trade potential, and economic strength.

Dumping Dumping is the sale of an exported product at a price lower than that charged for the same or a like product in the "home" market of the exporter. This practice is regarded as a form of price discrimination that can potentially harm the importing nation's competing industries. Dumping may occur as a result of

exporter business strategies that include (1) trying to increase an overseas market share, (2) temporarily distributing products in overseas markets to offset slack demand in the home market, (3) lowering unit costs by exploiting large-scale production, and (4) attempting to maintain stable prices during periods of exchange rate fluctuations.

Historically, the dumping of goods has presented serious problems in international trade. As a result, dumping has led to significant disagreements among countries and diverse views about its harmfulness. Some trade economists view dumping as harmful only when it involves the use of "predatory" practices that intentionally try to eliminate competition and gain monopoly power in a market. They believe that predatory dumping rarely occurs and that antidumping rules are a protectionist tool whose cost to consumers and import-using industries exceeds the benefits to the industries receiving protection.

Recently, the United States accused Vietnam of dumping textile products on the U.S. market. The U.S. imports about $4 billion worth of garments from Vietnam each year.[29] To date, the dumping claim has not been resolved.

Countertrade Global trade does not always involve cash. Countertrade is a fast-growing way to conduct global business. In **countertrade**, all or part of the payment for goods or services is in the form of other goods or services. Countertrade is thus a form of barter (swapping goods for goods), an age-old practice whose origins have been traced back to cave dwellers. The U.S. Department of Commerce says that roughly 30 percent of all global trade is countertrade. In fact, both India and China have made billion-dollar government purchasing lists, with most of the goods to be paid for by countertrade.

One common type of countertrade is straight barter. For example, PepsiCo sends Pepsi syrup to Russian bottling plants and in payment gets Stolichnaya vodka, which is then marketed in the West. Another form of

floating exchange rates prices of different currencies move up and down based on the demand for and the supply of each currency

dumping the sale of an exported product at a price lower than that charged for the same or a like product in the "home" market of the exporter

countertrade a form of trade in which all or part of the payment for goods or services is in the form of other goods or services

100 BEST GLOBAL BRANDS[2]

1. Coca-Cola
2. IBM
3. Microsoft
4. GE
5. Nokia
6. McDonald's
7. Google
8. Toyota
9. Intel
10. Disney

countertrade is the compensation agreement. Typically, a company provides technology and equipment for a plant in a developing nation and agrees to take full or partial payment in goods produced by that plant. For example, General Tire Company supplied equipment and know-how for a Romanian truck tire plant. In turn, General Tire sold the tires it received from the plant in the United States under the Victoria brand name. Both sides benefit even though they don't use cash.

LO 6 The Impact of the Internet

In many respects "going global" is easier than it has ever been before. Opening an e-commerce site on the Internet immediately puts a company in the international marketplace. Sophisticated language translation software can make any site accessible to people around the world. Global shippers such as UPS, FedEx, and DHL help solve international e-commerce distribution complexities. E4X, Inc. offers software to ease currency conversions by allowing customers to pay in the currency of their choice. E4X collects the payment from the customer and then pays the site in U.S. dollars. Nevertheless, the promise of "borderless commerce" and the global "Internet economy" are still being restrained by the old brick-and-mortar rules, regulations, and habits. For example, Lands' End is not allowed to mention its unconditional refund policy on its e-commerce site in Germany because German retailers, which normally do not allow returns after 14 days, sued and won a court ruling blocking mention of it.

Opening an e-commerce site on the Internet . . .

. . . immediately puts a company in the international marketplace.

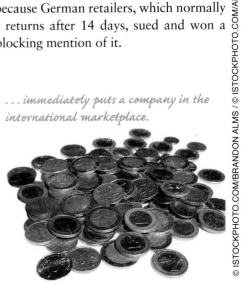

STUDY TOOLS CHAPTER 5

Located at back of the textbook
- ❑ **Rip out Chapter Review Card**

Located at 4ltrpress.cengage.com/mktg
- ❑ **Review Key Terms Flash Cards (Print or Online)**
- ❑ **Download Audio and Visual Summaries for on-the-go-review**
- ❑ **Complete both Practice Quizzes to prepare for tests**
- ❑ **Play "Beat the Clock" and "Quizbowl" to master concepts**
- ❑ **Complete "Crossword Puzzle" to review key terms**
- ❑ **Watch the video on "Method" for a real company example on Developing a Global Vision**

"It's easy to read, it outlines important topics, and it's relevant. Thanks for the good stuff on the website, I think it will **really help with tests**.

– Thomas Scholtes, Student at University of Maryland, College Park

REVIEW

HE DID

MKTG4 puts a multitude of study aids at your fingertips. After reading the chapters, check out these resources for further help:

- **Chapter Review cards**, found in the back of your book, include all learning outcomes, definitions, and visual summaries for each chapter.

- **Online printable flash cards** give you three additional ways to check your comprehension of key marketing concepts.

Other great ways to help you study include **interactive marketing games, podcasts, audio downloads,** and **online tutorial quizzes with feedback**.

You can find it all at **4ltrpress.cengage.com**.

"Consumers' product and service preferences are constantly changing."

Learning Outcomes

LO 1 Explain why marketing managers should understand consumer behavior 73

LO 2 Analyze the components of the consumer decision-making process 74–78

LO 3 Explain the consumer's postpurchase evaluation process 78–79

LO 4 Identify the types of consumer buying decisions and discuss the significance of consumer involvement 79–81

LO 5 Identify and understand the cultural factors that affect consumer buying decisions 82–85

LO 6 Identify and understand the social factors that affect consumer buying decisions 85–89

LO 7 Identify and understand the individual factors that affect consumer buying decisions 89–91

LO 8 Identify and understand the psychological factors that affect consumer buying decisions 91–97

LO1 The Importance of Understanding Consumer Behavior

AFTER YOU FINISH THIS CHAPTER GO TO PAGE 97 FOR STUDY TOOLS

Consumers' product and service preferences are constantly changing. Marketing managers must understand these desires in order to create a proper marketing mix for a well-defined market. So it is critical that marketing managers have a thorough knowledge of consumer behavior. **Consumer behavior** describes how consumers make purchase decisions and how they use and dispose of the purchased goods or services. The study of consumer behavior also includes factors that influence purchase decisions and product use.

Understanding how consumers make purchase decisions can help marketing managers in several ways. For example, if a manager knows through research that gas mileage is the most important attribute for a certain target market, the manufacturer can redesign a car to meet that criterion. If the firm cannot change the design in the short run, it can use promotion in an effort to change consumers' decision-making criteria, for example, by promoting style, durability, and cargo capacity.

consumer behavior processes a consumer uses to make purchase decisions, as well as to use and dispose of purchased goods or services; also includes factors that influence purchase decisions and product use

What do you think?

Shopping just boils down to "buy" or "don't buy."

1   2   3   4   5   6   7

STRONGLY DISAGREE   STRONGLY AGREE

Find out what others think at 4ltrpress.cengage.com/mktg

© ISTOCKPHOTOS.COM/PAUL PIEBINGA

73

LO2 The Consumer Decision-Making Process

When buying products, particularly new or expensive items, consumers generally follow the **consumer decision-making process** shown in Exhibit 6.1: (1) need recognition, (2) information search, (3) evaluation of alternatives, (4) purchase, and (5) post-purchase behavior. These five steps represent a general process that can be used as a guide for studying how consumers make decisions. It is important to note, though, that consumers' decisions do not always proceed in order through all of these steps. In fact, the consumer may end the process at any time or may not even make a purchase. The section on the types of consumer buying decisions later in the chapter discusses why a consumer's progression through these steps may vary. We begin, however, by examining the basic purchase process in greater detail.

Need Recognition

The first stage in the consumer decision-making process is need recognition. **Need recognition** occurs when consumers are faced with an imbalance between actual and desired states that arouses and activates the consumer decision-making process. A **want** is the new way that a consumer goes about addressing a need. For example, have you ever gotten blisters from an old running shoe? Or maybe you have seen a television commercial for a new sports car and wanted to buy it. Need recognition is triggered when a consumer is exposed to either an internal or an external **stimulus**. *Internal stimuli* are occurrences you experience, such as hunger or thirst. For example, you may hear your stomach growl and then realize that you are hungry. *External stimuli* are influences from an outside source such as someone's recommendation of a new restaurant, the color of an automobile, the design of a package, a brand name mentioned by a friend, or an advertisement on television or radio.

A marketing manager's objective is to get consumers to recognize an imbalance between their present status and their preferred state. Advertising and sales promotion often provide this stimulus. Surveying buyer preferences provides marketers with infor-

consumer decision-making process a five-step process used by consumers when buying goods or services

need recognition result of an imbalance between actual and desired states

want recognition of an unfulfilled need and a product that will satisfy it

stimulus any unit of input affecting one or more of the five senses: sight, smell, taste, touch, hearing

EXHIBIT 6.1
Consumer Decision-Making Process

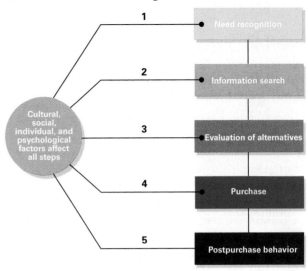

mation about consumer needs and wants that can be used to tailor products and services. Marketing managers can create wants on the part of the consumer. For example, when college students move into their own apartment or dorm room, they often need to furnish it and want new furniture rather than hand-me-downs from their parents. A want can be for a specific product, or it can be for a certain attribute or feature of a product. In this example, the college students not only need home furnishings, but also want items that reflect their personal sense of style. Similarly, consumers may want ready-to-eat meals, drive-through dry-cleaning service, and Internet shopping to fill their need for convenience.

Another way marketers create new products and services to meet wants is by observing trends in the marketplace. IKEA, the home furnishing giant, watches the home decor trends and then creates affordable, trendy furniture. For example, marketers at IKEA realized that Generation Y consumers prefer furniture that is stylish, easy to clean, multifunctional, and portable. As a result, IKEA uses "bold orange, pink and green colors." The wood boasts a lacquered finish that can be wiped clean and doesn't need polish. IKEA also offers a space-saving, multifunction desk that can be converted into a dining table; it has wheels so that it can be easily moved.

Consumers recognize unfulfilled wants in various ways. The two most common occur when a current product isn't performing properly and when the consumer is about to run out of something that is generally kept on hand. Consumers may also recognize unfulfilled wants if they become aware of a product that seems superior to the one currently used. Such wants are usually created by advertising and other promotional activities. For example, aware of the popularity of MP3s and consumers' desire to take their music with them, car stereo manufacturers such as Sonicblue and Kenwood have added MP3 interfaces.

Marketers selling their products in global markets must carefully observe the needs and wants of consumers in various regions. Unilever hit on an unrecognized need of European consumers when it introduced Persil Tablets, premeasured laundry detergent in tablet form. Although the tablets are more expensive than regular detergents, Unilever found that European consumers considered laundry a chore and wanted the process to be as simple and uncomplicated as possible. Unilever launched the tablets as a less messy and more convenient alternative. The laundry tablets were an immediate success in the United Kingdom and enabled Unilever's Persil brand to beat out rival Procter & Gamble's best-selling Ariel powder detergent.[1]

Information Search

After recognizing a need or want, consumers search for information about the various alternatives available to satisfy it. For example, as gasoline prices increase, many people are searching for information on vehicles that use alternatives to gasoline, such as Honda's hybrid models. An information search can occur internally, externally, or both. In an **internal information search**, the person recalls information stored in the memory. This stored information stems largely from previous experience with a product. For example, while traveling with your family, you encounter a hotel where you stayed during spring break earlier that year. By searching your memory, you can probably remember whether the hotel had clean rooms and friendly service.

In contrast, an **external information search** seeks information in the outside environment. There are two basic types of external information sources: nonmarketing-controlled and marketing-controlled. A **nonmarketing-controlled information source** is not associated with marketers promoting a product. These information sources include personal experiences (trying or observing a new product); personal sources (family, friends, acquaintances, and coworkers who may recommend a product or service); and public sources, such as Underwriters Laboratories, *Consumer Reports*, and other rating organizations that comment on products and services. For example, if you are in the mood to go to the movies, you may search your

memory for past experiences at various cinemas when determining which one to go to (personal experience). To choose which movie you will see, you may rely on the recommendation of a friend or family member (personal sources). Alternatively, you may read the critical reviews in the newspaper or online (public sources). Marketers gather information on how these information sources work and use it to attract customers. For example, car manufacturers know that younger customers are likely to get information from friends and family, so they try to develop enthusiasm for their products via word of mouth.

Living in the digital age has changed the way consumers get nonmarketing-controlled information. It can be from blogs, bulletin boards, activists, Web sites, Web forums, consumer opinion sites such as www.consumerreview.com, www.tripadvisor.com or www.epinions.com. The average American spends at least six hours per week online, according to many estimates. Nearly 94 percent of U.S. consumers regularly or occasionally research products online before making an offline purchase, and nearly half of those consumers then share the information and advice they gleaned online with other consumers.[2]

The latest research has examined how consumers use information picked up on the Internet. For example, in Web forums the information seeker has normally never met the information provider or ever interacted with the person before. Researchers found that an information provider's response speed, the extent to which the provider's previous responses within the forum had been positively evaluated by others, and the breadth of the provider's previous responses across different but related topics affected the information seeker's judgment about the value of the information. So, for example, if other information seekers had found the provider trustworthy, then the current seeker tended to believe the information.[3]

A **marketing-controlled information source** is biased toward a specific product because it originates with marketers promoting that product. Marketing-controlled information sources include mass-media advertising (radio, newspaper, television, and magazine advertising), sales promotion (contests, displays, premiums, and so forth), salespeople, product labels

internal information search the process of recalling past information stored in the memory

external information search the process of seeking information in the outside environment

nonmarketing-controlled information source a product information source that is not associated with advertising or promotion

marketing-controlled information source a product information source that originates with marketers promoting the product

and packaging, and the Internet. Many consumers, however, are wary of the information they receive from marketing-controlled sources, believing that most marketing campaigns stress the product's positive attributes and ignore its faults. These sentiments tend to be stronger among better educated and higher income consumers. Some marketing-controlled information sources can shift out of marketers' control, however, when there is bad news to report. Toy maker Mattel, Inc. has made headlines for its recall of toys with lead paint contamination or powerful magnets that can cause illness or even death in children who ingest them. Newspaper stories across the country, in this instance a nonmarketing-controlled information source, recounted the many toy recalls Mattel has had to make in the past. Mattel then used marketing-controlled information sources to try to combat the negative publicity. Damage control for Mattel took the form of full-page ads in *The New York Times* and *The Wall Street Journal*, as well as video coverage on its own and Yahoo!'s Web sites, with an apology and assurances of future safety of its products from Bob Eckert, Mattel's chair and CEO.

The extent to which an individual conducts an external search depends on his or her perceived risk, knowledge, prior experience, and level of interest in the good or service. Generally, as the perceived risk of the purchase increases, the consumer enlarges the search and considers more alternative brands. For example, suppose that you want to purchase a surround sound system for your home stereo. The decision is relatively risky because of the expense and technical nature of the stereo system, so you are motivated to search for information about models, prices, options, compatibility with existing entertainment products, and capabilities. You may decide to compare attributes of many speaker systems because the value of the time expended finding the "right" stereo will be less than the cost of buying the wrong system.

A consumer's knowledge about the product or service will also affect the extent of an external information search. A consumer who is knowledgeable and well informed about a potential purchase is less likely to search for additional information. In addition, the more knowledgeable consumers are, the more efficiently they will conduct the search process, thereby requiring less time to search. For example, many consumers know that AirTran and other discount

airlines have much lower fares, so they generally use the discounters and do not even check fares at other airlines.

The extent of a consumer's external search is also affected by confidence in one's decision-making ability. A confident consumer not only has sufficient stored information about the product but also feels self-assured about making the right decision. People lacking this confidence will continue an information search even when they know a great deal about the product. Consumers with prior experience in buying a certain product will have less perceived risk than inexperienced consumers. Therefore, they will spend less time searching and limit the number of products that they consider.

A third factor influencing the external information search is product experience. Consumers who have had a positive prior experience with a product are more likely to limit their search to items related to the positive experience. For example, when flying, consumers are likely to choose airlines with which they have had positive experiences, such as consistent on-time arrivals, and avoid airlines with which they had a negative experience, such as lost luggage.

Finally, the extent of the search is positively related to the amount of interest a consumer has in a product. A consumer who is more interested in a product will spend more time searching for information and alternatives. For example, suppose you are a dedicated runner who reads jogging and fitness magazines and catalogs. In searching for a new pair of running shoes, you may enjoy reading about the new brands available and spend more time and effort than other buyers in deciding on the right shoe.

The consumer's information search should yield a group of brands, sometimes called the buyer's **evoked set** (or **consideration set**), which are the consumer's most preferred alternatives. From this set, the buyer will further evaluate the alternatives and make a choice. Consumers do not consider all brands available in a product category, but they do seriously consider a much smaller set. For example, from the many brands of pizza available, consumers are likely to consider only the alternatives that fit their price range, location, take-out/delivery needs, and taste preferences. Having too many choices can, in fact, confuse consumers and cause them to delay the decision to buy or, in some instances, cause them not to buy at all.

Evaluation of Alternatives and Purchase

After getting information and constructing an evoked set of alternative products, the consumer is ready to make a decision. A consumer will use the information stored in memory and obtained from outside sources to develop a set of criteria. Recent research has shown that exposure to certain cues in your everyday environment can effect decision criteria and purchase. For example, when NASA landed the Pathfinder spacecraft on Mars it captured media attention worldwide. The candy maker Mars also noted a rather unusual increase in sales. Although the Mars bar takes its name from the company's founder and not the planet, consumers apparently responded to news about the planet Mars by purchasing more Mars bars. In a recent lab experiment, participants who used an orange (green) pen chose more orange (green) products. Thus, conceptual cues or primers (the pen color) influenced product evaluations and purchase likelihood.[4]

The environment, internal information, and external information help consumers evaluate and compare alternatives. One way to begin narrowing the number of choices in the evoked set is to pick a product attribute and then exclude all products in the set that don't have that attribute. For example, assume Jane and Jill, both college sophomores, are looking for their first apartment. They need a two-bedroom apartment, reasonably priced and located near campus. They want the apartment to have a swimming pool, washer and dryer, and covered parking. Jane and Jill begin their search with all apartments in the area and then systematically eliminate possibilities that lack the features they need. Hence, if there are 50 alternatives in the area, they may reduce their list to just 10 apartments that possess all of the desired attributes. Another way to narrow the number of choices is to use cutoffs. Cutoffs are either minimum or maximum levels of an attribute that an alternative must pass to be considered. Suppose Jane and Jill set a maximum of $1,000 to spend on combined rent. Then all apartments with rent higher than $1,000 will be eliminated, further reducing the list of apartments from ten to eight. A final way to narrow the choices is to rank the attributes under consideration in order of importance and evaluate the products based on how well each performs on the most important attributes. To reach a final decision on one of the remaining eight apartments, Jane and Jill may decide proximity to campus is the most important attribute. As a result, they will choose to rent the apartment closest to campus.

If new brands are added to an evoked set, the consumer's evaluation of the existing brands in that set changes. As a result, certain brands in the original set may become more desirable. Suppose Jane and Jill find two apartments located equal distance from campus, one priced at $800 and the other at $750. Faced with this choice, they may decide that the $800 apartment is too expensive given that a comparable apartment is cheaper. If they add a $900 apartment to the list, however, then they may perceive the $800 apartment as more reasonable and decide to rent it.

The purchase decision process described above is a piecemeal process. That is, the evaluation is made by examining alternative advantages and disadvantages along important product attributes. A different way consumers can evaluate a product is according to a categorization process. The evaluation of an alternative depends upon the particular category to which it is assigned. Categories can be very general (motorized forms of transportation), or they can be very specific (Harley-Davidson motorcycles). Typically, these categories are associated with some degree of liking or disliking. To the extent that the product can be assigned membership to a particular category, it will receive an evaluation similar to that attached to the category. If you go to the grocery store and see a new organic food on the shelf, you may evaluate it on your liking and opinions of organic food.

So, when consumers rely on a categorization process, a product's evaluation depends on the particular category to which it is perceived as belonging. Given this, companies need to understand whether consumers are using categories that evoke the desired evaluations. Indeed, how a product is categorized can strongly influence consumer demand. For example, what products come to mind when you think about the "morning beverages" category? To the soft drink industry's dismay, far too few consumers include sodas in this category. Several attempts have been made at getting soft drinks on the breakfast table, but with little success.

Brand extensions, in which a well-known and respected brand name from one product category is extended into other product categories, is one way companies employ categorization to their advantage. Brand extensions are a common business practice. Disney took a name built on cartoon characters and amusement parks and extended it to the cruise line industry. Kimberly-Clark, the maker of Huggies, the best-selling brand of disposable diapers in the United States, has extended the Huggies' name to disposable washcloths and liquid soap for babies, and Huggies toiletries. Coca-Cola has Coke, Diet Coke, Coke Zero, Cherry Coke, Diet Cherry Coke, Caffeine-free Coke, and the list goes on.[5]

To Buy or Not to Buy Ultimately, the consumer has to decide whether to buy or not buy. Specifically, consumers must decide:

1. Whether to buy
2. When to buy
3. What to buy (product type and brand)
4. Where to buy (type of retailer, specific retailer, online or in store)
5. How to pay

When a person is buying an expensive or complex item, it is often a *fully planned purchase* based upon a lot of information. People rarely buy a new home simply on impulse. Often consumers will make a *partially planned purchase* where they know the product category they want to buy (shirts, pants, reading lamp, car floor mats) but wait until they get to the store to choose a specific style or brand. Finally, there is the *unplanned purchase* where people buy on impulse. Research has found that up to 68 percent of the items bought during major shopping trips and 54 percent on smaller shopping trips are unplanned.[6]

LO 3 Postpurchase Behavior

When buying products, consumers expect certain outcomes from the purchase. How well these expectations are met determines whether the consumer is satisfied or dissatisfied with the purchase. For example, if a person bids on a used car stereo from eBay and wins, he may have fairly low expectations regarding performance. If the stereo's performance turns out to be of superior quality, then the person's satisfaction will be high because his expectations were exceeded. Conversely, if the person bid on a new car stereo expecting superior quality and performance, but the stereo broke within one month, he would be very dissatisfied because his expectations were not met. Price often influences the level of expectations for a product or service.

For the marketer, an important element of any postpurchase evaluation is reducing any lingering doubts that the decision was sound. When people recognize inconsistency between their values or opinions and their behavior, they tend to feel an inner tension called **cognitive dissonance**. For example, suppose a person who normally tans in a tanning bed decides to try a new "airbrush" tanning method, called "Hollywood" or "mystic" tanning. Mystic tanning costs $30 to $50, significantly more than "fake tanner" or a tanning bed. Prior to spending more on the tan, the person may feel inner tension or anxiety, which is a feeling of dissonance. This feeling occurs because she knows the product has some disadvantages, such as being expensive, and some advantages, such as being free of harmful ultraviolet rays. In this case, the disadvantage of higher cost battles the advantage of no harmful UV rays.

Consumers try to reduce dissonance by justifying their decision. They may seek new information that reinforces positive ideas about the purchase, avoid information that contradicts their decision, or revoke the original decision by returning the product. To ensure satisfaction, thereby reducing dissonance, consumers using the "mystic tanning" mentioned above may ask several friends about their experiences, do online research, and talk with the tanning booth representative to obtain additional information about the procedure. In some instances, people deliberately seek contrary information in order to refute it and reduce dissonance. Dissatisfied customers sometimes rely on word of mouth to reduce cognitive dissonance, by letting friends and family know they are displeased.

Marketing managers can help reduce dissonance through effective communication with purchasers. For example, a customer service manager may slip a note inside the package congratulating the buyer on making a wise decision. Postpurchase letters sent by manufacturers and dissonance-reducing statements in instruction booklets may help customers feel at ease with their purchase. Advertising that displays the product's superiority over competing brands or guarantees can also help relieve the possible dissonance of someone who has already bought the product. In the tanning example, the tanning salon

THE SHOE HAS TO FIT

Shoppers love Zappos, an online shoe and clothing company, for its free shipping and returns, 365-day return policy, and 24/7 customer service. But those are only part of the Zappos experience. It has a service-oriented culture that starts in the hiring process. Half of the initial interview is dedicated to finding out if potential hires have the right technical skills for the job, but the other half is about making sure they're a good cultural fit. "Getting customers excited about the service they had at Zappos has to come naturally," a Zappos manager says. "You can't teach it; you have to hire for it."

Once hired, all new employees, regardless of position, are required to complete a four-week customer loyalty training program. Then, during the second week of training, the CEO offers $2,000 to anyone who wants to quit. Only about 1 percent of the trainees actually take the offer.

may offer a 100 percent money-back guarantee. The Web site www.mystictan.com explains the procedure and even shows endorsements from various celebrities. Because the company offers this additional information and communicates effectively with its customers, its customers are more likely to understand the procedure and the expected results; hence, it is likely that the outcome will meet or exceed their expectations rather than being disappointing.

LO 4 Types of Consumer Buying Decisions and Consumer Involvement

All consumer buying decisions generally fall along a continuum of three broad categories: routine response behavior, limited decision making, and extensive decision making (see Exhibit 6.2). Goods and services in these three categories can best be described in terms of five factors: level of consumer involvement, length

of time to make a decision, cost of the good or service, degree of information search, and the number of alternatives considered. The level of consumer involvement is perhaps the most significant determinant in classifying buying decisions. **Involvement** is the amount of time and effort a buyer invests in the search, evaluation, and decision processes of consumer behavior.

Frequently purchased, low-cost goods and services are generally associated with **routine response behavior**. These goods and services can also be called low-involvement products because consumers spend little time on search and decision before making the purchase. Usually, buyers are familiar with several different brands in the product category but stick with one brand. For example, a person may routinely buy Tropicana orange juice. Consumers engaged in routine response behavior normally don't experience need recognition until they are exposed to advertising or see the product displayed on a store shelf. Consumers buy first and evaluate later, whereas the reverse is true for extensive decision making. A consumer who has previously purchased a whitening toothpaste and was satisfied with it will probably walk to the toothpaste aisle and select that same brand without spending 20 minutes examining all other alternatives.

involvement the amount of time and effort a buyer invests in the search, evaluation, and decision processes of consumer behavior

routine response behavior the type of decision making exhibited by consumers buying frequently purchased, low-cost goods and services; requires little search and decision time

EXHIBIT 6.2
Continuum of Consumer Buying Decisions

	Routine	Limited	Extensive
Involvement	low	low to moderate	high
Time	short	short to moderate	long
Cost	low	low to moderate	high
Information Search	internal only	mostly internal	internal and external
Number of Alternatives	one	few	many

And people who first use extensive decision making may then use limited or routine decision making for future purchases. For example, when a family gets a new puppy, they will spend a lot of time and energy trying out different toys to determine which one the dog prefers. Once the new owners learn that the dog prefers a bone to a ball, however, the purchase no longer requires extensive evaluation and will become routine.

limited decision making the type of decision making that requires a moderate amount of time for gathering information and deliberating about an unfamiliar brand in a familiar product category

extensive decision making the most complex type of consumer decision making, used when buying an unfamiliar, expensive product or an infrequently bought item; requires use of several criteria for evaluating options and much time for seeking information

Limited decision making typically occurs when a consumer has previous product experience but is unfamiliar with the current brands available. Limited decision making is also associated with lower levels of involvement (although higher than routine decisions) because consumers expend only moderate effort in searching for information or in considering various alternatives. But what happens if the consumer's usual brand of whitening toothpaste is sold out? Assuming that toothpaste is needed, the consumer will be forced to choose another brand. Before making a final decision, the consumer will likely evaluate several other brands based on their active ingredients, their promotional claims, and the consumer's prior experiences.

Consumers practice **extensive decision making** when buying an unfamiliar, expensive product or an infrequently bought item. This process is the most complex type of consumer buying decision and is associated with high involvement on the part of the consumer. This process resembles the model outlined in Exhibit 6.1. These consumers want to make the right decision, so they want to know as much as they can about the product category and available brands. People usually experience the most cognitive dissonance when buying high-involvement products. Buyers use several criteria for evaluating their options and spend much time seeking information. Buying a home or a car, for example, requires extensive decision making.

The type of decision making that consumers use to purchase a product does not necessarily remain constant. For instance, if a routinely purchased product no longer satisfies, consumers may practice limited or extensive decision making to switch to another brand.

Factors Determining the Level of Consumer Involvement

The level of involvement in the purchase depends on the following five factors:

▶▶ *Previous experience*: When consumers have had previous experience with a good or service, the level of involvement typically decreases. After repeated product trials, consumers learn to make quick choices. Because consumers are familiar with the product and know whether it will satisfy their needs, they become less involved in the purchase. For example, a consumer purchasing cereal has many brands to choose from—just think of any grocery store cereal aisle. If the consumer always buys the same brand because it satisfies his hunger, then he has a low level of involvement. When a consumer purchases cereal for the first time, however, it likely will be a much more involved purchase.

▶▶ *Interest*: Involvement is directly related to consumer interests, as in cars, music, movies, bicycling, or electronics. Naturally, these areas of interest vary from one individual to another. A person highly involved in bike racing will be more interested in the type of bike she owns and will spend quite a bit of time evaluating different bikes. If a person wants a bike only for recreation, however, he may be fairly uninvolved in the purchase and just look for a bike from the most convenient location.

▶▶ *Perceived risk of negative consequences*: As the perceived risk in purchasing a product increases, so does a consumer's level of involvement. The types of risks that concern consumers include financial risk, social risk, and psychological risk. First, financial risk is exposure to loss of wealth or purchasing power. Because high risk is associated with high-priced purchases, consumers tend to become extremely involved. Therefore, price and involvement are usually directly related: As price increases, so does the level of involvement. For example, someone who is purchasing a new car for the first time (higher perceived risk) will spend a lot of time and effort making this purchase. Second, consumers take social risks when they buy products that can affect people's social opinions of them (for example, driving an old, beat-up car or wearing unstylish clothes). Third, buyers undergo psychological risk if they feel that making the wrong decision might cause some concern or anxiety. For example, some consumers feel guilty about eating foods that are not healthy, such as regular ice cream rather than fat-free frozen yogurt.

▶▶ *Situation*: The circumstances of a purchase may temporarily transform a low-involvement decision into a high-involvement one. High involvement comes into play when the consumer perceives risk in a specific situation. For example, an individual might routinely buy low-priced brands of liquor and wine. When the boss visits, however, the consumer might make a high-involvement decision and buy more prestigious brands.

▶▶ *Social visibility*: Involvement also increases as the social visibility of a product increases. Products often on social display include clothing (especially designer labels), jewelry, cars, and furniture. All these items make a statement about the purchaser and, therefore, carry a social risk.

Marketing Implications of Involvement

Marketing strategy varies according to the level of involvement associated with the product. For high-involvement product purchases, marketing managers have several responsibilities. First, promotion to the target market should be extensive and informative. A good ad gives consumers the information they need for making the purchase decision and specifies the benefits and unique advantages of owning the product. For example, a recent two-page ad for Toyota's Camry Hybrid provides extensive information on the personal and planet-wide benefits of choosing their vehicle. Photos of a wide-eyed young girl and a globe are meant to appeal to the customer's care for the future, while captions on interior photos of the car and its engine note the vehicle's unique technology that "drives just like a regular car," benefits which might appeal to the consumer's need for performance.[7] Another ad featured in earlier pages of the same magazine shows the Camry Hybrid being driven along a country road, surrounded by green pastures and grazing horses. The ad is meant to appeal to the consumer who cares that the vehicle is built in the United States and that Toyota is committed to America, its air, its communities, and its future.

For low-involvement product purchases, consumers may not recognize their wants until they are in the store. Therefore, in-store promotion is an important tool when promoting low-involvement products. Marketing managers focus on package design so the product will be eye-catching and easily recognized on the shelf. Examples of products that take this approach are Campbell's soups, Tide detergent, Velveeta cheese, and Heinz ketchup. In-store displays also stimulate sales of low-involvement products. A good display can explain the product's purpose and prompt recognition of a want. Displays of health and beauty aid items in supermarkets have been known to increase sales many times above normal. Coupons, cents-off deals, and two-for-one offers also effectively promote low-involvement items.

Linking a product to a higher-involvement issue is another tactic that marketing managers can use to increase the sales or positive publicity of a low-involvement product. For example, in response to government and consumer concerns about childhood obesity, food manufacturers that advertise to children, such as Kellogg's, Hershey, McDonald's, and General Mills, have pledged to devote at least half of their marketing to the promotion of healthy dietary choices and lifestyles. In Kellogg's case, nearly $206 million in advertising dollars is at stake.[8]

LO 5–LO 8 Factors Influencing Consumer Buying Decisions

The consumer decision-making process does not occur in a vacuum. On the contrary, underlying cultural, social, individual, and psychological factors strongly influence the decision process. These factors have an effect from the time a consumer perceives a stimulus through postpurchase behavior. Cultural factors, which include culture and values, subculture, and social class, exert a broad influence over consumer decision making. Social factors sum up the social interactions between a consumer and influential groups of people, such as reference groups, opinion leaders, and family members. Individual factors, which include gender, age, family life-cycle stage, personality, self-concept, and lifestyle, are unique to each individual and play a major role in the type of products and services consumers want. Psychological factors determine how consumers perceive and interact with their environments and influence the ultimate decisions consumers make. They include perception, motivation, learning, beliefs, and attitudes. Exhibit 6.3 summarizes these influences.

EXHIBIT 6.3
Factors that Affect the Consumer Decision-Making Process

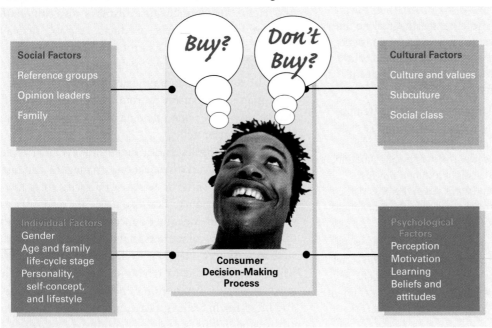

Social Factors

Reference groups

Opinion leaders

Family

Cultural Factors

Culture and values

Subculture

Social class

Buy?

Don't Buy?

Individual Factors

Gender

Age and family life-cycle stage

Personality, self-concept, and lifestyle

Consumer Decision-Making Process

Psychological Factors

Perception

Motivation

Learning

Beliefs and attitudes

© PHOTODISC/GETTY IMAGES

LO 5 Cultural Influences on Consumer Buying Decisions

Of all the factors that affect consumer decision making, cultural factors exert the broadest and deepest influence. Marketers must understand the way people's culture and its accompanying values, as well as their subculture and social class, influence their buying behavior.

Culture and Values

Culture is the essential character of a society that distinguishes it from other cultural groups. The underlying elements of every culture are the values, language, myths, customs, rituals, and laws that shape the behavior of the people, as well as the material artifacts, or products, of that behavior as they are transmitted from one generation to the next.

Culture is pervasive. Cultural values and influences are the ocean in which individuals swim, and yet most are completely unaware that it is there.

culture the set of values, norms, attitudes, and other meaningful symbols that shape human behavior and the artifacts, or products, of that behavior as they are transmitted from one generation to the next

value the enduring belief that a specific mode of conduct is personally or socially preferable to another mode of conduct

What people eat, how they dress, what they think and feel, and what language they speak are all dimensions of culture. It encompasses all the things consumers do without conscious choice because their culture's values, customs, and rituals are ingrained in their daily habits.

Culture is functional. Human interaction creates values and prescribes acceptable behavior for each culture. By establishing common expectations, culture gives order to society. Sometimes these expectations are enacted into laws. For example, drivers in our culture must stop at a red light. Other times these expectations are taken for granted: grocery stores and hospitals are open 24 hours, whereas banks are open only during bankers' hours.

Culture is learned. Consumers are not born knowing the values and norms of their society. Instead, they must learn what is acceptable from family and friends. Children learn the values that will govern their behavior from parents, teachers, and peers. As members of our society, they learn to shake hands when they greet someone, to drive on the right-hand side of the road, and to eat pizza and drink Coca-Cola.

Culture is dynamic. It adapts to changing needs and an evolving environment. The rapid growth of technology in today's world has accelerated the rate of cultural change. Television has changed entertainment patterns and family communication and has heightened public awareness of political and other news events. Automation has increased the amount of leisure time we have and, in some ways, has changed the traditional work ethic. Cultural norms will continue to evolve because of our need for social patterns that solve problems.

The most defining element of a culture is its **values**—the enduring beliefs shared by a society that a specific mode of conduct is personally or socially preferable to another mode of conduct. People's value systems have a great effect on their consumer behavior. Consumers with similar value systems tend to react alike to prices and other marketing-related inducements. Values also correspond to consumption patterns. For example, Americans place a high value on convenience. This value has created lucrative markets for products such as breakfast bars, energy bars, and nutrition bars that allow consumers to eat on the go. Values can also influence consumers' television viewing habits or the magazines they read. For instance, people who strongly object to violence avoid crime shows, and those who oppose pornography do not buy *Hustler*.

Understanding Cultural Differences

As more companies expand their operations globally, the need to understand the cultures of foreign countries becomes more important. A firm has little chance of selling products in a culture that it does not understand. Like people, products have cultural values and rules that influence their perception and use. Culture, therefore, must be understood before the behavior of individuals within the cultural context can be understood. Colors, for example, may have different meanings in global markets than they do at home. In China, white is the color of mourning, and brides wear red. In the United States, black is for mourning, and brides wear white.

Language is another important aspect of culture that global marketers must consider. When translating product names, slogans, and promotional messages into foreign languages, they must be careful not to convey the wrong message. General Motors discovered too late that Nova (the name of an economical car) literally means "doesn't go" in Spanish; Coors encouraged its English-speaking customers to "Turn it loose," but the phrase in Spanish means "Suffer from diarrhea."

Although marketers expanding into global markets generally adapt their products and business formats to the local culture, some fear that increasing globalization, as well as the proliferation of the Internet, will result in a homogeneous world culture of the future. U.S. companies in particular, they fear, are Americanizing the world by exporting bastions of American culture, such as McDonald's fast-food restaurants, Starbucks coffeehouses, Microsoft software, and American movies and entertainment.

Subculture

A culture can be divided into subcultures on the basis of demographic characteristics, geographic regions, national and ethnic background, political beliefs, and religious beliefs. A **subculture** is a homogeneous group of people who share elements of the overall culture as well as cultural elements unique to their own group. Within subcultures, people's attitudes, values, and purchase decisions are even more similar than they are within the broader culture. Within subcultures, people's attitudes, values, and purchase decisions are even more similar than they are within the broader culture. Subcultural differences may result in considerable variation within a culture in what, how, when, and where people buy goods and services.

In the United States alone, countless subcultures can be identified. Many are concentrated geographically. People who belong to the Church of Jesus Christ of Latter-Day Saints, for example, are clustered mainly in Utah; Cajuns are located in the bayou regions of southern Louisiana. Many Hispanics live in states bordering Mexico, whereas the majority of Chinese, Japanese, and Korean Americans are found on the West Coast. Other subcultures are geographically dispersed. Computer hackers, people who are hearing or visually impaired, Harley-Davidson bikers, military families, university professors, and gays may be found throughout the country. Yet they have identifiable attitudes, values, and needs that distinguish them from the larger culture.

Once marketers identify subcultures, they can design special marketing to serve their needs. Some companies launch simultaneous campaigns to reach different subcultures. According to the U.S. Census Bureau, the Hispanic population is the largest and fastest-growing subculture, increasing four times as fast as the general population. To tap into this large and growing segment, marketers have been forming partnerships with broadcasters that have an established Latino audience. The Univision Radio network covers approximately 73 percent of the U.S. Hispanic population and has over 10 million listeners weekly. State Farm has partnered with Julie Stav, the leading financial expert to the Latino community, to sponsor evening broadcasts of her hugely successful Spanish-language radio show. When Sweden-based furniture manufacturer IKEA found that it wasn't capturing the large Latino demographic in U.S. cities, it started advertising in Spanish. It also launched a series of commercials featuring Latina soap opera stars on Telemundo—the second-largest U.S. Spanish-language broadcaster. IKEA saw immediate results with more Latinos in their stores.[9]

subculture a homogeneous group of people who share elements of the overall culture as well as unique elements of their own group

EXHIBIT 6.4
U.S. Social Classes

Upper Classes		
Capitalist class	1%	People whose investment decisions shape the national economy; income mostly from assets, earned or inherited; university connections
Upper middle class	14%	Upper-level managers, professionals, owners of medium-sized businesses; well-to-do, stay-at-home homemakers who decline occupational work by choice; college-educated; family income well above national average
Middle Classes		
Middle class	33%	Middle-level white-collar, top-level blue-collar; education past high school typical; income somewhat above national average; loss of manufacturing jobs has reduced the population of this class
Working class	32%	Middle-level blue-collar, lower-level white-collar; income below national average; largely working in skilled or semi-skilled service jobs
Lower Classes		
Working poor	11–12%	Low-paid service workers and operatives; some high school education; below mainstream in living standard; crime and hunger are daily threats
Underclass	8–9%	People who are not regularly employed and who depend primarily on the welfare system for sustenance; little schooling; living standard below poverty line

SOURCE: Adapted from Richard P. Coleman, "The Continuing Significance of Social Class to Marketing," *Journal of Consumer Research*, December 1983, 267; Dennis Gilbert and Joseph A. Kahl, *The American Class Structure: A Synthesis* (Homewood, IL: Dorsey Press, 1982), ch. 11, http://en.wikipedia.org/wiki/social_structure_of_the_united_states, May 2006.

Social Class

The United States, like other societies, has a social class system. A **social class** is a group of people who are considered nearly equal in status or community esteem, who regularly socialize among themselves both formally and informally, and who share behavioral norms.

A number of techniques have been used to measure social class, and a number of criteria have been used to define it. One view of contemporary U.S. status structure is shown in Exhibit 6.4.

As you can see from Exhibit 6.4, the upper and upper middle classes comprise the small segment of affluent and wealthy Americans. In terms of consumer buying patterns, the affluent are more likely to own their own home and purchase new cars and trucks and are less likely to smoke. The very rich flex their financial muscles by spending more on vacation homes, vacations and cruises, and housekeeping and gardening services. The most affluent consumers are more likely to attend art auctions and galleries, dance performances, operas, the theater, museums, concerts, and sporting events. Marketers often pay attention to the superwealthy. For example, the Mercedes-Benz Maybach 62, touted as the "world's most luxurious car," is aimed at this group. Priced at $375,000, the car features electronic doors, reclining seats with footrests, a workstation with media capability, a champagne cooler, and lots more. Similarly, New York-based designer Calvin Stewart sells A.P.O. jeans featuring fully customized denim embellished with diamond, gold, and platinum details—starting at $1,000 a pair. The majority of Americans today define themselves as middle class, regardless of their actual income or educational attainment. This phenomenon most likely occurs because working-class Americans tend to aspire to the middle-class lifestyle while some of those who do achieve affluence may downwardly aspire to respectable middle-class status as a matter of principle.

The working class is a distinct subset of the middle class. Interest in organized labor is one of the most common attributes among the working class. This group often rates job security as the most important reason for taking a job. The working-class person depends heavily on relatives and the community for economic and emotional support.

Lifestyle distinctions between the social classes are greater than the distinctions within a given class. The most significant difference between the classes occurs between the middle and lower classes, where there is a major shift in lifestyles. Members of the lower class have incomes at or below the poverty level.

Social class is typically measured as a combination of occupation, income, education, wealth, and other variables. For instance, affluent upper-class consumers are more likely to be salaried executives or self-employed professionals with at least an under-

social class a group of people in a society who are considered nearly equal in status or community esteem, who regularly socialize among themselves both formally and informally, and who share behavioral norms

graduate degree. Working-class or middle-class consumers are more likely to be hourly service workers or blue-collar employees with only a high school education. Educational attainment, however, seems to be the most reliable indicator of a person's social and economic status. Those with college degrees or graduate degrees are more likely to fall into the upper classes, while those people with some college experience fall closest to traditional concepts of the middle class.

Marketers are interested in social class for two main reasons. First, social class often indicates which medium to use for advertising. Suppose an insurance company seeks to sell its policies to middle-class families. It might advertise during the local evening news because middle-class families tend to watch more television than other classes do. If the company wanted to sell more policies to upscale individuals, it might place a print ad in a business publication like *The Wall Street Journal*. The Internet, long the domain of more educated and affluent families, is becoming an increasingly important advertising outlet for advertisers hoping to reach blue-collar workers and homemakers. As the middle class rapidly adopts the medium, marketers have to do more research to find out which Web sites will reach their audience.

Second, knowing what products appeal to which social classes can help marketers determine where to best distribute their products. Affluent Americans, a fifth of the U.S. population, were responsible for nearly half of all new car and truck sales and more than half of hotel stays and vacation homes. This same group spent nearly twice as much as less-affluent Americans on restaurant fare, alcohol, sporting events, plays, and club memberships.[10]

For the first time in a long while, however, industry analysts are seeing shares of discount chains faring better than their full-priced and upscale counterparts. These days, analysts say, the big-box and discount retailers' greatest challenge has been courting consumers who fall in the middle-income level. The result is a fiercely competitive retail environment where discount retailers have focused less on their core, low-income consumers, who are most impacted by rising housing and gas costs. Overall, however, shares of discount chains are faring better during this particular penny-pinching economy than their full-priced and upscale counterparts, because discount retailers have focused on getting current customers to purchase a wider array of products in the store, rather than trying to attract new shoppers.[11]

LO 6 Social Influences on Consumer Buying Decisions

Many consumers seek out the opinions of others to reduce their search and evaluation effort or uncertainty, especially as the perceived risk of the decision increases. Consumers may also seek out others' opinions for guidance on new products or services, products with image-related attributes, or products where attribute information is lacking or uninformative. Specifically, consumers interact socially with reference groups, opinion leaders, and family members to obtain product information and decision approval.

Reference Groups

All the formal and informal groups that influence the buying behavior of an individual are that person's **reference groups**. Consumers may use products or brands to identify with or become a member of a group. They learn from observing how members of their reference groups consume, and they use the same criteria to make their own consumer decisions.

Reference groups can be categorized very broadly as either direct or indirect (see Exhibit 6.5). Direct reference groups are face-to-face membership groups that touch people's lives directly. They can be either primary or secondary. **Primary membership groups** include all groups with which people interact regularly

EXHIBIT 6.5
Types of Reference Groups

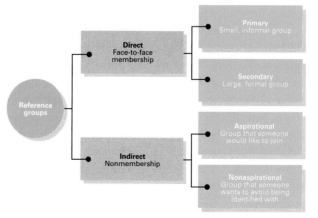

in an informal, face-to-face manner, such as family, friends, and coworkers. In contrast, people associate with **secondary membership groups** less consistently and more formally. These groups might include clubs, professional groups, and religious groups.

Consumers also are influenced by many indirect, nonmembership reference groups they do not belong to. **Aspirational reference groups** are those a person would like to join. To join an aspirational group, a person must at least conform to the norms of that group. (**Norms** are the values and attitudes deemed acceptable by the group.) Thus, a person who wants to be elected to public office may begin to dress more conservatively, as other politicians do. He or she may go to many of the restaurants and social engagements that city and business leaders attend and try to play a role that is acceptable to voters and other influential people. Similarly, teenagers today may dye their hair and experiment with body piercing and tattoos. Athletes are an aspirational group for several market segments. To appeal to the younger market, Coca-Cola signed basketball star LeBron James to be the spokesperson for its Sprite and Powerade brands, and Nike signed a sneaker deal with him reportedly worth $90 million. Coca-Cola and Nike assumed James would encourage consumers to drink Coke brands and buy Nike shoes because they would like to identify with James.

Nonaspirational reference groups, or dissociative groups, influence our behavior when we try to maintain distance from them. A consumer may avoid buying some types of clothing or car, going to certain restaurants or stores, or even buying a home in a certain neighborhood in order to avoid being associated with a particular group.

The activities, values, and goals of reference groups directly influence consumer behavior. For marketers, reference groups have three important implications: (1) they serve as information sources and influence perceptions; (2) they affect an individual's aspiration levels; and (3) their norms either constrain or stimulate consumer behavior. For example, research firms devoted to uncovering what's cool in the teen market have identified a couple of influential groups among today's teens based on their interests in clothes, music, and activities. Tracking these groups reveals how

products become cool and how groups influence the adoption of cool products by other groups. A trend or fad often starts with teens who have the most innovative tastes. These teens are on the cutting edge of fashion and music, and they wear their attitude all over their bodies in the form of tattoos, body piercing, studded jewelry, or colored tresses. Certain fads embraced by these "Edgers" will spark an interest in the small group of teens researchers call "Influencers," who project the look other teens covet. Influencers also create their own trends in music and clothing choices. Once a fad is embraced and adopted by Influencers, the look becomes cool and desirable. The remaining groups that comprise the majority of the teen population will not embrace a fad until it gets its seal of approval from the Influencers.

Understanding the effect of reference groups on a product is important for marketers as they track the life cycle of their products. Retailer Abercrombie & Fitch noticed it was beginning to lose its target audience of college students when its stores began attracting large numbers of high school students trying to be more like the college students. To solve the problem, A&F created its Hollister store chain specifically for high school students. The retailer also opened a chain called Abercrombie for a target market of boys and girls, ages seven to fourteen. Another A&F chain, Ruehl, offers Greenwich Village-inspired clothing for the post-college-age market.

Research has shown that reference groups are particularly powerful in influencing purchases of fragrances, wine, snack food, candy, clothing, and sodas.[12] People with well-formed networks of somewhat overlapping reference groups and those with strong personal values are less susceptible to reference group influences.[13]

Opinion Leaders

Reference groups frequently include individuals known as group leaders, or **opinion leaders**—those who influence others. Obviously, it is important for marketing managers to persuade such people to purchase their goods or services. Many products and services that are integral parts of Americans' lives today got their initial boost from opinion leaders. For example, DVDs and SUVs (sport-utility vehicles) were purchased by opinion leaders well ahead of the general public.

Opinion leaders are often the first to try new products and services out of pure curiosity. They are typically self-indulgent and status seeking, making them more likely to explore unproven but intriguing

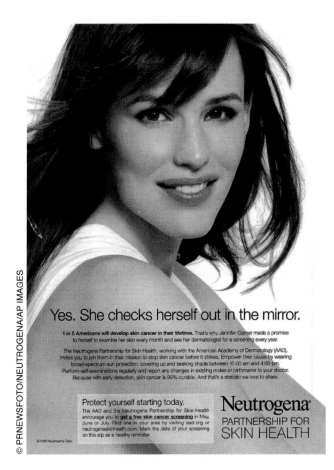

Yes. She checks herself out in the mirror.

1 in 5 Americans will develop skin cancer in their lifetime. That's why Jennifer Garner made a promise to herself to examine her skin every month and see her dermatologist for a screening every year.

The Neutrogena Partnership for Skin Health, working with the American Academy of Dermatology (AAD), invites you to join them in their mission to stop skin cancer before it strikes. Empower their cause by wearing broad-spectrum sun protection, covering up and seeking shade between 10:00 am and 4:00 pm. Perform self-examinations regularly and report any changes in existing moles or birthmarks to your doctor. Because with early detection, skin cancer is 99% curable. And that's a statistic we love to share.

Protect yourself starting today.
The AAD and the Neutrogena Partnership for Skin Health encourage you to **get a free skin cancer screening** in May, June or July. Find one in your area by visiting aad.org or neutrogenaskinhealth.com. Mark the date of your screening on this slip as a healthy reminder.

Neutrogena®
PARTNERSHIP FOR
SKIN HEALTH

products and services.[14] Technology companies have found that teenagers, because of their willingness to experiment, are key opinion leaders for the success of new technologies.

Opinion leadership is a casual, face-to-face phenomenon and is usually inconspicuous, so locating opinion leaders can be a challenge. Thus, marketers often try to create opinion leaders. They may use high school cheerleaders to model new fall fashions or civic leaders to promote insurance, new cars, and other merchandise. On a national level, companies sometimes use movie stars, sports figures, and other celebrities to promote products, hoping they are appropriate opinion leaders. The effectiveness of celebrity endorsements varies, though, depending largely on how credible and attractive the spokesperson is and how familiar people are with him or her. Endorsements are most likely to succeed if a reasonable association between the spokesperson and the product can be established.

Respected organizations such as the American Heart Association and the American Cancer Society may also serve as opinion leaders. Marketers may seek endorsements from them as well as from schools, churches, cities, the military, and fraternal organizations as a form of group opinion leadership. Sales-people often ask to use opinion leaders' names as a means of achieving greater personal influence in a sales presentation.

How Blogs Are Defining Today's Opinion Leaders

Increasingly, marketers are looking to Web logs, or blogs, as they're commonly called, to find opinion leaders. A new blog is created every second of every day according to Technorati, a blog-monitoring site, so it's getting harder to separate the true opinion leaders from intermediate Web users who are just looking to share random thoughts or vacation photos with family and friends. As of this printing, Technorati monitors 36.3 million blogs, Feedster monitors 80 million, and Nielsen BuzzMetrics boasts coverage of more than 25 million blogs.[15] The fashion industry used to dismiss bloggers as irrelevant and small-time, effectively limiting their access to hot events during semi-annual fashion week shows. Now, however, fashion bloggers have the attention of the fashion establishment because many are claiming bigger followings than traditional media. Still, not all fashion blogs are equal. Bloggers from FashionTribes.com and Bagtrends.com received tickets to some fall 2006 shows, but shopology.com and Coutorture.com were denied access because their audiences were too small.[16]

One way marketers are identifying true opinion leaders is by looking to teen blogs to identify the social trends that are shaping consumer behavior. During the research phase of development for its teen-targeted RED Blogs service, AOL discovered that over 50 percent of teens do not mind sharing their feelings in public forums. This is especially evident at social networking sites like MySpace, Facebook, and Xanga, where teens and twenty-somethings post extensive personal profiles, photo collections, links to user groups they belong to, and detailed descriptions of their social events.

Raised with MTV, 500-channel cable services, a rapidly maturing Internet, and ever-expanding cell phone capabilities, teens have unprecedented access to the world around them. Furthermore, they are no longer passive observers of the culture their parents have created. They can follow their favorite bands, actors, or athletes via their Web sites and blogs and expect to interact with them instead of just admiring them from afar. With their unprecedented ability to network and communicate with each other, young people rely on each others' opinions more than marketing messages when making purchase decisions. And blogs

AMERICAN TEENS HAVE A TOTAL INCOME OF $80 BILLION OF THEIR OWN, AND **PARENTS SPEND** AN ADDITIONAL $110 BILLION EACH YEAR **ON THEM.**

socialization process how cultural values and norms are passed down to children

are becoming a key way that teens communicate their opinions. Consequently, today's marketers are reading teen blogs, developing products that meet the very specific needs that teens express there, and learning unique and creative ways to put key influencers in charge of marketing their brands for them.

Family

The family is the most important social institution for many consumers, strongly influencing values, attitudes, self-concept—and buying behavior. For example, a family that strongly values good health will have a grocery list distinctly different from that of a family that views every dinner as a gourmet event. Moreover, the family is responsible for the **socialization process**, the passing down of cultural values and norms to children. Children learn by observing their parents' consumption patterns, and so they will tend to shop in a similar pattern.

Decision-making roles among family members tend to vary significantly, depending on the type of item purchased. Family members assume a variety of roles in the purchase process. *Initiators* suggest, initiate, or plant the seed for the purchase process. The initiator can be any member of the family. For example, Sister might initiate the product search by asking for a new bicycle as a birthday present. *Influencers* are those members of the family whose opinions are valued. In our example, Mom might function as a price-range watchdog, an influencer whose main role is to veto or approve price ranges. Brother may give his opinion on certain makes of bicycles. The *decision maker* is the family member who actually makes the decision to buy or not to buy. For example, Dad or Mom is likely to choose the final brand and model of bicycle to buy after seeking further information from Sister about cosmetic features such as color and then imposing additional criteria of his or her own, such as

durability and safety. The *purchaser* (probably Dad or Mom) is the one who actually exchanges money for the product. Finally, the consumer is the actual user—Sister, in the case of the bicycle.

Marketers should consider family purchase situations along with the distribution of consumer and decision-maker roles among family members. Ordinary marketing views the individual as both decision maker and consumer. Family marketing adds several other possibilities: sometimes more than one family member or all family members are involved in the decision; sometimes only children are involved in the decision; sometimes more than one consumer is involved; and sometimes the decision maker and the consumer are different people. In most households when parental joint decisions are being made, spouses consider their partner's needs and perceptions to maintain decision fairness and harmony.[17] This tends to minimize family conflict. Research also shows that in harmonious households the spouse that has "won" a previous decision is less likely to use strong influence in a subsequent decision.[18] This balancing factor is key in maintaining long-term family harmony.

Children can have great influence over the purchase decisions of their parents. In many families, with both parents working and short on time, children are encouraged to participate. In addition, children in single-parent households become more involved in family decisions at an earlier age. Children are especially influential in decisions about food and eating out. Exactly how much of an influence kids have varies depending on factors such as age, race, socioeconomic status, and region. For example, Restaurants & Institutions' New American Diner study shows that children age 5 or younger frequently influence restaurant visits, while children ages 6 to 18 have only occasional influence. Females, Generation Xers, Asian-Americans, and Midwesterners are most likely to say children influence which restaurants they visit.[19] Children influence purchase decisions for many more products and services than food. Even though they are usually not the actual purchasers of such items, children often participate in decisions about toys, clothes, vacations, recreation, automobiles, and many other products. And if those children happen to be teenagers? American teens have a total income of $80 billion of their own, and parents spend an additional $110 billion each year on them. Recent data shows that while teens make up only 7 percent of the U.S. population, they actually contribute to 11 percent of U.S. spending.[20]

Traditionally, children learn about consumption from their parents. In today's technologically overloaded world, that trend is reversing. Teenagers and adult children often contribute information and influence the purchase of parents' technology products.[21] Often they even help with installation and show the parents how to use the product!

LO7 Individual Influences on Consumer Buying Decisions

A person's buying decisions are also influenced by personal characteristics that are unique to each individual, such as gender; age and life cycle stage; and personality, self-concept, and lifestyle. Individual characteristics are generally stable over the course of one's life. For instance, most people do not change their gender, and the act of changing personality or lifestyle requires a complete reorientation of one's life. In the case of age and life cycle stage, these changes occur gradually over time.

Gender

Physiological differences between men and women result in different needs, such as health and beauty products. Just as important are the distinct cultural, social, and economic roles played by men and women and the effects that these

have on their decision-making processes. For example, many networks have programming targeted to women, while Spike TV calls itself the "first network for men." Two magazines are geared to men who like to shop: *Details* is an upscale fashion magazine for affluent men in their 20s and 30s; *Complex* is a magazine for younger men whose fashions range from hiphop and skateboarding to mainstream style.

Trends in gender marketing are influenced by the changing roles of men and women in society. For example, men used to rely on the women in their lives to shop for them. Today, however, more men are shopping for themselves. The number of men shopping online was up to 57 percent in 2007 from 38 percent in 2006. Census Bureau figures show that in March 2003, the latest year for which census statistics are available, there were 299,000 married-family households in which the husband was at home with at least one child under six. This figure was up 29 percent from 1993.[22] Men who have begun staying at home with their young children have noticed how few baby items, such as diaper bags, are made with a man's use in mind. One man went so far as to create his own product line, at dadgear.com. The first year the products hit the market, revenue was slightly higher than $40,000; projected revenue for 2006 was $800,000 to $1 million.[23] Whether because of the advent of online shopping or retailers wising up to the way men like to shop, today more men are comfortable shopping for themselves. A study commissioned by GQ found that 84 percent of men said they purchase their own clothes, compared with 65 percent four years ago.[24]

Age and Family Life-Cycle Stage

The age and family life-cycle stage of a consumer can have a significant impact on consumer behavior. How old a consumer is generally indicates what products he or she may be interested in purchasing. Consumer tastes in food, clothing, cars, furniture, and recreation are often age related.

Related to a person's age is his or her place in the family life cycle. As Chapter 7 explains in more detail, the *family life cycle* is an orderly series of stages through which consumers' attitudes and behavioral tendencies evolve through maturity, experience, and changing income and status.

personality a way of organizing and grouping the consistencies of an individual's reactions to situations

self-concept how consumers perceive themselves in terms of attitudes, perceptions, beliefs, and self-evaluations

Marketers often define their target markets in terms of family life cycle, such as "young singles," "young married with children," and "middle-aged married without children." For instance, young singles spend more than average on alcoholic beverages, education, and entertainment. New parents typically increase their spending on health care, clothing, housing, and food and decrease their spending on alcohol, education, and transportation. Households with older children spend more on food, entertainment, personal care products, and education, as well as cars and gasoline. After their children leave home, spending by older couples on vehicles, women's clothing, health care, and long-distance calls typically increases. For instance, the presence of children in the home is the most significant determinant of the type of vehicle that's driven off the new car lot. Parents are the ultimate need-driven car consumers, requiring larger cars and trucks to haul their children and all their belongings. It comes as no surprise then that for all households with children, SUVs rank either first or second among new-vehicle purchases, followed by minivans.

Marketers should also be aware of the many non-traditional life-cycle paths that are common today and provide insights into the needs and wants of such consumers as divorced parents, lifelong singles, and childless couples. Three decades ago, married couples with children under the age of 18 accounted for about half of U.S. households. Today, such families make up only 23 percent of all households, while people living alone or with nonfamily members represent more than 30 percent. Furthermore, according to the U.S. Census Bureau, the number of single-mother households grew by 25 percent over the last decade. The shift toward more single-parent households is part of a broader societal change that has put more women on the career track. Although many marketers continue to be wary of targeting nontraditional families, Charles Schwab targeted single mothers in an advertising campaign featuring Sarah Ferguson, the Duchess of York and a divorced mom. The idea was to appeal to single mothers' heightened awareness of the need for financial self-sufficiency.

Life Events Another way to look at the life cycle is to look at major events in one's life over time. Life-changing events can occur at any time. A few examples are: death of a spouse, moving to a different place, birth or adoption of a child, retirement, getting fired, divorce, and marriage. Typically, such events are quite stressful and consumers often take steps to minimize that stress. Many times such life-changing events will mean new consumption patterns.[25] A recent divorcee may try to improve his or her appearance by joining a health club and dieting. A person moving to a different city will need a new dentist, grocery store, auto service center and doctor, to name a few shops and service providers. Marketers realize that life-events often mean a chance to gain a new customer. The Welcome Wagon offers a number of free gifts and services for area newcomers. Lowe's sends out a discount coupon to those moving to a new community. And when you put your home on the market, very quickly you start getting flyers from moving companies promising a great price on moving your household goods.

Personality, Self-Concept, and Lifestyle

Each consumer has a unique personality. **Personality** is a broad concept that can be thought of as a way of organizing and grouping how an individual typically reacts to situations. Thus, personality combines psychological makeup and environmental forces. It includes people's underlying dispositions, especially their most dominant characteristics. Although personality is one of the least useful concepts in the study of consumer behavior, some marketers believe that personality influences the types and brands of products purchased. For instance, the type of car, clothes, or jewelry a consumer buys may reflect one or more personality traits.

Self-concept, or self-perception, is how consumers perceive themselves. Self-concept includes attitudes, perceptions, beliefs, and self-evaluations. Although self-concept may change, the change is often gradual. Through self-concept, people define their identity, which in turn provides for consistent and coherent behavior.

© INSPIRESTOCK/JUPITERIMAGES

GENERALLY, WE TRY TO RAISE OUR REAL SELF-IMAGE TOWARD OUR IDEAL.

Self-concept combines the **ideal self-image** (the way an individual would like to be) and the **real self-image** (how an individual actually perceives himself or herself). Generally, we try to raise our real self-image toward our ideal (or at least narrow the gap). Consumers seldom buy products that jeopardize their self-image. For example, someone who sees herself as a trendsetter wouldn't buy clothing that doesn't project a contemporary image.

Human behavior depends largely on self-concept. Because consumers want to protect their identity as individuals, the products they buy, the stores they patronize, and the credit cards they carry support their self-image. No other product quite reflects a person's self-image as much as the car he or she drives. For example, many young consumers do not like family sedans like the Honda Accord or Toyota Camry and say they would buy one for their mom, but not for themselves. Likewise, younger parents may avoid purchasing minivans because they do not want to sacrifice the youthful image they have of themselves just because they have new responsibilities. To combat decreasing sales, marketers of the Nissan Quest minivan decided to reposition it as something other than a "mom mobile" or "soccer mom car." They chose the ad copy "Passion built it. Passion will fill it up," followed by "What if we made a minivan that changed the way people think of minivans?"

By influencing the degree to which consumers perceive a good or service to be self-relevant, marketers can affect consumers' motivation to learn about, shop for, and buy a certain brand. Marketers also consider self-concept important because it helps explain the relationship between individuals' perceptions of themselves and their consumer behavior.

Many companies now use psychographics to better understand their market segments. For many years, marketers selling products to mothers conveniently assumed that all moms were fairly homogeneous and concerned about the same things—the health and well-being of their children—and that they could all be reached with a similar message. But recent lifestyle research has shown that there are traditional, blended, and nontraditional moms, and companies like Procter & Gamble and Pillsbury are using strategies to reach these different types of mothers. Psychographics is also effective with other market segments. Psychographics and lifestyle segmentation are discussed in more detail in Chapter 7.

ideal self-image
the way an individual would like to be

real self-image the way an individual actually perceives himself or herself

perception the process by which people select, organize, and interpret stimuli into a meaningful and coherent picture

selective exposure the process whereby a consumer notices certain stimuli and ignores others

LO 8 Psychological Influences on Consumer Buying Decisions

An individual's buying decisions are further influenced by psychological factors: perception, motivation, learning, and beliefs and attitudes. These factors are what consumers use to interact with their world. They are the tools consumers use to recognize their feelings, gather and analyze information, formulate thoughts and opinions, and take action. Unlike the other three influences on consumer behavior, psychological influences can be affected by a person's environment because they are applied on specific occasions. For example, you will perceive different stimuli and process these stimuli in different ways depending on whether you are sitting in class concentrating on the instructor, sitting outside of class talking to friends, or sitting in your dorm room watching television.

Perception

The world is full of stimuli. A stimulus is any unit of input affecting one or more of the five senses: sight, smell, taste, touch, and hearing. The process by which we select, organize, and interpret these stimuli into a meaningful and coherent picture is called **perception**. In essence, perception is how we see the world around us and how we recognize that we need some help in making a purchasing decision.

People cannot perceive every stimulus in their environment. Therefore, they use **selective exposure** to decide which stimuli to notice and which to ignore. A typical consumer is exposed to more than 2,500

selective distortion a process whereby a consumer changes or distorts information that conflicts with his or her feelings or beliefs

selective retention a process whereby a consumer remembers only that information that supports personal beliefs

advertising messages a day, but notices only between 11 and 20.

The familiarity of an object, contrast, movement, intensity (such as increased volume), and smell are cues that influence perception. Consumers use these cues to identify and define products and brands. The shape of a product's packaging, such as Coca-Cola's signature contour bottle, for instance, can influence perception. Color is another cue, and it plays a key role in consumers' perceptions. Packaged foods manufacturers use color to trigger unconscious associations for grocery shoppers who typically make their shopping decisions in the blink of an eye. Ampacet, a world leader in color additives for plastics, reported in 2007 that nature-inspired colors and organic values were becoming more popular as the economy and global focus shifted from the tech-boom to bio- or eco-boom. Ecological consequences and concerns have resulted in marketing initiatives such as "going green." Packaging colors like natural greens, earthy browns, and strong yellows are in, as well as metallics such as steely silver, carbon black, gold, and copper. Color researchers speculate that technological overload has led to resurgence in the appreciation of simplistic luxury. Color names for fabrics and makeup reflect that trend with names such as Grounded, Champagne Chic, and Serene Blue.[26]

What is perceived by consumers may also depend on the stimuli's vividness or shock value. Graphic warnings of the hazards associated with a product's use are perceived more readily and remembered more accurately than less vivid warnings or warnings that are written in text. "Sexier" ads excel at attracting the attention of younger consumers. Companies like Calvin Klein and Guess use sensuous ads intended to create a fantasy or mood to capture the attention of the target audience. Fragrance advertisements often make promises of the "outcome" of wearing their product, often the promise of a role transformation on the part of the wearer. David Rubin, brand development director for Axe deodorant, says Axe's theme from the very start has been "giving guys an edge in the mating game."[27]

Two other concepts closely related to selective exposure are selective distortion and selective retention. **Selective distortion** occurs when consumers change or distort information that conflicts with their feelings or beliefs. For example, suppose a college student buys a Sonicblue Rio MP3 player. After the pur-

chase, if the student gets new information about an alternative brand, such as an Apple iPod, he or she may distort the information to make it more consistent with the prior view that the Sonicblue Rio is just as good as the iPod, if not better. Business travelers who fly often may distort or discount information about airline crashes because they must use air travel constantly in their jobs.

ONE STUDY FOUND THAT THE JUST-NOTICEABLE DIFFERENCE IN A STIMULUS IS ABOUT A 20 PERCENT CHANGE. FOR EXAMPLE, CONSUMERS WILL LIKELY NOTICE A 20 PERCENT PRICE DECREASE MORE QUICKLY THAN A 15 PERCENT DECREASE.

Selective retention is remembering only information that supports personal feelings or beliefs. The consumer forgets all information that may be inconsistent. After reading a pamphlet that contradicts one's political beliefs, for instance, a person may forget many of the points outlined in it. Similarly, consumers may see a news report on suspected illegal practices by their favorite retail store but soon forget the reason the store was featured on the news.

Which stimuli will be perceived often depends on the individual. People can be exposed to the same stimuli under identical conditions but perceive them very differently. For example, two people viewing a television commercial may have different interpretations of the advertising message. One person may be thoroughly engrossed by the message and become highly motivated to buy the product. Thirty seconds after the ad ends, the second person may not be able to recall the content of the message or even the product advertised.

Marketing Implications of Perception Marketers must recognize the importance of cues, or signals, in consumers' perception of products. Marketing managers first identify the important attributes, such as price or quality, that the targeted consumers want in a product and then design signals to communicate these attributes. For example, consumers will pay more for candy in expensive-looking foil packages. But shiny labels on wine bottles signify less expensive wines; dull labels indicate more expensive wines. Marketers also often use price as a signal to consumers that the product is of higher quality than competing products. Gibson Guitar Corporation briefly cut prices on many of its guitars to compete with Japanese rivals Yamaha and Ibanez but found that it sold more guitars when it charged more for them. Consumers perceived that the higher price indicated a better quality instrument.[28] Of course, brand names send signals to consumers. The brand names of Close-Up toothpaste, DieHard batteries, and Caress moisturizing soap, for example, identify important product qualities. Names chosen for search engines and sites on the Internet, such as Yahoo!, Amazon.com, and Excite, are intended to convey excitement, intensity, and vastness. Companies may even change their names to send a message to consumers. As today's utility companies increasingly enter unregulated markets, many are shaking their stodgy "Power & Light & Electric" names in favor of those that let consumers know they are not just about electricity anymore, such as Reliant Resources, Entergy, and Cinergy.

Consumers also associate quality and reliability with certain brand names. Companies watch their brand identity closely, in large part because a strong link has been established between perceived brand value and customer loyalty. Brand names that consistently enjoy high perceived value from consumers include Kodak, Disney, National Geographic, Mercedes-Benz, and Fisher-Price. Naming a product after a place can also add perceived value by association. Brand names using the words Santa Fe, Dakota, or Texas convey a sense of openness, freedom, and youth, but products named after other locations might conjure up images of pollution and crime. Marketing managers are also interested in the *threshold level of perception*: the minimum difference in a stimulus that the consumer will notice. This concept is sometimes referred to as the "just-noticeable difference." For example, how much would Apple have to drop the price of its iPod Shuffle before consumers recognized it as a bargain—$25? $50? or more? One study found that the just-noticeable difference in a stimulus is about a 20 percent change. For example, consumers will likely notice a 20 percent price decrease more quickly than a 15 percent decrease. This marketing principle can be applied to other marketing variables as well, such as package size or loudness of a broadcast advertisement.[29]

Besides changing such stimuli as price, package size, and volume, marketers can change the product or attempt to reposition its image. But marketers must be careful when adding features. How many new services will discounter Target need to add before consumers perceive it as a full-service department store? How many sporty features will General Motors have to add to a basic two-door sedan before consumers start perceiving it as a sports car?

Marketing managers who intend to do business in global markets should be aware of how foreign consumers perceive their products. For instance, in Japan, product labels are often written in English or French, even though they may not translate into anything meaningful. Many Japanese associate foreign words on product labels with the exotic, the expensive, and high quality.

Marketers have often been suspected of sending advertising messages subconsciously to consumers in what is known as *subliminal perception*. The controversy began when a researcher claimed to have increased popcorn and Coca-Cola sales at a movie theater after flashing "Eat popcorn" and "Drink Coca-Cola" on the screen every five seconds for 1/300th of a second, although the audience did not consciously recognize the messages. Almost immediately consumer protection groups became concerned that advertisers were brainwashing consumers, and this practice was pronounced illegal in California and Canada. Although the researcher later admitted to making up the data and scientists have been unable to replicate the study since, consumers are still wary of hidden messages that advertisers may be sending.

Motivation

By studying motivation, marketers can analyze the major forces influencing consumers to buy or not buy products. When you buy a product, you usually do so to fulfill some kind of need. These needs become motives when aroused sufficiently. For instance, suppose this morning you were so hungry before class that you needed to eat something. In response to that need, you stopped at McDonald's for an Egg McMuffin. In other words, you were motivated by hunger to stop at McDonald's. **Motives** are the driving forces that cause a person to take action to satisfy specific needs.

motive a driving force that causes a person to take action to satisfy specific needs

EXHIBIT 6.6
Maslow's Hierarchy of Needs

Self-actualization needs
Self-development, self-realization

Esteem needs
Self-esteem, recognition, status

Social needs
Sense of belonging, love

Safety needs
Security, protection

Physiological needs
Hunger, thirst

Maslow's hierarchy of needs
a method of classifying human needs and motivations into five categories in ascending order of importance: physiological, safety, social, esteem, and self-actualization

Why are people driven by particular needs at particular times? One popular theory is **Maslow's hierarchy of needs**, shown in Exhibit 6.6, which arranges needs in ascending order of importance: physiological, safety, social, esteem, and self-actualization. As a person fulfills one need, a higher level need becomes more important.

The most basic human needs are *physiological*—that is, the needs for food, water, and shelter. Because they are essential to survival, these needs must be satisfied first. Ads showing a juicy hamburger or a runner gulping down Gatorade after a marathon are examples of appeals to satisfy the physiological needs of hunger and thirst.

Safety needs include security and freedom from pain and discomfort. Marketers sometimes appeal to consumers' fears and anxieties about safety to sell their products. For example, aware of the aging population's health fears, the retail medical imaging centers Heart Check America and HealthScreen America advertise that they offer consumers a full body scan for early detection of health problems such as coronary disease and cancer. On the other hand, some companies or industries advertise to allay consumer fears. For example, in the wake of the September 11 terrorist attacks, the airline industry found itself having to conduct an image campaign to reassure consumers about the safety of air travel.

After physiological and safety needs have been fulfilled, *social needs*—especially love and a sense of belonging—become the focus. Love includes acceptance by one's peers, as well as sex and romantic love. Marketing managers probably appeal more to this need than to any other. Ads for clothes, cosmetics, and vacation packages suggest that buying the product can bring love. The need to belong is also a favorite of marketers, especially those marketing products to teens. Teens consider Apple's iPod to be not only their favorite branded product, but also as defining their generation. Other such brands include American Eagle Outfitters, Axe, Baby Phat, Facebook, Google, Hollister, MTV, MySpace, Vans, and YouTube. The VP of Research at MTV says marketers need to understand a new dynamic in the "millennial generation" consumer. The relationship this generation has with their parents is completely different from previous generations. Parents can be a best friend. Brands that become too focused on "influential" teens can miss that parents can be the biggest influencer on this age group, especially when it comes to big-ticket items.[30]

Love is acceptance without regard to one's contribution. Esteem is acceptance based on one's contribution to the group. *Self-esteem needs* include self-respect and a sense of accomplishment. Esteem needs also include prestige, fame, and recognition of one's accomplishments. Mont Blanc pens, Mercedes-Benz automobiles, and Neiman Marcus stores all appeal to esteem needs.

The highest human need is *self-actualization*. It refers to finding self-fulfillment and self-expression, reaching the point in life at which "people are what they

feel they should be." Maslow felt that very few people ever attain this level. Even so, advertisements may focus on this type of need. For example, American Express ads convey the message that acquiring its card is one of the highest attainments in life. Microsoft appealed to consumers' needs for self-actualization when it chose "Your Potential. Our Passion" as the Windows XP slogan; similarly, the U.S. Army changed its slogan from "Be all that you can be" to "Army of One."

Learning

Almost all consumer behavior results from **learning**, which is the process that creates changes in behavior through experience and practice. It is not possible to observe learning directly, but we can infer when it has occurred by a person's actions. For example, suppose you see an advertisement for a new and improved cold medicine. If you go to the store that day and buy that remedy, we infer that you have learned something about the cold medicine.

There are two types of learning: experiential and conceptual. *Experiential learning* occurs when an experience changes your behavior. For example, if the new cold medicine does not relieve your symptoms, you may not buy that brand again. *Conceptual learning*, which is not acquired through direct experience, is the second type of learning. Assume, for example, that you are standing at a soft drink machine and notice a new diet flavor with an artificial sweetener. Because someone has told you that diet beverages leave an aftertaste, you choose a different drink. You have learned that you would not like this new diet drink without ever trying it.

Reinforcement and repetition boost learning. Reinforcement can be positive or negative. If you see a vendor selling frozen yogurt (stimulus), buy it (response), and find the yogurt to be quite refreshing (reward), your behavior has been positively reinforced. On the other hand, if you buy a new flavor of yogurt and it does not taste good (negative reinforcement), you will not buy that flavor of yogurt again (response). Without positive or negative reinforcement, a person will not be motivated to repeat the behavior pattern or to avoid it. Thus, if a new brand evokes neutral feelings, some marketing activity, such as a price change or an increase in promotion, may be required to induce further consumption. Learning theory is helpful in reminding marketers that concrete and timely actions are what reinforce desired consumer behavior.

Repetition is a key strategy in promotional campaigns because it can lead to increased learning. Most marketers use repetitious advertising so that consumers will learn what their unique advantage is over the competition. Generally, to heighten learning, advertising messages should be spread out over time rather than clustered together.

A related learning concept useful to marketing managers is **stimulus generalization**. In theory, stimulus generalization occurs when one response is extended to a second stimulus similar to the first. Marketers often use a successful, well-known brand name for a family of products because it gives consumers familiarity with and knowledge about each product in the family. Such brand-name families spur the introduction of new products and facilitate the sale of existing items. Jell-O frozen pudding pops rely on the familiarity of Jell-O gelatin; Clorox bathroom cleaner relies on familiarity with Clorox bleach; and Dove shampoo relies on familiarity with Dove soap. Branding is examined in more detail in Chapter 10.

Another form of stimulus generalization occurs when retailers or wholesalers design their packages to resemble well-known manufacturers' brands. Such imitation often confuses consumers, who buy the imitation thinking it's the original.

The opposite of stimulus generalization is **stimulus discrimination**, which means learning to differentiate among similar products. Consumers may perceive one product as more rewarding or stimulating. For example, some consumers prefer Coca-Cola and others prefer Pepsi. Many insist they can taste a difference between the two brands.

With some types of products—such as aspirin, gasoline, bleach, and paper towels—marketers rely on promotion to point out brand differences that consumers would otherwise not recognize. This process, called *product differentiation*, is discussed in more detail in Chapter 8. Usually, product differentiation is based on superficial differences. For example, Bayer tells consumers that it's the aspirin "doctors recommend most."

Beliefs and Attitudes

Beliefs and attitudes are closely linked to values. A **belief** is an organized pattern of knowledge that an individual holds as true about his or her world. A consumer may believe that Sony's camcorder makes the

learning a process that creates changes in behavior, immediate or expected, through experience and practice

stimulus generalization a form of learning that occurs when one response is extended to a second stimulus similar to the first

stimulus discrimination a learned ability to differentiate among similar products

belief an organized pattern of knowledge that an individual holds as true about his or her world

best home videos, tolerates hard use, and is reasonably priced. These beliefs may be based on knowledge, faith, or hearsay. Consumers tend to develop a set of beliefs about a product's attributes and then, through these beliefs, form a *brand image*—a set of beliefs about a particular brand. In turn, the brand image shapes consumers' attitudes toward the product.

An **attitude** is a learned tendency to respond consistently toward a given object, such as a brand. Attitudes rest on an individual's value system, which represents personal standards of good and bad, right and wrong, and so forth; therefore, attitudes tend to be more enduring and complex than beliefs.

For an example of the nature of attitudes, consider the differing attitudes of consumers around the world toward the practice of purchasing on credit. Americans have long been enthusiastic about charging goods and services and are willing to pay high interest rates for the privilege of postponing payment. To many European consumers, doing what amounts to taking out a loan—even a small one— to pay for anything seems absurd. Germans especially are reluctant to buy on credit. Italy has a sophisticated credit and banking system well suited to handling credit cards, but Italians prefer to carry cash, often huge wads of it. Although most Japanese consumers have credit cards, card purchases amount to less than 1 percent of all consumer transactions. The Japanese have long looked down on credit purchases, but acquire cards to use while traveling abroad.

If a good or service is meeting its profit goals, positive attitudes toward the product merely need to be reinforced. If the brand is not succeeding, however, the marketing manager must strive to change target consumers' attitudes toward it. Changes in attitude tend to grow out of an individual's attempt to reconcile long-held values with a constant stream of new information. This change can be accomplished in three ways: changing beliefs about the brand's attributes, changing the relative importance of these beliefs, and adding new beliefs.

Changing Beliefs and Attributes The first technique is to turn neutral, negative, or incorrect beliefs about product attributes into positive ones. Assume 24 Hour Fitness does a survey among persons considering joining a health club. They find that most respondents believe that 24 Hour Fitness offers fewer classes and less variety than Shapes, Curves for Women, or Lifestyle Family Fitness. In fact, 24 Hour Fitness offers greater variety and more classes than any other health and fitness center. Thus, target consumers have incorrect beliefs about the service's attributes (number of classes and variety). So 24 Hour Fitness must advertise and do other forms of promotion, such as an open house, to correct the misimpressions.

Changing beliefs about a service can be more difficult because service attributes are intangible. Convincing consumers to switch hairstylists or lawyers or to go to a mall dental clinic can be much more difficult than getting them to change brands of razor blades.

Image, which is also largely intangible, significantly determines service patronage. Usually changing beliefs about a product attribute is easier. For example, GE has created a new lightbulb, a compact fluorescent lamp (CFL), that uses one-third the energy of a traditional bulb, lasts nearly ten times longer, and can save up to $30 in energy costs over its lifetime. GE's new campaign urges the use of its new bulb by appealing to Americans' burgeoning ecological awareness, while exhibiting its own "care" for the world's resources. How could the consumer possibly resist when GE has made it so easy to participate? If every American swapped one standard bulb for a CFL, it would collectively prevent burning 30 billion pounds of coal and remove two million cars worth of greenhouse gas emissions from the atmosphere.[31] Service marketing is explored in detail in Chapter 11.

Changing the Importance of Beliefs The second approach to modifying attitudes is to change the relative importance of beliefs about an attribute. Cole Haan, originally a men's shoe outfitter, used boats and cars in its ads for years to associate the brand with active lifestyles, an important attribute for men. Now that it is selling women's products, such as handbags and shoes, some of its ads use models and emphasize how the products look, an important attribute for women. The company hopes the ads will change customers' perceptions and beliefs that it only sells men's products.[32] Marketers can also emphasize the importance of some beliefs over others. For example, when consumers think of full-sized SUVs, good gas mileage doesn't often come to mind. Now, Cadillac wants to raise the importance of fuel efficiency to buyers of full-size SUVs. The promotion for the 2009 Escalade Hybrid says, "Finally, a full-size luxury SUV confident enough to talk about fuel efficiency."[33]

Adding New Beliefs

The third approach to transforming attitudes is to add new beliefs. Although changes in consumption patterns often come slowly, cereal marketers are betting that consumers will eventually warm up to the idea of cereal as a snack. A print ad for General Mills's Cookie-Crisp cereal features a boy popping the sugary nuggets into his mouth while he does his homework. Koch Industries, the manufacturer of Dixie paper products, is also attempting to add new beliefs about the uses of its paper plates and cups with an advertising campaign aimed at positioning its product as a "home cleanup replacement." Commercials pitch Dixie paper plates as an alternative to washing dishes after everyday meals and not just for picnics.

U.S. companies attempting to market their goods overseas may need to help consumers add new beliefs about a product in general. Coca-Cola and PepsiCo have both found it challenging to sell their diet cola brands to consumers in India partly because diet foods of any kind are a new concept in that country where malnutrition was widespread not too many years ago. Indians also have deep-rooted attitudes that anything labeled "diet" is meant for a sick person, such as a diabetic. As a general rule, most Indians are not diet-conscious, preferring food prepared in the traditional manner that tastes good. Indians are also suspicious of the artificial sweeteners used in diet colas. India's Health Ministry has required warning labels on cans and bottles of Diet Coke and Diet Pepsi saying "Not Recommended for Children."[34]

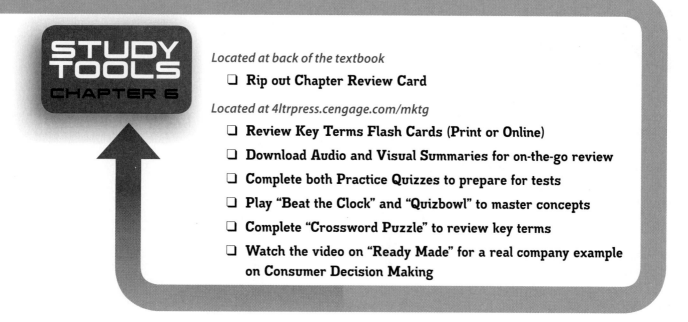

STUDY TOOLS CHAPTER 6

Located at back of the textbook

❑ **Rip out Chapter Review Card**

Located at 4ltrpress.cengage.com/mktg

❑ **Review Key Terms Flash Cards (Print or Online)**

❑ **Download Audio and Visual Summaries for on-the-go review**

❑ **Complete both Practice Quizzes to prepare for tests**

❑ **Play "Beat the Clock" and "Quizbowl" to master concepts**

❑ **Complete "Crossword Puzzle" to review key terms**

❑ **Watch the video on "Ready Made" for a real company example on Consumer Decision Making**

Business Marketing

"The key characteristic distinguishing business products from consumer products is intended use, not physical form."

LO1 What Is Business Marketing?

AFTER YOU FINISH THIS CHAPTER GO TO PAGE 114 FOR STUDY TOOLS

Business marketing is the marketing of goods and services to individuals and organizations for purposes other than personal consumption. The sale of a personal computer to your college or university is an example of business marketing. Business products include those that are used to manufacture other products, become part of another product, or aid the normal operations of an organization. The key characteristic distinguishing business products from consumer products is intended use, not physical characteristics. A product that is purchased for personal or family consumption or as a gift is a consumer good. If that same product, such as a personal computer or a cell phone, is bought for use in a business, it is a business product. A survey by *BtoB Magazine* revealed that the three primary marketing goals of U.S. business marketers are customer acquisition (62%), creating brand awareness (19%), and customer retention (12%).[1]

The size of the business market in the United States and most other countries substantially exceeds that of the consumer market. In the business market, a single customer can account for a huge volume of purchases. For example, General Motors' purchasing department spends more than $125 billion per year on goods and services. General Electric, DuPont, and IBM spend over $60 million per day on business purchases.[2] The top ten business marketing brands in 2008, according to *BtoB Magazine* are American Express, Bank of America, Cisco Systems, FedEx

business marketing the marketing of goods and services to individuals and organizations for purposes other than personal consumption

What do you think?

Salespeople make shopping an uncomfortable experience.

1   2   3   4   5   6   7
STRONGLY DISAGREE   STRONGLY AGREE

Find out what others think at 4ltrpress.cengage.com/mktg

© YURI ARCURS/SHUTTERSTOCK.COM

Corp., General Electric Co., Google, Microsoft Corp., UPS, AT&T, and IBM Corp.[3]

LO 2 Business Marketing on the Internet

The use of the Internet to facilitate activities between organizations is called **business-to-business electronic commerce** (B-to-B or B2B e-commerce). This method of conducting business has evolved and grown rapidly throughout its short history. In 1995, the commercial Web sites that did exist were static. Only a few had data-retrieval capabilities. Frames, tables, and styles were not available. Security of any sort was rare, and streaming video did not exist. In 2005, there were more than one billion Internet users worldwide. In 2008, the United States alone was expected to account for over $1 trillion of B2B e-commerce.[4] Before the Internet, customers had to call Dow Chemical and request a specification sheet for the products they were considering. The information would arrive a few days later by mail. After choosing a product, the customer could then place an order by calling Dow (during business hours, of course). Now, such information is available through MyAccount@Dow, which provides information tailored to the customer's requirements, such as secure internal monitoring of a customer's chemical tank levels. When tanks reach a predetermined level, reordering can be automatically triggered.[5]

Companies selling to business buyers face the same challenges as all marketers including determining who, exactly, the market is and how best to reach them. This is particularly difficult in business marketing because business has rapidly moved online and overseas.[6]

Each year, BtoBonline.com identifies ten business marketing Web sites that are particularly good examples of how companies can use the Web to communicate with customers. Exhibit 7.1 identifies the ten great Web sites for 2009. Many of these companies have been recognized in past

business-to-business electronic commerce the use of the Internet to facilitate the exchange of goods, services, and information between organizations

stickiness a measure of a Web site's effectiveness; calculated by multiplying the frequency of visits times the duration of a visit times the number of pages viewed during each visit (site reach)

years for effectively communicating with their target markets.[7]

In addition to Web sites, what Web 2.0 technologies are companies using? According to a poll taken during a webcast regarding online marketing, 64 percent reported using blogs, 61 percent use podcasts and video, 47 percent use social networks, 38 percent use RSS feeds, 22 percent use threaded discussion, and 11 percent use wikis.[8]

Measuring Online Success

Three of the most important measurements of online success are recency, frequency, and monetary value. *Recency* relates to the fact that customers who have made a purchase recently are more likely to purchase again in the near future than customers who haven't purchased for a while. *Frequency* data help marketers identify frequent purchasers who are definitely more likely to repeat their purchasing behavior in the future. The *monetary value* of sales is important because big spenders can be the most profitable customers for a business.

NetGenesis has developed a number of equations that can help online marketers better understand their data. For example, combining frequency data with the length of time a visitor spent on the Web site (duration) and the number of site pages viewed during each visit (total site reach) can provide an analytical measure for your site's **stickiness** factor.

$$STICKINESS = FREQUENCY \times DURATION \times SITE\ REACH$$

By measuring the stickiness factor of a Web site before and after a design or function change, the marketer can quickly determine whether visitors embraced the change. By adding purchase information to determine the level of stickiness needed to provide a desired purchase volume, the marketer gains an even more precise understanding of how a site change affected business. An almost endless number of factor combinations can be created to provide a quantitative method for determining buyer behavior online. First, though, the marketer must determine what measures are required and which factors can be combined to arrive at those measurements.[9]

EXHIBIT 7.1
Ten Great Web Sites

URL	Company	Target Audience
basecamphq.com	37signals	Businesses with fewer than ten employees
www.adp.com	ADP	Businesses, employees, prospective job-seekers, investors, industry analysts, and media
www.gettyimages.com	Getty Images, Inc.	Agencies, media companies, and bloggers
www.getharvest.com	Iridesco	Businesses with fewer than ten people
www.mcmaster.com	McMaster-Carr	Manufacturers and large commercial facilities
www.officedepot.com	Office Depot	Individual entrepreneurs and small- to mid-size businesses
www.ouncelabs.com	Ounce Labs, Inc.	C-level executives, IT staffers, security analysts, and software developers
www.plyboo.com	Smith & Fong Co.	Interior designers, architectural community, and homeowners
www.spiceworks.com	Spiceworks	IT professionals in small- to mid-size businesses; companies with fewer than 500 employees
www.trane.com/commercial	Trane	Building executives and owners, contractors, engineers, facility managers, job seekers, and media

SOURCE: "10 Great Web Sites: Overview," *BtoB Magazine,* online, September 14, 2009.

disintermediation
the elimination of intermediaries such as wholesalers or distributers from a marketing channel

Companies have had to transition from "We have a Web site because our customer does" to having a store that attracts, interests, satisfies, and retains customers. New applications that provide additional information about present and potential customers, increase efficiency, lower costs, increase supply chain efficiency, or enhance customer retention, loyalty, and trust are being developed each year. Chapter 21, Customer Relationship Management, describes several of these applications.

One term in Exhibit 7.2 that may be unfamiliar is **disintermediation**, which means eliminating

Trends in B2B Internet Marketing

According to James Soto, president of the business marketing agency Industrial Strength Marketing, "the number one thing to keep in mind in terms of trends in B2B Internet marketing is the shift of sourcing to the Net." His firm has found that 90 percent of business buyers go to the Internet at some point during the buying process, and over 50 percent start the buying process online.[10]

An Internet marketing technique that hasn't yet lived up to its potential is RSS (Real Simple Syndication) feeds. RSS feeds are used to publish frequently updated materials such as blogs, news headlines, audio, and video in a standard format. Web feeds benefit publishers by letting them syndicate content automatically. They benefit readers who want to subscribe to timely updates or aggregated information from various sources.[11]

A recent survey revealed that 7 out of 10 business marketers do not consider RSS feeds in their campaigns. However 71 percent of technology buyers reported using feeds.[12]

Over the past decade marketers have become more and more sophisticated in the use of the Internet. Exhibit 7.2 compares three prominent Internet business marketing strategy initiatives from the late 1990s compared to five that are currently being pursued.

EXHIBIT 7.2
Evolution of E-Business Initiatives

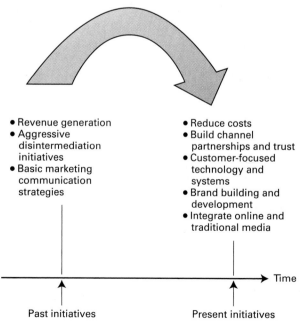

- Revenue generation
- Aggressive disintermediation initiatives
- Basic marketing communication strategies

- Reduce costs
- Build channel partnerships and trust
- Customer-focused technology and systems
- Brand building and development
- Integrate online and traditional media

Time

Past initiatives   Present initiatives

SOURCE: Andrew J. Rohm and Fareena Sultan, "The Evolution of E-Business," *Marketing Management,* January/February, 2004, p. 35. Used by permission.

reintermediation
the reintroduction of an intermediary between producers and users

intermediaries such as wholesalers or distributors from a marketing channel.[13] A prime example of disintermediation is Dell, Inc., which sells directly to business buyers and consumers. Large retailers such as Wal-Mart use a disintermediation strategy to help reduce costs and prices.

A few years ago, many people thought that the Internet would eliminate the need for distributors. Why would customers pay a distributor's markup when they could buy directly from the manufacturer with a few mouse clicks? Yet Internet disintermediation has occurred less frequently than many expected. The reason is that distributors often perform important functions such as providing credit, aggregation of supplies from multiple sources, delivery, and processing returns.

Many business customers, especially small firms, depend on knowledgeable distributors for information and advice that is not available to them online. You will notice in Exhibit 7.2 that building channel partnerships and trust has replaced aggressive disintermediation initiatives as a priority for most firms. Some firms have followed disintermediation with **reintermediation**, the reintroduction of an intermediary between producers and users. They realized that providing direct online purchasing only was similar to having only one store in a city selling a popular brand.

LO3 Relationship Marketing and Strategic Alliances

As explained in Chapter 1, relationship marketing is a strategy that entails seeking and establishing ongoing partnerships with customers. Relationship marketing has become an important business marketing strategy as customers have become more demanding and competition has become more intense. Loyal customers are also more profitable than those who are price-sensitive and perceive little or no difference among brands or suppliers.

That is why firms such as online printing company Mimeo.com focus on continually improving processes for communicating with customers once they place their first order. To help retain clients, the company has developed an automated system that sends out e-mails or triggers a live contact each time a customer places an order or asks a question.[14]

Building long-term relationships with customers offers companies a way to build competitive advantage that is hard for competitors to copy. For example, the FedEx Powership program includes a series of automated shipping, tracking, and invoicing systems that save customers time and money while solidify-

© MARTIN TAKIGAWA/UPPERCUT IMAGES/GETTY IMAGES

DISINTERMEDIATION = CUT OUT THE MIDDLE MAN

KEEP 'EM COMING BACK?

While **b-to-b marketers** are increasingly focused on improving relationships with customers, they still have a long way to go in implementing effective, consistent customer retention practices. A study by the Chief Marketing Officer Council found that only one-third of global marketers have strategies in place to win back dormant or lost customers; only half have strategies to further penetrate key account relationships. Only 6.8 percent of marketers said they have excellent knowledge of the customer when it comes to demographic, behavioral, and psychographic data, while 51.9 percent said they have fair to little knowledge of the customer.[15]

ing their loyalty to FedEx. This produces a win-win situation.

Strategic Alliances

A **strategic alliance**, sometimes called a **strategic partnership**, is a cooperative agreement between business firms. Strategic alliances can take the form of licensing or distribution agreements, joint ventures, research and development consortia, and partnerships. They may be between manufacturers, manufacturers and customers, manufacturers and suppliers, and manufacturers and channel intermediaries.

Business marketers form strategic alliances to strengthen operations and better compete. Office Depot has formed an alliance with Netbizz Office Supplies, an office supplies provider in Singapore. The alliance is intended to allow customers to use the Office Depot international network for their multicountry supply needs. Singapore is a key market for many global companies and this alliance offers a convenient procurement solution for both current and new customers.[16]

Sometimes alliance partners are fierce competitors. For instance, in the face of rising fuel prices, the express-delivery service DHL has formed an alliance with rival company UPS. Under the agreement, UPS provides all airlift services for DHL in the United States. According to one DHL executive, "the customer doesn't actually see a difference at all . . . unless they pay attention to the color of the partner's planes.[17]

Other alliances are formed between companies that operate in completely different industries. Choice Hotels and 1-800-Flowers share call-center employees because doing so is a cheaper alternative than outsourcing. When one company experiences increased demand for its products and services, it can call on its partner's employees rather than add staff or use a temporary agency. At a given time, as many as 100 call-center agents may be taking orders for the other company. Both companies report higher employee retention and better recruitment.[18]

For an alliance to succeed in the long term, it must be built on commitment and trust. **Relationship commitment** means that a firm believes that an ongoing relationship with some other firm is so important that it warrants maximum efforts at maintaining it indefinitely.[19] A perceived breakdown in commitment by one of the parties often leads to a breakdown in the relationship.

Trust exists when one party has confidence in an exchange partner's reliability and integrity.[20] Some alliances fail when participants lack trust in their trading partners. For instance, General Motors, Ford, DaimlerChrysler, Nissan Motor Company, and Renault SA created an Internet automobile parts exchange, called Covisint, that they hoped would make $300 billion

strategic alliance (strategic partnership) a cooperative agreement between business firms

relationship commitment a firm's belief that an ongoing relationship with another firm is so important that the relationship warrants maximum efforts at maintaining it indefinitely

trust the condition that exists when one party has confidence in an exchange partner's reliability and integrity

keiretsu a network of interlocking corporate affiliates

original equipment manufacturers (OEMs) individuals and organizations that buy business goods and incorporate them into the products that they produce for eventual sale to other producers or to consumers

in sales per year. But the auto industry is characterized by mistrust between buyers and sellers. And, after being forced to accept price concessions for years, suppliers were reluctant to participate in the exchange.

Relationships in Other Cultures

Although the terms *relationship marketing* and *strategic alliances* are fairly new, and popularized mostly by American business executives and educators, the concepts have long been familiar in other cultures. Businesses in China, Japan, Korea, Mexico, and much of Europe rely heavily on personal relationships. Chapter 21 explores customer relationship management in detail.

In Japan, for example, exchange between firms is based on personal relationships that are developed through what is called *amae*, or indulgent dependency. *Amae* is the feeling of nurturing concern for, and dependence upon, another. Reciprocity and personal relationships contribute to *amae*. Relationships between companies can develop into a **keiretsu**—a network of interlocking corporate affiliates. Within a keiretsu, executives may sit on the boards of their customers or their suppliers. Members of a keiretsu trade with each other whenever possible and often engage in joint product development, finance, and marketing activity. For example, the Toyota Group keiretsu includes 14 core companies and another 170 that receive preferential treatment. Toyota holds an equity position in many of these 170 member firms and is represented on many of their boards of directors.

Many American firms have found that the best way to compete in Asian countries is to form relationships with Asian firms. For example, General Motors' joint venture with Shanghai Motors produces Buicks, Chevrolets and Cadillacs. German automaker Volkswagen also has an alliance with Shanghai Motors to produce the Passat.[21]

LO4 Major Categories of Business Customers

The business market consists of four major categories of customers: producers, resellers, governments, and institutions.

Producers

The producer segment of the business market includes profit-oriented individuals and organizations that use purchased goods and services to produce other products, to incorporate into other products, or to facilitate the daily operations of the organization. Examples of producers include construction, manufacturing, transportation, finance, real estate, and food service firms. In the United States, there are more than 13 million firms in the producer segment of the business market. Some of these firms are small, and others are among the world's largest businesses.

Producers are often called **original equipment manufacturers** or **OEMs**. This term includes all individuals and organizations that buy business goods and incorporate them into the products that they produce for eventual sale to other producers or to consumers. Companies such as General Motors that buy steel, paint, tires, and batteries are said to be OEMs.

Resellers

The reseller market includes retail and wholesale businesses that buy finished goods and resell them for a profit. A retailer sells mainly to final consumers; wholesalers sell mostly to retailers and other organizational customers. There are approximately 1.5 million retailers and 500,000 wholesalers operating in the United States. Consumer-product firms like Procter & Gamble, Kraft Foods, and Coca-Cola sell directly to large retailers and retail chains and through wholesalers to smaller retail units. Retailing is explored in detail in Chapter 15.

Business product distributors are wholesalers that buy business products and resell them to business customers. They often carry thousands of items in stock and employ sales forces to call on business customers. Businesses that wish to buy a gross of pencils or a hundred pounds of fertilizer typically purchase these items from local distributors rather than directly from manufacturers such as Empire Pencil or Dow Chemical.

Governments

A third major segment of the business market is government. Government organizations include thousands of federal, state, and local buying units. They make up what may be the largest single market for goods and services in the world.

Contracts for government purchases are often put out for bid. Interested vendors submit bids (usually sealed) to provide specified products during a particular time. Sometimes the lowest bidder is awarded the contract. When the lowest bidder is not awarded the contract, strong evidence must be presented to justify the decision. Grounds for rejecting the lowest bid include lack of experience, inadequate financing, or poor past performance. Bidding allows all potential suppliers a fair chance at winning government contracts and helps ensure that public funds are spent wisely.

Federal Government Name just about any good or service and chances are that someone in the federal government uses it. The U.S. federal government buys goods and services valued at more than $600 billion per year, making it the world's largest customer.

Although much of the federal government's buying is centralized, no single federal agency contracts for all the government's requirements, and no single buyer in any agency purchases all that the agency needs. We can view the federal government as a combination of several large companies with overlapping responsibilities and thousands of small independent units. One popular source of information about government procurement is *Commerce Business Daily*. Until recently, businesses hoping to sell to the federal government found the document unorganized, and it often arrived too late to be useful. The online version (www.cbd-net.com) is timelier and lets contractors find leads using keyword searches. Other examples of publications designed to explain how to do business with the federal government include *Doing Business with the General Services Administration*, *Selling to the Military*, and *Selling to the U.S. Air Force*.

State, County, and City Government Selling to states, counties, and cities can be less frustrating for both small and large vendors than selling to the federal government. Paperwork is typically simpler and more manageable than it is at the federal level. On the other hand, vendors must decide which of the more than 82,000 government units are likely to buy their wares. State and local buying agencies include school districts, highway departments, government-operated hospitals, and housing agencies.

Institutions

The fourth major segment of the business market consists of institutions that seek to achieve goals other than the standard business goals of profit, market share, and return on investment. This segment includes schools, hospitals, colleges and universities, churches, labor unions, fraternal organizations, civic clubs, foundations, and other so-called nonbusiness organizations. Xerox offers educational and medical institutions the same prices as government agencies (the lowest that Xerox offers) and has a separate sales force that calls on these customers.

> **North American Industry Classification System (NAICS)** a detailed numbering system developed by the United States, Canada, and Mexico to classify North American business establishments by their main production processes

LO5 The North American Industry Classification System

The **North American Industry Classification System (NAICS)** is an industry classification system introduced in 1997 to replace the standard industrial classification system (SIC). NAICS (pronounced *nakes*) is a system for classifying North American business establishments. The system, developed jointly by the United States, Canada, and Mexico, provides a common industry classification system for the North American Free Trade Agreement (NAFTA) partners. Goods- or service-producing firms that use identical or similar production processes are grouped together.

NAICS is an extremely valuable tool for business marketers engaged in analyzing, segmenting, and targeting markets. Each classification group is relatively homogeneous in terms of raw materials required, components used, manufacturing processes employed, and problems faced. The more digits in a code, the more homogeneous the group is. Therefore, if a supplier understands the needs and requirements of a few

THE U.S. FEDERAL GOVERNMENT IS THE WORLD'S LARGEST CUSTOMER.

derived demand the demand for business products

joint demand the demand for two or more items used together in a final product

firms within a classification, requirements can be projected for all firms in that category. The number, size, and geographic dispersion of firms can also be identified. This information can be converted to market potential estimates, market share estimates, and sales forecasts. It can also be used for identifying potential new customers. NAICS codes can help identify firms that may be prospective users of a supplier's goods and services. For a complete listing of all NAICS codes, see www.naics.com/search/htm.

UNLIKE CONSUMER DEMAND, BUSINESS DEMAND IS DERIVED, INELASTIC, JOINT, AND FLUCTUATING.

products to be used in producing their customers' products. For instance, the number of drills or lathes that a manufacturing firm needs is "derived from," or based upon the demand for products that are produced using these machines. Because demand is derived, business marketers must carefully monitor demand patterns and changing preferences in final consumer markets, even though their customers are not in those markets. Moreover, business marketers must carefully monitor their customers' forecasts, because derived demand is based on expectations of future demand for those customers' products.

Some business marketers not only monitor final consumer demand and customer forecasts but also try to influence final consumer demand. Aluminum producers use television and magazine advertisements to point out the convenience and recycling opportunities that aluminum offers to consumers who can choose to purchase soft drinks in either aluminum or plastic containers.

How NAICS Works

The more digits in the NAICS code, the more homogeneous the groups are at that level.

NAICS Level	NAICS Code	Description
Sector	51	Information
Subsector	513	Broadcasting and telecommunications
Industry group	5133	Telecommunications
Industry	51332	Wireless telecommunications carriers, except satellite
Industry subdivision	513321	Paging

LO 6 Business versus Consumer Markets

The basic philosophy and practice of marketing are the same whether the customer is a business organization or a consumer. Business markets do, however, have characteristics different from consumer markets.

Demand

Consumer demand for products is quite different from demand in the business market. Unlike consumer demand, business demand is derived, inelastic, joint, and fluctuating.

Derived Demand The demand for business products is called **derived demand** because organizations buy

Inelastic Demand The demand for many business products is inelastic with regard to price. *Inelastic demand* means that an increase or decrease in the price of the product will not significantly affect demand for the product. This will be discussed further in Chapter 19.

The price of a product used in the production of, or as part of, a final product is often a minor portion of the final product's total price. Therefore, demand for the final consumer product is not affected. If the price of automobile paint or spark plugs rises significantly, say, 200 percent in one year, do you think the number of new automobiles sold that year will be affected? Probably not.

Joint Demand **Joint demand** occurs when two or more items are used together in a final product. For example, a decline in the availability of memory chips will slow production of microcomputers, which will in turn reduce the demand for disk drives. Likewise, the demand for Apple operating systems exists as long as there is demand for Apple computers. Sales of the two products are directly linked.

Fluctuating Demand The demand for business products—particularly new plants and equipment—tends to be less stable than the demand for consumer products. A small increase or decrease in consumer demand can produce a much larger change in demand for the facilities and equipment needed to make the consumer product. Economists refer to this phenomenon as the **multiplier effect** (or **accelerator principle**).

Cummins Engine Company, a producer of heavy-duty diesel engines, uses sophisticated surface grinders to make parts. Suppose Cummins is using twenty surface grinders. Each machine lasts about ten years. Purchases have been timed so two machines will wear out and be replaced annually. If the demand for engine parts does not change, two grinders will be bought this year. If the demand for parts declines slightly, only eighteen grinders may be needed and Cummins won't replace the worn ones. However, suppose that next year demand returns to previous levels plus a little more. To meet the new level of demand, Cummins will need to replace the two machines that wore out in the first year, the two that wore out in the second year, plus one or more additional machines. The multiplier effect works this way in many industries, producing highly fluctuating demand for business products.

Purchase Volume

Business customers buy in much larger quantities than consumers. Just think how large an order Kellogg's typically places for the wheat bran and raisins used to manufacture Raisin Bran. Imagine the number of tires that DaimlerChrysler buys at one time.

Number of Customers

Business marketers usually have far fewer customers than consumer marketers. The advantage is that it is a lot easier to identify prospective buyers, monitor current customers' needs and levels of satisfaction, and personally attend to existing customers. The main disadvantage is that each customer becomes crucial—especially for those manufacturers that have only one customer. In many cases, this customer is the U.S. government. The success or failure of one bid can make the difference between prosperity and bankruptcy. After five years of development, testing, and politicking, the Pentagon awarded Lockheed Martin a multi-decade contract to build 3,000 jet fighter airplanes. Boeing Aircraft Company, the only other bidder on the $200 billion contract, immediately announced plans for substantial layoffs.

Location of Buyers

Business customers tend to be much more geographically concentrated than consumers. For instance, more than half the nation's business buyers are located in California, Illinois, Michigan, New Jersey, New York,

Ohio, and Pennsylvania. The aircraft and microelectronics industries are concentrated on the West Coast, and many of the firms that supply the automobile manufacturing industry are located in and around Detroit.

Distribution Structure

Many consumer products pass through a distribution system that includes the producer, one or more wholesalers, and a retailer. In business marketing, however, because of many of the characteristics already mentioned, channels of distribution for business marketing are typically shorter. Direct channels, where manufacturers market directly to users, are much more common. The use of direct channels has increased dramatically in the past decade with the introduction of various Internet buying and selling schemes. One such technique is called a **business-to-business online exchange**, which is an electronic trading floor that provides companies with integrated links to their customers and suppliers. The goal of B2B exchanges is to simplify business purchasing and make them more efficient. For example, Exostar, the aerospace industry's online exchange,

has over 12,000 participating suppliers and conducts more than 20,000 transactions each week.[22] Exchanges such as Exostar facilitate direct channel relationships between producers and their customers.

Nature of Buying

Unlike consumers, business buyers usually approach purchasing rather formally. Businesses use professionally trained purchasing agents or buyers who spend their entire career purchasing a limited number of items. They get to know the items and the sellers well. Some professional purchasers earn the designation of Certified Purchasing Manager (CPM) after participating in a rigorous certification program.

Nature of Buying Influence

Typically, more people are involved in a single business purchase decision than in a consumer purchase. Experts from fields as varied as quality control, marketing, and finance, as well as professional buyers and users, may be grouped in a buying center (discussed later in this chapter).

Type of Negotiations

Consumers are used to negotiating price on automobiles and real estate. In most cases, however, American consumers expect sellers to set the price and other conditions of sale, such as time of delivery and credit terms. In contrast, negotiating is common in business marketing. Buyers and sellers negotiate product specifications, delivery dates, payment terms, and other pricing matters. Sometimes these negotiations occur during many meetings over several months. Final contracts are often very long and detailed.

Use of Reciprocity

Business purchasers often choose to buy from their own customers, a practice known as **reciprocity**. For example, General Motors buys engines for use in its automobiles and trucks from Borg Warner, which in turn buys many of the automobiles and trucks it needs from GM. This practice is neither unethical nor illegal unless one party coerces the other and the result is unfair competition. Reciprocity is generally considered a reasonable business practice. If all possible suppliers sell a similar product for about the same price,

doesn't it make sense to buy from those firms that buy from you?

Use of Leasing

Consumers normally buy products rather than lease them. But businesses commonly lease expensive equipment such as computers, construction equipment and vehicles, and automobiles. Leasing allows firms to reduce capital outflow, acquire a seller's latest products, receive better services, and gain tax advantages.

The lessor, the firm providing the product, may be either the manufacturer or an independent firm. The benefits to the lessor include greater total revenue from leasing compared to selling and an opportunity to do business with customers who cannot afford to buy.

Primary Promotional Method

Business marketers tend to emphasize personal selling in their promotion efforts, especially for expensive items, custom-designed products, large-volume purchases, and situations requiring negotiations. The sale of many business products requires a great deal of personal contact. Personal selling is discussed in more detail in Chapter 18.

 **LO7 Types of Business Products**

Business products generally fall into one of the following seven categories, depending on their use: major equipment, accessory equipment, raw materials, component parts, processed materials, supplies, and business services.

Major Equipment

Major equipment includes such capital goods as large or expensive machines, mainframe computers, blast furnaces, generators, airplanes, and buildings. (These items are also commonly called **installations**.) Major equipment is depreciated over time rather than charged as an expense in the year it is purchased. In addition, major equipment is often custom-designed for each customer. Personal selling is an important part of the marketing strategy for major equipment because distribution channels are almost always direct from the producer to the business user.

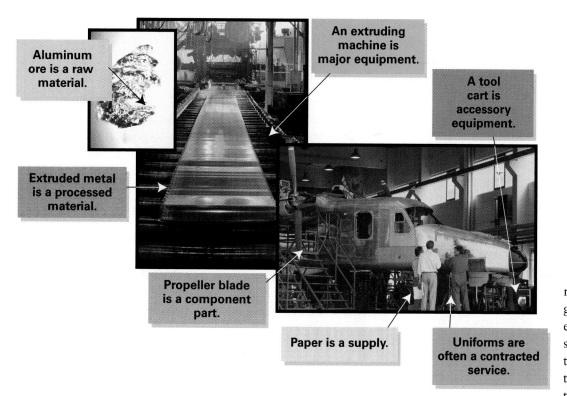

Aluminum ore is a raw material.

An extruding machine is major equipment.

A tool cart is accessory equipment.

Extruded metal is a processed material.

Propeller blade is a component part.

Paper is a supply.

Uniforms are often a contracted service.

accessory equipment goods, such as portable tools and office equipment, that are less expensive and shorter-lived than major equipment

raw materials unprocessed extractive or agricultural products, such as mineral ore, lumber, wheat, corn, fruits, vegetables, and fish

component parts either finished items ready for assembly or products that need very little processing before becoming part of some other product

Accessory Equipment

Accessory equipment is generally less expensive and shorter-lived than major equipment. Examples include portable drills, power tools, microcomputers, and fax machines. Accessory equipment is often charged as an expense in the year it is bought rather than depreciated over its useful life. In contrast to major equipment, accessories are more often standardized and are usually bought by more customers. These customers tend to be widely dispersed. For example, all types of businesses buy microcomputers.

Local industrial distributors (wholesalers) play an important role in the marketing of accessory equipment because business buyers often purchase accessories from them. Regardless of where accessories are bought, advertising is a more vital promotional tool for accessory equipment than for major equipment.

Raw Materials

Raw materials are unprocessed extractive or agricultural products—for example, mineral ore, timber, wheat, corn, fruits, vegetables, and fish. Raw materials become part of finished products. Extensive users, such as steel or lumber mills and food canners, generally buy huge quantities of raw materials. Because there is often a large number of relatively small sellers of raw mate-

rials, none can greatly influence price or supply. Thus, the market tends to set the price of raw materials, and individual producers have little pricing flexibility. Promotion is almost always via personal selling, and distribution channels are usually direct from producer to business user.

Component Parts

Component parts are either finished items ready for assembly or products that need very little processing before becoming part of some other product. Caterpillar diesel engines are component parts used in heavy-duty trucks. Other examples include spark plugs, tires, and electric motors for automobiles. A special feature of component parts is that they can retain their identity after becoming part of the final product. For example, automobile tires are clearly recognizable as part of a car. Moreover, because component parts often wear out, they may need to be replaced several times during the life of the final product. Thus, there are two important markets for many component parts: the original equipment manufacturer (OEM) market and the replacement market.

The availability of component parts is often a key factor in OEMs meeting their production deadlines. For example, Boeing Co. has had to delay final assembly of Boeing 787 Dreamliners by at least 15 months because of slower than expected completion of components prior to their arrival at the final assembly line. In addition to delayed sales and customer disappointment and dissatisfaction, Boeing will have to pay millions of dollars of penalty payments to customers.[23]

The difference between unit costs and selling prices in the OEM market is often small, but profits can be substantial because of volume buying.

The replacement market is composed of organizations and individuals buying component parts to replace worn-out parts. Because components often retain their identity in final products, users may choose to replace a component part with the same brand used by the manufacturer—for example, the same brand of automobile tires or battery. The replacement market operates differently from the OEM market, however. Whether replacement buyers are organizations or individuals, they tend to demonstrate the characteristics of consumer markets that were shown in Learning Outcome 6. Consider, for example, an automobile replacement part. Purchase volume is usually small and there are many customers, geographically dispersed, who typically buy from car dealers or parts stores. Negotiations do not occur, and neither reciprocity nor leasing is usually an issue.

Manufacturers of component parts often direct their advertising toward replacement buyers. Cooper Tire & Rubber, for example, makes and markets component parts—automobile and truck tires—for the replacement market only. General Motors and other car makers compete with independent firms in the market for replacement automobile parts.

Processed Materials

Processed materials are products used directly in manufacturing other products. Unlike raw materials, they have had some processing. Examples include sheet metal, chemicals, specialty steel, lumber, corn syrup, and plastics. Unlike component parts, processed materials do not retain their identity in final products.

Most processed materials are marketed to OEMs or to distributors servicing the OEM market. Processed materials are generally bought according to customer specifications or to some industry standard, as is the case with steel and ply-

wood. Price and service are important factors in choosing a vendor.

Supplies

Supplies are consumable items that do not become part of the final product—for example, lubricants, detergents, paper towels, pencils, and paper. Supplies are normally standardized items that purchasing agents routinely buy. Supplies typically have relatively short lives and are inexpensive compared to other business goods. Because supplies generally fall into one of three categories—maintenance, repair, or operating supplies—this category is often referred to as MRO items. Competition in the MRO market is intense. Bic and Paper Mate, for example, battle for business purchases of inexpensive ballpoint pens.

Business Services

Business services are expense items that do not become part of a final product. Businesses often retain outside providers to perform janitorial, advertising, legal, management consulting, marketing research, maintenance, and other services. Hiring an outside provider makes sense when it costs less than hiring or assigning an employee to perform the task and when an outside provider is needed for particular expertise.

LO 8 Business Buying Behavior

As you probably have already concluded, business buyers behave differently from consumers. Understanding how purchase decisions are made in organizations is a first step in developing a business selling strategy. Business buying behavior has five important aspects: buying centers, evaluative criteria, buying situations, business ethics, and customer service.

Buying Centers

In many cases, more than one person is involved in a purchase decision. Identifying who these people are and the roles that they play greatly enhances the salesperson's chances for success.[24]

A **buying center** includes all those people in an organization who become involved in the purchase decision. Membership and influence vary from company to company. For instance, in engineering-dominated firms like Bell Helicopter, the buying center may consist almost entirely of engineers. In marketing-oriented firms like Toyota and IBM, marketing and engineering have almost equal authority. In consumer goods firms like Procter & Gamble, product managers and other marketing decision makers may dominate the buying center. In a small manufacturing company, almost everyone may be a member.

The number of people involved in a buying center varies with the complexity and importance of a purchase decision. The composition of the buying group will usually change from one purchase to another and sometimes even during various stages of the buying process. To make matters more complicated, buying centers do not appear on formal organization charts.

For example, even though a formal committee may have been set up to choose a new plant site, it is only part of the buying center. Other people, like the company president, often play informal yet powerful roles. In a lengthy decision-making process, such as finding a new plant location, some members may drop out of the buying center when they can no longer play a useful role. Others whose talents are needed then become part of the center. No formal announcement of "who is in" and "who is out" is ever made.

Roles in the Buying Center As in family purchasing decisions, several people may play a role in the business purchase process.

BUSINESS PURCHASING ROLES:

▶▶ *Initiator:* the person who first suggests making a purchase.

▶▶ *Influencers/evaluators:* people who influence the buying decision. They often help define specifications and provide information for evaluating options. Technical personnel are especially important as influencers.

▶▶ *Gatekeepers:* group members who regulate the flow of information. Frequently, the purchasing agent views the gatekeeping role as a source of his or her power. A secretary may also act as a gatekeeper by determining which vendors get an appointment with a buyer.

▶▶ *Decider:* the person who has the formal or informal power to choose or approve the selection of the supplier or brand. In complex situations, it is often difficult to determine who makes the final decision.

▶▶ *Purchaser:* the person who actually negotiates the purchase. It could be anyone from the president of the company to the purchasing agent, depending on the importance of the decision.

▶▶ *Users:* members of the organization who will actually use the product. Users often initiate the buying process and help define product specifications.

Implications of Buying Centers for the Marketing Manager Successful vendors realize the importance of identifying who is in the decision-making unit, each member's relative influence in the buying decision, and each member's evaluative criteria. Successful selling strategies often focus on determining the most important buying influences and tailoring sales presentations to the evaluative criteria most important to these buying-center members. For example, Loctite Corporation, the manufacturer of Super Glue and industrial adhesives and sealants, found that engineers were the most important influencers and deciders in adhesive and sealant purchase decisions. As a result, Loctite focused its marketing efforts on production and maintenance engineers.

> **buying center** all those people in an organization who become involved in the purchase decision

Evaluative Criteria

Business buyers evaluate products and suppliers against three important criteria: quality, service, and price—in that order.

Quality In this case, quality refers to technical suitability. A superior tool can do a better job in the production process, and superior packaging can increase dealer and consumer acceptance of a brand. Evaluation of quality also applies to the salesperson and the salesperson's firm. Business buyers want to deal with reputable salespeople and companies that are financially responsible. Quality improvement should be part of every organization's marketing strategy.

Service Almost as much as they want satisfactory products, business buyers want satisfactory service. A purchase offers several opportunities for service. Suppose a vendor is selling heavy equipment. Prepurchase service could include a survey of the buyer's needs. After thorough analysis of the survey findings, the vendor could prepare a report and recommendations in the form of a purchasing proposal. If a purchase results, postpurchase service might consist of installing the equipment and training those who will be using it. Postsale services may also include maintenance and repairs. Another service that business buyers seek is dependability of supply. They must be able to count on delivery of what was ordered when it is scheduled to be delivered. Buyers also welcome services that help them sell their finished products. Services of this sort are especially appropriate when the seller's product is an identifiable part of the buyer's end product.

Price Business buyers want to buy at low prices—at the lowest prices, under most circumstances. However, a buyer who pressures a supplier to cut prices to a point where the supplier loses money on the sale almost forces shortcuts on quality. The buyer also may, in effect, force the supplier to quit selling to him or her. Then a new source of supply will have to be found.

Buying Situations

Often business firms, especially manufacturers, must decide whether to make something or buy it from an outside supplier. The decision is essentially one of economics. Can an item of similar quality be bought at a lower price elsewhere? If not, is manufacturing it in-house the best use of limited company resources? For example, Briggs & Stratton Corporation, a major manufacturer of four-cycle engines, might be able to save $150,000 annually on outside purchases by spending $500,000 on the equipment needed to produce gas throttles internally. Yet Briggs & Stratton could also use that $500,000 to upgrade its carburetor assembly line, which would save $225,000 annually. If a firm does decide to buy a product instead of making it, the purchase will be a new buy, a modified rebuy, or a straight rebuy.

New Buy A **new buy** is a situation requiring the purchase of a product for the first time. For example, suppose a manufacturing company needs a better way to page its managers while they are working on the shop floor. Currently, each of the several managers has a distinct ring, for example, two short and one long, that sounds over the plant intercom whenever he or she is being paged by anyone in the factory. The company decides to replace its buzzer system of paging with handheld wireless radio technology that will allow managers to communicate immediately with the department initiating the page. This situation represents the greatest opportunity for new vendors. No long-term relationship has been established for this

product, specifications may be somewhat fluid, and buyers are generally more open to new vendors.

If the new item is a raw material or a critical component part, the buyer cannot afford to run out of supply. The seller must be able to convince the buyer that the seller's firm can consistently deliver a high-quality product on time.

Modified Rebuy A **modified rebuy** is normally less critical and less time-consuming than a new buy. In a modified-rebuy situation, the purchaser wants some change in the original good or service. It may be a new color, greater tensile strength in a component part, more respondents in a marketing research study, or additional services in a janitorial contract.

Because the two parties are familiar with each other and credibility has been established, buyer and seller can concentrate on the specifics of the modification. But in some cases, modified rebuys are open to outside bidders. The purchaser uses this strategy to ensure that the new terms are competitive. An example would be the manufacturing company buying radios with a vibrating feature for managers who have trouble hearing the ring over the factory noise. The firm may open the bidding to examine the price/quality offerings of several suppliers.

Straight Rebuy A **straight rebuy** is a situation vendors prefer. The purchaser is not looking for new information or other suppliers. An order is placed and the product is provided as in previous orders. Usually, a straight rebuy is routine because the terms of the purchase have been agreed to in earlier negotiations. An example would be the previously cited manufacturing company purchasing additional radios for new managers from the same supplier on a regular basis.

One common instrument used in straight-rebuy situations is the purchasing contract. Purchasing contracts are used with products that are bought often and in high volume. In essence, the purchasing contract makes the buyer's decision-making routine and promises the salesperson a sure sale. The advantage to the buyer is a quick, confident decision and, to the salesperson, reduced or eliminated competition. Suppliers must remember not to take straight-rebuy relationships for granted. Retaining existing customers is much easier than attracting new ones.

Business Ethics

As we noted in Chapter 3, ethics refers to the moral principles or values that generally govern the conduct of an individual or a group. Ethics can also be viewed as the standard of behavior by which conduct is judged.

CODE OF ETHICS AT LOCKHEED MARTIN

© ISTOCKPHOTO.COM/JACOB WACKERHAUSEN

Lockheed Martin's *Code of Ethics and Business Conduct* provides guidance on the company's expectations for all employees, contracted labor, agents, consultants, members of the Board of Directors, and others when representing or acting for the corporation.

According to Chairman, President, and Chief Executive Officer Robert J. Stevens, "all of us have a shared responsibility to maintain the highest standard of integrity and ensure that we sustain a place where we are proud to work. If you are faced with an ethical dilemma, you have the responsibility to speak up and seek resolution. We must all be accountable for acting with integrity and upholding the values of the Corporation." The Code includes three key components: a culture of integrity, our vision, and our values.

A Culture of Integrity

Lockheed Martin is committed to dealing honestly and fairly with our employees, customers, suppliers, shareholders and the communities in which we live and work. Our success depends on maintaining a culture of integrity.

Our Vision and Our Values

Lockheed Martin holds each director, executive, leader, employee, and agent accountable for upholding Our Vision, Our Values, and Our Code. In so doing, we ensure that Lockheed Martin's business will be conducted consistent with the high ethical standards that we demand from each other, and that others have the right to demand from us.

Discuss the similarities and differences in Lockheed Martin's Code and the American Marketing Association's statement of ethics called its "Ethical Norms and Values for Marketers" at marketingpower.com/AboutAMA.

Although we have heard a lot about corporate misbehavior in recent years, most people, and most companies, follow ethical practices. To help achieve this, over half of all major corporations offer ethics training to employees. Many companies also have codes of ethics that help guide buyers and sellers.

Customer Service

Business marketers are increasingly recognizing the benefits of developing a formal system to monitor customer opinions and perceptions of the quality of customer service. Companies such as McDonald's, L.L. Bean, and Lexus build their strategies not only around products but also around a few highly developed service skills. These companies understand that keeping current customers satisfied is just as important as attracting new ones, if not more so. Leading-edge firms are obsessed not only with delivering high-quality customer service but also with measuring satisfaction, loyalty, relationship quality, and other indicators of nonfinancial performance.

Most firms find it necessary to develop measures unique to their own strategy, value propositions, and target market. For example, Anderson Corporation assesses the loyalty of its

KEEPING CURRENT CUSTOMERS SATISFIED IS JUST AS IMPORTANT AS ATTRACTING NEW ONES, IF NOT MORE SO.

trade customers by their willingness to continue carrying its windows and doors, recommend its products to colleagues and customers, increase their volume with the company, and put its products in their own homes. Basically, each firm's measures should not only ask "What are your expectations?" and "How are we doing?" but should also reflect what the firm wants its customers to do.

Some customers are more valuable than others. They may have greater value because they spend more, buy higher-margin products, have a well-known name, or have the potential of becoming a bigger customer in the future. Some companies selectively provide different levels of service to customers based on their value to the business. By giving the most valuable customers superior service, a firm is more likely to keep them happy, hopefully increasing retention of these high-value customers and maximizing the total business value they generate over time.

To achieve this goal, the firm must be able to divide customers into two or more groups based on their value. It must also create and apply policies that govern how service will be allocated among groups. Policies might establish which customers' phone calls get "fast tracked" and which customers are directed to use the Web and/or voice self-service, how specific e-mail questions are routed, and who is given access to online chat and who isn't.[26]

Providing different customers with different levels of service is a very sensitive matter. It must be handled

IF YOU ORDER IT WE WILL COME.

FOOD AND DRINKS ON DEMAND. THIS IS HOW TO FLY.

GRAB A SEAT AT VIRGINAMERICA.COM
SAN FRANCISCO : LAS VEGAS : LOS ANGELES : NEW YORK : SAN DIEGO : SEATTLE : WASHINGTON, D.C.

Virgin america

© AP IMAGES/PRNEWSFOTO/VIRGIN AMERICA

very carefully and very discreetly to avoid offending lesser value, but still important customers.

STUDY TOOLS
CHAPTER 7

Located at back of the textbook

❏ **Rip out Chapter Review Card**

Located at 4ltrpress.cengage.com/mktg

❏ **Review Key Terms Flash Cards (Print or Online)**

❏ **Download Audio and Visual Summaries for on-the-go review**

❏ **Complete both Practice Quizzes to prepare for tests**

❏ **Play "Beat the Clock" and "Quizbowl" to master concepts**

❏ **Complete "Crossword Puzzle" to review key terms**

❏ **Watch the video on "Ready Made" for a real company example on Business Marketing**

The podcasts are the best thing in the world! If one week I don't have enough time to read the chapter for the lesson, it is so easy to listen to it on my way to University on the train, so I can at least have a basic knowledge of that chapter before the lecture, and I can catch up with my reading later. The images in the chapters are engaging, and it makes you feel like you are in the midst of the Marketing World.

– Sandra DeWitt, Student at University of Notre Dame Fremantle, Australia

LISTEN UP!

SHE DID

MKTG4 was designed for students just like you – busy people who want choices, flexibility, and multiple learning options.

MKTG4 delivers concise, focused information in a fresh and contemporary format. And…

MKTG4 gives you a variety of online learning materials designed with you in mind.

At **4ltrpress.cengage.com**, you'll find electronic resources such as **video podcasts, audio downloads,** and **interactive quizzes** for each chapter.

These resources will help supplement your understanding of core marketing concepts in a format that fits your busy lifestyle. Visit **4ltrpress.cengage.com** to learn more about the multiple resources available to help you succeed!

CHAPTER **8** | **Segmenting and Targeting Markets**

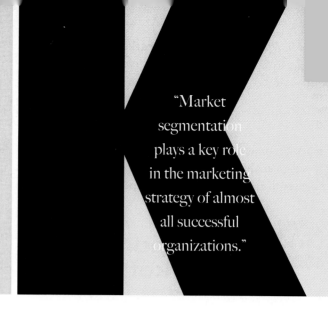

> "Market segmentation plays a key role in the marketing strategy of almost all successful organizations."

LO1   Market Segmentation

AFTER YOU FINISH THIS CHAPTER GO TO PAGE 132 FOR STUDY TOOLS

The term market means different things to different people. We are all familiar with the supermarket, stock market, labor market, fish market, and flea market. All these types of markets share several characteristics. First, they are composed of people (consumer markets) or organizations (business markets). Second, these people or organizations have wants and needs that can be satisfied by particular product categories. Third, they have the ability to buy the products they seek. Fourth, they are willing to exchange their resources, usually money or credit, for desired products. In sum, a **market** is (1) people or organizations with (2) needs or wants and with (3) the ability and (4) the willingness to buy. A group of people or an organization that lacks any one of these characteristics is not a market.

Within a market, a **market segment** is a subgroup of people or organizations sharing one or more characteristics that cause them to have similar product needs. At one extreme, we can define every person and every organization in the world as a market segment because each is unique. At the other extreme, we can define the entire consumer market as one large market segment and the business market as another large segment. All people have some similar characteristics and needs, as do all organizations.

> **market** people or organizations with needs or wants and the ability and willingness to buy
>
> **market segment** a subgroup of people or organizations sharing one or more characteristics that cause them to have similar product needs

What do you think?

It's pretty obvious when advertising is aimed at a certain group.

1   2   3   4   5   6   7
STRONGLY DISAGREE   STRONGLY AGREE

© WORLDFOTO/ALAMY

Find out what others think at 4ltrpress.cengage.com/mktg

market segmentation the process of dividing a market into meaningful, relatively similar, and identifiable segments or groups

From a marketing perspective, market segments can be described as somewhere between the two extremes. The process of dividing a market into meaningful, relatively similar, and identifiable segments or groups is called **market segmentation**. The purpose of market segmentation is to enable the marketer to tailor marketing mixes to meet the needs of one or more specific segments.

LO 2 The Importance of Market Segmentation

Until the 1960s, few firms practiced market segmentation. When they did, it was more likely a haphazard effort than a formal marketing strategy. Before 1960, for example, the Coca-Cola Company produced only one beverage and aimed it at the entire soft drink market. Today, Coca-Cola offers more than a dozen different products to market segments based on diverse consumer preferences for flavors and calorie and caffeine content. Coca-Cola offers traditional soft drinks, energy drinks (including POWERade), flavored teas, fruit drinks (Fruitopia), and water (Dasani).

Market segmentation plays a key role in the marketing strategy of almost all successful organizations and is a powerful marketing tool for several reasons. Most important, nearly all markets include groups of people or organizations with different product needs and preferences. Market segmentation helps marketers define customer needs and wants more precisely. Because market segments differ in size and potential, segmentation helps decision makers to more accurately define marketing objectives and better allocate resources. In turn, performance can be better evaluated when objectives are more precise.

Chico's, a successful women's fashion retailer, thrives by marketing to women ages 35 to 55 who like to wear comfortable, yet stylish, clothing. It sells private-label clothing that comes in just a few nonjudgmental sizes: zero (standard sizes 4–6), one (8–10), two (10–12), and three (14–16). Another example is Best Buy, which identifies the needs of customers depending on their geographic location. For example, the store in Baytown, Texas caters to Eastern European workers from cargo ships or oil tankers that are temporarily docked at the city's busy port. These workers don't have a lot of time to shop, so the Baytown Best Buy moved the iPods from the back corner of the store to the front, paired them with overseas power converters and made the signage simpler.[1]

LO 3 Criteria for Successful Segmentation

Marketers segment markets for three important reasons. First, segmentation enables marketers to identify groups of customers with similar needs and to analyze the characteristics and buying behavior of these groups. Second, segmentation provides marketers with information to help them design marketing mixes specifically matched with the characteristics and desires of one or more segments. Third, segmentation is consistent with the marketing concept of satisfying customer wants and needs while meeting the organization's objectives.

To be useful, a segmentation scheme must produce segments that meet four basic criteria:

1. **Substantiality:** A segment must be large enough to warrant developing and maintaining a special marketing mix. This criterion does not necessarily mean that a segment must have many potential customers. Marketers of custom-designed homes and business buildings, commercial airplanes, and large computer systems typically develop marketing programs tailored to each potential customer's needs. In most cases, however, a market segment needs many potential customers to make commercial sense. In the 1980s, home banking failed because not enough people owned personal computers. Today, a larger number of people own computers, and home banking is a thriving industry.

© ISTOCKPHOTO.COM/ROB BELKNAP

2 **Identifiability and measurability**: Segments must be identifiable and their size measurable. Data about the population within geographic boundaries, the number of people in various age categories, and other social and demographic characteristics are often easy to get, and they provide fairly concrete measures of segment size. Suppose that a social service agency wants to identify segments by their readiness to participate in a drug and alcohol program or in prenatal care. Unless the agency can measure how many people are willing, indifferent, or unwilling to participate, it will have trouble gauging whether there are enough people to justify setting up the service.

3 **Accessibility**: The firm must be able to reach members of targeted segments with customized marketing mixes. Some market segments are hard to reach—for example, senior citizens (especially those with reading or hearing disabilities), individuals who don't speak English, and the illiterate.

4 **Responsiveness**: Markets can be segmented using any criteria that seem logical. Unless one market segment responds to a marketing mix differently from other segments, however, that segment need not be treated separately. For instance, if all customers are equally price-conscious about a product, there is no need to offer high-, medium-, and low-priced versions to different segments.

LO4 Bases for Segmenting Consumer Markets

Marketers use **segmentation bases**, or **variables**, which are characteristics of individuals, groups, or organizations, to divide a total market into segments. The choice of segmentation bases is crucial because an inappropriate segmentation strategy may lead to lost sales and missed profit opportunities. The key is to identify bases that will produce substantial, measurable, and accessible segments that exhibit different response patterns to marketing mixes.

Markets can be segmented using a single variable, such as age group, or several variables, such as age group, gender, and education. Although it is less precise, single-variable segmentation has the advantage of being simpler and easier to use than multiple-variable segmentation. The disadvantages of multiple-variable segmentation are that it is often harder to use than single-variable segmentation; usable secondary data are less likely to be available; and as the number of segmentation bases increases, the size of individual segments decreases. Nevertheless, the current trend is toward using more rather than fewer variables to segment most markets. Multiple-variable segmentation is clearly more precise than single-variable segmentation.

Consumer goods marketers commonly use one or more of the following characteristics to segment markets: geography, demographics, psychographics, benefits sought, and usage rate.

Geographic Segmentation

Geographic segmentation refers to segmenting markets by region of a country or the world, market size, market density, or climate. Market density means the number of people within a unit of land, such as a census tract. Climate is commonly used for geographic segmentation because of its dramatic impact on residents' needs and purchasing behavior. Snow blowers, water and snow skis, clothing, and air-conditioning and heating systems are products with varying appeal, depending on climate.

Consumer goods companies take a regional approach to marketing for four reasons. First, many firms need to find new ways to generate sales because of sluggish and intensely competitive markets. Second, computerized checkout stations with scanners give retailers an accurate assessment of which brands sell best in their region. Third, many packaged-goods manufacturers are introducing new regional brands intended to appeal to local preferences. Fourth, a more regional approach allows consumer goods companies

> **segmentation bases (variables)**
> characteristics of individuals, groups, or organizations
>
> **geographic segmentation**
> segmenting markets by region of a country or the world, market size, market density, or climate

© ISTOCKPHOTO.COM/ROB BELKNAP

to react more quickly to competition. For example, research showed Saks Fifth Avenue's customers differ significantly at stores around the country. At the New York store, Saks' core shopper is a woman in her mid-forties with a classic style. By contrast, core shoppers at its Birmingham, Alabama store are more brand-savvy, fashion-loving, and slightly younger.[2] Macy's is another retailer that uses geographic segmentation. The company has changed the merchandise mix so that 15 percent of the merchandise in stores reflects local preferences of its customers.[3]

Demographic Segmentation

Marketers often segment markets on the basis of demographic information because it is widely available and often related to consumers' buying and consuming behavior. Some common bases of **demographic segmentation** are age, gender, income, ethnic background, and family life cycle.

Age Segmentation   Marketers use a variety of terms to refer to different age groups. Examples include newborns, infants, young children, tweens, Generation Y (teens, young adults), Generation X, baby boomers, and seniors. Age segmentation can be an important tool, as a brief exploration of the market potential of several age segments illustrates.

Through allowances, earnings, and gifts, children account for, and influence, a great deal of consumption. For example, tweens (ages 8–14) in the United States spend billions of their own dollars each year on purchases for themselves, and also have considerable influence over major family purchase decisions. They are technology savvy and very social consumers.[4] Tweens desire to be kids but also want some of the fun of being a teenager. Many retailers serve this market with clothing that is similar in style to that worn by teenagers and young adults.

Generation Y, or the Millennial generation, spans the age group 14–29. This group also has formidable purchasing power. They like to try whatever is new and trendy, tend to change their minds quickly about things, and covet status brands.[5] The teens in this group spend most of their money on clothing, entertainment, and food. They are aware of brands and also of marketing strategies; therefore, obvious marketing techniques won't work. They are environmentally conscious and say they would shop at an environmentally friendly retailer more often and spend more money if services, products, and brands were environmentally friendly.[6]

Generation X is the group that was born after the baby boomers. Members of Generation X tend to be disloyal to brands and skeptical of big business. Many of them are becoming parents, and they make purchasing decisions with thought for and input from their families. Xers desire an experience, not just a product. For example, Starbucks developed a market for expensive coffee by encompassing it in the coffee-drinking experience that appeals to this consumer segment.[7]

People born between 1946 and 1964 are often called "baby boomers." Boomers spend $2.1 trillion a year and represent half of all spending in the United States. For the next 18 years, one baby boomer will turn 60 every seven seconds. They make up 49 percent of affluent households, and they want attention and service when they shop.[8] This group spends big money on products such as travel, electronics, and automobiles. Baby boomers are not particularly brand loyal, and they are a very diverse group. Some may be the parents of a baby, while others are empty nesters.

Consumers in their early sixties and older represent people who are part of the War Generation (ages 61 to 66), the Depression Generation (ages 67 to 76) and the G.I. Generation (age 77 and up). Many in this group view retirement not as a passive time, but as an active time they use to explore new knowledge, travel, volunteer, and spend time with family and friends. They are living longer and are healthier than older consumers twenty years ago.

Gender Segmentation   In the United States, women handle 75 percent of family finances and make or influence 80 percent of consumer purchases. They buy 51 percent of the new electronics sold, 75 percent of over-the-counter drugs, and 65 percent of new cars. That means that women are making decisions when it comes to the purchase of a huge variety of goods and services, not just the packaged goods that have traditionally been marketed to them.[9]

Women are buying and playing video games in rapidly increasing numbers. Forty percent of gamers are women and they outnumber under-17 males by nearly two to one in the gaming world. The video game industry has been forced to respond by developing more games with female protagonists and changing its advertising strategy. A recent commercial for EA sports featured real video gamers—some of them women—instead of actors, and presented video game playing as an interactive social activity.[10] Other marketers that traditionally focused most of their attention on males are also recognizing the potential of the female market segment. For example, the number of women

© ISTOCKPHOTO.COM/STEFAN HERMANS

shopping at hardware stores such as Home Depot and Lowe's Home Improvement Warehouse has been rising in recent years. Home Depot is testing a new store concept that is designed to attract more women shoppers. These stores will focus more on upscale home décor and organization, using showrooms that are more extravagant and carry more products.[11]

Marketers of products such as clothing, cosmetics, personal-care items, magazines, jewelry, and gifts still commonly segment markets by gender. For instance, one Internet retailer, CoolStuffForDads.com targets shoppers with a wide variety of gifts that men would enjoy.[12] Grocers have tapped into the roughly 18 percent of men who shop for groceries by marketing directly to them. A recent study found that compared to women, men place a higher priority on location and convenience, don't like loyalty cards, and often vary from their lists, creating opportunities for grocers to encourage impulse buys.[13]

Income Segmentation Income is a popular demographic variable for segmenting markets because income level influences consumers' wants and determines their buying power. Many markets are segmented by income, including the markets for housing, clothing, automobiles, and food. Wholesale clubs Costco and Sam's Club appeal to many income segments. According to a Nielsen study, affluent households (those that earn more than $100,000 annually) are twice as likely to shop warehouse stores compared to households that earn $20,000 or less a year, and the affluent shopper spends an average $46 more than the lower-income shopper

per trip.[14] High-income customers looking for luxury want outstanding customer service. For example, fashion companies use computer technology to customize upscale products that are designed specifically for their wealthy customers' needs.[15] Other companies try to appeal to low-income customers. Casual Male has launched a big-and-tall brand of men's apparel aimed at the lower-income market. Procter & Gamble has introduced Bounty Basic paper towels and Charmin Basic bath tissue to attract more price-sensitive consumers.[16]

Ethnic Segmentation In the past, ethnic groups in the United States were expected to conform to a homogenized, Anglo-centric ideal. This was evident both in the marketing of mass-marketed products and in the selective way that films, television, advertisements, and popular music portrayed America's diverse population. Until the 1970s, ethnic foods were rarely sold except in specialty stores. The racial barrier in entertainment lasted nearly as long, except for supporting movie and television roles—often based on stereotypes dating back to the nineteenth century.[17] Increasing numbers of ethnic minorities, along with increased buying power, have changed this. Hispanic Americans, African Americans, and Asian Americans are the three largest ethnic groups in the United States. In 2006, these three groups accounted for 88 million people, and by 2010 are expected to represent about a third of the total U.S. population.[18] Today, companies such as Procter & Gamble, Allstate Insurance, Bank of America, and Reebok have developed multicultural marketing initiatives designed to better understand and serve the wants and preferences of U.S. minority groups. Many consumer goods companies spend 5 to 10 percent of their marketing budgets specifically targeting multicultural consumers. This proportion will likely increase in the future as ethnic groups represent larger and larger percentages of the U.S. population.[19]

Family Life-Cycle Segmentation The demographic factors of gender, age, and income often do not sufficiently explain why consumer buying behavior varies. Frequently, consumption patterns among people of the same age and gender differ because they are in different stages of the family life cycle. The **family life cycle (FLC)** is a series of stages determined by a combination of age, marital status, and the presence or absence of children.

The life-cycle stage consisting of the married-couple household, used to be considered the traditional family in the United States. Today, however, married

> **family life cycle (FLC)** a series of stages determined by a combination of age, marital status, and the presence or absence of children

psychographic segmentation
market segmentation on the basis of personality, motives, lifestyles, and geodemographics

geodemographic segmentation
segmenting potential customers into neighborhood lifestyle categories

couples make up just about half of households, down from nearly 80 percent in the 1950s. This means that the 86 million single adults in the United States could soon define the new majority. Already, unmarried Americans make up 42 percent of the workforce, 40 percent of homebuyers, and one of the most potent consumer groups on record. Exhibit 8.1 illustrates numerous FLC patterns and shows how families' needs, incomes, resources, and expenditures differ at each stage. The horizontal flow shows the traditional family life cycle. The lower part of the exhibit gives some of the characteristics and purchase patterns of families in each stage of the traditional life cycle. The exhibit also acknowledges that about half of all first marriages end in divorce. When young marrieds move into the young divorced stage, their consumption patterns often revert back to those of the young single stage of the cycle. About four out of five divorced persons remarry by middle age and reenter the traditional life cycle, as indicated by the "recycled flow" in the exhibit. Consumers are especially receptive to marketing efforts at certain points in the life cycle.

> RESEARCH HAS FOUND THAT THE OVERRIDING FACTOR IN DESCRIBING BABY BOOMER SUBSEGMENTS IS THE PRESENCE OF CHILDREN IN THE HOUSE. THE NIELSEN STUDY DISCOVERED EIGHT SPECIFIC SEGMENTS: FOUR SEGMENTS WITH CHILDREN UNDER 18 REPRESENTED ABOUT 40 PERCENT OF THE BOOMERS, AND FOUR SEGMENTS WITHOUT CHILDREN REPRESENTED 60 PERCENT.[20]

Psychographic Segmentation

Age, gender, income, ethnicity, family life-cycle stage, and other demographic variables are usually helpful in developing segmentation strategies, but often they don't paint the entire picture. Demographics provide the skeleton, but psychographics add meat to the bones. **Psychographic segmentation** is market segmentation on the basis of the following variables:

PSYCHOGRAPHIC SEGMENTATION VARIABLES:

▶▶ *Personality*: Personality reflects a person's traits, attitudes, and habits. According to a national survey by Roper, almost half of Americans believe their cars match their personalities: SUVs deliver the heady feeling of being independent and above it all. Convertibles epitomize wind-in-the-hair freedom; and off-roaders convey outdoor adventure. About 25 percent of people surveyed say that their cars make them feel powerful.[21]

▶▶ *Motives*: Marketers of baby products and life insurance appeal to consumers' emotional motives—namely, to care for their loved ones. Using appeals to economy, reliability, and dependability, carmakers like Subaru and Suzuki target customers with rational motives. Carmakers like Mercedes-Benz, Jaguar, and Cadillac appeal to customers with status-related motives.

▶▶ *Lifestyles*: Lifestyle segmentation divides people into groups according to the way they spend their time, the importance of the things around them, their beliefs, and socioeconomic characteristics such as income and education. For example, the companies behind the sport Nordic walking are targeting couch potatoes and other nonathletic types. They hope to make the activity appealing to those for whom regular exercise has been a challenge.[22] PepsiCo is promoting its low-calorie, vitamin-enhanced water, Aquafina Alive, to consumers who are health conscious.[23]

▶▶ *Geodemographics*: **Geodemographic segmentation** clusters potential customers into neighborhood lifestyle categories. It combines geographic, demographic, and lifestyle segmentations. Geodemographic segmentation helps marketers develop marketing programs tailored to prospective buyers who live in small geographic regions, such as neighborhoods, or who have very specific lifestyle and demographic characteristics. H-E-B Grocery Company, a 304-store, Texas-based supermarket chain, specializes in developing its own branded products designed to meet the needs and tastes of specific communities. In the Rio Grande Valley, where summers are hot and many residents don't have air conditioning, H-E-B markets its own brand of rubbing oil that helps cool the skin while adding moisturizers. Along the southern border, the grocer stocks *discos*, large metal disks that Mexican Americans use to cook brisket. In Detroit, Home Depot has stores in some neighborhoods that have charcoal barbeque grills, while others offer gas grills.[24]

Psychographic variables can be used individually to segment markets or be combined with other variables to provide more detailed descriptions of market segments. One combination approach is the Claritas PRIZM Lifestyle software program that divides Americans into sixty-six "clusters," or consumer types, all with catchy names. The clusters combine basic demographic data such as age, ethnicity, and income with lifestyle information, such as magazine and sports preferences, taken from consumer surveys. For example, the "Kids and Cul-de-Sacs" group consists of upscale, married couples with children who live in recently built subdivisions. These families have a median household income of $70,233, tend to own a Honda Odyssey, and are likely to spend large sums of money for child-centered products and services such as video games and Chuck E. Cheese. The "Bohemian Mix" cluster is made up of urbanites under age 35. These young singles, couples, students, and professionals have a median income of $51,100, are early adopters in many product categories, tend to shop at Banana Republic and are likely to read *Vanity Fair* magazine.[25] The program also predicts to which neighborhoods

EXHIBIT 8.1
Family Life Cycle

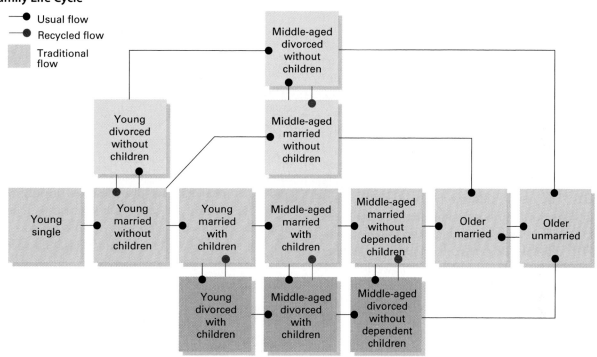

Young single	Young married or divorced without children	Young married or divorced with children	Middle-aged married or divorced with or without children	Middle-aged married or divorced without children	Older married	Older unmarried
Few financial burdens	Better off financially than they will be in near future	Home purchasing at peak	Financial position still better	Home ownership at peak	Drastic cut in income	Drastic cut in income
Fashion opinion leaders	Highest purchase rate and highest average purchase of durables	Liquid assets low	More wives work	Most satisfied with financial position and money saved	Keep home	Special need for attention, affection, and security
Recreation-oriented	Buy: cars, refrigerators, stoves, sensible and durable furniture, vacations	Dissatisfied with financial position and amount of money saved	Some children get jobs	Interested in travel, recreation, self-education	Buy: medical appliances, medical care, products that aid health, sleep, and digestion	Buy: same medical and product needs as other older group
Buy: basic kitchen equipment, basic furniture, cars, equipment for mating game, vacations		Interested in new products	Hard to influence with advertising	Make gifts and contributions		
		Like advertised products	High average purchase of durables	Not interested in new products		
		Buy: washers, dryers, televisions, baby food, chest rubs, cough medicine, vitamins, dolls, wagons, sleds, skates	Buy: new and more tasteful furniture, auto travel, unnecessary appliances, boats, dental	Buy: vacations, luxuries, home improvements		

benefit segmentation the process of grouping customers into market segments according to the benefits they seek from the product

usage-rate segmentation dividing a market by the amount of product bought or consumed

80/20 principle a principle holding that 20 percent of all customers generate 80 percent of the demand

across the country these clusters are likely to gravitate.

Benefit Segmentation

Benefit segmentation is the process of grouping customers into market segments according to the benefits they seek from the product. Most types of market segmentation are based on the assumption that this variable and customers' needs are related. Benefit segmentation is different because it groups potential customers on the basis of their needs or wants rather than some other characteristic, such as age or gender. The snack-food market, for example, can be divided into six benefit segments: nutritional snackers, weight watchers, guilty snackers, party snackers, indiscriminate snackers, and economical snackers.

Customer profiles can be developed by examining demographic information associated with people seeking certain benefits. This information can be used to match marketing strategies with selected target markets. The many different types of performance energy bars with various combinations of nutrients are aimed at consumers looking for different benefits. For example, PowerBar is designed for athletes looking for long-lasting fuel, while PowerBar Protein Plus is aimed at those who want extra protein for replenishing muscles after strength training. Carb Solutions High Protein Bars are for those on low-carb diets; Luna Bars are targeted to women who want a bar with fewer calories, soy protein, and calcium; and Clif Bars are for people who want a natural bar with ingredients like rolled oats, soybeans, and organic soy flour.

Usage-Rate Segmentation

Usage-rate segmentation divides a market by the amount of product bought or consumed. Categories vary with the product, but they are likely to include some combination of the following: former users, potential users, first-time users, light or irregular users,

medium users, and heavy users. Segmenting by usage rate enables marketers to focus their efforts on heavy users or to develop multiple marketing mixes aimed at different segments. Because heavy users often account for a sizable portion of all product sales, some marketers focus on the heavy-user segment.

The **80/20 principle** holds that 20 percent of all customers generate 80 percent of the demand. Although the percentages usually are not exact, the general idea often holds true. For example, in the fast-food industry, the heavy user accounts for only one of five fast-food patrons but makes about 60 percent of all visits to fast-food restaurants. The needs of heavy users differs from the needs of other usage-rate groups. They have intense needs for product and service selection and a variety of types of information, as well as an emotional attachment to the product category. Individuals in this group spend four to fourteen times as much in their favored product category than do light users.[26]

Developing customers into heavy users is the goal behind many frequency/loyalty programs like the airlines' frequent flyer programs. Many supermarkets and other retailers have also designed loyalty programs that reward the heavy-user segment with deals available only to them, such as in-store coupon dispensing systems, loyalty card programs, and special price deals on selected merchandise.

LO5 Bases for Segmenting Business Markets

The business market consists of four broad segments: producers, resellers, government, and institutions. (For a detailed discussion of the characteristics of these segments, see Chapter 6.) Whether marketers focus on only one or on all four of these segments, they are likely to find diversity among potential cus-

20 PERCENT OF ALL CUSTOMERS GENERATE 80 PERCENT OF THE DEMAND.

tomers. Thus, further market segmentation offers just as many benefits to business marketers as it does to consumer-product marketers.

Company Characteristics

Company characteristics, such as geographic location, type of company, company size, and product use, can be important segmentation variables. Some markets tend to be regional because buyers prefer to purchase from local suppliers, and distant suppliers may have difficulty competing in terms of price and service. Therefore, firms that sell to geographically concentrated industries benefit by locating close to their markets.

Segmenting by customer type allows business marketers to tailor their marketing mixes to the unique needs of particular types of organizations or industries. Many companies are finding this form of segmentation to be quite effective. For example, Home Depot, one of the largest do-it-yourself retail businesses in the United States, has targeted professional repair and remodeling contractors in addition to consumers. Procter & Gamble is beginning to target business customers by focusing on janitors, fast-food workers, maids, and launderers with products specific to each group's cleaning needs.[27] Volume of purchase (heavy, moderate, light) is a commonly used basis for business segmentation. Another is the buying organization's size, which may affect its purchasing procedures, the types and quantities of products it needs, and its responses to different marketing mixes. Banks frequently offer different services, lines of credit, and overall attention to commercial customers based on their size. Many products, especially raw materials like steel, wood, and petroleum, have diverse applications. How customers use a product may influence the amount they buy, their buying criteria, and their selection of vendors. For example, a producer of springs may have customers that use the product in applications as diverse as making machine tools, bicycles, surgical devices, office equipment, telephones, and missile systems.

Buying Processes

Many business marketers find it helpful to segment customers and prospective customers on the basis of how they buy. For example, companies can segment some business markets by ranking key purchasing criteria, such as price, quality, technical support, and service. Atlas Corporation has developed a commanding position in the industrial door market by providing customized products in just four weeks, which is much faster than the industry average of twelve to fifteen weeks. Atlas's primary market is companies with an immediate need for customized doors.

The purchasing strategies of buyers may provide useful segments. Two purchasing profiles that have been identified are satisficers and optimizers. **Satisficers** contact familiar suppliers and place the order with the first one to satisfy product and delivery requirements. **Optimizers** consider numerous suppliers (both familiar and unfamiliar), solicit bids, and study all proposals carefully before selecting one.

The personal characteristics of the buyers themselves (their demographic characteristics, decision style, tolerance for risk, confidence level, job responsibilities, and so on) influence their buying behavior and thus offer a viable basis for segmenting some business markets. IBM computer buyers, for example, are sometimes characterized as being more risk averse than buyers of less expensive computers that perform essentially the same functions. In advertising, therefore, IBM stresses its reputation for high quality and reliability.

satisficers business customers who place an order with the first familiar supplier to satisfy product and delivery requirements

optimizers business customers who consider numerous suppliers, both familiar and unfamiliar, solicit bids, and study all proposals carefully before selecting one

LO 6 Steps in Segmenting a Market

The purpose of market segmentation, in both consumer and business markets, is to identify marketing opportunities.

1 **Select a market or product category for study:** Define the overall market or product category to be studied. It may be a market in which the firm already competes, a new but related market or product category, or a totally new one. For instance, Anheuser-Busch closely examined the beer market before introducing Michelob Light and Bud Light. Anheuser-Busch also carefully studied the market for salty snacks before introducing the Eagle brand.

2 **Choose a basis or bases for segmenting the market:** This step requires managerial insight, creativity, and market knowledge. There are no scientific procedures for selecting segmentation variables. However, a successful segmentation scheme must produce segments that meet the four basic criteria discussed earlier in this chapter.

target market
a group of people or organizations for which an organization designs, implements, and maintains a marketing mix intended to meet the needs of that group, resulting in mutually satisfying exchanges

undifferentiated targeting strategy
a marketing approach that views the market as one big market with no individual segments and thus uses a single marketing mix

3 **Select segmentation descriptors:** After choosing one or more bases, the marketer must select the segmentation descriptors. Descriptors identify the specific segmentation variables to use. For example, if a company selects demographics as a basis of segmentation, it may use age, occupation, and income as descriptors. A company that selects usage segmentation needs to decide whether to go after heavy users, nonusers, or light users.

4 **Profile and analyze segments:** The profile should include the segments' size, expected growth, purchase frequency, current brand usage, brand loyalty, and long-term sales and profit potential. This information can then be used to rank potential market segments by profit opportunity, risk, consistency with organizational mission and objectives, and other factors important to the firm.

5 **Select target markets:** Selecting target markets is not a part of but a natural outcome of the segmentation process. It is a major decision that influences and often directly determines the firm's marketing mix. This topic is examined in greater detail later in this chapter.

6 **Design, implement, and maintain appropriate marketing mixes:** The marketing mix has been described as product, place (distribution), promotion, and pricing strategies intended to bring about mutually satisfying exchange relationships with target markets. These topics are explored in detail in Chapters 10 through 20.

Markets are dynamic, so it is important that companies proactively monitor their segmentation strategies over time. Often, once customers or prospects have been assigned to a segment, marketers think their task is done. Once customers are assigned to an age segment, for example, they stay there until they reach the next age bracket or category, which could be ten years in the future. Thus, the segmentation classifications are static, but the customers and prospects are changing. Dynamic segmentation approaches adjust to fit the changes that occur in customers' lives. Abercrombie & Fitch, an apparel store that targets teenagers, has opened a new store called Ruehl No. 925 that caters to 20–35-year-olds, and Aéropostale owns P.S., which stocks clothing for boys and girls aged seven to twelve.

LO7 Strategies for Selecting Target Markets

So far this chapter has focused on the market segmentation process, which is only the first step in deciding whom to approach about buying a product. The next task is to choose one or more target markets. A **target market** is a group of people or organizations for which an organization designs, implements, and maintains a marketing mix intended to meet the needs of that group, resulting in mutually satisfying exchanges. Because most markets will include customers with different characteristics, lifestyles, backgrounds, and income levels, it is unlikely that a single marketing mix will attract all segments of the market. Thus, if a marketer wishes to appeal to more than one segment of the market, it must develop different marketing mixes. For example, Buick targets people in their sixties with the Lucerne sedan, a luxury car with a V8 engine and extras like OnStar service. The company also targets younger, Generation Y customers with the Enclave, a crossover SUV. The three general strategies for selecting target markets—undifferentiated, concentrated, and multisegment targeting—are illustrated in Exhibit 8.2, which also illustrates the advantages and disadvantages of each targeting strategy.

Undifferentiated Targeting

A firm using an **undifferentiated targeting strategy** essentially adopts a mass-market philosophy, viewing the market as one big market with no individual segments. The firm uses one marketing mix for the entire market. A firm that adopts an undifferentiated targeting strategy assumes that individual customers have similar needs that can be met with a common marketing mix.

The first firm in an industry sometimes uses an undifferentiated targeting strategy. With no competition, the firm may not need to tailor marketing mixes to the preferences of market segments. Henry Ford's famous comment about the Model T is a classic example of an undifferentiated targeting strategy: "They can have their car in any color they want, as long as it's black." At one time, Coca-Cola used this strategy with a single product and a single size of its familiar green bottle. Marketers of commodity products, such as flour and sugar, are also likely to use an undifferentiated targeting strategy.

EXHIBIT 8.2
Advantages and Disadvantages of Target Marketing Strategies

Targeting Strategy	Advantages	Disadvantages
Undifferentiated Targeting	• Potential savings on production/ marketing costs	• Unimaginative product offerings • Company more susceptible to competition
Concentrated Targeting	• Concentration of resources • Can better meet the needs of a narrowly defined segment • Allows some small firms to better compete with larger firms • Strong positioning	• Segments too small, or changing • Large competitors may more effectively market to niche segment
Multisegment Targeting	• Greater financial success • Economies of scale in producing/marketing	• High costs • Cannibalization

One advantage of undifferentiated marketing is the potential for saving on production and marketing. Because only one item is produced, the firm should be able to achieve economies of mass production. Also, marketing costs may be lower when there is only one product to promote and a single channel of distribution. Too often, however, an undifferentiated strategy emerges by default rather than by design, reflecting a failure to consider the advantages of a segmented approach. The result is often sterile, unimaginative product offerings that have little appeal to anyone.

Another problem associated with undifferentiated targeting is that it makes the company more susceptible to competitive inroads. Hershey lost a big share of the candy market to Mars and other candy companies before it changed to a multisegment targeting strategy. Coca-Cola forfeited its position as the leading seller of cola drinks in supermarkets to PepsiCo in the late 1950s, when Pepsi began offering several sizes of containers.

You might think a firm producing a standard product like toilet tissue would adopt an undifferentiated strategy. However, this market has industrial segments and consumer segments. Industrial buyers want an economical, single-ply product sold in boxes of a hundred rolls. The consumer market demands a more versatile product in smaller quantities. Within the consumer market, the product is differentiated with designer print or no print, cushioned or noncushioned, and economy priced or luxury priced. Fort Howard Corporation, the market share leader in industrial toilet paper, does not even sell to the consumer market.

Undifferentiated marketing can succeed in certain situations, though. A small grocery store in a small, isolated town may define all of the people that live in the town as its target market. It may offer one marketing mix and generally satisfy everyone in town. This strategy is not likely to be as effective if there are three or four grocery stores in town.

Concentrated Targeting

With a **concentrated targeting strategy**, a firm selects a market **niche** (one segment of a market) for targeting its marketing efforts. Because the firm is appealing to a single segment, it can concentrate on understanding the needs, motives, and satisfactions of that segment's members and on developing and maintaining a highly specialized marketing mix. Some firms find that concentrating resources and meeting the needs of a narrowly defined market segment is more profitable than spreading resources over several different segments.

For example, Starbucks became successful by focusing on consumers who want gourmet coffee products. America Online (AOL) became one of the world's leading Internet providers by targeting Internet newcomers.

Small firms often adopt a concentrated targeting strategy to compete effectively with much larger firms. For example, Enterprise Rent-A-Car rose to number one in the car rental industry by catering to people with cars in the shop. It has now expanded into the airport rental market. Some other firms use a concentrated strategy to establish a strong position in a desirable market segment. Porsche, for instance, targets an upscale automobile market through "class appeal, not mass appeal."

Concentrated targeting violates the old adage "Don't put all your eggs in one basket." If the chosen segment is

concentrated targeting strategy a strategy used to select one segment of a market for targeting marketing efforts

niche one segment of a market

too small or if it shrinks because of environmental changes, the firm may suffer negative consequences. For instance, OshKosh B'Gosh, Inc. was highly successful selling children's wear in the 1980s. It was so successful, however, that the children's line came to define OshKosh's image to the extent that the company could not sell clothes to anyone else. Attempts at marketing older children's clothing, women's casual clothes, and maternity wear were all abandoned. Recognizing it was in the children's wear business, the company expanded into products such as kids' shoes, children's eyewear, and plush toys.

A concentrated strategy can also be disastrous for a firm that is not successful in its narrowly defined target market. Before Procter & Gamble introduced Head & Shoulders shampoo, several small firms were already selling antidandruff shampoos. Head & Shoulders was introduced with a large promotional campaign, and the new brand captured over half the market immediately. Within a year, several of the firms that had been concentrating on this market segment went out of business.

Multisegment Targeting

A firm that chooses to serve two or more well-defined market segments and develops a distinct marketing mix for each has a **multisegment targeting strategy**. For example, CitiCard offers its mtvU College Card to students who want to earn rewards geared towards their age group, its Platinum Select Card to those who want no annual fee and a competitive interest rate, its Diamond Preferred Rewards Card to customers who want to earn free rewards like travel and brand-name merchandise, and its Citi AAdvantage Card to those who want to earn American Airlines Advantage frequent flyer miles to redeem for travel. Many credit-card companies even have programs specifically designed for tweens, teens, and college students. Wal-Mart has historically followed a concentrated strategy that targeted lower-income segments. Recently, however, the company has segmented its customers into three core groups based on the type of value they seek at the stores. "Brand Aspirationals" are low-income customers who like to buy brand names such as KitchenAid, "Price-Sensitive Affluents" are wealthier shoppers who love deals, and "Value-Price Shoppers" like low prices and can't afford much more.[29]

Multisegment targeting offers many potential benefits to firms, including greater sales volume, higher profits, larger market share, and economies of scale in manufacturing and marketing. Yet it may also involve greater product design, production, promotion, inventory, marketing research, and management costs. Before deciding to use this strategy, firms should compare the

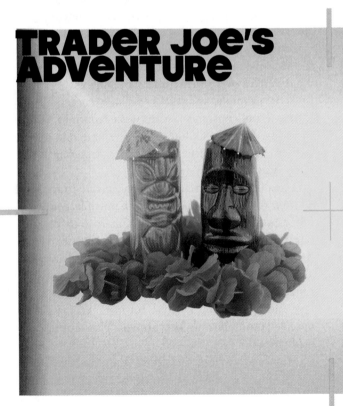

TRADER JOE'S ADVENTURE

A trip to **Trader Joe's** is an adventure, and the food and beverage retailer is a brand with a cult-like following. It carries more than 2,000 unique grocery items (compared to the approximately 30,000 items a typical supermarket carries) under their house label. The company has a tasting panel that tries every product before they buy it; if customers buy something and then don't like it, they can return it for a no-hassle refund. However, a customer can ask an employee about a product, and he or she will find the product and join the customer in a taste test.

Their staff are friendly, knowledgeable, and happy to see customers. A popular radio ad for the company features its CEO making fun of other supermarkets that have put in flat screen television for customers to watch at check out counters. At Trader Joe's, he says, customers can entertain themselves by actually talking to employees.[28]

benefits and costs of multisegment targeting to those of undifferentiated and concentrated targeting.

Another potential cost of multisegment targeting is **cannibalization**, which occurs when sales of a new product cut into sales of a firm's existing products. In many cases, however, companies prefer to steal sales from their own brands rather than lose sales to a competitor. Also, in today's fast-paced world of Internet business, some companies are willing to cannibalize existing business to build new business.

LO 8 One-to-One Marketing

Most businesses today use a mass-marketing approach designed to increase *market share* by selling their products to the greatest number of people. For many businesses, however, it is more efficient and profitable to use one-to-one marketing to increase *share of customer*—in other words, to sell more products to each customer. **One-to-one marketing** is an individualized marketing method that utilizes customer information to build long-term, personalized, and profitable relationships with each customer. The goal is to reduce costs through customer retention and increase revenue through customer loyalty.

The difference between one-to-one marketing and the traditional mass-marketing approach can be compared to shooting a rifle and a shotgun. If you have good aim, a rifle is the more efficient weapon to use. A shotgun, on the other hand, increases your odds of hitting the target when it is more difficult to focus. Instead of scattering messages far and wide across the spectrum of mass media (the shotgun approach), one-to-one marketers look for opportunities to communicate with each individual customer (the rifle approach).

Teen retailer Karmaloop developed a system on their Web site that allows customers to pre-select by brand or clothing category what types of merchandise they wanted to get e-mails about.[30] Lands' End also engages in one-to-one marketing by custom designing clothing. On Lands' End's Web site, customers provide information by answering a series of questions that takes about 20 minutes. Customer sizing information is saved, and reordering is simple. Customers who customize have been found to be more loyal. Several factors suggest that personalized communications and product customization will continue to expand as more companies understand why and how their customers make and execute purchase decisions.

At least four trends will lead to the continuing growth of one-to-one marketing: *personalization*, *time savings*, *loyalty*, and *technology*.

- ▸▸ *First*, one-size-fits-all marketing is no longer relevant. Consumers want to be treated as the individuals they are, with their own unique sets of needs and wants. By its personalized nature, one-to-one marketing can fulfill this desire.

- ▸▸ *Second*, direct and personal marketing efforts will continue to grow to meet the needs of consumers who no longer have the time to spend shopping and making purchase decisions. With the personal and targeted nature of one-to-one marketing, consumers can spend less time making purchase decisions and more time doing the things that are important.

- ▸▸ *Third*, consumers will be loyal only to those companies and brands that have earned their loyalty and reinforced it at every purchase occasion. One-to-one marketing techniques focus on finding a firm's best customers, rewarding them for their loyalty, and thanking them for their business.

- ▸▸ *Fourth*, mass-media approaches will decline in importance as advances in market research and database technology allow marketers to collect detailed information on their customers. New technology offers one-to-one marketers a more cost-effective way to reach customers and enables businesses to personalize their messages. For example, MyYahoo.com greets each user by name and offers information in which the user has expressed interest. Similarly, RedEnvelope.com helps customers keep track of special occasions and offers personalized gift recommendations. With the help of database technology, one-to-one marketers can track their customers as individuals, even if they number in the millions.

One-to-one marketing is a huge commitment and often requires a 180-degree turnaround for marketers who spent the last half of the twentieth century developing and implementing mass-marketing efforts. Although mass marketing will probably continue to be used, especially to create brand awareness or to remind consumers of a product, the advantages of one-to-one marketing cannot be ignored.

LO 9 Positioning

The development of any marketing mix depends on **positioning**, a process that influences potential customers'

cannibalization a situation that occurs when sales of a new product cut into sales of a firm's existing products

one-to-one marketing an individualized marketing method that utilizes customer information to build long-term, personalized, and profitable relationships with each customer

positioning developing a specific marketing mix to influence potential customers' overall perception of a brand, product line, or organization in general

overall perception of a brand, product line, or organization in general. **Position** is the place a product, brand, or group of products occupies in consumers' minds relative to competing offerings. Consumer goods marketers are particularly concerned with positioning. Procter & Gamble, for example, markets eleven different laundry detergents, each with a unique position, such as allergen-free, softening, or ultra-concentrated.

Positioning assumes that consumers compare products on the basis of important features. Marketing efforts that emphasize irrelevant features are therefore likely to misfire. For example, Crystal Pepsi and a clear version of Coca-Cola's Tab failed because consumers perceived the "clear" positioning as more of a marketing gimmick than a benefit.

Effective positioning requires assessing the positions occupied by competing products, determining the important dimensions underlying these positions, and choosing a position in the market where the organization's marketing efforts will have the greatest impact. Callaway Golf positions its new line of clubs and balls as innovative and technologically superior, using the tag line "A better game by design."[31] As the previous example illustrates, **product differentiation** is a positioning strategy that many firms use to distinguish their products from those of competitors. The distinctions can be either real or perceived. Tandem Computer designed machines with two central processing units and two memories for computer systems that can never afford to be down or lose their databases (for example, an airline reservation system). In this case, Tandem used product differentiation to create a product with very real advantages for the target market. However, many everyday products, such as bleaches, aspirin, unleaded regular gasoline, and some soaps, are differentiated by such trivial means as brand names, packaging, color, smell, or "secret" additives. The marketer attempts to convince consumers that a particular brand is distinctive and that they should demand it over competing brands.

Some firms, instead of using product differentiation, position their products as being similar to competing products or brands. Two examples of this positioning include artificial sweeteners advertised as tasting like sugar or margarine tasting like butter.

Perceptual Mapping

Perceptual mapping is a means of displaying or graphing, in two or more dimensions, the location of products, brands, or groups of products in customers' minds. For example, Saks, Inc., the tiny department store chain, stumbled in sales when it tried to attract a younger core customer. To recover, Saks invested in research to determine its core customers in its 54 stores across the country. The perceptual map in Exhibit 8.3 shows how Saks, Inc. uses customer demographics, such as age, spending habits, and shopping patterns, to build a matrix that charts the best mix of clothes and accessories to stock in each store.

Positioning Bases

Firms use a variety of bases for positioning, including the following:

▸▸ *Attribute*: A product is associated with an attribute, product feature, or customer benefit. Kleenex has designed a tissue that contains substances to kill germs in an effort to differentiate its product from competing tissues.[32]

▸▸ *Price and quality*: This positioning base may stress high price as a signal of quality or emphasize low price as an indication of value. Neiman Marcus uses the high-price strategy; Wal-Mart has successfully followed the low-price and value strategy. The mass merchandiser Target has developed an interesting position based on price

EXHIBIT 8.3
Perceptual Map and Positioning Strategy for Saks' Department Stores

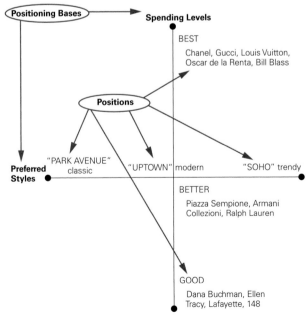

SOURCE: Vanessa O'Connell, "Park Avenue Classic or Soho Trendy?" *The Wall Street Journal*, April 20, 2007, B1.

and quality. It is an "upscale discounter," sticking to low prices but offering higher quality and design than most discount chains.

▸▸ *Use or application*: Stressing uses or applications can be an effective means of positioning a product with buyers. Danone introduced its Kahlúa liqueur using advertising to point out 228 ways to consume the product. Snapple introduced a new drink called "Snapple a Day" that is intended for use as a meal replacement.

▸▸ *Product user*: This positioning base focuses on a personality or type of user. Zale Corporation has several jewelry store concepts, each positioned to a different user. The Zales stores cater to middle-of-the-road consumers with traditional styles. Its Gordon's stores appeal to a slightly older clientele with a contemporary look.

▸▸ *Product class*: The objective here is to position the product as being associated with a particular category of products; for example, positioning a margarine brand with butter. Alternatively, products can be disassociated with a category. Del Monte introduced Fruit Chillers, a shelf-stable sorbet that consumers freeze themselves when they're ready to eat it. Fruit Chillers are sold next to single-serve fruit cups, positioned as fruit rather than as a frozen dessert.[33]

▸▸ *Competitor*: Positioning against competitors is part of any positioning strategy. Avis Rent A Car positioning as number 2 compared to Hertz exemplifies positioning against specific competitors.

▸▸ *Emotion*: Positioning using emotion focuses on how the product makes customers feel. A number of companies use this approach. For example, Nike's "Just Do It" campaign didn't tell consumers what "it" is, but most got the emotional message of achievement and courage. Budweiser's advertising featuring talking frogs and lizards emphasized fun. Sears is drawing on the nostalgia of its brand name by remodeling a store outside Atlanta to resemble its stores of the past. The focus is on tapping into Sears' heritage, and its legacy as America's store.[34]

Repositioning

Sometimes products or companies are repositioned in order to sustain growth in slow markets or to correct positioning mistakes. **Repositioning** is changing consumers' perceptions of a brand in relation to competing brands. For example, Procter & Gamble increased its baby-care business in the early 2000s when they changed Pampers' position from being about dryness to being about helping Mom with her baby's development. P&G also repositioned Olay from being a pink liquid that moisturizes to a product that helps women look better and feel better as they age.[35]

An entire industry of firms that need to think about repositioning is the supermarket industry. For more than a decade, Wal-Mart has been expanding in both rural and metro areas. The result has generally been devastating to competitors, especially independent grocers. Consulting firm Retail Forward predicts that two supermarkets will go out of business for every Wal-Mart Supercenter that opens in the United States. The Strategic Resource Group adds twenty-seven leading national and regional supermarket operators have either gone bankrupt or have liquidated since Wal-Mart went national with Supercenters.[36] Because Wal-Mart owns the low price position, competitors have to establish viable alternative positions.

H-E-B stores in Hispanic areas in Texas are tailoring their product mix to appeal to this market segment. Its Central Market format offers an upscale experience with unique products and very high-quality perishables. Research shows that more than half of all families with incomes between $50,000 and $100,000 are willing to pay more for high-quality items in a more pleasant shopping environment.[37] Safeway is trying to avoid Wal-Mart by repositioning itself as upscale with about half its stores converted to "Lifestyle" markets with wood floors, on-site bakeries, and high-end private label brands.[38] It is too early to tell if any of these repositioning strategies will be successful. Clearly, though, competing head-on with a company whose positioning statement is "Always the low price" is not a good idea.

repositioning
changing consumers' perceptions of a brand in relation to competing brands

20

Percent of customers responsible for 80% of a company's demand

$2.1 trillion

Amount baby boomers spend annually (half of all U.S. spending!)

2

Number of supermarkets that go out of business for each Wal-Mart Supercenter built

6

Number of steps in segmenting a market

11

Number of laundry detergents marketed by Procter & Gamble, each targted to a different segment

STUDY TOOLS
CHAPTER 8

Located at back of the textbook

❑ **Rip out Chapter Review Card**

Located at 4ltrpress.cengage.com/mktg

❑ **Review Key Terms Flash Cards (Print or Online)**
❑ **Download Audio and Visual Summaries for on-the-go review**
❑ **Complete both Practice Quizzes to prepare for tests**
❑ **Play "Beat the Clock" and "Quizbowl" to master concepts**
❑ **Complete "Crossword Puzzle" to review key terms**
❑ **Watch the video on "Ready Made" for a real company example on Segmenting and Targeting Markets**

"It's easy to read, it outlines important topics, and it's relevant. Thanks for the good stuff on the website, I think it will **really help with tests**.

– Thomas Scholtes, Student at University of Maryland, College Park

REVIEW

HE DID

MKTG4 puts a multitude of study aids at your fingertips. After reading the chapters, check out these resources for further help:

• **Chapter Review cards**, found in the back of your book, include all learning outcomes, definitions, and visual summaries for each chapter.

• **Online printable flash cards** give you three additional ways to check your comprehension of key marketing concepts.

Other great ways to help you study include **interactive marketing games, podcasts, audio downloads,** and **online tutorial quizzes with feedback**.

You can find it all at **4ltrpress.cengage.com**.

CHAPTER 9

Decision Support Systems

and Marketing Research

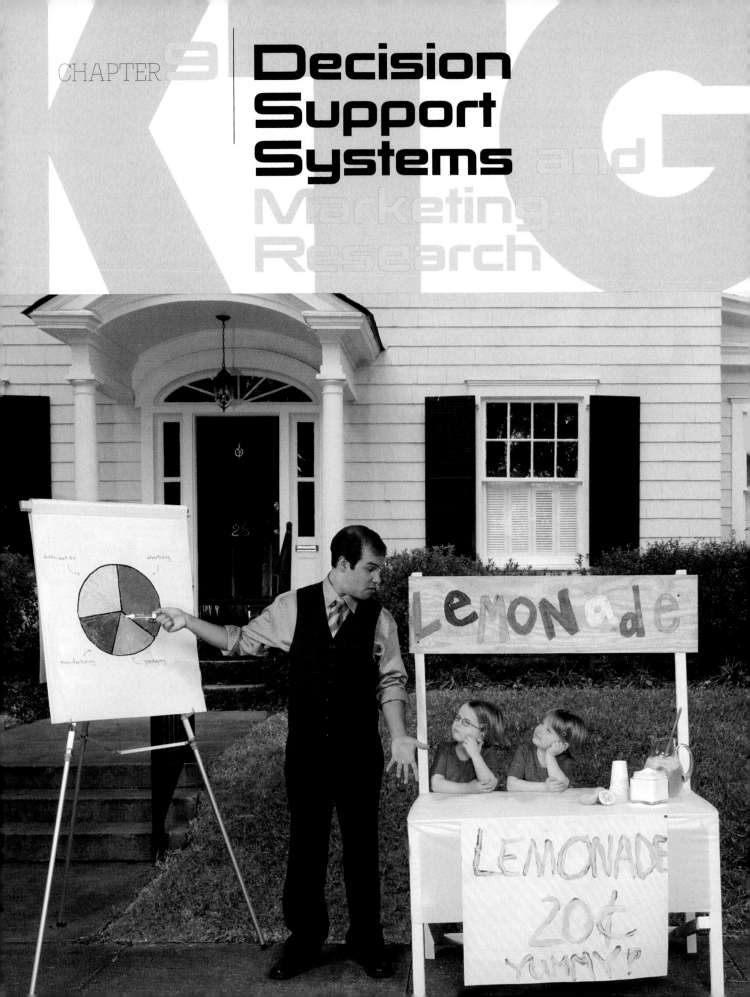

Learning Outcomes

"Whether a research project costs $200 or $2 million, the same general process should be followed."

LO 1 Marketing Decision Support Systems

AFTER YOU FINISH THIS CHAPTER GO TO PAGE 151 FOR STUDY TOOLS

Accurate and timely information is the lifeblood of marketing decision making. Good information can help an organization maximize sales and efficiently use scarce company resources. To prepare and adjust marketing plans, managers need a system for gathering everyday information about developments in the marketing environment—that is, for gathering marketing information. The system most commonly used these days for gathering **marketing information** is called a *marketing decision support system.*

A marketing **decision support system (DSS)** is an interactive, flexible, computerized information system that enables managers to obtain and manipulate information as they are making decisions. A DSS bypasses the information-processing specialist and gives managers access to useful data from their own desks.

These are the characteristics of a true DSS:

▸▸ *Interactive*: Managers give simple instructions and see immediate results. The process is under their direct control; no computer programmer is needed. Managers don't have to wait for scheduled reports.

▸▸ *Flexible*: A DSS can sort, regroup, total, average, and manipulate the data in various ways. It will shift gears as the user changes topics, matching information to the problem at

marketing information
everyday information about developments in the marketing environment that managers use to prepare and adjust marketing plans

decision support system (DSS)
an interactive, flexible computerized information system that enables managers to obtain and manipulate information as they are making decisions

What do you think?

The Internet has made me more likely to take surveys for companies.

1 2 3 4 5 6 7
STRONGLY DISAGREE   STRONGLY AGREE

© SHEER PHOTO, INC./DIGITAL VISION/GETTY IMAGES

database marketing the creation of a large computerized file of customers' and potential customers' profiles and purchase patterns

marketing research the process of planning, collecting, and analyzing data relevant to a marketing decision

hand. For example, the CEO can see highly aggregated figures, and the marketing analyst can view very detailed breakouts.

▸▸ *Discovery oriented*: Managers can probe for trends, isolate problems, and ask "what if" questions.

▸▸ *Accessible*: Managers who aren't skilled with computers can easily learn how to use a DSS. Novice users should be able to choose a standard, or default, method of using the system. They can bypass optional features so they can work with the basic system right away while gradually learning to apply its advanced features.

Perhaps the fastest-growing use of DSSs is for **database marketing**, which is the creation of a large computerized file of customers' and potential customers' profiles and purchase patterns. It is usually the key tool for successful one-to-one marketing, which relies on very specific information about a market.

LO 2 The Role of Marketing Research

Marketing research is the process of planning, collecting, and analyzing data relevant to a marketing decision. The results of this analysis are then communicated to management. Thus, marketing research is the function that links the consumer, customer, and public to the marketer through information. Marketing research plays a key role in the marketing system. It provides decision makers with data on the effectiveness of the current marketing mix and insights for necessary changes. Furthermore, marketing research is a main data source for both management information systems and DSS. In other words, the findings of a marketing research project become data in a DSS.

Marketing research has three roles: descriptive, diagnostic, and predictive. Its *descriptive* role includes gathering and presenting factual statements. For example, what is the historic sales trend in the industry? What are consumers' attitudes toward a prod-

uct and its advertising? Its *diagnostic* role includes explaining data, such as determining the impact on sales of a change in the design of the package. Its *predictive* function is to address "what if" questions. For example, how can the researcher use the descriptive and diagnostic research to predict the results of a planned marketing decision?

LO 3 Steps in a Marketing Research Project

EXHIBIT 9.1
The Marketing Research Process

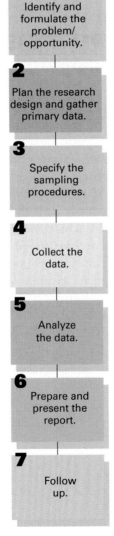

1 Identify and formulate the problem/opportunity.

2 Plan the research design and gather primary data.

3 Specify the sampling procedures.

4 Collect the data.

5 Analyze the data.

6 Prepare and present the report.

7 Follow up.

Virtually all firms that have adopted the marketing concept engage in some marketing research because it offers decision makers many benefits. Some companies spend millions on marketing research; others, particularly smaller firms, conduct informal, limited-scale research studies.

Whether a research project costs $200 or $2 million, the same general process should be followed. The marketing research process is a scientific approach to decision making that maximizes the chance of getting accurate and meaningful results. Exhibit 9.1 traces the seven steps in the research process, which begins with the recognition of a marketing problem or opportunity. As changes occur in the firm's external environment, marketing managers are faced with the questions, "Should we change the existing marketing mix?" and, if so, "How?" Marketing research may be used to evaluate product, promotion, distribution, or pricing alternatives.

Though famous for its well-known line of household lubricants, San Diego–based WD-40 Co. has repositioned one of its product lines as essential bathroom cleaners—the result of a research process.

Sales of the company's six household product brands (including X-14) make up a sizable percentage—more than 31 percent—of the overall portfolio.[1] However, rival brands were more popular. Which elements in the company's marketing mix could be adjusted to gain more share of the cleaning products market?

WD-40's X-14 line is not new, but its repositioning helped the $287 million company find the brand's niche. Marketing research measured product effectiveness against competitors' products, and found that its Trigger Bathroom Cleaner scored a 91 percent approval rating, placing it higher than four other competing brands. The research also found that consumers engage in two types of cleaning—weekly deep cleanings and quick daily cleanings. WD-40 decided that its best bet for X-14 was a "bathroom expert" line of products and created a new cohesive packaging design characterized by various blues, purples, and reds to convey its new message. Not only did WD-40's research help reposition the X-14 line, it also supplied insights for use in future product development.

The WD-40 story illustrates an important point about problem/opportunity definition. The **marketing research problem** is information oriented. It involves determining what information is needed and how that information can be obtained efficiently and effectively. The **marketing research objective**, then, is to provide insightful decision-making information. This requires specific pieces of information needed to solve the marketing research problem. Managers must combine this information with their own experience and other information to make a proper decision. WD-40's marketing research problem was to gather information on how consumers clean and how they shop for cleaning products. The marketing research objectives were to identify a better positioning strategy for X-14 and to identify opportunities to add new items to the X-14 brand.

In contrast, the **management decision problem** is action oriented. Management problems tend to be much broader in scope and far more general than marketing research problems, which must be narrowly defined and specific if the research effort is to be successful. Sometimes several research studies must be conducted to solve a broad management problem. The management decision problem was: "How do we grow sales of X-14 family brand?" Management then decided to reposition X-14 as The Bathroom Expert—the centerpiece around which its new product line reenters the market.

Secondary Data

A valuable tool throughout the research process but particularly in the problem/opportunity identification stage is **secondary data**—data previously collected for any purpose other than the one at hand. Secondary information originating within the company includes documents such as annual reports, reports to stockholders, product testing results perhaps made available to the news media, and house periodicals composed by the company's personnel for communication to employees, customers, or others. Often this information is incorporated into a company's internal database.

Innumerable outside sources of secondary information also exist, principally in the forms of government departments and agencies (federal, state, and local) that compile and publish summaries of business data. Trade and industry associations also publish secondary data. Still more data are available in business periodicals and other news media that regularly publish studies and articles on the economy, specific industries, and even individual companies. The unpublished summarized secondary information from these sources corresponds to internal

Using marketing research helped the WD-40 Company successfully reposition its X-14 cleaning products in the marketplace. The research also identified opportunities to extend the X-14 brand.

reports, memos, or special-purpose analyses with limited circulation. Economic considerations or priorities in the organization may preclude publication of these summaries. Most of the sources listed above can be found on the Internet.

Secondary data save time and money if they help solve the researcher's problem. Even if the problem is not solved, secondary data have other advantages. They can aid in formulating the problem statement and suggest research methods and other types of data needed for solving the problem. In addition, secondary data can pinpoint the kinds of people to approach and their locations and serve as a basis of comparison for other data. The disadvantages of secondary data stem mainly from a mismatch between the researcher's unique problem and the purpose for which the secondary data were originally gathered, which are typically different. For example, a company wanted to determine the market potential for a fireplace log made of coal rather than compressed wood by-products. The researcher found plenty of secondary data about total wood consumed as fuel, quantities consumed in each state, and types of wood burned. Secondary data were also available about consumer attitudes and purchase patterns of wood by-product fireplace logs. The wealth of secondary data provided the researcher with many insights into the artificial log market. Yet nowhere was there any information that would tell the firm whether consumers would buy artificial logs made of coal.

The quality of secondary data may also pose a problem. Often secondary data sources do not give detailed information that would enable a researcher to assess their quality or relevance. Whenever possible, a researcher needs to address these important questions: Who gathered the data? Why were the data obtained? What methodology was used? How were classifications (such as heavy users versus light users) developed and defined? When was the information gathered?

The New Age of Secondary Information: The Internet

Although necessary in almost any research project, gathering secondary data has traditionally been a tedious and boring job. The researcher often had to write to government agencies, trade associations, or other secondary data providers and then wait days or weeks for a reply that might never come. Often, one or more trips to the library were required and the researcher might find that needed reports were checked out or missing. Now, however, the rapid development of the Internet has eliminated much of the drudgery associated with the collection of secondary data.

Marketing Research Aggregators

The **marketing research aggregator** industry is a $120 million business that is growing about 6 percent a year. Companies in this field acquire, catalog, reformat, segment, and resell reports already published by large and small marketing research firms. Even Amazon.com has added a marketing research aggregation area to its high-profile e-commerce site.

The role of aggregator firms is growing because their databases of research reports are getting bigger and more comprehensive—and more useful—as marketing research firms get more comfortable using resellers as a sales channel. Meanwhile, advances in Web technology are making the databases easier to search and deliveries speedier. By slicing and repackaging research reports into narrower, more specialized sections for resale to small- and medium-sized clients that often cannot afford to commission their own studies or buy full reports, the aggregators are essentially nurturing a new target market for the information.

Prior to the emergence of research aggregators, a lot of marketing research was available only through premium-priced subscription services. For example, a seventeen-chapter, $2,800 report from Wintergreen Research, Inc. was recently broken up and sold (on AllNetResearchers.com) for $350 per chapter, significantly boosting the overall revenue generated by

SECONDARY DATA SAVE TIME AND MONEY IF THEY HELP **SOLVE** THE RESEARCHER'S **PROBLEM.**

the report. In addition to AllNetResearch.com, other major aggregators are mindbranch.com, aarkstore.com, and usadata.com.

Planning the Research Design and Gathering Primary Data

Good secondary data can help researchers conduct a thorough situation analysis. With that information, researchers can list their unanswered questions and rank them. Researchers must then decide the exact information required to answer the questions. The **research design** specifies which research questions must be answered, how and when the data will be gathered, and how the data will be analyzed. Typically, the project budget is finalized after the research design has been approved.

Sometimes research questions can be answered by gathering more secondary data; otherwise, primary data may be needed. **Primary data**, or information collected for the first time, are used for solving the particular problem under investigation. The main advantage of primary data is that they will answer a specific research question that secondary data cannot answer. For example, suppose Pillsbury has two new recipes for refrigerated dough for sugar cookies. Which one will consumers like better? Secondary data will not help answer this question. Instead, targeted consumers must try each recipe and evaluate the taste, texture, and appearance of each cookie. Moreover, primary data are current and researchers know the source. Sometimes researchers gather the data themselves rather than assign projects to outside companies. Researchers also specify the methodology of the research. Secrecy can be maintained because the information is proprietary. In contrast, much secondary data is available to all interested parties for relatively small fees or free.

Gathering primary data is expensive; costs can range from a few thousand dollars for a limited survey to several million for a nationwide study. For instance, a nationwide, 15-minute telephone interview with 1,000 adult males can cost $50,000 for everything, including a data analysis and report. Because primary data gather-

ing is so expensive, firms may cut back on the number of in-person interviews to save money and use an Internet study instead. Larger companies that conduct many research projects use another cost-saving technique. They *piggyback* studies, or gather data on two different projects using one questionnaire. Nevertheless, the disadvantages of primary data gathering are usually offset by the advantages. It is often the only way of solving a research problem. And with a variety of techniques available for research—including surveys, observations, and experiments—primary research can address almost any marketing question.

Survey Research The most popular technique for gathering primary data is **survey research**, in which a researcher interacts with people to obtain facts, opinions, and attitudes. Exhibit 9.2 summarizes the characteristics of traditional forms of survey research.

In-Home Personal Interviews Although in-home personal interviews often provide high-quality information, they tend to be very expensive because of the interviewers' travel time and mileage costs. Therefore, they are rapidly disappearing from the American and European researcher's survey toolbox. They are, however, still popular in many countries around the globe.

Mall Intercept Interviews The **mall intercept interview** is conducted in the common area of a shopping mall or in a market research office within the mall. To conduct this type of interview, the research firm rents office space in the mall or pays a significant daily fee. One drawback is that it is hard to get a representative sample of the population. One advantage is the ability of the interviewer to probe when necessary—a technique used to clarify a

> **research design** specifies which research questions must be answered, how and when the data will be gathered, and how the data will be analyzed
>
> **primary data** information that is collected for the first time; used for solving the particular problem under investigation
>
> **survey research** the most popular technique for gathering primary data, in which a researcher interacts with people to obtain facts, opinions, and attitudes
>
> **mall intercept interview** a survey research method that involves interviewing people in the common areas of shopping malls

A NATIONWIDE, 15-MINUTE TELEPHONE INTERVIEW WITH 1,000 ADULT MALES CAN COST $50,000.

EXHIBIT 9.2
Characteristics of Traditional Forms of Survey Research

Characteristic	In-Home Personal Interviews	Mall Intercept Interviews	Central-Location Telephone Interviews	Self-Administered and One-Time Mail Surveys	Mail Panel Surveys	Executive Interviews	Focus Groups
Cost	High	Moderate	Moderate	Low	Moderate	High	Low
Time span	Moderate	Moderate	Fast	Slow	Relatively slow	Moderate	Fast
Use of interviewer probes	Yes	Yes	Yes	No	Yes	Yes	Yes
Ability to show concepts to respondent	Yes (also taste tests)	Yes (also taste tests)	No	Yes	Yes	Yes	No
Management control over interviewer	Low	Moderate	High	N/A	N/A	Moderate	High
General data quality	High	Moderate	High to moderate	Moderate to low	Moderate	High	Moderate
Ability to collect large amounts of data	High	Moderate	Moderate to low	Low to moderate	Moderate	Moderate	Moderate
Ability to handle complex questionnaires	High	Moderate	High, if computer-aided	Low	Low	High	N/A

computer-assisted personal interviewing an interviewing method in which the interviewer reads the questions from a computer screen and enters the respondent's data directly into the computer

computer-assisted self-interviewing an interviewing method in which a mall interviewer intercepts and directs willing respondents to nearby computers where the respondent reads questions off a computer screen and directly keys his or her answers into a computer

central-location telephone (CLT) facility a specially designed phone room used to conduct telephone interviewing

person's response and ask for more detailed information.

Mall intercept interviews must be brief. Only the shortest ones are conducted while respondents are standing. Usually, researchers invite respondents to their office for interviews, which are still generally less than fifteen minutes long. The overall quality of mall intercept interviews is about the same as telephone interviews.

Marketing researchers are applying computer technology in mall interviewing. The first technique is **computer-assisted personal interviewing**. The researcher conducts in-person interviews, reads questions to the respondent off a computer screen, and directly keys the respondent's answers into the computer. A second approach is **computer-assisted self-interviewing**. A mall interviewer intercepts and directs willing respondents to nearby computers. Each respondent reads questions off a computer screen and directly

keys his or her answers into a computer. The third use of technology is fully automated self-interviewing. Respondents are guided by interviewers or independently approach a centrally located computer station or kiosk, read questions off a screen, and directly key their answers into the station's computer.

Telephone Interviews Telephone interviews costs less than personal interviews, but cost is rapidly increasing due to respondent refusals to participate. Most telephone interviewing is conducted from a specially designed phone room called a **central-location telephone (CLT) facility**. A phone room has many phone lines, individual interviewing stations, sometimes monitoring equipment, and headsets. The research firm typically will interview people nationwide from a single location. The federal "Do Not Call" law does not apply to survey research.

Most CLT facilities offer computer-assisted interviewing. The interviewer reads the questions from a computer screen and enters the respondent's data directly into the computer, saving time. Hallmark Cards found that an interviewer administered a printed questionnaire for its Shoebox Greeting cards in twenty-eight minutes. The same questionnaire administered with computer assistance took only eighteen minutes. The researcher can stop the survey at any point and immediately print out the survey results, allowing the research design to be refined as necessary.

Mail Surveys Mail surveys have several benefits: relatively low cost, elimination of interviewers and field supervisors, centralized control, and actual or promised anonymity for respondents (which may draw more candid responses). A disadvantage is that mail questionnaires usually produce low response rates because certain elements of the population tend to respond more than others. The resulting sample may therefore not represent the surveyed population. Another serious problem with mail surveys is that no one probes respondents to clarify or elaborate on their answers.

Mail panels offer an alternative to the one-shot mail survey. A mail panel consists of a sample of households recruited to participate by mail for a given period. Panel members often receive gifts in return for their participation. Essentially, the panel is a sample used several times. In contrast to one-time mail surveys, the response rates from mail panels are high. Rates of 70 percent (of those who agree to participate) are not uncommon.

Executive Interviews An **executive interview** involves interviewing businesspeople, at their offices, concerning industrial products or services, a process which is very expensive. First, individuals involved in the purchase decision for the product in question must be identified and located, which can itself be expensive and time-consuming. Once a qualified person is located, the next step is to get that person to agree to be interviewed and to set a time for the interview.

Finally, an interviewer must go to the particular place at the appointed time. Long waits are frequently encountered; cancellations are not uncommon. This type of survey requires the very best interviewers because they are frequently interviewing on topics that they know very little about.

Focus Groups A **focus group** is a type of personal interviewing. Often recruited by random telephone screening, seven to ten people with certain desired characteristics form a focus group. These qualified consumers are usually offered an incentive (typically $30 to $50) to participate in a group discussion. The meeting place (sometimes resembling a living room, sometimes featuring a conference table) has audiotaping and perhaps videotaping equipment. It also likely has a viewing room with a one-way mirror so that cli-

ents (manufacturers or retailers) may watch the session. During the session, a moderator, hired by the research company, leads the group discussion. Focus groups can be used to gauge consumer response to a product or promotion and are occasionally used to brainstorm new product ideas or to screen concepts for new products.

Questionnaire Design All forms of survey research require a questionnaire. Questionnaires ensure that all respondents will be asked the same series of questions. Questionnaires include three basic types of questions: open-ended, closed-ended, and scaled-response. An **open-ended question** encourages an answer phrased in the respondent's own words. Researchers get a rich array of information based on the respondent's frame of reference (What do you think about the new flavor?). In contrast, a **closed-ended question** asks the respondent to make a selection from a limited list of responses. Closed-ended questions can either be what marketing researchers call *dichotomous* (Do you like the new flavor? Yes or No.) or *multiple choice*. A **scaled-response question** is a closed-ended question designed to measure the intensity of a respondent's answer. The "What do you think?" question that opened the chapter is a scaled-response question.

Closed-ended and scaled-response questions are easier to tabulate than open-ended questions because response choices are fixed. On the other hand, unless the researcher designs the closed-ended question very carefully, an important choice may be omitted.

A good question must be clear and concise and avoid ambiguous language. The answer to the question "Do you live within ten minutes of here?" depends on the mode of transportation (maybe the person walks), driving speed, perceived time, and other factors. Language should also be clear. As such, jargon should be avoided, and wording should be geared to the target audience. A question such as "What is the level of efficacy of your preponderant dishwasher powder?" would probably be greeted by a lot of blank stares. It would be much simpler to say "Are you (1) very satisfied, (2) somewhat satisfied, or (3) not satisfied with your current brand of dishwasher powder?"

Stating the survey's purpose at the beginning of the interview may improve clarity, but it may also increase

executive interview a type of survey that involves interviewing businesspeople at their offices concerning industrial products or services

focus group seven to ten people who participate in a group discussion led by a moderator

open-ended question an interview question that encourages an answer phrased in the respondent's own words

closed-ended question an interview question that asks the respondent to make a selection from a limited list of responses

scaled-response question a closed-ended question designed to measure the intensity of a respondent's answer

EXHIBIT 9.3
Observational Situations

Situation	Example
People watching people	Observers stationed in supermarkets watch consumers select frozen Mexican dinners; the purpose is to see how much comparison shopping people do at the point of purchase.
People watching phenomena	Observer stationed at an intersection counts traffic moving in various directions.
Machines watching people	Movie or videotape cameras record behavior as in the people-watching-people example above.
Machines watching phenomena	Traffic-counting machines monitor traffic flow.

observation research a research method that relies on four types of observation: people watching people, people watching an activity, machines watching people, and machines watching an activity

mystery shoppers researchers posing as customers who gather observational data about a store

ethnographic research the study of human behavior in its natural context; involves observation of behavior and physical setting

the chances of receiving biased responses. Many times respondents will try to provide answers that they believe are "correct" or that the interviewer wants to hear. To avoid bias at the question level, researchers should avoid leading questions and adjectives that cause respondents to think of the topic in a certain way.

Finally, to ensure clarity, the interviewer should avoid asking two questions in one; for example, "How did you like the taste and texture of the Pepperidge Farm coffee cake?" This should be divided into two questions, one concerning taste and the other texture.

Observation Research In contrast to survey research, **observation research** depends on watching what people do. Specifically, it can be defined as the systematic process of recording the behavioral patterns of people, objects, and occurrences without questioning them. A market researcher using the observation technique witnesses and records information as events occur or compiles evidence from records of past events. Carried a step further, observation may involve watching people or phenomena and may be conducted by human observers or machines. Examples of these various observational situations are shown in Exhibit 9.3.

Two common forms of people-watching-people research are one-way mirror observations and mystery shoppers.

At the Fisher-Price Play Laboratory, children are invited to spend twelve sessions playing with toys. Toy designers watch through one-way mirrors to see how children react to Fisher-Price's and other makers' toys. A one-way mirror allows the researchers to see the participants, but they cannot see the researchers. Fisher-Price, for example, had difficulty designing a toy lawn mower that children would play with. A designer, observing behind the mirror, noticed the children's fascination with soap bubbles. He then created a lawn mower that spewed soap bubbles. It sold over a million units in the first year.

Mystery shoppers are researchers posing as customers who gather observational data about a store (e.g., are the shelves neatly stocked?) and collect data about customer/employee interactions. The interaction is not an interview, and communication occurs only so that the mystery shopper can observe the actions and comments of the employee. Mystery shopping is, therefore, classified as an observational marketing research method even though communication is often involved.

Ethnographic Research Ethnographic research comes to marketing from the field of anthropology. The technique is becoming increasingly popular in commercial marketing research. **Ethnographic research**, or the study of human behavior in its natural context, involves observation of behavior and physical setting. Ethnographers directly observe the population they are studying. As "participant observers," ethnographers can use their intimacy with the people they are studying to gain richer, deeper insights into culture and behavior—in short, what makes people do what they do.

Marriott hired IDEO, Inc., an ethnographic research firm, to rethink the hotel experience for an increasingly important customer: the young, tech-savvy road warrior. To better understand Marriott's customers, IDEO dispatched a team of seven consultants, including a designer, anthropologist, writer, and architect, on a six-week trip. They learned that hotels are not good at serving small groups of business travelers and that Marriott lacked places where guests could comfortably combine work with pleasure outside their rooms. Having studied IDEO's findings, Marriott announced plans to reinvent the lobbies of its Marriott and Renaissance Hotels, creating a social zone, with small tables, brighter lights, and wireless Web access.[2]

Virtual Shopping Advances in computer technology have enabled researchers to simulate an actual retail

the original people selected to be interviewed either refused to cooperate or were inaccessible.

Frame error, another type of sampling error, arises if the sample drawn from a population differs from the target population. For instance, suppose a telephone survey is conducted to find out Chicago beer drinkers' attitudes toward Coors. If a Chicago telephone directory is used as the *frame* (the device or list from which the respondents are selected), the survey will contain a frame error. Not all Chicago beer drinkers have a phone, and many phone numbers are unlisted. An ideal sample (for example, a sample with no frame error) matches all important characteristics of the target population to be surveyed. Could you find a perfect frame for Chicago beer drinkers?

Random error occurs when the selected sample is an imperfect representation of the overall population. Random error represents how accurately the chosen sample's true average (mean) value reflects the population's true average (mean) value. For example, we might take a random sample of beer drinkers in Chicago and find that 16 percent regularly drink Coors beer. The next day we might repeat the same sampling procedure and discover that 14 percent regularly drink Coors beer. The difference is due to random error. Error is common to all surveys, yet it is often not reported or is underreported. Typically, the only error mentioned in a written report is sampling error.

Collecting the Data

Marketing research field service firms collect most primary data. A **field service firm** specializes in interviewing respondents on a subcontracted basis. Many have offices, often in malls, throughout the country. A typical marketing research study involves data collection in several cities, which requires the marketer to work with a comparable number of field service firms. Besides conducting interviews, field service firms provide focus-group facilities, mall intercept locations, test product storage, and kitchen facilities to prepare test food products.

Analyzing the Data

After collecting the data, the marketing researcher proceeds to the next step in the research process: data analysis. The purpose of this analysis is to interpret and draw conclusions from the mass of collected data. The marketing researcher tries to organize and analyze those data by using one or more techniques common to marketing research: one-way frequency counts, cross-tabulations, and more sophisticated statistical analysis. Of these three techniques, one-way frequency counts are the simplest. One-way frequency tables simply record the responses to a question. For example, the answers to the question "What brand of microwave popcorn do you buy most often?" would provide a one-way frequency distribution. One-way frequency tables are always done in data analysis, at least as a first step, because they provide the researcher with a general picture of the study's results. A **cross-tabulation** lets the analyst look at the responses to one question in relation to the responses to one or more other questions. For example, what is the association between gender and the brand of microwave popcorn bought most frequently?

Researchers can use many other more powerful and sophisticated statistical techniques, such as hypothesis testing, measures of association, and regression analysis. A description of these techniques goes beyond the scope of this book but can be found in any good marketing research textbook. The use of sophisticated statistical techniques depends on

Popcorn Cross-Tab

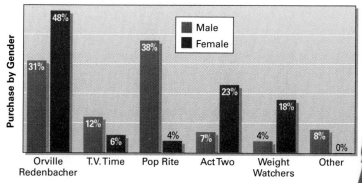

© ISTOCKPHOTO.COM/NINA SHANNON

the researchers' objectives and the nature of the data gathered.

Preparing and Presenting the Report

After data analysis has been completed, the researcher must prepare the report and communicate the conclusions and recommendations to management. This is a key step in the process. If the marketing researcher wants managers to carry out the recommendations, he or she must convince them that the results are credible and justified by the data collected.

Researchers are usually required to present both written and oral reports on the project. Today, the written report is no more than a copy of the Power-Point slides used in the oral presentation. Both reports should be tailored to the audience. They should begin with a clear, concise statement of the research objectives, followed by a complete, but brief and simple, explanation of the research design or methodology employed. A summary of major findings should come next. The conclusion of the report should also present recommendations to management.

Most people who enter marketing will become research users rather than research suppliers. Thus, they must know what to notice in a report. As with many other items we purchase, quality is not always readily apparent. Nor does a high price guarantee superior quality. The basis for measuring the quality of a marketing research report is the research proposal. Did the report meet the objectives established in the proposal? Was the methodology outlined in the proposal followed? Are the conclusions based on logical deductions from the data analysis? Do the recommendations seem prudent, given the conclusions?

Following Up

The final step in the marketing research process is to follow up. The researcher should determine why management did or did not carry out the recommendations in the report. Was sufficient decision-making information included? What could have been done to make the report more useful to management? A good rapport between the product manager, or whoever authorized the project, and the market researcher is essential. Often they must work together on many studies throughout the year.

Typically, the research process flows rather smoothly from one step to the next in the United States. However, conducting research in international markets can create a whole host of problems and challenges.

LO 4 The Profound Impact of the Internet on Marketing Research

Today, about one-fifth of the world's population is online. In the United States, 70 percent of the population is online, spanning every ethnic, socioeconomic, and educational divide. Most managers accept that online research can, under appropriate conditions, accurately represent U.S. consumers as a whole. Nonadopters of the Internet tend to be older, low-income consumers (aged 65 + with household income less than $30,000), who do not tend to be the target market for many goods and services.[6]

More than 90 percent of America's marketing research companies conduct some form of online research.[7] Online survey research has replaced computer-assisted telephone interviewing (CATI) as the most popular mode of data collection, though there is no evidence of this or other traditional survey methods being completely replaced by online surveys.[8] Internet data collection is also rated as having the greatest potential for further growth.

Advantages of Internet Surveys

The huge growth in the popularity of Internet surveys is the result of the many advantages offered by the Internet. The specific advantages of Internet surveys are related to many factors:

▸ *Rapid development, real-time reporting:* Internet surveys can be broadcast to thousands of potential respondents simultaneously. Respondents complete surveys simultaneously; then results are tabulated and posted for corporate clients to view as the returns arrive. The result: survey results can be in a client's hands in significantly less time than would be required for traditional surveys.

▸ *Dramatically reduced costs:* The Internet can cut costs by 25 to 40 percent and provide results in half the time it takes to do traditional telephone surveys. Traditional survey methods are labor-intensive efforts incurring training, telecommunications, and management costs. Electronic methods eliminate these completely. While costs for traditional survey techniques rise proportionally with the number of interviews desired, electronic solicitations can grow in volume with little increase in project costs.

THE CHALLENGES OF GLOBAL MARKETING RESEARCH

In multicultural, multilingual research, questionnaires must be designed especially carefully. People in some cultures better relate to conversational interviewing styles than fixed questionnaire order. Some cultures require sensitive questions to be in a different order than others. In some places, people will only talk in particular settings. In Bosnia and Herzegovina, for example, questionnaires have to be administered in a neutral location not affiliated with any local ethnic group. In South Africa, many villages lack addresses and roads, and sampling has to be designed using satellite maps.[9]

© ISTOCKPHOTO.COM/KUTAY TANIR

▸▸ *Personalized questions and data*: Internet surveys can be highly personalized for greater relevance to each respondent's own situation, thus speeding the response process.

▸▸ *Improved respondent participation*: Internet surveys take half as much time to complete as phone interviews, can be accomplished at the respondent's convenience (after work hours), and are much more stimulating and engaging. As a result, Internet surveys enjoy much higher response rates.

▸▸ *Contact with the hard-to-reach*: Certain groups—doctors, high-income professionals, top management in Global 2000 firms—are among the most surveyed on the planet and the most difficult to reach. Many of these groups are well represented online. Internet surveys provide convenient anytime/anywhere access that makes it easy for busy professionals to participate.

Uses of the Internet by Marketing Researchers

Marketing researchers are using the Internet to administer surveys, conduct focus groups, and perform a variety of other types of marketing research.

Methods of Conducting Online Surveys There are several basic methods for conducting online surveys: Web survey systems; survey design and web hosting sites; and online panel providers.

Web Survey Systems Web survey systems are software systems specifically designed for Web questionnaire construction and delivery. They consist of an integrated questionnaire designer, Web server, database, and data delivery program, designed for use by non-programmers. The Web server distributes the questionnaire and files responses in a database. The user can query the server at any time via the Web for completion statistics, descriptive statistics on responses, and graphical displays of data. Some popular online survey research software packages are Sawtooth CiW, Infopoll, SurveyMonkey, and SurveyPro.

Survey Design and Web Hosting Sites Several Web sites allow the researcher to design a survey online without loading design software. The survey is then administered on the design site's server. Some offer tabulation and analysis packages as well. Two popular sites that offer Web hosting are WebSurveyor and Perseus.

Online Panel Providers Often researchers use online panel providers for a ready-made sample population. Online panel providers such as Survey Sampling and e-Rewards pre-recruit people who agree to participate in online market research surveys.

Some online panels are created for specific industries and may have a few thousand panel members, while the large commercial online panels have millions of people waiting to be surveyed. When people join online panels, they answer an extensive profiling questionnaire that enables the panel provider to target research efforts to panel members who meet specific criteria.

Online Focus Groups A relatively recent development in qualitative research is the online or cyber focus group. A number of organizations are currently offering this new means of conducting focus groups. The process is fairly simple. The research firm builds a database of respondents via a screening questionnaire on its Web site. When a client comes to a firm with a need for a particular focus group, the firm goes to its database and identifies individuals who appear to qualify. It sends an e-mail message to these individuals, asking them to log on to a particular site at a particular time scheduled for the group. The firm pays them an incentive for their participation.

The firm develops a discussion guide similar to the one used for a conventional focus group, and a moderator runs the group by typing in questions online for all to see. The group operates in an environment similar to that of a chat room so that all participants see all questions and all responses. The firm captures the complete text of the focus group and makes it available for review after the group has finished.

The huge popularity of social networking sites like myspace.com and facebook.com convinced market researchers at Procter & Gamble to build their own social networking community. P&G's site, show-

cased in Yahoo.com's health section, doesn't promote specific P&G products. Instead, P&G offers a forum where women can "meet" to discuss health issues. In return, P&G's market researchers will monitor discussions on the site to learn more about its consumers—and how to market to them.[10]

The Moderator's Role The basic way the moderator communicates with respondents in an online focus group is by typing all questions, instructions, and probes into the text-entry area of the chat room in real-time (live, on-the-spot). An advantage of the freestyle method is that it forces the moderator to adapt to the group rather than use a series of canned questions. A disadvantage is that typing everything freestyle (or even copying and pasting from a separate document) takes time.

Online focus groups also allow respondents to view things such as a concept statement, a mockup of a print ad, or a short product demonstration on video. The moderator simply provides a URL reference for the respondents to go to in another browser window. One of the risks of doing this, however, is that once respondents open another browser, they have "left the room" and the moderator may lose their attention; researchers must hope that respondents will return within the specified amount of time.

More advanced virtual focus group software reserves a frame (section) of the screen for stimuli to be shown. Here, the moderator has control over what is shown in the stimulus area. The advantage of this approach is that the respondent does not have to do any work to see the stimuli.

Types of Online Focus Groups There are two basic types of online focus groups:

1 *Real-time online focus groups*: These are live, interactive sessions with four to six participants and a moderator in a chat room format. The typical session does not last longer than forty-five to fifty minutes. The technique is best for simple, straightforward issues that can be covered in a limited amount of time. The results tend to be superficial compared to in-person focus groups—but this is acceptable for certain types of projects. Typically, three to four groups are recommended as a minimum. Clients can view the chat room as the session unfolds and communicate with the moderator. A variation of real-time online focus groups includes video capabilities, which allow participants to see and hear each other courtesy of Web cams attached to their PCs. Both verbal and nonverbal reactions can be recorded.

2 *Time-extended online focus groups*: These sessions follow a message board format and usually last five to ten

days. The fifteen to twenty participants must comment at least two or three times per day and spend fifteen minutes a day logged in to the discussion. The moderator reviews respondents' comments several times per day (and night) and probes or redirects the discussion as needed. This technique provides three to four times as much content as the average in-person focus group. Time-extended online focus groups give participants time to reflect, talk to others, visit a store, or check the pantry. This extra time translates into richer content and deeper insights. Clients can view the online content as it is posted and may communicate with the moderator at any time.[11]

Advantages of Online Focus Groups Many advantages are claimed for cyber groups:

▸▸ *Better participation rates*: Typically, online focus groups can be conducted over the course of days; once participants are recruited, they are less likely to pull out due to time conflicts.

▸▸ *Cost-effectiveness*: Face-to-face focus groups incur costs for facility rental, airfare, hotel, and food. None of these costs is incurred with online focus groups.

▸▸ *Broad geographic scope*: Time is flexible online; respondents can be gathered from all over the world.

▸▸ *Accessibility*: Online focus groups give you access to individuals who otherwise might be difficult to recruit (e.g., business travelers, senior executives, mothers with infants).

▸▸ *Honesty*: From behind their screen names, respondents are anonymous to other respondents and tend to talk more freely about issues that might create inhibitions in a face-to-face group.

Web Community Research

A Web community is a carefully selected group of consumers who agree to participate in an ongoing dialogue with a particular corporation.[12] All community interaction takes place on a custom-designed Web site. During the life of the community—which may last anywhere from six months to a year or more—community members respond to questions posed by the corporation on a regular basis. In addition to responding to the corporation's questions, community members talk to one another about topics that are of interest to them.

The popularity and power of Web communities initially came from several key benefits. They:

▸▸ engage customers in a space where they are comfortable, allowing clients to interact with them on a deeper level

▸▸ achieve customer-derived innovations

▸▸ establish brand advocates who are emotionally invested in a company's success

▸▸ offer real-time results, enabling clients to explore ideas that normal time constraints prohibit

Additionally, Web communities help companies create a customer-focused organization by putting employees into direct contact with consumers from the comfort of their own desks, as well as providing cost-effective, flexible research.

The Role of Blogs in Marketing Research Cutting-edge, technology-driven, marketing research companies, like Nielsen BuzzMetrics (formerly Intelliseek), are now using more refined Internet search technologies to monitor, interpret, and report on comments, opinions, and feedback generated on blogs.[13] Arguably, the most revolutionary product is BuzzMetrics' BlogPulse, which monitors key words and phrases, detects authors' sentiments, classifies data in terms of relevance, and unearths specific facts and data points about the brands, products, or companies that are the subject of bloggers' attention. Major clients such as Sony, AOL, Porsche, Yahoo!, and VH1 use Blog-Pulse to monitor consumers' opinions about their products or services on a daily, or even hourly, basis. BlogPulse can also identify the Internet's most influential bloggers, which is something marketers dearly love to know.

Other Uses of the Internet by Marketing Researchers The Internet revolution in marketing research has had an impact on more than just the way surveys and focus groups are conducted. The management of the research process and the dissemination of information have also been greatly enhanced by the Internet. Several key areas have been affected:

▸▸ *The distribution of requests for proposals (RFPs) and proposals*: Companies can now quickly and efficiently send RFPs to a select e-mail list of research suppliers. In turn, research suppliers can develop proposals and e-mail them back to clients in a matter of hours.

▸▸ *Collaboration between the client and the research supplier in the management of a research project*: Now a researcher and client may both be looking at a proposal, RFP, report, or some type of statistical analysis at the same time on their respective computer screens while discussing it over the telephone. Changes to the research plan can be discussed and made immediately.

▸▸ *Data management and online analysis*: Clients can access their survey via the research supplier's secure Web site and monitor the data gathering in real time. The client can use sophisticated tools to actually do data analysis as the survey develops, allowing on-the-fly modifications to the elements of the project.

▶▶ *Publication and distribution of reports:* Reports can be published to the Web directly from numerous software programs, which means that results can be made available to appropriate managers worldwide on an almost instantaneous basis.

▶▶ *Viewing of oral presentations of marketing research surveys by widely scattered audiences:* By placing oral presentations on password-protected Web sites, managers throughout the world can see and hear the actual client presentation.[14]

LO5 Scanner-Based Research

Scanner-based research is a system for gathering information from a single group of respondents by continuously monitoring the advertising, promotion, and pricing they are exposed to and the things they buy. The variables measured are advertising campaigns, coupons, displays, and product prices. The result is a huge database of marketing efforts and consumer behavior.

The two major scanner-based suppliers are Information Resources, Inc. (IRI) and the A. C. Nielsen Company. Each has about half of the market. However, IRI is the founder of scanner-based research. IRI's first product is called **BehaviorScan**. A household panel (a group of 3,000 long-term participants in the research

project) has been recruited and maintained in each BehaviorScan town. Panel members shop with an ID card, which is presented at the checkout in scanner-equipped grocery stores and drugstores, allowing IRI to track electronically each household's purchases, item by item, over time. It uses microcomputers to measure television viewing in each panel household and can send special commercials to panel member television sets. With such a measure of household purchasing, it is possible to manipulate marketing variables, such as television advertising or consumer promotions, or to introduce a new product and analyze real changes in consumer buying behavior.

IRI's most successful product is **InfoScan**—a scanner-based sales-tracking service for the consumer packaged-goods industry. Retail sales, detailed consumer purchasing information (including measurement of store loyalty and total grocery basket expenditures), and promotional activity by manufacturers and retailers are monitored and evaluated for all bar-coded products. Data are collected weekly from more than 34,000 supermarkets, drugstores, and mass merchandisers.[15]

LO6 When Should Marketing Research Be Conducted?

When managers have several possible solutions to a problem, they should not instinctively call for marketing research. In fact, the first decision to make is whether to conduct marketing research at all.

Some companies have been conducting research in certain markets for many years. Such firms understand the characteristics of target customers and their likes and dislikes about existing products. Under these circumstances, further research would be repetitive and waste money. Procter & Gamble, for example, has extensive knowledge of the coffee market. After it conducted initial taste tests with Folgers Instant Coffee, P&G went into national distribution without further research. Sara Lee followed the same strategy with its frozen croissants, as did Quaker Oats with Chewy Granola Bars. This tactic, however, can backfire. Marketers may think they understand a particular market thoroughly and so bypass market research for a product, only to have the product fail and be withdrawn from the market.

If information were available and free, managers would rarely refuse more, but because marketing information can require a great deal of time and expense to accumulate, they might decide to forego additional information. Ultimately, the willingness to acquire additional decision-making information depends on managers' perceptions of its quality, price, and timing. Research should be undertaken only when the expected value of the information is greater than the cost of obtaining it.

LO 7 Competitive Intelligence

Derived from military intelligence, competitive intelligence is an important tool for helping a firm overcome a competitor's advantage. Specifically, competitive intelligence can help identify the advantage and play a major role in determining how it was achieved.

Competitive intelligence (CI) helps managers assess their competitors and their vendors in order to become a more efficient and effective competitor. Intelligence is analyzed information. It becomes decision-making intelligence when it has implications for the organization. For example, a primary competitor may have plans to introduce a product with performance standards equal to those of the company gathering the information but with a 15 percent cost advantage. The new product will reach the market in eight months. This intelligence has important decision-making and policy consequences for management. Competitive intelligence and environmental scanning (where management gathers data about the external environment—see Chapter 2) combine to create marketing intelligence. Marketing intelligence is then used as input into a marketing decision support system.

A survey of sports business professionals in each of five major professional leagues (the National Basketball Association, the National Football League, Major League Baseball, the National Hockey League, and Major League Soccer) indicated that 62 percent of all teams report that they maintain a CI function and nearly two-thirds of all teams have employed a CI function for three years or more. The CI assists in player personnel decisions and the identification of market opportunities.[16]

Clearly, the Internet is an important resource for gathering competitive intelligence, but noncomputer sources can be equally valuable. Some examples include company salespeople, industry experts, CI consultants, government agencies, Uniform Commercial Code filings, suppliers, periodicals, the Yellow Pages, and industry trade shows.

competitive intelligence (CI) an intelligence system that helps managers assess their competition and vendors in order to become more efficient and effective competitors

STUDY TOOLS CHAPTER 9

Located at back of the textbook
❑ **Rip out Chapter Review Card**

Located at 4ltrpress.cengage.com/mktg
❑ **Review Key Terms Flash Cards (Print or Online)**
❑ **Download Audio and Visual Summaries for on-the-go review**
❑ **Complete both Practice Quizzes to prepare for tests**
❑ **Play "Beat the Clock" and "Quizbowl" to master concepts**
❑ **Complete "Crossword Puzzle" to review key terms**
❑ **Watch the video on "Ready Made" for a real company example on Decision Support Systems and Marketing Research**

CHAPTER 10 Product Concepts

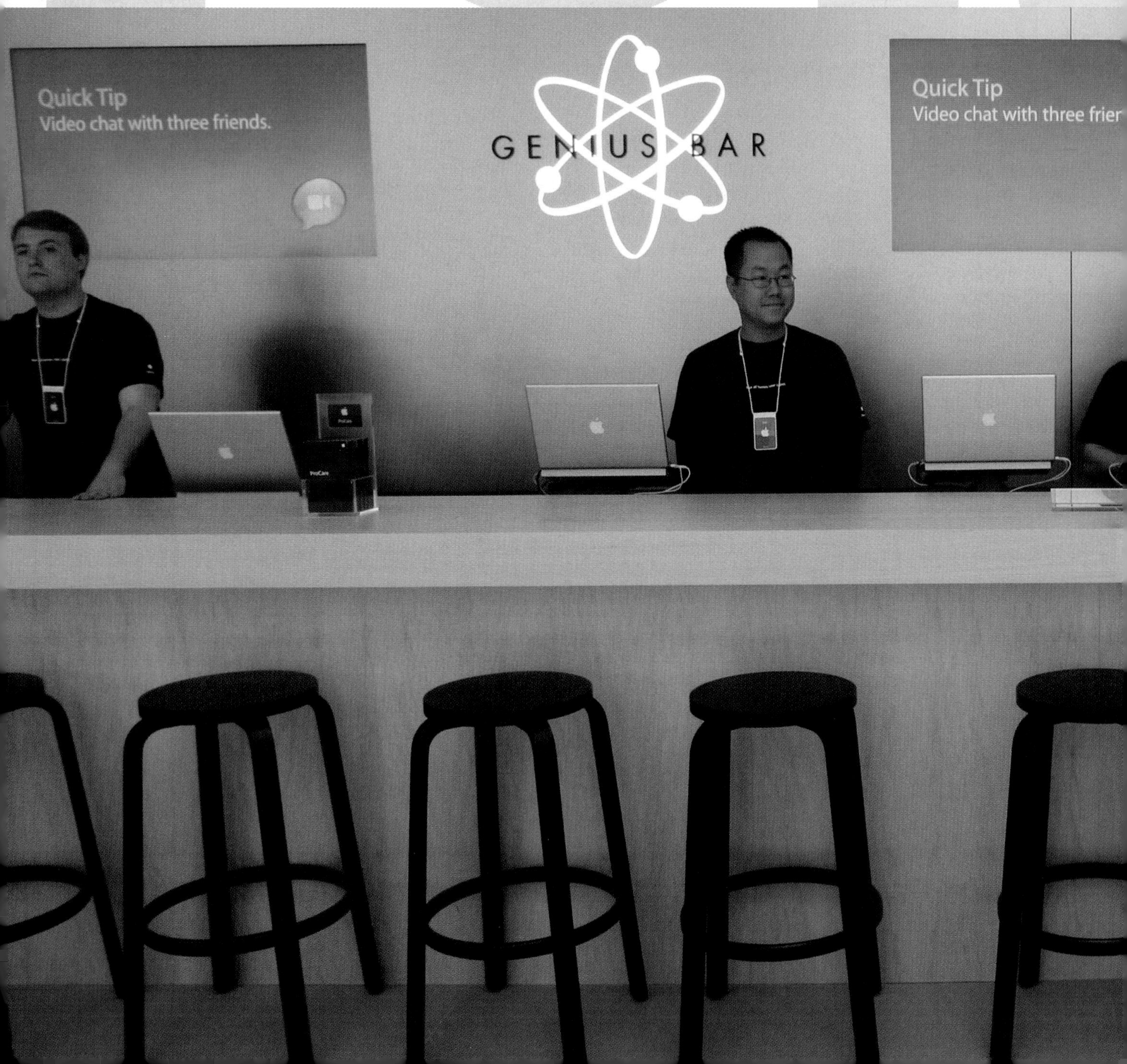

"The product is the starting point in creating a marketing mix."

AFTER YOU FINISH THIS CHAPTER GO TO PAGE 164 FOR STUDY TOOLS

© BRIAN SNYDER/REUTERS/LANDOV

LO 1 What Is a Product?

The product offering, the heart of an organization's marketing program, is usually the starting point in creating a marketing mix. A marketing manager cannot determine a price, design a promotion strategy, or create a distribution channel until the firm has a product to sell. Moreover, an excellent distribution channel, a persuasive promotion campaign, and a fair price have no value when the product offering is poor or inadequate.

A **product** may be defined as everything, both favorable and unfavorable, that a person receives in an exchange. A product may be a tangible good like a pair of shoes, a service like a haircut, an idea like "don't litter," or any combination of these three. Packaging, style, color, options, and size are some typical product features. Just as important are intangibles such as service, the seller's image, the manufacturer's reputation, and the way consumers believe others will view the product.

To most people, the term *product* means a tangible good. However, services and ideas are also products. (Chapter 12 focuses specifically on the unique aspects of marketing services.) The marketing process identified in Chapter 1 is the same whether the product marketed is a good, a service, an idea, or some combination of these.

> **product** everything, both favorable and unfavorable, that a person receives in an exchange

What do you think?

I pay attention to which brands I choose.

| 1 | 2 | 3 | 4 | 5 | 6 | 7 |

STRONGLY DISAGREE   STRONGLY AGREE

Find out what others think at 4ltrpress.cengage.com/mktg

LO 2 Types of Consumer Products

Products can be classified as either business (industrial) or consumer products, depending on the buyer's intentions. The key distinction between the two types of products is their intended use. If the intended use is a business purpose, the product is classified as a business or industrial product. As explained in Chapter 7, a **business product** is used to manufacture other goods or services, to facilitate an organization's operations, or to resell to other customers. A **consumer product** is bought to satisfy an individual's personal wants. Sometimes the same item can be classified as either a business or a consumer product, depending on its intended use. Examples include lightbulbs, pencils and paper, and computers.

We need to know about product classifications because business and consumer products are marketed differently. They are marketed to different target markets and tend to use different distribution, promotion, and pricing strategies.

Chapter 7 examined seven categories of business products: major equipment, accessory equipment, component parts, processed materials, raw materials, supplies, and services. The current chapter examines an effective way of categorizing consumer products. Although there are several ways to classify them, the most popular approach includes these four types: convenience products, shopping products, specialty products, and unsought products. This approach classifies products according to how much effort is normally used to shop for them.

Convenience Products

A **convenience product** is a relatively inexpensive item that merits little shopping effort—that is, a consumer is unwilling to shop extensively for such an item. Candy, soft drinks, aspirin, small hardware items, dry cleaning, and car washes fall into the convenience product category.

Consumers buy convenience products regularly, usually without much planning. Nevertheless, consumers do know the brand names of popular convenience products, such as Coca-Cola, Bayer aspirin, and Right Guard deodorant. Convenience products normally require wide distribution in order to sell sufficient quantities to meet profit goals. For example, the gum Dentyne Ice is available everywhere, including Wal-Mart, Walgreens, gas stations, newsstands, and vending machines.

Shopping Products

A **shopping product** is usually more expensive than a convenience product and is found in fewer stores. Consumers usually buy a shopping product only after comparing several brands or stores on style, practicality, price, and lifestyle compatibility. They are willing to invest some effort into this process to get the desired benefits.

There are two types of shopping products: homogeneous and heterogeneous. Consumers perceive *homogeneous* shopping products as basically similar—for example, washers, dryers, refrigerators, and televisions. With homogeneous shopping products, consumers typically look for the lowest-priced brand that has the desired features. For example, they might compare Kenmore, Whirlpool, and General Electric refrigerators.

In contrast, consumers perceive *heterogeneous* shopping products as essentially different—for example, furniture, clothing, housing, and universities. Consumers often have trouble comparing heterogeneous shopping products because the prices, quality, and features vary so much. The benefit of comparing heterogeneous shopping products is "finding the best product or brand for me"; this decision is often highly individual. For example, it would be difficult to compare a small, private college with a large, public university.

Specialty Products

When consumers search extensively for a particular item and are very reluctant to accept substitutes, that item is a **specialty product**. Omega watches, Rolls-Royce automobiles, Bose speakers, Ruth's Chris Steak House, and highly specialized forms of medical care are generally considered specialty products.

Marketers of specialty products often use selective, status-conscious advertising to maintain their product's exclusive image. Distribution is often limited to one or a very few outlets in a geographic area.

Brand names and quality of service are often very important.

Unsought Products

A product unknown to the potential buyer or a known product that the buyer does not actively seek is referred to as an **unsought product**. New products fall into this category until advertising and distribution increase consumer awareness of them.

Some goods are always marketed as unsought items, especially needed products we do not like to think about or care to spend money on. Insurance, burial plots, and similar items require aggressive personal selling and highly persuasive advertising. Salespeople actively seek leads to potential buyers. Because consumers usually do not seek out this type of product, the company must go directly to them through a salesperson, direct mail, or direct-response advertising.

LO 3 Product Items, Lines, and Mixes

Rarely does a company sell a single product. More often, it sells a variety of things. A **product item** is a specific version of a product that can be designated as a distinct offering among an organization's products. Campbell's cream of chicken soup is an example of a product item (see Exhibit 10.1).

A group of closely related product items is a **product line**. For example, the column in Exhibit 10.1 titled "Soups" represents one of Campbell's product lines. Different container sizes and shapes also distinguish items in a product line. Diet Coke, for example, is available in cans and various plastic containers. Each size and each container are separate product items.

An organization's **product mix** includes all the products it sells. All Campbell's products—soups, sauces, frozen entrées, beverages, and biscuits—constitute its product mix. Each product item in the product mix may require a separate marketing strategy. In some cases, however, product lines and even entire product mixes share some marketing strategy components. Nike promoted all of its product items and lines with the theme "Just Do It." Organizations derive several benefits from organizing related items into product lines.

Product mix width (or breadth) refers to the number of product lines an organization offers. In Exhibit 10.1, for example, the width of Campbell's product mix is five product lines. **Product line depth** is the number of product items in a product line. As shown in Exhibit 10.1, the sauces product line consists of four product items; the frozen entrée product line includes three product items.

Firms increase the *width* of their product mix to diversify risk. To generate sales and boost profits, firms spread risk across many product lines rather than depend on only one or two. Firms also widen their product mix to capitalize on established reputations. The Oreo cookie brand has been extended to include items such as breakfast cereal, ice cream, Jell-O pudding, and cake mix.

Firms increase the *depth* of their product lines to attract buyers with different preferences, to increase sales and profits by further segmenting the market, to capitalize on economies of scale in production and

unsought product
a product unknown to the potential buyer or a known product that the buyer does not actively seek

product item a specific version of a product that can be designated as a distinct offering among an organization's products

product line a group of closely related product items

product mix all products that an organization sells

product mix width the number of product lines an organization offers

product line depth the number of product items in a product line

EXHIBIT 10.1
Campbell's Product Lines and Product Mix

	Width of the Product Mix				
DEPTH	**Soups**	**Sauces**	**Frozen Entrées**	**Beverages**	**Biscuits**
	Cream of Chicken	Mild Cheese	Chicken á la King	Tomato Juice	Arnott's:
	Cream of Mushroom	Alfredo	Beef Stew	V-8 Juice	Water Cracker
	Vegetable Beef	Italian Tomato	Chicken Lasagna	V-8 Splash	Butternut Snap
	Chicken Noodle	Marinara			Chocolate Chip
	Tomato				Fruit Oat
	Bean with Bacon				White Fudge
	Minestrone				
	Clam Chowder				
	French Onion				
	more . . .				

Depth of the Product Lines

marketing, and to even out seasonal sales patterns. Coca-Cola and PepsiCo are introducing soft drinks in the United States using the natural, plant-based sweetener, stevia. These companies are targeting consumers looking for healthier sweetener alternatives.[1]

BENEFITS OF PRODUCT LINES

▶▶ *Advertising economies*: Product lines provide economies of scale in advertising. Several products can be advertised under the umbrella of the line. Campbell's can talk about its soup being "M'm, M'm, Good!" and promote the entire line.

▶▶ *Package uniformity*: A product line can benefit from package uniformity. All packages in the line may have a common look and still keep their individual identities. Again, Campbell's soup is a good example.

▶▶ *Standardized components*: Product lines allow firms to standardize components, thus reducing manufacturing and inventory costs. For example, General Motors uses the same parts on many automobile makes and models.

▶▶ *Efficient sales and distribution*: A product line enables sales personnel for companies like Procter & Gamble to provide a full range of choices to customers. Distributors and retailers are often more inclined to stock the company's products if it offers a full line. Transportation and warehousing costs are likely to be lower for a product line than for a collection of individual items.

▶▶ *Equivalent quality*: Purchasers usually expect and believe that all products in a line are about equal in quality. Consumers expect that all Campbell's soups and all Gillette razors will be of similar quality.

Adjustments to Product Items, Lines, and Mixes

Over time, firms change product items, lines, and mixes to take advantage of new technical or product developments or to respond to changes in the environment. They may adjust by modifying products, repositioning products, or extending or contracting product lines.

Product Modification Marketing managers must decide if and when to modify existing products. **Product modification** changes one or more of a product's characteristics:

▶▶ *Quality modification*: change in a product's dependability or durability. Reducing a product's quality may let the manufacturer lower the price and appeal to target markets unable to

product modification
changing one or more of a product's characteristics

planned obsolescence the practice of modifying products so those that have already been sold become obsolete before they actually need replacement

afford the original product. Conversely, increasing quality can help the firm compete with rival firms. Increasing quality can also result in increased brand loyalty, greater ability to raise prices, or new opportunities for market segmentation. Inexpensive ink-jet printers have improved in quality to the point that they produce photo-quality images, competing with camera film.

▶▶ *Functional modification*: change in a product's versatility, effectiveness, convenience, or safety. Campbell's offers Swanson Broth in "chef" size cartons for serious cooks and 16-ounce packages for simple side dishes.[2] Newman's Own demonstrates the versatility of its pasta sauce in the ad below.

▶▶ *Style modification*: aesthetic product change, rather than a quality or functional change. Clothing and auto manufacturers commonly use style modifications to motivate customers to replace products before they are worn out.

Planned obsolescence is a term commonly used to describe the practice of modifying products so that those that have already been sold become obsolete before they actually need replacement. For example, products such as printers and cell phones become obsolete because technology changes so quickly.

Some argue that planned obsolescence is wasteful; some claim it is unethical. Marketers respond that consumers favor style modifications because they like changes in the appearance of goods such as clothing and cars. Marketers also contend that consumers, not

manufacturers and marketers, decide when styles are obsolete.

Repositioning Repositioning, as Chapter 8 explained, involves changing consumers' perceptions of a brand. Kool-Aid, the soft drink brand that has stood for fun and refreshment for many years, is adding better-for-you options by introducing new and reformulated products. They are repositioning the brand as supporting a healthier family lifestyle.[3] Changing demographics, declining sales, or changes in the social environment often motivate firms to reposition established brands. Procter & Gamble is redesigning its Dawn liquid detergent line, including adding new products, sizes and graphics. For example, its Dawn Plus line will be positioned as a tough cleaning brand, reformulated with an added enzyme to fight stuck-on foods.[4]

Product Line Extensions A **product line extension** occurs when a company's management decides to add products to an existing product line in order to compete more broadly in the industry. Kraft extended a number of its popular Nabisco brands by adding small-portioned packages. Procter & Gamble extended its Febreze Fabric Refresher line with Febreze Fabric Refresher To Go aimed at travelers.[5]

YOUR BRAND'S OVEREXTENDED WHEN . . .

» Some products in the line do not contribute to profits because of low sales or cannibalize sales of other items in the line.

» Manufacturing or marketing resources are disproportionately allocated to slow-moving products.

» Some items in the line are obsolete because of new product entries in the line or new products offered by competitors.

Product Line Contraction Sometimes, marketers can get carried away with product extensions (Does the world really need thirty-one varieties of Head & Shoulders shampoo?). Contracting product lines is a strategic way to deal with overextension. When Steve Jobs took over Apple, the company sold more than forty products. He immediately simplified by cutting the product line down to four computers—two desktop and two laptops that Apple could focus on perfecting. This move helped Apple double its market share.[6]

Three major benefits are likely when a firm contracts overextended product lines. First, resources become concentrated on the most important products. Second, managers no longer waste resources trying to improve the sales and profits of poorly performing products. Third, new product items have a greater chance of being successful because more financial and human resources are available to manage them.

LO 4 Branding

The success of any business or consumer product depends in part on the target market's ability to distinguish one product from another. Branding is the main tool marketers use to distinguish their products from the competition's.

A **brand** is a name, term, symbol, design, or combination thereof that identifies a seller's products and differentiates them from competitors' products. A **brand name** is that part of a brand that can be spoken, including letters (GM, YMCA), words (Chevrolet), and numbers (WD-40, 7-Eleven). The elements of a brand that cannot be spoken are called the **brand mark**—for example, the well-known Mercedes-Benz and Delta Air Lines symbols.

Benefits of Branding

Branding has three main purposes: product identification, repeat sales, and new-product sales. The most important purpose is *product identification*. Branding allows marketers to distinguish their products from all others. Many brand names are familiar to consumers and indicate quality.

The term **brand equity** refers to the value of company and brand names. A brand that has high awareness, perceived quality, and brand loyalty among customers has high brand equity. Starbucks, Volvo, and Dell are companies with high brand equity. A brand with strong brand equity is a valuable asset. For example, when Tiffany & Co. created a line of more affordable silver jewelry to broaden its offerings to the upper-middle classes, it took a gamble with its reputation as an upscale luxury brand. Tiffany's managers began to worry about alienating its core clientele—the older, affluent, and conservative customer who prizes exclusivity. Tiffany decided to protect its brand equity by raising prices on its silver

product line extension adding additional products to an existing product line in order to compete more broadly in the industry

brand a name, term, symbol, design, or combination thereof that identifies a seller's products and differentiates them from competitors' products

brand name that part of a brand that can be spoken, including letters, words, and numbers

brand mark the elements of a brand that cannot be spoken

brand equity the value of company and brand names

jewelry beyond the reach of "aspirational" customers while aggressively courting its affluent customers. Still, Tiffany lost some wealthy customers who complained that "everyone has Tiffany jewelry now."[7]

The term **global brand** refers to a brand that obtains at least a third of its earnings from outside its home country, is recognizable outside its home base of customers, and has publicly available marketing and financial data. Yum! Brands, which owns Pizza Hut, KFC, and Taco Bell, is a good example of a company that has developed strong global brands. Yum believes that it has to adapt its restaurants to local tastes and different cultural and political climates. In Japan, for instance, KFC sells tempura crispy strips. In northern England, KFC focuses on gravy and potatoes, and in Thailand it offers rice with soy or sweet chili sauce.

The best generator of *repeat sales* is satisfied customers. Branding helps consumers identify products they wish to buy again and avoid those they do not. **Brand loyalty**, a consistent preference for one brand over all others, is quite high in some product categories. More than half the users in product categories such as cigarettes, mayonnaise, toothpaste, coffee, headache remedies, bath soap, and ketchup are loyal to one brand. Many students come to college and purchase the same brands they used at home rather than choosing by price. Brand identity is essential to developing brand loyalty.

The third main purpose of branding is to *facilitate new-product sales*. Having a well-known and respected company and brand name is extremely useful when introducing new products.

Branding Strategies

Firms face complex branding decisions. Firms may choose to follow a policy of using manufacturers' brands, private (distributor) brands, or both. In either case, they must then decide among a policy of individual branding (different brands for different products), family branding (common names for different products), or a combination of individual branding and family branding.

Manufacturers' Brands versus Private Brands The brand name of a manufacturer—such as Kodak, La-Z-Boy, and Fruit of the Loom—is called a **manufacturer's brand**. Sometimes "national brand" is used as a synonym for "manufacturer's brand." This term is not always accurate, however, because many manufacturers serve only regional markets. Using "manufacturer's brand" more precisely defines the brand's owner.

A **private brand**, also known as a private label or store brand, is a brand name owned by a wholesaler or a retailer. Private brands include Wal-Mart's Ol' Roy dog food, which has surpassed Nestlé's Purina as the world's top-selling dog food, and the George line of apparel, which has knocked Liz Claiborne's clothing out of Wal-Mart. Part of the reason for the success of private brands is due to perceptions about quality. A survey conducted for the Private Label Manufacturers Association found that 41 percent of shoppers identify themselves as frequent buyers of store brands, and seven out of ten feel the private-label products they buy are as good as, if not better than, their national brand counterparts.[8]

Retailers love consumers' greater acceptance of private brands. Because overhead is low and there are no marketing costs, private-label products bring 10 percent higher margins, on average, than manufacturers' brands. More than that, a trusted store brand can differentiate a chain from its competitors. Exhibit 10.2 illustrates key issues that wholesalers and retailers should consider in deciding whether to sell manufacturers' brands or private brands. Many firms offer a combination of both. Instead of marketing private brands as cheaper and inferior to manufacturer's brands, many retailers are creating and promoting their own **captive brands**. These brands carry no evidence of the store's affiliation, are manufactured by a third party, and are sold exclusively at the chains. This strategy allows the retailer to ask a price similar to manufacturer's brands, and they are typically displayed alongside mainstream products. For example, bioInfusion, a line of hair care products only available at Walgreens, has grown to become one of the top brands in the entire hair care category.[9]

Individual Brands versus Family Brands Many companies use different brand names for different products, a practice referred to as **individual branding**. Companies use individual brands when their products vary greatly in use or performance. For instance, it would not make sense to use the same brand name for a pair of dress socks and a baseball bat. Procter

EXHIBIT 10.2
Comparison of Manufacturers' and Private Brands from the Reseller's Perspective

Key Advantages of Carrying Manufacturers' Brands	Key Advantages of Carrying Private Brands
• Heavy advertising to the consumer by manufacturers such as Procter & Gamble helps develop strong consumer loyalties.	• A wholesaler or retailer can usually earn higher profits on its own brand. In addition, because the private brand is exclusive, there is less pressure to mark down the price to meet competition.
• Well-known manufacturers' brands, such as Kodak and Fisher-Price, can attract new customers and enhance the dealer's (wholesaler's or retailer's) prestige.	• A manufacturer can decide to drop a brand or a reseller at any time or even become a direct competitor to its dealers.
• Many manufacturers offer rapid delivery, enabling the dealer to carry less inventory.	• A private brand ties the customer to the wholesaler or retailer. A person who wants a DieHard battery must go to Sears.
• If a dealer happens to sell a manufacturer's brand of poor quality, the customer may simply switch brands and remain loyal to the dealer.	• Wholesalers and retailers have no control over the intensity of distribution of manufacturers' brands. Wal-Mart store managers don't have to worry about competing with other sellers of Sam's American Choice products or Ol' Roy dog food. They know that these brands are sold only in Wal-Mart and Sam's Club stores.

& Gamble targets different segments of the laundry detergent market with Bold, Cheer, Dash, Dreft, Era, Gain, Ivory Snow, Oxydol, Solo, and Tide.

No one grows Ketchup like Heinz.

IMAGE COURTESY OF THE ADVERTISING ARCHIVES

In contrast, a company that markets several different products under the same brand name is using a **family brand**. Sony's family brand includes radios, television sets, stereos, and other electronic products. The Heinz brand name is attached to products such as ketchup, mustard, and pickles.

Cobranding Cobranding entails placing two or more brand names on a product or its package. Three common types of cobranding are ingredient branding, cooperative branding, and complementary branding. *Ingredient branding* identifies the brand of a part that makes up the product, for example, Procter & Gamble has developed Mr. Clean Disinfecting Wipes with Febreze (a scent) Freshness. Febreze is also cobranded with Tide, Bounce, and Downy.[10] *Cooperative branding* occurs when two brands receiving equal treatment (in the context of an advertisement) borrow on each other's brand equity. A promotional contest jointly sponsored by Ramada Inn, American Express, and Continental Airlines used cooperative branding. Guests at Ramada who paid with an American Express card were automatically entered in the contest and were eligible to win more than a hundred getaways for two at any Ramada in the continental United States and round-trip airfare from Continental. Finally, with *complementary branding*, products are advertised or marketed together to suggest usage, such as a spirits brand (Seagram's) and a compatible mixer (7-Up).

family brand marketing several different products under the same brand name

cobranding placing two or more brand names on a product or its package

Cobranding is a useful strategy when a combination of brand names enhances the prestige or perceived value of a product or when it benefits brand owners and users. Cobranding may be used to increase a company's presence in markets where it has little or no market share. For example, Coach was able to build a presence in a whole new category when its leather upholstery with logo was used in Lexus automobiles.[11]

Trademarks

A **trademark** is the exclusive right to use a brand or part of a brand. Others are prohibited from using the brand without permission. A **service mark** performs the same function for services, such as H&R Block and Weight Watchers. Parts of a brand or other product identification may qualify for trademark protection. Some examples are:

▸ *Sounds,* such as General Electric Broadcasting Company's ship's bell clock sound and the MGM lion's roar.

▸ *Shapes,* such as the Jeep front grille and the Coca-Cola bottle.

▸ *Ornamental color or design,* such as the decoration on Nike tennis shoes, the black-and-copper color combination of a Duracell battery, Levi's small tag on the left side of the rear pocket of its jeans, or the cutoff black cone on the top of Cross pens.

▸ *Catchy phrases,* such as Prudential's "Own a piece of the rock," Mountain Dew's "Do the Dew," and Nike's "Just Do It!".

▸ *Abbreviations,* such as Bud, Coke, or The Met.

It is important to understand that trademark rights come from use rather than registration. An intent-to-use application is filed with the U.S. Patent and Trademark Office, and a company must have a genuine intention to use the mark when it files and actually use it within three years of the application being granted. Trademark protection typically lasts for ten years.[12] To renew the trademark, the company must prove it is using the mark. Rights to a trademark last as long as the mark is used. Normally, if the firm does not use it for two years, the trademark is considered abandoned, and a new user can claim exclusive ownership of the mark.

In November 1999, legislation went into effect that explicitly applies trademark law to the online world. This law includes financial penalties for those who violate trademarked products or register an otherwise trademarked term as a domain name.[13]

Companies that fail to protect their trademarks face the possibility that their product names will become generic. A **generic product name** identifies a product by class or type and cannot be trademarked. Former brand names that were not sufficiently protected by their owners and were subsequently declared to be generic product names by U.S. courts include aspirin, cellophane, linoleum, thermos, kerosene, monopoly, cola, and shredded wheat.

Companies such as Rolls-Royce, Cross, Xerox, Levi Strauss, Frigidaire, and McDonald's aggressively enforce their trademarks. Rolls-Royce, Coca-Cola, and Xerox even run newspaper and magazine ads stating that their names are trademarks and should not be used as descriptive or generic terms. Some companies, such as Apple and Google threaten lawsuits against competitors that violate trademarks, such as using the word "pod" in naming a new product (only the Apple iPod has that naming privilege), or using the phrase "to google," unless you are specifically referring to Google's services.[14]

Despite severe penalties for trademark violations, trademark infringement lawsuits are not uncommon. Serious conflict can occur when brand names resemble one another too closely. The celebrity chef Wolfgang Puck filed a lawsuit against Wolfgang Zweiner when Zweiner opened Wolfgang's Steakhouse and confused fans began calling to make reservations at what they thought was the new Puck restaurant.[15]

Companies must also contend with fake or unauthorized brands. Knockoffs of trademarked clothing lines are easy to find in cheap shops all over the world,

RIGHTS TO A TRADEMARK LAST AS LONG AS THE MARK IS USED.

PACKAGING HAS A MEASURABLE EFFECT ON SALES.

and loose imitations are found in some reputable department stores as well. Hasbro sued the makers of the online game Scrabulous for copyright infringement on its Scrabble game. Scrabulous was an obvious copy of Scrabble, including the rules, game pieces, and board colors.[16]

In Europe, you can sue counterfeiters only if your brand, logo, or trademark is formally registered. Until recently, formal registration was required in each country in which a company sought protection. A company can now register its trademark in all European Union (EU) member countries with one application.

LO 5 Packaging

Packages have always served a practical function—that is, they hold contents together and protect goods as they move through the distribution channel. Today, however, packaging is also a container for promoting the product and making it easier and safer to use.

Packaging Functions

The three most important functions of packaging are to contain and protect products, promote products, and facilitate the storage, use, and convenience of products. A fourth function of packaging that is becoming increasingly important is to facilitate recycling and reduce environmental damage.

Containing and Protecting Products The most obvious function of packaging is to contain products that are liquid, granular, or otherwise divisible. Packaging also enables manufacturers, wholesalers, and retailers to market products in specific quantities, such as ounces.

Physical protection is another obvious function of packaging. Most products are handled several times between the time they are manufactured, harvested, or otherwise produced and the time they are consumed or used. Many products are also shipped, stored, and inspected several times between production and consumption. Some, like milk, need to be refrigerated. Others, like beer, are sensitive to light. Still others, like medicines and bandages, need to be kept sterile. Packages protect products from breakage, evaporation, spillage, spoilage, light, heat, cold, infestation, and many other conditions.

Promoting Products Packaging does more than identify the brand, list the ingredients, specify features, and give directions. A package differentiates a product from competing products and may associate a new product with a family of other products from the same manufacturer. Welch's repackaged its line of grape juice–based jams, jellies, and juices to unify the line and get more impact on the shelf.

Packages use designs, colors, shapes, and materials to try to influence consumers' perceptions and buying behavior. For example, marketing research shows that health-conscious consumers are likely to think that any food is probably good for them as long as it comes in green packaging. Packaging can also influence consumer perceptions of quality and/or prestige. And packaging has a measurable effect on sales. Quaker Oats revised the package for Rice-a-Roni without making any other changes in marketing strategy and experienced a 44 percent increase in sales in one year.

Facilitating Storage, Use, and Convenience Wholesalers and retailers prefer packages that are easy to ship, store, and stock on shelves. They also like packages that protect products, prevent spoilage or breakage, and extend the product's shelf life.

Consumers' requirements for storage, use, and convenience cover many dimensions. Consumers are constantly seeking items that are easy to handle, open, and reclose, although some consumers want packages that are tamperproof or childproof. Research indicates that hard-to-open packages are among consumers' top complaints.[17] Surveys conducted by *Sales & Marketing Management* magazine revealed that consumers dislike—and avoid buying—leaky ice cream boxes, overly heavy or fat vinegar bottles, immovable pry-up lids on glass bottles, key-opener sardine cans, and hard-to-pour cereal boxes. Such packaging innovations as zipper tear strips, hinged lids, tab slots, screw-on tops, and pour spouts were introduced to solve these and other problems. Easy openings are especially important for kids and aging baby boomers.

Some firms use packaging to segment markets. For example, a C&H sugar carton with an easy-to-pour, reclosable top is targeted to consumers who don't do a lot of baking and are willing to pay at least twenty cents more for the package. Different size packages appeal to heavy, moderate, and light users. Campbell's soup is packaged in single-serving cans aimed at the elderly and singles market segments. Packaging convenience can increase a product's utility and, therefore, its market share and profits.

Facilitating Recycling and Reducing Environmental Damage One of the most important packaging issues today is compatibility with the environment. In a recent study of consumers, a majority said they would give up the following conveniences if it would benefit the environment: packaging designed for easy stacking/storing, packaging that can be used for cooking, and packaging designed for easy transport.[18] Some firms use their packaging to target environmentally concerned market segments. The French winery Boisset Family Estates recently introduced Tetra Pak cartons of its

French Rabbit chardonnay to offer consumers a playful and eco-friendly alternative to glass bottles. When the cartons sold well, other companies followed suit.[19] Groups like the Sustainable Packaging Coalition assist companies in creating perpetually recycled packaging so that materials don't ever end up in landfills, damaging the ecosystem.[20]

Labeling

An integral part of any package is its label. Labeling generally takes one of two forms: persuasive or informational. **Persuasive labeling** focuses on a promotional theme or logo, and consumer information is secondary. Note that the standard promotional claims—such as "new," "improved," and "super"—are no longer very persuasive. Consumers have been saturated with "newness" and thus discount these claims.

Informational labeling, in contrast, is designed to help consumers make proper product selections and lower their cognitive dissonance after the purchase. Sears attaches a "label of confidence" to all its floor coverings. This label gives such product information as

GREENWASHING

Companies that use more resources to promote their products as environmentally friendly than to implement environmentally sound practices are greenwashing. Companies greenwash consumers with:

- ◎ *Hidden trade-offs:* "energy efficient" electronics may contain hazardous materials.
- ◎ *Unsupported claims:* "certified organic" shampoos lack verifiable certification.
- ◎ *Vague claims:* "100% natural" products with naturally occurring yet hazardous ingredients.
- ◎ *Irrelevant claims:* advertising CFC-free products, though CFCs were banned twenty years ago.
- ◎ *Lying:* products may claim to be certified by an internationally recognized environmental standard, but aren't.

Avoid being greenwashed by looking for third-party accreditation, such as Ecologo, that provides an insignia to help consumers know that an independent, credible, and expert third party has verified a product's green qualifications.

SOURCES: "Greenwash," *Wikipedia.com*, January 11, 2009; David Roberts, "Another Inconvenient Truth," *Fast Company*, March 2008, 70; "The Six Sins of Greenwashing," TerraChoice Environmental Marketing Inc., November 2007.

durability, color, features, cleanability, care instructions, and construction standards. Most major furniture manufacturers affix labels to their wares that explain the products' construction features, such as type of frame, number of coils, and fabric characteristics. The Nutritional Labeling and Education Act of 1990 mandated detailed nutritional information on most food packages and standards for health claims on food packaging. An important outcome of this legislation has been guidelines from the Food and Drug Administration for using terms such as *low fat*, *light*, *reduced cholesterol*, *low sodium*, *low calorie*, *low carb*, and *fresh*. Getting the right information is very important to consumers—so much so that almost 75 percent said they would be willing to pay extra, for example, to have products display country of origin information.[21]

Universal Product Codes

The **universal product codes (UPCs)** that appear on most items in supermarkets and other high-volume outlets were first introduced in 1974. Because the numerical codes appear as a series of thick and thin vertical lines, they are often called *bar codes*. The lines are read by computerized optical scanners that match codes with brand names, package sizes, and prices. They also print information on cash register tapes and help retailers rapidly and accurately prepare records of customer purchases, control inventories, and track sales. The UPC system and scanners are also used in single-source research (see Chapter 9).

LO 6 Global Issues in Branding and Packaging

When planning to enter a foreign market with an existing product, a firm has three options for handling the brand name:

▸▸ *One brand name everywhere*: This strategy is useful when the company markets mainly one product and the brand name does not have negative connotations in any local market. The Coca-Cola Company uses a one-brand-name strategy in more than 195 countries around the world. The advantages of a one-brand-name strategy are greater identification of the product from market to market and ease of coordinating promotion from market to market.

▸▸ *Adaptations and modifications*: A one-brand-name strategy is not possible when the name cannot be pro-

nounced in the local language, when the brand name is owned by someone else, or when the brand name has a negative or vulgar connotation in the local language. The Iranian detergent "Barf," for example, might encounter some problems in the U.S. market.

▸▸ *Different brand names in different markets*: Local brand names are often used when translation or pronunciation problems occur, when the marketer wants the brand to appear to be a local brand, or when regulations require localization. Gillette's Silkience hair conditioner is called Soyance in France and Sientel in Italy. Coca-Cola's Sprite brand had to be renamed Kin in Korea to satisfy a government prohibition on the unnecessary use of foreign words.

In addition to global branding decisions, companies must consider global packaging needs. Three aspects of packaging that are especially important in international marketing are labeling, aesthetics, and climate considerations. The major *labeling* concern is properly translating ingredient, promotional, and instructional information on labels. Care must also be employed in meeting all local labeling requirements. Several years ago, an Italian judge ordered that all bottles of Coca-Cola be removed from retail shelves because the ingredients were not properly labeled. Labeling is also harder in countries like Belgium and Finland, which require it to be bilingual.

Package *aesthetics* may also require some attention. Even though simple visual elements of the brand, such as a symbol or logo, can be a standardizing element across products and countries, marketers must stay attuned to cultural traits in host countries. For example, colors may have different connotations. Red is associated with witchcraft in some countries, green may be a sign of danger, and white may be symbolic of death. Aesthetics also influence package size. Soft drinks are not sold in six-packs in countries that lack refrigeration. In some countries, products such as detergent may be bought only in small quantities because of a lack of storage space. Other products, such as cigarettes, may be bought in small quantities, and even single units, because of the low purchasing power of buyers.

Extreme climates and long-distance shipping necessitate sturdier and more durable packages for goods sold overseas. Spillage, spoilage, and breakage are all more important concerns when products are shipped long distances or frequently handled during shipping and storage. Packages may also have to ensure a longer product life if the time between production and consumption lengthens significantly.

warranty a confirmation of the quality or performance of a good or service

express warranty a written guarantee

implied warranty an unwritten guarantee that the good or service is fit for the purpose for which it was sold

Just as a package is designed to protect the product, a **warranty** protects the buyer and gives essential information about the product. A warranty confirms the quality or performance of a good or service. An **express warranty** is a written guarantee. Express warranties range from simple statements—such as "100 percent cotton" (a guarantee of quality) and "complete satisfaction guaranteed" (a statement of performance)—to extensive documents written in technical language. In contrast, an **implied warranty** is an unwritten guarantee that the good or service is fit for the purpose for which it was sold. All sales have an implied warranty under the Uniform Commercial Code.

Congress passed the Magnuson-Moss Warranty–Federal Trade Commission Improvement Act in 1975 to help consumers understand warranties and get action from manufacturers and dealers. A manufacturer that promises a full warranty must meet certain minimum standards, including repair "within a reasonable time and without charge" of any defects and replacement of the merchandise or a full refund if the product does not work "after a reasonable number of attempts" at repair. Any warranty that does not live up to this tough prescription must be "conspicuously" promoted as a limited warranty.

195 Number of countries where the Coke brand name is used

1/3 Amount of a brand's revenue that has to come from international sources before it can be considered a global brand

44 Percent sales increase that Rice-a-Roni experienced when it upgraded its package

4 Types of consumer products; functions of packaging

1974 Year the bar code was introduced

STUDY TOOLS CHAPTER 10

Located at back of the textbook
- ❏ **Rip out Chapter Review Card**

Located at 4ltrpress.cengage.com/mktg
- ❏ **Review Key Terms Flash Cards (Print or Online)**
- ❏ **Download Audio and Visual Summaries for on-the-go review**
- ❏ **Complete both Practice Quizzes to prepare for tests**
- ❏ **Play "Beat the Clock" and "Quizbowl" to master concepts**
- ❏ **Complete "Crossword Puzzle" to review key terms**
- ❏ **Watch the video on "Kodak" for a real company example on Product Concepts**

Mattel updated Barbie's packaging to keep her fresh and familiar.

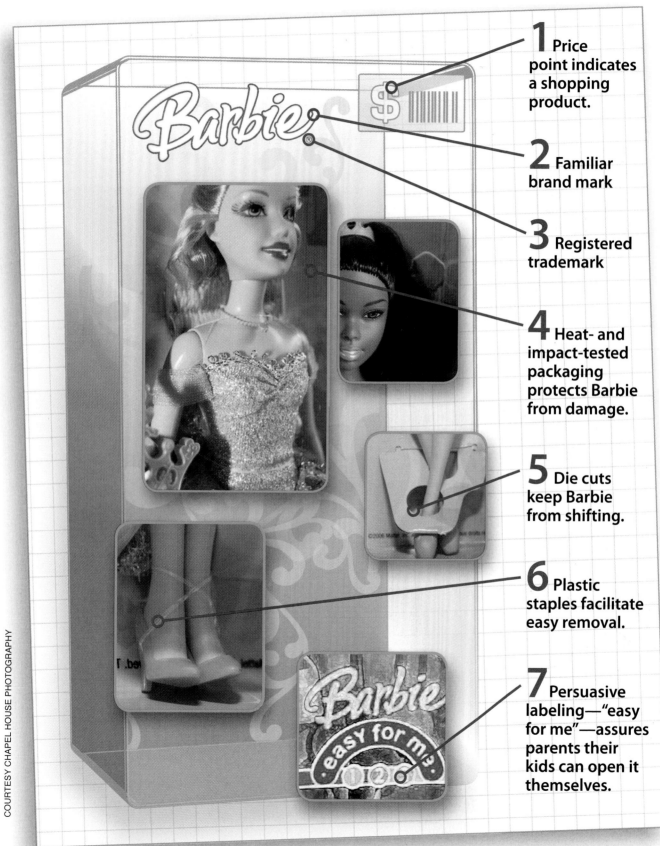

1 Price point indicates a shopping product.

2 Familiar brand mark

3 Registered trademark

4 Heat- and impact-tested packaging protects Barbie from damage.

5 Die cuts keep Barbie from shifting.

6 Plastic staples facilitate easy removal.

7 Persuasive labeling—"easy for me"—assures parents their kids can open it themselves.

"The average fast-moving consumer goods company introduces 70 to 80 new products per year."

LO 1 The Importance of New Products

AFTER YOU FINISH THIS CHAPTER GO TO PAGE 179 FOR STUDY TOOLS

New products are important to sustain growth, increase revenues and profits, and replace obsolete items. Research by *Business Week* and the Boston Consulting Group revealed that the world's twenty-five most innovative companies have higher average stock returns and higher average revenue growth than companies that were not included in this group.[1] The *Business Week*-Boston Consulting Group's list includes firms such as Apple, Inc., Nintendo Corporation, Boeing Company, Nokia, and Microsoft Corporation.[2] These firms are known for innovative products. Other firms on the list are known for innovative business models, innovative customer experience, and/or innovative processes.[3]

new product a product new to the world, the market, the producer, the seller, or some combination of these

Categories of New Products

The term **new product** is somewhat confusing because its meaning varies widely. Actually, the term has several "correct" definitions. A product can be new to the world, to the market, to the producer or seller, or some combination of these. There are six categories of new products:

▸▸ *New-to-the-world products (also called discontinuous innovations)*: These products create an entirely new market. New-to-the-world products represent the smallest category of new products.

What do you think?

Getting the newest products is always extremely exciting.

1	2	3	4	5	6	7

STRONGLY DISAGREE   STRONGLY AGREE

Find out what others think at 4ltrpress.cengage.com/mktg

▶▶ *New product lines*: These products, which the firm has not previously offered, allow it to enter an established market. For example, Disney Consumer Products recently added a new line of fragrances targeting boys ages 4–11 in Latin communities under the brand names Pirates of the Caribbean and Buzz Lightyear.[4]

▶▶ *Additions to existing product lines*: This category includes new products that supplement a firm's established line. Nintendo added to its product line by introducing Wii Fit—an exercise and weight-loss system aimed at busy mothers—to its Wii line of gaming consoles.

▶▶ *Improvements or revisions of existing products*: The "new and improved" product may be significantly or slightly changed. Procter & Gamble's Tide Coldwater is an example. The product is concentrated so that packaging materials are reduced. By not requiring hot water, Tide Coldwater requires less energy to wash a load of clothes and would reduce carbon emissions by 34 tons per year if every U.S. household used the product.[5]

▶▶ *Repositioned products*: These are existing products targeted at new markets or market segments, or repositioned to change the current market's perception of the product. Sometimes repositioning is intended to boost sales of a product with declining sales. For example, Harley-Davidson, Inc. is targeting a younger generation of riders who like bikes that are lighter and faster than the heavy (and very expensive) hog for which Harley is famous. And Harley now makes bikes that are lower to the ground with narrower seats and adjustable handlebars to make bikes more comfortable for smaller riders, such as women.[6]

▶▶ *Lower-priced products*: This category refers to products that provide performance similar to competing brands at a lower price. Hewlett-Packard Laser Jet 3100 is a scanner, copier, printer, and fax machine combined. This new product is priced lower than many conventional color copiers and much lower than the combined price of the four items purchased separately.

LO 2 The New-Product Development Process

The management consulting firm Booz Allen Hamilton has studied the new-product development process for more than thirty years. Analyzing five major studies undertaken during this period, the firm has con-

EXHIBIT 11.1
New-Product Development Process

1	New-product strategy
2	Idea generation
3	Idea screening
4	Business analysis
5	Development
6	Test marketing
7	Commercialization
	New product

cluded that the companies most likely to succeed in developing and introducing new products are those that take the following actions:

▶▶ Make the long-term commitment needed to support innovation and new-product development.

▶▶ Use a company-specific approach, driven by corporate objectives and strategies, with a well-defined new-product strategy at its core.

▶▶ Capitalize on experience to achieve and maintain competitive advantage.

▶▶ Establish an environment—a management style, organizational structure, and degree of top-management support—conducive to achieving company-specific new-product and corporate objectives.

Most companies follow a formal new-product development process, usually starting with a new-product strategy. Exhibit 11.1 traces the seven-step process, which is discussed in detail in this section. The exhibit is funnel-shaped to highlight the fact that each stage acts as a screen. The purpose is to filter out unworkable ideas.

New-Product Strategy

A **new-product strategy** links the new-product development process with the objectives of the marketing department, the business unit, and the corporation. A new-product strategy must be compatible with these objectives, and in turn, all three of the objectives must be consistent with one another.

A new-product strategy is part of the organization's overall marketing strategy. It sharpens the focus and provides general guidelines for generating, screening, and evaluating new-product ideas. The new-product strategy specifies the roles that new products must play in the organization's overall plan and describes the characteristics of products the organization wants to offer and the markets it wants to serve.

The importance of having a well-thought-out new-product strategy is illustrated by a Dun & Bradstreet finding that for each successful new product introduced, a company needs between fifty and sixty other new-product ideas somewhere in its new-product development process.[7] Procter & Gamble has made a public commitment to introduce $20 billion worth of "sustainable, innovative products" between 2008 and 2013.[8]

Idea Generation

New-product ideas come from many sources, including customers, employees, distributors, competitors, vendors, research and development (R&D), and consultants.

> FOR EACH SUCCESSFUL NEW PRODUCT INTRODUCED, A COMPANY NEEDS BETWEEN FIFTY AND SIXTY OTHER NEW-PRODUCT IDEAS SOMEWHERE IN ITS NEW-PRODUCT DEVELOPMENT PROCESS.

▸▸ *Customers*: The marketing concept suggests that customers' wants and needs should be the springboard for developing new products. Many of today's most innovative and successful marketers have taken the approach of introducing fewer new products, but taking the necessary steps to ensure these "chosen few" are truly unique, better, and, above all, really do address unmet consumer needs. How do they do that? Many firms rely on "co-creation," inventing new products along with their customers.[9] At MyStarbucks.com, customers can make suggestions, other customers can vote on and discuss them, and Starbucks can see which ideas gain support.[10] Dell Computers has a similar site, called IdeaStorm.com, that has led to a host of new offerings.[11] Some companies are using Web 2.0 tools to get consumers more involved in new-product development (see box below). This approach is far from an intuitive extension of previous new-product development and advertising practices.

▸▸ *Employees*: Marketing personnel—advertising and marketing research employees, as well as salespeople—often create new-product ideas because they analyze and are involved in the marketplace. Encouraging employees from different divisions to exchange ideas is also a useful strategy. The developers of Mr. Clean AutoDry turned to scientists who worked on PuR water purification and Cascade dishwashing detergent to learn how to dry dishes without spotting.[12]

NEW PRODUCT DEVELOPMENT USING WEB 2.0 TOOLS

Web 2.0 is the set of tools that allows people to build social and business connections, share information, and collaborate on projects online (such as Wikipedia and Facebook). Now marketers are beginning to use those tools to collaborate with consumers on product development, service enhancement, and promotions. Community members can help companies identify what consumers are looking for as well as suggest innovations. One company developed some prototypes based on their community's suggestions and got an enthusiastic response: members clamored to know if they'd get the first purchase opportunity.[13]

Some firms reward employees for coming up with creative new ideas. For example, McDonald's has a team of seventy employees that tests new equipment ideas and procedures at its Innovation Center in Romeoville, Illinois.[14] According to the results of a survey by Prophet, a management consulting firm, 80 percent of "model innovators" encourage employees to be curious, 76 percent systematically encourage risk taking, 64 percent make it a priority to provide time and space for the development of new ideas, and 60 percent have incentive systems encouraging employees to contribute to innovation efforts.[15]

▸▸ *Distributors*: A well-trained sales force routinely asks distributors about needs that are not being met. Because they are closer to end users, distributors are often more aware of customer needs than are manufacturers. The inspiration for Rubbermaid's Sidekick, a litter-free lunch box, came from a distributor who suggested that the company place some of its plastic containers inside a lunch box and sell the box as an alternative to plastic wrap and paper bags.

The survey by Prophet mentioned in the previous paragraph found that 75 percent of model innovators actively involve their vendors and suppliers in new product development.[16] Procter & Gamble has reported that its innovation productivity has increased 60 percent due to external collaborations.[17]

▸▸ *Vendors*: 7-Eleven, Inc. regularly forges partnerships with vendors to create proprietary products. Coca-Cola invented the flavor blue vanilla for a 7-Eleven Slurpee® drink and the matching Blue Vanilla Laffy Taffy Rope candy was developed by Nestlé's Wonka division exclusively for 7-Eleven.

▸▸ *Competitors*: No firms rely solely on internally generated ideas for new products. A big part of any organization's marketing intelligence system should be monitoring the performance of competitors' products. One purpose of competitive monitoring is to determine which, if any, of the competitors' products should be copied. There is plenty of information about competitors on the Internet. For example, AltaVista (www.altavista.digital.com) is a powerful index tool that can be used to locate information about products and companies. Fuld & Company's competitive intelligence guide provides links to a variety of market intelligence sites.

▸▸ *Research and development*: R&D is carried out in four distinct ways. You learned about basic research and applied research in Chapter 4. The other two ways are product development and product modification. **Product development** goes beyond applied research by converting applications into marketable products. *Product modification* makes cosmetic or functional changes in existing products. Many new-product breakthroughs come from R&D activities. Procter & Gamble, the world's largest household goods manufacturer, has 9,000 research and development employees.[18]

Some companies are establishing innovation laboratories to complement or even replace traditional R&D programs. Idea labs focus on substantially increasing the speed of innovation. Motorola's MOTORAZR telephone was developed in an innovation lab called Moto City, located about fifty miles from company headquarters. Most of the development work was done by a team of engineers, designers, and marketers who worked in open spaces and waist-high cubicles. Many normal practices, such as soliciting input from regional managers around the world, were omitted to foster teamwork and speed development.[19] Boeing, Wrigley, Procter & Gamble, and the Mayo Clinic all use innovation labs.

▸▸ *Consultants*: Outside consultants are always available to examine a business and recommend product ideas. Examples include the Weston Group; Booz Allen Hamilton; and Management Decisions. Traditionally, consultants determine whether a company has a balanced portfolio of products and, if not, what new-product ideas are needed to offset the imbalance.

Creativity is the wellspring of new-product ideas, regardless of who comes up with them. A variety of approaches and techniques have been developed to stimulate creative thinking. The two considered most useful for generating new-product ideas are brainstorming and focus-group exercises. The goal of **brainstorming** is to get a group to think of unlimited ways to vary a product or solve a problem. Group members avoid criticism of an idea, no matter how ridiculous it may seem. Objective evaluation is postponed. The sheer quantity of ideas is what matters. As noted in Chapter 9, an objective of focus-group interviews is to stimulate insightful comments through group interaction. Focus groups usually consist of seven to ten people. Sometimes consumer focus groups generate excellent new-product ideas. In the industrial market, machine tools, keyboard designs, aircraft interiors, and backhoe accessories have evolved from focus groups.

Idea Screening

After new ideas have been generated, they pass through the first filter in the product development process. This stage, called **screening**, eliminates ideas that are inconsistent with the organization's new-product strategy or are obviously inappropriate for some other reason. The new-product committee, the new-product department, or some other formally appointed group performs the screening review. General Motors' Advanced Portfolio Exploration Group (APEx) knows that only one out of every twenty new car concepts developed by the group will ever become a reality. That's not a bad percentage. In the pharmaceutical business the percentage is much lower. Most new-product ideas are rejected at the screening stage.

Concept tests are often used at the screening stage to rate concept (or product) alternatives. A **concept test** evaluates a new-product idea, usually before any prototype has been created. Typically, researchers get consumer reactions to descriptions and visual representations of a proposed product.

Concept tests are considered fairly good predictors of success for line extensions. They have also been relatively precise predictors of success for new products that are not copycat items, are not easily classified into existing product categories, and do not require major changes in consumer behavior—such as Betty Crocker Tuna Helper and Libby's Fruit Float. However, concept tests are usually inaccurate in predicting the success of new products that create new consumption patterns and require major changes in consumer behavior—such as microwave ovens, VCRs, computers, and word processors.

Business Analysis

New-product ideas that survive the initial screening process move to the **business analysis** stage, where preliminary figures for demand, cost, sales, and profitability are calculated. For the first time, costs and revenues are estimated and compared. Depending on the nature of the product and the company, this process may be simple or complex.

The newness of the product, the size of the market, and the nature of the competition all affect the accuracy of revenue projections. In an established market like soft drinks, industry estimates of total market size are available. Forecasting market share for a new entry is a bigger challenge.

Analyzing overall economic trends and their impact on estimated sales is especially important in product categories that are sensitive to fluctuations in the business cycle. If consumers view the economy as uncertain and risky, they will put off buying durable goods such as major home appliances, automobiles, and homes. Likewise, business buyers postpone major equipment purchases if they expect a recession. Understanding the market potential is important because costs increase dramatically once a product idea enters the development stage.

COMMON QUESTIONS IN THE BUSINESS ANALYSIS STAGE:

▶▶ What is the likely demand for the product?

▶▶ What impact would the new product probably have on total sales, profits, market share, and return on investment?

▶▶ How would the introduction of the product affect existing products? Would the new product cannibalize existing products?

▶▶ Would current customers benefit from the product?

▶▶ Would the product enhance the image of the company's overall product mix?

▶▶ Would the new product affect current employees in any way? Would it lead to increasing or reducing the size of the workforce?

▶▶ What new facilities, if any, would be needed?

▶▶ How might competitors respond?

▶▶ What is the risk of failure? Is the company willing to take the risk?

Development

In the early stage of **development**, the R&D or engineering department may develop a prototype of the product. During this stage, the firm should start sketching a marketing strategy. The marketing department should decide on the product's packaging, branding, labeling, and so forth. In addition, it should map out preliminary promotion, price, and distribution strategies. The feasibility of manufacturing the product at an acceptable cost should be thoroughly examined. The development stage can last a long time and thus be very expensive. It took ten years

screening the first filter in the product development process, which eliminates ideas that are inconsistent with the organization's new-product strategy or are obviously inappropriate for some other reason

concept test a test to evaluate a new-product idea, usually before any prototype has been created

business analysis the second stage of the screening process where preliminary figures for demand, cost, sales, and profitability are calculated

development the stage in the product development process in which a prototype is developed and a marketing strategy is outlined

to develop Crest toothpaste, fifteen years to develop the Polaroid Colorpack camera and the Xerox copy machine, eighteen years to develop Minute Rice, and fifty-one years to develop television. Gillette developed three shaving systems over a twenty-seven-year period (TracII, Atra, and Sensor) before introducing the Mach3 in 1998 and Fusion in 2006.[20]

The development process works best when all the involved areas (R&D, marketing, engineering, production, and even suppliers) work together rather than sequentially, a process called **simultaneous product development**. This approach allows firms to shorten the development process and reduce costs. With simultaneous product development, all relevant functional areas and outside suppliers participate in all stages of the development process. Rather than proceeding through highly structured stages, the cross-functional team operates in unison. Involving key suppliers early in the process capitalizes on their knowledge and enables them to develop critical component parts.

The Internet is a useful tool for implementing simultaneous product development. On the Net, multiple partners from a variety of locations can meet regularly to assess new-product ideas, analyze markets and demographics, and review cost information. Ideas judged to be feasible can quickly be converted into new products. Without the Internet it would be impossible to conduct simultaneous product development from different parts of the world. Global R&D is important for two reasons. First, large companies have become global and are no longer focused only on one market. Global R&D is necessary to connect with customers in different parts of the world. Second, companies want to tap into the world's best talent—which isn't always found in the United States.[21]

Some firms use online brain trusts to solve technical problems. InnoCentive, Inc. is a network of 80,000 self-selected science problem solvers in 173 countries. Its clients include Boeing, DuPont, and Procter & Gamble. Procter & Gamble has another program called the Connect-and-Develop Model. When the company selects an idea for development, it no longer tries to develop it from the ground up with its own resources and time. Instead, it issues a brief to its network of think-

THE DEVELOPMENT STAGE CAN LAST A LONG TIME AND THUS BE VERY EXPENSIVE. IT TOOK TEN YEARS TO DEVELOP CREST TOOTHPASTE, FIFTEEN YEARS TO DEVELOP THE POLAROID COLORPACK CAMERA AND THE XEROX COPY MACHINE, EIGHTEEN YEARS TO DEVELOP MINUTE RICE, AND FIFTY-ONE YEARS TO DEVELOP TELEVISION.

ers, researchers, technology entrepreneurs, and inventors around the world, hoping to generate dialog, suggestions, and solutions.[22]

Innovative firms are also gathering a variety of R&D input from customers online. Threadless, a tee-shirt company, and Ryz, an athletic shoe manufacturer, ask consumers to vote online for their favorites. The companies use these results to determine the products they sell over the Internet.[23]

Laboratory tests are often conducted on prototype models during the development stage. User safety is an important aspect of laboratory testing, which actually subjects products to much more severe treatment than is expected by end users. The Consumer Product Safety Act of 1972 requires manufacturers to conduct a "reasonable testing program" to ensure that their products conform to established safety standards.

Many products that test well in the laboratory are also tried out in homes or businesses. Examples of product categories well suited for such use tests include human and pet food products, household cleaning products, and industrial chemicals and supplies. These products are all relatively inexpensive, and their performance characteristics are apparent to users. For example, Procter & Gamble tests a variety of personal and home-care products in the community around its Cincinnati, Ohio headquarters.

Test Marketing

After products and marketing programs have been developed, they are usually tested in the marketplace. **Test marketing** is the limited introduction of a product and a marketing program to determine the reactions of potential customers in a market situation. Test marketing allows management to evaluate alternative strategies and to assess how well the various aspects of the marketing mix fit together. Even established products are test marketed to assess new marketing strategies.

The cities chosen as test sites should reflect market conditions in the new product's projected market area. Yet no "magic city" exists that can universally represent market conditions, and a product's success in one city doesn't guarantee that it will be a nationwide hit. When selecting test market cities, researchers should therefore find locations where the demographics and purchasing habits mirror the overall market. The company should also have good distribution in test cities.

Moreover, test locations should be isolated from the media. If the television stations in a particular market reach a very large area outside that market, the advertising used for the test product may pull in many consumers from outside the market. The product may then appear more successful than it really is.

The High Costs of Test Marketing Test marketing frequently takes one year or longer, and costs can exceed $1 million. Some products remain in test markets even longer. Despite the cost, many firms believe it is better to fail in a test market than in a national introduction. Because test marketing is so expensive, some companies do not test line extensions of well-known brands. For example, because its Sara Lee brand is well known, Consolidated Foods Kitchen faced little risk in distributing its frozen croissants nationally.

The high cost of test marketing is not just financial. One unavoidable problem is that test marketing exposes the new product and its marketing mix to competitors before its introduction. Thus, the element of surprise is lost. Competitors can also sabotage or "jam" a testing program by introducing their own sales promotion, pricing, or advertising campaign. The purpose is to hide or distort the normal conditions that the testing firm might expect in the market.

Alternatives to Test Marketing Many firms are looking for cheaper, faster, safer alternatives to traditional test marketing. In the early 1980s, Information Resources, Inc. pioneered one alternative: single-source research

EXTENSIVE THOUGHT AND PLANNING WENT INTO DESIGNING AND LAUNCHING HEINEKEN PREMIUM LIGHT BEER. THE PROCESS INCLUDED 9 PACKAGING PROPOSALS, 24 BREW FORMULAS, 39 DESIGN SCHEMES, AND 199 POTENTIAL NAMES.[24]

under true market conditions. Research firms offer simulated market tests for $25,000 to $100,000, compared to $1 million or more for full-scale test marketing.

In Japan, soft-drink makers do little in the way of market research. They just release about 1,000 new drinks each year and see which ones sell. Japan's beverage market is crowded, but the three new drinks that make the list each year can sell half a billion cans. Industry analysts consider Japan a kind of global beverage testing ground.[25]

The Internet also offers a fast, cost-effective way to conduct test marketing. Procter & Gamble uses the Internet to assess customer demand for potential new products. Many products that are not available in grocery stores or drugstores can be sampled from P&G's corporate Web site (www.pg.com).[26]

Despite these alternatives, most firms still consider test marketing essential for most new products. The high price of failure simply prohibits the widespread introduction of most new products without testing.

Commercialization

The final stage in the new-product development process is **commercialization**, the decision to market a product. The decision to commercialize the product sets several tasks in motion: ordering production materials and equipment, starting production, building inventories, shipping the product to field distribution points, training the sales force, announcing the new product to the trade, and advertising to potential customers.

The time from the initial commercialization decision to the product's actual introduction varies. It can range from a few weeks for simple products that use existing equipment to several years for technical products that require custom manufacturing equipment. And the total cost of development and initial introduction can be staggering. Gillette spent $750 million

using supermarket scanner data (discussed in Chapter 8). A typical supermarket scanner test costs about $300,000. Another alternative to traditional test marketing is **simulated (laboratory) market testing**. Advertising and other promotional materials for several products, including the test product, are shown to members of the product's target market. These people are then taken to shop at a mock or real store, where their purchases are recorded. Shopper behavior, including repeat purchasing, is monitored to assess the product's likely performance

simulated (laboratory) market testing the presentation of advertising and other promotional materials for several products, including a test product, to members of the product's target market

commercialization the decision to market a product

developing MACH3, and the first-year marketing budget for the new three-bladed razor was $300 million.

The most important factor in successful new-product introduction is a good match between the product and market needs—as the marketing concept would predict. Successful new products deliver a meaningful and perceivable benefit to a sizable number of people or organizations and are different in some meaningful way from their intended substitutes. Firms that routinely experience success in new-product introductions tend to share the following characteristics:

- A history of listening carefully to customers
- An obsession with producing the best product possible
- A vision of what the market will be like in the future
- Strong leadership
- A commitment to new-product development
- A project-based team approach to new-product development
- Getting every aspect of the product development process right

LO 3 Global Issues in New-Product Development

Increasing globalization of markets and competition provides a reason for multinational firms to consider new-product development from a worldwide perspective. A firm that starts with a global strategy is better able to develop products that are marketable worldwide. In many multinational corporations, every product is developed for potential worldwide distribution, and unique market requirements are built in whenever possible.

Some global marketers design their products to meet regulations in their major markets and then, if necessary, meet smaller markets' requirements country by country. Nissan develops lead-country car models that, with minor changes, can be sold in most markets. With this approach, Nissan has been able to reduce the number of its basic models from forty-eight to eighteen. Some products, however, have little potential for global market penetration without modification. In other cases, companies cannot sell their product at affordable prices and still make a profit in many countries. GE Healthcare engineers figured out a way to develop the MAC 400, a portable electrocardiograph machine selling for $1,500 in India. The MAC 400 was based upon technology developed for a U.S. machine that sold for $5.4 million.[27]

LO 4 The Spread of New Products

Managers have a better chance of successfully marketing products if they understand how consumers learn about and adopt products.

FRUGAL ENGINEERING

Deere & Co. is pursuing U.S. hobby farmers thanks to innovations at its research facility in India. The move to India was unexpected: Deere is known in the United States for its heavy-duty farm equipment and big (and expensive) construction gear, but Deere saw potential for another market once its Indian engineers came up with a few no-frills models sturdy enough to handle the rigors of commercial farming for the lower-budget Indian farmers. Even still, Deere didn't consider selling the low-cost models in the United States until Indian competitor Mahindra & Mahindra targeted farming hobbyists and bargain hunters here. Now about half the tractors Deere manufactures in India make their way overseas.[28]

Diffusion of Innovation

An **innovation** is a product perceived as new by a potential adopter. It really doesn't matter whether the product is "new to the world" or some other category of new product. If it is new to a potential adopter, it is an innovation in this context. **Diffusion** is the process by which the adoption of an innovation spreads.

Five categories of adopters participate in the diffusion process:

» *Innovators*: the first 2.5 percent of all those who adopt the product. Innovators are eager to try new ideas and products, almost as an obsession. In addition to having higher incomes, they are more worldly and more active outside their community than noninnovators. They rely less on group norms and are more self-confident. Because they are well educated, they are more likely to get their information from scientific sources and experts. Innovators are characterized as being venturesome.

» *Early adopters*: the next 13.5 percent to adopt the product. Although early adopters are not the very first, they do adopt early in the product's life cycle. Compared to innovators, they rely much more on group norms and values. They are also more oriented to the local community, in contrast to the innovators' worldly outlook. Early adopters are more likely than innovators to be opinion leaders because of their closer affiliation with groups. Early adopters are a new product's best friends.[29] The respect of others is a dominant characteristic of early adopters.

» *Early majority*: the next 34 percent to adopt. The early majority weighs the pros and cons before adopting a new product. They are likely to collect more information and evaluate more brands than early adopters, therefore extending the adoption process. They rely on the group for information but are unlikely to be opinion leaders themselves. Instead, they tend to be opinion leaders' friends and neighbors. The early majority is an important link in the process of diffusing new ideas because they are positioned between earlier and later adopters. A dominant characteristic of the early majority is deliberateness.

» *Late majority*: the next 34 percent to adopt. The late majority adopts a new product because most of their friends have already adopted it. Because they also rely on group norms, their adoption stems from pressure to conform. This group tends to be older and below average in income and education. They depend mainly on word-of-mouth communication rather than on the mass media. The dominant characteristic of the late majority is skepticism.

» *Laggards*: the final 16 percent to adopt. Like innovators, laggards do not rely on group norms. Their independence is rooted in their ties to tradition. Thus, the past heavily influences their decisions. By the time laggards adopt an innovation, it has probably been outmoded and replaced by something else. For example, they may have bought their first black-and-white television set after color television was already widely diffused. Laggards have the longest adoption time and the lowest socioeconomic status. They tend to be suspicious of new products and alienated from a rapidly advancing society. The dominant value of laggards is tradition. Marketers typically ignore laggards, who do not seem to be motivated by advertising or personal selling and are virtually impossible to reach online.

Note that some product categories may never be adopted by 100 percent of the population. The adopter categories refer to all of those who will eventually adopt a product, not the entire population.

Product Characteristics and the Rate of Adoption

Five product characteristics can be used to predict and explain the rate of acceptance and diffusion of a new product:

» *Complexity*: the degree of difficulty involved in understanding and using a new product. The more complex the product, the slower is its diffusion.

» *Compatibility*: the degree to which the new product is consistent with existing values and product knowledge, past experiences, and current needs. Incompatible products diffuse more slowly than compatible products.

product life cycle (PLC) a concept that provides a way to trace the stages of a product's acceptance, from its introduction (birth) to its decline (death)

▸▸ *Relative advantage*: the degree to which a product is perceived as superior to existing substitutes. Because it can store and play back thousands of songs, the iPod has a clear relative advantage over the portable CD player.

▸▸ *Observability*: the degree to which the benefits or other results of using the product can be observed by others and communicated to target customers. For instance, fashion items and automobiles are highly visible and more observable than personal-care items.

▸▸ *"Trialability"*: the degree to which a product can be tried on a limited basis. It is much easier to try a new toothpaste or breakfast cereal than a new automobile or microcomputer.

Marketing Implications of the Adoption Process

Two types of communication aid the diffusion process: *word-of-mouth communication* among consumers and communication from marketers to consumers. Word-of-mouth communication within and across groups speeds diffusion. Opinion leaders discuss new products with their followers and with other opinion leaders. Marketers must therefore ensure that opinion leaders have the types of information desired in the media that they use. Suppliers of some products, such as professional and health-care services, rely almost solely on word-of-mouth communication for new business.

The second type of communication aiding the diffusion process is *communication directly from the marketer to potential adopters*. Messages directed toward early adopters should normally use different appeals than messages directed toward the early majority, the late majority, or the laggards. Early adopters are more important than innovators because they make up a larger group, are more socially active, and are usually opinion leaders.

As the focus of a promotional campaign shifts from early adopters to the early majority and the late majority, marketers should study the dominant characteristics, buying behavior, and media characteristics of these target markets. Then they should revise messages and media strategy to fit. The diffusion model helps guide marketers in developing and implementing promotion strategy.

LO 5 Product Life Cycles

The **product life cycle (PLC)** is one of the most familiar concepts in marketing. Few other general concepts have been so widely discussed. Although some researchers and consultants have challenged the theoretical basis and managerial value of the PLC, many believe it is a useful marketing management diagnostic tool and a general guide for marketing planning in various "life-cycle" stages.[30]

The product life cycle is a biological metaphor that traces the stages of a product's acceptance, from its introduction (birth) to its decline (death). As Exhibit 11.2 shows, a product progresses through four major stages: introduction, growth, maturity, and decline.

The PLC concept can be used to analyze a brand, a product form, or a product category. The PLC for a product form is usually longer than the PLC for

EXHIBIT 11.2
Four Stages of the Product Life Cycle

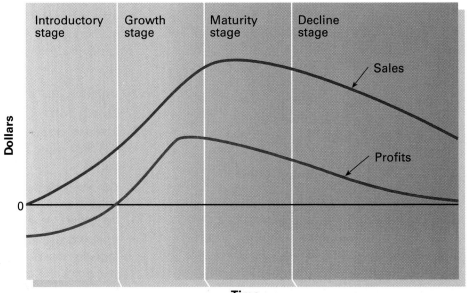

any one brand. The exception would be a brand that was the first and last competitor in a product form market. In that situation, the brand and product form life cycles would be equal in length. Product categories have the longest life cycles. A **product category** includes all brands that satisfy a particular type of need such as shaving products, passenger automobiles, or soft drinks.

EXHIBIT 11.3
Product Life Cycles for Styles, Fashions, and Fads

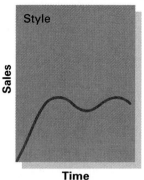

Style — Sales / Time

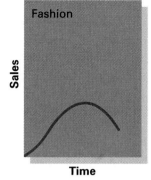

Fashion — Sales / Time

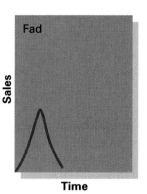

Fad — Sales / Time

The time a product spends in any one stage of the life cycle may vary dramatically. Some products, such as fad items, move through the entire cycle in weeks. Others, such as electric clothes washers and dryers, stay in the maturity stage for decades. Exhibit 11.2 illustrates the typical life cycle for a consumer durable good, such as a washer or dryer. In contrast, Exhibit 11.3 illustrates typical life cycles for styles (such as formal, business, or casual clothing), fashions (such as miniskirts or baggy jeans), and fads (such as leopard-print clothing). Changes in a product, its uses, its image, or its positioning can extend that product's life cycle.

The PLC concept does not tell managers the length of a product's life cycle or its duration in any stage. It does not dictate marketing strategy. It is simply a tool to help marketers forecast future events and suggest appropriate strategies.

Introductory Stage

The **introductory stage** of the PLC represents the full-scale launch of a new product into the marketplace. Computer databases for personal use, room-deodorizing air-conditioning filters, and wind-powered home electric generators are all product categories that have recently entered the product life cycle. A high failure rate, little competition, frequent product modification, and limited distribution typify the introductory stage of the PLC.

Marketing costs in the introductory stage are normally high for several reasons. High dealer margins are often needed to obtain adequate distribution, and incentives are needed to get consumers to try the new product. Advertising expenses are high because of the need to educate consumers about the new product's benefits. Production costs are also often high in this stage, as product and manufacturing flaws are identified and corrected and efforts are undertaken to develop mass-production economies.

Sales normally increase slowly during the introductory stage. Moreover, profits are usually negative because of R&D costs, factory tooling, and high introduction costs. The length of the introductory phase is largely determined by product characteristics, such as the product's advantages over substitute products, the educational effort required to make the product known, and management's commitment of resources to the new item. A short introductory period is usually preferred to help reduce the impact of negative earnings and cash flows. As soon as the product gets off the ground, the financial burden should begin to diminish. Also, a short introduction helps dispel some of the uncertainty as to whether the new product will be successful.

Promotion strategy in the introductory stage focuses on developing product awareness and informing consumers about the product category's potential benefits. At this stage, the communication challenge is to stimulate primary demand—demand for the product in general rather than for a specific brand. Intensive personal selling is often required to gain acceptance for the product among wholesalers and retailers. Promotion of convenience products often requires heavy consumer sampling and couponing. Shopping and specialty products demand educational advertising and personal selling to the final consumer.

Growth Stage

If a product category survives the introductory stage, it advances to the **growth stage** of the life cycle. In this stage, sales typically grow at an increasing rate, many competitors enter the market, and large companies may start to acquire small pioneering firms.

product category all brands that satisfy a particular type of need

introductory stage the full-scale launch of a new product into the marketplace

growth stage the second stage of the product life cycle when sales typically grow at an increasing rate, many competitors enter the market, large companies may start to acquire small pioneering firms, and profits are healthy

Profits rise rapidly in the growth stage, reach their peak, and begin declining as competition intensifies. Emphasis switches from primary demand promotion (e.g., promoting personal digital assistants, or PDAs) to aggressive brand advertising and communication of the differences between brands (e.g., promoting Casio versus Palm and Visor).

Distribution becomes a major key to success during the growth stage, as well as in later stages. Manufacturers scramble to sign up dealers and distributors and to build long-term relationships. Without adequate distribution, it is impossible to establish a strong market position.

Maturity Stage

A period during which sales increase at a decreasing rate signals the beginning of the **maturity stage** of the life cycle. New users cannot be added indefinitely, and sooner or later the market approaches saturation. Normally, this is the longest stage of the product life cycle. Many major household appliances are in the maturity stage of their life cycles.

For shopping products such as durable goods and electronics, and many specialty products, annual models begin to appear during the maturity stage. Product lines are lengthened to appeal to additional market segments. Service and repair assume more important roles as manufacturers strive to distinguish their products from others. Product design changes tend to become stylistic (How can the product be made different?) rather than functional (How can the product be made better?).

As prices and profits continue to fall, marginal competitors start dropping out of the market. Dealer margins also shrink, resulting in less shelf space for mature items, lower dealer inventories, and a general reluctance to promote the product. Thus, promotion to dealers often intensifies during this stage in order to retain loyalty.

Heavy consumer promotion by the manufacturer is also required to maintain market share. Cut-throat competition during this stage can lead to price wars. Another characteristic of the maturity stage is the emergence of "niche marketers" that target narrow, well-defined, underserved segments of a market. Starbucks Coffee targets its gourmet line at the only segment of the coffee market that is growing: new, younger, more affluent coffee drinkers.

Decline Stage

A long-run drop in sales signals the beginning of the **decline stage**. The rate of decline is governed by how rapidly consumer tastes change or substitute products are adopted. Many convenience products and fad items lose their market overnight, leaving large inventories of unsold items, such as designer jeans. Others die more slowly. According to a report from the International Federation of the Phonographic Industry, CD sales in the United States fell by 14 percent in 2007. They have fallen 30 percent worldwide in the past three years.[31] It appears that the popularity of iTunes and other digital download options are rapidly making CDs obsolete.

Some firms have developed successful strategies for marketing products in the decline stage of the product life cycle. They eliminate all nonessential marketing expenses and let sales decline as more and more customers discontinue purchasing the products. Eventually, the product is withdrawn from the market.

Some firms practice what management sage Peter Drucker has called "organized abandonment," which is based upon a periodic audit of all goods and services that a firm markets. One key question is, if we weren't already marketing the product, would we be willing to introduce it now? If the answer is "no," the product should be carefully considered as a candidate for elimination from the product mix.[32]

Implications for Marketing Management

The product life cycle concept encourages marketing managers to plan so that they can take the initiative instead of reacting to past events. The PLC is especially useful as a predicting or forecasting tool. Because products pass through distinctive stages, it is often possible to estimate a product's location on the

EXHIBIT 11.4
Relationships between the Diffusion Process and the Product Life Cycle

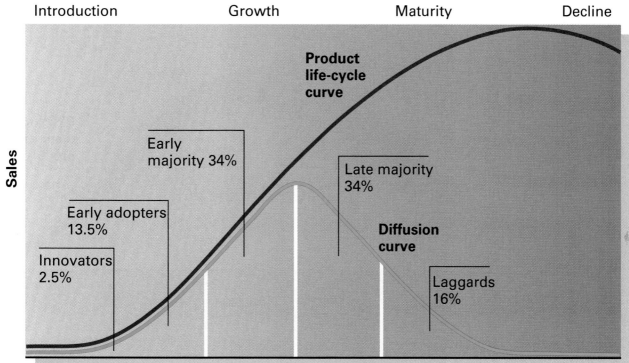

Product life-cycle curve: Time
Diffusion curve: Percentage of total adoptions by category

curve using historical data. Profits, like sales, tend to follow a predictable path over a product's life cycle.

Exhibit 11.4 shows the relationship between the adopter categories and stages of the PLC. Note that the various categories of adopters first buy products in different stages of the life cycle. Almost all sales in the maturity and decline stages represent repeat purchasing.

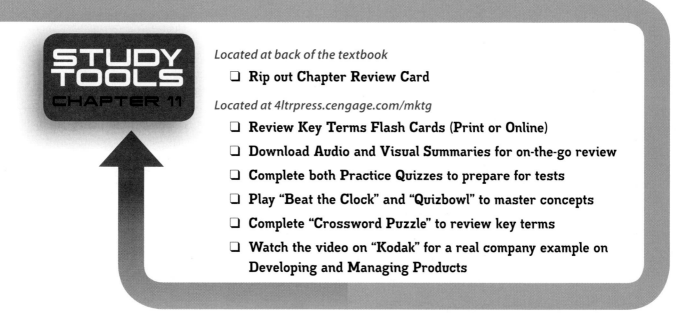

STUDY TOOLS CHAPTER 11

Located at back of the textbook
- ❏ **Rip out Chapter Review Card**

Located at 4ltrpress.cengage.com/mktg
- ❏ **Review Key Terms Flash Cards (Print or Online)**
- ❏ **Download Audio and Visual Summaries for on-the-go review**
- ❏ **Complete both Practice Quizzes to prepare for tests**
- ❏ **Play "Beat the Clock" and "Quizbowl" to master concepts**
- ❏ **Complete "Crossword Puzzle" to review key terms**
- ❏ **Watch the video on "Kodak" for a real company example on Developing and Managing Products**

A PRODUCT LIFE CYCLE: VCR

VCR sales dropped rapidly in the face of growing DVD competition.

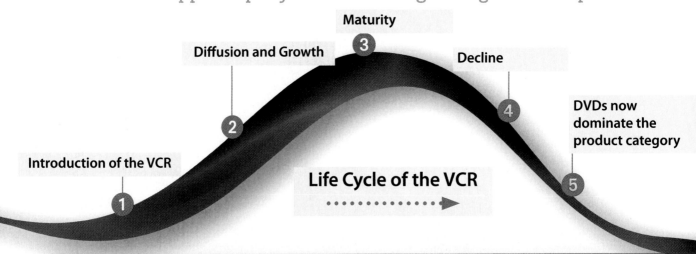

Maturity ③

Diffusion and Growth ②

Decline ④

DVDs now dominate the product category ⑤

Introduction of the VCR ①

Life Cycle of the VCR ⋯⋯⋯⋯⋯▶

1977 VHS first sold in the United States

1992 100 millionth VCR sold

1997 First DVD titles released in the United States

2000 VCR sales peak at 23 million units

2001 DVD dollar sales surpass VHS sales

2006 More households own DVD players than VCRs

☐ 525/60   PCM 1, 2   ☐ STEREO   ☐ MON
☐ 625/50   PCM 3, 4   ☐ STEREO   ☐ MON

"Overall, I enjoy the textbook and feel that **you have made it as easy as possible to succeed in this course by providing numerous study aids online.**"

– Ben Larkins, Student at Middle Tennessee State University

GET ONLINE

HE DID

Discover your **MKTG4** online experience at **4ltrpress.cengage.com**.

You'll find everything you need to succeed in your class.

- Interactive Quizzes
- PowerPoint® Slides
- Printable Flash Cards
- Podcasts
- Videos
- Animated Flash Games and Quizzes
- And more

4ltrpress.cengage.com

CHAPTER **12** | Services and Nonprofit Organization Marketing

" [The service sector] will be responsible for more than half of all new job growth through the year 2016."

LO The Importance of Services

AFTER YOU FINISH THIS CHAPTER GO TO PAGE 194 FOR STUDY TOOLS

A **service** is the result of applying human or mechanical efforts to people or objects. Services involve a deed, a performance, or an effort that cannot be physically possessed. Today, the service sector substantially influences the U.S. economy, and according to the Bureau of Labor Statistics, will be responsible for more than half of all new job growth through the year 2016.[1] The demand for services is expected to continue. Much of this demand results from demographics. An aging population will need nurses, home health care workers, physical therapists, and social workers. Demand for information managers, such as computer engineers and systems analysts, will also increase. There is also a growing market for service companies worldwide.

> **service** the result of applying human or mechanical efforts to people or objects

The marketing process described in Chapter 1 is the same for all types of products, whether they are goods or services. In addition, although a comparison of goods and services marketing can be beneficial, in reality it is hard to distinguish clearly between manufacturing and service firms. Indeed, many manufacturing firms can point to service as a major factor in their success. For example, maintenance and repair services offered by the manufacturer are important to buyers of copy machines. Nevertheless, services have some unique characteristics that distinguish them from goods, and marketing strategies need to be adjusted for these characteristics.

What do you think?

Most jobs have something to do with service.

| 1 | 2 | 3 | 4 | 5 | 6 | 7 |

STRONGLY DISAGREE   STRONGLY AGREE

How Services Differ from Goods

intangibility the inability of services to be touched, seen, tasted, heard, or felt in the same manner that goods can be sensed

search quality a characteristic that can be easily assessed before purchase

experience quality a characteristic that can be assessed only after use

credence quality a characteristic that consumers may have difficulty assessing even after purchase because they do not have the necessary knowledge or experience

inseparability the inability of the production and consumption of a service to be separated; consumers must be present during the production

heterogeneity the variability of the inputs and outputs of services, which causes services to tend to be less standardized and uniform than goods

perishability the inability of services to be stored, warehoused, or inventoried

Services have four unique characteristics that distinguish them from goods. Services are intangible, inseparable, heterogeneous, and perishable.

Intangibility

The basic difference between services and goods is that services are intangible performances. Because of their **intangibility**, they cannot be touched, seen, tasted, heard, or felt in the same manner that goods can be sensed.

Evaluating the quality of services before or even after making a purchase is harder than evaluating the quality of goods because, compared to goods, services tend to exhibit fewer search qualities. A **search quality** is a characteristic that can be easily assessed before purchase—for instance, the color of an appliance or automobile. At the same time, services tend to exhibit more experience and credence qualities. An **experience quality** is a characteristic that can be assessed only after use, such as the quality of a meal in a restaurant. A **credence quality** is a characteristic that consumers may have difficulty assessing even after purchase because they do not have the necessary knowledge or experience. Medical and consulting services are examples of services that exhibit credence qualities.

These characteristics also make it harder for marketers to communicate the benefits of an intangible service than to communicate the benefits of tangible goods. Thus, marketers often rely on tangible cues to communicate a service's nature and quality. For example, Travelers' Insurance Company uses an umbrella symbol as a tangible reminder of the protection that insurance provides.

The facilities that customers visit, or from which services are delivered, are a critical tangible part of the total service offering. Messages about the organization are communicated to customers through such elements as the decor, the clutter or neatness of service areas, and the staff's manners and dress.

Inseparability

Goods are produced, sold, and then consumed. In contrast, services are often sold, produced, and consumed at the same time. In other words, their production and consumption are inseparable activities. This **inseparability** means that, because consumers must be present during the production of services like haircuts or surgery, they are actually involved in the production of the services they buy. That type of consumer involvement is rare in goods manufacturing.

Simultaneous production and consumption also means that services normally cannot be produced in a centralized location and consumed in decentralized locations, as goods typically are. Services are also inseparable from the perspective of the service provider. Thus, the quality of service that firms are able to deliver depends on the quality of their employees.

Heterogeneity

One great strength of McDonald's is consistency. Whether customers order a Big Mac in Chicago or Seattle, they know exactly what they are going to get. This is not the case with many service providers. Because services have greater **heterogeneity** or variability of inputs and outputs, they tend to be less standardized and uniform than goods. For example, physicians in a group practice or barbers in a barber shop differ within each group in their technical and interpersonal skills. Because services tend to be labor-intensive and production and consumption are inseparable, consistency and quality control can be hard to achieve.

Standardization and training help increase consistency and reliability. Every morning, the staff of the Ritz-Carlton hotels meets for a daily "Lineup," during which an inspirational quote is read aloud, people are introduced to each other, and an employee recites one of the company's twelve service values. This ritual occurs at the beginning of each shift in every department for all 32,000 employees at the company's seventy hotels.[2]

Perishability

The fourth characteristic of services is their **perishability**, which means that they cannot be stored, warehoused, or inventoried. An empty hotel room or airplane seat produces no revenue that day. The revenue is lost. Yet service organizations are often forced to turn away full-price customers during peak periods.

AN EMPTY HOTEL ROOM PRODUCES NO REVENUE.

© ISTOCKPHOTO.COM/TERRY J. ALCORN

One of the most important challenges in many service industries is finding ways to synchronize supply and demand. The philosophy that some revenue is better than none has prompted many hotels to offer deep discounts on weekends and during the off-season.

LO3 Service Quality

Because of the four unique characteristics of services, service quality is more difficult to define and measure than is the quality of tangible goods. Business executives rank the improvement of service quality as one of the most critical challenges facing them today.

Research has shown that customers evaluate service quality by the following five components:[3]

- **Reliability:** the ability to perform the service dependably, accurately, and consistently. Reliability is performing the service right the first time. This component has been found to be the one most important to consumers.

- **Responsiveness:** the ability to provide prompt service. Examples of responsiveness include calling the customer back quickly, serving lunch fast to someone who is in a hurry, or mailing a transaction slip immediately. The ultimate in responsiveness is offering service twenty-four hours a day, seven days a week.

- **Assurance:** the knowledge and courtesy of employees and their ability to convey trust. Skilled employees who treat customers with respect and make customers feel that they can trust the firm exemplify assurance.

- **Empathy:** caring, individualized attention to customers. Firms whose employees recognize customers and learn their specific requirements are providing empathy.

- **Tangibles:** the physical evidence of the service. The tangible parts of a service include the physical facilities, tools, and equipment used to provide the service, and the appearance of personnel.

Overall service quality is measured by combining customers' evaluations for all five components.

reliability the ability to perform a service dependably, accurately, and consistently

responsiveness the ability to provide prompt service

assurance the knowledge and courtesy of employees and their ability to convey trust

empathy caring, individualized attention to customers

tangibles the physical evidence of a service, including the physical facilities, tools, and equipment used to provide the service

gap model a model identifying five gaps that can cause problems in service delivery and influence customer evaluations of service quality

The Gap Model of Service Quality

A model of service quality called the **gap model** identifies five gaps that can cause problems in service delivery and influence customer evaluations of service quality.[4] These gaps are illustrated in Exhibit 12.1:

- *Gap 1:* the gap between what customers want and what management thinks customers want. This gap results from a lack of understanding or a misinterpretation of the customers' needs, wants, or desires. A firm that does little or no customer satisfaction research is likely to experience this gap. To close gap 1, firms must stay attuned to customer wishes by doing research on customer needs and satisfaction.

- *Gap 2:* the gap between what management thinks customers want and the quality specifications that management develops to provide the service. Essentially, this gap is the result of management's inability to translate customers' needs into delivery systems within the firm. For example, when KFC once rated its managers' success according to "chicken efficiency," or how much chicken they threw away at closing, consumers who came in late would either have to wait for chicken to be cooked or settle for chicken several hours old.

- *Gap 3:* the gap between the service quality specifications and the service that is actually provided. If both gaps 1 and 2 have been closed, then gap 3 is due to the inability of management and employees to do what should be done. Management needs to ensure that employees have the skills and the proper tools to perform their jobs. Other techniques that help to close gap 3 are training employees so they know what management expects and encouraging teamwork.

EXHIBIT 12.1
Gap Model of Service Quality

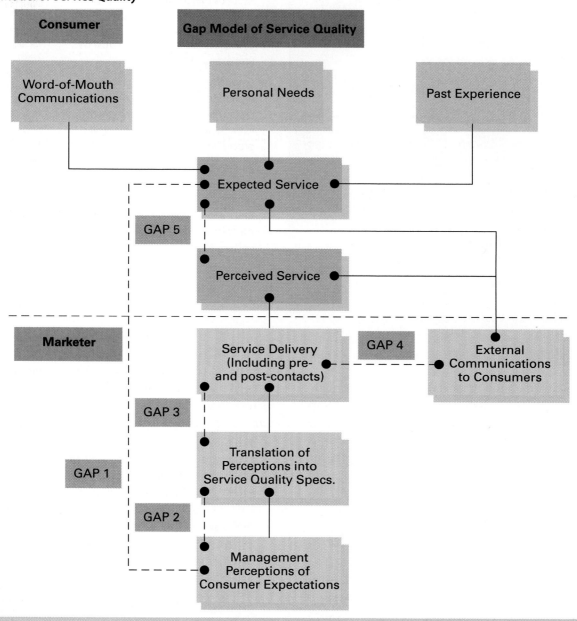

The gap analysis model measures consumer perceptions of service quality. Managers use the model to analyze sources of quality problems and to understand how service quality can be improved.

▶▶ *Gap 4*: the gap between what the company provides and what the customer is told it provides. This is clearly a communication gap. It may include misleading or deceptive advertising campaigns promising more than the firm can deliver or doing "whatever it takes" to get the business. To close this gap, companies need to create realistic customer expectations through honest, accurate communication about what the firms can provide.

▶▶ *Gap 5*: the gap between the service that customers receive and the service they want. This gap can be positive or negative. For example, if a patient expects to wait twenty minutes in the physician's office before seeing the physician but waits only ten minutes, the patient's evaluation of service quality will be high. However, a forty-minute wait would result in a lower evaluation.

When one or more of these gaps is large, service quality is perceived as low. As the gaps shrink, service quality perception improves.

LO4 Marketing Mixes for Services

Services' unique characteristics—intangibility, inseparability of production and consumption, heterogeneity, and perishability—make marketing more challenging. Elements of the marketing mix (product, place, promotion, and pricing) need to be adjusted to meet the special needs created by these characteristics.

Product (Service) Strategy

A product, as defined in Chapter 10, is everything a person receives in an exchange. In the case of a service organization, the product offering is intangible and consists in large part of a process or a series of processes. Product strategies for service offerings include decisions on the type of process involved, core and supplementary services, standardization or customization of the service product, and the service mix.

Service as a Process Two broad categories of things get processed in service organizations: people and objects. In some cases, the process is physical, or tangible, while in others the process is intangible. Based on these characteristics, service processes can be placed into one of four categories:[5]

▸▸ *People processing* takes place when the service is directed at a customer. Examples are transportation services and health care.

▸▸ *Possession processing* occurs when the service is directed at customers' physical possessions. Examples are lawn care, dry cleaning, and veterinary services.

▸▸ *Mental stimulus* processing refers to services directed at people's minds. Examples are theater performances and education.

▸▸ *Information processing* describes services that use technology or brainpower directed at a customer's assets. Examples are insurance and consulting.

Because customers' experiences and involvement differ for each of these types of services, marketing strategies may also differ. For example, people-processing services require customers to enter the *service factory*, which is a physical location, such as an aircraft, a physician's office, or a hair salon. In contrast, possession-processing services typically do not require the presence of the customer in the service factory. Marketing strategies for the former would therefore focus more on an attractive, comfortable physical environment and employee training on employee-customer interaction issues than would strategies for the latter.

Core and Supplementary Service Products The service offering can be viewed as a bundle of activities that includes the **core service**, which is the most basic benefit the customer is buying, and a group of **supplementary services** that support or enhance the core service. Exhibit 12.2 illustrates these concepts for an overnight stay at a luxury hotel. The core service is overnight rental of a bedroom, which involves people processing. The supplementary services, some of which involve information processing, include reservations, check-ins and check-outs, room service, and meals.

In many service industries, the core service becomes a commodity as competition increases. Thus, firms usually emphasize supplementary services to create a competitive advantage. On the other hand, some firms are positioning themselves in the marketplace by greatly reducing supplementary services.

Customization/Standardization An important issue in developing the service offering is whether to customize or standardize it. Customized services are more flexible and respond to individual customers' needs. They also usually command a higher price. Standardized services are more efficient and cost less.

> **core service** the most basic benefit the consumer is buying
>
> **supplementary services** a group of services that support or enhance the core service

© ISTOCKPHOTO.COM/AUKE HOLWERDA

EXHIBIT 12.2
Core and Supplementary Services for a Luxury Hotel

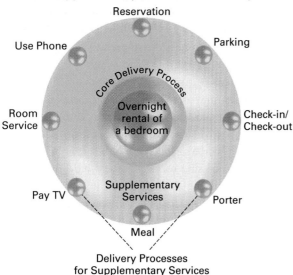

Reservation

Use Phone

Parking

Core Delivery Process

Overnight rental of a bedroom

Room Service

Check-in/ Check-out

Pay TV

Supplementary Services

Porter

Meal

Delivery Processes for Supplementary Services

SOURCE: Lovelock, Christopher H.; Wirtz, Jochen, *Services Marketing*, 6th, ©2007. Electronically reproduced by permission of Pearson Education, Inc., Upper Saddle River, New Jersey.

mass customization a strategy that uses technology to deliver customized services on a mass basis

Instead of choosing to either standardize or customize a service, a firm may incorporate elements of both by adopting an emerging strategy called **mass customization**. Mass customization uses technology to deliver customized services on a mass basis, which results in giving each customer whatever she or he asks for. For example, the Lands' End Web site offers women advice on which swimsuits will flatter their shapes and encourages them to mix and match more than 216 combinations of colors and styles.[6]

The Service Mix Most service organizations market more than one service. For example, TruGreen offers lawn care, shrub care, carpet cleaning, and industrial lawn services. Each organization's service mix represents a set of opportunities, risks, and challenges. Each part of the service mix should make a different contribution to achieving the firm's goals. To succeed, each service may also need a different level of financial support. Designing a service strategy therefore means deciding what new services to introduce to which target market, what existing services to maintain, and what services to eliminate.

Place (Distribution) Strategy

Distribution strategies for service organizations must focus on such issues as convenience, number of outlets, direct versus indirect distribution, location, and scheduling. A key factor influencing the selection of a service provider is *convenience*. For example, infirm or elderly patients would probably prefer to use a doctor who makes house calls.

An important distribution objective for many service firms is the number of outlets to use or the *number of outlets* to open during a certain time. Generally, the intensity of distribution should meet, but not exceed, the target market's needs and preferences. Having too few outlets may inconvenience customers; having too many outlets may boost costs unnecessarily. Intensity of distribution may also depend on the image desired. Having only a few outlets may make the service seem more exclusive or selective.

The next service distribution decision is whether to distribute services to end users *directly* or *indirectly* through other firms. Because of the intangible nature of services, many service firms have to use direct distribution or franchising. Examples include legal, medical, accounting, and personal-care services. The newest form of direct distribution is the Internet. Most major airlines are now using online services to sell tickets directly to consumers, which results in lower distribution costs for the airlines. Other firms with standardized service packages have developed indirect channels using independent intermediaries. For example, Bank of America offers teller and loan services to customers in small satellite facilities at Albertsons grocery stores in Texas.

The *location* of a service most clearly reveals the relationship between its target market strategy and distribution strategy. For time-dependent service providers such as airlines, physicians, and dentists, *scheduling* is often a more important factor.

Promotion Strategy

Consumers and business users have more trouble evaluating services than goods because services are less tangible. In turn, marketers have more trouble promoting intangible services than tangible goods. Here are four promotion strategies they can try:

▸ *Stressing tangible cues:* A tangible cue is a concrete symbol of the service offering. To make their intangible services more tangible, hotels turn down the bedcovers and put mints on the pillows. DoubleTree hotels offer their guests a warm chocolate chip cookie as they check in.

▸ *Using personal information sources:* A personal information source is someone consumers are familiar with (such as a celebrity) or someone they admire or can relate to personally. Service firms may seek to simulate positive word-of-mouth communication among present and prospective customers by using real customers in their ads.

- *Creating a strong organizational image*: One way to create an image is to manage the evidence, including the physical environment of the service facility, the appearance of the service employees, and the tangible items associated with a service (such as stationery, bills, and business cards). For example, McDonald's Golden Arches are instantly recognizable. Another way to create an image is through branding.
- *Engaging in postpurchase communication*: Postpurchase communication refers to the follow-up activities that a service firm might engage in after a customer transaction. Postcard surveys, telephone calls, and other types of follow-up show customers that their feedback matters.

Many Web sites use cookies to build relationships with returning customers. (A cookie is a small file that gets stored on your computer every time you visit a Web site.) For example, every time "Abi" visits a particular Web site, the site looks on her computer for its cookie. The site can then "recognize" her as a returning customer.

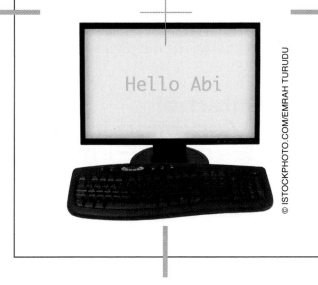

© ISTOCKPHOTO.COM/EMRAH TURUDU

Price Strategy

Considerations in pricing a service are similar to the pricing considerations to be discussed in Chapters 19 and 20. However, the unique characteristics of services present two special pricing challenges.

First, in order to price a service, it is important to define the unit of service consumption. For example, should pricing be based on completing a specific service task (cutting a customer's hair), or should it be time based (how long it takes to cut a customer's hair)? Some services include the consumption of goods, such as food and beverages. Restaurants charge customers for food and drink rather than the use of a table and chairs.

Second, for services that are composed of multiple elements, the issue is whether pricing should be based on a "bundle" of elements or whether each element should be priced separately. A bundled price may be preferable when consumers dislike having to pay "extra" for every part of the service (e.g., paying extra for baggage or food on an airplane), and it is simpler for the firm to administer. Alternatively, customers may not want to pay for service elements they do not use. Many furniture stores now have "unbundled" delivery charges from the price of the furniture. Customers who wish to can pick up the furniture at the store, saving on the delivery fee.

Marketers should set performance objectives when pricing each service. Three categories of pricing objectives have been suggested:[7]

- *Revenue-oriented pricing* focuses on maximizing the surplus of income over costs. A limitation of this approach is that determining costs can be difficult for many services.
- *Operations-oriented pricing* seeks to match supply and demand by varying prices. For example, matching hotel demand to the number of available rooms can be achieved by raising prices at peak times and decreasing them during slow times.
- *Patronage-oriented pricing* tries to maximize the number of customers using the service. Thus, prices vary with different market segments' ability to pay, and methods of payment (such as credit) are offered that increase the likelihood of a purchase.

A firm may need to use more than one type of pricing objective. In fact, all three objectives probably need to be included to some degree in a pricing strategy, although the importance of each type may vary depending on the type of service provided, the prices that competitors are charging, the differing ability of various customer segments to pay, or the opportunity to negotiate price. For customized services (such as construction services), customers may also have the ability to negotiate a price.

LO 5 Relationship Marketing in Services

Many services involve ongoing interaction between the service organization and the customer. Thus, they can

internal marketing treating employees as customers and developing systems and benefits that satisfy their needs

benefit from relationship marketing, the strategy described in Chapter 1, as a means of attracting, developing, and retaining customer relationships. The idea is to develop strong loyalty by creating satisfied customers who will buy additional services from the firm and are unlikely to switch to a competitor. Satisfied customers are also likely to engage in positive word-of-mouth communication, thereby helping to bring in new customers.

Many businesses have found that it is more cost-effective to hang on to the customers they have than to focus only on attracting new ones. A bank executive, for example, found that increasing customer retention by 2 percent can have the same effect on profits as reducing costs by 10 percent.

Services that purchasers receive on a continuing basis (e.g., cable television, banking, insurance) can be considered membership services. This type of service naturally lends itself to relationship marketing. When services involve discrete transactions (e.g., in a movie theater, at a restaurant, or on public transportation), it may be more difficult to build membership-type relationships with customers. Nevertheless, services involving discrete transactions may be transformed into membership relationships using marketing tools. For example, the service could be sold in bulk (e.g., a theater series subscription or a commuter pass on public transportation). Or a service firm could offer special benefits to customers who choose to register with the firm (e.g., loyalty programs for hotels and airlines). The service firm that has a more formalized relationship with its customers has an advantage because it knows who its customers are and how and when they use the services offered.[8]

Relationship marketing can be practiced at three levels:[9]

▶▶ *Level 1*: The firm uses pricing incentives to encourage customers to continue doing business with it. Frequent flyer programs are an example of level 1 relationship marketing. This level of relationship marketing is the least effective in the long term because its price-based advantage is easily imitated by other firms.

▶▶ *Level 2*: This level of relationship marketing also uses pricing incentives but seeks to build social bonds with customers. The firm stays in touch with customers, learns about their needs, and designs services to meet those needs. Level 2 relationship marketing is often more effective than level 1 relationship marketing.

© TIM BOYLE/GETTY IMAGES

▶▶ *Level 3*: At this level, the firm again uses financial and social bonds but adds structural bonds to the formula. Structural bonds are developed by offering value-added services that are not readily available from other firms. Hertz's #1 Club Gold program allows members to call and reserve a car, board a courtesy bus at the airport, tell the driver their name, and get dropped off in front of their car. Marketing programs like this one have the strongest potential for sustaining long-term relationships with customers.

LO 6 Internal Marketing in Service Firms

Services are performances, so the quality of a firm's employees is an important part of building long-term relationships with customers. Employees who like their jobs and are satisfied with the firm they work for are more likely to deliver superior service to customers. In other words, a firm that makes its employees happy has a better chance of retaining customers. Thus, it is critical that service firms practice **internal marketing**, which means treating employees as customers and developing systems and benefits that satisfy their needs. To satisfy employees, companies have designed and instituted a wide variety of programs such as flextime, on-site daycare, and concierge services. Starbucks claims to be in the people business rather than the coffee business and prides itself on its stellar customer service. Its top executives believe that the key to great service is to create an environment of respect and appreciation for all employees.[10] Travelocity keeps its employees engaged in their work by sending them weekly e-mails and hosting a monthly lunch where employees can express their concerns.[11]

LO 7 Global Issues in Services Marketing

The international marketing of services is a major part of global business, and the United States has become the world's largest exporter of services. Competition in international services is increasing rapidly, however. To be successful in the global marketplace, service firms must first determine the nature of their core product. Then the marketing mix elements (additional services, place, promotion, pricing, distribution) should be designed to take into account each country's cultural, technological, and political environment.

Because of their competitive advantages, many U.S. service industries have been able to enter the global marketplace. U.S. banks, for example, have advantages in customer service and collections management.

LO 8 Nonprofit Organization Marketing

A **nonprofit organization** is an organization that exists to achieve some goal other than the usual business goals of profit, market share, or return on investment. Both nonprofit organizations and private-sector service firms market intangible products and both often require the customer to be present during the production process. Both for-profit and nonprofit services

vary greatly from producer to producer and from day to day, even from the same producer.

Few people realize that nonprofit organizations account for more than 20 percent of the economic activity in the United States. The cost of government (i.e., taxes), the predominant form of nonprofit organization, has become the biggest single item in the American family budget—more than housing, food, or health care. Together, federal, state, and local governments collect tax revenues that amount to more than a third of the U.S. gross domestic product. In addition to government entities, nonprofit organizations include hundreds of thousands of private museums, theaters, schools, and churches.

What Is Nonprofit Organization Marketing?

Nonprofit organization marketing is the effort by nonprofit organizations to bring about mutually satisfying exchanges with target markets. Although these organizations vary substantially in size and purpose and operate in different environments, most perform the following marketing activities:

▸▸ Identify the customers they wish to serve or attract (although they usually use another term, such as *clients*, *patients*, *members*, or *sponsors*)

▸▸ Explicitly or implicitly specify objectives

▸▸ Develop, manage, and eliminate programs and services

▸▸ Decide on prices to charge (although they use other terms, such as *fees*, *donations*, *tuition*, *fares*, *fines*, or *rates*)

▸▸ Schedule events or programs, and determine where they will be held or where services will be offered

▸▸ Communicate their availability through brochures, signs, public service announcements, or advertisements

Often, the nonprofit organizations that carry out these functions do not realize they are engaged in marketing.

nonprofit organization an organization that exists to achieve some goal other than the usual business goals of profit, market share, or return on investment

nonprofit organization marketing the effort by nonprofit organizations to bring about mutually satisfying exchanges with target markets

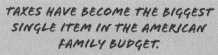

TAXES HAVE BECOME THE BIGGEST SINGLE ITEM IN THE AMERICAN FAMILY BUDGET.

© ISTOCKPHOTO.COM/VALENTIN MOSICHEV / © ISTOCKPHOTO.COM/SEAN MCDERMID

Unique Aspects of Nonprofit Organization Marketing Strategies

Like their counterparts in business organizations, nonprofit managers develop marketing strategies to bring about mutually satisfying exchanges with target markets. However, marketing in nonprofit organizations is unique in many ways—including the setting of marketing objectives, the selection of target markets, and the development of appropriate marketing mixes.

Objectives In the private sector, the profit motive is both an objective for guiding decisions and a criterion for evaluating results. Nonprofit organizations do not seek to make a profit for redistribution to owners or shareholders. Rather, their focus is often on generating enough funds to cover expenses.

Most nonprofit organizations are expected to provide equitable, effective, and efficient services that respond to the wants and preferences of multiple constituencies. These include users, payers, donors, politicians, appointed officials, the media, and the general public. Nonprofit organizations cannot measure their success or failure in strictly financial terms.

The lack of a financial "bottom line" and the existence of multiple, diverse, intangible, and sometimes vague or conflicting objectives make prioritizing objectives, making decisions, and evaluating performance hard for nonprofit managers. They must often use approaches different from the ones commonly used in the private sector.

Target Markets Three issues relating to target markets are unique to nonprofit organizations:

▸ *Apathetic or strongly opposed targets*: Private-sector organizations usually give priority to developing those market segments that are most likely to respond to particular offerings. In contrast, nonprofit organizations must often target those who are apathetic about or strongly opposed to receiving their services, such as vaccinations and psychological counseling.

▸ *Pressure to adopt undifferentiated segmentation strategies*: Nonprofit organizations often adopt undifferentiated strategies (see Chapter 8) by default. Sometimes they fail to recognize the advantages of targeting, or an undifferentiated approach may appear to offer economies of scale and low per-capita costs. In other instances, nonprofit organizations are pressured or required to serve the maximum number of people by targeting the average user.

▸ *Complementary positioning*: The main role of many nonprofit organizations is to provide services, with available resources, to those who are not adequately served by private-sector organizations. As a result, the nonprofit organization must often complement, rather than com-

Product
- Benefit complexity
- Benefit strength
- Involvement

Promotion
- Professional volunteers
- Sales promotion activities
- Public service advertisements

Place
- Special facilities

Price
- Pricing objectives
- Nonfinancial pricing
- Indirect payment
- Separation between payers and users
- Below-cost pricing

pete with, the efforts of others. The positioning task is to identify underserved market segments and to develop marketing programs that match their needs rather than to target the niches that may be most profitable. For example, a university library may see itself as complementing the services of the public library, rather than as competing with it.

Product Decisions There are three product-related distinctions between business and nonprofit organizations:

▸ *Benefit complexity*: Nonprofit organizations often market complex behaviors or ideas. Examples include the need to exercise or eat right, and the need to quit smoking. The benefits that a person receives are complex, long term, and intangible, and therefore are more difficult to communicate to consumers.

▸ *Benefit strength*: The benefit strength of many nonprofit offerings is quite weak or indirect. What are the direct, personal benefits to you of driving 55 miles per hour or donating blood? In contrast, most private-sector service organizations can offer customers direct, personal benefits in an exchange relationship.

▸ *Involvement*: Many nonprofit organizations market products that elicit very low involvement ("Prevent forest fires") or very high involvement ("Stop smoking"). The typical range for private-sector goods is much narrower. Traditional promotional tools may be inadequate to motivate adoption of either low- or high-involvement products.

Place (Distribution) Decisions A nonprofit organization's capacity for distributing its service offerings to potential customer groups when and where they want them is typically a key variable in determining the success of those service offerings. For example, many large universities have one or more satellite campus locations to provide easier access for students in other areas. Some educational institutions also offer classes to students at off-campus locations via interactive video technology or at home via the Internet.

The extent to which a service depends on fixed facilities has important implications for distribution decisions. Services like rail transit and lake fishing can be delivered only at specific points. Many nonprofit services, however, do not depend on special facilities.

Promotion Decisions Many nonprofit organizations are explicitly or implicitly prohibited from advertising, thus limiting their promotion options. Most federal agencies fall into this category. Other nonprofit organizations simply do not have the resources to retain advertising agencies, promotion consultants, or marketing staff. However, nonprofit organizations have a few special promotion resources to call on:

▸▸ *Professional volunteers*: Nonprofit organizations often seek out marketing, sales, and advertising professionals to help them develop and implement promotion strategies. In some instances, an advertising agency donates its services in exchange for potential long-term benefits. Donated services create goodwill, personal contacts, and general awareness of the donor's organization, reputation, and competency.

▸▸ *Sales promotion activities*: Sales promotion activities that make use of existing services or other resources are increasingly being used to draw attention to the offerings of nonprofit organizations. Sometimes nonprofit charities even team up with other companies for promotional activities.

▸▸ *Public service advertising*: A **public service advertisement (PSA)** is an announcement that promotes a program of a federal, state, or local government or of a nonprofit organization. Unlike a commercial advertiser, the sponsor of the PSA does not pay for the time or space. Instead, it is donated by the medium. The Advertising Council's PSAs are some of the most memorable advertisements of all time. For example, Smokey the Bear reminded everyone to be careful not to start forest fires.

Pricing Decisions Five key characteristics distinguish the pricing decisions of nonprofit organizations from those of the profit sector:

▸▸ *Pricing objectives*: The main pricing objective in the profit sector is revenue or, more specifically, profit maxi-

Drunk Driving

Buzzed Driving

Buzzed driving is drunk driving.

mization, sales maximization, or target return on sales or investment. Many nonprofit organizations must also be concerned about revenue. Often, however, nonprofit organizations seek to either partially or fully defray costs rather than to achieve a profit for distribution to stockholders. Nonprofit organizations also seek to redistribute income—for instance, through taxation and sliding-scale fees. Moreover, they strive to allocate resources fairly among individuals or households or across geographic or political boundaries.

▸▸ *Nonfinancial prices*: In many nonprofit situations, consumers are not charged a monetary price but instead must absorb nonmonetary costs. The importance of those costs is illustrated by the large number of eligible citizens who do not take advantage of so-called free services for the poor. In many public assistance programs, about half the people who are eligible don't participate. Nonmonetary costs include time, embarrassment, and effort.

▸▸ *Indirect payment*: Indirect payment through taxes is common to marketers of "free" services, such as libraries, fire protection, and police protection. Indirect payment is not a common practice in the profit sector.

public service advertisement (PSA) an announcement that promotes a program of a federal, state, or local government or of a nonprofit organization

▸▸ *Separation between payers and users*: By design, the services of many charitable organizations are provided for those who are relatively poor and largely paid for by those who are better off financially. Although examples of separation between payers and users can be found in the profit sector (such as insurance claims), the practice is much less prevalent.

▸▸ *Below-cost pricing*: An example of below-cost pricing is university tuition. Virtually all private and public colleges and universities price their services below full cost.

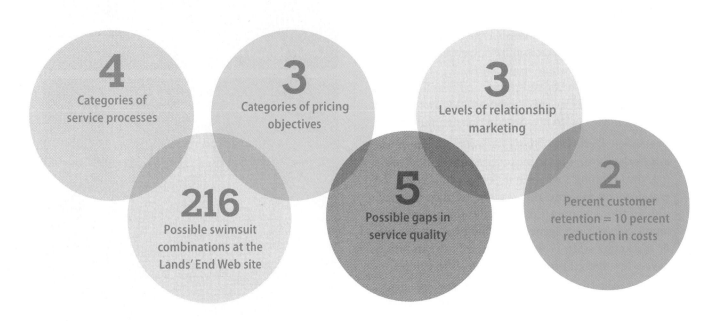

4 Categories of service processes

3 Categories of pricing objectives

3 Levels of relationship marketing

216 Possible swimsuit combinations at the Lands' End Web site

5 Possible gaps in service quality

2 Percent customer retention = 10 percent reduction in costs

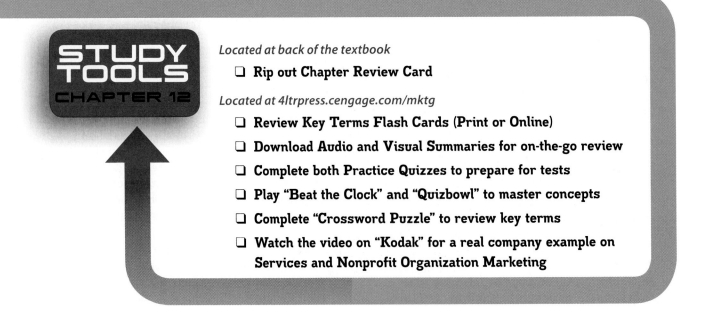

STUDY TOOLS
CHAPTER 12

Located at back of the textbook
❑ **Rip out Chapter Review Card**

Located at 4ltrpress.cengage.com/mktg
❑ **Review Key Terms Flash Cards (Print or Online)**
❑ **Download Audio and Visual Summaries for on-the-go review**
❑ **Complete both Practice Quizzes to prepare for tests**
❑ **Play "Beat the Clock" and "Quizbowl" to master concepts**
❑ **Complete "Crossword Puzzle" to review key terms**
❑ **Watch the video on "Kodak" for a real company example on Services and Nonprofit Organization Marketing**

"The podcasts are the best thing in the world! If one week I don't have enough time to read the chapter for the lesson, it is so easy to listen to it on my way to University on the train, so I can at least have a basic knowledge of that chapter before the lecture, and I can catch up with my reading later. The images in the chapters are engaging, and it makes you feel like you are in the midst of the Marketing World."

– Sandra DeWitt, Student at University of Notre Dame Fremantle, Australia

LISTEN UP!

SHE DID

MKTG4 was designed for students just like you – busy people who want choices, flexibility, and multiple learning options.

MKTG4 delivers concise, focused information in a fresh and contemporary format. And...

MKTG4 gives you a variety of online learning materials designed with you in mind.

At **4ltrpress.cengage.com,** you'll find electronic resources such as **video podcasts, audio downloads,** and **interactive quizzes** for each chapter.

These resources will help supplement your understanding of core marketing concepts in a format that fits your busy lifestyle. Visit **4ltrpress.cengage.com** to learn more about the multiple resources available to help you succeed!

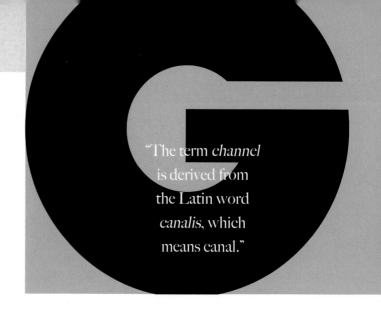

"The term *channel* is derived from the Latin word *canalis*, which means canal."

LO1 Marketing Channels

AFTER YOU FINISH THIS CHAPTER GO TO PAGE 210 FOR STUDY TOOLS

A marketing channel can be viewed as a large canal or pipeline through which products, their ownership, communication, financing and payment, and accompanying risk flow to the consumer. Formally, a **marketing channel** (also called a **channel of distribution**) is a business structure of interdependent organizations that reach from the point of product origin to the consumer with the purpose of moving products to their final consumption destination. Marketing channels facilitate the physical movement of goods through the supply chain, representing "place" or "distribution" in the marketing mix (product, price, promotion, and place) and encompassing the processes involved in getting the right product to the right place at the right time.

Many different types of organizations participate in marketing channels. **Channel members** (also called *intermediaries*, *resellers*, and *middlemen*) negotiate with one another, buy and sell products, and facilitate the change of ownership between buyer and seller

marketing channel (channel of distribution) a set of interdependent organizations that eases the transfer of ownership as products move from producer to business user or consumer

channel members all parties in the marketing channel that negotiate with one another, buy and sell products, and facilitate the change of ownership between buyer and seller in the course of moving the product from the manufacturer into the hands of the final consumer

What do you think?

The way a product gets to me is only important if it isn't working correctly.

| 1 | 2 | 3 | 4 | 5 | 6 | 7 |
STRONGLY DISAGREE STRONGLY AGREE

Find out what others think at 4ltrpress.cengage.com/mktg

in the course of moving the product from the manufacturer into the hands of the final consumer. An important aspect of marketing channels is the joint effort of all channel members to create a continuous and seamless supply chain. The **supply chain** is the connected chain of all of the business entities, both internal and external to the company, that perform or support the marketing channel functions. As products move through the supply chain, channel members facilitate the distribution process by providing specialization and division of labor, overcoming discrepancies, and providing contact efficiency.

Providing Specialization and Division of Labor

According to the concept of *specialization and division of labor*, breaking down a complex task into smaller, simpler ones and allocating them to specialists will create greater efficiency and lower average production costs. Manufacturers achieve economies of scale through the use of efficient equipment capable of producing large quantities of a single product.

Marketing channels can also attain economies of scale through specialization and division of labor by aiding producers who lack the motivation, financing, or expertise to market directly to end users or consumers. In some cases, as with most consumer convenience goods, such as soft drinks, the cost of marketing directly to millions of consumers—taking and shipping individual orders—is prohibitive. For this reason, producers hire channel members, such as wholesalers and retailers, to do what the producers are not equipped to do or what channel members are better prepared to do. Channel members can do some things more efficiently than producers because they have built good relationships with their customers. Therefore, their specialized expertise enhances the overall performance of the channel.

Overcoming Discrepancies

Marketing channels also aid in overcoming discrepancies of quantity, assortment, time, and space created by economies of scale in production. For example, assume that Pillsbury can efficiently produce its Hungry Jack instant pancake mix only at a rate of 5,000 units in a typical day. Not even the most ardent pancake fan could consume that amount in a year, much less in a day. The quantity produced to achieve low unit costs has created a **discrepancy of quantity**, which is the difference between the amount of product produced and the amount an end user wants to buy. By storing the product and distributing it in the appropriate amounts, marketing channels overcome quantity discrepancies by making products available in the quantities that consumers desire.

Mass production creates not only discrepancies of quantity but also discrepancies of assortment. A

CAPTURING A BIGGER SLICE OF THE PIE

In early 2008, Papa John's, a 2,700-unit national pizza restaurant chain, introduced a new marketing and ordering channel where customers order pizza from a cell phone or PDA via text message. From an online account, customers tap in their pizza preference using an abbreviated code. Their order is delivered to a pre-programmed address and paid for with information filed in a database. By keeping a database of customer purchase behavior, customers receive promotions according to past preferences, a result of better customer awareness. Papa John's share has risen to 6.9 percent of the market since implementing the new system, and the company is optimistic that these new channels will allow it to continue to compete strongly with the "big boys" of pizza delivery.

discrepancy of assortment occurs when a consumer does not have all of the items needed to receive full satisfaction from a product. For pancakes to provide maximum satisfaction, several other products are required to complete the assortment. At the very least, most people want a knife, fork, plate, butter, and syrup. Even though Pillsbury is a large consumer-products company, it does not come close to providing the optimal assortment to go with its Hungry Jack pancakes. To overcome discrepancies of assortment, marketing channels assemble in one place many of the products necessary to complete a consumer's needed assortment.

A **temporal discrepancy** is created when a product is produced but a consumer is not ready to buy it. Marketing channels overcome temporal discrepancies by maintaining inventories in anticipation of demand. For example, manufacturers of seasonal merchandise, such as Christmas or Halloween decorations, are in operation all year even though consumer demand is concentrated during certain months of the year.

Furthermore, because mass production requires many potential buyers, markets are usually scattered over large geographic regions, creating a **spatial discrepancy**. Often global, or at least nationwide, markets are needed to absorb the outputs of mass producers. Marketing channels overcome spatial discrepancies by making products available in locations convenient to consumers. For example, if all the Hungry Jack pancake mix is produced in Boise, Idaho, then Pillsbury must use an intermediary to distribute the product to other regions of the United States.

Consider the example illustrated in Exhibit 13.1. Four consumers each want to buy a television set. Without a retail intermediary like Best Buy, television manufacturers JVC, Zenith, Sony, Toshiba, and RCA would each have to make four contacts to reach the four buyers who are in the target market, for a total of twenty transactions. However, when Best Buy acts as an intermediary between the producer and consumers, each producer has to make only one contact, reducing the number of transactions to nine. Each producer sells to one retailer rather than to four consumers. In turn, consumers buy from one retailer instead of from five producers. Information technology has enhanced contact efficiency by making information on products and services easily available over the Internet. Shoppers can find the best bargains without physically searching for them.

LO 2 Channel Intermediaries and Their Functions

Intermediaries in a channel negotiate with one another, facilitate the change of ownership between buyers and sellers, and physically move products

Providing Contact Efficiency

The third need fulfilled by marketing channels is that they provide contact efficiency by reducing the number of stores customers must shop in to complete their purchases. Suppose you had to buy your milk at a dairy and your meat at a stockyard. You would spend a great deal of time, money, and energy just shopping for a few groceries. Supply chains simplify distribution by cutting the number of transactions required to get products from manufacturers to consumers and making an assortment of goods available in one location.

EXHIBIT 13.1
How Marketing Channels Reduce the Number of Required Transactions

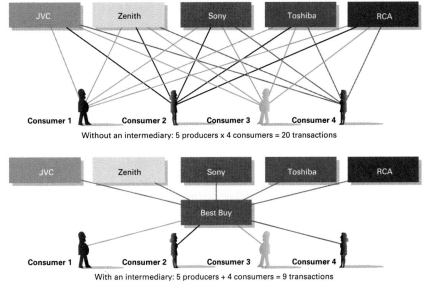

Without an intermediary: 5 producers x 4 consumers = 20 transactions

With an intermediary: 5 producers + 4 consumers = 9 transactions

retailer a channel intermediary that sells mainly to consumers

merchant wholesaler an institution that buys goods from manufacturers and resells them to businesses, government agencies, and other wholesalers or retailers and that receives and takes title to goods, stores them in its own warehouses, and later ships them

agents and brokers wholesaling intermediaries who do not take title to a product but facilitate its sale from producer to end user by representing retailers, wholesalers, or manufacturers

logistics the efficient and cost-effective forward and reverse flow as well as storage of goods, services, and related information, into, through, and out of channel member companies

from the manufacturer to the final consumer. The most prominent difference separating intermediaries is whether they take title to the product. *Taking title* means they own the merchandise and control the terms of the sale—for example, price and delivery date. Retailers and merchant wholesalers are examples of intermediaries that take title to products in the marketing channel and resell them. **Retailers** are firms that sell mainly to consumers. Retailers will be discussed in more detail in Chapter 15.

Merchant wholesalers are organizations that facilitate the movement of products and services from the manufacturer to producers, resellers, governments, institutions, and retailers. All merchant wholesalers take title to the goods they sell, and most of them operate one or more warehouses where they receive goods, store them, and later reship them. Customers are mostly small- or medium-sized retailers, but merchant wholesalers also market to manufacturers and institutional clients.

Other intermediaries do not take title to goods and services they market but do facilitate the exchange of ownership between sellers and buyers. **Agents and brokers** simply facilitate the sale of a product from producer to end user by representing retailers, wholesalers, or manufacturers. Title reflects ownership, and ownership usually implies control. Unlike wholesalers, agents or brokers only facilitate sales and generally have little input into the terms of the sale. They do, however, get a fee or commission based on sales volume. For example, when selling a home, the owner usually hires a real estate agent who then brings potential buyers to see the house. The agent facilitates the sale by bringing the buyer and owner together, but never actually takes ownership of the home.

Variations in channel structures are due in large part to variations in the numbers and types of wholesaling intermediaries. Generally, product characteristics, buyer considerations, and market conditions determine the type of intermediary the manufacturer should use.

» *Product characteristics* that may require a certain type of wholesaling intermediary include whether the product is standardized or customized, the complexity of the product, and the gross margin of the product. For example, a customized product such as insurance is sold through an insurance agent or broker who may represent one or multiple companies. In contrast, a standardized product such as gum is sold through a merchant wholesaler that takes possession of the gum and reships it to the appropriate retailers.

» *Buyer considerations* affecting the wholesaler choice include how often the product is purchased and how long the buyer is willing to wait to receive the product. For example, at the beginning of the school term, a student may be willing to wait a few days for a textbook to get a lower price by ordering online. Thus, this type of product can be distributed directly. But, if the student waits to buy the book until right before an exam and needs the book immediately, it will have to be purchased at the school bookstore.

» *Market characteristics* determining the wholesaler type include how many buyers are in the market and whether they are concentrated in a general location or are widely dispersed. Gum and textbooks, for example, are produced in one location and consumed in many other locations. Therefore, a merchant wholesaler is needed to distribute the products. In contrast, in a home sale, the buyer and seller are localized in one area, which facilitates the use of an agent/broker relationship.

Channel Functions Performed by Intermediaries

Retailing and wholesaling intermediaries in marketing channels perform several essential functions that make the flow of goods between producer and buyer possible. The three basic functions that intermediaries perform are summarized in Exhibit 13.2.

Transactional functions involve contacting and communicating with prospective buyers to make them aware of existing products and explain their features, advantages, and benefits. Intermediaries in the channel also provide *logistical* functions. **Logistics** is the efficient and cost-effective forward and reverse flow and storage of goods, services, and related information, into, through, and out of channel member companies. Logistics functions typically include transportation and storage of assets, as well as their sorting, accumulation, consolidation, and/or allocation for the purpose of conforming to customer requirements. For example, grading agricultural products typifies the sorting-out process, while consolidation of many lots of grade A eggs from different sources into one lot illustrates the accumulation process. Supermarkets or other retailers perform the assorting function by assembling thousands of different items that

EXHIBIT 13.2
Marketing Channel Functions Performed by Intermediaries

Type of Function	Description
Transactional Functions	**Contacting and promoting**: Contacting potential customers, promoting products, and soliciting orders
	Negotiating: Determining how many goods or services to buy and sell, type of transportation to use, when to deliver, and method and timing of payment
	Risk taking: Assuming the risk of owning inventory
Logistical Functions	**Physically distributing**: Transporting and sorting goods to overcome temporal and spatial discrepancies
	Storing: Maintaining inventories and protecting goods
	Sorting: Overcoming discrepancies of quantity and assortment by
	Sorting out: Breaking down a heterogeneous supply into separate homogeneous stocks
	Accumulating: Combining similar stocks into a larger homogeneous supply
	Allocating: Breaking a homogeneous supply into smaller and smaller lots ("breaking bulk")
	Assorting: Combining products into collections or assortments that buyers want available at one place
Facilitating Functions	**Researching**: Gathering information about other channel members and consumers
	Financing: Extending credit and other financial services to facilitate the flow of goods through the channel to the final consumer

match their customers' desires. Similarly, while large companies typically have direct channels, many small companies depend on wholesalers to promote and distribute their products.

The third basic channel function, *facilitating*, includes research and financing. Research provides information about channel members and consumers by getting answers to key questions: Who are the buyers? Where are they located? Why do they buy? Financing ensures that channel members have the money to keep products moving through the channel to the ultimate consumer.

Although individual members can be added to or deleted from a channel, someone must still perform these essential functions. They can be performed by producers, end users, or consumers, channel intermediaries such as wholesalers and retailers, and sometimes nonmember channel participants. For example, if a manufacturer decides to eliminate its private fleet of trucks, it must still have a way to move the goods to the wholesaler. This task may be accomplished by the wholesaler, which may have its own fleet of trucks, or by a nonmember channel participant, such as an independent trucking firm. Nonmembers also provide many other essential functions that may at one time have been provided by a channel member. For exam-

ple, research firms may perform the research function; advertising agencies may provide the promotion function; transportation and storage firms, the physical distribution function; and banks the financing function.

direct channel a distribution channel in which producers sell directly to consumers

LO 3 Channel Structures

A product can take many routes to reach its final consumer. Marketers search for the most efficient channel from the many alternatives available. Marketing a consumer convenience good such as gum or candy differs from marketing a specialty good like a Prada handbag. The next sections discuss the structures of typical and alternative marketing channels, for consumer and business-to-business products.

Channels for Consumer Products

Exhibit 13.3 illustrates the four ways manufacturers can route products to consumers. Producers use the **direct channel** to sell directly to consumers. Direct marketing activities—including telemarketing, mail-order

© AP PHOTO/MATT SLOCUM

A retailer channel is most common when the retailer is large, such as JCPenney, and can buy in large quantities directly from the manufacturer. Large retailers often bypass a wholesaler.

and catalog shopping, and forms of electronic retailing such as online shopping and shop-at-home television networks—are a good example of this type of channel structure. There are no intermediaries. Producer-owned stores and factory outlet stores—like Sherwin-Williams, Polo Ralph Lauren, Oneida, and WestPoint Home—are examples of direct channels.

By contrast, an *agent/broker channel* is fairly complicated and typically used in markets with many small manufacturers and many retailers that lack the resources to find each other. Agents or brokers bring manufacturers and wholesalers together for negotiations, but they do not take title to merchandise. Ownership passes directly to one or more wholesalers and then to retailers. Finally, retailers sell to the ultimate consumer of the product. For example, a food broker represents buyers and sellers of grocery products. The broker acts on behalf of many different producers and negotiates the sale of their products to wholesalers that specialize in foodstuffs. These wholesalers in turn sell to grocers and convenience stores.

Most consumer products are sold through distribution channels similar to the other two alternatives: the retailer channel and the wholesaler channel. A retailer channel is most common when the retailer is large and can buy in large quantities directly from the manufacturer. Wal-Mart, Sears, and car dealers are examples of retailers that often bypass a wholesaler. A *wholesaler channel* is commonly used for low-cost items that are frequently purchased, such as candy, cigarettes, and magazines.

Channels for Business and Industrial Products

As Exhibit 13.4 illustrates, five channel structures are common in business and industrial markets. First, direct channels are typical in business and industrial markets. For example, manufacturers buy large quantities of raw materials, major equipment, processed materials, and supplies directly from other manufacturers. Manufacturers that require suppliers to meet detailed technical specifications often prefer direct channels. The direct communication required between General Motors and its suppliers, for example, along with the tremendous size of the orders, makes anything but a direct channel impractical. The channel from producer to government buyers is also a direct channel. Since much government buying is done through bidding, a direct channel is attractive.

Companies selling standardized items of moderate or low value often rely on *industrial distributors*. In many ways, an industrial distributor is like a supermarket for organizations. Industrial distributors are wholesalers and channel members that buy and take title to products. Moreover, they usually keep inventories of their products and sell and

EXHIBIT 13.3
Marketing Channels for Consumer Products

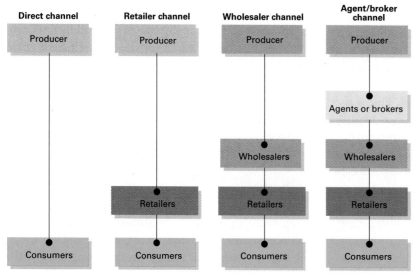

service them. Often small manufacturers cannot afford to employ their own sales force. Instead, they rely on manufacturers' representatives or selling agents to sell to either industrial distributors or users.

The Internet has enabled virtual distributors to emerge and forced traditional industrial distributors to expand

EXHIBIT 13.4
Channels for Business and Industrial Products

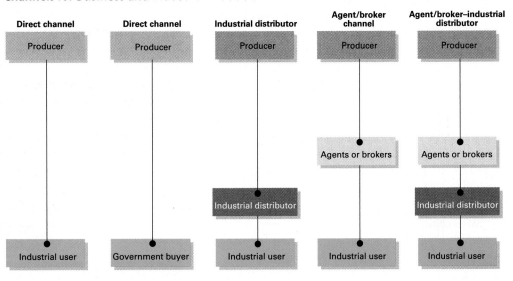

their business model. Many manufacturers and consumers are bypassing distributors and going direct, often via the Internet. Companies looking to drop the intermediary from the supply chain have created exchanges. Retailers use the Worldwide Retail Exchange to make purchases that in the past would have required telephone, fax, or face-to-face sales calls, and in so doing save approximately 15 percent in their purchasing costs. Finally, a third type of Internet marketplace is a "private exchange." A private exchange is when a company creates a network so it can connect its business with that of its suppliers. Some large companies prefer private exchanges because they provide tighter security over transactions, especially when negotiating complex contracts.

Alternative Channel Arrangements

Rarely does a producer use just one type of channel to move its product. It usually employs several different or alternative channels, which include multiple channels, nontraditional channels, and strategic channel alliances.

Multiple Channels When a producer selects two or more channels to distribute the same product to target markets, this arrangement is called **dual distribution** (or **multiple distribution**). As more people embrace online shopping, an increasing number of retailers are using multiple distribution channels. For example, companies such as the Limited, which includes Express, Victoria's Secret, and Bath and Body Works, sell in-store, online, and through catalogs.

Nontraditional Channels

Often nontraditional channel arrangements help differentiate a firm's product from the competition. Nontraditional channels include the Internet, mail-order channels, or infomercials. Although nontraditional channels may limit a brand's coverage, they can give a producer serving a niche market a way to gain market access and customer attention without having to establish channel intermediaries. Nontraditional channels can also provide another avenue of sales for larger firms. For example, a London publisher sells short stories through vending machines in the London Underground. Instead of the traditional book format, the stories are printed like folded maps, making them an easy-to-read alternative for commuters.

Strategic Channel Alliances

Companies often form **strategic channel alliances**, which enable them to use another manufacturer's already-established channel. Alliances are used most often when the creation of marketing channel relationships may be too expensive and time-consuming. Fifteen years ago, Starbucks contracted with PepsiCo to develop and bottle a Starbucks brand of ready-to-drink (RTD) coffee. The resulting Frappuccino and DoubleShot were an immediate success. Today, PepsiCo is still the sole distributor for Starbucks RTD beverages, and Starbucks has continued access to the thousands of outlets where Pepsi is sold.[1]

dual distribution (multiple distribution) the use of two or more channels to distribute the same product to target markets

strategic channel alliance a cooperative agreement between business firms to use the other's already established distribution channel

Alliances can also prove more efficient when a company wants to broaden its market reach. In their eagerness to expand, for example, Coca-Cola's two largest U.S. bottlers formed alliances with smaller, faster-growing beverage brands, such as Honest Tea and Arizona iced teas, to distribute their products alongside Coke products. Conversely, Coca-Cola bypassed these same large distributors and began to channel some of its newer, noncarbonated drinks through other distribution systems with a different market base.[2]

Strategic channel alliances are proving to be more successful for growing businesses than mergers and acquisitions. This is especially true in global markets where cultural differences, distance, and other barriers can prove challenging.

An increasing number of retailers use multiple channels of distribution. For example, Sears purchased Lands' End, a traditional direct business-to-consumer clothing manufacturer. Now Lands' End products are available in Sears's stores, and Sears credit cards are accepted on the Lands' End Web site.

LO 4 Making Channel Strategy Decisions

Devising a marketing channel strategy requires several critical decisions. Managers must decide what role distribution will play in the overall marketing strategy. In addition, they must be sure that the channel strategy chosen is consistent with product, promotion, and pricing strategies. In making these decisions, marketing managers must determine what factors will influence the choice of channel and what level of distribution intensity will be appropriate.

Factors Affecting Channel Choice

Managers must answer many questions before choosing a marketing channel. The final choice depends on the analysis of several factors, which often interact. These factors can be grouped as market factors, product factors, and producer factors.

Market Factors Among the most important market factors affecting the choice of distribution channel are target customer considerations. Specifically, managers should answer the following questions: Who are the potential customers? What do they buy? Where do they buy? When do they buy? How do they buy? Additionally, the choice of channel depends on whether the producer is selling to consumers or to industrial customers. Industrial customers' buying habits are very different from those of consumers. Industrial customers tend to buy in larger quantities and require more customer service.

The geographic location and size of the market are also important to channel selection. As a rule, if the target market is concentrated in one or more specific areas, then direct selling through a sales force is appropriate. When markets are more widely dispersed, intermediaries would be less expensive. The size of the market also influences channel choice. Generally, larger markets require more intermediaries.

Product Factors Products that are more complex, customized, and expensive tend to benefit from shorter and more direct marketing channels. These types of products sell better through a direct sales force. Examples include pharmaceuticals, scientific instruments, airplanes, and mainframe computer systems. On the other hand, the more standardized a product is, the longer its distribution channel can be and the greater the number of intermediaries that can be involved. For example, with the exception of flavor and shape, the formula for chewing gum is about the same from producer to producer. Chewing gum is also very inexpensive. As a result, the distribution channel for gum tends to involve many wholesalers and retailers.

The product's life cycle is also an important factor in choosing a marketing channel. In fact, the choice of channel may change over the life of the product. As products become more common and less intimidating to potential users, producers tend to look for alternative channels.

Another factor is the delicacy of the product. Perishable products such as vegetables and milk have a relatively short life span. Fragile products like china and crystal require a minimum amount of handling. Therefore, both require fairly short marketing channels. Online retailers such as eBay facilitate the sale of unusual or difficult-to-find products that benefit from a direct channel.

Producer Factors Several factors pertaining to the producer itself are important to the selection of a marketing channel. In general, producers with large financial, managerial, and marketing resources are better able to use more direct channels. These producers have the ability to hire and train their own sales force, warehouse their own goods, and extend credit to their customers. Smaller or weaker firms, on the other hand, must rely on intermediaries to provide these services for them. Compared to producers with only one or two product lines, producers that sell several products in a related area are able to choose channels that are more direct. Sales expenses then can be spread over more products.

A producer's desire to control pricing, positioning, brand image, and customer support also tends to influence channel selection. For instance, firms that sell products with exclusive brand images, such as designer perfumes and clothing, usually avoid channels in which discount retailers are present. Manufacturers of upscale products,

Intensive distribution is susceptible to errors when intermediaries are expected to handle products in a pre-specified manner detailed in buyer-seller agreements. For example, Scholastic executives were alarmed when copies of the final book in the Harry Potter series were mistakenly released a day earlier than the widely publicized release date.

© AP PHOTO/MARK BAKER

such as Gucci (handbags) and Godiva (chocolates), may sell their wares only in expensive stores in order to maintain an image of exclusivity. Many producers have opted to risk their image, however, and test sales in discount channels. Levi Strauss expanded its distribution to include JCPenney, Sears, and Wal-Mart.

Levels of Distribution Intensity

Organizations have three options for intensity of distribution: intensive distribution, selective distribution, or exclusive distribution.

Intensive Distribution **Intensive distribution** is a form of distribution aimed at maximum market coverage. The manufacturer tries to have the product available in every outlet where potential customers might want to buy it. If buyers are unwilling to search for a product (as is true of convenience goods and operating supplies), the product must be very accessible to buyers. A low-value product that is purchased frequently may require a lengthy channel. For example, candy, chips, and other snack foods, which are found in almost every type of retail store, are typically sold to retailers in small quantities by food or candy wholesalers.

Most manufacturers pursuing an intensive distribution strategy sell to a large percentage of the wholesalers willing to stock their products. Retailers' willingness (or unwillingness) to handle items tends to control the manufacturer's ability to achieve intensive distribution. For example, a retailer already carrying ten brands of gum may show little enthusiasm for one more brand.

Selective Distribution **Selective distribution** is achieved by screening dealers and retailers to eliminate all but a few in any single area. Because only a few are chosen, the consumer must seek out the product. For example, when Heeling Sports Ltd. launched Heelys, thick-soled sneakers with a wheel embedded in each heel, the company hired a group of forty teens to perform Heelys exhibitions in targeted malls, skate parks, and college campuses across the country to create demand. Then the company made the decision to avoid large stores like Target and to distribute the shoes only through selected mall retailers and skate and surf shops in order to position the product as "cool and kind of irreverent." Selective distribution strategies often hinge on a manufacturer's desire to maintain a superior product image so as to be able to charge a premium price. DKNY clothing, for instance, is sold only in select retail outlets, mainly full-price department stores. Manufacturers sometimes expand selective

intensive distribution a form of distribution aimed at having a product available in every outlet where target customers might want to buy it
selective distribution a form of distribution achieved by screening dealers to eliminate all but a few in any single area

distribution strategies, believing that doing so will enhance revenues without diminishing their product's image. For example, Playboy Energy, a new energy drink manufactured and bottled by the media enterprise of the same name, uses selective distribution to position itself as a higher-end option versus the more intensively distributed competitor Red Bull.[3] The drink has been introduced in luxurious nightclubs and upscale bars only in Boston, Las Vegas, Los Angeles, and Miami in order to draw the attention of "elite" customers prior to its broader release in grocery and convenience stores in the future.

Recently, a high-tech form of selective distribution has emerged whereby products are pushed through to the membership of exclusive virtual social networks. ScionSpeak was developed as a social network Internet portal where Toyota Scion owners could design and share their own unique graffiti-type artwork which then could be airbrushed onto the body of their cars. This type of service is among the first to leverage the power of social network Web sites as a product distribution medium.[4]

Exclusive Distribution The most restrictive form of market coverage is **exclusive distribution**, which entails only one or a few dealers within a given area. Because buyers may have to search or travel extensively to buy the product, exclusive distribution is usually confined to consumer specialty goods, a few shopping goods, and major industrial equipment. Products such as Rolls-Royce automobiles, Chris-Craft power boats, and Pettibone tower cranes are distributed under exclusive arrangements.

Retailers and wholesalers may be unwilling to commit the time and money necessary to promote and service a product unless the manufacturer guarantees them an exclusive territory. This arrangement shields the dealer from direct competition and enables it to be the main beneficiary of the manufacturer's promotion efforts in that geographic area. With exclusive distribution, channels of

communication are usually well established because the manufacturer works with a limited number of dealers rather than many accounts.

Exclusive distribution also takes place within a retailer's store rather than a geographic area—for example, when a retailer agrees not to sell a manufacturer's competing brands. Mossimo, traditionally an apparel wholesaler, developed an agreement with Target to design clothing and related items sold exclusively at Target stores.

LO 5 Types of Channel Relationships

A marketing channel is more than a set of institutions linked by economic ties. Social relationships play an important role in building unity among channel members. Marketing managers should carefully consider the types of relationships they choose to foster between their company and other companies, and in doing so, pay close attention to the benefits and hazards associated with each relationship type. Relationships among channel members range from "loose" to "tight," taking the form of a continuum stretching from single transactions to complex interdependent relationships such as partnerships or alliances. The choice of relationship type is important for channel management because each relationship type carries with it different levels of time, financial, and resource investment. Three basic types of relationships, organized by degree of closeness, are:

▸▸ **Arm's-length relationships** are considered by channel members to be temporary or one-time-only and often arise from a sudden or unique need. These relationships are characterized by the companies' unwillingness or lack of ability to develop a closer type of relationship. Both parties typically retain their independence and pursue only their own interests while attempting to benefit from the goods or services provided by the other.

▸▸ **Cooperative relationships**, generally administered using some kind of formal contract, are used when a company wants less ambiguity but doesn't want the long term and/or capital investment necessary in an integrated relationship. Cooperative relationships tend to be more flexible than integrated relationships, but

© ISTOCKPHOTO.COM/TOMML

are more structured than arm's-length relationships, and include nonequity agreements such as franchising and licensing, as well as joint ventures and strategic alliances.

▸▸ **Integrated relationships** are closely bonded relationships characterized by formal arrangements that explicitly define the relationships to the involved channel members. There is vertical integration, where all of the related channel members are owned by a single legal entity, and supply chains, which are several companies acting as one. Supply chains are discussed in detail in Chapter 14.

Based on these descriptions, it seems that integrated relationships would be the preferred relationship type in almost all company-to-company channel settings. However, highly integrated relationships also come with some significant costs and/or hazards. For example, the single-owner model is somewhat risky because a large amount of capital assets must be purchased or leased (requiring a potentially huge initial cash outlay), and the failure of any portion of the business may result in not only the economic loss of that portion, but may also reduce the value of the other business units (or render them totally worthless). Because these tradeoffs are sometimes hard to justify, companies often look for the sort of "happy medium" of cooperative relationships.

LO6 Managing Channel Relationships

In addition to considering the multiple different types of channel relationships and their costs and benefits, managers must also be aware of the social dimensions that are constantly impacting their relationships. The basic social dimensions of channels are power, control, leadership, conflict, and partnering.

THE SOCIAL DIMENSIONS OF CHANNELS:

▸▸ Power
▸▸ Control
▸▸ Leadership
▸▸ Conflict
▸▸ Partnering

Channel Power, Control, and Leadership

Channel power is a channel member's ability to control or influence the behavior of other channel members. **Channel control** occurs when one channel member's power affects another member's behavior. To achieve control, a channel member assumes channel leadership and exercises authority and power. This member is termed the **channel leader**, or **channel captain**. In one marketing channel, a manufacturer may be the leader because it controls new-product designs and product availability. In another, a retailer may be the channel leader because it wields power and control over the retail price, inventory levels, and postsale service.

Channel Conflict

Inequitable channel relationships often lead to **channel conflict**, which is a clash of goals and methods among the members of a distribution channel. In a broad context, conflict may not be bad. Often it arises because staid, traditional channel members refuse to keep pace with the times. Removing an outdated intermediary may result in reduced costs for the entire channel. The Internet has forced many intermediaries to offer services such as merchandise tracking and inventory availability online.

Conflicts among channel members can be due to many different situations and factors. Oftentimes, conflict arises because channel members have conflicting goals. For instance, athletic footwear retailers want to sell as many shoes as possible in order to maximize profits, regardless of whether the shoe is manufactured by Nike, Adidas, or Saucony, but the Nike manufacturer wants a certain sales volume and market share in each market.

Conflict can also arise when channel members fail to fulfill expectations of other channel members—for example, when a franchisee does not follow the rules set down by the franchisor, or when communications channels break down between channel members. Further, ideological differences and different perceptions of reality can also cause conflict among channel members. For instance, when it comes to return policies, a retailer's "the customer is always right" perspective will likely conflict with a wholesaler or manufacturer's

integrated relationship a relationship between companies that is tightly connected, with linked processes across and between firm boundaries, and high levels of trust and interfirm commitment

channel power the capacity of a particular marketing channel member to control or influence the behavior of other channel members

channel control a situation that occurs when one marketing channel member intentionally affects another member's behavior

channel leader (channel captain) a member of a marketing channel that exercises authority and power over the activities of other channel members

channel conflict a clash of goals and methods between distribution channel members

perspective that people try to get something for nothing.

Conflict within a channel can be either horizontal or vertical. **Horizontal conflict** occurs among channel members on the same level, such as two or more different wholesalers or two or more different retailers that handle the same manufacturer's brands. This type of channel conflict is found most often when manufacturers practice dual or multiple distribution strategies. When Apple changed its distribution strategy and began opening its own stores, it angered Apple's traditional retail partners, some of whom ultimately filed lawsuits against the company. Horizontal conflict can also occur when some channel members feel that other members on the same level are being treated differently by the manufacturer.

Many marketers and customers regard horizontal conflict as healthy competition. Much more serious is **vertical conflict**, which occurs between different levels in a marketing channel, most typically between the manufacturer and wholesaler or the manufacturer and retailer. Producer-versus-wholesaler conflict occurs when the producer chooses to bypass the wholesaler and deal directly with the consumer or retailer.

Dual distribution strategies can also cause vertical conflict in the channel. For example, high-end fashion designers who traditionally sold their products through luxury retailers such as Neiman Marcus and Saks Fifth Avenue, began to open their own boutiques in shopping centers anchored by luxury retailers. The retailers therefore lost revenue on many luxury items. Producers and retailers may also disagree over the terms of the sale or other aspects of the business relationship. When Procter & Gamble introduced "everyday low pricing" to its retail channel members, a strategy designed to standardize wholesale prices and eliminate most trade promotions, many retailers retaliated. Some cut the variety of P&G sizes they carried or eliminated marginal brands. Others moved P&G brands from prime shelf space to less visible shelves.

Channel Partnering

Regardless of the locus of power, channel members rely heavily on one another. **Channel partnering**, or **channel cooperation**, is the joint effort of all channel members to create a channel that serves customers and creates a competitive advantage. Channel partnering is vital if each member is to gain something from other members. By cooperating, retailers, wholesalers, manufacturers, and suppliers can speed up inventory replenishment, improve customer service, and reduce the total costs of the marketing channel.

Channel alliances and partnerships help managers create the parallel flow of materials and information required to leverage the channel's intellectual, material, and marketing resources. The rapid growth in channel partnering is due to new enabling technology and the need to lower costs.

LO 7 Channels and Distribution Decisions for Global Markets

With the spread of free-trade agreements and treaties in recent decades, such as the European Union and the North American Free Trade Agreement (NAFTA), global marketing channels and management of the channels have become increasingly

© ISTOCKPHOTO.COM/ELNUR AMIKISHIYEV

important to U.S. companies that export their products or manufacture abroad.

Developing Global Marketing Channels

Executives should recognize the unique cultural, economic, institutional, and legal aspects of each market before trying to design marketing channels in foreign countries. Manufacturers introducing products in global markets have to decide whether the product will be marketed directly, mostly by company salespeople, or through independent foreign intermediaries, such as agents and distributors. Using company salespeople generally provides more control and is less risky than using foreign intermediaries. However, setting up a sales force in a foreign country also entails a greater commitment, both financially and organizationally.

Marketers should be aware that channel structures and types abroad may differ from those in the United States. For instance, the more highly developed a nation is economically, the more specialized its channel types. Therefore, a marketer wishing to sell in Germany or Japan will have several channel types to choose from. Conversely, developing countries such as Ethiopia, India, and Venezuela have limited channel types available, and they tend to shun the large-scale formats popular in the United States and Western Europe.

Marketers must also be aware that many countries have "gray" marketing channels in which products are distributed through unauthorized channel intermediaries. It is estimated that sales of counterfeit luxury items like Prada handbags and Big Bertha golf clubs have reached almost $2 billion a year. The Internet has also proved to be a way for pirates to circumvent authorized distribution channels, especially in the case of popular prescription drugs.

LO8 Channels and Distribution Decisions for Services

The fastest-growing part of our economy is the service sector. Although distribution in the service sector is difficult to visualize, the same skills, techniques, and strategies used to manage inventory can also be used to manage service inventory—for instance, hospital beds, bank accounts, or airline seats. The quality of the planning and execution of distribution can have a major impact on costs and customer satisfaction.

One thing that sets service distribution apart from traditional manufacturing distribution is that, in a service environment, production and consumption are simultaneous. In manufacturing, a production setback can often be remedied by using safety stock or a faster mode of transportation. Such substitution is not possible with a service. The benefits of a service are also relatively intangible—that is, a consumer normally can't see the benefits of a service, such as a doctor's physical exam, but normally can see the benefits provided by a product—for example, cold medicine relieving a stuffy nose.

Because service industries are so customer oriented, customer service is a priority. To manage customer relationships, many service providers, such as insurance carriers, physicians, hair salons, and financial services, use technology to schedule appointments, manage accounts, and disburse information. Service distribution focuses on three main areas:

▸▸ *Minimizing wait times:* Minimizing the amount of time customers wait in line is a key factor in maintaining the quality of service. People tend to overestimate the amount of time they spend waiting in line, researchers report, and unexplained waiting seems longer than explained waits.

▸▸ *Managing service capacity:* If service firms don't have the capacity to meet demand, they must either turn down some prospective customers, let service levels slip, or expand capacity. For instance, at tax time a tax preparation firm may have so many customers desiring its services that it has to either turn business away or add temporary offices or preparers.

▸▸ *Improving service delivery:* Service firms are now experimenting with different distribution channels for their services. Choosing the right distribution channel can increase the times that services are available or add to customer convenience. The Internet is fast becoming an alternative channel for delivering services. Consumers can now purchase plane tickets, plan a vacation cruise, reserve a hotel room, pay bills, purchase mutual funds, and receive electronic newspapers in cyberspace.

UPS by the Numbers
Delivery of packages and documents:

4.0 billion
packages annually

15.8 million
packages daily by ground

2.3 million
packages daily by air

268
jet aircraft fleet
(9th largest in the world)

200+
countries and territories
(EVERY address in North
America and Europe)

8 million
daily customers

93,637
ground delivery fleet

source:
www.ups.com

STUDY TOOLS CHAPTER 13

Located at back of the textbook
- ❏ **Rip out Chapter Review Card**

Located at 4ltrpress.cengage.com/mktg
- ❏ **Review Key Terms Flash Cards (Print or Online)**
- ❏ **Download Audio and Visual Summaries for on-the-go review**
- ❏ **Complete both Practice Quizzes to prepare for tests**
- ❏ **Play "Beat the Clock" and "Quizbowl" to master concepts**
- ❏ **Complete "Crossword Puzzle" to review key terms**
- ❏ **Watch the video on "Sephora" for a real company example on Marketing Channels**

" They are written in **concise, down-to-earth language.** There are tons of pictures and interesting blurbs of information. It's very relevant to my life. It's nice to have a book/website that seems to **reach out to students and actually care** about how we learn and try to tailor to our needs as much as possible. Thank you for this. "

– Alice Brent, Student at Arizona State University

SPEAK UP! THEY DID

MKTG4 was built on a simple principle: to create a new teaching and learning solution that reflects the way today's faculty teach and the way you learn.

Through conversations, focus groups, surveys, and interviews, we collected data that drove the creation of the current version of MKTG4 that you are using today. But it doesn't stop there – in order to make MKTG4 an even better learning experience, we'd like you to SPEAK UP and tell us how MKTG4 worked for you.

What did you like about it?
What would you change?
Are there additional ideas you have that would help us build a better product for next semester's principles of marketing students?

At **4ltrpress.cengage.com** you'll find all of the resources you need to succeed in principles of marketing – **video podcasts, audio downloads, flash cards, interactive quizzes**, and more!

Speak Up! Go to **4ltrpress.cengage.com**.

"In today's marketplace, products are being driven by consumers."

LO 1 Supply Chains and Supply Chain Management

AFTER YOU FINISH THIS CHAPTER GO TO **PAGE 224** FOR **STUDY TOOLS**

Many modern companies are turning to supply chain management for competitive advantage. A company's **supply chain** includes all of the companies involved in all of the upstream and downstream flows of products, services, finances, and information, from initial suppliers (the point of origin) to the ultimate customer (the point of consumption). The goal of **supply chain management** is to coordinate and integrate all of the activities performed by supply chain members into a seamless process, from the source to the point of consumption, ultimately giving supply chain managers "total visibility" of the supply chain both inside and outside the firm. The philosophy behind supply chain management is that by visualizing the entire supply chain, supply chain managers can maximize strengths and efficiencies at each level of the process to create a highly competitive, customer-driven supply system that is able to respond immediately to changes in supply and demand.

Supply chain management is completely customer driven. In the mass-production era, manufacturers produced standardized products that were "pushed"

supply chain the connected chain of all of the business entities, both internal and external to the company, that perform or support the logistics function

supply chain management a management system that coordinates and integrates all of the activities performed by supply chain members into a seamless process, from the source to the point of consumption, resulting in enhanced customer and economic value

What do you think?

I purchase more merchandise online than in stores.

1 STRONGLY DISAGREE   2   3   4   5   6   7 STRONGLY AGREE

Find out what others think at 4ltrpress.cengage.com/mktg

RESEARCH HAS SHOWN A CLEAR RELATIONSHIP BETWEEN SUPPLY CHAIN PERFORMANCE AND PROFITABILITY.

down through the supply channel to the consumer. In today's marketplace, however, products are being driven by customers, who expect to receive product configurations and services matched to their unique needs. The focus is on pulling products into the marketplace and partnering with members of the supply chain to enhance customer value. New supply chain relationships between the automobile manufacturers and the after-market auto-parts industry make it possible to customize an automobile.[1]

This reversal of the flow of demand from a "push" to a "pull" has resulted in a radical reformulation of both market expectations and traditional marketing, production, and distribution functions. Integrated channel partnerships allow companies to respond with the unique product configuration and mix of services demanded by the customer. Today, supply chain management is both a *communicator* of customer demand that extends from the point of sale all the way back to the supplier, and a *physical flow* process that engineers the timely and cost-effective movement of goods through the entire supply pipeline.

Benefits of Supply Chain Management

Supply chain management is a key means of differentiation for a firm and a critical component in marketing and corporate strategy. Companies that focus on supply chain management commonly report lower inventory, transportation, warehousing, and packaging costs; greater supply chain flexibility; improved customer service; and higher revenues. Research has shown a clear relationship between supply chain performance and profitability.

LO 2 Supply Chain Integration

A key principle of supply chain management is that multiple firms work together to perform tasks as a single, unified system, rather than as several individual companies acting in isolation. Companies in a world-class supply chain combine their resources, capabilities, and innovations such that they are used for the best interest of the entire chain as a whole, with the goal being that overall performance of the supply chain will be greater than the sum of its parts. As firms become increasingly supply chain oriented, they develop management practices that are consistent with this systems approach.

Management practices that are reflective of a highly coordinated effort between supply chain partners are said to be "integrated." In other words, supply chain integration occurs when multiple firms in a supply chain coordinate their activities and processes so that they are seamlessly linked to one another in an effort to satisfy the customer. In a world-class supply chain, the customer may not know where the business activities of one firm or business unit end, and where those of another begin—all of the participating firms and business units appear to be reading from the same script.

In the practice of world-class supply chain management, six types of integration are sought by firms interested in providing top-level service to customers:[2]

▸▸ *Relationship integration* is the ability of two or more companies to develop social connections that serve to guide their interactions when working together. More specifically, relationship integration is the capability to develop and maintain a shared mental framework across companies that describes how they will depend on one another when working together. This includes the ways in which they will collaborate on activities or projects so that the customer gains the maximum amount of total value possible from the supply chain.

▸▸ *Measurement integration* reflects the idea that performance assessments should be transparent and measurable across the borders of different business units and firms, and also assess the performance of the supply chain as a whole while holding each individual firm or business unit accountable for meeting its own goals.

▶▶ *Technology and planning integration* refers to the creation and maintenance of information technology systems that connect managers across and through the firms in the supply chain; it requires information hardware and software systems that can exchange information when needed between customers, suppliers, and internal operational areas of each of the supply chain partners.

▶▶ *Material and service supplier integration* requires firms to link seamlessly to those outsiders that provide goods and services to them, so that they can streamline work processes and thereby provide smooth, high-quality customer experiences. Both sides need to have a common vision of the total value creation process and be willing to share the responsibility for satisfying customer requirements to make supplier integration successful.

▶▶ *Internal operations integration* is the result of capabilities development toward the goal of linking internally performed work into a seamless process that stretches across departmental and/or functional boundaries, with the goal of satisfying customer requirements.

▶▶ *Customer integration* is a competency that enables firms to offer long-lasting, distinctive, value-added offerings to those customers who represent the greatest value to the firm or supply chain. Highly customer-integrated firms assess their own capabilities and then match them to customers whose desires they can meet and who offer large enough sales potential for the linkage to be profitable over the long term.

Firms' success in achieving each of these types of integration is very important. Highly integrated supply chains (those that are successful in achieving many or all of these types of integration) have been shown to be better at satisfying customers, managing costs, delivering high-quality products, enhancing productivity, and utilizing company or business unit assets, all of which translate into greater profitability for the firms and their partners working together in the supply chain.

LO 3 The Key Processes of Supply Chain Management

When firms practice good supply chain management, their functional departments or areas, such as marketing, research and development, and/or production, are integrated both within and across the linked firms. Integration, then, is "how" excellent supply chain management works. The business processes on which the linked firms work together represent the "what" of supply chain management—they are the objects of focus on which firms, departments, areas, and people work together when seeking to reduce supply chain costs or generate additional revenues. **Business processes** are composed of bundles of interconnected activities that stretch across firms in the supply chain; they represent key areas that some or all of the involved firms are constantly working on in order to reduce costs and/or generate revenues for everyone throughout supply chain management.

business processes bundles of interconnected activities that stretch across firms in the supply chain

customer relationship management process allows companies to prioritize their marketing focus on different customer groups according to each group's long-term value to the company or supply chain

There are eight critical business processes on which supply chain managers must focus:

1 customer relationship management
2 customer service management
3 demand management
4 order fulfillment
5 manufacturing flow management
6 supplier relationship management
7 product development and commercialization
8 returns management.[3]

Customer Relationship Management

The **customer relationship management process** (discussed further in Chapter 21) allows companies to prioritize their marketing focus on different customer groups according to each group's long-term value to the company or supply chain. Once higher-value customers are identified, firms should focus on providing customized products and better service to this group than to others. The customer relationship management process includes both segmentation of customers by value and the generation of customer loyalty for the most attractive segments—key activities that are enabled through customer integration. This process provides a set of comprehensive principles for the initiation and maintenance of customer relationships and is often carried out with the assistance of specialized CRM (Customer Relationship Management) computer software.

customer service management process presents a multi-company, unified response system to the customer whenever complaints, concerns, questions, or comments are voiced

demand management process seeks to align supply and demand throughout the supply chain by anticipating customer requirements at each level and creating demand-related plans of action prior to actual customer purchasing behavior

order fulfillment process a highly integrated process, often requiring persons from multiple companies and multiple functions to come together and coordinate to create customer satisfaction at a given place and time

Customer Service Management

Whereas the customer relationship management process is designed to identify and build relationships with good customers, the customer service management process is designed to ensure that those customer relationships remain strong. The **customer service management process** presents a multi-company, unified response system to the customer whenever complaints, concerns, questions, or comments are voiced. When the process is well-executed, it can have a strong positive impact on revenues, often as a result of quick positive response to negative customer feedback, and sometimes even in the form of additional sales gained through the additional customer contact. Customers expect service from the moment a product is purchased until it is disposed of, and the customer service management process allows for touch points between the buyer and seller throughout this life cycle. The use of customer care software enables companies to enhance their customer service management process.

Demand Management

The **demand management process** seeks to align supply and demand throughout the supply chain by anticipating customer requirements at each level and creating demand-related plans of action prior to actual customer purchasing behavior. At the same time, demand management seeks to minimize the costs of serving multiple types of customers who have variable wants and needs. In other words, the demand management process allows companies in the supply chain to satisfy customers in the most efficient and effective ways possible. The activities such as customer data collection, forecasting of future demand, and the development of activities that serve to "smooth out" demand help bring available inventory into alignment with customer desires. Though it is very difficult to predict exactly what items and quantities customers will buy prior to purchase, demand management can ease the pressure on the production process and allow companies to satisfy most of their customers through greater flexibility in manufacturing, marketing, and sales programs. However, much of the uncertainty in demand planning can be mitigated by conducting collaborative planning, forecasting, and replenishment (CPFR) activities with the company's customers and suppliers. One animal food company adopting CPFR reduced its forecasting error by 6 percent, which enabled it to cut prices paid by customers almost 4 percent in less than a year's time.[4]

Order Fulfillment

One of the most fundamental processes in supply chain management is the order fulfillment process, which involves generating, filling, delivering, and providing on-the-spot service for customer orders. The **order fulfillment process** is a highly integrated process, often requiring persons from multiple companies and multiple functions to come together and coordinate to create customer satisfaction at a given place and time. The best order fulfillment processes reduce the time between order and customer receipt as much as possible, while ensuring that the customer receives exactly what he/she wanted. The shorter lead times are beneficial in that they allow firms to carry reduced inventory levels and free up cash that can be used on other projects. Overall, the order fulfillment process involves understanding both internal capabilities and external customer needs, and matching

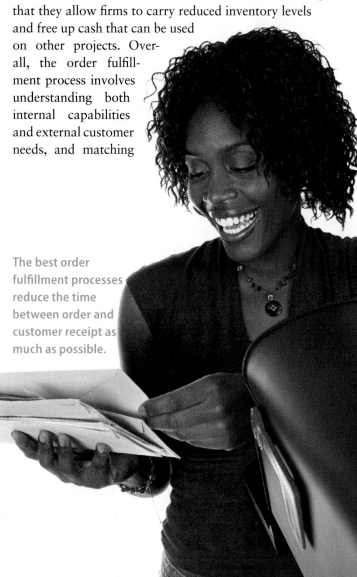

The best order fulfillment processes reduce the time between order and customer receipt as much as possible.

© ISTOCKPHOTO.COM/SEAN LOCKE

these together so that the supply chain maximizes profits while minimizing costs and waste.

When the order fulfillment process is managed diligently, the amount of time between order placement and receipt of the customer's payment following order shipment (known as the order-to-cash cycle) is minimized as much as possible. Since many firms do not view order fulfillment as a core competency (versus, for example, product development or marketing), they often outsource this function to a third-party logistics firm (3PL) that specializes in the order fulfillment process. The 3PL becomes a semi-permanent part of the firm's supply chain assigned to manage one or more specialized functions. When employed for the purposes of order fulfillment, the 3PL is contracted to manage the firm's order fulfillment process from beginning to end, thereby freeing up the firm's time and resources so that they can be expended on core business activities.

Manufacturing Flow Management

The **manufacturing flow management process** is concerned with ensuring that firms in the supply chain have the needed resources to manufacture with flexibility and to move products through a multi-stage production process. Firms with flexible manufacturing have the ability to create a wide variety of goods and/or services with minimized costs associated with changing production techniques. The manufacturing flow process includes much more than simple production of goods and services—it means creating flexible agreements with suppliers and shippers so that unexpected demand bursts can be accommodated.

The goals of the manufacturing flow management process are centered on leveraging the capabilities held by multiple members of the supply chain to improve overall manufacturing output in terms of quality, delivery speed, and flexibility, all of which tie to profitability.

Supplier Relationship Management

The **supplier relationship management process** is closely related to the manufacturing flow management process and contains several characteristics that parallel the customer relationship management process. The manufacturing flow management process is highly dependent on supplier relationships for flexibility. Furthermore, in a way similar to that found in the customer relationship management process, supplier relationship management provides structural support for developing and maintaining relationships with suppliers. Thus, integrating these two ideas, supplier relationship management supports manufacturing flow by identifying and maintaining relationships with highly valued suppliers. Just as firms benefit from developing close-knit and integrated relationships with customers, close-knit and integrated relationships with suppliers provide a means through which performance advantages can be gained.

The management of supplier relationships is a key step toward ensuring that firms' manufacturing resources are available, and thereby the supplier relationship management process has a direct impact on each supply chain member's bottom-line financial performance.

Product Development and Commercialization

The **product development and commercialization process** (discussed in detail in Chapter 11) includes the group of activities that facilitates the joint development and marketing of new offerings among a group of supply chain partner firms. In many cases, new products and services are not the sole responsibility of a single firm that serves as inventor, engineer, builder, marketer, and sales agent, but rather, they are often the product of a multi-company collaboration with multiple firms and business units playing unique roles in new product development, testing, and launch activities, among others. The capability for developing and introducing new offerings quickly is key for competitive success versus rival firms, and so it is often advantageous to involve many supply chain partners in the effort. The process requires the close cooperation of suppliers and customers who provide input throughout the process and serve as advisors and co-producers for the new offering(s).

Returns Management

The final supply chain management process deals with incidents where customers choose to return a product to the retailer or supplier, thus creating a reversed flow of goods within the supply chain. The **returns management process** enables firms to manage volumes

manufacturing flow management process concerned with ensuring that firms in the supply chain have the needed resources to manufacture with flexibility and to move products through a multi-stage production process

supplier relationship management process closely related to the manufacturing flow management process and contains several characteristics that parallel the customer relationship management process

product development and commercialization process includes the group of activities that facilitates the joint development and marketing of new offerings among a group of supply chain partner firms

returns management process enables firms to manage volumes of returned product efficiently, while minimizing returns-related costs and maximizing the value of the returned assets to the firms in the supply chain

of returned product efficiently, while minimizing returns-related costs and maximizing the value of the returned assets to the firms in the supply chain. Returns have the potential to impact a firm's financial position in a major and negative way if mishandled. Certain industries, such as apparel e-retailing, can reach up to 40 percent of sales volume in returns.

In addition to the value of managing returns from a pure asset-recovery perspective, many firms are discovering that returns management also creates additional marketing and customer service touch points that can be leveraged for added customer value above and beyond normal sales and promotion-driven encounters. Handling returns gives the company an additional opportunity to please the customer, and customers who have positive experiences with the returns management process can become very confident buyers who are willing to reorder, since they know any problems they encounter with purchases will be quickly and fairly rectified. In addition, the returns management process allows the firm to recognize weaknesses in product design and/or areas for potential improvement through the direct customer feedback that initiates the process.

LO4 Managing the Logistical Components of the Supply Chain

Critical to any supply chain is orchestrating the physical means through which products move through it. **Logistics** is the process of strategically managing the efficient flow and storage of raw materials, in-process inventory, and finished goods from point of origin to point of consumption. As mentioned earlier, supply chain management coordinates and integrates all of the activities performed by supply chain members into a seamless process. The supply chain consists of several interrelated and integrated logistical components: (1) sourcing and procurement of raw materials and supplies, (2) production scheduling, (3) order processing, (4) inventory control, (5) warehousing and materials-handling, and (6) transportation.

The **logistics information system** is the link connecting all of the logistics components of the supply chain. The components of the system include, for example, software for materials acquisition and handling, warehouse-management and enterprise-wide solutions, data storage and integration in data warehouses, mobile communications, electronic data interchange, RFID chips, and the Internet. Working together, the components of the logistics information system are the fundamental enablers of successful supply chain management.

The **supply chain team**, in concert with the logistics information system, orchestrates the movement of goods, services, and information from the source to the consumer. Supply chain teams typically cut across organizational boundaries, embracing all parties who participate in moving the product to market. The best supply chain teams also move beyond the organization to include the external partici-

Certain industries, such as apparel e-retailing, can reach up to 40 percent of sales volume in returns.

© ISTOCKPHOTO.COM/MARIA TOUTOUDAKI

pants in the chain, such as suppliers, transportation carriers, and third-party logistics suppliers. Members of the supply chain communicate, coordinate, and cooperate extensively.

Sourcing and Procurement

One of the most important links in the supply chain is that between the manufacturer and the supplier. Purchasing professionals are on the front lines of supply chain management. Purchasing departments plan purchasing strategies, develop specifications, select suppliers, and negotiate price and service levels.

The goal of most sourcing and procurement activities is to reduce the costs of raw materials and supplies. Purchasing professionals have traditionally relied on tough negotiations to get the lowest price possible from suppliers of raw materials, supplies, and components. Perhaps the biggest contribution purchasing can make to supply chain management, however, is in the area of vendor relations. Companies can use the purchasing function to strategically manage suppliers in order to reduce the total cost of materials and services. Through enhanced vendor relations, buyers and sellers can develop cooperative relationships that reduce costs and improve efficiency with the aim of lowering prices and enhancing profits. By integrating suppliers into their companies' businesses, purchasing managers have become better able to streamline purchasing processes, manage inventory levels, and reduce overall costs of the sourcing and procurement operations.

> The supply chain consists of several interrelated and integrated logistical components:
> 1. sourcing and procurement of raw materials and supplies,
> 2. production scheduling,
> 3. order processing,
> 4. inventory control,
> 5. warehousing and materials-handling, and
> 6. transportation.

Production Scheduling

In traditional mass-market manufacturing, production begins when forecasts call for additional products to be made or when inventory control systems signal low inventory levels. The firm then makes a product and transports the finished goods to its own warehouses or those of intermediaries, where the goods wait to be ordered by retailers or customers. For example, many types of convenience goods, such as toothpaste, deodorant, and detergent, are manufactured based on past sales and demand and then sent to retailers to resell. Production scheduling based on pushing a product down to the consumer obviously has its disadvantages, the most notable being that companies risk making products that may become obsolete or that consumers don't want in the first place.

In a customer "pull" manufacturing environment, which is growing in popularity, production of goods or services is not scheduled until an order is placed by the customer specifying the desired configuration. This process, known as **mass customization**, or **build-to-order**, uniquely tailors mass-market goods and services to the needs of the individuals who buy them. Companies as diverse as BMW, Dell, Levi Strauss, Mattel, and a host of Web-based businesses are adopting mass customization to maintain or obtain a competitive edge.

As more companies move toward mass customization—and away from mass marketing—of goods, the need to stay on top of consumer demand is forcing manufacturers to make their supply chains more flexible. Flexibility is critical to a manufacturer's success when dramatic swings in demand occur. To meet consumers' demand for customized products, companies are forced to adapt their manufacturing approach or even create a completely new process. For years,

mass customization (build-to-order) a production method whereby products are not made until an order is placed by the customer; products are made according to customer specifications

T-Mobile's myTouch 3G's marketing focuses on being fully customizeable by working with Skinit to help customers create their own personalized, fully individual shells for their phones.

Nike sold its shoes through specialty retailers to hard-core runners who cared little what the shoes looked like. Over time, however, runners began to demand more stylish designs and technologically advanced footwear. To keep pace with rapidly changing fashions and trends, Nike launched NikeID, a set of specialty stores and a Web site through which consumers can design and order athletic shoes.[5]

Just-in-Time Manufacturing An important manufacturing process common today among manufacturers is just-in-time manufacturing. Borrowed from the Japanese, **just-in-time production (JIT)**, sometimes called *lean production*, requires manufacturers to work closely with suppliers and transportation providers to get necessary items to the assembly line or factory floor at the precise time they are needed for production. For the manufacturer, JIT means that raw materials arrive at the assembly line in guaranteed working order "just in time" to be installed, and finished products are generally shipped to the customer immediately after completion. For the supplier, JIT means supplying customers with products in just a few days, or even a few hours, rather than weeks. For the ultimate consumer, JIT means lower costs, shorter lead times, and products that more closely meet the consumer's needs. For example, Zara, a European clothing manufacturer and retailer with more than 600 stores in forty-eight countries, uses the JIT process to ensure that its stores are stocked with the latest fashion trends. Using its salespeople to track which fashions are selling fastest, the company can increase production of hot items and ship them to its stores in just a few days. Because Zara stores do not maintain large inventories, they can respond quickly to fashion trends and offer their products for less, giving Zara a distinct advantage over more traditional retailers that place orders months in advance.[6]

Order Processing

The order is often the catalyst that sets the supply chain in motion, especially in build-to-order environments. The **order processing system** processes the requirements of the customer and sends the information into the supply chain via the logistics information system. The order goes to the manufacturer's ware-house. If the product is in stock, the order is filled and arrangements are made to ship it. If the product is not in stock, it triggers a replenishment request that finds its way to the factory floor.

Proper order processing is critical to good service. As an order enters the system, management must monitor two flows: the flow of goods and the flow of information. Good communication among sales representatives, office personnel, and warehouse and shipping personnel is essential to correct order processing. Shipping incorrect merchandise or partially filled orders can create just as much dissatisfaction as stockouts or slow deliveries. The flow of goods and information must be continually monitored so that mistakes can be corrected before an invoice is prepared and the merchandise shipped.

Order processing is becoming more automated through the use of computer technology known as **electronic data interchange (EDI)**. The basic idea of EDI is to replace the paper documents that usually accompany business transactions, such as purchase orders and invoices, with electronic transmission of the needed information. A typical EDI message includes all the information that would traditionally be included on a paper invoice, such as product code, quantity, and transportation details. The information is usually sent via private networks, which are more secure and

Most trading partners that adopt EDI do so for increased efficiencies and cost savings. Sometimes pressures from larger trading partners force smaller trading partners to use EDI. For instance, Wal-Mart will not do business with a supplier that doesn't agree to use its preferred EDI processes.

reliable than the networks used for standard e-mail messages. Most important, the information can be read and processed by computers, significantly reducing costs and increasing efficiency. Companies that use EDI can reduce inventory levels, improve cash flow, streamline operations, and increase the speed and accuracy of information transmission. EDI also creates a closer relationship between buyers and sellers.

Retailers like Wal-Mart and Target have become major users of EDI because logistics speed and accuracy are crucial competitive tools in the overcrowded retail environment. EDI works hand in hand with retailers' *efficient consumer response programs* to ensure the right products are on the shelf, in the right styles and colors, at the right time, through improved inventory, ordering, and distribution techniques.

Inventory Control

The **inventory control system** develops and maintains an adequate assortment of materials or products to meet a manufacturer's or a customer's demands. Inventory decisions, for both raw materials and finished goods, have a big impact on supply chain costs and the level of service provided. If too many products are kept in inventory, costs increase—as do risks of obsolescence, theft, and damage. If too few products are kept on hand, then the company risks product shortages and angry customers, and ultimately lost sales. The goal of inventory management, therefore, is to keep inventory levels as low as possible while maintaining an adequate supply of goods to meet customer demand.

Managing inventory from the supplier to the manufacturer is called **materials requirement planning (MRP)**, or **materials management**. This system also encompasses the sourcing and procurement operations, signaling when raw materials, supplies, or components will need to be replenished for the production of more goods. The system that manages the finished goods inventory from manufacturer to end user is commonly referred to as **distribution resource planning (DRP)**.

Both inventory systems use various inputs, such as sales forecasts, available inventory, outstanding orders, lead times, and mode of transportation to be used, to determine what needs to be done to

replenish goods at all points in the supply chain. Marketers identify demand at each level in the supply chain, from the retailer back up the chain to the manufacturer, and use EDI to transmit important information throughout the channel.

As you would expect, JIT has a significant impact on reducing inventory levels. Because supplies are delivered exactly when they are needed on the factory floor, little inventory of any kind is needed, and companies can order materials in smaller quantities. Those lower inventory levels can give firms a competitive edge through the flexibility to halt production of existing products in favor of those gaining popularity with consumers. Savings also come from having less capital tied up in inventory and from the reduced need for storage facilities.

Warehousing and Materials-Handling

Although JIT manufacturing processes may eliminate the need to warehouse many raw materials, manufacturers may often keep some safety stock on hand in the event of an emergency, such as a strike at a supplier's plant or a catastrophic event that temporarily stops the flow of raw materials to the production

inventory control system a method of developing and maintaining an adequate assortment of materials or products to meet a manufacturer's or a customer's demand

materials requirement planning (MRP) (materials management) an inventory control system that manages the replenishment of raw materials, supplies, and components from the supplier to the manufacturer

distribution resource planning (DRP) an inventory control system that manages the replenishment of goods from the manufacturer to the final consumer

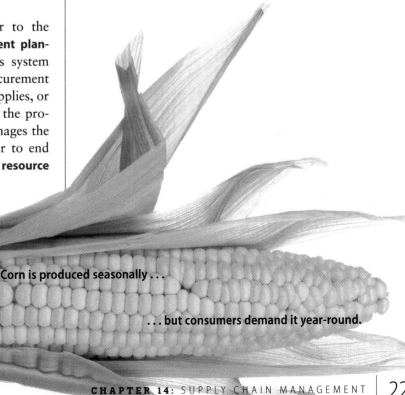

Corn is produced seasonally . . .

. . . but consumers demand it year-round.

line. Likewise, the final user may not need or want the goods at the same time the manufacturer produces and wants to sell them. Products such as grain and corn are produced seasonally, but consumers demand them year-round. Other products, such as Christmas ornaments and turkeys, are produced year-round, but consumers do not want them until autumn or winter. Therefore, management must have a storage system to hold these products until they are shipped.

Storage helps manufacturers manage supply and demand, or production and consumption. It provides time utility to buyers and sellers, which means that the seller stores the product until the buyer wants or needs it. But, storing additional product does have disadvantages, including the costs of insurance on the stored product, taxes, obsolescence or spoilage, theft, and warehouse operating costs. Another drawback is opportunity costs—that is, the opportunities lost because money is tied up in stored product instead of being used for something else.

Because businesses are focusing on cutting supply chain costs, the warehousing industry is investing in services using sophisticated tracking technology such as materials-handling systems. An effective **materials-handling system** moves inventory into, within, and out of the warehouse quickly with minimal handling. With a manual, nonautomated materials-handling system, a product may be handled more than a dozen times. Each time it is handled, the cost and risk of damage increase; each lifting of a product stresses its package. Consequently, most manufacturers today have moved to automated systems. Scanners quickly identify goods entering and leaving a warehouse through bar-coded labels affixed to the packaging. Automatic storage and retrieval systems store and pick goods in the warehouse or distribution center. Automated materials-handling systems decrease product handling, ensure accurate placement of product, and improve the accuracy of order picking and the rates of on-time shipment. Efficient central planning can be crucial when supply costs rise. Facing increased cheese and flour prices, Papa John's International recently centralized its inventory, storage, and transportation planning. The new program reduces waste and supplies all 3,263 pizza restaurants. The switch from individual to centralized planning helped Papa John's cut inventory levels by 17 percent and warehouse space by 33 percent in one year.[7]

EXHIBIT 14.1
Criteria for Ranking Modes of Transportation

	Highest				Lowest
Relative Cost	Air	Truck	Rail	Pipe	Water
Transit Time	Water	Rail	Pipe	Truck	Air
Reliability	Pipe	Truck	Rail	Air	Water
Capability	Water	Rail	Truck	Air	Pipe
Accessibility	Truck	Rail	Air	Water	Pipe
Traceability	Air	Truck	Rail	Water	Pipe

Transportation

Transportation typically accounts for 5 to 10 percent of the price of goods. Supply chain logisticians must decide which mode of transportation to use to move products from supplier to producer and from producer to buyer. These decisions are, of course, related to all other logistics decisions. The five major modes of transportation are railroads, motor carriers, pipelines, water transportation, and airways. Supply chain managers generally choose a mode of transportation on the basis of several criteria:

▶▶ *Cost*: The total amount a specific carrier charges to move the product from the point of origin to the destination

▶▶ *Transit time*: The total time a carrier has possession of goods, including the time required for pickup and delivery, handling, and movement between the point of origin and the destination

▶▶ *Reliability*: The consistency with which the carrier delivers goods on time and in acceptable condition

▶▶ *Capability*: The ability of the carrier to provide the appropriate equipment and conditions for moving specific kinds of goods, such as those that must be transported in a controlled environment (e.g., under refrigeration)

▶▶ *Accessibility*: A carrier's ability to move goods over a specific route or network

▶▶ *Traceability*: The relative ease with which a shipment can be located and transferred

The mode of transportation used depends on the needs of the shipper as they relate to these six criteria. Exhibit 14.1 compares the basic modes of transportation based on these criteria.

In many cases, especially in a JIT manufacturing environment, the transportation network replaces the warehouse or eliminates the expense of storing inventories as goods are timed to arrive the moment they're needed on the assembly line or for shipment to customers.

Electronic Distribution

Electronic distribution is the most recent development in the logistics arena. Broadly defined, **electronic distribution** includes any kind of product or service that can be distributed electronically, whether over traditional forms such as fiber-optic cable or through satellite transmission of electronic signals. Companies like eTrade, iTunes, and Movies.com have built their business models around electronic distribution.

Green Supply Chain Management

In response to the need for firms to both gain cost savings and act as leaders in protecting the natural environment, many are adopting green supply chain management principles as a key part of their supply chain strategy. Green supply chain management involves the integration of environmentally-conscious thinking into all phases of key supply chain management processes. Such activities include green materials sourcing, the design of products with consideration given to their environmental impact based on packaging, shipment and use, as well as end-of-life management for products including easy recycling and/or clean disposal. By enacting green supply chain management principles, firms hope to simultaneously generate cost savings and protect our natural resources from excess pollution, damage, and/or wastefulness.

Global Logistics and Supply Chain Management

Global markets present their own sets of logistical challenges. It is critical for importers of any size to understand and cope with the legalities of trade in other countries. Shippers and distributors must be aware of the permits, licenses, and registrations they may need to acquire and, depending on the type of product they are importing, the tariffs, quotas, and other regulations that apply in each country. This multitude of different rules is why multinational companies are so committed to working through the World Trade Organization to develop a global set of rules and to encourage countries to participate.

Transportation can also be a major issue for companies dealing with global supply chains. Uncertainty regarding shipping usually tops the list of reasons companies, especially smaller ones, resist international markets. In some instances, poor infrastructure makes transportation dangerous and unreliable. And the process of moving goods across the borders of even the most industrialized nations can still be complicated by government regulations.

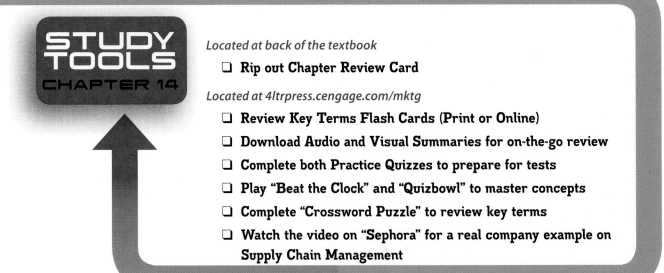

STUDY TOOLS CHAPTER 14

Located at back of the textbook
- ❏ **Rip out Chapter Review Card**

Located at 4ltrpress.cengage.com/mktg
- ❏ **Review Key Terms Flash Cards (Print or Online)**
- ❏ **Download Audio and Visual Summaries for on-the-go review**
- ❏ **Complete both Practice Quizzes to prepare for tests**
- ❏ **Play "Beat the Clock" and "Quizbowl" to master concepts**
- ❏ **Complete "Crossword Puzzle" to review key terms**
- ❏ **Watch the video on "Sephora" for a real company example on Supply Chain Management**

"It's easy to read, it outlines important topics, and it's relevant. Thanks for the good stuff on the website, I think it will **really help with tests**.

– Thomas Scholtes, Student at University of Maryland, College Park

REVIEW

HE DID

MKTG4 puts a multitude of study aids at your fingertips. After reading the chapters, check out these resources for further help:

• **Chapter Review cards**, found in the back of your book, include all learning outcomes, definitions, and visual summaries for each chapter.

• **Online printable flash cards** give you three additional ways to check your comprehension of key marketing concepts.

Other great ways to help you study include **interactive marketing games, podcasts, audio downloads,** and **online tutorial quizzes with feedback**.

You can find it all at **4ltrpress.cengage.com**.

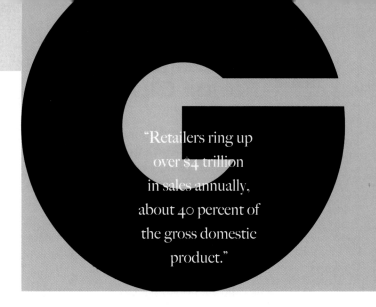

"Retailers ring up over $4 trillion in sales annually, about 40 percent of the gross domestic product."

AFTER YOU FINISH THIS CHAPTER GO TO PAGE 243 FOR STUDY TOOLS

LO 1 The Role of Retailing

Retailing—all the activities directly related to the sale of goods and services to the ultimate consumer for personal, nonbusiness use—has enhanced the quality of our daily lives. When we shop for groceries, hair styling, clothes, books, and many other products and services, we are involved in retailing. The millions of goods and services provided by retailers mirror the needs and styles of U.S. society.

Retailing affects all of us directly or indirectly. The retailing industry is one of the largest employers; over 1.6 million U.S. retailers employ more than 24 million people—about one in five American workers.[1] Retail trade accounts for 11.6 percent of all U.S. employment, and almost 13 percent of all businesses are considered retail under NAICS.[2] At the store level, retailing is still largely a mom-and-pop business. Almost nine out of ten retail companies employ fewer than twenty employees, and, according to the National Retail Federation, over 90 percent of all retailers operate just one store.[3]

The U.S. economy is heavily dependent on retailing. Retailers ring up over $4 trillion in sales annually, about 40 percent of the gross domestic product (GDP).[4] Although most retailers are quite small, a few giant organizations dominate the industry, most notably Wal-Mart, whose annual U.S. sales are greater than the next five U.S. retail giants' sales combined.

retailing all the activities directly related to the sale of goods and services to the ultimate consumer for personal, nonbusiness use

What do you think?

I enjoy seeing mall exhibits while shopping.

1 2 3 4 5 6 7
STRONGLY DISAGREE   STRONGLY AGREE

Find out what others think at 4ltrpress.cengage.com/mktg

© ISTOCKPHOTO.COM/NIKADA

LO 2 Classification of Retail Operations

A retail establishment can be classified according to its ownership, level of service, product assortment, and price. Specifically, retailers use the latter three variables to position themselves in the competitive marketplace. (As noted in Chapter 8, positioning is the strategy used to influence how consumers perceive one product in relation to all competing products.) These three variables can be combined in several ways to create distinctly different retail operations. Exhibit 15.1 lists the major types of retail stores discussed in this chapter and classifies them by level of service, product assortment, price, and gross margin.

Ownership

Retailers can be broadly classified by form of ownership: independent, part of a chain, or franchise outlet. Retailers owned by a single person or partnership and not operated as part of a larger retail institution are **independent retailers**. Around the world, most retailers are independent, operating one or a few stores in their community. Local florists and ethnic food markets typically fit this classification.

Chain stores are owned and operated as a group by a single organization. Under this form of ownership, many administrative tasks are handled by the home office for the entire chain. The home office also buys most of the merchandise sold in the stores. Gap and Starbucks are examples of chains.

Franchises are owned and operated by individuals but are licensed by a larger supporting organization, such as Subway and Quiznos. The franchising approach combines the advantages of independent ownership with those of the chain store organization.

Level of Service

The level of service that retailers provide can be classified along a continuum, from full service to self-service. Some retailers, such as exclusive clothing stores, offer high levels of service. They provide alterations, credit, delivery, consulting, liberal return policies, layaway, gift wrapping, and personal shopping. Retailers like factory outlets and warehouse clubs offer virtually no services.

Product Assortment

The third basis for positioning or classifying stores is by the breadth and depth of their product line. Specialty stores—for example, Best Buy, Toys "R" Us, or Gamestop—have the most concentrated product assortments, usually carrying single or narrow product lines, but in considerable depth. On the other end of the spectrum, full-line discounters typically carry broad assortments of merchandise with limited depth. For example, Target carries automotive supplies, household cleaning products, and pet food. Typically, though, it carries only four or five brands of dog food. In contrast, a specialty pet store, like Petsmart, may carry as many as twenty brands in a large variety of flavors, shapes, and sizes.

Other retailers, such as factory outlet stores, may carry only part of a single line. Nike stores sell only certain items of its own brand. Discount specialty stores like Home Depot or Rack Room Shoes carry a broad assortment in concentrated product lines, such as building and home supplies or shoes.

Price

Price is a fourth way to position retail stores. Traditional department stores and specialty stores typically charge the full "suggested retail price." In contrast, discounters, factory outlets, and off-price retailers use low prices to lure shoppers.

The last column in Exhibit 15.1 shows the typical **gross margin**—how much the retailer makes as a percentage of sales after the cost of goods sold is subtracted. The level of gross margin and the price level generally match. For example, a traditional jew-

EXHIBIT 15.1
Types of Stores and Their Characteristics

Type of Retailer	Level of Service	Product Assortment	Price	Gross Margin
Department store	Moderately high to high	Broad	Moderate to high	Moderately high
Specialty store	High	Narrow	Moderate to high	High
Supermarket	Low	Broad	Moderate	Low
Convenience store	Low	Medium to narrow	Moderately high	Moderately high
Drugstore	Low to moderate	Medium	Moderate	Low
Full-line discount store	Moderate to low	Medium to broad	Moderately low	Moderately low
Discount specialty store	Moderate to low	Medium to broad	Moderately low to low	Moderately low
Warehouse clubs	Low	Broad	Low to very low	Low
Off-price retailer	Low	Medium to narrow	Low	Low
Restaurant	Low to high	Narrow	Low to high	Low to high

elry store has high prices and high gross margins. A factory outlet has low prices and low gross margins. Markdowns on merchandise during sale periods and price wars among competitors, in which stores lower prices on certain items in an effort to win customers, cause gross margins to decline.

LO 3 Major Types of Retail Operations

Traditionally, there have been several distinct types of retail stores, with each offering a different product assortment, type of service, and price level, according to its customers' shopping preferences. In a recent trend, however, retailers are experimenting with alternative formats that make it harder to classify them. For instance, supermarkets are expanding their nonfood items and services, discounters are adding groceries, drugstores are becoming more like convenience stores, and department stores are experimenting with smaller stores. Nevertheless, many stores still fall into the basic types.

Department Stores

A **department store** carries a wide variety of shopping and specialty goods, including apparel, cosmetics, housewares, electronics, and sometimes furniture. Purchases are generally made within each department rather than at one central checkout area. Each department is treated as a separate buying center to achieve economies in promotion, buying, service, and control. Each department is usually headed by a **buyer**, a department head who not only selects the merchandise for his or her department but may also be responsible for promotion and for personnel. For a consistent, uniform store image, central management sets broad policies about the types of merchandise carried and price ranges. Central management is also responsible for the overall advertising program, credit policies, store expansion, customer service, and so on. Large independent department stores are rare today. Most are owned by national chains. Macy's (formerly known as Federated Department Stores, Inc.), JCPenney, Sears, Dillard's, and Nordstrom are some of the largest U.S. department store chains.

Specialty Stores

Specialty store formats allow retailers to refine their segmentation strategies and tailor their merchandise to specific target markets. A **specialty store** is not only a type of store but also a method of retail operations—namely, specializing in a given type of merchandise. Examples include children's clothing, baked goods, and pet supplies. A typical specialty store carries a deeper but narrower assortment of specialty merchandise than does a department store. Generally, specialty stores' knowledgeable sales clerks offer more attentive customer service. The format has become very powerful in the apparel market and other areas. In fact, consumers buy more clothing from specialty stores than from any other type of retailer. The Children's Place, Williams-Sonoma, and Foot Locker are examples of successful chain specialty retailers.

Consumers usually consider price to be secondary in specialty outlets. Instead, the distinctive merchandise, the store's physical appearance, and the caliber of the staff determine its popularity. Because of their attention to the

department store a store housing several departments under one roof

buyer a department head who selects the merchandise for his or her department and may also be responsible for promotion and personnel

specialty store a retail store specializing in a given type of merchandise

customer and limited product line, manufacturers often favor introducing new products in small specialty stores before moving on to larger retail and department stores.

Supermarkets

U.S. consumers spend about a tenth of their disposable income in **supermarkets**. Supermarkets are large, departmentalized, self-service retailers that specialize in food and some nonfood items. Supermarkets have experienced declining sales in recent years. Some of this decline has been the result of increased competition from discounters Wal-Mart and Sam's Clubs. But demographic and lifestyle changes have also affected the supermarket industry, as families eat out more or are just too busy to prepare meals at home.

Conventional supermarkets are being replaced by bigger *superstores*, which are usually twice the size of supermarkets. Superstores meet the needs of today's customers for convenience, variety, and service by offering one-stop shopping for many food and nonfood needs, as well as many services—including pharmacies, flower shops, salad bars, in-store bakeries, takeout food sections, sit-down restaurants, health food sections, video rentals, dry-cleaning services, shoe repair, photo processing, and banking. Some even offer family dentistry or optical shops, and many now have gas stations. This tendency to offer a wide variety of nontraditional goods and services under one roof is called **scrambled merchandising**.

To stand out in an increasingly competitive marketplace, many supermarket chains are tailoring marketing strategies to appeal to specific consumer segments. Most notable is the shift toward *loyalty marketing programs* that reward loyal customers carrying frequent shopper cards with discounts or gifts. Once scanned at the checkout, frequent shopper cards help supermarket retailers electronically track shoppers' buying habits.

Drugstores

Drugstores stock pharmacy-related products and services as their main draw, but they also carry an extensive selection of over-the-counter (OTC) medications, cosmetics, health and beauty aids, seasonal merchandise, specialty items such as greeting cards and a limited selection of toys, and some nonrefrigerated convenience foods. As competition has increased from mass merchandisers and supermarkets with their own pharmacies, as well as from direct-mail prescription services, drugstores have added services such as 24-hour, drive-through pharmacies and low-cost health clinics staffed by nurse practitioners.

Demographic trends in the United States look favorable for the drugstore industry. The average 60-year-old purchases fifteen prescriptions per year, nearly twice as many as the average 30-year-old. Because baby boomers are attentive to their health and keenly sensitive about their looks, the increased traffic at the pharmacy counter in the future should also spur sales in other traditionally strong drugstore merchandise categories, most notably OTC drugs, vitamins, and health and beauty aids.

Convenience Stores

A **convenience store** can be defined as a miniature supermarket, carrying only a limited line of high-turnover convenience goods. These self-service stores are typically located near residential areas and are open twenty-four hours, seven days a week. Convenience stores offer exactly what their name implies: convenient location, long hours, fast service. However, prices are almost always higher at a convenience store than at a supermarket. Thus, the customer pays for the convenience.

In response to recent heavy competition from gas stations and supermarkets, convenience store operators have changed their strategy. They have expanded

Food is a customer magnet for supercenters.

Save even more Was $3.50

2 for $5.00

their offerings of nonfood items with video rentals and health and beauty aids and added upscale sandwich and salad lines and more fresh produce. Some convenience stores are even selling Pizza Hut, Subway, and Taco Bell products prepared in the store.

Discount Stores

A **discount store** is a retailer that competes on the basis of low prices, high turnover, and high volume. Discounters can be classified into four major categories: full-line discount stores, specialty discount stores, warehouse clubs, and off-price discount retailers.

Full-Line Discount Stores Compared to traditional department stores, **full-line discount stores** offer consumers very limited service and carry a much broader assortment of well-known, nationally branded "hard goods," including housewares, toys, automotive parts, hardware, sporting goods, and garden items, as well as clothing, bedding, and linens. As with department stores, national chains dominate the discounters. Full-line discounters are often called mass merchandisers. **Mass merchandising** is the retailing strategy whereby retailers use moderate to low prices on large quantities of merchandise and lower levels of service to stimulate high turnover of products.

Wal-Mart is the largest full-line discount store in terms of sales. Today, it has more than 7,200 stores on four continents, and its pioneering retail strategy of "everyday low pricing" is now widely copied by retailers the world over. Wal-Mart has also become a formidable retailing giant in online shopping, concentrating on toys and electronics. With tie-ins to its stores across the country, Wal-Mart offers online shopping with in-store kiosks linking to the site and the ability to handle returns and exchanges from Internet sales at its physical stores.[5]

Supercenters combine a full line of groceries and general merchandise with a wide range of services, including pharmacy, dry cleaning, portrait studios, photo finishing, hair salons, optical shops, and restaurants—all in one location. For supercenter operators such as Target, food is a customer magnet that sharply increases the store's overall volume, while taking customers away from traditional supermarkets.

Specialty Discount Stores Another discount niche includes the single-line **specialty discount stores**—for example, stores selling sporting goods, electronics, auto parts, office supplies, housewares, or toys. These stores offer a nearly complete selection of single-line merchandise and use self-service, discount prices, high volume, and high turnover to their advantage. Spe-

cialty discount stores are often termed **category killers** because they so heavily dominate their narrow merchandise segment. Examples include Best Buy in electronics, Staples and Office Depot in office supplies, and IKEA in home furnishings.

Category killers have emerged in other specialty segments as well, creating retailing empires in highly fragmented mom-and-pop markets. For instance, the home improvement industry, which for years was served by professional builders and small hardware stores, is now dominated by Home Depot and Lowe's. Category-dominant retailers like these serve their customers by offering a large selection of merchandise, stores that make shopping easy, and low prices every day, which eliminates the need for time-consuming comparison shopping.

Warehouse Membership Clubs **Warehouse membership clubs** sell a limited selection of brand-name appliances, household items, and groceries. These are usually sold in bulk from warehouse outlets on a cash-and-carry basis to members only. Individual members of warehouse clubs are charged low or no membership fees. Warehouse club members tend to be better educated and more affluent and have larger households than regular supermarket shoppers. These core customers use warehouse clubs to stock up on staples; then they go to specialty outlets or food stores for perishables. Currently, the leading stores in this category are Wal-Mart's Sam's Club, Costco, and BJ's Wholesale Club.

Off-Price Retailers An **off-price retailer** sells at prices 25 percent or more below traditional department store prices because it pays cash for its stock and usually doesn't ask for return privileges. Off-price retailers buy manufacturers' overruns at cost or even less. They also absorb goods from bankrupt stores, irregular merchandise, and unsold end-of-season output. Nevertheless, much off-price retailer merchandise is first-quality, current goods. Because buyers for off-price retailers purchase only what is available or

discount store a retailer that competes on the basis of low prices, high turnover, and high volume

full-line discount store a retailer that offers consumers very limited service and carries a broad assortment of well-known, nationally branded "hard goods"

mass merchandising a retailing strategy using moderate to low prices on large quantities of merchandise and lower levels of service to stimulate high turnover of products

supercenter a retail store that combines groceries and general merchandise goods with a wide range of services

specialty discount store a retail store that offers a nearly complete selection of single-line merchandise and uses self-service, discount prices, high volume, and high turnover

category killers specialty discount stores that heavily dominate their narrow merchandise segment

warehouse membership clubs limited-service merchant wholesalers that sell a limited selection of brand-name appliances, household items, and groceries on a cash-and-carry basis to members, usually small businesses and groups

off-price retailer a retailer that sells at prices 25 percent or more below traditional department store prices because it pays cash for its stock and usually doesn't ask for return privileges

what they can get a good deal on, merchandise styles and brands often change monthly. Today, there are hundreds of off-price retailers, the best known being T.J. Maxx, Ross Stores, Marshalls, HomeGoods, and Tuesday Morning.

Factory outlets are an interesting variation on the off-price concept. A **factory outlet** is an off-price retailer that is owned and operated by a manufacturer. Thus, it carries one line of merchandise—its own. Each season, from 5 to 10 percent of a manufacturer's output does not sell through regular distribution channels because it consists of closeouts (merchandise being discontinued), factory seconds, and canceled orders. With factory outlets, manufacturers can regulate where their surplus is sold, and they can realize higher profit margins than they would by disposing of the goods through independent wholesalers and retailers. Factory outlet malls typically locate in out-of-the-way rural areas or near vacation destinations. Most are situated ten to fifteen miles from urban or suburban shopping areas so that manufacturers don't alienate their department store accounts by selling the same goods virtually next door at a discount. Recently, the weakening U.S. economy has encouraged several high-end designers and upscale retailers to open separate luxury outlets, including Saks Fifth Avenue Off 5th. These stores offer a mixture of discounted designer items and special outlet lines, and they target a different crowd of aspirational shoppers.[6]

factory outlet an off-price retailer that is owned and operated by a manufacturer

nonstore retailing shopping without visiting a store

Restaurants

Restaurants straddle the line between retailing establishments and service establishments. Restaurants do sell tangible products—food and drink— but they also provide a valuable service for consumers in the form of food preparation and food service. Most restaurants could even fall into the definition of a specialty retailer given that most concentrate their menu offerings on a distinctive type of cuisine—for example, Olive Garden Italian restaurants and Starbucks coffeehouses.

Eating out is an important part of Americans' daily activities and is growing in strength. According to the National Restaurant Association, more than 70 billion meals are eaten in restaurants or cafeterias annually. This means that Americans consume an average of 5.8 commercially prepared meals per week. Food away from home accounts for about 48 percent of the annual household food budget. The trend toward eating out has been fueled by the increase in working mothers and dual-income families who have more money to eat out and less time to shop and prepare meals at home.[7]

The restaurant industry is one of the most entrepreneurial of businesses and one of the most competitive. Because barriers to entering the restaurant industry are low, the opportunity appeals to many people. The risks, however, are great. About 50 percent of all new restaurants fail within the first year of operation. Restaurants face competition not only from other restaurants but also from the consumer who can easily choose to cook at home. Competition has fostered innovation and ever-changing menus in most segments of the restaurant industry. Many restaurants are now competing directly with supermarkets by offering takeout and delivery in an effort to capture more of the home meal replacement market.

LO 4 Nonstore Retailing

The retailing methods discussed so far have been in-store methods, in which customers must physically shop at stores. In contrast, **nonstore retailing** is shopping without visiting a store. Because consumers demand convenience, nonstore retailing is currently growing faster than in-store retailing. The major forms of nonstore retailing are automatic vending, direct retailing, direct marketing, and electronic retailing.

Automatic Vending

A low-profile yet important form of retailing is **automatic vending**, the use of machines to offer goods for sale—for example, the soft drink, candy, or snack vending machines found in college cafeterias and office buildings. Vending is the most pervasive retail business in the United States, with about 11.5 million vending machines—only 12,000 accepting credit cards—selling billions of dollars worth of goods annually.[8] Consumers are willing to pay higher prices for products from a convenient vending machine than for the same products in a traditional retail setting.

Retailers are constantly seeking new opportunities to sell via vending. Many vending machines today sell nontraditional kinds of merchandise, DVDs, digital cameras, perfumes, and even ice-cream. Vending machines at McCarran International Airport in Las Vegas sell iPods, Coty's celebrity fragances, and Rosetta Stone's language software; they make an annual average of $42,000 per square foot.[9]

Direct Retailing

In **direct retailing**, representatives sell products door-to-door, office-to-office, or at home sales parties. Companies like Avon and The Pampered Chef have used this approach for years. But recently direct retailers' sales have suffered as women have entered the workforce. Although most direct sellers like Avon and Tupperware still advocate the party plan method, the realities of the marketplace have forced them to be more creative in reaching their target customer. Direct sales representatives now hold parties in offices, parks, and even parking lots. Others hold informal gatherings where shoppers can drop in at their convenience or offer self-improvement classes. Many direct retailers are also turning to direct mail, telephone, or more traditional retailing venues to find new avenues to their customers and increase sales. Avon, for instance, has begun opening cosmetic kiosk counters, called Avon Beauty Centers, in malls and strip centers. Avon has also launched a new brand—Mark, a beauty "experience" for young women. Most Mark representatives are students who typically sell the product as an after-school part-time job. Prospective representatives and consumers can buy products or register to be a representative in person, online, or over the phone.[10]

Direct retailers are also using the Internet as a channel to reach more customers and increase sales. Amway launched Quixtar.com, an online channel for its products that generated over $1 billion in revenues

in its first year. Customers access the site using a unique referral number for each Amway rep, a system that ensures that the reps earn their commissions.

Direct Marketing

Companies spent approximately $183 billion on direct marketing in 2008, and their efforts generated an estimated $1.2 trillion in sales.[11] **Direct marketing**, sometimes called **direct-response marketing**, refers to the techniques used to get consumers to make a purchase from their home, office, or other nonretail setting. Those techniques include telemarketing, direct mail, catalogs and mail order, and electronic retailing. Shoppers using these methods are less bound by traditional shopping situations. Time-strapped consumers and those who live in rural or suburban areas are most likely to be direct-response shoppers because they value the convenience and flexibility that direct marketing provides.

Telemarketing **Telemarketing** is the use of the telephone to sell directly to consumers. It consists of outbound sales calls, usually unsolicited, and inbound calls—that is, orders through toll-free 800 numbers or fee-based 900 numbers.

Rising postage rates and decreasing long-distance phone rates have made *outbound* telemarketing into an attractive direct-marketing technique. Skyrocketing field sales costs have also led marketing managers to use outbound telemarketing. Searching for ways to keep costs under control, marketing managers have learned

© STOCKBYTE/GETTY IMAGES

how to pinpoint prospects quickly, zero in on serious buyers, and keep in close touch with regular customers. Meanwhile, they are reserving expensive, time-consuming, in-person calls for closing sales. So many consumers complained about outbound telemarketing, however, that Congress passed legislation establishing a national "do not call" list of consumers who do not want to receive unsolicited telephone calls. In addition, Congress passed laws requiring e-mail marketers to allow recipients to opt out of mass e-mails (spam). The laws also prohibit marketers from camouflaging their identity through false return addresses and misleading subject lines. A problem with the telemarketing law, however, is that it exempted nonprofits, so some companies have set up nonprofit subsidiaries to continue their calling activities. Some industry experts say the lists help them by eliminating nonbuyers, but others believe this legislation could have a long-term negative effect on telemarketing sales.[12]

Inbound telemarketing programs, which use 800 and 900 numbers, are mainly used to take orders, generate leads, and provide customer service. Inbound 800 telemarketing has successfully supplemented direct-response television, radio, and print advertising for more than twenty-five years. The more recently introduced 900 numbers, which customers pay to call, are gaining popularity as a cost-effective way for companies to target customers. One of the major benefits of 900 numbers is that they allow marketers to generate qualified responses. Although the charge may reduce the total volume of calls, the calls that do come are from customers who have a true interest in the product.

Direct Mail Direct mail can be the most efficient or the least efficient retailing method, depending on the quality of the mailing list and the effectiveness of the mailing piece. With direct mail, marketers can precisely target their customers according to demographics, geographics, and even psychographics. Good mailing lists come from an internal database or are available from list brokers for about $35 to $150 per thousand names.

Direct mailers are becoming more sophisticated in targeting the "right" customers. Using statistical methods to analyze census data, lifestyle and financial information, and past purchase and credit history, direct mailers can pick out those most likely to buy their products. So, despite increases in postal rates and raw material and logistics costs, U.S. direct mail services totaled $56 billion in 2007.[13]

Catalogs and Mail Order Consumers can now buy just about anything through the mail, from the mun-

CATALOGS IN THE DIGITAL AGE

With e-commerce booming and environmentalists cracking down on waste, it would seem printed catalogs face certain doom. However, this might not be the case. Marketers mailed 17 billion catalogs last year, which amounts to 56 catalogs per person in the United States. A recent study concluded that customers who received a catalog spent 28 percent more money on that retailer's Web site. Though some companies are moving to an "iCatalog," the 12,524 catalogs available in print vastly outnumber the digital. Apparently, receiving a physical, visual reminder to visit a company's Web site makes catalogs more important than ever, and there is no substitute for the enticement of those glossy images.[14]

dane to the outlandish. Although women make up the bulk of catalog shoppers, the percentage of male catalog shoppers has recently soared. As changing demographics have shifted more of the shopping responsibility to men, they are viewing shopping via catalog, mail order, and the Internet as more sensible than a trip to the mall. Often, interested consumers will flip through a traditional paper catalog to get ideas before placing their orders online. Many shoppers like retail Web sites because they can recommend products and offer customized packages.

Successful catalogs usually are created and designed for highly segmented markets. Certain types of retailers are using mail order successfully. For example, computer manufacturers have discovered that mail order is a lucrative way to sell personal computers to home and small-business users, evidenced by the huge successes of Dell, which has used its direct business model to become a $59 billion company and the number-one PC seller worldwide. With a global market share of almost 20 percent, it sells about $50 million in computers and equipment online every day.[15]

Electronic Retailing

Electronic retailing includes online retailing and the twenty-four-hour, shop-at-home television networks.

CONSUMER TOP TEN FAVORITE e-COMMERCE SITES

1. Amazon.com
2. WalMart.com
3. eBay.com
4. BestBuy.com
5. JCPenney.com
6. Target.com
7. Kohls.com
8. Google.com
9. Overstock.com
10. Sears.com

SOURCE: STORES, September 2009, www.stores.org.

Online Retailing For years, shopping at home meant looking through catalogs and then placing an order over the telephone. For many people today, however, it now means turning on a computer, surfing retail Web sites, and selecting and ordering products online with the click of a mouse. **Online retailing**, or *e-tailing*, is a type of shopping available to consumers with personal computers and access to the Internet. More than 70 percent of Americans have Internet access either at home or at work.

Online retailing has exploded in the last several years as consumers have found this type of shopping convenient and, in many instances, less costly. Consumers can shop without leaving home, choose from a wide selection of merchants, use shopping comparison services to search the Web for the best price, and then have the items delivered to their doorsteps. For example, Like.com uses a visual search engine technology that makes it possible to search for a product from a photo. If a customer wants a pair of boots worn by a celebrity, for instance, that customer can search for the boots on Like.com by the celebrity's name, the color of the boots, or even a magazine photo of the particular boots.[16] As a result of improved technology and convenience, online shopping continues to grow at a rapid pace, with online sales accounting for roughly 8 percent of total retail sales. Online retailing is also increasing in popularity outside the United States.

Most traditional retailers have now jumped on the Internet bandwagon, allowing shoppers to purchase the same merchandise found in their stores from their Web site. Online retailing also fits well with traditional catalog companies, such as Lands' End and Eddie Bauer, that already have established distribution networks.

As the popularity of online retailing grows, it is becoming critical that retailers be online and that their stores, Web sites, and catalogs be integrated. Customers expect to find the same brands, products, and prices whether they purchase online, on the phone, or in a store. Therefore, retailers are increasingly using in-store kiosks to help tie the channels together for greater customer service.

Popular e-tailers don't necessarily have to have a physical presence in the market. Bluefly.com, Zappos.com, and eBay have created tremendously successful formulas without selling in a single retail store.

Shop-at-Home Networks The shop-at-home television networks are specialized forms of direct-response marketing. These shows display merchandise, with the retail price, to home viewers. Viewers can phone in their orders directly on a toll-free line and shop with a credit card. The shop-at-home industry has quickly grown into a multi-billion-dollar business with a loyal customer following. Shop-at-home networks can reach nearly every home with a television set. The best-known shop-at-home networks are HSN (formerly the Home Shopping Network) and the QVC (Quality, Value, Convenience) Network. Home shopping networks attract a broad audience through diverse programming and product offerings and are now adding new products to appeal to more affluent audiences. HSN features a range of personalities selling their own brands and products. For instance, the celebrity chef Wolfgang Puck demonstrates the benefits of his gourmet cookware. The network employs 4,000 people and is worth $3 billion.[17]

LO 5 Franchising

A *franchise* is a continuing relationship in which a franchiser grants to a franchisee the business rights to operate or to sell a product. The **franchisor** originates the trade name, product, methods of operation, and

online retailing a type of shopping available to consumers with personal computers and access to the Internet

franchisor the originator of a trade name, product, methods of operation, and so on that grants operating rights to another party to sell its product

franchisee an individual or business that is granted the right to sell another party's product

so on. The **franchisee**, in return, pays the franchisor for the right to use its name, product, or business methods. A franchise agreement between the two parties usually lasts for ten to twenty years, at which time the agreement can be renewed if both parties are agreeable.

To be granted the rights to a franchise, a franchisee usually pays an initial, one-time franchise fee. The amount of this fee depends solely on the individual franchisor, but it generally ranges from $50,000 to $250,000 or higher. In addition to this initial franchise fee, the franchisee is expected to pay royalty fees, usually in the range of 3 to 7 percent of gross revenues. The franchisee may also be expected to pay advertising fees, which usually cover the cost of promotional materials and, if the franchise organization is large enough, regional or national advertising. A McDonald's franchise, for example, costs an initial $45,000 per store plus a monthly fee based upon the restaurant's sales performance and base rent. In addition, a new McDonald's franchisee can expect start-up costs for equipment and pre-opening expenses to range from $511,000 to over $1 million. The size of the restaurant facility, area of the country, inventory, selection of kitchen equipment, signage, and style of decor and landscaping affect new restaurant costs.[18] Fees such as these are typical for all major franchisers, including Burger King and Subway.

> A NEW MCDONALD'S FRANCHISEE CAN EXPECT START-UP COSTS FOR EQUIPMENT AND PRE-OPENING EXPENSES TO RANGE FROM $511,000 TO OVER $1 MILLION.

Two basic forms of franchises are used today: product and trade name franchising and business format franchising. In *product and trade name franchising*, a dealer agrees to sell certain products provided by a manufacturer or a wholesaler. This approach has been used most widely in the auto and truck, soft drink bottling, tire, and gasoline service industries. For example, a local tire retailer may hold a franchise to sell Michelin tires.

Business format franchising is an ongoing business relationship between a franchisor and a franchisee. Typically, a franchiser "sells" a franchisee the rights to use the franchisor's format or approach to doing business. This form of franchising has rapidly expanded since the 1950s through retailing, restaurant, food-service, hotel and motel, printing, and real estate franchises.

TOP 20 FRANCHISORS

1. Subway
2. McDonald's
3. Liberty Tax Service
4. Sonic Drive-In Restaurants
5. InterContinental Hotels Group
6. Ace Hardware Corp.
7. Pizza Hut
8. The UPS Store/Mail Boxes Etc.
9. Circle K
10. Papa John's International, Inc.
11. Jiffy Lube International, Inc.
12. Instant Tax Service
13. Baskin-Robbins, USA Co.
14. KFC Corp.
15. Jani-King
16. Dairy Queen
17. Super 8 WorldWide
18. Arby's
19. JAN-PRO Franchising International, Inc.
20. Taco Bell Corp.

SOURCE: "2009 Franchise 500 Rankings" at http://www.entrepreneur.com, accessed December 9, 2009.

LO 6 Retail Marketing Strategy

Retailers must develop marketing strategies based on overall goals and strategic plans. Retailing goals might include more traffic, higher sales of a specific item, a more upscale image, or heightened public awareness of the retail operation. The strategies that retailers use to obtain their goals might include a sale, an updated decor, or a new advertisement. The key tasks in strategic retailing are defining and selecting a target market and developing the retailing mix to successfully meet the needs of the chosen target market.

Defining a Target Market

The first and foremost task in developing a retail strategy is to define the target market. This process begins with market segmentation, the topic of Chapter 8. Successful retailing has always been based on knowing the customer. Sometimes retailing chains flounder when management loses sight of the customers the stores should be serving. For example, Gap built a retail empire by offering updated, casual classics like white shirts and khaki pants that appealed to everyone from high school through middle age, but began losing customers when it shifted toward trendier fashions with a limited appeal.

Target markets in retailing are often defined by demographics, geographics, and psychographics. For instance, Bluefly.com, a discount fashion e-tailer, targets both men and women in their thirties, who have a higher-than-average income, read fashion magazines, and favor high-end designers. By understanding who its customers are, the company has been able to tailor its Web site to appeal specifically to its audience. The result is a higher sales rate than most e-tailers.[19] Determining a target market is a prerequisite to creating the retailing mix. For example, Target's merchandising approach for sporting goods is to match its product assortment to the demographics of the local store and region.

Choosing the Retailing Mix

Retailers combine the elements of the retailing mix to come up with a single retailing method to attract the target market. The **retailing mix** consists of six Ps: the four Ps of the marketing mix (product, place, promotion, and price) plus presentation and personnel (see Exhibit 15.2).

The combination of the six Ps projects a store's image, which influences consumers' perceptions. Using these impressions of stores, shoppers position one store against another. A retail marketing manager must make sure that the store's positioning is compatible with the target customers' expectations. As discussed at the begin-

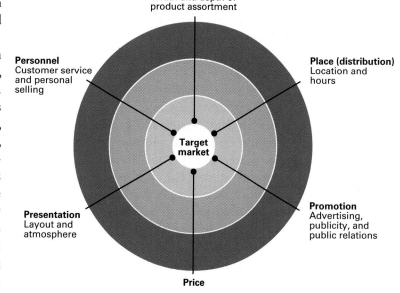

EXHIBIT 15.2
The Retailing Mix

Product
Width and depth of product assortment

Place (distribution)
Location and hours

Promotion
Advertising, publicity, and public relations

Price

Presentation
Layout and atmosphere

Personnel
Customer service and personal selling

Target market

ning of the chapter, retail stores can be positioned on three broad dimensions: service provided by store personnel, product assortment, and price. Management should use everything else—place, presentation, and promotion—to fine-tune the basic positioning of the store.

The Product Offering The first element in the retailing mix is the **product offering**, also called the *product*

retailing mix a combination of the six Ps—product, place, promotion, price, presentation, and personnel—to sell goods and services to the ultimate consumer

product offering the mix of products offered to the consumer by the retailer; also called the *product assortment* or *merchandise mix*

© ISTOCKPHOTO.COM/ALVIN BURROWS

assortment or *merchandise mix*. Retailers decide what to sell on the basis of what their target market wants to buy. They can base their decision on market research, past sales, fashion trends, customer requests, and other sources. A recent approach, called *data mining*, uses complex mathematical models to help retailers make better product mix decisions. Dillard's, Target, and Wal-Mart use data mining to determine which products to stock at what price, how to manage markdowns, and how to advertise to draw target customers.

Developing a product offering is essentially a question of the width and depth of the product assortment. *Width* refers to the assortment of products offered; *depth* refers to the number of different brands offered within each assortment. Price, store design, displays, and service are important to consumers in determining where to shop, but the most critical factor is merchandise selection. This reasoning also holds true for online retailers. Amazon.com, for instance, is building the world's biggest online department store so that shoppers can get whatever they want with one click on their Web browsers. Like a traditional department store or mass merchandiser, Amazon offers considerable width in its product assortment with millions of different items, including books, music, toys, videos, tools and hardware, health and beauty aids, electronics, and software. Conversely, online specialty retailers, such as 1-800-Flowers.com and Polo.com clothing, focus on a single category of merchandise, hoping to attract loyal customers with a larger depth of products at lower prices and better customer service. Many online retailers purposely focus on single product line niches that could never garner enough foot traffic to support a traditional brick-and-mortar store. For instance, Fridgedoor.com claims to be the single largest stop for all things magnetic: novelty magnets, custom magnets, and magnetic supplies. It is the Web's largest refrigerator magnet retailer, with more than 1,500 different types of magnets for sale.[20]

After determining what products will satisfy target customers' desires, retailers must find sources of supply and evaluate the products. When the right products are found, the retail buyer negotiates a purchase contract. The buying function can either be performed in-house or be delegated to an outside firm. The goods must then be moved from the seller to the retailer, which means shipping, storing, and stocking the inventory. The trick is to manage the inventory by cutting prices to move slow goods and by keeping adequate supplies of hot-selling items in stock. As in all good systems, the final step is to evaluate the entire process to seek more efficient methods and eliminate problems and bottlenecks.

Promotion Strategy Retail promotion strategy includes advertising, public relations and publicity, and sales promotion. The goal is to help position the store in consumers' minds. Retailers design intriguing ads, stage special events, and develop promotions aimed at their target markets. Today's grand openings are a carefully orchestrated blend of advertising, merchandising, goodwill, and glitter. All the elements of an opening—press coverage, special events, media advertising, and store displays—are carefully planned.

Retailers' advertising is carried out mostly at the local level. Local advertising by retailers usually provides specific information about their stores, such as location, merchandise, hours, prices, and special sales. In contrast, national retail advertising generally focuses on image. For example, Target has used its "sign of the times" advertising campaign to effectively position itself as the "chic place to buy cheap."

Target's advertising campaign also takes advantage of cooperative advertising, another popular retail advertising practice. Traditionally, marketers would pay retailers to feature their products in store mailers, or a marketer would develop a television campaign for the product and simply tack on several retailers' names at the end. But Target's advertising makes use of a more collaborative trend by integrating products such as Tide laundry detergent or Coca-Cola into the actual campaign. Another common form of cooperative advertising involves promotion of exclusive products. For example, Target hires famous young designers for temporary partnerships, during which they develop reasonably priced product lines available exclusively at Target stores.

The Proper Location The retailing axiom "location, location, location" has long emphasized the importance of place to the retail mix. The location decision is important first because the retailer is making a large, semipermanent commitment of resources that can reduce its future flexibility. Second, the location will affect the store's future growth and profitability.

Site location begins by choosing a community. Important factors to consider are the area's economic growth potential, the amount of competition, and geography. For instance, retailers like T.J. Maxx and Wal-Mart often build stores in new communities that are still under development. On the other hand, while population growth is an important consideration for fast-food restaurants, most also look for an area with other fast-food restaurants because being located in clusters helps to draw customers for each restaurant. However, even after careful research, the perfect position can be elusive in the face of changing markets. For example, Wendy's found, when attempting to enter the competitive breakfast business, that its locations weren't positioned on the right side of the road to attract the bulk of commuters looking for breakfast.[21] Finally, for many retailers geography remains the most important factor in choosing a community. For example, Starbucks looks for densely populated urban communities for its stores.

After settling on a geographic region or community, retailers must choose a specific site. In addition to growth potential, the important factors to consider are neighborhood socioeconomic characteristics, traffic flows, land costs, zoning regulations, and public transportation. A particular site's visibility, parking, entrance and exit locations, accessibility, and safety and security issues are also important considerations. Additionally, a retailer should consider how its store will fit into the surrounding environment. Retail decision makers probably would not locate a Dollar General store next door to a Neiman Marcus department store.

Retailers face one final decision about location: whether to have a freestanding unit or to become a tenant in a shopping center or mall.

Freestanding Stores An isolated, freestanding location can be used by large retailers like Wal-Mart or Target and sellers of shopping goods like furniture and cars because they are "destination" stores. **Destination stores** are stores consumers seek out and purposely plan to visit. An isolated store location may have the advantages of low site cost or rent and no nearby

competitors. On the other hand, it may be hard to attract customers to a freestanding location, and no other retailers are around to share costs.

Freestanding units are increasing in popularity as retailers strive to make their stores more convenient to access, more enticing to shop, and more profitable. Freestanding sites now account for more than half of all retail construction starts in the United States as more and more retailers are deciding not to locate in pedestrian malls. Perhaps the greatest reason for developing a freestanding site is greater visibility. Retailers often feel they get lost in huge centers and malls, but freestanding units can help stores develop an identity with shoppers. Also, an aggressive expansion plan may not allow time to wait for shopping centers to be built. Drugstore chains like Walgreens have been purposefully relocating their existing shopping center stores to freestanding sites, especially street corner sites for drive-through accessibility.

Shopping Centers Shopping centers first appeared in the 1950s when the U.S. population started migrating to the suburbs. The first shopping centers were *strip centers*, typically located along busy streets. They usually included a supermarket, a variety store, and perhaps a few specialty stores. Then *community shopping centers* emerged, with one or two small department stores, more specialty stores, a couple of restaurants, and several apparel stores. These community shopping centers provided off-street parking and a broader variety of merchandise.

Regional malls offering a much wider variety of merchandise started appearing in the mid-1970s. Regional malls are either entirely enclosed or roofed to allow shopping in any weather. Most are landscaped with trees, fountains, sculptures, and the like to enhance the shopping environment. They have acres of free parking. The *anchor stores* or *generator stores* (often major department stores) are usually located at opposite ends of the mall to create heavy foot traffic.

According to shopping center developers, *lifestyle centers* are emerging as the newest generation of shopping centers. Lifestyle centers typically combine outdoor shopping areas comprised of upscale retailers and restaurants, with plazas, fountains, and pedestrian streets. They appeal to retail developers looking for an alternative to the traditional shopping mall, a concept rapidly losing favor among shoppers.

destination stores
stores that consumers purposely plan to visit

Apple stores use large open tables to display company products, making it easier for visitors to play with them.

atmosphere the overall impression conveyed by a store's physical layout, decor, and surroundings

Store within a Store Many smaller specialty lines are opening shops inside larger stores to expand their retail opportunities without risking investment in a separate store. FAO Schwarz, for example, has opened toy boutiques in hundreds of Macy's department stores.[22]

Pop-up Shops Pop-up shops, tiny, temporary stores that stay in one location only for a few months, are a growing trend. They help retailers reach a wide market while avoiding high rent at retail locations. Levi's recently ran a fifteen-square-foot pop-up shop for two months within the American Rag Cie's denim store.[23]

Retail Prices Another important element in the retailing mix is price. Retailing's ultimate goal is to sell products to consumers, and the right price is critical in ensuring sales. Because retail prices are usually based on the cost of the merchandise, an essential part of pricing is efficient and timely buying.

Price is also a key element in a retail store's positioning strategy. Higher prices often indicate a level of quality and help reinforce the prestigious image of retailers, as they do for Lord & Taylor and Neiman Marcus. On the other hand, discounters and off-price retailers, such as Target and T.J. Maxx, offer a good value for the money. There are even stores, such as Dollar Tree, where everything costs $1. Dollar Tree's single-price-point strategy is aimed at getting custom-

ers to make impulse purchases through what analysts call the "wow factor"—the excitement of discovering that an item costs only a dollar.

Presentation of the Retail Store The presentation of a retail store helps determine the store's image and positions the retail store in consumers' minds. For instance, a retailer that wants to position itself as an upscale store would use a lavish or sophisticated presentation.

The main element of a store's presentation is its **atmosphere**, the overall impression conveyed by a store's physical layout, decor, and surroundings. The atmosphere might create a relaxed or busy feeling, a sense of luxury or efficiency, a friendly or cold attitude, a sense of organization or clutter, or a fun or serious mood. Urban Outfitters stores, targeted to Generation Y consumers, use raw concrete, original brick, rusted steel, and unfinished wood to convey an urban feel.

The layout of retail stores is a key factor in their success. The goal is to use all of the store's space effectively, including aisles, fixtures, merchandise displays, and nonselling areas. In addition to making shopping easy and convenient for the customer, an effective layout has a powerful influence on traffic patterns and purchasing behavior. Kohl's uses a unique circular store layout, which encourages customers to pass all of a store's departments to reach the checkout lanes. Even though stores are on the small side, the store

© ISTOCKPHOTO.COM/4X6

layout, together with over-merchandising strategies, generates an average of over $300 in sales per square foot (this is a standard industry measurement) in the chain's 930 stores.[24]

Layout also includes where products are placed in the store. Many technologically advanced retailers are using a technique called *market-basket analysis* to sift through the data collected by their point-of-purchase scanning equipment. The analysis looks for products that are commonly purchased together to help retailers find ideal locations for each product. Wal-Mart uses market-basket analysis to determine where in the store to stock products for customer convenience. Kleenex tissues, for example, are in the paper-goods aisle and beside the cold medicines.

These are the most influential factors in creating a store's atmosphere:

▸▸ *Employee type and density*: Employee type refers to an employee's general characteristics—for instance, neat, friendly, knowledgeable, or service oriented. Density is the number of employees per thousand square feet of selling space. Whereas low employee density creates a "do-it-yourself," casual atmosphere, high employee density denotes readiness to serve the customer's every whim.

▸▸ *Merchandise type and density*: A prestigious retailer like Nordstrom or Neiman Marcus carries the best brand names and displays them in a neat, uncluttered arrangement. Discounters and off-price retailers often carry seconds or out-of-season goods crowded into small spaces and hung on long racks by category—tops, pants, skirts, etc.—creating the impression that "We've got so much stuff, we're practically giving it away."

▸▸ *Fixture type and density*: Fixtures can be elegant (rich woods), trendy (chrome and smoked glass), or consist of old, beat-up tables, as in an antiques store. The fixtures should be consistent with the general atmosphere the store is trying to create.

▸▸ *Sound*: Sound can be pleasant or unpleasant for a customer. Music can entice customers to stay in the store longer and buy more or eat quickly and leave a table for others. It can also control the pace of the store traffic, create an image, and attract or direct the shopper's attention.

▸▸ *Odors*: Smell can either stimulate or detract from sales. Research suggests that people evaluate merchandise more positively, spend more time shopping, and are generally in a better mood when an agreeable odor is present. Retailers use fragrances as an extension of their retail strategy.

▸▸ *Visual factors*: Colors can create a mood or focus attention and therefore are an important factor in atmosphere. Red, yellow, and orange are considered warm colors and are used when a feeling of warmth and closeness is desired. Cool colors like blue, green, and violet are used to open up closed-in places and create an air of elegance and cleanliness. Many retailers have found that natural lighting, either from windows or skylights, can lead to increased sales. Outdoor lighting can also affect consumer patronage.

Personnel and Customer Service People are a unique aspect of retailing. Most retail sales involve a customer–salesperson relationship, if only briefly. When customers shop at a grocery store, the cashiers check and bag their groceries. When customers shop at a prestigious clothier, the salesclerks may assist in the fitting process, offer alteration services, wrap purchases, and even serve champagne. Sales personnel provide their customers with the amount of service prescribed by the retail strategy of the store.

Retail salespeople serve another important selling function: They persuade shoppers to buy. They must therefore be able to persuade customers that what they are selling is what the customer needs. Salespeople are trained in two common selling techniques: trading up and suggestion selling. Trading up means persuading customers to buy a higher-priced item than they originally intended to purchase. To avoid selling customers something they do not need or want, however, salespeople should take care when practicing trading-up techniques. Suggestion selling, a common practice among most retailers, seeks to broaden customers' original purchases with related items. For example, if you buy a new printer at Office Depot, the sales representative will ask if you would like to purchase paper, a USB cable, and/or extra ink cartridges. Suggestion selling and trading up should always help shoppers recognize true needs rather than sell them unwanted merchandise.

Providing great customer service is one of the most challenging elements in the retail mix because customer expectations for service vary greatly. What customers expect in a department store is very different from what they expect in a discount store. Customer expectations also change. Ten years ago, shoppers wanted personal one-on-one attention.

Suggestion selling seeks to broaden customers' original purchases with related items, such as USB cords, paper, or extra ink when buying a printer.

Today, most customers are happy to help themselves as long as they can easily find what they need.

Customer service is also critical for online retailers. Online shoppers expect a retailer's Web site to be user-friendly, with readily available products and an easy return process. Therefore, customer-friendly retailers like Bluefly.com design their sites to give their customers the information they need regarding new products and sales. Other companies like Amazon.com and LandsEnd.com offer product recommendations and personal shoppers. Some retailers with online, catalog, and traditional brick-and-mortar stores, such as Lands' End and Williams-Sonoma, now allow customers to return goods bought through the catalog or online to their traditional store to make returns easier.

LO 7 New Developments in Retailing

In an effort to better serve their customers and attract new ones, retailers are constantly adopting new strategies. Two recent developments are interactivity and m-commerce.

Interactivity

Adding interactivity to the retail environment is one of the most popular strategies in retailing in the past few years. Small retailers as well as national chains are using interactivity in stores to differentiate themselves from the competition. The new interactive trend gets customers involved rather than just catching their eye. For example, Build-a-Bear enables customers to make their own stuffed animals by choosing which animals to stuff and then dressing and naming it.

M-Commerce

M-commerce (mobile e-commerce) enables consumers using wireless mobile devices to connect to the Internet and shop. M-commerce enjoyed early success overseas and has been gaining acceptance and popularity in the United States. Essentially, m-commerce goes beyond text message advertisements to allow consumers to purchase goods and services using wireless mobile devices, such as mobile telephones, pagers, personal digital assistants (PDAs), and handheld computers. M-commerce users adopt the new technology because it saves time and offers more convenience in a greater number of locations. Vending machines are an important venue for m-commerce. Both PepsiCo and Coca-Cola have developed smart vending technologies. Coca-Cola's Intelligent Vending, a "cashless" payment system, accepts credit cards, RFID devices, and hotel room keys, and can be accessed via cell phone.[25]

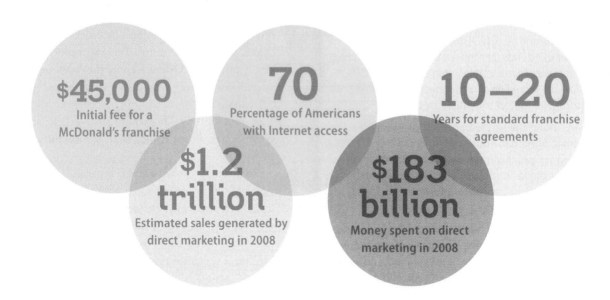

$45,000 Initial fee for a McDonald's franchise

70 Percentage of Americans with Internet access

10–20 Years for standard franchise agreements

$1.2 trillion Estimated sales generated by direct marketing in 2008

$183 billion Money spent on direct marketing in 2008

M-COMMERCE GROWTH POTENTIAL

The past few months have seen a veritable explosion in the number of consumers using mobile technology to do their shopping. This is a part of a bigger trend in which mobile technology allows people to do tasks on-the-go that they used to at a desktop computer. While at least eleven major companies, ranging from Polo Ralph Lauren to Sears, currently offer shopping on mobile phones, there is huge growth potential. Thus far, purchases from mobile phones account for just 2 percent of online sales, and web-capable smartphones make up only 10 percent of the U.S. market. Both figures are expected to grow markedly in the coming months and years. For this reason, Nick Taylor, the president of Usablenet, a firm that guides retailers in providing mobile web content, argues that mobile shopping is not a passing trend. "Anyone in the Fortune 1000 or Internet Retail 500, to the extent that you believe your company needs a Web site, you should have a mobile site."

© ISTOCKPHOTO.COM

STUDY TOOLS CHAPTER 15

Located at back of the textbook

❑ **Rip out Chapter Review Card**

Located at 4ltrpress.cengage.com/mktg

❑ **Review Key Terms Flash Cards (Print or Online)**

❑ **Download Audio and Visual Summaries for on-the-go review**

❑ **Complete both Practice Quizzes to prepare for tests**

❑ **Play "Beat the Clock" and "Quizbowl" to master concepts**

❑ **Complete "Crossword Puzzle" to review key terms**

❑ **Watch the video on "Sephora" for a real company example on Retailing**

"Few goods or services can survive in the marketplace without effective promotion."

AFTER YOU FINISH THIS CHAPTER GO TO PAGE 259 FOR STUDY TOOLS

LO 1 The Role of Promotion in the Marketing Mix

Few goods or services, no matter how well developed, priced, or distributed, can survive in the marketplace without effective **promotion**—communication by marketers that informs, persuades, and reminds potential buyers of a product in order to influence an opinion or elicit a response.

Promotional strategy is a plan for the optimal use of the elements of promotion: advertising, public relations, personal selling, and sales promotion. As Exhibit 16.1 shows, the marketing manager determines the goals of the company's promotional strategy in light of the firm's overall goals for the marketing mix—product, place (distribution), promotion, and price. Using these overall goals, marketers combine the elements of the promotional strategy (the promotional mix) into a coordinated plan. The promotion plan then becomes an integral part of the marketing strategy for reaching the target market.

The main function of a marketer's promotional strategy is to convince target customers that the goods and services offered provide a competitive advantage over the competition. A **competitive advantage** is the set of unique features of a company and its products that are perceived by the target market as significant and superior to the competition. Such features can include

promotion
communication by marketers that informs, persuades, and reminds potential buyers of a product in order to influence an opinion or elicit a response

promotional strategy a plan for the optimal use of the elements of promotion: advertising, public relations, personal selling, and sales promotion

competitive advantage the unique set of features of a company and its products that are perceived by the target market as significant and superior to the competition

What do you think?

Time taken to communicate is time well spent.

1 2 3 4 5 6 7

STRONGLY DISAGREE   STRONGLY AGREE

EXHIBIT 16.1
Role of Promotion in the Marketing Mix

promotional mix the combination of promotional tools—including advertising, public relations, personal selling, and sales promotion—used to reach the target market and fulfill the organization's overall goals

advertising impersonal, one-way mass communication about a product or organization that is paid for by a marketer

public relations the marketing function that evaluates public attitudes, identifies areas within the organization the public may be interested in, and executes a program of action to earn public understanding and acceptance

high product quality, rapid delivery, low prices, excellent service, or a feature not offered by the competition. For example, fast-food restaurant Subway promises fresh sandwiches that are better for you than a hamburger or pizza. Subway effectively communicates its competitive advantage through advertising featuring longtime "spokes-eater" Jared Fogle, who lost weight by eating at Subway every day.[1] Thus, promotion is a vital part of the marketing mix, informing consumers of a product's benefits and thereby positioning the product in the marketplace.

LO 2 The Promotional Mix

Most promotional strategies use several ingredients—which may include advertising, public relations, sales promotion, and personal selling—to reach a target market. That combination is called the **promotional mix**. The proper promotional mix is the one that management believes will meet the needs of the target market and fulfill the organization's overall goals. The more funds allocated to each promotional ingredient and the more managerial emphasis placed on each technique, the more important that element is thought to be in the overall mix.

Advertising

Almost all companies selling a good or a service use advertising, whether in the form of a multimillion-dollar campaign or a simple classified ad in a newspaper. **Advertising** is any form of impersonal paid communication in which the sponsor or company is identified. Traditional media—such as television, radio, newspapers, magazines, books, direct mail, billboards, and transit cards (advertisements on buses and taxis and at bus stops)—are most commonly used to transmit advertisements to consumers. With the increasing fragmentation of traditional media choices, marketers are using new methods, such as Web sites, e-mail, blogs, and interactive video kiosks located in department stores and supermarkets, to send their advertisements to consumers. However, as the Internet becomes a more vital component of many companies' promotion and marketing mix, consumers and lawmakers are increasingly concerned about possible violations of consumers' privacy. Social networking sites, such as Facebook, are having to reexamine their privacy policies.

One of the primary benefits of advertising is its ability to communicate to a large number of people at one time. Cost per contact, therefore, is typically very low. Advertising has the advantage of being able to reach the masses (e.g., through national television networks), but it can also be microtargeted to small groups of potential customers, such as television ads on a targeted cable network. Although the *cost per contact* in advertising is very low, the *total cost* to advertise is typically very high. This hurdle tends to restrict advertising on a national basis. Chapter 17 examines advertising in greater detail.

Public Relations

Concerned about how they are perceived by their target markets, organizations often spend large sums to build a positive public image. **Public relations** is the marketing function that evaluates public attitudes, identifies areas within the organization the public may be interested in, and executes a program of action to earn public understanding and acceptance. Public relations helps an organization communicate with its customers, suppliers, stockholders, government officials, employees, and the community in which it operates. Marketers use public relations not only to maintain a positive image but also to educate the public about the company's goals and objectives, introduce new products, and help support the sales effort.

In recent years, soft drink companies such as Coca-Cola have been criticized for contributing to

WHO'S PEEPING AT YOUR FACE-BOOK? PRIVACY CONCERNS AND SOCIAL NETWORKS

Millions of people have embraced social networking sites such as Facebook (70 million users) and MySpace (110 million users), but there are privacy concerns. Facebook uses outside developers to create widgets and apps that allow the developers to see the user's personal information to develop their applications. When a user installs an app, the developer can see everything but contact information. There are things you can do to protect your privacy, but the problem is the lack of a privacy policy for social networks. Consumer advocates and the Center for Digital Democracy are urging the Federal Trade Commission to develop a policy surrounding third-party applications.[2]

childhood obesity. In response, Coca-Cola spent $4 million to develop the "Live It" children's fitness campaign, which includes campaign posters, pedometers, nutrition education materials, and prizes for children who meet the program's exercise goal. The goal is to offset a push by the Center for Science in the Public Interest to persuade the Food and Drug Administration to require labels on sodas warning about obesity, tooth decay, and diabetes.[3]

A public relations program can generate favorable **publicity**—public information about a company, product, service, or issue appearing in the mass media as a news item. Organizations generally do not pay for the publicity and are not identified as the source of the information, but they can benefit tremendously from

it. The online retailer Bag Borrow or Steal attracted attention from consumers and the media when it was mentioned in the movie *Sex and the City*. The company took advantage of its screen time by highlighting bags featured in the film and holding a sweepstakes for movie tickets.[4]

Although organizations do not directly pay for publicity, it should not be viewed as free. Preparing news releases, staging special events, and persuading media personnel to broadcast or print publicity messages costs money. Public relations and publicity are examined further in Chapter 17.

Sales Promotion

Sales promotion consists of all marketing activities—other than personal selling, advertising, and public relations—that stimulate consumer purchasing and dealer effectiveness. Sales promotion is generally a short-run tool used to stimulate immediate increases in demand. Sales promotion can be aimed at end consumers, trade customers, or a company's employees. Sales promotions include free samples, contests, premiums, trade shows, vacation giveaways, and coupons.

For example, Sephora, a Paris-based make-up producer, recently opened a training center called Sephora University. The center's primary purpose is to train employees, but Sephora also holds customer training events to promote its new products. Women pay to attend after-hours classes, where they can watch demonstration makeovers, listen to cosmetics experts, enjoy wine and brownies, and order products for themselves at the end of the night.[5]

Often marketers use sales promotion to improve the effectiveness of other ingredients in the promotional mix, especially advertising and personal selling. Research shows that sales promotion complements advertising by yielding faster sales responses.[6]

publicity public information about a company, product, service, or issue appearing in the mass media as a news item

sales promotion marketing activities—other than personal selling, advertising, and public relations—that stimulate consumer buying and dealer effectiveness

personal selling
a purchase situation involving a personal, paid-for communication between two people in an attempt to influence each other

communication the process by which meanings are exchanged or shared through a common set of symbols

interpersonal communication
direct, face-to-face communication between two or more people

mass communication the communication of a concept or message to large audiences

Personal Selling

Personal selling is a purchase situation involving a personal, paid-for communication between two people in an attempt to influence each other. In this dyad, both the buyer and the seller have specific objectives they wish to accomplish. The buyer may need to minimize cost or assure a quality product, for instance, while the salesperson may need to maximize revenue and profits.

Traditional methods of personal selling include a planned presentation to one or more prospective buyers for the purpose of making a sale. Whether it takes place face to face or over the phone, personal selling attempts to persuade the buyer to accept a point of view. For example, a car salesperson may try to persuade a car buyer that a particular model is superior to a competing model in certain features, such as gas mileage. Once the buyer is somewhat convinced, the salesperson may attempt to elicit some action from the buyer, such as a test-drive or a purchase. Frequently, in this traditional view of personal selling, the objectives of the salesperson are at the expense of the buyer, creating a win-lose outcome.

More current notions on personal selling emphasize the relationship that develops between a salesperson and a buyer. Initially, this concept was more typical in business-to-business selling situations, involving the sale of products like heavy machinery or computer systems. More recently, both business-to-business and business-to-consumer selling focus on building long-term relationships rather than on making a one-time sale.

Relationship selling emphasizes a win-win outcome and the accomplishment of mutual objectives that benefit both buyer and salesperson in the long term. Rather than focusing on a quick sale, relationship selling attempts to create a long-term, committed relationship based on trust, increased customer loyalty, and a continuation of the relationship between the salesperson and the customer. Personal selling, like other promotional mix elements, is increasingly dependent on the Internet. Most companies use their Web sites to attract potential buyers seeking information on products and services and to drive customers to their physi-

cal locations where personal selling can close the sale. Personal selling is discussed further in Chapter 18.

LO 3 Marketing Communication

Promotional strategy is closely related to the process of communication. As humans, we assign meaning to feelings, ideas, facts, attitudes, and emotions. **Communication** is the process by which meanings are exchanged or shared through a common set of symbols. When a company develops a new product, changes an old one, or simply tries to increase sales of an existing good or service, it must communicate its selling message to potential customers. Marketers communicate information about the firm and its products to the target market and various publics through its promotion programs.

Communication can be divided into two major categories: interpersonal communication and mass communication. **Interpersonal communication** is direct, face-to-face communication between two or more people. When communicating face to face, people see the other person's reaction and can respond almost immediately. A salesperson speaking directly with a client is an example of an interpersonal marketing communication.

Mass communication involves communicating a concept or message to large audiences. A great deal of marketing communication is directed to consumers as a whole, usually through a mass medium such as television or newspapers. When a company advertises, it generally does not personally know the people with whom it is trying to communicate. Furthermore, the company is unable to respond immediately to consumers' reactions to its message. Instead, the marketing manager must wait to see whether people are reacting positively or negatively to the mass-communicated promotion. Any clutter from competitors' messages or other distractions in the environment can reduce the effectiveness of the mass-communication effort.

© AP PHOTO/CHRIS CARLSON

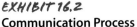

EXHIBIT 16.2
Communication Process

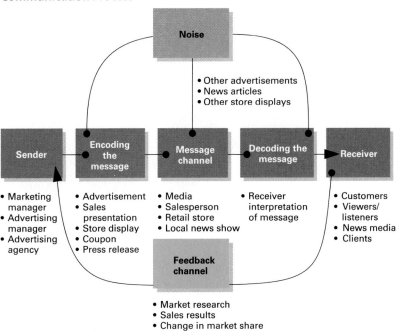

sender the originator of the message in the communication process

encoding the conversion of a sender's ideas and thoughts into a message, usually in the form of words or signs

channel a medium of communication—such as a voice, radio, or newspaper—for transmitting a message

noise anything that interferes with, distorts, or slows down the transmission of information

The Communication Process

Marketers are both senders and receivers of messages. As *senders*, marketers attempt to inform, persuade, and remind the target market to adopt courses of action compatible with the need to promote the purchase of goods and services. As *receivers*, marketers attune themselves to the target market in order to develop the appropriate messages, adapt existing messages, and spot new communication opportunities. In this way, marketing communication is a two-way, rather than one-way, process. The two-way nature of the communication process is shown in Exhibit 16.2.

The Sender and Encoding The **sender** is the originator of the message in the communication process. In an interpersonal conversation, the sender may be a parent, a friend, or a salesperson. For an advertisement or press release, the sender is the company or organization itself. For example, the Swedish brand Absolut vodka launched a marketing campaign using the theme "In an Absolut World." At the outset, the objective of the campaign was to increase Absolut's market share in the crowded and increasingly competitive U.S. vodka market. To appeal to this market, Absolut had to differentiate its message from the "rational benefits" (such as best taste or smooth feel) being claimed by so many of the upstarts in the vodka category. Thus, Absolut launched a new campaign using the phrase "Absolut World" to promote the mes-

sage that their vodka is the brand for customers who want to challenge the status quo by taking on bold and optimistic new worldviews. The new ads assert that Absolut vodka is in a class by itself—indeed, in a world of its own, an "Absolut World." The ad campaign also invites Absolut's consumers to visualize a world that appeals to them—even a world that may be idealized or "fantastic."[7]

Encoding is the conversion of the sender's ideas and thoughts into a message, usually in the form of words or signs. For example, Absolut's marketers encoded the message by creating a series of life-size outdoor ads, television commercials, wrapped buildings, and other media that imagined an "Absolut World" where factories emit harmless bubbles instead of smoke, ATMs dispense "free" money, politicians' noses grow if they lie, and people in bars wear buttons labeling their dating status and mindset.[8]

A basic principle of encoding is that what matters is not what the source says but what the receiver hears. One way of conveying a message that the receiver will hear properly is to use concrete words and pictures.

Message Transmission Transmission of a message requires a **channel**—a voice, radio, newspaper, computer, or other communication medium. A facial expression or gesture can also serve as a channel.

Reception occurs when the message is detected by the receiver and enters his or her frame of reference. In a two-way conversation such as a sales pitch given by a sales representative to a potential client, reception is normally high. In contrast, the desired receivers may or may not detect the message when it is mass communicated because most media are cluttered by **noise**—anything that interferes with, distorts, or slows down the transmission of information. In some media overcrowded with advertisers, such as newspapers and television, the noise level is high and the reception level is low. For example, competing network advertisements, other entertainment option advertisements, or other programming on the

receiver the person who decodes a message

decoding interpretation of the language and symbols sent by the source through a channel

feedback the receiver's response to a message

network itself might hamper reception of the "Absolut World" advertising campaign message. Transmission can also be hindered by situational factors such as physical surroundings like light, sound, location, and weather; the presence of other people; or the temporary moods consumers might bring to the situation. Mass communication may not even reach all the right consumers. Some members of the target audience were likely watching television when Absolut's commercials were shown, but others probably were not.

The Receiver and Decoding Marketers communicate their message through a channel to customers, or **receivers**, who will decode the message. **Decoding** is the interpretation of the language and symbols sent by the source through a channel. Common understanding between two communicators, or a common frame of reference, is required for effective communication. Therefore, marketing managers must ensure a proper match between the message to be conveyed and the target market's attitudes and ideas.

Even though a message has been received, it will not necessarily be properly decoded—or even seen, viewed, or heard—because of selective exposure, distortion, and retention. Even when people receive a message, they tend to manipulate, alter, and modify it to reflect their own biases, needs, knowledge, and culture. Differences in age, social class, education, culture, and ethnicity can lead to miscommunication. Further, because people don't always listen or read carefully, they can easily misinterpret what is said or written. In fact, researchers have found that consumers misunderstand a large proportion of both printed and televised communications. Bright colors and bold graphics have been shown to increase consumers' comprehension of marketing communication. Even these techniques are not foolproof, however.

Marketers targeting consumers in foreign countries must also worry about the translation and possible miscommunication of their promotional messages by other cultures. Global marketers must decide whether to standardize or customize the message for each global market in which they sell. While Absolut's marketers used the "World" message globally, they tailored the ads to reflect how people in various regions might envision an "Absolut World." In Germany, consumers were given a firsthand experience of the "Absolut World." For one week, a fleet of Porsche taxis chauffeured passengers quickly—and for free—around Berlin, Ham-

burg, and Munich. By the end of that week, the taxis had generated over 15 million media contacts through television, print, and online news coverage.[9]

Feedback In interpersonal communication, the receiver's response to a message is direct **feedback** to the source. Feedback may be verbal, as in saying "I agree," or nonverbal, as in nodding, smiling, frowning, or gesturing.

Because mass communicators like Absolut's are often cut off from direct feedback, they must rely on market research or analysis of viewer responses for indirect feedback. Absolut might use such measurements as the percentage of television viewers who recognized, recalled, or stated that they were exposed to Absolut's messages. Indirect feedback enables mass communicators to decide whether to continue, modify, or drop a message. Web sites also facilitate feedback. For example, Absolut could capture consumer feedback in e-mails, discussion boards, blogs, and other tools from their Web site.

The Communication Process and the Promotional Mix

The four elements of the promotional mix differ in their ability to affect the target audience. For instance, promotional mix elements may communicate with the consumer directly or indirectly. The message may flow one way or two ways. Feedback may be fast or slow, a little or a lot. Likewise, the communicator may have varying degrees of control over message delivery, content, and flexibility. Exhibit 16.3 outlines characteristics among the promotional mix elements with respect to mode of communication, marketer's control over the communication process, amount and speed of feedback, direction of message flow, marketer's control

© ISTOCKPHOTO.COM/SUPRIJONO SUHARJOTO

EXHIBIT 16.3

Characteristics of the Elements in the Promotional Mix

	Advertising	Public Relations	Sales Promotion	Personal Selling
Mode of Communication	Indirect and impersonal	Usually indirect and impersonal	Usually indirect and impersonal	Direct and face-to-face
Communicator Control over Situation	Low	Moderate to low	Moderate to low	High
Amount of Feedback	Little	Little	Little to moderate	Much
Speed of Feedback	Delayed	Delayed	Varies	Immediate
Direction of Message	One-way	One-way	Mostly one-way	Two-way
Control over Message Content	Yes	No	Yes	Yes
Identification of Sponsor	Yes	No	Yes	Yes
Speed in Reaching Large Audience	Fast	Usually fast	Fast	Slow
Message Flexibility	Same message to all audiences	Usually no direct control over message audiences	Same message to varied targets	Tailored to prospective buyer

over the message, identification of the sender, speed in reaching large audiences, and message flexibility.

From Exhibit 16.3, you can see that most elements of the promotional mix are indirect and impersonal when used to communicate with a target market, providing only one direction of message flow. For example, advertising, public relations, and sales promotion are generally impersonal, one-way means of mass communication. Because they provide no opportunity for direct feedback, it is more difficult to adapt these promotional elements to changing consumer preferences, individual differences, and personal goals.

Personal selling, on the other hand, is personal, two-way communication. The salesperson receives immediate feedback from the consumer and can adjust the message in response. Personal selling, however, is very slow in dispersing the marketer's message to large audiences. A salesperson can only communicate to one person or a small group of people at one time.

The Impact of Web 2.0 on Marketing Communication

The Internet and related technologies are having a profound impact on marketing communication, including the promotional mix. Web 2.0 tools include blogs (online journals), podcasting (online radio shows), vodcasts (online videos and newscasts), and social networks such as MySpace and Facebook. In the beginning, these tools were primarily used by individuals to express themselves. But soon, businesses began to see that these tools could be used to engage with consumers as well. The

rise of blogging, for example, has created a completely new way for marketers to manage their image, connect with consumers, and generate interest in and desire for their companies' products. Measuring blogging activity remains challenging. According to Technorati, the first blog search engine, there were more than 28 million blogs online in 2006.[10] But by early 2008, there were too many blogs to generate a consistent number. While research companies agree that there are millions of blogs, comScore Media Metrix says that as of August 2008, there were 189 million blogs (counting Facebook) and Universal McCann reports there were 184 million blogs.[11] As part of their annual State of the Blogosphere, Technorati says the real trend is with the Active Blogosphere that tends to influence the mainstream media. Brands also permeate the blogosphere. Four of five bloggers post brand or product reviews so even if a company does not have a formal social media strategy, chances are the brand is still out in the blogosphere thanks to the millions of bloggers. As such, companies are now reaching out to the most influential bloggers. Indeed, more than one third have been approached to be a brand advocate.

Blogging alters the marketing communication process for the promotional elements that rely on mass communication—advertising, public relations, and sales promotion—by moving them away from impersonal, indirect communication toward a personalized, direct communication model.

Blogs can be divided into two broad categories: corporate and professional blogs versus noncorporate blogs (such as personal blogs). Corporate blogs are sponsored by a company or one of its brands and maintained by one or more of the company's employees. **Corporate blogs** disseminate marketing-controlled information. (See Chapter 6.) Because blogs are designed to change daily, corporate blogs are dynamic and highly flexible, giving marketers the opportunity to adapt their messages more frequently than any other communication channel. Initially, blogs were maintained by only the most technology-savvy companies, but today, companies as diverse as Coca-Cola, Starwood Hotels, Honda, and Guinness have all launched corporate blogs. Undoubtedly, many more will appear in the near future.

In contrast, **noncorporate blogs** are independent and not associated with the marketing efforts of any particular company or brand. As such, noncorporate blogs contain nonmarketing-controlled information and so are percieved to be independent and more authentic than a corporate blog. For example, mcchronicles.blogspot.com is a blog site that specifies that it is "about [but] not affiliated with, McDonald's." The site is dedicated to gathering customers' views on the "McDonald's Brand Experience" around the globe. So, even though McChronicles is dedicated to one brand, it is a noncorporate blog.[12]

Both corporate and noncorporate blogs have had an impact on the communication model depicted in Exhibit 16.2. That model shows the feedback channel as primarily impersonal and numbers driven. Corporate blogs allow marketers to personalize the feedback channel by opening the door for direct conversation with consumers. The result is an unfiltered feedback channel. In 2006, Enrico Minoli, CEO of

Ducati, the Italian motorcycle brand, launched a blog at http://blog.ducati.com. He vowed to write "openly about what's going on at Ducati." Within three days, his posting had generated ninety-nine responses from motorcycle enthusiasts from Greece to Daytona Beach, who all seemed most pleased that the CEO himself was a motorbike enthusiast. Minoli's blog put a face on the impersonal nature of a large corporation.[13]

Noncorporate blogs have also personalized the feedback channel. But while corporate blogs create a *direct*, personalized feedback channel for masses of consumers, noncorporate blogs represent an *indirect*, personalized feedback channel.

LO 4 The Goals and Tasks of Promotion

People communicate with one another for many reasons. They seek amusement, ask for help, give assistance or instructions, provide information, and express ideas and thoughts. Promotion, on the other hand, seeks to modify behavior and thoughts in some way. For example, promoters may try to persuade consumers to eat at Burger King rather than at McDonald's. Promotion also strives to reinforce existing behavior—for instance, getting consumers to continue dining at Burger King once they have switched. The source (the seller) hopes to project a favorable image or to motivate purchase of the company's goods and services.

Promotion can perform one or more of three tasks: *inform* the target audience, *persuade* the target audience, or *remind* the target audience. Often a marketer will try to accomplish two or more of these tasks at the same time.

Informing

Informative promotion seeks to convert an existing need into a want or to stimulate interest in a new product. It is generally more prevalent during the early stages of the product life cycle. People typically will not buy a product or service or support a non-profit organization until they know its purpose and its ben-

efits to them. Informative messages are important for promoting complex and technical products such as automobiles, computers, and investment services. For example, Philips's original advertisement for the Magnavox flat-screen television focused on how to use the flat-screen TV.[14] Informative promotion is also important for a "new" brand being introduced into an "old" product class. The new product cannot establish itself against more mature products unless potential buyers are aware of it, value its benefits, and understand its positioning in the marketplace.

Persuading

Persuasive promotion is designed to stimulate a purchase or an action. Persuasion normally becomes the main promotion goal when the product enters the growth stage of its life cycle. By this time, the target market should have general product awareness and some knowledge of how the product can fulfill its wants. Therefore, the promotional task switches from informing consumers about the product category to persuading them to buy the company's brand rather than the competitor's. At this time, the promotional message emphasizes the product's real and perceived competitive advantages, often appealing to emotional needs such as love, belonging, self-esteem, and ego satisfaction. For example, advertisements for the Philips Magnavox flat-screen television focused on the product's benefits such as technological features, like HDTV and Dolby digital surround sound, and the superiority of the brand.[15]

Persuasion can also be an important goal for very competitive mature product categories such as many household items and soft drinks. In a marketplace characterized by many competitors, the promotional message often encourages brand switching and aims to convert some buyers into loyal users. Critics believe that some promotional messages and techniques can be too persuasive, causing consumers to buy products and services they really don't need.

Reminding

Reminder promotion is used to keep the product and brand name in the public's mind. This type of promotion prevails during the maturity stage of the life cycle. It assumes that the target market has already been persuaded of the merits of the good or service. Its purpose is simply to trigger a memory. Crest toothpaste and other consumer products often use reminder promotion.

AIDA concept a model that outlines the process for achieving promotional goals in terms of stages of consumer involvement with the message; the acronym stands for *attention, interest, desire,* and *action*

LO 5 Promotional Goals and the AIDA Concept

The ultimate goal of any promotion is to get someone to buy a good or service or, in the case of nonprofit organizations, to take some action (for instance, donate blood). A classic model for reaching promotional goals is called the **AIDA concept**.[16] The acronym stands for *attention, interest, desire,* and *action*—the stages of consumer involvement with a promotional message.

This model proposes that consumers respond to marketing messages in a cognitive (thinking), affective (feeling), and conative (doing) sequence. First, a promotion manager may focus on attracting a consumer's *attention* by training a salesperson to use a friendly greeting and approach, or by using loud volume, bold headlines, movement, bright colors, and the like in an advertisement. Next, a good sales presentation, demonstration, or advertisement creates *interest* in the product and then, by illustrating how the product's features will satisfy the consumer's needs, arouses *desire*. Finally, a special offer or a strong closing sales pitch may be used to obtain purchase *action*.

The AIDA concept assumes that promotion propels consumers along the following four steps in the purchase-decision process:

1 *Attention:* The advertiser must first gain the attention of the target market. A firm cannot sell something if the market does not know that the good or service exists. When Apple introduced the iPod, the company needed to create awareness and gain attention for the new product, so Apple advertised and promoted it extensively through ads on television, in magazines, and on the Internet. Because the iPod was a brand extension of the Apple computer, it required less effort than an entirely

new brand would have. At the same time, because the iPod was an innovative new product line, the promotion had to get customers' attention and create awareness of a new idea from an established company.

2 *Interest*: Simple awareness of a brand seldom leads to a sale. The next step is to create interest in the product. A print ad cannot tell potential customers all the features of the iPod. Thus, Apple had to arrange iPod demonstrations and target messages to innovators and early adopters to create interest in the new portable music players.

3 *Desire*: Potential customers for the Apple iPod may like the concept of a portable music player, but they may not feel it is necessarily better than a portable music player with fewer features. Therefore, Apple had to create brand preference with its iTunes Music Store, extended-life battery, clock and alarm, calendar and to-do list, photo storage, and other features. Specifically, Apple had to convince potential customers that the iPod was the best solution to meet their desire for a portable digital music player.

4 *Action*: Some potential target market customers may have been convinced to buy an iPod but had not yet made the actual purchase. To motivate them to take action, Apple continued advertising to more effectively communicate the features and benefits and also used promotions and price discounts.

Most buyers involved in high-involvement purchase situations pass through the four stages of the AIDA model on the way to making a purchase. The promoter's task is to determine where on the purchase ladder most of the target consumers are located and design a promotion plan to meet their needs. For example, if Apple learned from its market research that many potential customers were in the desire stage but had not yet bought an iPod for some reason, then Apple could place advertising on Google and perhaps in video games, to target younger individuals, who are the primary target market, with messages to motivate them to buy an iPod.

The AIDA concept does not explain how all promotions influence purchase decisions. The model suggests that promotional effectiveness can be measured in terms of consumers progressing from one stage to the next. However, the order of stages in the model, as well as whether consumers go through all steps, has been much debated. A purchase can occur without interest or desire, perhaps when a low-involvement product is bought on impulse. Regardless of the order of the stages or consumers' progres-

sion through these stages, the AIDA concept helps marketers by suggesting which promotional strategy will be most effective.[17] Strategy is often a matter of timing. DreamWorks made great use of the AIDA model with its successful marketing campaign for the film *Kung Fu Panda*. It started marketing early to build awareness of the film, used humor and a graphic novel to keep viewers interested, and then showed a trailer before *Indiana Jones and the Kingdom of the Crystal Skull* so that audiences would want to buy tickets.[18]

AIDA and the Promotional Mix

Exhibit 16.4 depicts the relationship between the promotional mix and the AIDA model. It shows that, although advertising does have an impact in the later stages, it is most useful in gaining attention for goods or services. In contrast, personal selling reaches fewer people at first. Salespeople are more effective at creating customer interest for merchandise or a service and at creating desire. For example, advertising may help a potential computer purchaser gain knowledge about competing brands, but the salesperson may be the one who actually encourages the buyer to decide a particular brand is the best choice. The salesperson also has the advantage of having the computer physically there to demonstrate its capabilities to the buyer.

Public relations has its greatest impact in gaining attention for a company, good, or service. Many companies can attract attention and build goodwill by sponsoring community events that benefit a worthy cause such as antidrug and antigang programs. Such sponsorships project a positive image of the firm and its products into the minds of consumers and potential consumers. Book publishers push to get their titles on the best-seller lists of major publications, such as *Publishers Weekly* or *The Wall Street Journal*. Book authors also make appearances on talk shows and at bookstores to personally sign books and speak to fans.

Sales promotion's greatest strength is in creating strong desire and purchase intent. Coupons and other price-off promotions are techniques used to persuade customers to buy new products. Frequent buyer sales promotion programs, popular among retailers, allow consumers to accumulate points or dol-

BUY ME!!

EXHIBIT 16.4

	Attention	Interest	Desire	Action
Advertising	●	●	○	●
Public Relations	●	●	○	●
Sales Promotion	○	○	●	○
Personal Selling	○	●	●	●

● Very effective ○ Somewhat effective ● Not effective

lars that can later be redeemed for goods. Frequent buyer programs tend to increase purchase intent and loyalty and encourage repeat purchases.

LO 6 Factors Affecting the Promotional Mix

Promotional mixes vary a great deal from one product and one industry to the next. Normally, advertising and personal selling are used to promote goods and services, supported and supplemented by sales promotion. Public relations helps develop a positive image for the organization and the product line. However, a firm may choose not to use all four promotional elements in its promotional mix, or it may choose to use them in varying degrees. The particular promotional mix chosen by a firm for a product or service depends on several factors: the nature of the product, the stage in the product life cycle, target market characteristics, the type of buying decision, funds available for promotion, and whether a push or a pull strategy will be used.

Nature of the Product

Characteristics of the product itself can influence the promotional mix. For instance, a product can be classified as either a business product or a consumer product. (Refer to Chapters 7 and 10.) As business products are often custom-tailored to the buyer's exact specifications, they are often not well suited to mass promotion. Therefore, producers of most business goods, such as computer systems or industrial machinery, rely more heavily on personal selling than on advertising. Advertising, however, still serves a purpose in promoting business goods. Advertising in trade media can help locate potential customers for the sales force. For example, print media advertising often includes coupons soliciting the potential customer to "fill this out for more detailed information."

In contrast, because consumer products generally are not custom-made, they do not require the selling efforts of a company representative who can tailor them to the user's needs. Thus, consumer goods are promoted mainly through advertising to create brand familiarity. Television and radio advertising, consumer-oriented magazines, and increasingly the Internet and other highly targeted media are used to promote consumer goods, especially nondurables. Sales promotion, the brand name, and the product's packaging are about twice as important for consumer goods as for business products. Persuasive personal selling is important at the retail level for goods such as automobiles and appliances.

The costs and risks associated with a product also influence the promotional mix. As a general rule, when the costs or risks of buying and using a product increase, personal selling becomes more important. In fact, inexpensive items cannot support the cost of a salesperson's time and effort unless the potential volume is high. On the other hand, expensive and complex machinery, cars, and new homes represent a considerable investment. A salesperson must assure buyers that they are spending their money wisely and not taking an undue financial risk.

Social risk is an issue as well. Many consumer goods are not products of great social importance because they do not reflect social position. People do not experience much social risk in buying a loaf of bread. However, buying many specialty products such as jewelry and clothing involves a social risk. Many consumers depend on sales personnel for guidance in making the "proper" choice.

Stage in the Product Life Cycle

The product's stage in its life cycle is a big factor in designing a promotional mix (see Exhibit 16.5). During the *introduction stage*, the basic goal of promotion is to inform the target audience that the product is available. Initially, the emphasis is on the general product class—for example, mobile phones. This emphasis gradually changes to gaining attention for a particular brand, such as Nokia, Samsung, Sony Ericsson, or Motorola. Typically, both extensive advertising and public relations inform the target audience of the product class or brand and heighten awareness levels. Sales promotion encourages early trial of the product, and personal selling gets retailers to carry the product.

When the product reaches the *growth stage* of the life cycle, the promotion blend may shift. Often a change is necessary because different types of potential buyers are targeted. Although advertising and public relations continue to be major elements of the promotional mix, sales promotion can be reduced because consumers need fewer incentives to purchase. The promotional strategy is to emphasize the product's differential advantage over the competition. Persuasive promotion is used to build and maintain brand loyalty during the growth stage. By this stage, personal selling has usually succeeded in getting adequate distribution for the product.

As the product reaches the *maturity stage* of its life cycle, competition becomes fiercer, and thus persuasive and reminder advertising are more strongly emphasized. Sales promotion comes back into focus as product sellers try to increase their market share.

All promotion, especially advertising, is reduced as the product enters the *decline stage*. Nevertheless, personal selling and sales promotion efforts may be maintained, particularly at the retail level.

Target Market Characteristics

A target market characterized by widely scattered potential customers, highly informed buyers, and brand-loyal repeat purchasers generally requires a promotional mix with more advertising and sales promotion and less personal selling. Sometimes, however, personal selling is required even when buyers are well informed and geographically dispersed. Although industrial installations may be sold to well-educated people with extensive work experience, salespeople must be present to explain the product and work out the details of the purchase agreement.

Often firms sell goods and services in markets where potential customers are hard to locate. Print advertising can be used to find them. The reader is invited to go online, call, or to mail in a reply card for more information. As the online queries, calls, or cards are received, salespeople are sent to visit the potential customers.

Type of Buying Decision

The promotional mix also depends on the type of buying decision—for example, a routine decision or a complex decision. For routine consumer decisions like buying toothpaste, the most effective promotion calls attention to the brand or reminds the consumer about the brand. Advertising and, especially, sales promotion are the most productive promotion tools to use for routine decisions.

If the decision is neither routine nor complex, advertising and public relations help establish awareness for the good or service. Suppose a man is looking for a bottle of wine to serve to his dinner guests. As a beer drinker, he is not familiar with wines, yet he has read an article in a popular magazine about the Robert Mondavi winery and seen an advertisement for the wine. He may be more likely to buy this brand because he is already aware of it. Online reviews are often important in this type of buying

EXHIBIT 16.5
Product Life Cycle and the Promotional Mix

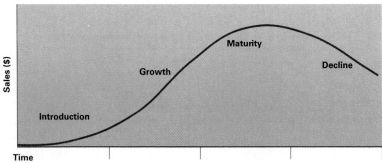

| Preintroduction publicity; small amounts of advertising near introduction | Heavy advertising and public relations to build awareness; sales promotion to induce trial; personal selling to obtain distribution | Heavy advertising and public relations to build brand loyalty; decreasing use of sales promotion; personal selling to maintain distribution | Advertising slightly decreased—more persuasive and reminder in nature; increased use of sales promotion to build market share; personal selling to maintain distribution | Advertising and public relations drastically decreased; sales promotion and personal selling maintained at low levels |

Though new cars can be researched online, consumers depend on a salesperson to help them reach a decision.

push strategy a marketing strategy that uses aggressive personal selling and trade advertising to convince a wholesaler or a retailer to carry and sell particular merchandise

pull strategy a marketing strategy that stimulates consumer demand to obtain product distribution

decision as well because the consumer has any number of other consumer's reviews easily accessible.

In contrast, consumers making complex buying decisions are more extensively involved. They rely on large amounts of information to help them reach a purchase decision. Personal selling is most effective in helping these consumers decide. For example, consumers thinking about buying a car typically research the car online using corporate and third-party Web sites. However, few people buy a car without visiting the dealership. They depend on a salesperson to provide the information they need to reach a decision. In addition to online resources, print advertising may also be used for high-involvement purchase decisions because it can often provide a large amount of information to the consumer.

Available Funds

Money, or the lack of it, may easily be the most important factor in determining the promotional mix. A small, undercapitalized manufacturer may rely heavily on free publicity if its product is unique. If the situation warrants a sales force, a financially strained firm may turn to manufacturers' agents, who work on a commission basis with no advances or expense accounts. Even well-capitalized organizations may not be able to afford the advertising rates of publications like *Time Magazine*, *Reader's Digest*, and *The Wall Street Journal*, or the cost of running television commercials on *Desperate Housewives*, *American Idol*, or the Super Bowl. The price of a high-profile advertisement in these media could support several salespeople for an entire year.

When funds are available to permit a mix of promotional elements, a firm will generally try to optimize its return on promotion dollars while minimizing the *cost per contact*, or the cost of reaching one member of the target market. In general, the cost per contact is very high for personal selling, public relations, and sales promotions like sampling and demonstrations. On the other hand, given the number of people national advertising reaches, it has a very low cost per contact. Usually, there is a trade-off among the funds available, the number of people in the target market, the quality of communication needed, and the relative costs of the promotional elements. There are plenty of low-cost options available to companies without a huge budget. Many of these include online strategies and public relations efforts, where the company relies on free publicity.

Push and Pull Strategies

The last factor that affects the promotional mix is whether a push or a pull promotional strategy will be used. Manufacturers may use aggressive personal selling and trade advertising to convince a wholesaler or a retailer to carry and sell their merchandise. This approach is known as a **push strategy** (see Exhibit 16.6). The wholesaler, in turn, must often push the merchandise forward by persuading the retailer to handle the goods. The retailer then uses advertising, displays, and other forms of promotion to convince the consumer to buy the "pushed" products. This concept also applies to services.

At the other extreme is a **pull strategy**, which stimulates consumer demand to obtain product distribution. Rather than trying to sell to the wholesaler, the manufacturer using a pull strategy focuses its promotional efforts on end consumers or opinion leaders. A classic example of a pull strategy is the heavy advertising and promotion of sugary breakfast cereals on children's television programs. The demand created from such major advertising campaigns is likely to "pull" demand from children (and then their parents) and encourage retailers to stock those cereals in their stores. As consumers begin demanding the product, the retailer orders the merchandise from the wholesaler. The wholesaler, confronted with rising demand, then places an order for the "pulled" merchandise from the manufacturer. Consumer demand pulls the product through the channel of distribution

EXHIBIT 16.6
Push Strategy versus Pull Strategy

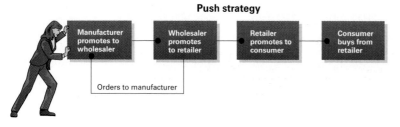

Push strategy

Manufacturer promotes to wholesaler → Wholesaler promotes to retailer → Retailer promotes to consumer → Consumer buys from retailer

Orders to manufacturer

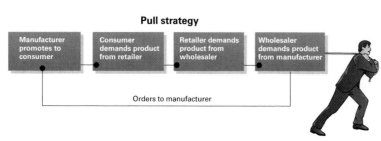

Pull strategy

Manufacturer promotes to consumer → Consumer demands product from retailer → Retailer demands product from wholesaler → Wholesaler demands product from manufacturer

Orders to manufacturer

integrated marketing communications (IMC) the careful coordination of all promotional messages for a product or a service to assure the consistency of messages at every contact point where a company meets the consumer

(see Exhibit 16.6). Heavy sampling, introductory consumer advertising, cents-off campaigns, and couponing are part of a pull strategy.

Rarely does a company use a pull or a push strategy exclusively. Instead, the mix will emphasize one of these strategies. For example, pharmaceutical companies generally use a push strategy, through personal selling and trade advertising, to promote their drugs and therapies to physicians. Sales presentations and advertisements in medical journals give physicians the detailed information they need to prescribe medication to their patients. Most pharmaceutical companies supplement their push promotional strategy with a pull strategy targeted directly to potential patients through advertisements in consumer magazines and on television.

LO7 Integrated Marketing Communications

Ideally, marketing communications from each promotional mix element (personal selling, advertising, sales promotion, and public relations) should be integrated—that is, the message reaching the consumer should be the same regardless of whether it is from an advertisement, a salesperson in the field, a magazine article, or a coupon in a newspaper insert.

From the consumer's standpoint, a company's communications are already integrated. Consumers do not think in terms of the four elements of promotion: advertising, sales promotion, public relations, and personal selling. Instead, everything is an "ad." The only people who recognize the distinctions among these communications elements are the marketers themselves. Unfortunately, many marketers neglect this fact when planning promotional messages and fail to integrate their communication efforts from one element to the next. The most common rift typically occurs between personal selling and the other elements of the promotional mix.

This unintegrated, disjointed approach to promotion has propelled many companies to adopt the concept of **integrated marketing communications (IMC)**. IMC is the careful coordination of all promotional messages—traditional advertising, direct marketing, interactive, public relations, sales promotion, personal selling, event marketing, and other communications—for a product or service to assure the consistency of messages at every contact point where a company meets the consumer. Following the concept of IMC, marketing managers carefully work out the roles that various promotional elements will play in the marketing mix. Timing of promotional activities is coordinated, and the results of each campaign are carefully monitored to improve future use of the promotional mix tools. Typically, a marketing communications director is appointed who has overall responsibility for integrating the company's marketing communications.

Movie marketing campaigns benefit greatly from an IMC approach. Those campaigns that are most integrated generally have more impact and make a deeper impression on potential moviegoers, leading to higher box-office sales. It is not uncommon for movie marketing to include premieres, fast-food tie-ins, toys, contests, games, books, music CDs, and even podcasts. Marketers for the film *The Da Vinci Code* also used games, interactive contests, even cereal to build excitement before its opening weekend.

The IMC concept has been growing in popularity for several reasons. First, the proliferation of thou-

FROM THE CONSUMER'S STANDPOINT, A COMPANY'S COMMUNICATIONS ARE ALREADY INTEGRATED.

sands of media choices beyond traditional television has made promotion a more complicated task. Instead of promoting a product just through mass-media options, like television and magazines, promotional messages today can appear in many varied sources. Further, the mass market has also fragmented—more selectively segmented markets and an increase in niche marketing have replaced the traditional broad market groups that marketers promoted to in years past. Finally, marketers have slashed their advertising spending in favor of promotional techniques that generate immediate sales responses and those that are more easily measured, such as direct marketing. Thus, the interest in IMC is largely a reaction to the scrutiny that marketing communications has come under and, particularly, to suggestions that uncoordinated promotional activity leads to a strategy that is wasteful and inefficient.

$4 Million
Amount spent on Coca-Cola's "Live It" campaign

15 Million
Number of media contacts generated by Abolut's taxis

4/5
Bloggers posting brand or product reviews

180 Million
Number of people on Facebook and MySpace

STUDY TOOLS
CHAPTER 16

Located at back of the textbook
- ❏ **Rip out Chapter Review Card**

Located at 4ltrpress.cengage.com/mktg
- ❏ **Review Key Terms Flash Cards (Print or Online)**
- ❏ **Download Audio and Visual Summaries for on-the-go review**
- ❏ **Complete both Practice Quizzes to prepare for tests**
- ❏ **Play "Beat the Clock" and "Quizbowl" to master concepts**
- ❏ **Complete "Crossword Puzzle" to review key terms**
- ❏ **Watch the video on "Vans" for a real company example on Integrated Marketing Communication**

Advertising and Public Relations

"General Motors, Procter & Gamble, and Time Warner each spend almost $10 million a day on national advertising in the United States alone."

AFTER YOU FINISH THIS CHAPTER GO TO PAGE 276 FOR STUDY TOOLS

© SERGE KROUGLIKOFF/ZEFA/CORBIS

LO 1   The Effects of Advertising

Advertising is defined in Chapter 16 as impersonal, one-way mass communication about a product or organization that is paid for by a marketer. It is a popular form of promotion, especially for consumer packaged goods and services. Advertising expenditures typically increase annually but were expected to decline in 2009, due to economic conditions. In recent years, thirty companies spent over $1 billion each, with the top 100 global marketers spending more than $108 billion overall on measured media. Among the top brands advertised by these companies were Procter & Gamble ($9.4 billion), Unilever ($5.3 billion), L'Oréal ($3.4 billion), and General Motors Company ($3.3 billion).[1]

Advertising and marketing services, agencies, and other firms that provide marketing and communications services to marketers, employ an estimated 750,000 people. About another 850,000 people work in media advertising, such as newspapers, broadcast and cable television, radio, magazines, and Internet media companies.[2] This represents a decrease in both areas primarily due to economic conditions and much lower newspaper employment.

The amount of money budgeted for advertising by some firms is staggering. AT&T, General Motors, Procter & Gamble, and Time Warner each spend almost $10 million a day on national advertising in the United States alone. If local advertising, sales promotion, and public relations are included, this figure rises much higher. More than 100 companies spend over $300 million each on advertising every year.[3] Spending on advertising varies by industry.

What do you think?

Television advertising helps me to know which brands have the features I am looking for.

1   2   3   4   5   6   7

STRONGLY DISAGREE   STRONGLY AGREE

Find out what others think at 4ltrpress.cengage.com/mktg

261

PEPSI'S NEW LOOK

Pepsi recently revealed its new logo—only the eleventh change since 1898. PepsiCo's top executives say they wanted to move the brand into the current culture of personalization. The new logo has a white band in the middle of the Pepsi circle that represents a series of smiles . . . a smile for Pepsi, a grin for Diet Pepsi, and a laugh for Pepsi Max. Branding experts are mixed: Some think the new look will make the logo less durable and classic while others feel that it is more adventurous and youthful. There is a minimalist feel that has captured the attention of the iPod generation with the idea of simple elegance. [4]

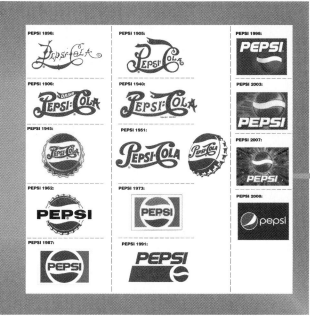

© PEPSI-COLA NORTH AMERICA BEVERAGES

Advertising and Market Share

Today's most successful brands of consumer goods, like Ivory soap and Coca-Cola, were built by heavy advertising and marketing investments long ago. Today's advertising dollars for successful consumer brands are spent on maintaining brand awareness and market share.

New brands with a small market share tend to spend proportionately more for advertising and sales promotion than those with a large market share, typically for two reasons. First, beyond a certain level of spending for advertising and sales promotion, diminishing returns set in. That is, sales or market share begins to decrease no matter how much is spent on advertising and sales promotion. This phenomenon is called the **advertising response function**. Understanding the advertising response function helps marketers use budgets wisely. A market leader like Johnson & Johnson's Neutrogena typically spends proportionately less on advertising than a newcomer like Jergens' Natural Glow Daily Moisturizer brand. Neutrogena has already captured the attention of the majority of its target market. It only needs to remind customers of its product.

The second reason that new brands tend to require higher spending for advertising and sales promotion is that a certain minimum level of exposure is needed to measurably affect purchase habits. If Jergens advertised Natural Glow Daily Moisturizer in only one or two publications and bought only one or two television spots, it would not achieve the exposure needed to penetrate consumers' perceptual defenses and affect purchase intentions.

The Effects of Advertising on Consumers

Advertising affects consumers' daily lives, informing them about products and services and influencing their attitudes, beliefs, and ultimately their purchases. Advertising affects the television programs people watch, the content of the newspapers they read, the politicians they elect, the medicines they take, and the toys their children play with. Consequently, the influence of advertising on the U.S. socioeconomic system has been the subject of extensive debate in nearly all corners of society.

Though advertising cannot change consumers' deeply rooted values and attitudes, advertising may succeed in transforming a person's negative attitude toward a product into a positive one. For instance, serious or dramatic advertisements are more effective at changing consumers' negative attitudes. Humorous ads, on the other hand, have been shown to be more effective at shaping attitudes when consumers already have a positive image of the advertised brand. [5]

Advertising also reinforces positive attitudes toward brands. When consumers have a neutral or favorable frame of reference toward a product or brand, advertising often positively influences them. When consumers are already highly loyal to a brand, they may buy more of it when advertising and promotion for that brand increase. [6] This is why market leaders spend billions of dollars annually to reinforce and remind their loyal customers about the benefits of their products. Coca-Cola Co. spent nearly $300 million advertising Coke in 2007. Johnson & Johnson spent $153 million advertising Tylenol in the same year.[7]

Advertising can also affect the way consumers rank a brand's attributes. For example, in years past, car ads emphasized such brand attributes as roominess, speed, and low maintenance. Today, however, car marketers have added safety, versatility, customization, and fuel efficiency to the list.

LO2 Major Types of Advertising

The firm's promotional objectives determine the type of advertising it uses. If the goal of the promotion plan is to build up the image of the company or the industry,

Institutional advertising is designed to promote, establish, change, or maintain a corporation's positive identity. Usually the audience isn't asked to do anything except maintain a favorable attitude toward the institution.

© AP IMAGES/PRNEWSFOTO/PEABODY ENERGY

ENERGY FOR THE 21ST CENTURY

COAL

Today's technologies can convert U.S. coal into:

Clean Electricity to power growing cities.

Transportation Fuels to keep our economy moving.

Natural Gas to warm homes and families in winter.

Hydrogen to energize fuel cells of tomorrow.

Yeah... coal can do that.

Today, coal fuels more than 50% of U.S. electricity. America has the largest coal reserves in the world... and greater use of this clean and affordable fuel can reduce our reliance on foreign oil and liquefied natural gas.

Peabody Energy (NYSE: BTU) is the world's largest provider of coal to fuel 21st Century energy solutions.

CoalCanDoThat.com

Peabody

institutional advertising may be used. In contrast, if the advertiser wants to enhance the sales of a specific good or service, **product advertising** is used.

Institutional Advertising

Historically, advertising in the United States has been product oriented. Today, however, companies market multiple products and need a different type of advertising. Institutional advertising, or corporate advertising, promotes the corporation as a whole and is designed to establish, change, or maintain the corporation's identity. It usually does not ask the audience to do anything but maintain a favorable attitude toward the advertiser and its goods and services.

A form of institutional advertising called **advocacy advertising** is typically used to safeguard against negative consumer attitudes and to enhance the company's credibility among consumers who already favor its position. Often corporations use advocacy advertising to express their views on controversial issues. At other times, firms' advocacy campaigns react to criticism or blame, some in direct response to criticism by the media. Other advocacy campaigns may try to ward off increased regulation, damaging legislation, or an unfavorable outcome in a lawsuit.

Product Advertising

Unlike institutional advertising, product advertising promotes the benefits of a specific good or service. The product's stage in its life cycle often determines which type of product advertising is used: pioneering advertising, competitive advertising, or comparative advertising.

Pioneering Advertising **Pioneering advertising** is intended to stimulate primary demand for a new product or product category. Heavily used during the introductory stage of the product life cycle, pioneering advertising offers consumers in-depth information about the benefits of the product class. Pioneering advertising also seeks to create interest. Pharmaceutical companies are the latest big players in pioneering advertising. For instance, one pharma giant, Pfizer, has steadily ramped up consumer advertising of a new drug, Lyrica, toward the controversial pain disorder fibromyalgia. In just six months Pfizer spent $46 million on a new ad campaign for Lyrica compared with $33 million the previous year.[8]

institutional advertising a form of advertising designed to enhance a company's image rather than promote a particular product

product advertising a form of advertising that touts the benefits of a specific good or service

advocacy advertising a form of advertising in which an organization expresses its views on controversial issues or responds to media attacks

pioneering advertising a form of advertising designed to stimulate primary demand for a new product or product category

Competitive Advertising Firms use competitive or brand advertising when a product enters the growth phase of the product life cycle and other companies begin to enter the marketplace. Instead of building demand for the product category, the goal of **competitive advertising** is to influence demand for a specific brand. Often promotion becomes less informative and appeals more to emotions during this phase. Advertisements may begin to stress subtle differences between brands, with heavy emphasis on building recall of a brand name and creating a favorable attitude toward the brand. Automobile advertising has long used very competitive messages, drawing distinctions based on such factors as quality, performance, and image.

Comparative Advertising **Comparative advertising** directly or indirectly compares two or more competing brands on one or more specific attributes. Some advertisers even use comparative advertising against their own brands. Products experiencing slow growth or those entering the marketplace against strong competitors are more likely to employ comparative claims in their advertising.

Before the 1970s, comparative advertising was allowed only if the competing brand was veiled and unidentified. In 1971, however, the Federal Trade Commission (FTC) fostered the growth of comparative advertising by saying that the advertising provided information to the customer and that advertisers were more skillful than the government in communicating this information. Federal rulings prohibit advertisers from falsely describing competitors' products and allow competitors to sue if ads show their products or mention their brand names in an incorrect or false manner. FTC rules also apply to advertisers making false claims about their own products.

The Mac versus PC ads for Apple use comparative advertising by portraying the stodgy PC against a hip, cool Mac.

LO3 Creative Decisions in Advertising

Advertising strategies are typically organized around an advertising campaign. An advertising campaign is a series of related advertisements focusing on a common theme, slogan, and set of advertising appeals. It is a specific advertising effort for a particular product that extends for a defined period of time.

Before any creative work can begin on an advertising campaign, it is important to determine what goals or objectives the advertising should achieve. An **advertising objective** identifies the specific communication task that a campaign should accomplish for a specified target audience during a specified period. The objectives of a specific advertising campaign often depend on the overall corporate objectives and the product being advertised.

The DAGMAR approach (Defining Advertising Goals for Measured Advertising Results) is one method of setting objectives. According to this method, all advertising objectives should precisely define the target audience, the desired percentage change in some specified measure of effectiveness, and the time frame in which that change is to occur.

Once objectives are defined, creative work can begin on the advertising campaign. Advertising campaigns often follow the AIDA model, which was discussed in Chapter 16. Depending on where consumers are in the AIDA process, the creative development of an advertising campaign might focus on creating attention, arousing interest, stimulating desire, or ultimately

© A. MILLER/WENN/NEWSCOM

leading to the action of buying the product. Specifically, creative decisions include identifying product benefits, developing and evaluating advertising appeals, executing the message, and evaluating the effectiveness of the campaign.

Identifying Product Benefits

A well-known rule of thumb in the advertising industry is "Sell the sizzle, not the steak"—that is, in advertising the goal is to sell the benefits of the product, not its attributes. An attribute is simply a feature of the product such as its easy-open package or special formulation. A benefit is what consumers will receive or achieve by using the product. A benefit should answer the consumer's question "What's in it for me?" Benefits might be such things as convenience or savings. A quick test to determine whether you are offering attributes or benefits in your advertising is to ask "So?" Consider this example:

▸▸ *Attribute*: "SoBe Lifewater has reformulated five delicious, low-calorie flavors—Blackberry Grape, Pomegranate Cherry, Orange Tangerine, Strawberry Kiwi and Passionfruit Citrus—each infused with a unique mix of antioxidant vitamins C & E, essential B vitamins and healthy herbal ingredients . . ." "So . . . ?"

▸▸ *Benefit*: "So . . . SoBe Lifewater is not only an enhanced water; it is a lifestyle unto itself . . . providing consumers the healthiest, most fun and refreshing products, delivering the incredibly positive benefits of hydration and unmatched brand experiences."[9]

Developing and Evaluating Advertising Appeals

An **advertising appeal** identifies a reason for a person to buy a product. Developing advertising appeals, a challenging task, is typically the responsibility of the creative people in the advertising agency. Advertising appeals typically play off consumers' emotions or address some need or want the consumer has.

Advertising campaigns can focus on one or more advertising appeals. Often the appeals are quite general, thus allowing the firm to develop a number of subthemes or mini campaigns using both advertising and sales promotion. Several possible advertising appeals are listed in Exhibit 17.1.

Choosing the best appeal from those developed normally requires market research. Criteria for evaluation include desirability, exclusiveness, and believability. The appeal first must make a positive impression on and be desirable to the target market. It must also be exclusive or unique; consumers must be able to distinguish the advertiser's message from competitors' messages. Most important, the appeal should be believable. An appeal that makes extravagant claims not only wastes promotional dollars but also creates ill will for the advertiser.

The advertising appeal selected for the campaign becomes what advertisers call its **unique selling proposition**. The unique selling proposition usually becomes the campaign's slogan. Red Bull's "Red Bull has wings" touts its benefits, including improved concentration and reaction time, improved performance and increased

EXHIBIT 17.1
Common Advertising Appeals

Profit	Lets consumers know whether the product will save them money, make them money, or keep them from losing money
Health	Appeals to those who are body-conscious or who want to be healthy; love or romance is used often in selling cosmetics and perfumes
Fear	Can center around social embarrassment, growing old, or losing one's health; because of its power, requires advertiser to exercise care in execution
Admiration	Frequently highlights celebrity spokespeople
Convenience	Is often used for fast-food restaurants and microwave foods
Fun and Pleasure	Are the keys to advertising vacations, beer, amusement parks, and more
Vanity and Egotism	Are used most often for expensive or conspicuous items such as cars and clothing
Environmental Consciousness	Centers around protecting the environment and being considerate of others in the community

EXHIBIT 17.2
Eleven Common Executional Styles for Advertising

Slice-of-Life	Depicts people in normal settings, such as at the dinner table or in their car. McDonald's often uses slice-of-life styles showing youngsters munching french fries and Happy Meals on family outings.
Lifestyle	Shows how well the product will fit in with the consumer's lifestyle. As their Volkswagen Jetta moves through the streets of the French Quarter, the Gen X drivers insert a techno music CD and marvel at how the rhythms of the world mimic the ambient vibe inside their vehicle.
Spokesperson/ Testimonial	Can feature a celebrity, company official, or typical consumer making a testimonial or endorsing a product. Sheryl Crow represented Revlon's Colorist hair coloring while Beyoncé Knowles was named the new face of American Express. Dell, Inc. founder Michael Dell touts his vision of the customer experience via Dell in television ads.
Fantasy	Creates a fantasy for the viewer built around use of the product. Carmakers often use this style to let viewers fantasize about how they would feel speeding around tight corners or down long country roads in their cars.
Humorous	Advertisers often use humor in their ads, such as Snickers' "Not Going Anywhere for a While" campaign featuring hundreds of souls waiting, sometimes impatiently, to get into heaven.
Real/Animated Product	Creates a character that represents the product in advertisements, such as the Energizer bunny or Starkist's Charlie the Tuna.
Symbols	GEICO's suave gecko and disgruntled cavemen became cult classics for the insurance company.
Mood or Image	Builds a mood or image around the product, such as peace, love, or beauty. De Beers ads depicting shadowy silhouettes wearing diamond engagement rings and diamond necklaces portrayed passion and intimacy while extolling that a "diamond is forever."
Demonstration	Shows consumers the expected benefit. Many consumer products use this technique. Laundry-detergent spots are famous for demonstrating how their product will clean clothes whiter and brighter. Fort James Corporation demonstrated in television commercials how its Dixie Rinse & ReUse disposable stoneware product line can stand up to the heat of a blowtorch and survive a cycle in a clothes washer.
Musical	Conveys the message of the advertisement through song. For example, Nike's ads depicted a marathoner's tortured feet and a surfer's thigh scarred by a shark attack while strains of Joe Cocker's "You Are So Beautiful" could be heard in the background.
Scientific	Uses research or scientific evidence to give a brand superiority over competitors. Pain relievers like Advil, Bayer, and Excedrin use scientific evidence in their ads.

endurance (www.redbull.com). Effective slogans often become so ingrained that consumers hearing the slogan can immediately conjure up images of the product.

Executing the Message

Message execution is the way an advertisement portrays its information. In general, the AIDA plan (see Chapter 16) is a good blueprint for executing an advertising message. Any ad should immediately draw the reader's, viewer's, or listener's attention. The advertiser must then use the message to hold interest, create desire for the good or service, and ultimately motivate a purchase.

The style in which the message is executed is one of the most creative elements of an advertisement. Exhibit 17.2 lists some examples of executional styles used by advertisers. Executional styles often dictate what type of media is to be employed to convey the message. Scientific executional styles lend themselves well to print advertising where more information can be conveyed. Testimonials by athletes are one of the more popular executional styles.

Injecting humor into an advertisement is a popular and effective executional style. Humorous executional styles are more often used in radio and television advertising than in print or magazine advertising where humor is less easily communicated. Humorous ads are typically used for lower-risk, low-involvement, routine purchases such as candy, cigarettes, and casual jeans than for higher-risk purchases or those that are expensive, durable, or flamboyant.[10]

Sometimes a company will modify its executional styles to make its advertising more effective. For decades, Procter & Gamble has advertised shampoo in China using a demonstrational executional style. Television ads showed how the science of shampoo worked and then a woman with nice, shiny hair. Because today's urban Chinese no longer make solely utilitarian purchases, P&G now uses emotional appeals in its advertisements. One shows a woman emerging from an animated cocoon as a sophisticated butterfly, while a voice purrs, "Head & Shoulders metamorphosis—new life for hair."[11]

Postcampaign Evaluation

Evaluating an advertising campaign can be the most demanding task facing advertisers. How to assess if the campaign led to an increase in sales or market share or elevated awareness of the product? Most advertising campaigns aim to create an image for the good or service instead of asking for action, so their real effect is unknown. So many variables shape the effectiveness of an ad that advertisers often must guess whether their money has been well spent. Nonetheless, marketers spend considerable time studying advertising effectiveness and its probable impact on sales, market share, or awareness.

Testing ad effectiveness can be done either before or after the campaign. Before a campaign is released, marketing managers use pretests to determine the best advertising appeal, layout, and media vehicle. After advertisers implement a campaign, they use several monitoring techniques to determine whether the campaign has met its original goals. Even if a campaign has been highly successful, advertisers still typically do a postcampaign analysis to identify how the campaign might have been more efficient and what factors contributed to its success.

LO 4 Media Decisions in Advertising

A major decision for advertisers is the choice of **medium**—the channel used to convey a message to a target market. **Media planning**, therefore, is the series of decisions advertisers make regarding the selection and use of media, allowing the marketer to optimally and cost-effectively communicate the message to the target audience. Specifically, advertisers must determine which types of media will best communicate the benefits of their product or service to the target audience and when and for how long the advertisement will run.

Promotional objectives and the appeal and executional style of the advertising strongly affect the selection of media. Both creative and media decisions are made at the same time: Creative work cannot be completed without knowing which medium will be used to convey the message to the target market. In many cases, the advertising objectives dictate the medium and the creative approach to be used. For example, if the objective is to demonstrate how fast a product operates, a television commercial that shows this action may be the best choice.

U.S. advertisers spend roughly $300 billion annually on media monitored by national reporting services—newspapers, magazines, Internet, radio, television, and outdoor media. The remainder is spent on unmonitored media, such as direct mail, trade exhibits, cooperative advertising, brochures, coupons, catalogs, and special events. Roughly 30 percent of every media dollar goes toward television ads, 20 percent toward magazines, and about 18 percent for newspaper ads. But these traditional mass-market mediums are declining in usage as more targeted mediums grow.

Media Types

Advertising media are channels that advertisers use in mass communication. The seven major advertising media are newspapers, magazines, radio, television, outdoor media, Yellow Pages, and the Internet. Exhibit 17.3 summarizes the advantages and disadvantages of some of these major channels. In recent years, however, alternative media channels have emerged that give advertisers innovative ways to reach their target audience and avoid advertising clutter.

Newspapers The advantages of newspaper advertising include geographic flexibility and timeliness. Because copywriters can usually prepare newspaper ads quickly and at a reasonable cost, local merchants can reach their target market almost daily. Because newspapers are generally a mass-market medium, however, they may not be the best vehicle for marketers trying to reach a very narrow market. Newspaper advertising also encounters a lot of distractions from competing ads and news stories; thus, one company's ad may not be particularly visible.

The main sources of newspaper ad revenue are local retailers, classified ads, and cooperative advertising. In **cooperative advertising**, the manufacturer and the retailer split the costs of advertising the

medium the channel used to convey a message to a target market

media planning the series of decisions advertisers make regarding the selection and use of media, allowing the marketer to optimally and cost-effectively communicate the message to the target audience

cooperative advertising an arrangement in which the manufacturer and the retailer split the costs of advertising the manufacturer's brand

EXHIBIT 17.3
Advantages and Disadvantages of Major Advertising Media

Medium	Advantages	Disadvantages
Newspapers	Geographic selectivity and flexibility; short-term advertiser commitments; news value and immediacy; year-round readership; high individual market coverage; co-op and local tie-in availability; short lead time	Little demographic selectivity; limited color capabilities; low pass-along rate; may be expensive
Magazines	Good reproduction, especially for color; demographic selectivity; regional selectivity; local market selectivity; relatively long advertising life; high pass-along rate	Long-term advertiser commitments; slow audience buildup; limited demonstration capabilities; lack of urgency; long lead time
Radio	Low cost; immediacy of message; can be scheduled on short notice; relatively no seasonal change in audience; highly portable; short-term advertiser commitments; entertainment carryover	No visual treatment; short advertising life of message; high frequency required to generate comprehension and retention; distractions from background sound; commercial clutter
Television	Ability to reach a wide, diverse audience; low cost per thousand; creative opportunities for demonstration; immediacy of messages; entertainment carryover; demographic selectivity with cable stations	Short life of message; some consumer skepticism about claims; high campaign cost; little demographic selectivity with network stations; long-term advertiser commitments; long lead times required for production; commercial clutter
Outdoor Media	Repetition; moderate cost; flexibility; geographic selectivity	Short message; lack of demographic selectivity; high "noise" level distracting audience
Internet	Fastest-growing medium; ability to reach a narrow target audience; relatively short lead time required for creating Web-based advertising; moderate cost	Difficult to measure ad effectiveness and return on investment; ad exposure relies on "click-through" from banner ads; not all consumers have access to the Internet

manufacturer's brand. One reason manufacturers use cooperative advertising is the impracticality of listing all their dealers in national advertising. Also, cooperative advertising encourages retailers to devote more effort to the manufacturer's lines.

Magazines Compared to the cost of other media, the cost per contact in magazine advertising is usually high. The cost per potential customer may be much lower, however, because magazines are often targeted to specialized audiences and thus reach more potential customers.

One of the main advantages of magazine advertising is its market selectivity. Magazines are published for virtually every market segment. For instance, *Lucky*, "The Magazine About Shopping," is a leading fashion magazine; *ESPN the Magazine* is a successful sports magazine; *Essence* is targeted toward African-American women; *Marketing News* is a trade magazine for the marketing professional; and *The Source* is a niche pub-lication geared to young urbanites with a passion for hip-hop music.

Radio Radio has several strengths as an advertising medium: selectivity and audience segmentation, a large out-of-home audience, low unit and production costs, timeliness, and geographic flexibility. Local advertisers are the most frequent users of radio advertising, contributing over three-quarters of all radio ad revenues. Like newspapers, radio also lends itself well to cooperative advertising.

As Americans become more mobile and pressed for time, network television and newspapers have lost viewers and readers, particularly in the youth market, but radio is experiencing a resurgence in popularity because its immediate, portable nature meshes so well with a fast-paced lifestyle. The ability to target specific demographic groups is a major selling point for radio stations, attracting advertisers pursuing narrowly defined audiences that are more likely to respond to certain kinds

© ISTOCKPHOTO.COM/JCAUNEDO

of ads and products. Radio listeners tend to listen habitually and at predictable times, with the most popular being "drive time," when commuters form a vast captive audience. Finally, satellite radio has attracted new audiences that are exposed to ads, which were not previously allowed on that format.

Television Television broadcasters include network television, independent stations, cable television, and a relative newcomer, direct broadcast satellite television. Network television reaches a wide and diverse market, and cable television and direct broadcast satellite systems, such as DirecTV and Dish Network, broadcast a multitude of channels devoted to highly segmented markets. Because of its targeted channels, cable television is often characterized as "narrowcasting" by media buyers.

Advertising time on television can be very expensive, especially for network and popular cable channels. Special events and first-run prime-time shows for top-ranked television programs command the highest rates for a typical thirty-second spot, with the least expensive ads costing about $300,000 and the more expensive ones $500,000. A thirty-second spot during the Super Bowl starts at $3 million.[12]

One of the more successful recent television formats to emerge is the **infomercial**, a thirty-minute or longer advertisement, which is relatively inexpensive to produce and air. Advertisers say the infomercial is an ideal way to present complicated information to potential customers, which other advertising vehicles typically don't allow time to do. Some companies are now producing infomercials with a more polished look, which is being embraced by mainstream marketers.

Probably the most significant trend to affect television advertising is the rise in popularity of digital video recorders (DVRs) like TiVo. For every hour of television programming, an average of fifteen minutes is dedicated to nonprogram material (ads, public service announcements, and network promotions), so the popularity of DVRs is hardly surprising among ad-weary viewers. Like marketers and advertisers, networks are also highly concerned about ad skipping. If consumers are not watching advertisements, then marketers will spend a greater proportion of their advertising budgets on alternative media, and a critical revenue stream for networks will disappear. In 2006, NBC ran a test to measure the effectiveness of running shorter blocks of advertising, seeming to acknowledge pressure from ad-skipping technology. Still, the company said it has no intention of changing its business model relative to advertising sales. The full impact of DVR technology on television as an advertis-

ing medium has yet to be determined, but research companies such as Nielsen have started to measure the number of people who record a show and watch at their convenience.[13] To combat new ad-skipping habits, some advertisers have been trying to catch viewers' attention with two-minute microseries that air during episodes of network shows and feature their products. Match.com and Revlon sponsor "Commuter Confidential," which stars four carpooling women who apply Revlon makeup and discuss their success with dates found on Match.com.[14]

> **infomercial** a thirty-minute or longer advertisement that looks more like a television talk show than a sales pitch

TIM GUNN GIVES TOTAL CARE

Procter & Gamble's Tide Total Care line, with its $60 million price tag, is Tide's largest product launch. To promote the innovative anti-aging laundry line, P&G is working with Ann Taylor to give away samples and lessons on prolonging clothing life spans. P&G even has the dapper Tim Gunn, fashion guru and Project Runway mentor, doing television spots and giving fashion tips online at www.tide.com/en-US/videos.jspx. His tips, called Dressed to the Sevens, cover everything from body shapes to clothing care—and give the customer the total care they can expect from Tide's new line.[15]

The Internet With ad revenues exceeding $26 billion annually, the Internet has become a solid advertising medium. Online advertising continues to grow at double-digit rates—well ahead of other advertising media.[16] In fact, online ad spending is expected to exceed $60 billion annually by 2012 and account

advergaming placing advertising messages in Web-based or video games to advertise or promote a product, service, organization, or issue

for 18 percent of all marketing expenditures.[17] Internet advertising provides an interactive, versatile platform that offers rich data on consumer usage, enabling advertisers to improve their ad targetability and achieve measurable results.[18]

Popular Internet sites and search engines generally sell advertising space to marketers to promote their goods and services. Internet surfers click on these ads to be linked to more information about the advertised product or service. Leading advertisers as well as companies whose ad budgets are not as large have also become big Internet advertisers.

One of the most popular approaches for Internet advertising is search engine ads. Marketers' primary objective in using search engine ads is to enhance brand awareness. They do this through paid placement of ads tied to key words used in search engines—when someone clicks on the ad, the advertiser pays the search engine a fee. Search engine advertising accounts for half of all money spent on Internet advertising. By 2011, marketers will likely spend $16.6 billion annually on search engine advertising.[19] Blogs are also an attractive medium for marketing messages. Budget Rent A Car recently bought ads on 177 blogs.[20]

Advergaming Advergaming is another popular Internet advertising format in which companies put ad messages in Web-based or video games to advertise or promote a product, service, organization, or issue. Sometimes the entire game amounts to a virtual commercial; other times advertisers sponsor games or buy ad space for a product placement in them. PepsiCo developed a multiplayer online game in which players get a chance to choose the next flavor of Mountain Dew. The site, dewmocracy.com, drew 700,000 unique visitors and 200,000 registered users who spent an average of twenty-eight minutes per gaming session. PepsiCo's "dewmocracy" advergame campaign taps into the explosive popularity of online connected game play, such as "World of Warcraft" with more than ten million paying subscribers.[21]

Outdoor Media Outdoor or out-of-home advertising is a flexible, low-cost medium that may take a variety of forms. Examples include billboards, skywriting, giant inflatables, mini billboards in malls and on bus stop shelters, signs in sports arenas, lighted moving signs in bus terminals and airports, and ads painted on cars, trucks, buses, water towers, manhole covers, drinking glass coasters, and even people, called "living advertising." The plywood scaffolding surrounding

downtown construction sites often holds ads, which in places like Manhattan's Times Square, can reach over a million viewers a day.

Outdoor advertising reaches a broad and diverse market and is, therefore, ideal for promoting convenience products and services as well as directing consumers to local businesses. One of outdoor's main advantages over other media is that its exposure frequency is very high, yet the amount of clutter from competing ads is very low. Outdoor advertising also can be customized to local marketing needs, which is why local businesses are the leading outdoor advertisers in any given region.

Alternative Media To cut through the clutter of traditional advertising media, advertisers are developing new media vehicles, like shopping carts in grocery stores, computer screen savers, DVDs, CDs, interactive kiosks in department stores, advertisements run before movies at the cinema, posters on bathroom stalls, and "advertainments"—mini movies that promote a product and are shown via the Internet.

Marketers are looking for more innovative ways to reach captive and often bored commuters. For instance, subway systems are now showing ads via lighted boxes installed along tunnel walls. Other advertisers seek consumers at home. Some marketers have begun replacing the irritating music played to callers waiting on hold for customer service with advertisements and movie trailers. This strategy generates revenue for the company being called and catches undistracted consumers for advertisers. The trick is to amuse and interest this captive audience without annoying them during their ten- to fifteen-minute wait.[22]

Video games are emerging as an excellent medium for reaching males ages 18 to 34. Massive, Inc. started a video game advertising network and established a partnership with Nielsen Entertainment, Inc. to provide ad ratings. Massive can insert ads with full motion and sound into games played on Internet-connected computers. This is a big improvement over previous ads, which had to be inserted when the games were made and therefore quickly became obsolete.[23]

Cell phones are particularly useful for reaching the youth market. Mobile advertising has substantial upside potential when you consider there are more than four billion cell phone users in the world. Today's GPS capability allows you to receive "location-based" advertising on your cell phone. For example, a nearby restaurant can alert you about specials when you're in the neighborhood. Cell phone advertising is less popular in the United States than in Europe and Asia, where cell phone owners utilize text messaging more often.[24]

U.S. CONSUMER INTEREST IN RECEIVING TYPES OF CELL PHONE ADS

▶▶ Free downloads (games, ring tones) in exchange for viewing ads	16%
▶▶ Promotion to enter code from product or advertisement	15%
▶▶ Loyalty/frequent shopper program tied to cell phone number	14%
▶▶ Audio commercial to offset directory assistance charge	12%
▶▶ Ads placed next to maps or directions	11%
▶▶ Ads placed in or near mobile games	7%
▶▶ Banner ads on mobile Web page	6%
▶▶ Text messages from advertiser	4%
▶▶ Cell phone call from advertiser	3%

SOURCE: Forrester Research

Media Selection Considerations

An important element in any advertising campaign is the **media mix**, the combination of media to be used. Media mix decisions are typically based on several factors: cost per contact, reach, frequency, target audience considerations, flexibility of the medium, noise level, and the life span of the medium.

Cost per contact is the cost of reaching one member of the target market. Naturally, as the size of the audience increases, so does the total cost. Cost per contact enables an advertiser to compare media vehicles, such as television versus radio or magazine versus newspaper, or more specifically *Newsweek* versus *Time*. An advertiser debating whether to spend local advertising dollars for television spots or radio spots could consider the cost per contact of each. The advertiser might then pick the vehicle with the lowest cost per contact to maximize advertising punch for the money spent.

Reach is the number of target consumers who are exposed to a commercial at least once during a specific period, usually four weeks. Media plans for product introductions and attempts at increasing brand awareness usually emphasize reach. For example, an advertiser might try to reach 70 percent of the target audience during the first three months

of the campaign. Reach is related to a medium's ratings, generally referred to in the industry as *gross ratings points*, or GRP. A television program with a higher GRP means that more people are tuning in to the show and the reach is higher. Accordingly, as GRP increases for a particular medium, so does cost per contact.

Because the typical ad is short-lived and because often only a small portion of an ad may be perceived at one time, advertisers repeat their ads so that consumers will remember the message. **Frequency** is the number of times an individual is exposed to a given message during a specific period. Advertisers use average frequency to measure the intensity of a specific medium's coverage. For example, Coca-Cola might want an average exposure frequency of five for its Powerade television ads. That means that each of the television viewers who saw the ad saw it an average of five times.

Media selection is also a matter of matching the advertising medium with the product's target market. If marketers are trying to reach teenage females, they might select *Seventeen* magazine. A medium's ability to reach a precisely defined market is its **audience selectivity**. Some media vehicles, like general newspapers and network television, appeal to a wide cross section of the population. Others—such as *Brides*, *Popular Mechanics*, *Architectural Digest*, *Lucky*, MTV, ESPN, and Christian radio stations—appeal to very specific groups.

The *flexibility* of a medium can be extremely important to an advertiser. For example, because of layouts and design, the lead time for magazine advertising is considerably longer than for other media types and so is less flexible. By contrast, radio and Internet advertising provide maximum flexibility. If necessary, an advertiser can change a radio ad on the day it is aired.

Noise level is the level of distraction to the target audience in a medium. Noise can be created by competing ads, as when a street is lined with billboards or when a television program is cluttered with competing ads. Whereas newspapers and magazines have a high noise level, direct mail is a private medium with a low noise level. Typically, no other advertising media or news stories compete for direct-mail readers' attention.

media mix the combination of media to be used for a promotional campaign

cost per contact the cost of reaching one member of the target market

reach the number of target consumers exposed to a commercial at least once during a specific period, usually four weeks

frequency the number of times an individual is exposed to a given message during a specific period

audience selectivity the ability of an advertising medium to reach a precisely defined market

Media have either a short or a long *life span*, which means that messages can either quickly fade or persist as tangible copy to be carefully studied. A radio commercial may last less than a minute, but advertisers can overcome this short life span by repeating radio ads often. In contrast, a magazine has a relatively long life span, which is further increased by a high pass-along rate.

Media planners have traditionally relied on the above factors in selecting an effective media mix, with reach, frequency, and cost often the overriding criteria. Well-established brands with familiar messages, however, probably need fewer exposures to be effective, while newer or unfamiliar brands likely need more exposures to become familiar. In addition, today's media planners have more media options than ever before. (Today, there are over 1,600 television stations across the country compared to forty years ago when there were three.)

The proliferation of media channels is causing *media fragmentation* and forcing media planners to pay as much attention to where they place their advertising as to how often the advertisement is repeated. That is, marketers should evaluate reach *and* frequency in assessing the effectiveness of advertising. In certain situations it may be important to reach potential consumers through as many media vehicles as possible. When this approach is considered, however, the budget must be large enough to achieve sufficient

levels of frequency to have an impact. In evaluating reach versus frequency, therefore, the media planner ultimately must select an approach that is most likely to result in the ad being understood and remembered when a purchase decision is being made.

Advertisers also evaluate the qualitative factors involved in media selection. These include such things as attention to the commercial and the program, involvement, program liking, lack of distractions, and other audience behaviors that affect the likelihood that a commercial message is being seen and, hopefully, absorbed. While advertisers can advertise their product in as many media as possible and repeat the ad as many times as they like, the ad still may not be effective if the audience is not paying attention. Research on audience attentiveness for television, for example, shows that the longer viewers stay tuned to a particular program, the more memorable they find the commercials. Contrary to long-held assumptions, "holding power" can be more important than ratings (the number of people tuning in to any part of the program) when selecting media vehicles. Top-ranked shows like *Heroes*, *Lost*, and *Grey's Anatomy* draw many viewers, but those viewers may be unlikely to remember the commercials they watch, perhaps because they are so intensely focused on the shows themselves. Advertising spots during less popular shows, which reach fewer viewers and cost less, may be more likely to make a memorable impression with a limited audience.

WELCOME TO BOLLYWOOD

© DREAM PICTURES/TAXI/GETTY IMAGES

With the smashing success of the film *Slumdog Millionaire*, Hollywood is taking notice of Bollywood. Bollywood, shorthand for the Indian movie industry in Mumbai, pumps out more movies (and less expensive movies) than Hollywood. Many of the new movies blend Indian themes and storylines with American cinematic styles. This new blend of entertainment could have huge marketing and advertising implications in the United States, especially for minority groups like the Desis. The Desis are the 2.5 million Americans of Indian, Pakistani, Bangladeshi, Sri Lankan, Bhutanese, and Nepalese descent. Desis come to the United States with knowledge of English, an appreciation of the culture, $76 billion of disposable income, and education. Some companies have already targeted the Desi subculture by focusing on their community because it is an important characteristic for the Desi.

Younger viewers' tendency to view their network shows via online video stream may also benefit marketers. Research suggests that consumers recall online commercials 60 to 90 percent of the time, while they remember roughly 25 percent of the advertisements they view on television.[25]

Additional research highlights the benefits of cross-media advertising campaigns. Viewers who encounter ads both on traditional television and online are most likely to remember and respond to them. Listerine ran a recent campaign on ABC and ABC.com and found that its mouthwash sales increased 33 percent more among viewers who saw the ad in both places.[26]

Media Scheduling

After choosing the media for the advertising campaign, advertisers must schedule the ads. A **media schedule** designates the medium or media to be used (such as magazines, television, or radio), the specific vehicles (such as *People* magazine, the show *Lost* on television, or the American Top 40 national radio program), and the insertion dates of the advertising.

There are four basic types of media schedules:

» Products in the later stages of the product life cycle, which are advertised on a reminder basis, use a **continuous media schedule**. A continuous schedule allows the advertising to run steadily throughout the advertising period. Examples include Ivory soap and Charmin toilet tissue, which may have an ad in the newspaper every Sunday and a television commercial on NBC every Wednesday at 7:30 P.M. over a three-month time period.

» With a **flighted media schedule**, the advertiser may schedule the ads heavily every other month or every two weeks to achieve a greater impact with an increased frequency and reach at those times. Movie studios might schedule television advertising on Wednesday and Thursday nights, when moviegoers are deciding which films to see that weekend.

» A **pulsing media schedule** combines continuous scheduling with flighting. Continuous advertising is simply heavier during the best sale periods. A retail department store may advertise on a year-round basis but place more advertising during certain sale periods such as Thanksgiving, Christmas, and back-to-school.

» Certain times of the year call for a **seasonal media schedule**. Products like cough syrup and sunscreen, which are used more during certain times of the year, tend to follow a seasonal strategy.

New research comparing continuous media schedules versus flighted ones finds that continuous schedules for television advertisements are more effective than flighting in driving sales. The research suggests that it may be more important to get exposure as close as possible to the time when someone is going to make a purchase. Therefore, the advertiser should maintain a continuous schedule over as long a period of time as possible. Often called *recency planning*, this theory of scheduling is now commonly used for scheduling television advertising for frequently purchased products, such as Coca-Cola or Tide detergent. Recency planning's main premise is that advertising works by influencing the brand choice of people who are ready to buy.

LO 5 Public Relations

Public relations is the element in the promotional mix that evaluates public attitudes, identifies issues that may elicit public concern, and executes programs to gain public understanding and acceptance. Public relations is a vital link in a progressive company's marketing communication mix. Marketing managers plan solid public relations campaigns that fit into overall marketing plans and focus on targeted audiences. These campaigns strive to maintain a positive image of the corporation in the eyes of the public. As such, they should capitalize on the factors that enhance the firm's image and minimize the factors that could generate a negative image.

Publicity is the effort to capture media attention— for example, through articles or editorials in publications or through human-interest stories on radio or

THE ADVERTISER SHOULD MAINTAIN A CONTINUOUS SCHEDULE OVER AS LONG A PERIOD OF TIME AS POSSIBLE.

media schedule designation of the media, the specific publications or programs, and the insertion dates of advertising

continuous media schedule a media scheduling strategy in which advertising is run steadily throughout the advertising period; used for products in the later stages of the product life cycle

flighted media schedule a media scheduling strategy in which ads are run heavily every other month or every two weeks, to achieve a greater impact with an increased frequency and reach at those times

pulsing media schedule a media scheduling strategy that uses continuous scheduling throughout the year coupled with a flighted schedule during the best sales periods

seasonal media schedule a media scheduling strategy that runs advertising only during times of the year when the product is most likely to be used

Get your new product right here, folks!

Get your new product right here, folks!

product placement a public relations strategy that involves getting a product, service, or company name to appear in a movie, television show, radio program, magazine, newspaper, video game, video or audio clip, book, or commercial for another product; on the Internet; or at special events

television programs. Corporations usually initiate publicity through a press release that furthers their public relations plans. A company about to introduce a new product or open a new store may send press releases to the media in the hope that the story will be published or broadcast. Savvy publicity can often create overnight sensations or build up a reserve of goodwill with consumers. Corporate donations and sponsorships can also create favorable publicity.

Public relations departments may perform any or all of the following functions:

▸ *Press relations*: placing positive, newsworthy information in the news media to attract attention to a product, a service, or a person associated with the firm or institution

▸ *Product publicity*: publicizing specific products or services

▸ *Corporate communication*: creating internal and external messages to promote a positive image of the firm or institution

▸ *Public affairs*: building and maintaining national or local community relations

▸ *Lobbying*: influencing legislators and government officials to promote or defeat legislation and regulation

▸ *Employee and investor relations*: maintaining positive relationships with employees, shareholders, and others in the financial community

▸ *Crisis management*: responding to unfavorable publicity or a negative event

Major Public Relations Tools

Public relations professionals commonly use several tools, many of which require an active role on the part of the public relations professional, such as writing press releases and engaging in proactive media relations. Sometimes, however, these techniques create their own publicity.

New-Product Publicity Publicity is instrumental in introducing new products and services. Publicity can help advertisers explain what's different about their new product by prompting free news stories or positive word of mouth about it. During the introductory period, an especially innovative new product often needs more exposure than conventional, paid advertising affords. Public relations professionals write press

releases or develop videos in an effort to generate news about their new product. They also jockey for exposure of their product or service at major events, on popular television and news shows, or in the hands of influential people. The Internet now helps marketers create their own events and spread excitement through consumer groups. For instance, BMW produced a mockumentary about a small German village attempting to launch a BMW 1 series coupe across the Atlantic to land in the United States. The humorous film drew lots of attention on auto blogs and stayed popular even after BMW explained that it was an ad.[27] Publicity stunts have been around for a long time and sometimes leave a lasting impression. For example, in 1903, newspaper publisher Henri Desgrange promoted a new bicycle race as a publicity stunt to publicize his newspaper. That race—the Tour de France—is still going strong more than 100 years later.[28]

Product Placement Marketers are increasingly using product placement to reinforce brand awareness and create favorable attitudes. **Product placement** is a strategy that involves getting one's product, service, or name to appear in a movie, television show, radio program, magazine, newspaper, video game, video or audio clip, book, or commercial for another product; on the Internet; or at special events. Including an actual product, such as a can of Pepsi, adds a sense of realism to a movie, television show, video game, book, or similar vehicle that cannot be created by a can simply marked "soda." Product placements are arranged through barter (trade of product for placement), through paid placements, or at no charge when the product is viewed as enhancing the vehicle it is placed in.

Product placement expenditures are about $5 billion annually, and that figure is growing about 30 percent annually due to increasing audience fragmentation and the spread of ad-skipping technology.[29] More than two-thirds of product placements are in movies and television shows, but placements in other alternative media are growing, particularly on the Internet and in video games. Digital technology now enables companies to "virtually" place their products in any audio or video production. Virtual placement not only reduces the cost of product placement for new productions but also enables companies to place things in previously produced programs, such as reruns of television shows. Overall, companies obtain valuable product exposure, brand reinforcement, and increased sales through product placement, often at a much lower cost than in mass media like television ads.

Consumer Education Some major firms believe that educated consumers are better, more loyal customers. Financial planning firms often sponsor free educational seminars on money management, retirement planning, and investing in the hope that the seminar participants will choose the sponsoring organization for their future financial needs.

Sponsorship Sponsorships are increasing both in number and as a proportion of companies' marketing budgets, with spending reaching $17 billion annually in the United States and Canada. Overall, global spending on sponsorships including North America was expected to exceed $44 billion in 2008. Probably the biggest reason for the increasing use of sponsorships is the difficulty of reaching audiences and differentiating a product from competing brands through the mass media.

With **sponsorship**, a company spends money to support an issue, cause, or event that is consistent with corporate objectives, such as improving brand awareness or enhancing corporate image. The biggest category is sports, which accounts for almost 70 percent of spending in sponsorships. Non-sports categories include entertainment tours and attractions, causes, arts, festivals, fairs and annual events, and association and membership organizations.[30]

Although the most popular sponsorship events are still those involving sports, music, or the arts, companies have recently been turning to more specialized events such as tie-ins with schools, charities, and other community service organizations. Marketers sometimes even create their own events tied around their product.

Corporations sponsor issues as well as events. Sponsorship issues are quite diverse, but the three most popular are education, health care, and social programs. Firms often donate a percentage of sales or profits to a worthy cause favored by their target market.

A special type of sponsorship, **cause-related marketing**, involves the association of a for-profit company with a nonprofit organization. Through the sponsorship, the company's product or service is promoted, and money is raised for the nonprofit. In a common type of cause-related sponsorship, a company agrees to donate a percentage of the purchase price for a particular item to a charity, but some arrangements are more complex. For example, schools around the United States collect Campbell's soup labels and General Mills cereal box tops because those companies will donate to the school a certain amount for every label or top submitted. Several studies indicate that some consumers consider a company's reputation when making purchasing decisions and that a company's community involvement boosts employee morale and loyalty.[31]

> **sponsorship** a public relations strategy in which a company spends money to support an issue, cause, or event that is consistent with corporate objectives, such as improving brand awareness or enhancing corporate image
>
> **cause-related marketing** a type of sponsorship involving the association of a for-profit company and a nonprofit organization; through the sponsorship, the company's product or service is promoted, and money is raised for the nonprofit

© PRNEWSFOTO/THE KROGER CO.

Internet Web Sites Companies increasingly are using the Internet in their public relations strategies. Company Web sites are used to introduce new products, promote existing products, obtain consumer feedback, post news releases, communicate legislative and regulatory information, showcase upcoming events, provide links to related sites, release financial information, interact with customers and potential customers, and perform many more marketing activities. Online reviews from opinion leaders and other consumers help marketers sway purchasing decisions in their favor. On Playstation.com, Sony has online support, events and promotions, game trailers, and new and updated product releases. The site also includes message boards where the gaming community exchanges tips on games, votes on lifestyle issues like music and videos, and learns about promotional events.[32]

Web sites are also key elements of integrated marketing communications strategies. For example, CBS integrated broadcast advertising with product placement by placing a bonus scene from *CSI: Miami* on its Web site featuring a plot twist that was not revealed to television viewers until later in the season. The bonus scene page was sponsored by General Motors' Hummer brand, which also appeared in the bonus scene itself.[33]

More and more often, companies are also using blogs—both corporate and noncorporate—as a tool to manage their public images. Noncorporate blogs cannot be controlled, but marketers must monitor them to be aware of and respond to negative information and encourage positive content. In addition to "getting the message out," companies are using blogs to create communities of consumers who feel positively about the brand. The hope is that positive attitude toward the brand will build into strong word-of-mouth marketing. Companies must exercise caution when diving into corporate blogging, however. Coca-Cola launched a blog authored by a fictional character that did little except parrot the company line. Consumers immediately saw the blog for what it was (a transparent public relations platform) and lambasted Coca-Cola for its insincerity.[34]

Managing Unfavorable Publicity

Although marketers try to avoid unpleasant situations, crises do happen. In our free-press environment, publicity is not easily controlled, especially in a crisis. **Crisis management** is the coordinated effort to handle the effects of unfavorable publicity, ensuring fast and accurate communication in times of emergency.

For example, in the wake of an FDA "Import Alert" on Chinese shrimp and concerns about the presence of antibiotics and carcinogens in farmed shrimp, Blue Horizon Organic Seafood has rushed to educate grocers and reassure consumers that its eco-friendly shrimp is safe to eat. The company has increased its sales of prepackaged frozen shrimp with labeling that describes its organic certification process.[35]

STUDY TOOLS CHAPTER 17

Located at back of the textbook

❑ **Rip out Chapter Review Card**

Located at 4ltrpress.cengage.com/mktg

❑ **Review Key Terms Flash Cards (Print or Online)**

❑ **Download Audio and Visual Summaries for on-the-go review**

❑ **Complete both Practice Quizzes to prepare for tests**

❑ **Play "Beat the Clock" and "Quizbowl" to master concepts**

❑ **Complete "Crossword Puzzle" to review key terms**

❑ **Watch the video on "Vans" for a real company example on Advertising and Public Relations**

"They are written in **concise, down-to-earth language.** There are tons of pictures and interesting blurbs of information. It's very relevant to my life. It's nice to have a book/website that seems to **reach out to students and actually care** about how we learn and try to tailor to our needs as much as possible. Thank you for this."

– Alice Brent, Student at Arizona State University

SPEAK UP!

THEY DID

MKTG4 was built on a simple principle: to create a new teaching and learning solution that reflects the way today's faculty teach and the way you learn.

Through conversations, focus groups, surveys, and interviews, we collected data that drove the creation of the current version of MKTG4 that you are using today. But it doesn't stop there – in order to make MKTG4 an even better learning experience, we'd like you to SPEAK UP and tell us how MKTG4 worked for you.

What did you like about it?
What would you change?
Are there additional ideas you have that would help us build a better product for next semester's principles of marketing students?

At **4ltrpress.cengage.com** you'll find all of the resources you need to succeed in principles of marketing – **video podcasts, audio downloads, flash cards, interactive quizzes,** and more!

Speak Up! Go to **4ltrpress.cengage.com**.

Sales Promotion and Personal Selling

"Advertising offers the consumer a reason to buy; sales promotion offers an incentive to buy."

AFTER YOU FINISH THIS CHAPTER GO TO PAGE 293 FOR STUDY TOOLS

LO1 Sales Promotion

In addition to using advertising, public relations, and personal selling, marketing managers can use sales promotion to increase the effectiveness of their promotional efforts. *Sales promotion* is marketing communication activities, other than advertising, personal selling, and public relations, in which a short-term incentive motivates consumers or members of the distribution channel to purchase a good or service immediately, either by lowering the price or by adding value.

Advertising offers the consumer a reason to buy; sales promotion offers an incentive to buy. Sales promotion is usually cheaper than advertising and easier to measure. A major national television advertising campaign often costs $5 million or more to create, produce, and place. In contrast, promotional campaigns using the Internet or direct marketing methods can cost less than half that amount. It is also very difficult to determine how many people buy a product or service as a result of radio or television ads. With sales promotion, marketers know the precise number of coupons redeemed or the number of contest entries.

Sales promotion is usually targeted toward either of two distinctly different markets. **Consumer sales promotion** is targeted to the ultimate consumer market. **Trade sales promotion** is directed to members of the marketing channel, such as wholesalers and retailers. Sales promotion expenditures have been steadily increasing over the past several years as a result of increased competition, the ever-expanding array of available media choices, consumers and retailers demanding

consumer sales promotion sales promotion activities targeting the ultimate consumer

trade sales promotion sales promotion activities targeting a marketing channel member, such as a wholesaler or retailer

What do you think?

The money I can save by using coupons does not amount to much.

STRONGLY DISAGREE   STRONGLY AGREE

Find out what others think at 4ltrpress.cengage.com/mktg

© ISTOCKPHOTO.COM/STEVE SNYDER

more deals from manufacturers, and the continued reliance on accountable and measurable marketing strategies. In addition, product and service marketers that have traditionally ignored sales promotion activities, such as power companies, have discovered the marketing power of sales promotion. In fact, annual expenditures on promotion marketing in the United States now exceed $400 billion. Direct mail is the most widely used promotional medium, accounting for 50 percent of annual promotional expenditures.[1]

The Objectives of Sales Promotion

Sales promotion usually has more effect on behavior than on attitudes. Immediate purchase is the goal of sales promotion, regardless of the form it takes. The objectives of a promotion depend on the general behavior of target consumers (see Exhibit 18.1). For example, marketers who are targeting loyal users of their product actually need to reinforce existing behavior or increase product usage. An effective tool for strengthening brand loyalty is the *frequent buyer program*, which rewards consumers for repeat purchases. Other types of promotions are more effective with customers prone to brand switching or with those who are loyal to a competitor's product. A cents-off coupon, free sample, or eye-catching display in a store will often entice shoppers to try a different brand.

Once marketers understand the dynamics occurring within their product category and have determined the particular consumers and consumer behaviors they want to influence, they can then go about selecting promotional tools to achieve these goals.

LO 2 Tools for Consumer Sales Promotion

Marketing managers must decide which consumer sales promotion devices to use in a specific campaign. The methods chosen must suit the objectives to ensure success of the overall promotion plan. The popular tools for consumer sales promotion discussed in the following pages have also been easily transferred to online versions to entice Internet users to visit sites, purchase products, or use services on the Web.

EXHIBIT 18.1

Types of Consumers and Sales Promotion Goals

Type of Buyer	Desired Results	Sales Promotion Examples
Loyal customers People who buy your product most or all of the time	Reinforce behavior, increase consumption, change purchase timing	• Loyalty marketing programs, such as frequent buyer cards or frequent shopper clubs • Bonus packs that give loyal consumers an incentive to stock up or premiums offered in return for proofs of purchase
Competitor's customers People who buy a competitor's product most or all of the time	Break loyalty, persuade to switch to your brand	• Sampling to introduce your product's superior qualities compared to their brand • Sweepstakes, contests, or premiums that create interest in the product
Brand switchers People who buy a variety of products in the category	Persuade to buy your brand more often	• Any promotion that lowers the price of the product, such as coupons, price-off packages, and bonus packs • Trade deals that help make the product more readily available than competing products
Price buyers People who consistently buy the least expensive brand	Appeal with low prices or supply added value that makes price less important	• Coupons, price-off packages, refunds, or trade deals that reduce the price of the brand to match that of the brand that would have been purchased

SOURCE: From *Sales Promotion Essentials*, 2nd ed., by Don E. Schultz, William A. Robinson, and Lisa A. Petrison. Reprinted by permission of NTC Publishing Group, 4255 Touhy Ave., Lincolnwood, IL 60048.

Coupons and Rebates

A **coupon** is a certificate that entitles consumers to an immediate price reduction when they buy the product. Coupons are a particularly good way to encourage product trial and repurchase. They are also likely to increase the amount of a product bought.

Almost 300 billion coupons are distributed to U.S. households annually, and this does not include the billions of coupons increasingly available over the Internet and in stores. Intense competition in the consumer packaged goods category and the annual introduction of over 1,200 new products have contributed to this trend. Though coupons are often criticized for reaching consumers who have no interest in the product or for encouraging repeat purchase by regular users, recent studies indicate that coupons promote new-product use and are likely to stimulate purchases.

Freestanding inserts (FSIs), the promotional coupons inserts found in newspapers, have been the traditional way of circulating printed coupons. But volume of FSI coupons distributed is declining. To overcome the diminishing redemption rates, marketers are using new couponing strategies. Shortening the time during which coupons can be redeemed creates a greater sense of urgency to redeem the coupon. Other tactics include de-emphasizing the use of coupons in favor of everyday low pricing and distributing single, all-purpose coupons that can be redeemed for several brands.[2]

In-store coupons have become popular because they are more likely to influence customers' buying decisions. Instant coupons on product packages, coupons distributed from on-shelf coupon-dispensing machines, and electronic coupons issued at the checkout counter now achieve much higher redemption rates because consumers are making more in-store purchase decisions.

Internet coupons are gaining in popularity, and coupon sites like coolsavings.com and valpak.com are emerging as major coupon distribution outlets.[3] For example, Kroger has launched "Coupons that you click. Not clip." on Kroger.com. Registered Kroger Plus card members just log on to the Web site and click on the coupons they want. Coupons are automatically loaded on to the Kroger Plus card and redeemed at checkout when the shopper's Kroger Plus card is scanned.[4] As marketing tactics grow more sophisticated, however, coupons are no longer viewed as a stand-alone tactic, but as an integral component of a larger promotional campaign.

Rebates are similar to coupons in that they offer the purchaser a price reduction; however, because the purchaser must mail in a rebate form and usually some proof of purchase, the reward is not as immediate. Manufacturers prefer rebates for several reasons. Rebates allow manufacturers to offer price cuts to consumers directly. Manufacturers have more control over rebate promotions because they can be rolled out and shut off quickly. Further, because buyers must fill out forms with their names, addresses, and other data, manufacturers use rebate programs to build customer databases. Perhaps the best reason of all to offer rebates is that although rebates are particularly good at enticing purchase, most consumers never bother to redeem them. The Federal Trade Commission estimates that only half of consumers eligible for rebates collect them.[5]

Premiums

A **premium** is an extra item offered to the consumer, usually in exchange for some proof that the promoted product has been purchased. Premiums reinforce the consumer's purchase decision, increase consumption, and persuade nonusers to switch brands. The best example of the use of premiums is McDonald's Happy Meal, which rewards children with a small toy.

Premiums can also include more product for the regular price, such as two-for-the-price-of-one bonus packs or packages that include more of the product. Kellogg's, for instance, added two more pastries to its Pop Tarts without increasing the price in an effort to

coupon a certificate that entitles consumers to an immediate price reduction when they buy the product

rebate a cash refund given for the purchase of a product during a specific period

premium an extra item offered to the consumer, usually in exchange for some proof of purchase of the promoted product

boost market share lost to private-label brands and new competitors. The promotion was so successful the company decided to keep the additional product in its regular packaging. Another possibility is to attach a premium to the product's package.

Loyalty Marketing Programs

Loyalty marketing programs, or **frequent buyer programs**, reward loyal consumers for making multiple purchases. The objective of loyalty marketing programs is to build long-term, mutually beneficial relationships between a company and its key customers.

There are almost 1.5 billion loyalty program memberships in the United States, with the average household participating in twelve programs.[6] Popularized by the airline industry through frequent flyer programs, loyalty marketing enables companies to strategically invest sales promotion dollars in activities designed to capture greater profits from customers already loyal to the product or company. One of the more successful recent premium promotions is Starbucks' Duetto Card, which combines a Visa credit card with a reloadable Starbucks card. The card allows members to collect "Duetto Dollars" that can be redeemed for anything they want to purchase at a Starbucks location.[7]

Studies show consumer loyalty is on the decline. According to research conducted by Gartner, more than 75 percent of consumers have more than one loyalty card that rewards them with redeemable points. Frequent shopper card programs offered by many retailers have exploded in popularity. Research from Forrester shows that 54 percent of primary grocery shoppers belong to two or more supermarket loyalty programs. Although this speaks to the popularity of loyalty cards, it also shows that customers are pledging "loyalty" to more than one store: 15 percent of primary grocery shoppers are cardholders in at least three programs.[8]

Cobranded credit cards are an increasingly popular loyalty marketing tool. In a recent year, almost one billion direct marketing appeals for a cobranded credit card were sent to potential customers in the United States. Target, Gap, Sony, and American Airlines are only a few of the companies sponsoring cobranded Visa, MasterCard, or American Express cards.

Through loyalty programs, shoppers receive discounts, alerts on new products, and other types of enticing offers. In exchange, retailers are able to build customer databases that help them better understand customer preferences.

Companies are increasingly using the Internet to build customer loyalty through e-mail and blogs. Over 80 percent of supermarket chains are using e-mail to register customers for their loyalty programs and to entice them with coupons, flyers, and promotional campaigns.[9] Blogs enable companies to build social networks around their brands. Starwood Hotels' corporate blog called TheLobby.com is open to the public, but its content is aimed specifically at members of the Starwood Preferred Guest loyalty program. Features include postings about special events at specific Starwood properties and how travelers can earn loyalty points through special promotions. The company's goal is to combine advertising with useful information to create a Web destination for its guests—and divert them away from other travel blogs that might contain negative postings about Starwood hotels.[10]

Contests and Sweepstakes

Contests and sweepstakes are generally designed to create interest in a good or service, often to encourage brand switching. *Contests* are promotions in which participants use some skill or ability to compete for prizes. A consumer contest usually requires entrants to answer questions, complete sentences, or write a paragraph about the product and submit proof of purchase. Winning a *sweepstakes*, on the other hand, depends on chance, and participation is free. Sweepstakes usually draw about ten times more entries than contests do.

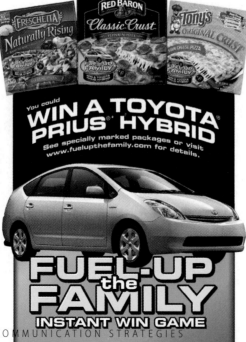

Freschetta, Red Baron, and Tony's pizzas' mega event "Fuel-Up the Family" gave consumers the opportunity to win a Toyota Prius. To participate, consumers entered the UPC from specially marked packages and played an instant win game on an interactive Web site.

While contests and sweepstakes may draw considerable interest and publicity, generally they are not effective tools for generating long-term sales. To increase their effectiveness, sales promotion managers must make certain the award will appeal to the target market. Offering several smaller prizes to many winners instead of one huge prize to just one person often will increase the effectiveness of the promotion, but there's no denying the attractiveness of a jackpot-type prize.

Sampling

Sampling allows the customer to try a product risk-free. Sampling can increase retail sales by as much as 40 percent, so it's no surprise that sampling has increased more than 20 percent annually in recent years.[11]

Samples can be directly mailed to the customer, delivered door-to-door, packaged with another product, or demonstrated or distributed at a retail store or service outlet. Sampling at special events is a popular, effective, and high-profile distribution method that permits marketers to piggyback onto fun-based consumer activities—including sporting events, college fests, fairs and festivals, beach events, and chili cook-offs.

Distributing samples to specific location types, such as health clubs, churches, or doctors' offices, is one of the most efficient methods of sampling. What better way to get consumers to try a product than to offer a sample exactly when it is needed most? If someone visits a health club regularly, chances are he or she is a good prospect for a health-food product or vitamin supplement. Health club instructors are handing out not only these products but also body wash, deodorant, and face cloths to sweating participants at the end of class. This method of distributing samples is working. In fact, one recent study found that sampling events produced an average 36 percent increase in sales soon afterward.[12] Online sampling is gaining momentum as Web communities bring people together with common interests in trying new products, often using blogs to spread the word. Nail polish company OPI used SheSpeaks.com to encourage trials of new lacquer nail polish pens. Consumers had to register and then order one of five color pens and coupons. Consumers also blogged about the new pens and passed along the coupons to friends.[13]

Point-of-Purchase Promotion

Point-of-purchase (P-O-P) display includes any promotional display set up at the retailer's location to build traffic, advertise the product, or induce impulse buy-

ing. Point-of-purchase displays include shelf "talkers" (signs attached to store shelves), shelf extenders (attachments that extend shelves so products stand out), ads on grocery carts and bags, end-aisle and floor-stand displays, television monitors at supermarket checkout counters, in-store audio messages, and audiovisual displays. One big advantage of P-O-P display is that it offers manufacturers a captive audience in retail stores. Another advantage is that between 70 and 80 percent of all retail purchase decisions are made in-store, so P-O-P displays can be very effective, increasing sales by as much as 65 percent. For example, when a Florida entrepreneur decided to join the growing niche vodka market, he didn't have a large advertising budget. Instead, he made the rounds of local bars and restaurants, hosting cocktail comparisons to drum up interest in his vodka brand. He managed to sell 3,200 cases.[14] Strategies to increase sales include adding header or riser cards, changing messages on base or case wraps, adding inflatable or mobile displays, and using signs that advertise the brand's sports, movie, or charity tie-in.[15]

Online Sales Promotion

Online sales promotions have expanded dramatically in recent years. Marketers are now spending billions of dollars annually on such promotions. Sales promotions online have proved effective and cost-efficient, generating response rates three to five times higher than off-line promotions. The most effective types of online sales promotions are free merchandise, sweepstakes, free shipping with purchases, and coupons.

Eager to boost traffic, Internet retailers are busy giving away free services or equipment, such as personal computers and travel, to lure consumers not only to their own Web sites but to

DID YOU USE THE PROMOTION CODE?

sampling a promotional program that allows the consumer the opportunity to try a product or service for free

point-of-purchase (P-O-P) display a promotional display set up at the retailer's location to build traffic, advertise the product, or induce impulse buying

the Internet in general. Another goal is to add potential customers to their databases.

Marketers have discovered that online coupon distribution provides another vehicle for promoting their products. In addition, e-coupons can help marketers lure new customers. Online coupons often have a redemption rate of more than 20 percent, as much as ten times higher than for traditional coupons.[16] In fact, nearly 50 percent of consumers who purchase something online use a coupon or discount promotional code. With the speed of compiling data online, marketers can conduct tests in real time and measure the results in time to offer last-minute promotions and react to changing market conditions.[17]

Online versions of loyalty programs are also popping up, and although many types of companies have these programs, the most successful are those run by hotel and airline companies.

LO 3 Tools for Trade Sales Promotion

Whereas consumer promotions pull a product through the channel by creating demand, trade promotions *push* a product through the distribution channel (see Chapter 13). When selling to members of the distribution channel, manufacturers use many of the same sales promotion tools used in consumer promotions—such as sales contests, premiums, and point-of-purchase displays. Several tools, however, are unique to manufacturers and intermediaries.

▸▸ *Trade allowances*: A **trade allowance** is a price reduction offered by manufacturers to intermediaries such as wholesalers and retailers. The price reduction or rebate is given in exchange for doing something specific, such as allocating space for a new product or buying something during special periods. For example, a local Best Buy outlet could receive a special discount for running its own promotion on Sony surround sound systems.

▸▸ *Push money*: Intermediaries receive **push money** as a bonus for pushing the manufacturer's brand through the distribution channel. Often the push money is directed toward a retailer's salespeople. LinoColor, the leading high-end scanner company, produces a Picture Perfect Rewards catalog filled with merchandise retailers can purchase with points accrued for every LinoColor scanner they sell.

▸▸ *Training*: Sometimes a manufacturer will train an intermediary's personnel if the product is rather complex—as frequently occurs in the computer and telecommunications industries. For example, representatives of a television manufacturer like Toshiba may train salespeople in how to demonstrate the new features of the latest models of televisions to consumers.

▸▸ *Free merchandise*: Often a manufacturer offers retailers free merchandise in lieu of quantity discounts. Occasionally, free merchandise is used as payment for trade allowances normally provided through other sales promotions. Instead of giving a retailer a price reduction for buying a certain quantity of merchandise, the manufacturer may throw in extra merchandise "free" (that is, at a cost that would equal the price reduction).

▸▸ *Store demonstrations*: Manufacturers can also arrange with retailers to perform an in-store demonstration. Food manufacturers often send representatives to grocery stores and supermarkets to let customers sample a product while shopping.

WOULD YOU LIKE A FREE SAMPLE OF STOVE TOP STUFFING?

▸▸ *Business meetings, conventions, and trade shows*: Trade association meetings, conferences, and conventions are an important aspect of sales promotion and a growing, multibillion-dollar market. At these shows, manufacturers, distributors, and other vendors have the chance to display their goods or describe their services to customers and potential customers.

Companies participate in trade shows to attract and identify new prospects, serve current customers, introduce new products, enhance corporate image, test the market response to new products, enhance corporate morale, and gather competitive product information.

Trade promotions are popular among manufacturers for many reasons. Trade sales promotion tools help manufacturers gain new distributors for their products, obtain wholesaler and retailer support for consumer sales promotions, build or reduce dealer inventories, and improve trade relations. Car manufacturers annually sponsor dozens of auto shows for consumers. The shows attract millions of consumers, providing dealers with increased store traffic as well as good leads.

LO 4 Personal Selling

As mentioned in Chapter 16, *personal selling* is a purchase situation involving a personal, paid-for communication between two people in an attempt to influence each other. In a sense, all businesspeople are salespeople. An individual may become a plant manager, a chemist, an engineer, or a member of any profession and yet still have to sell. During a job search, applicants must "sell" themselves to prospective employers in an interview.

ADVANTAGES OF PERSONAL SELLING

▸▸ Personal selling provides a detailed explanation or demonstration of the product. This capability is especially needed for complex or new goods and services.

▸▸ The sales message can be varied according to the motivations and interests of each prospective customer. Moreover, when the prospect has questions or raises objections, the salesperson is there to provide explanations. In contrast, advertising and sales promotion can only respond to the objections the copywriter thinks are important to customers.

▸▸ Personal selling can be directed only to qualified prospects. Other forms of promotion include some unavoidable waste because many people in the audience are not prospective customers.

▸▸ Personal selling costs can be controlled by adjusting the size of the sales force (and resulting expenses) in one-person increments. On the other hand, advertising and sales promotion must often be purchased in fairly large amounts.

▸▸ Perhaps the most important advantage is that personal selling is considerably more effective than other forms of promotion in obtaining a sale and gaining a satisfied customer.

EXHIBIT 18.2
Comparison of Personal Selling and Advertising/Sales Promotion

Personal selling is more important if . . .	Advertising and sales promotion are more important if . . .
The product has a high value.	The product has a low value.
It is a custom-made product.	It is a standardized product.
There are few customers.	There are many customers.
The product is technically complex.	The product is easy to understand.
Customers are concentrated.	Customers are geographically dispersed.
Examples: insurance policies, custom windows, airplane engines	**Examples:** soap, magazine subscriptions, cotton T-shirts

Personal selling offers several advantages over other forms of promotion. Personal selling may also work better than other forms of promotion given certain customer and product characteristics. Generally speaking, personal selling becomes more important as the number of potential customers decreases, as the complexity of the product increases, and as the value of the product grows (see Exhibit 18.2). For highly complex goods, such as business jets or private communication systems, a salesperson is needed to determine the prospective customer's needs, explain the product's basic advantages, and propose the exact features and accessories that will meet the client's needs. Personal selling can also be a good strategy for high-end luxuries; designer Michael Kors recently sold $575,000 worth of clothing during a four-hour luncheon with select customers.[18]

LO 5 Relationship Selling

Until recently, marketing theory and practice concerning personal selling focused almost entirely on a planned presentation to prospective customers for the sole purpose of making the sale. Marketers were most concerned with making a one-time sale and then moving on to the next prospect. Traditional personal selling methods attempted to persuade the buyer to accept a point of view or convince the buyer to take some action. Frequently, the objectives of the salesperson were at the expense of the buyer, creating a win-lose outcome.

Although this type of sales approach has not disappeared entirely, it is being used less and less often by professional salespeople.

In contrast, modern views of personal selling emphasize the relationship that develops between a salesperson and a buyer. **Relationship selling**, or **consultative selling**, is a multistage process that emphasizes personalization and empathy as key ingredients in identifying prospects and developing them as long-term, satisfied customers. With relationship selling, the objective is to build long-term branded relationships with consumers/buyers, so the focus is on building mutual trust between the buyer and seller through the delivery of anticipated, long-term, value-added benefits to the buyer.

Relationship or consultative salespeople, therefore, become consultants, partners, and problem solvers for their customers. They strive to build long-term relationships with key accounts by developing trust over time. The emphasis shifts from a one-time sale to a long-term relationship in which the salesperson works with the customer to develop solutions for enhancing the customer's bottom line. Research has shown that positive customer-salesperson relationships contribute to trust, increased customer loyalty, and the intent to continue the relationship with the salesperson.[19] Thus, relationship selling promotes a win-win situation for both buyer and seller.

IT COSTS BUSINESSES SIX TIMES MORE TO GAIN A NEW CUSTOMER THAN TO RETAIN A CURRENT ONE.

The end result of relationship selling tends to be loyal customers who purchase from the company time after time. A relationship selling strategy focused on retaining customers costs a company less than constantly prospecting and selling to new customers.

Relationship selling is more typical with selling situations for industrial-type goods, such as heavy machinery or computer systems, and services, such as airlines and insurance, than for consumer goods. Exhibit 18.3 lists the key differences between traditional personal selling and relationship or consultative selling. These differences will become more apparent as we explore the personal selling process later in the chapter.

LO 6 Steps in the Selling Process

Completing a sale actually requires several steps. The **sales process**, or **sales cycle**, is simply the set of steps a salesperson goes through to sell a particular product or service. The sales process or cycle can be unique for each product or service, depending on the features of the product or service, characteristics of customer segments, and internal processes in place within the firm, such as how leads are gathered.

Some sales take only a few minutes, but others may take much longer to complete. Sales of technical

EXHIBIT 18.3

Key Differences between Traditional Selling and Relationship Selling

Traditional Personal Selling	Relationship or Consultative Selling
Sell products (goods and services)	Sell advice, assistance, and counsel
Focus on closing sales	Focus on improving the customer's bottom line
Limited sales planning	Consider sales planning as top priority
Spend most contact time telling customers about product	Spend most contact time attempting to build a problem-solving environment with the customer
Conduct "product-specific" needs assessment	Conduct discovery in the full scope of the customer's operations
"Lone wolf" approach to the account	Team approach to the account
Proposals and presentations based on pricing and product features	Proposals and presentations based on profit impact and strategic benefits to the customer
Sales follow-up is short term, focused on product delivery	Sales follow-up is long term, focused on long-term relationship enhancement

SOURCE: Robert M. Peterson, Patrick L. Schul, and George H. Lucas, Jr., "Consultative Selling: Walking the Walk in the New Selling Environment," National Conference on Sales Management, *Proceedings*, March 1996.

© COMSTOCK IMAGES/JUPITERIMAGES

products like a Boeing or Airbus airplane and customized goods and services typically take many months, perhaps even years, to complete. On the other end of the spectrum, sales of less technical products like stationery are generally more routine and may take only a few days. Whether a salesperson spends a few minutes or a few years on a sale, there are seven basic steps in the personal selling process, outlined further in the following sections.

Seven Steps in the Personal Selling Process

1. Generating leads
2. Qualifying leads
3. Approaching the customer and probing needs
4. Developing and proposing solutions
5. Handling objections
6. Closing the sale
7. Following up

Like other forms of promotion, these steps of selling follow the AIDA concept discussed in Chapter 16. Once a salesperson has located a prospect with the authority to buy, he or she tries to get the prospect's attention. A thorough needs assessment turned into an effective sales proposal and presentation should generate interest. After developing the customer's initial desire (preferably during the presentation of the sales proposal), the salesperson seeks action in the close by trying to get an agreement to buy. Follow-up after the sale, the final step in the selling process, not only lowers cognitive dissonance (refer to Chapter 6) but also may open up opportunities to discuss future sales. Effective follow-up will also lead to repeat business in which the process may start all over again at the needs assessment step.

Traditional selling and relationship selling follow the same basic steps. They differ in the relative importance placed on key steps in the process. Traditional selling efforts are transaction oriented, focusing on generating as many leads as possible, making as many presentations as possible, and closing as many sales as possible. Minimal effort is placed on asking questions to identify customer needs and wants or matching these needs and wants to the benefits of the product or service. In contrast, salespeople practicing relationship selling emphasize an up-front investment in the time and effort needed to uncover each customer's specific needs and wants and meet them with the product or service offering. By doing their homework up front, salespeople create the conditions necessary for a relatively straightforward close. Look at each step of the selling process individually.

Step 1: Generating Leads

Initial groundwork must precede communication between the potential buyer and the salesperson. **Lead generation**, or **prospecting**, is the identification of those firms and people most likely to buy the seller's offerings. These firms or people become "sales leads" or "prospects."

Sales leads can be obtained in several different ways, most notably through advertising, trade shows and conventions, or direct mail and telemarketing programs. Favorable publicity also helps to create leads. Company records of past client purchases are another excellent source of leads. Many sales professionals are also securing valuable leads from their firm's Web site.

Another way to gather a lead is through a **referral**—a recommendation from a customer or business associate. The advantages of referrals over other forms of prospecting include highly qualified leads, higher closing rates, larger initial transactions, and shorter sales cycles. Referrals typically are as much as ten times more productive in generating sales than are cold calls. Unfortunately, although most clients are willing to give referrals, many salespeople do not ask for them. Effective sales training can help to overcome this reluctance to ask for referrals. To increase the number of referrals, some companies even pay or send small gifts to customers or suppliers that provide referrals.

Networking is using friends, business contacts, coworkers, acquaintances, and fellow members in professional and civic organizations to identify potential clients. Indeed, a number of national networking clubs have been started for the sole purpose of generating leads and providing valuable business advice. Increasingly, sales professionals are also using online networking sites such as LinkedIn to connect with targeted leads and clients around the world, twenty-four hours a day. Some of LinkedIn's

lead generation (prospecting) identification of those firms and people most likely to buy the seller's offerings

referral a recommendation to a salesperson from a customer or business associate

networking a process of finding out about potential clients from friends, business contacts, coworkers, acquaintances, and fellow members in professional and civic organizations

© ISTOCKPHOTO.COM/ALF ERTSLAND

© ISTOCKPHOTO.COM/RYAN BALDERAS

estimated thirty million users have reported response rates between 50 and 60 percent, versus 3 percent from direct marketing efforts.[20]

Before the advent of more sophisticated methods of lead generation, such as direct mail and telemarketing, most prospecting was done through **cold calling**—a form of lead generation in which the salesperson approaches potential buyers without any prior knowledge of the prospects' needs or financial status. Although cold calling is still used in generating leads, many sales managers have realized the inefficiencies of having their top salespeople use their valuable selling time searching for the proverbial "needle in a haystack." Passing the job of cold calling to a lower-cost employee, typically an internal sales support person, allows salespeople to spend more time and use their relationship-building skills on prospects who have already been identified.

Step 2: Qualifying Leads

When a prospect shows interest in learning more about a product, the salesperson has the opportunity to follow up, or qualify, the lead. Personally visiting unqualified prospects wastes valuable salesperson time and company resources. Often many leads go unanswered because salespeople are given no indication as to how qualified the leads are in terms of interest and ability to purchase. Unqualified prospects give vague or incomplete answers to a salesperson's specific questions, try to evade questions on budgets, and request changes in standard procedures like prices or terms of sale. In contrast, qualified leads are real prospects who answer questions, value your time, and are realistic about money and when they are prepared to buy. Salespeople who are given accurate information on qualified leads are more than twice as likely to follow up.[21]

Lead qualification involves determining whether the prospect has three things:

▸ *A recognized need*: The most basic criterion for determining whether someone is a prospect for a product is a need that is not being satisfied. The salesperson should first consider prospects who are aware of a need but should not disregard prospects who have not yet recognized that they have one. With a little more information about the product, they may decide they do have a need for it. Preliminary interviews and questioning can often provide the salesperson with enough information to determine whether there is a need.

▸ *Buying power*: Buying power involves both authority to make the purchase decision and access to funds to pay for it. To avoid wasting time and money, the salesperson needs to identify the purchasing authority and the ability to pay before making a presentation. Organizational charts and information about a firm's credit standing can provide valuable clues.

▸ *Receptivity and accessibility*: The prospect must be willing to see the salesperson and be accessible to the salesperson. Some prospects simply refuse to see salespeople. Others, because of their stature in their organization, will see only a salesperson or sales manager with similar stature.

Often the task of lead qualification is handled by a telemarketing group or a sales support person who *prequalifies* the lead for the salesperson. Prequalification systems free sales representatives from the time-consuming task of following up on leads to determine need, buying power, and receptiveness. Prequalification systems may even set up initial appointments with the prospect for the salesperson. The result is more time for the sales force to spend in front of interested customers. Software is increasingly being utilized in lead qualification.

Companies are increasingly using their Web sites to qualify leads. When qualifying leads online, companies want visitors to register, indicate the products and services they are interested in, and provide information on their time frame and resources. Leads from the Internet can then be prioritized (those indicating a short time frame, for instance, given a higher priority) and then transferred to salespeople. Enticing visitors to register also enables companies to customize future electronic interactions.

Step 3: Approaching the Customer and Probing Needs

Before approaching customers, the salesperson should learn as much as possible about the prospect's organization and its buyers. This process, called the **preapproach**, describes the "homework" that must be done by the salesperson before contacting the prospect. This may include visiting company Web sites, consulting standard reference sources such as Moody's, Standard & Poor's, or Dun & Bradstreet, or contacting acquaintances or others who may have information about the prospect. Another preapproach task is to determine whether the actual approach should be a personal visit, a phone call, a letter, or some other form of communication.

During the sales approach, the salesperson either talks to the prospect or secures an appointment for a future time in which to probe the prospect further as to his or her needs. Relationship selling theorists suggest that salespeople should begin developing mutual trust with their prospect during the approach. Salespeople must sell themselves before they can sell the product. Small talk that projects sincerity and some suggestion of friendship is encouraged to build rapport with the prospect, but remarks that could be construed as insincere should be avoided.

The salesperson's ultimate goal during the approach is to conduct a **needs assessment** to find out as much as possible about the prospect's situation. The salesperson should be determining how to maximize the fit between what he or she can offer and what the prospective customer wants. As part of the needs assessment, the consultative salesperson must know everything there is to know about the following:

» *The product or service*: Product knowledge is the cornerstone for conducting a successful needs analysis. The consultative salesperson must be an expert on his or her product or service, including technical specifications, the product's features and benefits, pricing and billing procedures, warranty and service support, performance comparisons with the competition, other customers' experiences with the product, and current advertising and promotional campaign messages. For example, a salesperson who is attempting to sell a Xerox copier to a doctor's office should be very knowledgeable about Xerox's selection of copiers, their attributes, capabilities, technological specifications, and postpurchase servicing.

» *Customers and their needs*: The salesperson should know more about customers than they know about themselves. That's the secret to relationship and consultative selling, where the salesperson acts not only as a supplier of products and services but also as a trusted consultant and adviser. The professional salesperson brings each client business-building ideas and solutions to problems. For example, if the Xerox salesperson is asking the "right" questions, then he or she

should be able to identify copy-related areas where the doctor's office is losing or wasting money. The Xerox salesperson can act as a "consultant" on how the doctor's office can save money and time, rather than just selling a copier.

» *The competition*: The salesperson must know as much about the competitor's company and products as he or she knows about his or her own company. *Competitive intelligence* includes many factors: who the competitors are and what is known about them; how their products and services compare; advantages and disadvantages; and strengths and weaknesses. For example, if the Canon copy machine is less expensive than the Xerox copier, the doctor's office may be leaning toward purchasing the Canon. But if the Xerox salesperson can point out that the cost of long-term maintenance and toner cartridges is lower for the Xerox copier, offsetting its higher initial cost, the salesperson may be able to persuade the doctor's office to purchase the Xerox copier.

» *The industry*: Knowing the industry involves active research on the part of the salesperson. This means attending industry and trade association meetings, reading articles published in industry and trade journals, keeping track of legislation and regulation that affect the industry, awareness of product alternatives and innovations from domestic and foreign competition, and having a feel for economic and financial conditions that may affect the industry. It is also important to be aware of economic downturns because businesses may be looking for less expensive financing options.

needs assessment
a determination of the customer's specific needs and wants and the range of options the customer has for satisfying them

Creating a *customer profile* during the approach helps salespeople optimize their time and resources. This profile is then used to help develop an intelligent analysis of the prospect's needs in preparation for the next step, developing and proposing solutions. Customer profile information is typically stored and manipulated using sales force automation software packages designed for use on laptop computers. Sales force automation software provides sales reps with a computerized and efficient method of collecting customer information for use during the entire sales process. Further, customer and sales data stored in a computer database can be easily shared among sales team members. The information can also be

THE **MORE** SALESPEOPLE **KNOW** ABOUT THEIR PROSPECTS, THE **BETTER** THEY CAN MEET THEIR NEEDS.

sales proposal a formal written document or professional presentation that outlines how the salesperson's product or service will meet or exceed the prospect's needs

sales presentation a formal meeting in which the salesperson presents a sales proposal to a prospective buyer

appended with industry statistics, sales or meeting notes, billing data, and other information that may be pertinent to the prospect or the prospect's company. The more salespeople know about their prospects, the better they can meet their needs.

Salespeople should wrap up their sales approach and need-probing mission by summarizing the prospect's need, problem, and interest. The salesperson should also get a commitment from the customer to some kind of action, whether it's reading promotional material or agreeing to a demonstration. This commitment helps qualify the prospect further and justify additional time invested by the salesperson. The salesperson should reiterate the action he or she promises to take, such as sending information or calling back to provide answers to questions. The date and time of the next call should be set at the conclusion of the sales approach as well as an agenda for the next call in terms of what the salesperson hopes to accomplish, such as providing a demonstration or presenting a solution.

Step 4: Developing and Proposing Solutions

Once the salesperson has gathered the appropriate information about the client's needs and wants, the next step is to determine whether his or her company's products or services match the needs of the prospective customer. The salesperson then develops a solution, or possibly several solutions, in which the salesperson's product or service solves the client's problems or meets a specific need.

These solutions are typically presented to the client in the form of a sales proposal presented at a sales presentation. A **sales proposal** is a written document or professional presentation that outlines how the company's product or service will meet or exceed the client's needs. The **sales presentation** is the formal meeting in which the salesperson has the opportunity

to present the sales proposal. The presentation should be explicitly tied to the prospect's expressed needs. Further, the prospect should be involved in the presentation by being encouraged to participate in demonstrations or by exposure to computer exercises, slides, video or audio, flipcharts, photographs, and the like. Technology has become an important part of presenting solutions for many salespeople.

Because the salesperson often has only one opportunity to present solutions, the quality of both the sales proposal and presentation can make or break the sale. Salespeople must be able to present the proposal and handle any customer objections confidently and professionally. For a powerful presentation, salespeople must be well prepared, use direct eye contact, ask open-ended questions, be poised, use hand gestures and voice inflection, focus on the customer's needs, incorporate visual elements that impart valuable information, know how to operate the audio/visual or computer equipment being used for the presentation, and make sure the equipment works.[22] Nothing dies faster than a boring presentation. Often customers are more likely to remember how salespeople present themselves than what they say.

Step 5: Handling Objections

Rarely does a prospect say "I'll buy it" right after a presentation. Instead, the prospect often raises objec-

tions or asks questions about the proposal and the product. The potential buyer may insist that the price is too high or that the good or service will not satisfy the present need.

One of the first lessons every salesperson learns is that objections to the product should not be taken personally as confrontations or insults. A good salesperson considers objections a legitimate part of the purchase decision. To handle objections effectively, the salesperson should anticipate specific objections such as concerns about price, fully investigate the objection with the customer, be aware of what the competition is offering, and, above all, stay calm. When Dell introduced its direct-selling model, salespeople anticipated that customers would worry that they would not receive the same level of service and dedication as they would get from a reseller. As a result, the salespeople included assurances about service and support following the sale in their sales presentations.

Often salespeople can use objections to close the sale. If the customer tries to pit suppliers against each other to drive down the price, the salesperson should be prepared to point out weaknesses in the competitor's offer and stand by the quality in his or her own proposal.

Step 6: Closing the Sale

At the end of the presentation, the salesperson should ask the customer how he or she would like to proceed. If the customer exhibits signs that he or she is ready to purchase and all questions have been answered and objections have been met, then the salesperson can try to close the sale. Customers often give signals during or after the presentation that they are ready to buy or are not interested. Examples include changes in facial expressions, gestures, and questions asked. The salesperson should look for these signals and respond appropriately.

Closing requires courage and skill. A salesperson should keep an open mind when asking for the sale and be prepared for either a yes or a no. The typical salesperson makes several hundred sales calls a year, many of which are repeat calls to the same client in an attempt to make a sale. Building a good relationship with the customer is very important. Often, if the salesperson has developed a strong relationship with the customer, only minimal efforts are needed to close a sale.

Negotiation often plays a key role in the closing of the sale. **Negotiation** is the process during which both the salesperson and the prospect offer special conces-

sions in an attempt to arrive at a sales agreement. For example, the salesperson may offer a price cut, free installation, or a trial order. Effective negotiators, however, avoid using price as a negotiation tool. Because companies spend millions on advertising and product development to create value, when salespeople give in to price negotiations too quickly, it decreases the value of the product. Instead, effective salespeople should emphasize value to the customer, rendering price a nonissue. Salespeople should also be prepared to ask for trade-offs and try to avoid giving unilateral concessions. Moreover, if the customer asks for a 5 percent discount, the salesperson should ask for something in return, such as higher volume or more flexibility in delivery schedules.

More and more U.S. companies are expanding their marketing and selling efforts into global markets. Salespeople selling in foreign markets should tailor their presentation and closing styles to each market. Different personalities and skills will be successful in some countries and absolute failures in others. For instance, if a salesperson is an excellent closer and always focuses on the next sale, doing business in Latin America might be difficult because people there want to take a long time building a personal relationship with their suppliers.

Step 7: Following Up

Salespeople's responsibilities do not end with making the sales and placing the orders. One of the most important

negotiation the process during which both the salesperson and the prospect offer special concessions in an attempt to arrive at a sales agreement

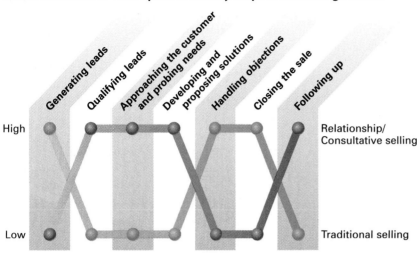

SOURCE: Robert Peterson, Patrick Schul, and George H. Lucas Jr., "Consultative Selling: Walking the Walk in the New Selling Enviroment," National Conference on Sales Management Proceedings, March 1996.

ing long-term relationships. Exhibit 18.4 depicts the time involved in the sales process and how those elements relate to the traditional and relationship selling approaches.

Most businesses depend on repeat sales, and repeat sales depend on thorough and continued follow-up by the salesperson. When customers feel abandoned, cognitive dissonance arises and repeat sales decline. Today, this issue is more pertinent than ever because customers are far less loyal to brands and vendors. Buyers are more inclined to look for the best deal, especially in the case of poor after-the-sale follow-up. Automated e-mail follow-up marketing—a combination of sales automation and Internet technology—is enhancing customer satisfaction as well as bringing in more business for some marketers. After the initial contact with a prospect, a software program automatically sends a series of personalized e-mail over a period of time.

follow-up the final step of the selling process, in which the salesperson ensures that delivery schedules are met, that the goods or services perform as promised, and that the buyers' employees are properly trained to use the products

aspects of their jobs is **follow-up**—the final step in the selling process, in which they must ensure that delivery schedules are met, that the goods or services perform as promised, and that the buyers' employees are properly trained to use the products.

In the traditional sales approach, follow-up with the customer is generally limited to successful product delivery and performance. A basic goal of relationship selling is to motivate customers to come back, again and again, by developing and nurtur-

The Impact of Technology on Personal Selling

Will the increasingly sophisticated technology now available at marketers' fingertips eliminate the need for

LOBBYING—IS IT JUST GOOD MARKETING?

According to the U.S. Senate, lobbying is the "practice of trying to persuade legislators to propose, pass or defeat legislation or to change existing laws. A lobbyist may work for a group, organization or industry and present information on legislative proposals to support his or her client's interest." Sounds a lot like what marketers do for their clients. A lobbyist's most powerful tools are the skills learned from personal selling. Leaders of the National Beer Wholesalers Association view lobbying as selling a product and routinely use basic marketing principles such as positioning, differentiation, repetition, and keeping their message simple. They even use personal selling principles to train their members who are meeting with Congress by using a sales kit called "Making the Capitol Hill Sales Call."[23]

© ISTOCKPHOTO.COM/CARLOS SANTA MARIA

salespeople? Experts agree that a relationship between the salesperson and customer will always be necessary. Technology, however, can certainly help to improve that relationship. Cell phones, laptops, pagers, e-mail, and electronic organizers allow salespeople to be more accessible to both clients and the company. Moreover, the Internet provides salespeople with vast resources of information on clients, competitors, and the industry. In fact, many companies are utilizing technology to stay more in touch with their own employees. For instance, when IBM held an electronic brainstorming session, a total of 52,600 employees logged on to the event to discuss issues of employee retention, work efficiency, quality, and teamwork.[24]

E-business, or buying, selling, marketing, collaborating with partners, and servicing customers electron-ically using the Internet, has had a significant impact on personal selling. Virtually all large companies and most medium and small companies are involved in e-commerce and consider it to be necessary to compete in today's marketplace. For customers, the Web has become a powerful tool, providing accurate and up-to-date information on products, pricing, and order status. The Internet also cost-effectively processes orders and services requests. Although on the surface the Internet might look like a threat to the job security of salespeople, the Web is actually freeing sales reps from tedious administrative tasks, like shipping catalogs, placing routine orders, or tracking orders. This leaves them more time to focus on the needs of their clients.

70–80%
Retail decisions that are made in-store

7
Basic steps in the personal selling process

$5 million
Cost of a major national television ad campaign

1.5 billion
Number of loyalty program memberships

12
Number of loyalty programs per household

$400 billion
Annual promotion marketing spending

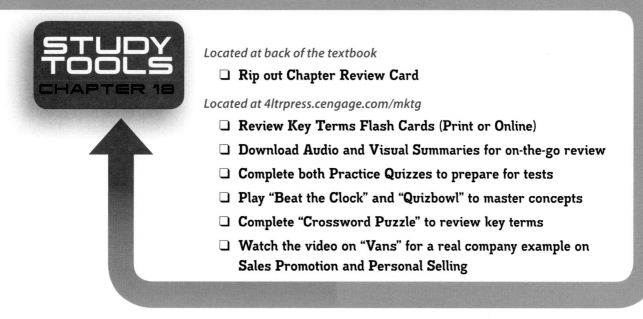

STUDY TOOLS CHAPTER 18

Located at back of the textbook
- ❑ **Rip out Chapter Review Card**

Located at 4ltrpress.cengage.com/mktg
- ❑ **Review Key Terms Flash Cards (Print or Online)**
- ❑ **Download Audio and Visual Summaries for on-the-go review**
- ❑ **Complete both Practice Quizzes to prepare for tests**
- ❑ **Play "Beat the Clock" and "Quizbowl" to master concepts**
- ❑ **Complete "Crossword Puzzle" to review key terms**
- ❑ **Watch the video on "Vans" for a real company example on Sales Promotion and Personal Selling**

> "Trying to set the right price is one of the most stressful and pressure-filled tasks of the marketing manager."

AFTER YOU FINISH THIS CHAPTER GO TO PAGE 310 FOR STUDY TOOLS

LO 1 The Importance of Price

Price means one thing to the consumer and something else to the seller. To the consumer, it is the cost of something. To the seller, price is revenue, the primary source of profits. In the broadest sense, price allocates resources in a free-market economy. Marketing managers are frequently challenged by the task of price setting.

price that which is given up in an exchange to acquire a good or service

What Is Price?

Price is that which is given up in an exchange to acquire a good or service. Price plays two roles in the evaluation of product alternatives: as a measure of sacrifice and as an information cue. To some degree, these are two opposing effects.[1]

The Sacrifice Effect of Price Price is, again, "that which is given up," which means what is sacrificed to get a good or service. In the United States, the sacrifice is usually money, but can be other things as well. It may also be time lost while waiting to acquire the good or service. Price might also include "lost dignity" for individuals who lose their jobs and must rely on charity.

The Information Effect of Price Consumers do not always choose the lowest priced product in a category, such as shoes, cars or wine, even when the products are otherwise similar. One explanation of this, based upon research, is that we infer quality information from price.[2] That is, higher quality equals higher price. The information effect of price may also extend to favorable price perceptions by others because

What do you think?

I enjoy the prestige of buying a high-priced brand.

1 2 3 4 5 6 7
STRONGLY DISAGREE   STRONGLY AGREE

Find out what others think at 4ltrpress.cengage.com/mktg   295

© ISTOCKPHOTO.COM/BLACKRED

revenue the price charged to customers multiplied by the number of units sold

profit revenue minus expenses

higher prices can convey the prominence and status of the purchaser to other people. Thus a Swatch and a Rolex both can accurately tell time but convey different meanings. The price-quality relationship will be discussed later in the chapter.

Value Is Based upon Perceived Satisfaction Consumers are interested in obtaining a "reasonable price." "Reasonable price" really means "perceived reasonable value" at the time of the transaction. The price paid is based on the satisfaction consumers *expect* to receive from a product and not necessarily the satisfaction they *actually* receive. Price can relate to anything with perceived value, not just money. When goods and services are exchanged, the trade is called *barter*.

The Importance of Price to Marketing Managers

Prices are the key to revenues, which in turn are the key to profits for an organization. **Revenue** is the price charged to customers multiplied by the number of units sold. Revenue is what pays for every activity of the company: production, finance, sales, distribution, and so on. What's left over (if anything) is **profit**. Managers usually strive to charge a price that will earn a fair profit.

Price x Units = Revenue

To earn a profit, managers must choose a price that is not too high or too low, a price that equals the perceived value to target consumers. If, in consumers' minds, a price is set too high, the perceived value will be less than the cost, and sale opportunities will be lost. Conversely, if a price is too low, the consumer may perceive it as a great value, but the firm loses revenue it could have earned.

Trying to set the right price is one of the most stressful and pressure-filled tasks of the marketing manager, as trends in the consumer market attest:

▸▸ Confronting a flood of new products, potential buyers carefully evaluate the price of each one against the value of existing products.

▸▸ The increased availability of bargain-priced private and generic brands has put downward pressure on overall prices.

▸▸ Many firms are trying to maintain or regain their market share by cutting prices.

▸▸ The Internet has made comparison shopping easier.

▸▸ The United States was in a recession from late 2007 until 2009.

In the business market, buyers are also becoming more price sensitive and better informed. Computerized information systems enable organizational buyers to compare price and performance with great ease and accuracy. Improved communication and the increased use of direct marketing and computer-aided selling have also opened up many markets to new competitors. Finally, competition in general is increasing, so some installations, accessories, and component parts are being marketed like indistinguishable commodities.

LO 2 Pricing Objectives

To survive in today's highly competitive marketplace, companies need pricing objectives that are specific, attainable, and measurable. Realistic pricing goals then require periodic monitoring to determine the effectiveness of the company's strategy. For convenience, pricing objectives can be divided into three categories: profit oriented, sales oriented, and status quo.

Profit-Oriented Pricing Objectives

Profit-oriented objectives include profit maximization, satisfactory profits, and target return on investment.

Profit Maximization *Profit maximization* means setting prices so that total revenue is as large as possible relative to total costs. Profit maximization does not always signify unreasonably high prices, however. Both price and profits depend on the type of competitive environment a firm faces, such as whether it is in a monopoly position (being the only seller) or in a much more competitive situation. Also, remember that a firm cannot charge a price higher than the product's perceived value. Many firms do not have the accounting data they need for maximizing profits.

Sometimes managers say that their company is trying to maximize profits—in other words, trying to make as much money as possible. Although this goal may sound impressive to stockholders, it is not good enough for planning.

In attempting to maximize profits, managers can try to expand revenue by increasing customer satisfaction, or they can attempt to reduce costs by operating more efficiently. A third possibility is to attempt to do both. Recent research has shown that striving to enhance customer satisfaction leads to greater profitability (and customer satisfaction) than following a cost reduction strategy or attempting to do both.[3] This means that companies should consider allocating more resources to customer service initiatives, loyalty programs, and customer relationship management programs and allocating fewer resources to programs that are designed to improve efficiency and reduce costs. Both types of programs, of course, are critical to the success of the firm.

Satisfactory Profits Satisfactory profits are a reasonable level of profits. Rather than maximizing profits, many organizations strive for profits that are satisfactory to the stockholders and management—in other words, a level of profits consistent with the level of risk an organization faces. In a risky industry, a satisfactory profit may be 35 percent. In a low-risk industry, it might be 7 percent.

Target Return on Investment The most common profit objective is a target **return on investment (ROI)**, sometimes called the firm's return on total assets. ROI measures management's overall effectiveness in generating profits with the available assets. The higher the firm's ROI, the better off the firm is. Many companies use a target ROI as their main pricing goal. In summary, ROI is a percentage that puts a firm's profits into perspective by showing profits relative to investment.

Return on investment is calculated as follows:

$$\text{Return on investment} = \frac{\text{Net profits after taxes}}{\text{Total assets}}$$

Assume that in 2008 Johnson Controls had assets of $4.5 million, net profits of $550,000, and a target ROI of 10 percent. This was the actual ROI:

$$\text{ROI} = \frac{\$550,000}{\$4,500,000}$$
$$= 12.2 \text{ percent}$$

As you can see, the ROI for Johnson Controls exceeded its target, which indicates that the company prospered in 2010.

Comparing the 12.2 percent ROI with the industry average provides a more meaningful picture, however. Any ROI needs to be evaluated in terms of the competitive environment, risks in the industry, and economic conditions. Generally speaking, firms seek ROIs in the 10 to 30 percent range. In some industries such as the grocery industry, however, a return of under 5 percent is common and acceptable.

A company with a target ROI can predetermine its desired level of profitability. The marketing manager can use the standard, such as 10 percent ROI, to determine whether a particular price and marketing mix are feasible. In addition, however, the manager must weigh the risk of a given strategy even if the return is in the acceptable range.

Sales-Oriented Pricing Objectives

Sales-oriented pricing objectives are based either on market share or on dollar or unit sales.

Market Share **Market share** is a company's product sales as a percentage of total sales for that industry. Sales can be reported in dollars or in units of product. It is very important to know whether market share is expressed in revenue or units because the results may be different. Consider four companies competing in an industry with 2,000 total unit sales and total industry revenue of $4 million (see Exhibit 19.1). Company A has the largest unit market share at 50 percent, but it has only 25 percent of the revenue market share. In contrast, company D has only a 15 percent unit share but the largest revenue share: 30 percent. Usually, market share is expressed in terms of revenue and not units.

Many companies believe that maintaining or increasing market

return on investment (ROI) net profit after taxes divided by total assets

market share a company's product sales as a percentage of total sales for that industry

© ISTOCKPHOTO.COM/ROB FRIEDMAN

EXHIBIT 19.1
Two Ways to Measure Market Share (Units and Revenue)

Company	Units Sold	Unit Price	Total Revenue	Unit Market Share	Revenue Market Share
A	1,000	$1.00	$1,000,000	50%	25%
B	200	4.00	800,000	10	20
C	500	2.00	1,000,000	25	25
D	300	4.00	1,200,000	15	30
Total	2,000		$4,000,000		

status quo pricing
a pricing objective that maintains existing prices or meets the competition's prices

share is an indicator of the effectiveness of their marketing mix. Larger market shares have indeed often meant higher profits, thanks to greater economies of scale, market power, and ability to compensate top-quality management. Conventional wisdom also says that market share and return on investment are strongly related. For the most part they are; however, many companies with low market share survive and even prosper. To succeed with a low market share, companies need to compete in industries with slow growth and few product changes—for instance, industrial supplies. Otherwise, they must vie in an industry that makes frequently bought items, such as consumer convenience goods.

The conventional wisdom about market share and profitability isn't always reliable, however. Because of extreme competition in some industries, many market share leaders either do not reach their target ROI or actually lose money. Procter & Gamble switched from market share to ROI objectives after realizing that profits don't automatically follow from a large market share. Still, the struggle for market share can be all-consuming for some companies.

For decades, Folgers and Maxwell House have been locked in a struggle to dominate the coffee market. Numerous promotions and product extensions and modifications have been tried to persuade coffee drinkers to switch brands (or stay with their current brand). At present, Procter & Gamble's Folgers (36 percent) has taken the lead from Kraft's Maxwell House (34 percent), but both companies face a new and increasingly formidable competitor for market share: Starbucks.

Research organizations like The Nielsen Company and Information Resources, Inc. provide excellent market share reports for many different industries. These reports enable companies to track their performance in various product categories over time.

Sales Maximization Rather than strive for market share, sometimes companies try to maximize sales. A firm with the objective of maximizing sales ignores profits, competition, and the marketing environment as long as sales are rising.

If a company is strapped for funds or faces an uncertain future, it may try to generate a maximum amount of cash in the short run. Management's task when using this objective is to calculate which price-quantity relationship generates the greatest cash revenue. Sales maximization can also be effectively used on a temporary basis to sell off excess inventory.

Maximization of cash should never be a long-run objective because cash maximization may mean little or no profitability.

Status Quo Pricing Objectives

Status quo pricing seeks to maintain existing prices or to meet the competition's prices. This third category of pricing objectives has the major advantage of requiring little planning. It is essentially a passive policy.

Often firms competing in an industry with an established price leader simply meet the competition's prices. These industries typically have fewer price wars than those with direct price competition. In other cases, managers regularly shop competitors' stores to ensure that their prices are comparable.

LO3 The Demand Determinant of Price

After marketing managers establish pricing goals, they must set specific prices to reach those goals. The price they set for each product depends mostly on two factors: the demand for the good or service and the cost to

WHEN **PRICING GOALS** ARE MAINLY SALES ORIENTED, **DEMAND CONSIDERATIONS** USUALLY DOMINATE.

the seller for that good or service. When pricing goals are mainly sales oriented, demand considerations usually dominate. Other factors, such as distribution and promotion strategies, perceived quality, needs of large customers, the Internet, and the stage of the product life cycle, can also influence price.

The Nature of Demand

Demand is the quantity of a product that will be sold in the market at various prices for a specified period. The quantity of a product that people will buy depends on its price. The higher the price, the fewer goods or services consumers will demand. Conversely, the lower the price, the more goods or services they will demand.

This trend is illustrated in the following graph of the demand per week for gourmet cookies at a local retailer at various prices. This graph is called a *demand curve* (Exhibit 19.2). The vertical axis of the graph shows different prices of gourmet cookies, measured in dollars per package. The horizontal axis measures the quantity of gourmet cookies that will

be demanded per week at each price. For example, at a price of $2.50, 50 packages will be sold per week; at $1.00, consumers will demand 120 packages—as the *demand schedule* (Exhibit 19.2) shows.

Notice how the demand curve slopes downward and to the right, which indicates that more gourmet cookies are demanded as the price is lowered. In other words, if cookie manufacturers put a greater quantity on the market, then their hope of selling all of it will be realized only by selling it at a lower price.

One reason more is sold at lower prices than at higher prices is that lower prices bring in new buyers. With each reduction in price, existing customers may also buy extra.

Supply is the quantity of a product that will be offered to the market by a supplier or suppliers at various prices for a specified period. The graph below illustrates the resulting *supply curve* (Exhibit 19.3) for gourmet cookies. Unlike the falling demand curve, the supply curve for gourmet cookies slopes upward

demand the quantity of a product that will be sold in the market at various prices for a specified period

supply the quantity of a product that will be offered to the market by a supplier at various prices for a specified period

---

EXHIBIT 19.2
Demand Curve and Demand Schedule for Gourmet Cookies

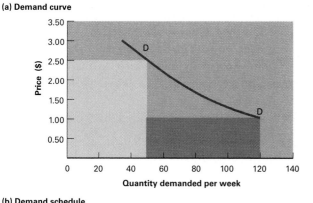

(a) Demand curve

(b) Demand schedule

Price per package of gourmet cookies ($)	Packages of gourmet cookies demanded per week
3.00	35
2.50	50
2.00	65
1.50	85
1.00	120

EXHIBIT 19.3
Supply Curve and Supply Schedule for Gourmet Cookies

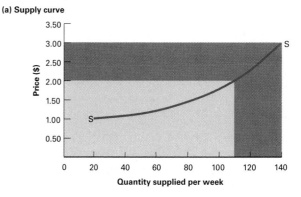

(a) Supply curve

(b) Supply schedule

Price per package of gourmet cookies ($)	Packages of gourmet cookies supplied per week
3.00	140
2.50	130
2.00	110
1.50	85
1.00	25

price equilibrium
the price at which demand and supply are equal

elasticity of demand consumers' responsiveness or sensitivity to changes in price

elastic demand a situation in which consumer demand is sensitive to changes in price

inelastic demand a situation in which an increase or a decrease in price will not significantly affect demand for the product

unitary elasticity a situation in which total revenue remains the same when prices change

and to the right. At higher prices, gourmet cookies manufacturers will obtain more resources (flour, eggs, chocolate) and produce more gourmet cookies. If the price consumers are willing to pay for gourmet cookies increases, producers can afford to buy more ingredients.

Output tends to increase at higher prices because manufacturers can sell more cookies and earn greater profits. The *supply schedule* in Exhibit 19.3b shows that at $2 suppliers are willing to place 110 packages of gourmet cookies on the market, but they will offer 140 packages at a price of $3.

How Demand and Supply Establish Prices At this point, combine the concepts of demand and supply to see how competitive market prices are determined. So far, the premise is that if the price is X, then consumers will purchase Y amount of gourmet cookies. The demand curve cannot predict consumption, nor can the supply curve alone forecast production. Instead, we need to look at what happens when supply and demand interact—as shown in Exhibit 19.4.

At a price of $3, the public would demand only 35 packages of gourmet cookies. However, suppliers stand ready to place 140 packages on the market at this price (data from the demand and supply schedules). If they do, they would create a surplus of 105 packages of gourmet cookies. How does a merchant eliminate a surplus? She lowers the price.

At a price of $1.00, 120 packages would be demanded, but only 25 would be placed on the market. A shortage of 95 units would be created. If a prod-

uct is in short supply and consumers want it, how do they entice the dealer to part with one unit? They offer more money—that is, pay a higher price.

Now let's examine a price of $1.50. At this price, 85 packages are demanded and 85 are supplied. When demand and supply are equal, a state called **price equilibrium** is achieved. A temporary price below equilibrium—say, $1.00—results in a shortage because at that price the demand for gourmet cookies is greater than the available supply. Shortages put upward pressure on price. As long as demand and supply remain the same, however, temporary price increases or decreases tend to return to equilibrium. At equilibrium, there is no inclination for prices to rise or fall.

Prices may fluctuate during a trial-and-error period as the market for a good or service moves toward equilibrium. Sooner or later, however, demand and supply will settle into proper balance.

Elasticity of Demand

To appreciate demand analysis, you should understand the concept of elasticity. **Elasticity of demand** refers to consumers' responsiveness or sensitivity to changes in price. **Elastic demand** occurs when consumers buy more or less of a product when the price changes. Conversely, **inelastic demand** means that an increase or a decrease in price will not significantly affect demand for the product.

Elasticity over the range of a demand curve can be measured by using this formula:

$$\text{Elasticity } (E) = \frac{\text{Percentage change in quantity demanded of good A}}{\text{Percentage change in price of good A}}$$

If *E* is greater than 1, demand is elastic.
If *E* is less than 1, demand is inelastic.
If *E* is equal to 1, demand is unitary.

Unitary elasticity means that an increase in sales exactly offsets a decrease in prices, so total revenue remains the same.

Elasticity can be measured by observing these changes in total revenue:

▸▸ If price goes down and revenue goes up, demand is elastic.

▸▸ If price goes down and revenue goes down, demand is inelastic.

▸▸ If price goes up and revenue goes up, demand is inelastic.

▸▸ If price goes up and revenue goes down, demand is elastic.

▸▸ If price goes up or down and revenue stays the same, elasticity is unitary.

EXHIBIT 19.4
Equilibrium Price for Gourmet Cookies

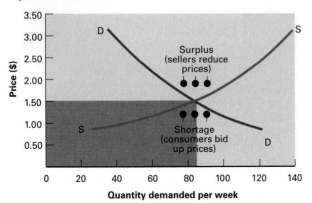

The demand curve for Sony DVD players is a very elastic demand curve. Decreasing the price of a Sony DVD player from $300 to $200 increases sales from 18,000 units to 59,000 units. Revenue increases from $5.4 million ($300 × 18,000) to $11.8 million ($200 × 59,000). The price decrease results in a large increase in sales and revenue.

Inelastic Demand When price and total revenue fall, demand is inelastic. When demand is inelastic, sellers can raise prices and increase total revenue. Often items that are relatively inexpensive but convenient tend to have inelastic demand. Auto inspection stickers have a completely inelastic demand curve. The state of Nevada dropped its used-car vehicle inspection fee from $20 to $10. Decreasing the price (inspection fee) 50 percent did not cause people to buy more used cars. Demand is completely inelastic for inspection fees, which are required by law.

Elastic Demand In the previous example of Sony DVD players, when the price is dropped from $300 to $200, total revenue increases by $6.4 million ($11.8 million minus $5.4 million). An increase in total revenue when price falls indicates that demand is elastic. Let's measure Sony's elasticity of demand when the price drops from $300 to $200 by applying the formula presented earlier:

$$E = \frac{\text{Change in quantity/(Sum of quantities/2)}}{\text{Change in price/(Sum of prices/2)}}$$

$$E = \frac{(59,000 - 18,000)/[(59,000 + 18,000)/2]}{(\$300 - \$200)/[(\$300 + \$200)/2]}$$

$$E = \frac{41,000/38,500}{\$100/\$250}$$

$$E = \frac{1.065}{.4}$$

$$E = 2.66$$

Because E is greater than 1, demand is elastic.

Factors That Affect Elasticity Several factors affect elasticity of demand, including the following:

▸▸ *Availability of substitutes*: When many substitute products are available, the consumer can easily switch from one product to another, making demand elastic. The same is true in reverse: a person with complete renal failure will pay whatever is charged for a kidney transplant because there is no substitute.

▸▸ *Price relative to purchasing power*: If a price is so low that it is an inconsequential part of an individual's budget, demand will be inelastic.

▸▸ *Product durability*: Consumers often have the option of repairing durable products rather than replacing them, thus prolonging their useful life. In other words, people are sensitive to the price increase, and demand is elastic.

▸▸ *A product's other uses*: The greater the number of different uses for a product, the more elastic demand tends to be. If a product has only one use, as may be true of a new medicine, the quantity purchased probably will not vary as price varies. A person will consume only the prescribed quantity, regardless of price. On the other hand, a product like steel has many possible applications. As its price falls, steel becomes more economically feasible in a wider variety of applications, thereby making demand relatively elastic.

▸▸ *Rate of inflation*: Recent research has found that when a country's inflation rate (the rate at which the price level is rising) is high, demand becomes more elastic. In other words, rising price levels make consumers more price sensitive. During inflationary periods consumers base their timing (when to buy) and quantity decisions on price promotions. This suggests that a brand gains additional sales or market share if the product is effectively promoted or if the marketing manager keeps the brand's price increases low relative to the inflation rate. [4]

LO 4 The Power of Yield Management Systems

When competitive pressures are high, a company must know when it can raise prices to maximize its revenues. More and more companies are turning to yield management systems to help adjust prices. First developed in the airline industry, **yield management systems (YMS)** use complex mathematical software to profitably fill unused capacity. The software employs techniques such as discounting early purchases, limiting early sales at these discounted prices, and overbooking capacity. YMS now are appearing in other services as well.

Yield management systems are spreading beyond service industries as their popularity increases. The lessons of airlines and hotels aren't entirely applicable to other industries, however, because plane seats and hotel beds are perishable—if they go empty, the revenue opportunity is lost forever. So it makes sense to slash prices to move toward capacity if it's possible to do so without reducing the prices that other customers pay. Cars and steel aren't so perishable, but the capacity to make them is. An underused factory is a lost revenue opportunity. So it makes sense to cut prices to use up capacity if it's possible to do so while getting other customers to pay full price.

Duane Reade now has Demand-Tec's algorithms determining prices for two-thirds of the items it sells. The prices of some cough medicines are up. (Sick people don't shop around.) The per-pill price of the fifty-pill bottles of certain pain relievers used to be lower than on the twenty-four-pill bottle. Now it's higher. The kind of people who buy jugs of pills are a bit less sensitive to a higher unit price.[5]

LO 5 The Cost Determinant of Price

Sometimes companies minimize or ignore the importance of demand and decide to price their products largely or solely on the basis of costs. Prices determined strictly on the basis of costs may be too high for the target market, thereby reducing or eliminating sales. On the other hand, cost-based prices may be too low, causing the firm to earn a lower return than it should. Nevertheless, costs should generally be part of any

price determination, if only as a floor below which a good or service must not be priced in the long run.

The idea of cost may seem simple, but it is actually a multifaceted concept, especially for producers of goods and services. A **variable cost** is a cost that varies with changes in the level of output; an example of a variable cost is the cost of materials. In contrast, a **fixed cost** does not change as output is increased or decreased. Examples include rent and executives' salaries.

To compare the cost of production to the selling price of a product, it is helpful to calculate costs per unit, or average costs. **Average variable cost (AVC)** equals total variable costs divided by quantity of output. **Average total cost (ATC)** equals total costs divided by output. As the graph in Exhibit 19.5(a) shows, AVC and ATC are basically U-shaped curves. In contrast, average fixed cost (AFC) declines continually as output increases because total fixed costs are constant.

Marginal cost (MC) is the change in total costs associated with a one-unit change in output. Exhibit 19.5(b) shows that when output rises from seven to eight units, the change in total cost is from $640 to $750; therefore, marginal cost is $110.

All the curves illustrated in Exhibit 19.5(a) have definite relationships:

▸▸ AVC plus AFC equals ATC.

▸▸ MC falls for a while and then turns upward, in this case with the fourth unit. At that point diminishing returns set in, meaning that less output is produced for every additional dollar spent on variable input.

▸▸ MC intersects both AVC and ATC at their lowest possible points.

▸▸ When MC is less than AVC or ATC, the incremental cost will continue to pull the averages down. Conversely, when MC is greater than AVC or ATC, it pulls the averages up, and ATC and AVC begin to rise.

▸▸ The minimum point on the ATC curve is the least cost point for a fixed-capacity firm, although it is not necessarily the most profitable point.

Costs can be used to set prices in a variety of ways. Markup pricing is relatively simple. Profit maximization pricing and break-even pricing make use of the more complicated concepts of cost.

Markup Pricing

Markup pricing, the most popular method used by wholesalers and retailers to establish a selling price, does not directly analyze the costs of production. Instead, **markup pricing** uses the cost of buying the product from the producer, plus amounts for profit

EXHIBIT 19.5
Hypothetical Set of Cost Curves and a Cost Schedule

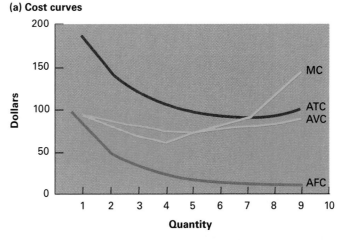

(a) Cost curves

(b) Cost schedule

	Total-cost data, per week			Average-cost data, per week			
(1) Total product (Q)	(2) Total fixed cost (TFC)	(3) Total variable cost (TVC)	(4) Total cost (TC)	(5) Average fixed cost (AFC)	(6) Average variable cost (AVC)	(7) Average total cost (ATC)	(8) Marginal cost (MC)
			$TC = TFC + TVC$	$AFC = \dfrac{TFC}{Q}$	$AVC = \dfrac{TVC}{Q}$	$ATC = \dfrac{TC}{Q}$	$(MC) = \dfrac{\text{change in TC}}{\text{change in Q}}$
0	$100	$ 0	$ 100	—	—	—	—
1	100	90	190	$100.00	$90.00	$190.00	$ 90
2	100	170	270	50.00	85.00	135.00	80
3	100	240	340	33.33	80.00	113.33	70
4	100	300	400	25.00	75.00	100.00	60
5	100	370	470	20.00	74.00	94.00	70
6	100	450	550	16.67	75.00	91.67	80
7	100	540	640	14.29	77.14	91.43	90
8	100	650	750	12.50	81.25	93.75	110
9	100	780	880	11.11	86.67	97.78	130
10	100	930	1,030	10.00	93.00	103.00	150

and for expenses not otherwise accounted for. The total determines the selling price.

A retailer, for example, adds a certain percentage to the cost of the merchandise received to arrive at the retail price. An item that costs the retailer $1.80 and is sold for $2.20 carries a markup of 40 cents, which is a markup of 22 percent of the cost ($.40 ÷ $1.80). Retailers tend to discuss markup in terms of its percentage of the retail price—in this example, 18 percent ($.40 ÷ $2.20). The difference between the retailer's cost and the selling price (40 cents) is the gross margin.

The formula for calculating the retail price given a certain desired markup is as follows:

$$\text{Retail price} = \frac{\text{Cost}}{1 - \text{Desired return on sales}}$$

$$= \frac{\$1.80}{1.00 - 0.18}$$

$$= \$2.20$$

If the retailer wants a 30 percent return, then:

$$\text{Retail price} = \frac{\$1.80}{1.00 - 0.30}$$

$$= \$2.57$$

The reason that retailers and others speak of markups on selling price is that many important figures in financial reports, such as gross sales and revenues, are sales figures, not cost figures.

To use markup based on cost or selling price effectively, the marketing manager must calculate an adequate gross margin—the amount added to cost to determine price. The margin must ultimately provide adequate funds to cover selling expenses and profit. Once an appropriate margin has been determined, the markup technique has the major advantage of being easy to employ.

Markups are often based on experience. For example, many small retailers mark up merchandise 100 percent over cost. (In other words, they double the cost.) This tactic is called **keystoning**. Some other factors that influence markups are the merchandise's appeal to customers, past response to the markup (an implicit demand consideration), the item's promotional value, the seasonality of the goods, their fashion appeal, the product's traditional selling price, and competition. Most retailers avoid any set markup because of such considerations as promotional value and seasonality.

PAY WHAT IT'S WORTH

Terra Bite Lounge, a coffee shop in Washington, has no prices listed on its wall menu. The customers pay what and whenever they like and leave the money in a locked box on the counter. Such a business model contradicts the basic concept of running a business: the exchange of goods for a set amount of money. However, a few businesses in Colorado, Utah, Washington, and other places have proven this model can be both a profitable and charitable way of doing business. Plus, the marketing buzz such a scheme generates can help a business stand out from the pack.[6]

EXHIBIT 19.6
Point of Profit Maximization

Quantity	Marginal Revenue (MR)	Marginal Cost (MC)	Cumulative Total Profit
0	—	—	—
1	$140	$ 90	$ 50
2	130	80	100
3	105	70	135
4	95	60	170
5	85	70	185
*6	80	80	185
7	75	90	170
8	60	110	120
9	50	130	40
10	40	150	(70)

*Profit maximization.

Profit Maximization Pricing

Producers tend to use more complicated methods of setting prices than distributors use. One is **profit maximization**, which occurs when marginal revenue equals marginal cost. You learned earlier that marginal cost is the change in total costs associated with a one-unit change in output. Similarly, **marginal revenue (MR)** is the extra revenue associated with selling an extra unit of output. As long as the revenue of the last unit produced and sold is greater than the cost of the last unit produced and sold, the firm should continue manufacturing and selling the product.

Exhibit 19.6 shows the marginal revenues and marginal costs for a hypothetical firm, using the cost data from Exhibit 19.5(b). The profit-maximizing quantity, where MR = MC, is six units. You might say, "If profit is zero, why produce the sixth unit? Why not stop at five?" In fact, you would be right. The firm, however, would not know that the fifth unit would produce zero profits until it determined that profits were no longer increasing. Economists suggest producing up to the point where MR = MC. If marginal revenue is just one penny greater than marginal costs, it will still increase total profits.

Break-Even Pricing

Now let's take a closer look at the relationship between sales and cost. **Break-even analysis** determines what sales volume must be reached before the company breaks even (its total costs equal total revenue) and no profits are earned.

The typical break-even model assumes a given fixed cost and a constant average variable cost. Suppose that Universal Sportswear, a hypothetical firm, has fixed costs of $2,000 and that the cost of labor and materials for each unit produced is 50 cents. Assume that it can sell up to 6,000 units of its product at $1 without having to lower its price.

Exhibit 19.7(a) illustrates Universal Sportswear's break-even point. As Exhibit 19.7(b) indicates, Universal Sportswear's total variable costs increase by 50 cents every time a new unit is produced, and total fixed costs remain constant at $2,000 regardless of the level of output. Therefore, for 4,000 units of output, Universal Sportswear has $2,000 in fixed costs and $2,000 in total variable costs (4,000 units × $.50), or $4,000 in total costs.

Revenue is also $4,000 (4,000 units × $1), giving a net profit of zero dollars at the break-even point of 4,000 units. Notice that once the firm gets past the break-even point, the gap between total revenue and total costs gets wider and wider because both functions are assumed to be linear.

The formula for calculating break-even quantities is simple:

$$\text{Break-even quantity} = \frac{\text{Total fixed costs}}{\text{Fixed cost contribution}}$$

Fixed cost contribution is the price minus the average variable cost. Therefore, for Universal Sportswear,

$$\text{Break-even quantity} = \frac{\$2,000}{(\$1.00 - \$.50)} = \frac{\$2,000}{\$.50}$$
$$= 4,000 \text{ units}$$

EXHIBIT 19.7

Costs, Revenues, and Break-Even Point for Universal Sportswear

(a) Break-even point

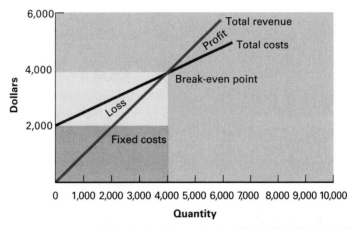

(b) Costs and revenues

Output	Total fixed costs	Average variable costs	Total variable costs	Average total costs	Average revenue (price)	Total revenue	Total costs	Profit or loss
500	$2,000	$0.50	$ 250	$4.50	$1.00	$ 500	$2,250	($1,750)
1,000	2,000	0.50	500	2.50	1.00	1,000	2,500	(1,500)
1,500	2,000	0.50	750	1.83	1.00	1,500	2,750	(1,250)
2,000	2,000	0.50	1,000	1.50	1.00	2,000	3,000	(1,000)
2,500	2,000	0.50	1,250	1.30	1.00	2,500	3,250	(750)
3,000	2,000	0.50	1,500	1.17	1.00	3,000	3,500	(500)
3,500	2,000	0.50	1,750	1.07	1.00	3,500	3,750	(250)
*4,000	2,000	0.50	2,000	1.00	1.00	4,000	4,000	0
4,500	2,000	0.50	2,250	.94	1.00	4,500	4,250	250
5,000	2,000	0.50	2,500	.90	1.00	5,000	4,500	500
5,500	2,000	0.50	2,750	.86	1.00	5,500	4,750	750
6,000	2,000	0.50	3,000	.83	1.00	6,000	5,000	1,000

*Break-even point

The advantage of break-even analysis is that it provides a quick estimate of how much the firm must sell to break even and how much profit can be earned if a higher sales volume is obtained. If a firm is operating close to the break-even point, it may want to see what can be done to reduce costs or increase sales. Moreover, in a simple break-even analysis, it is not necessary to compute marginal costs and marginal revenues because price and average cost per unit are assumed to be constant. Also, because accounting data for marginal cost and revenue are frequently unavailable, it is convenient not to have to depend on that information.

Break-even analysis is not without several important limitations. Sometimes it is hard to know whether a cost is fixed or variable. If labor wins a tough guaranteed-employment contract, are the resulting expenses a fixed cost? More important than cost determination is the fact that simple break-even analysis ignores demand. How does Universal Sportswear know it can sell 4,000 units at $1? Could it sell the same 4,000 units at $2 or even $5? Obviously, this information would profoundly affect the firm's pricing decisions.

LO 6 Other Determinants of Price

Other factors besides demand and costs can influence price. For example, the stages in the product life cycle, the competition, the product distribution strategy, the promotion strategy, and the perceived quality can all affect pricing.

Stages in the Product Life Cycle

As a product moves through its life cycle (see Chapter 11), the demand for the product and the competitive conditions tend to change:

▸▸ *Introductory stage*: Management usually sets prices high during the introductory stage. One reason is that it hopes to recover its development costs quickly. In addition, demand originates in the core of the market (the customers whose needs ideally match the product's attributes) and thus is relatively inelastic. On the other hand, if the target market is highly price sensitive, management often finds it better to price the product at the market level or lower.

▸▸ *Growth stage*: As the product enters the growth stage, prices generally begin to stabilize for several reasons.

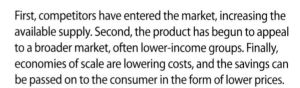

First, competitors have entered the market, increasing the available supply. Second, the product has begun to appeal to a broader market, often lower-income groups. Finally, economies of scale are lowering costs, and the savings can be passed on to the consumer in the form of lower prices.

▸▸ *Maturity stage*: Maturity usually brings further price decreases as competition increases and inefficient, high-cost firms are eliminated. Distribution channels become a significant cost factor, however, because of the need to offer wide product lines for highly segmented markets, extensive service requirements, and the sheer number of dealers necessary to absorb high-volume production. The manufacturers that remain in the market toward the end of the maturity stage typically offer similar prices. At this stage, price increases are usually cost initiated, not demand initiated. Nor do price reductions in the late phase of maturity stimulate much demand. Because demand is limited and producers have similar cost structures, the remaining competitors will probably match price reductions.

▸▸ *Decline stage*: The final stage of the life cycle may see further price decreases as the few remaining competitors try to salvage the last vestiges of demand. When only one firm is left in the market, prices begin to stabilize. In fact, prices may eventually rise dramatically if the product survives and moves into the specialty goods category, as horse-drawn carriages and vinyl records have.

The Competition

Competition varies during the product life cycle, of course, and so at times it may strongly affect pricing decisions. Although a firm may not have any competition at first, the high prices it charges may eventually induce another firm to enter the market.

Often, in hotly competitive markets, price wars break out. Amazon.com has been increasing its online presence by offering more than just books, looking to become the go-to online e-tailer. Wal-Mart answered

In its marketing and in its dealings with its suppliers, Wal-Mart sends a clear message to competitors that it will not be undersold.

© AP PHOTO/TONY DEJAK

Amazon's expansion by selling its most anticipated hardcovers online for just $10 apiece (an average hardcover sells for about $25). Later that day, Amazon matched the price. The battle continued until the prices stabilized with books selling for $9 at Amazon, $8.99 at Target, and $8.98 at Wal-Mart. These prices have caused concern about the perceived value of books and the ability of independent bookstores to compete with the large chains selling the same books for up to 74 percent less than the list price.[7]

Distribution Strategy

An effective distribution network can often overcome other minor flaws in the marketing mix.[8] For example, although consumers may perceive a price as being slightly higher than normal, they may buy the product anyway if it is being sold at a convenient retail outlet.

Adequate distribution for a new product can often be attained by offering a larger-than-usual profit margin to distributors. A variation on this strategy is to give dealers a large trade allowance to help offset the costs of promotion and further stimulate demand at the retail level.

Manufacturers have gradually been losing control within the distribution channel to wholesalers and retailers, which often adopt pricing strategies that serve their own purposes. For instance, some distributors are **selling against the brand**: They place well-known brands on the shelves at high

© AP IMAGES/PRNEWSFOTO/ORBITZ, INC.

prices while offering other brands—typically, their private-label brands, such as Kroger canned pears—at lower prices. Of course, sales of the higher-priced brands decline.

Wholesalers and retailers may also go outside traditional distribution channels to buy gray-market goods. As explained previously, distributors obtain the goods through unauthorized channels for less than they would normally pay, so they can sell the goods with a bigger-than-normal markup or at a reduced price. Imports seem to be particularly susceptible to gray marketing. Although consumers may pay less for gray-market goods, they often find that the manufacturer won't honor the warranty.

Manufacturers can regain some control over price by using an exclusive distribution system, by franchising, or by avoiding doing business with price-cutting discounters. Manufacturers can also package merchandise with the selling price marked on it or place goods on consignment. The best way for manufacturers to control prices, however, is to develop brand loyalty in consumers by delivering quality and value.

The Impact of the Internet and Extranets

The Internet, **extranets** (private electronic networks), and wireless setups are linking people, machines, and companies around the globe—and connecting sellers and buyers as never before. These links are enabling

selling against the brand stocking well-known branded items at high prices in order to sell store brands at discounted prices

extranet a private electronic network that links a company with its suppliers and customers

If you want to buy an airline ticket, where do you go? Straight to your preferred airline's Web site? Or do you do some comparison shopping on a site like Orbitz?

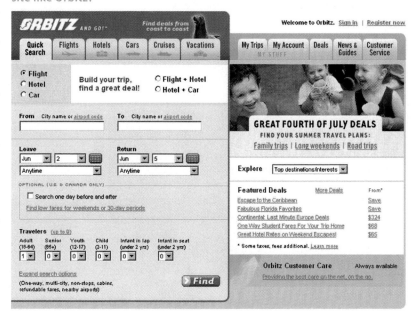

buyers to quickly and easily compare products and prices, putting them in a better bargaining position. At the same time, the technology allows sellers to collect detailed data about customers' buying habits, preferences, and even spending limits so that sellers can tailor their products and prices.

Using Shopping Bots A shopping bot is a program that searches the Web for the best price for a particular item that you wish to purchase. *Bot* is short for *robot*. Shopping bots theoretically give pricing power to the consumer. The more information that the shopper has, the more efficient his or her purchase decision will be.

There are two general types of shopping bots. The first is the broad-based type that searches a wide range of product categories such as MySimon.com, Dealtime.com, Bizrate.com, Pricegrabber.com, and PriceScan.com. These sites operate using a Yellow Pages type of model, in that they list every retailer they can find. The second is the niche-oriented type that searches for only one type of product such as computer equipment (CNET.com), books (Bookfinder.com), or airfare prices (Farecast.com).[9]

Most shopping bots give preferential listings to those e-retailers that pay for the privilege. These so-called merchant partners receive about 60 percent of the click-throughs.[10] Typically, the bot lists its merchant partners first, not the retailer offering the lowest price.

Internet Auctions The Internet auction business is huge. Among the most popular consumer auction sites are the following:

▸ *www.ebay.com*: The most popular auction site
▸ *www.bidz.com*: Buys closeout deals in very large lots and offers them online in its no-reserve auctions

Even though consumers are spending billions on Internet auctions, business-to-business auctions are likely to be the dominant form in the future. Recently, Whirlpool began holding online auctions. Participants bid on the price of the items that they would supply to Whirlpool, but with a twist: they had to include the date when Whirlpool would have to pay for the items. The company wanted to see which suppliers would offer the longest grace period before requiring payment. Five auctions held over five months helped Whirlpool uncover savings of close to $2 million and more than doubled the grace period.

Whirlpool's success is a sign that the business-to-business auction world is shifting from haggling over prices to niggling over parameters of the deal. Warranties, delivery dates, transportation methods, customer support, financing options, and quality have all become bargaining chips.

INTERNET SHOPPING SAFETY

Americans report millions of online fraud losses each year to the FBI. The average dollar loss per complaint is nearly $700. In order to shop online, Internet shoppers need to be aware that online auction fraud, non-delivery of goods, and credit card fraud can happen to anyone. Despite the risks, eBay.com users worldwide trade $2,000 worth of goods on the site every second. Beginning in April 2010, sellers will have to meet minimum standards requirements to continue selling on eBay. By removing unsatisfactory sellers, eBay hopes to provide more satisfactory service for everyone.[11] Why do eBay.com users worldwide trade $2,000 worth of goods on the site every second? What does an auction site like eBay have to do to protect consumers and keep them coming back?

Promotion Strategy

Price is often used as a promotional tool to increase consumer interest. The weekly flyers sent out by grocery stores in the Sunday newspaper, for instance, advertise many products with special low prices. Crested Butte Ski Resort in Colorado made the unusual offer of free skiing between Thanksgiving and Christmas. Its only revenues were voluntary contributions from lodging and restaurant owners who benefited from the droves of skiers taking advantage of the promotion. Lodging during the slack period is now booked solid, and Crested Butte Resort no longer loses money during this time of the year.

Pricing can be a tool for trade promotions as well. For example, Levi's Dockers (casual men's pants) are very popular. Sensing an opportunity, rival pants-maker Bugle Boy began offering similar pants at cheaper wholesale prices, which gave retailers a bigger gross margin than they were getting with Dockers. Levi Strauss had to either lower prices or risk its $400 million annual Dockers sales. Although Levi Strauss intended its cheapest Dockers to retail for $35, it started selling Dockers to retailers for $18 a pair. Retailers could then advertise Dockers at a very attractive retail price of $25.

Demands of Large Customers

Manufacturers find that their large customers such as department stores often make specific pricing demands that the suppliers must agree to. Department stores are making greater-than-ever demands on their suppliers to cover the heavy discounts and markdowns on their own selling floors. They want suppliers to guarantee their stores' profit margins, and they insist on cash rebates if the guarantee isn't met. They are also exacting fines for violations of ticketing, packing, and shipping rules. Cumulatively, the demands are nearly wiping out profits for all but the very biggest suppliers, according to fashion designers and garment makers.

In 2008, with gas, grain, and dairy prices exploding, you'd think the biggest seller of corn flakes and Cocoa Puffs would be getting hit by rising food costs. But Wal-Mart temporarily rolled back prices on hundreds of food items by as much as 30 percent. How? By pressuring vendors to take costs out of the supply chain. "When our grocery suppliers bring price increases, we don't just accept them," says Pamela Kohn, Wal-Mart's general merchandise manager for perishables.[12]

The Relationship of Price to Quality

As mentioned at the beginning of the chapter, when a purchase decision involves great uncertainty, consumers tend to rely on a high price as a predictor of good quality. Reliance on price as an indicator of quality seems to occur for all products, but it reveals itself more strongly for some items than for others.[13] Among the products that benefit from this phenomenon are coffee, aspirin, salt, floor wax, shampoo, clothing, furniture, whiskey, and many services. In the absence of other information, people typically assume that prices are higher because the products contain better materials, because they are made more carefully, or, in the case of professional services, because the provider has more expertise.

Research has found that products that are perceived to be of high quality tend to benefit more from price promotions than products perceived to be of lower quality.[14] However, when perceived high- and lower-quality products are offered in settings where consumers have difficulty making comparisons, then price promotions have an equal effect on sales. Comparisons are more difficult in end-of-aisle displays, feature advertising, and the like.

Knowledgeable merchants take these consumer attitudes into account when devising their pricing strategies. **Prestige pricing** is charging a high price to help promote a high-quality image. A successful prestige pricing strategy requires a retail price that is reasonably consistent with consumers' expectations. No one goes shopping at a Gucci's shop in New York and expects to pay $9.95 for a pair of loafers. In fact, demand would fall drastically at such a low price. In addition to prestige pricing, research has found two other basic effects associated with the price quality relationship: hedonistic and allocative effects.[15] High purchase prices may create feelings of pleasure and excitement associated with consuming higher priced products. This is the hedonistic effect. Hedonistic consumption refers to pursuing emotional responses associated with using a product, such as pleasure, excitement, arousal, good feelings, and fun.

The allocative effect refers to the notion that consumers must allocate their budgets across alternative goods and services. The more you spend on one product the less you have to spend on all others. Consumers sensitive to the allocative effects likely prefer low prices. However, managers must be aware that setting low prices or lowering prices with a discount may lower perceptions of product quality, prestige value,

> **prestige pricing**
> charging a high price to help promote a high-quality image

and hedonistic value. This is because of the negative cues associated with lower selling prices.[16]

Some of the latest research on price-quality relationships has focused on consumer durable goods. The researchers first conducted a study to ascertain the dimensions of quality. These are (1) ease of use; (2) versatility (the ability of a product to perform more functions, or be more flexible); (3) durability; (4) serviceability (ease of obtaining quality repairs); (5) performance; and (6) prestige. The researchers found that when consumers focused on prestige and/or durability to assess quality, price was a strong indicator of perceived overall quality. Price was less important as an indicator of quality if the consumer was focusing on one of the other four dimensions of quality.[17]

L'ORÉAL PLAYS THE PRICE-QUALITY CARD IN INDIA

In India, most beauty products sell for less than a dollar. L'Oréal SA is betting its future there on products costing three to twenty times as much. The French cosmetics giant has embarked on a strategy that sharply differs from that of its rivals. Having failed to turn a profit selling low-priced shampoo in India, it now hopes to capture the growing ranks of middle-class Indian women by luring them upscale. In shops across the country, L'Oréal's offerings include a $5.60 Garnier Nutrisse hair dye, a $17 L'Oréal Paris face powder, and a $25 Vichy sunscreen.[18]

© ISTOCKPHOTO.COM/RUSLAN OLINCHUK

STUDY TOOLS
CHAPTER 19

Located at back of the textbook

❑ **Rip out Chapter Review Card**

Located at 4ltrpress.cengage.com/mktg

❑ **Review Key Terms Flash Cards (Print or Online)**

❑ **Download Audio and Visual Summaries for on-the-go review**

❑ **Complete both Practice Quizzes to prepare for tests**

❑ **Play "Beat the Clock" and "Quizbowl" to master concepts**

❑ **Complete "Crossword Puzzle" to review key terms**

❑ **Watch the video on "Acid" for a real company example on Pricing Concepts**

CHAPTER **20** | **Setting the Right Price**

SALE $3.99

> "All pricing objectives have trade-offs that managers must weigh."

AFTER YOU FINISH THIS CHAPTER GO TO **PAGE 327** FOR **STUDY TOOLS**

LO 1
How to Set a Price on a Product

Setting the right price on a product is a four-step process, illustrated in Exhibit 20.1 on the next page and discussed throughout this chapter:

1. Establish pricing goals.
2. Estimate demand, costs, and profits.
3. Choose a price strategy to help determine a base price.
4. Fine-tune the base price with pricing tactics.

Establish Pricing Goals

The first step in setting the right price is to establish pricing goals. Recall from Chapter 19 that pricing objectives fall into three categories: profit oriented, sales oriented, and status quo. These goals are derived from the firm's overall objectives. A good understanding of the marketplace and of the consumer can sometimes tell a manager very quickly whether a goal is realistic.

All pricing objectives have trade-offs that managers must weigh. A profit maximization objective may require a bigger initial investment than the firm can commit or wants to commit. Reaching the desired market share often means sacrificing short-term profit because without careful management, long-term profit goals may not be met. Meeting the competition is the easiest pricing goal to implement. But can managers really afford to ignore demand and costs, the life-cycle stage, and other considerations? When creating pricing objectives, managers must consider these trade-offs

What do you think?

A person can save a lot of money by shopping around for bargains.

1 STRONGLY DISAGREE   2   3   4   5   6   7 STRONGLY AGREE

in light of the target customer, the environment, and the company's overall objectives.

Estimate Demand, Costs, and Profits

Chapter 19 explained that total revenue is a function of price and quantity demanded and that quantity demanded depends on elasticity. The types of questions managers consider when conducting marketing research on demand and elasticity are key.

EXHIBIT 20.1
Steps in Setting the Right Price on a Product

Establish pricing goals.

↓

Estimate demand, costs, and profits.

↓

Choose a price strategy to help determine a base price.

↓

Fine-tune the base with pricing tactics.

↓

Results lead to the right price.

QUESTIONS FOR MARKET RESEARCH ON DEMAND AND ELASTICITY

▸▸ What price is so low they would question its quality?

▸▸ What is the highest price at which the product would still be a bargain?

▸▸ What is the price at which the product is starting to get expensive?

▸▸ What is the price at which the product becomes too expensive to consider buying?[1]

After establishing pricing goals, managers should estimate total revenue at a variety of prices. Next, they should determine corresponding costs for each price. They are then ready to estimate how much profit, if any, and how much market share can be earned at each possible price. Managers can study the options in light of revenues, costs, and profits. In turn, this information can help determine which price can best meet the firm's pricing goals.

Choose a Price Strategy

The basic, long-term pricing framework for a good or service should be a logical extension of the pricing objectives. The marketing manager's chosen **price strategy** defines the initial price and gives direction for price movements over the product life cycle.

The price strategy sets a competitive price in a specific market segment, based on a well-defined positioning strategy. Changing a price level from premium to super premium may require a change in the product itself, the target customers served, the promotional strategy, or the distribution channels.

A company's freedom in pricing a new product and devising a price strategy depends on the market conditions and the other elements of the marketing mix. If a firm launches a new item resembling several others already on the market, its pricing freedom will be restricted. To succeed, the company will probably have to charge a price close to the average market price. In contrast, a firm that introduces a totally new product with no close substitutes will have considerable pricing freedom.

Despite its strategic value, pricing research is an under-used tool. McKinsey & Company's Pricing Benchmark Survey estimated that only about 15 percent of companies do serious pricing research.[2]

Strategic pricing decisions tend to be made without an understanding of the likely buyer or the competitive response. Managers often make tactical pricing decisions without reviewing how they may fit into the firm's overall pricing or marketing strategy. Many companies make pricing decisions and changes without an existing process for managing the pricing activity. As a result, many of them do not have a serious pricing strategy and do not conduct pricing research to develop their strategy.[3]

Companies that do serious planning for creating a price strategy can select from three basic approaches: price skimming, penetration pricing, and status quo pricing.

Price Skimming Price skimming is sometimes called a "market-plus" approach to pricing because it denotes a high price relative to the prices of competing products. The term **price skimming** is derived from the phrase "skimming the cream off the top." Companies often use this strategy for new products when the product is perceived by the target market as having unique advantages. Often companies will use skimming and then lower prices over time. This is called "sliding down the demand curve." Hardcover book publishers, such as HarperCollins, lower the price when the books are re-released in paperback. Other manufacturers maintain skimming prices throughout a product's life cycle. A manager of the factory that produces Chanel purses (retailing for over $2,000 each) told one of your authors that it takes back unsold inventory and

© ISTOCKPHOTO.COM/SHIRONOSOV

destroys it rather than sell it at a discount.

Price skimming works best when the market is willing to buy the product even though it carries an above-average price. Firms can also effectively use price skimming when a product is well protected legally, when it represents a technological breakthrough, or when it has in some other way blocked the entry of competitors. Managers may follow a skimming strategy when production cannot be expanded rapidly because of technological difficulties, shortages, or constraints imposed by the skill and time required to produce a product. As long as demand is greater than supply, skimming is an attainable strategy.

A successful skimming strategy enables management to recover its product development costs quickly. Even if the market perceives an introductory price as too high, managers can lower the price. Firms often feel it is better to test the market at a high price and then lower the price if sales are too slow. Successful skimming strategies are not limited to products. Well-known athletes, lawyers, and hairstylists are experts at price skimming. Naturally, a skimming strategy will encourage competitors to enter the market.

Penetration Pricing Penetration pricing is at the opposite end of the spectrum from skimming. **Penetration pricing** means charging a relatively low price for a product as a way to reach the mass market. The low price is designed to capture a large share of a substantial market, resulting in lower production costs. If a marketing manager has made obtaining a large market share the firm's pricing objective, penetration pricing is a logical choice.

Penetration pricing does mean lower profit per unit, however. Therefore, to reach the break-even point, it requires a higher volume of sales than would a skimming policy. The recovery of product development costs may be slow. As you might expect, penetration pricing tends to discourage competition.

A penetration strategy tends to be effective in a price-sensitive market. Price should decline more rapidly when demand is elastic because the market can be expanded through a lower price. Also, price sensitivity and greater competitive pressure should lead to a lower initial price and a relatively slow decline in the price later or to a stable low price.

Although Wal-Mart is typically associated with penetration pricing, other chains have done an excellent job of following this strategy as well. Dollar stores, those bare-bones, strip-mall chains that sell staples at cut-rate prices, are now the fastest-growing retailers in America. Dollar chains can put small stores right in downtown neighborhoods, where their shoppers live. Parking is usually a snap, and shoppers can be in and out in less time than it takes to hike across a jumbo Wal-Mart lot.[4]

Another form of extreme penetration pricing that has dramatically increased sales during the recent economic downturn is salvage or surplus grocers. Salvage grocers sell "close-outs" which include products that manufacturers have discontinued, seasonal items that are outdated and goods that are near the date when manufacturers expect freshness to wane. Many such grocers also sell products that were damaged in transit but remain edible, such as a dented box of Cheerios. Prices tend to be significantly lower than those at conventional stores and big discounters like Wal-Mart Stores, Inc.[5]

If a firm has a low fixed cost structure and each sale provides a large contribution to those fixed costs, penetration pricing can boost sales and provide large increases in profits—but only if the market size grows or if competitors choose not to respond. Low prices can attract additional buyers to the market. The increased sales can justify production expansion or the adoption of new technologies, both of which can reduce costs. And, if firms have excess capacity, even low-priced business can provide incremental dollars toward fixed costs.

Penetration pricing can also be effective if an experience curve will cause costs per unit to drop significantly. The experience curve proposes that per-unit

> **penetration pricing** a pricing policy whereby a firm charges a relatively low price for a product initially as a way to reach the mass market

THE BIG ADVANTAGE OF PENETRATION PRICING IS THAT IT TYPICALLY DISCOURAGES OR BLOCKS COMPETITION FROM ENTERING A MARKET.

status quo pricing charging a price identical to or very close to the competition's price.

unfair trade practice acts laws that prohibit wholesalers and retailers from selling below cost

costs will go down as a firm's production experience increases. Manufacturers that fail to take advantage of these effects will find themselves at a competitive cost disadvantage relative to others that are further along the curve.

The big advantage of penetration pricing is that it typically discourages or blocks competition from entering a market. The disadvantage is that penetration means gearing up for mass production to sell a large volume at a low price. If the volume fails to materialize, the company will face huge losses from building or converting a factory to produce the failed product.

Penetration pricing can also prove disastrous for a prestige brand that adopts the strategy in an effort to gain market share and fails. When Omega—once a more prestigious brand than Rolex—was trying to improve the market share of its watches, it adopted a penetration pricing strategy that destroyed the watches' brand image by flooding the market with lower-priced products. Omega never gained sufficient share on its lower-priced/lower-image competitors to justify destroying its brand image and high-priced position with upscale buyers.

Status Quo Pricing The third basic price strategy a firm may choose is **status quo pricing**, also called meeting the competition or going rate pricing (see also Chapter 19). It means charging a price identical to or very close to the competition's price.

Although status quo pricing has the advantage of simplicity, its disadvantage is that the strategy may ignore demand or cost or both. If the firm is

comparatively small, however, meeting the competition may be the safest route to long-term survival.

LO 2 The Legality and Ethics of Price Strategy

As we mentioned in Chapter 4, some pricing decisions are subject to government regulation. Among the issues that fall into this category are unfair trade practices, price fixing, price discrimination, and predatory pricing.

Unfair Trade Practices

In over half the states, **unfair trade practice acts** put a floor under wholesale and retail prices. Selling below cost in these states is illegal. Wholesalers and retailers must usually take a certain minimum percentage markup on their combined merchandise cost and transportation cost. The most common markup figures are 6 percent at the retail level and 2 percent at the wholesale level. If a specific wholesaler or retailer can provide "conclusive proof" that operating costs are lower than the minimum required figure, lower prices may be allowed.

The intent of unfair trade practice acts is to protect small local firms from giants like Wal-Mart, which operates very efficiently on razor-thin profit margins. State enforcement of unfair trade practice laws has generally been lax, however, partly because low prices benefit local consumers.

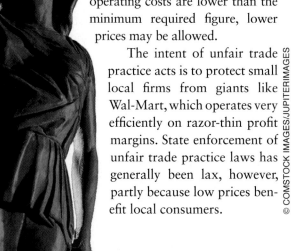

Price Fixing

Price fixing is an agreement between two or more firms on the price they will charge for a product. Suppose two or more executives from competing firms meet to decide how much to charge for a product or to decide which of them will submit the lowest bid on a certain contract. Such practices are illegal under the Sherman Act and the Federal Trade Commission Act. Offenders have received fines and sometimes prison terms. Price fixing is one area where the law is quite clear, and the Justice Department's enforcement is vigorous. In August 2007, British Airways pleaded guilty and was sentenced to pay a $300-million fine for conspiring to fix cargo rates for international air shipments and conspiring to fix passenger fuel surcharges for long-haul flights. In October 2008, the Justice Department announced that a former British Airways executive will serve eight months in jail and pay a $20,000 criminal fine for conspiracy to fix rates on international air cargo shipments.[6]

International price fixing by private entities can be prosecuted under the antitrust laws of many countries. In 2006, France fined thirteen perfume brands and three vendors for price collusion. Other international cartels have been prosecuted for controlling the prices and output of citric acid, graphite electrodes, and bulk vitamins.[7]

Most price-fixing cases focus on high prices charged to customers. A reverse form of price fixing occurs when powerful buyers force their suppliers' prices down. Recently, Maine blueberry growers alleged that four big processors conspired to push down the price they would pay for fresh wild berries. A state court jury agreed and awarded millions in damages.[8] Some price-fixing accusations are less clear-cut. For instance, Leegin Creative Leather Products sought to control its brand image by insisting that retailers charge a certain minimum price for its products. Leegin sued a boutique, Kay's Kloset, for offering its products at a lower price. The suit was decided in favor of Kay's, but appeals are ongoing and may influence the pricing and retail strategies of luxury goods companies trying to control their brand image.[9]

Price Discrimination

The Robinson-Patman Act of 1936 prohibits any firm from selling to two or more different buyers, within a reasonably short time, commodities (not services) of like grade and quality at different prices where the result would be to substantially lessen competition. The act also makes it illegal for a seller to offer two buyers different supplementary services and for buyers to use their purchasing power to force sellers into granting discriminatory prices or services.

SIX ELEMENTS NEEDED FOR A VIOLATION OF THE ROBINSON-PATMAN ACT TO OCCUR:

1. There must be price discrimination; that is, the seller must charge different prices to different customers for the same product.

2. The transaction must occur in interstate commerce.

3. The seller must discriminate by price among two or more purchasers; that is, the seller must make two or more actual sales within a reasonably short time.

4. The products sold must be commodities or other tangible goods.

5. The products sold must be of like grade and quality, not necessarily identical. If the goods are truly interchangeable and substitutable, then they are of like grade and quality.

6. There must be significant competitive injury.

The Robinson-Patman Act provides three defenses for the seller charged with price discrimination (in each case the burden is on the defendant to prove the defense):

▶▶ *Cost*: A firm can charge different prices to different customers if the prices represent manufacturing or quantity discount savings.

▶▶ *Market conditions*: Price variations are justified if designed to meet fluid product or market conditions. Examples include the deterioration of perishable goods, the obsolescence of seasonal products, a distress sale under court order, and a legitimate going-out-of-business sale.

▶▶ *Competition*: A reduction in price may be necessary to stay even with the competition. Specifically, if a competitor undercuts the price quoted by a seller to a buyer, the law authorizes the seller to lower the price charged to the buyer for the product in question.

Predatory Pricing

Predatory pricing is the practice of charging a very low price for a product with the intent of driving competitors out of business or out of a market. Once competitors have been driven out, the firm raises its prices. This practice is illegal under the Sherman Act and the Federal Trade Commission Act. To prove predatory pricing, the Justice Department must show that the predator, the destructive company, explicitly tried to ruin a competitor and that the predatory price was below the predator's average variable cost.

Prosecutions for predatory pricing suffered a major setback when a federal judge threw out a predatory pricing suit filed by the Justice Department against American Airlines. The Justice Department argued that the definition should be updated and that the test should be whether there was any business justification, other than driving away competitors, for American's aggressive pricing. Under that definition, the Justice Department attorneys thought they had a great case. Whenever a fledgling airline tried to get a toehold in the Dallas market, American would meet its fares and add flights. As soon as the rival retreated, American would jack its fares back up.

Under the average variable cost definition, however, the case would have been almost impossible to win. The reason is that like the high-tech industry, the airline industry has high fixed costs and low marginal costs. Once a flight is scheduled, the marginal cost of providing a seat for an additional passenger is almost zero. Thus, it is very difficult to prove that an airline is pricing below its average variable cost. The judge was not impressed by the Justice Department's argument, however, and stuck to the average variable cost definition of predatory pricing.

LO 3 Tactics for Fine-Tuning the Base Price

After managers understand both the legal and the marketing consequences of price strategies, they should set a **base price**, the general price level at which the company expects to sell the good or service. The general price level is correlated with the pricing policy: above the market (price skimming), at the market (status quo pricing), or below the market (penetration pricing). The final step, then, is to fine-tune the base price.

Fine-tuning techniques are short-run approaches that do not change the general price level. They do, however, result in changes within a general price level. These pricing tactics allow the firm to adjust for competition in certain markets, meet ever-changing government regulations, take advantage of unique demand situations, and meet promotional and positioning goals. Fine-tuning pricing tactics include various sorts of discounts, geographic pricing, and other pricing tactics.

price Discounts, Allowances, Rebates, and Value-Based Pricing

A base price can be lowered through the use of discounts and the related tactics of allowances, rebates, low or zero percent financing, and value-based pricing. Managers use the various forms of discounts to encourage customers to do what they would not ordinarily do, such as paying cash rather than using credit, taking delivery out of season, or performing certain functions within a distribution channel.[10] The following are of the most common tactics:

▸ *Quantity discounts*: When buyers get a lower price for buying in multiple units or above a specified dollar amount, they are receiving a **quantity discount**. A **cumulative quantity discount** is a deduction from list price that applies to the buyer's total purchases made during a specific period; it is intended to encourage customer loyalty. In contrast, a **noncumulative quantity discount** is a deduction from list price that applies to a single order rather than to the total volume of orders placed during a certain period. It is intended to encourage orders in large quantities.

▸ *Cash discounts*: A **cash discount** is a price reduction offered to a consumer, an industrial user, or a market-

---

predatory pricing the practice of charging a very low price for a product with the intent of driving competitors out of business or out of a market

base price the general price level at which the company expects to sell the good or service

quantity discount a price reduction offered to buyers buying in multiple units or above a specified dollar amount

cumulative quantity discount a deduction from list price that applies to the buyer's total purchases made during a specific period

noncumulative quantity discount a deduction from list price that applies to a single order rather than to the total volume of orders placed during a certain period

cash discount a price reduction offered to a consumer, an industrial user, or a marketing intermediary in return for prompt payment of a bill

ing intermediary in return for prompt payment of a bill. Prompt payment saves the seller carrying charges and billing expenses and allows the seller to avoid bad debt.

▶▶ *Functional discounts*: When distribution channel intermediaries, such as wholesalers or retailers, perform a service or function for the manufacturer, they must be compensated. This compensation, typically a percentage discount from the base price, is called a **functional discount** (or **trade discount**). Functional discounts vary greatly from channel to channel, depending on the tasks performed by the intermediary.

▶▶ *Seasonal discounts*: A **seasonal discount** is a price reduction for buying merchandise out of season. It shifts the storage function to the purchaser. Seasonal discounts also enable manufacturers to maintain a steady production schedule year-round.

▶▶ *Promotional allowances*: A **promotional allowance** (also known as a **trade allowance**) is a payment to a dealer for promoting the manufacturer's products. It is both a pricing tool and a promotional device. As a pricing tool, a promotional allowance is like a functional discount. If, for example, a retailer runs an ad for a manufacturer's product, the manufacturer may pay half the cost.

▶▶ *Rebates*: A **rebate** is a cash refund given for the purchase of a product during a specific period. The advantage of a rebate over a simple price reduction for stimulating demand is that a rebate is a temporary inducement that can be taken away without altering the basic price structure. A manufacturer that uses a simple price reduction for a short time may meet resistance when trying to restore the price to its original, higher level.

▶▶ *Zero percent financing*: During the mid and late-2000s, new-car sales receded. To get people back into the automobile showrooms, manufacturers offered zero percent financing, which enabled purchasers to borrow money to pay for new cars with no interest charge. The tactic created a huge increase in sales but not without cost to the manufacturers. A five-year interest-free car loan represented a cost of over $3,000 on a typical vehicle sold during the zero percent promotion. Automakers were still offering such incentives in 2009.

Value-Based Pricing **Value-based pricing**, also called *value pricing*, is a pricing strategy that has grown out of the quality movement. Instead of figuring prices based on costs or competitors' prices, it starts with the customer, considers the competition, and then determines the appropriate price. The basic assumption is that the firm is customer driven, seeking to understand the attributes customers want in the goods and services they buy and the value of that bundle of attributes to customers. Because very few firms operate in a pure monopoly, however, a marketer using value-based pricing must also determine the value of competitive offerings to customers. Customers determine the value of a product (not just its price) relative to the value of alternatives. In value-based pricing, therefore, the price of the product

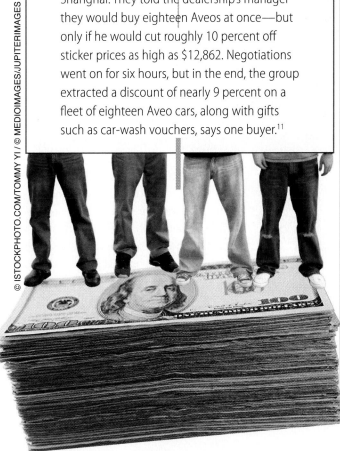

GANGING UP FOR DISCOUNTS

Chinese shoppers have long been known as hard-nosed bargainers. Now, some have started shopping in teams to haggle for bigger markdowns. One Saturday morning, eighteen people met, as planned via a chat room, at a Chevy showroom in downtown Shanghai. They told the dealership's manager they would buy eighteen Aveos at once—but only if he would cut roughly 10 percent off sticker prices as high as $12,862. Negotiations went on for six hours, but in the end, the group extracted a discount of nearly 9 percent on a fleet of eighteen Aveo cars, along with gifts such as car-wash vouchers, says one buyer.[11]

© ISTOCKPHOTO.COM/TOMMY YI / © MEDIOIMAGES/JUPITERIMAGES

is set at a level that seems to the customer to be a good price compared with the prices of other options.

Because of Wal-Mart's strong market entry into groceries, value-based pricing is being adopted as a defensive move by rival supermarkets. Shoppers in competitive markets are seeing prices fall as Wal-Mart pushes rivals to match its value prices. A number of regional grocery chains have switched to value pricing. In the past, they offered weekly specials to attract shoppers and then made up the lost profit by keeping nonsale prices substantially higher. Now, stores like Costco and Wal-Mart have conditioned consumers to expect inexpensive goods every day.

The recession of 2008–2009 has given food companies an opportunity to push value-pricing on certain lines. Just because a product is value-priced does not necessarily mean it is low profit margin. For example, powdered Kool-Aid beverages are inexpensive to make and are extremely profitable. For the first time in over a decade, Kraft is advertising Kool-Aid on television. The commercial shows that four pitchers of Kool-Aid cost the same as a two-liter bottle of soda. At the end, a voice-over says, "Kool-Aid: delivering more smiles per gallon."

Campbell's and Kraft are promoting their value-priced products instead of premium items like Campbell's Pepperidge Farm cookies and Kraft's Wheat Thins crackers. Kraft and Campbell's are promoting soup and grilled cheese sandwiches as a wallet-friendly meal "your family will love."[12]

Pricing Products Too Low

Sometimes managers price their products too low, thereby reducing company profits. This seems to happen for two reasons. First, managers attempt to buy market share through aggressive pricing. Usually, however, these price cuts are quickly met by competitors. Thus, any gain in market share is short-lived, and overall industry profits end up falling. Second, managers have a natural tendency to want to make decisions that can be justified objectively.

The problem is that companies often lack hard data on the complex determinants of profitability, such as the relationship between price changes and sales volumes, the link between demand levels and costs, and the likely responses of competitors to price changes. In contrast, companies usually have rich, unambiguous information on costs, sales, market share, and competitors' prices. As a result, managers tend to make pricing decisions based on current costs, projected short-term share gains, or current competitor prices rather than on long-term profitability.

The problem of "underpricing" can be solved by linking information about price, cost, and demand within the same decision support system. The demand data can be developed via marketing research. This will enable managers to get the hard data they need to calculate the effects of pricing decisions on profitability. Parker Hannifin Corporation makes industrial components used in everything from the space shuttle to a mechanism for tilting the model steamship used in the movie *Titanic*. It was good, but it was stuck in a profit-margin rut. It couldn't seem to improve its return on invested capital. Like most U.S. manufacturers, Parker used a "cost-plus" pricing method—calculating how much it cost to make a product and adding a flat percentage on top, usually 35 percent. Then its new CEO, Donald Washkewicz, decided to start thinking less like a "widget maker" and more like a retailer.[13] That meant that Parker Hannifin started determining its prices by what a consumer was willing to pay, instead of what a product costs to make. Washkewicz had his new "pricing gurus" determine which of their products were high-volume commodities with a competitive market, and which were customized products, with limited or no competition. Then they determined which products offered some unique value, such as faster delivery or better design. Parker's strategic pricing process led to some price cuts in their basic products and price increases of more than 25 percent in their custom products. Parker's net income soared, from $130 million in 2002 to $830 million in 2007. Its return on investment capital has risen from 7 percent to 21 percent in that same amount of time.[14]

© BRT PHOTO/ALAMY

Geographic Pricing

Because many sellers ship their wares to a nationwide or even a worldwide market, the cost of freight can greatly affect the total cost of a product. Sellers may use several different geographic pricing tactics to moderate the impact of freight costs on distant customers. The following methods of geographic pricing are the most common:

▸ *FOB origin pricing*: **FOB origin pricing**, also called *FOB factory* or *FOB shipping point*, is a price tactic that requires the buyer to absorb the freight costs from the shipping point ("free on board"). The farther buyers are from sellers, the more they pay, because transportation costs generally increase with the distance merchandise is shipped.

▸ *Uniform delivered pricing*: If the marketing manager wants total costs, including freight, to be equal for all purchasers of identical products, the firm will adopt uniform delivered pricing, or "postage stamp" pricing. With **uniform delivered pricing**, the seller pays the actual freight charges and bills every purchaser an identical, flat freight charge.

▸ *Zone pricing*: A marketing manager who wants to equalize total costs among buyers within large geographic areas—but not necessarily all of the seller's market area—may modify the base price with a zone-pricing tactic. **Zone pricing** is a modification of uniform delivered pricing. Rather than using a uniform freight rate for the entire United States (or its total market), the firm divides it into segments or zones and charges a flat freight rate to all customers in a given zone. The U.S. Postal Service's parcel post rate structure is probably the best-known zone-pricing system in the country.

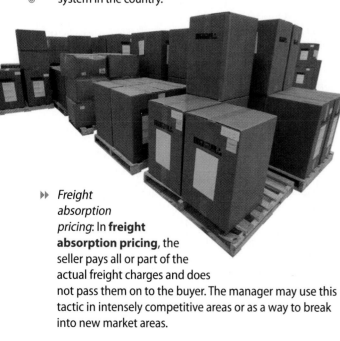

▸ *Freight absorption pricing*: In **freight absorption pricing**, the seller pays all or part of the actual freight charges and does not pass them on to the buyer. The manager may use this tactic in intensely competitive areas or as a way to break into new market areas.

▸ *Basing-point pricing*: With **basing-point pricing**, the seller designates a location as a basing point and charges all buyers the freight cost from that point, regardless of the city from which the goods are shipped. Thanks to several adverse court rulings, basing-point pricing has waned in popularity. Freight fees charged when none were actually incurred, called *phantom freight*, have been declared illegal.

Other Pricing Tactics

Unlike geographic pricing, other pricing tactics are unique and defy neat categorization. Managers use these tactics for various reasons—for example, to stimulate demand for specific products, to increase store patronage, and to offer a wider variety of merchandise at a specific price point. "Other" pricing tactics include a single-price tactic, flexible pricing, professional services pricing, price lining, leader pricing, bait pricing, odd–even pricing, price bundling, and two-part pricing.

Single-Price Tactic A merchant using a **single-price tactic** offers all goods and services at the same price (or perhaps two or three prices). A relatively recent example of a single-price strategy is that of online music downloads. Many online music suppliers offer a flat rate of 99 cents per song. Yahoo! Music Unlimited offers unlimited access to over two million songs for "6 bucks a month."[15] A new music service from Amazon.com sells music downloads with no restrictions on how consumers use the files. Consumers are able to listen to songs from Amazon on any device, including the iPod.[16]

Single-price selling removes price comparisons from the buyer's decision-making process. The retailer enjoys the benefits of a simplified pricing system and minimal clerical errors. However, continually rising costs are a headache for retailers following this strategy. In times of inflation, they must frequently raise the selling price.

Flexible Pricing **Flexible pricing** (or **variable pricing**) means that different customers pay different prices for essentially the same merchandise bought in equal quantities. This tactic is often found in the

---

FOB origin pricing a price tactic that requires the buyer to absorb the freight costs from the shipping point ("free on board")

uniform delivered pricing a price tactic in which the seller pays the actual freight charges and bills every purchaser an identical, flat freight charge

zone pricing a modification of uniform delivered pricing that divides the United States (or the total market) into segments or zones and charges a flat freight rate to all customers in a given zone

freight absorption pricing a price tactic in which the seller pays all or part of the actual freight charges and does not pass them on to the buyer

basing-point pricing a price tactic that charges freight from a given (basing) point, regardless of the city from which the goods are shipped

single-price tactic a price tactic that offers all goods and services at the same price (or perhaps two or three prices)

flexible pricing (variable pricing) a price tactic in which different customers pay different prices for essentially the same merchandise bought in equal quantities

Car dealerships follow flexible price strategies, including trade-ins. A popular promotion offers employee pricing for customers.

© FRANK POLICH/REUTERS/LANDOV

price lining the practice of offering a product line with several items at specific price points

sale of shopping goods, specialty merchandise, and most industrial goods except supply items. Car dealers and many appliance retailers commonly follow the practice. It allows the seller to adjust for competition by meeting another seller's price. Thus, a marketing manager with a status quo pricing objective might readily adopt the tactic. Flexible pricing also enables the seller to close a sale with price-conscious consumers.

The obvious disadvantages of flexible pricing are the lack of consistent profit margins, the potential ill will of high-paying purchasers, the tendency for salespeople to automatically lower the price to make a sale, and the possibility of a price war among sellers.

Trade-Ins Flexible pricing and trade-ins often go hand-in-hand. About 57 percent of all new car sales involve a trade-in.[17] Trade-ins occur for other products as well, such as musical instruments, sporting goods, jewelry, and some appliances. If a trade-in is involved, the consumer must negotiate two prices, one for the new product and one for the existing product. The existence of a trade-in raises several questions for the purchaser. For example, will the new product's price differ depending on whether there is a trade-in? Are consumers better off trading in their used product toward the purchase of the new one from the same retailer, or should they keep the two transactions separate by dealing with different retailers? Several car buying guides, such as Edmunds.com and Autotrader.

com advise consumers to keep the two transactions separate.[18]

Recent research found that trade-in customers tend to care more about the trade-in value they receive than the price they pay for the new product. Thus, these buyers tend to pay more than purchasers without a trade-in. Analysis of data from the automobile market found that, on average, trade-in customers end up paying $452 more than customers who simply buy a new car from a dealer.[19]

Professional Services Pricing Professional services pricing is used by people with lengthy experience, training, and often certification by a licensing board—for example, lawyers, physicians, and family counselors. Professionals sometimes charge customers at an hourly rate, but sometimes fees are based on the solution of a problem or performance of an act (such as an eye examination) rather than on the actual time involved.

Those who use professional pricing have an ethical responsibility not to overcharge a customer. Because demand is sometimes highly inelastic, such as when a person requires heart surgery to survive, there may be a temptation to charge "all the traffic will bear."[20]

Price Lining When a seller establishes a series of prices for a type of merchandise, it creates a price line. **Price lining** is the practice of offering a product line with several items at specific price points. The Limited may offer women's dresses at $40, $70, and $100, with no merchandise marked at prices between those figures. Instead of a normal demand curve running from $40 to $100, The Limited has three demand points (prices). Theoretically, the "curve" exists only because people would buy goods at the in-between prices if it were possible to do so.

Price lining reduces confusion for both the salesperson and the consumer. The buyer may be offered a wider variety of merchandise at each established price. Price lines may also enable a seller to reach several market segments. For buyers, the question of price may be quite simple: all they have to do is find a suitable product at the predetermined price. Moreover, price lining is a valuable tactic for the marketing manager, because the firm may be able to carry a smaller total inventory than it could without price lines. The results may include fewer markdowns, simplified purchasing, and lower inventory carrying charges.

Price lines also present drawbacks, especially if costs are continually rising. Sellers can offset rising costs in three ways. First, they can begin stocking lower-quality merchandise at each price point. Second, sellers can change the prices, although frequent price line changes confuse buyers. Third, sellers can accept lower profit margins and hold quality and prices constant. This third alternative has short-run benefits, but its long-run handicaps may drive sellers out of business.

Leader Pricing Leader pricing (or **loss-leader pricing**) is an attempt by the marketing manager to attract customers by selling a product near or even below cost in the hope that shoppers will buy other items once they are in the store. This type of pricing appears weekly in the newspaper advertising of supermarkets. Leader pricing is normally used on well-known items that consumers can easily recognize as bargains. The goal is not necessarily to sell large quantities of leader items, but to try to appeal to customers who might shop elsewhere.[21] Wal-Mart is using $9 books as a loss-leader to entice customers away from Amazon.com for their online shopping.

Leader pricing is not limited to products. Health clubs offer a one-month free trial as a loss leader.

Bait Pricing In contrast to leader pricing, which is a genuine attempt to give the consumer a reduced price, bait pricing is deceptive. **Bait pricing** tries to get the consumer into a store through false or misleading price advertising and then uses high-pressure selling to persuade the consumer to buy more expensive merchandise. You may have seen this ad or a similar one:

REPOSSESSED . . . Singer slant-needle sewing machine . . . take over 8 payments of $5.10 per month . . . ABC Sewing Center.

This is bait. When a customer goes in to see the machine, a salesperson says that it has just been sold or else shows the prospective buyer a piece of junk. Then the salesperson says, "But I've got a really good deal on this fine new model." This is the switch that may cause a susceptible consumer to walk out with a $400 machine. The Federal Trade Commission considers bait pricing a deceptive act and has banned its use in interstate commerce. Most states also ban bait pricing, but sometimes enforcement is lax.

Odd–Even Pricing Odd–even pricing (or **psychological pricing**) means pricing at odd-numbered prices to connote a bargain and pricing at even-numbered prices to imply quality. For years, many retailers have priced their products in odd numbers—for example, $99.95—to make consumers feel they are paying

a lower price for the product. Even-numbered pricing is often used for "prestige" items, such as a fine perfume at $100 a bottle or a good watch at $500. The demand curve for such items would also be sawtoothed, except that the outside edges would represent even-numbered prices and, therefore, elastic demand.

Price Bundling Price bundling is marketing two or more products in a single package for a special price. For example, Microsoft offers "suites" of software that bundle spreadsheets, word processing, graphics, electronic mail, Internet access, and groupware for networks of microcomputers.

Price bundling can stimulate demand for the bundled items if the target market perceives the price as a good value.

Services like hotels and airlines sell a perishable commodity (hotel rooms and airline seats) with relatively constant fixed costs. Bundling can be an important income stream for these businesses because the variable cost tends to be low—for instance, the cost of cleaning a hotel room. Therefore, most of the revenue can help cover fixed costs and generate profits.

Bundling has also been used in the telecommunications industry. Companies offer local service, long distance, DSL Internet service, wireless, and even cable television in various menus of bundling. Telecom companies use bundling as a way to protect their market share and fight off competition by locking customers into a group of services. For consumers, comparison shopping may be difficult since they may not be able to determine how much they are really paying for each component of the bundle. A related price tactic is **unbundling**, or reducing the bundle of services that comes with the basic product. To help hold the line on costs, some stores require customers to pay for gift wrapping.

Clearly, price bundling can influence consumers' purchase behavior. But what about the decision to consume a particular bundled product or service? Some of the latest research has focused on how people consume certain bundled products or services. According to this research, the key to consumption behavior is how closely consumers can link the costs and benefits of the exchange.[22] In complex transactions like a

leader pricing (loss-leader pricing) a price tactic in which a product is sold near or even below cost in the hope that shoppers will buy other items once they are in the store

bait pricing a price tactic that tries to get consumers into a store through false or misleading price advertising and then uses high-pressure selling to persuade consumers to buy more expensive merchandise

odd–even pricing (psychological pricing) a price tactic that uses odd-numbered prices to connote bargains and even-numbered prices to imply quality

price bundling marketing two or more products in a single package for a special price

unbundling reducing the bundle of services that comes with the basic product

two-part pricing a price tactic that charges two separate amounts to consume a single good or service

holiday package, it may be unclear which costs are paying for which benefits. In such cases, consumers tend to mentally downplay their up-front costs for the bundled product, so they may be more likely to forgo a benefit that's part of the bundle, like a free dinner.

Similarly, when people buy season tickets to a concert series, sporting event, or other activity, the sunk costs (price of the bundle) and the pending benefit (going to see an event) become decoupled. This reduces the likelihood of consumption of the event over time.

Theatergoers who purchase tickets to a single play are almost certain to use those tickets. This is consistent with the idea that in a one-to-one transaction (i.e., one payment, one benefit), the costs and benefits of that transaction are tightly coupled, resulting in strong sunk cost pressure to consume the pending benefit.

A theater manager might expect a no-show rate of 20 percent when the percentage of season ticket holders is high, but a no-show rate of only 5 percent when the percentage of season ticket holders is low. With a high number of season ticket holders, a manager could oversell performances and maximize the revenue for the theater. The surge in petroleum prices in 2007–2008 forced airlines to unbundle in a dramatic fashion. Now everything from checking luggage to soft drinks to pillows and blankets comes at a price. United Airlines thinks that it can earn $1 billion a year with its new menu of fees.[23] British-based Easy Jet doesn't offer assigned seats. However, now for $15 extra a passenger can have "Speedy Boarding," which lets you board first and get a choice of seats. Jet Blue, in a recent quarter, collected $40 million by charging extra for seats with more legroom.

The physical format of the transaction also figures in. A ski lift pass in the form of a booklet of tickets strengthens the cost-benefit link for consumers, whereas a single pass for multiple ski lifts weakens that link.

Though price bundling of services can result in a lower rate of total consumption of that service, the same is not necessarily true for products. Consider the purchase of an expensive bottle of wine. When the wine is purchased as a single unit, its cost and eventual benefit are tightly coupled. As a result, the cost of the wine will be important, and a person will likely reserve that wine for a special occasion. When purchased as part of a bundle (e.g., as part of a case of wine), however, the cost and benefit of that individual bottle of wine will likely become decoupled, reducing the impact of the cost on eventual consumption. Thus, in contrast to the price bundling of services, the price bundling of physical goods could lead to an increase in product consumption.

Two-Part Pricing **Two-part pricing** means establishing two separate charges to consume a single good or service. Health clubs charge a membership fee and a flat fee each time a person uses certain equipment or facilities.

Consumers sometimes prefer two-part pricing because they are uncertain about the number and the types of activities they might use at places like an amusement park. Also, the people who use a service most often pay a higher total price. Two-part pricing can increase a seller's revenue by attracting consumers who would not pay a high fee even for unlimited use. For example, a health club might be able to sell only 100 memberships at $700 annually with unlimited use of facilities, for a total revenue of $70,000. However, it could sell 900 memberships at $200 with a guarantee of using the racquetball courts ten times a month. Every use over ten would require the member to pay a $5 fee. Thus, membership revenue would provide a base of $180,000, with some additional usuage fees throughout the year.

Research has shown that when consumers are thinking of buying a good or service with two–part pricing they may mentally process the base price, such as a membership fee, more thoroughly than the extra fee or surcharge (playing a game of tennis). Thus, they can underestimate the total price compared with when prices are not partitioned.[24] The researchers also found that low-perceived benefit components should be priced

This health club is trying to get new members in the door with a reduced membership fee.

relatively low and vice versa. Consumers find a higher total price more acceptable when the high-benefit component is priced high than when the low benefit component is priced high. For example, assume John joins a health club and swims at the club four times a month. John really enjoys working out and views being a member of the club as part of a healthy life style (high value). He also swims after a workout once a week to unwind and relax. Swimming is not that important to John, but is enjoyable (low value). If the club charges $60 a month dues and $5 per swim, John perceived this as acceptable. According to the research, John would find it less attractive if the monthly dues were $40 and each swim was $10. Yet the total cost is the same!

Consumer Penalties

More and more businesses are adopting **consumer penalties**—extra fees paid by consumers for violating the terms of a purchase agreement. Businesses impose consumer penalties for two reasons: They will allegedly (1) suffer an irrevocable revenue loss and/or (2) incur significant additional transaction costs should customers be unable or unwilling to complete their purchase obligations. For the company, these customer payments are part of doing business in a highly competitive marketplace. With profit margins in many companies increasingly coming under pressure, organizations are looking to stem losses resulting from customers not meeting their obligations. However, the perceived unfairness of a penalty may affect some consumers' willingness to patronize a business in the future.

LO 4 Product Line Pricing

Product line pricing is setting prices for an entire line of products. Compared to setting the right price on

a single product, product line pricing encompasses broader concerns. In product line pricing, the marketing manager tries to achieve maximum profits or other goals for the entire line rather than for a single component of the line.

Relationships among Products

The manager must first determine the type of relationship that exists among the various products in the line:

- ▸▸ If items are *complementary*, an increase in the sale of one good causes an increase in demand for the complementary product, and vice versa. For example, the sale of ski poles depends on the demand for skis, making these two items complementary.

- ▸▸ Two products in a line can also be *substitutes* for each other. If buyers buy one item in the line, they are less likely to buy a second item in the line.

- ▸▸ A *neutral* relationship can also exist between two products. In other words, demand for one of the products is unrelated to demand for the other.

Joint Costs

Joint costs are costs that are shared in the manufacturing and marketing of several products in a product line. These costs pose a unique problem in product pricing (e.g., the production of compact discs that combine photos and music).

Any assignment of joint costs must be somewhat subjective because costs are actually shared. Suppose a company produces two products, X and Y, in a common production process, with joint costs allocated on a weight basis. Product X weighs 1,000 pounds, and product Y weighs 500 pounds. Thus, costs are allocated on the basis of $2 for X for every $1 for Y. Gross margins (sales less the cost of goods sold) might then be as follows:

	Product X	Product Y	Total
Sales	$20,000	$6,000	$26,000
Less: cost of goods sold	15,000	7,500	22,500
Gross margin	$ 5,000	($1,500)	$ 3,500

This statement reveals a loss of $1,500 on product Y. However, the firm must realize that overall it earned a $3,500 profit on the two items in the line. Also, weight may not be the right way to allocate the joint costs. Instead, the firm might use other bases, including market value or quantity sold.

LO5 Pricing during Difficult Economic Times

Pricing is always an important aspect of marketing, but it is especially crucial in times of inflation and recession. The firm that does not adjust to economic trends may lose ground that it can never make up.

Inflation

When the economy is characterized by high inflation, special pricing tactics are often necessary. They can be subdivided into cost-oriented and demand-oriented tactics.

Cost-Oriented Tactics One popular cost-oriented tactic is *culling products with a low profit margin* from the product line. However, this tactic may backfire for three reasons:

▸ A high volume of sales on an item with a low profit margin may still make the item highly profitable.

▸ Eliminating a product from a product line may reduce economies of scale, thereby lowering the margins on other items.

▸ Eliminating the product may affect the price-quality image of the entire line.

Another popular cost-oriented tactic is **delayed-quotation pricing**, which is used for industrial installations and many accessory items. Price is not set on the product until the item is either finished or delivered. Long production lead times force many firms to adopt this policy during periods of inflation. Builders of nuclear power plants, ships, airports, and office towers sometimes use delayed-quotation tactics.

Escalator pricing is similar to delayed-quotation pricing in that the final selling price reflects cost increases incurred between the time an order is placed and the time delivery is made. An escalator clause allows for price increases (usually across the board) based on the cost of living index or some other formula. As with any price increase, management's ability to implement such a policy is based on inelastic demand for the product. Often it is used only for extremely complex products that take a long time to produce or with new customers.

Another tactic growing in popularity is to hold prices constant but add new fees.

Any cost-oriented pricing policy that tries to maintain a fixed gross margin under all conditions can lead to a vicious circle. For example, a price increase will result in decreased demand, which in turn increases production costs (because of lost economies of scale). Increased production costs require a further price increase, leading to further diminished demand, and so on.

Demand-Oriented Tactics Demand-oriented pricing tactics use price to reflect changing patterns of demand caused by inflation or high interest rates. Cost changes are considered, of course, but mostly in the context of how increased prices will affect demand.

Price shading is the use of discounts by salespeople to increase demand for one or more products in a line. Often shading becomes habitual and is done routinely without much forethought. To make the demand for a good or service more inelastic and to create buyer dependency, a company can use several strategies:

▸ *Cultivate selected demand:* Marketing managers can target prosperous customers who will pay extra for convenience or service. In cultivating close relationships with affluent organizational customers, marketing managers should avoid putting themselves at the mercy of a dominant firm. They can more easily raise prices when an account is readily replaceable. Finally, in companies where engineers exert more influence than purchasing departments do, performance is favored over price. Often a preferred vendor's pricing range expands if other suppliers prove technically unsatisfactory.

▸ *Create unique offerings:* Marketing managers should study buyers' needs. If the seller can design distinctive goods or services uniquely fitting buyers' activities, equipment, and procedures, a mutually beneficial relationship will evolve. By satisfying targeted buyers in a superior way, marketing managers can make them dependent. Cereal manufacturers have been able to pass along costs by marketing unique value-added or multi-ingredient cereals.

▸ *Change the package design:* Another way companies pass on higher costs is to shrink product sizes but keep prices the same. When Wrigley introduced its "Slim Pack" to replace its traditional packages of Juicy Fruit, Big Red, and other brands, it reduced the number of sticks per pack from seventeen to fifteen, but left the $1.09 sticker intact. Breyers and Edy's reduced

Wrigley changed its gum packaging to hold fifteen sticks in a slim, modern package, including their newer brands, such as 5 gum.

their ice cream containers from 1.75 to 1.5 quarts but did not lower prices. Blue Bell ice cream plans to counter with a promotional campaign that its containers are still a full half gallon.[25]

▸▸ *Heighten buyer dependence*: Owens Corning Fiberglass supplies an integrated insulation service that includes commercial and scientific training for distributors and seminars for end users. This practice freezes out competition and supports higher prices.

Recession

As discussed in Chapter 4, a recession is a period of reduced economic activity, such as occurred in the United States in 2008–2009. Reduced demand for goods and services, along with higher rates of unemployment, is a common trait of a recession. Yet astute marketers can often find opportunity during recessions. A recession is an excellent time to build market share because competitors are struggling to make ends meet.

Two effective pricing tactics to hold or build market share during a recession are value-based pricing and bundling. *Value-based pricing*, discussed earlier in the chapter, stresses to customers that they are getting a good value for their money. Sony has created a value-priced television called the Bravia M series. It was created by Sony engineers in Mexico using mostly off-the-shelf parts. They are $200 cheaper than comparable Sony sets.[26]

Bundling or *unbundling* can also stimulate demand during a recession. If features are added to a bundle, consumers may perceive the offering as having greater value. Conversely, companies can unbundle offerings and lower base prices to stimulate demand.

Recessions are a good time for marketing managers to study the demand for individual items in a product line and the revenue they produce. Pruning unprofitable items can save resources to be better used elsewhere.

Prices often fall during a recession as competitors try desperately to maintain demand for their wares. Even if demand remains constant, falling prices mean lower profits or no profits. Falling prices, therefore, are a natural incentive to lower costs. During the past recession, companies implemented new technology to improve efficiency and then slashed payrolls. They also discovered that suppliers were an excellent source of cost savings; the cost of purchased materials accounts for slightly more than half of most U.S. manufacturers' expenses. Specific strategies that companies use with suppliers include the following:

▸▸ *Renegotiating contracts*: Sending suppliers letters demanding price cuts of 5 percent or more; putting out for rebid the contracts of those that refuse to cut costs.

▸▸ *Offering help*: Dispatching teams of experts to suppliers' plants to help reorganize and suggest other productivity-boosting changes; working with suppliers to make parts simpler and cheaper to produce.

▸▸ *Keeping the pressure on*: To make sure that improvements continue, setting annual, across-the-board cost reduction targets, often of 5 percent or more a year.

▸▸ *Paring down suppliers*: To improve economies of scale, slashing the overall number of suppliers, sometimes by up to 80 percent, and boosting purchases from those that remain.

STUDY TOOLS
CHAPTER 20

Located at back of the textbook

❑ **Rip out Chapter Review Card**

Located at 4ltrpress.cengage.com/mktg

❑ **Review Key Terms Flash Cards (Print or Online)**

❑ **Download Audio and Visual Summaries for on-the-go review**

❑ **Complete both Practice Quizzes to prepare for tests**

❑ **Play "Beat the Clock" and "Quizbowl" to master concepts**

❑ **Complete "Crossword Puzzle" to review key terms**

❑ **Watch the video for real company examples on Setting the Right Price**

> "CRM is often described as a closed-loop system that builds relationships with customers."

LO 1 — What Is Customer Relationship Management?

AFTER YOU FINISH THIS CHAPTER GO TO PAGE 341 FOR STUDY TOOLS

Customer relationship management (CRM) is the ultimate goal of a new trend in marketing that focuses on understanding customers as individuals instead of as part of a group. To do so, marketers are making their communications more customer-specific. This movement initially was popularized as one-to-one marketing. But CRM is a much broader approach to understanding and serving customer needs than is one-to-one marketing.

Customer relationship management is a company wide business strategy designed to optimize profitability, revenue, and customer satisfaction by focusing on highly defined and precise customer groups. This is accomplished by organizing the company around customer segments, establishing and tracking customer interactions with the company, fostering customer-satisfying behaviors, and linking all processes of the company from its customers through its suppliers. The difference between CRM and traditional mass marketing can be compared to shooting a rifle and a shotgun. Instead of scattering messages far and wide across the spectrum of mass media (the shotgun approach), CRM marketers now are homing in on ways to effectively communicate with each individual customer (the rifle approach).

customer relationship management (CRM) a company wide business strategy designed to optimize profitability, revenue, and customer satisfaction by focusing on highly defined and precise customer groups

What do you think?

I often complain when I'm dissatisfied with a business or a product because I feel it is my duty to do so.

1   2   3   4   5   6   7
STRONGLY DISAGREE   STRONGLY AGREE

Find out what others think at 4ltrpress.cengage.com/mktg

© ISTOCKPHOTO.COM/ROBERT CHURCHILL

The Customer Relationship Management Cycle

On the surface, CRM may resemble a simplistic customer service strategy. But, though customer service is part of the CRM process, it is only a small part of a totally integrated approach to building customer relationships. CRM is often described as a closed-loop system that builds relationships with customers. Exhibit 21.1 illustrates this closed-loop system, one that is continuous and circular with no predefined starting or end point.[1]

To initiate the CRM cycle, a company must first *identify customer relationships with the organization*. This may simply entail learning who the customers are or where they are located, or it may require more detailed information about the products and services they are using. Bridgestone/Firestone, a tire manufacturer and tire service company, uses a CRM system called OnDemand5, which initially gathers information from a point-of-sale interaction.[2] The types of information gathered include basic demographic information, how frequently consumers purchase goods, how much they purchase, and how far they drive.

Next, the company must *understand the interactions with current customers*. Companies accomplish this by collecting data on all types of communications a customer has with the company. Using its OnDemand5 system, Bridgestone/Firestone adds information based on additional interactions with the consumer, such as multiple visits to a physical store location and purchasing history. In this phase, companies build on the initial information collected and develop a more useful database.

EXHIBIT 21.1
A Simple Flow Model of the Customer Relationship Management System

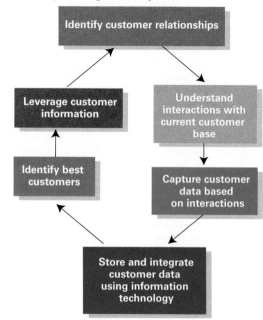

Using this knowledge of its customers and their interactions, the company then *captures relevant customer data on interactions*. As an example, Bridgestone/Firestone can collect information such as the date of the last communication with a customer, how often the customer makes purchases, and whether the customer redeemed coupons sent through direct mail.

How can marketers realistically analyze and communicate with individual customers? The answer lies in how information technology is used to implement the CRM system. Fundamentally, a CRM approach is no more than the relationship cultivated by a salesperson with the customer. A successful salesperson builds a relationship over time, constantly thinks about what the customer needs and wants, and is mindful of the trends and patterns in the customer's purchase history. The salesperson may also inform, educate, and instruct the customer about new products, technology, or applications in anticipation of the customer's future needs or requirements.

This kind of thoughtful attention is the basis of successful CRM systems. Information technology is used not only to enhance the collection of customer data, but also to *store and integrate customer data* throughout the company and, ultimately, to "get to know" customers on a personal basis. Customer data are the firsthand responses that are obtained from customers through investigation or by asking direct questions. These initial data, which might include individual answers to questionnaires, responses on warranty cards, or lists of purchases recorded by electronic cash registers, have not yet been analyzed or interpreted.

The value of customer data depends on its consistency and on the system used to store it. Obtaining high-quality, actionable data from various sources is a key element in any CRM system. Bridgestone/Firestone accomplishes this by managing all information in a central database accessible by marketers. Different kinds of database management software are available, from extremely high-tech, expensive, custom-designed databases to standardized programs.

Every customer wants to be a company's main priority. Yet not all customers are equally important in the eyes of a business. Consequently, the company must identify *its profitable and unprofitable customers*. Data mining is an analytical process that compiles actionable data about the purchase habits of a firm's current and potential customers. Essentially, data mining transforms customer data into customer information a company can use to make managerial decisions. Bridgestone/Firestone uses OnDemand5 to analyze its data to determine which customers qualify for the MasterCare Select program.

Once customer data are analyzed and transformed into usable information, the information must be *leveraged*. The CRM system sends the customer information to all areas of a business because the customer interacts with all aspects of the business. Essentially, the company is trying to enhance customer relationships by getting the right information to the right person in the right place at the right time.

Bridgestone/Firestone utilizes the information in its database to develop different marketing campaigns

for each type of customer. Customers are also targeted by promotions aimed at increasing store visits, upgrades to higher-end tires, and purchases of additional services. Since the company customized its mailings to each type of customer, visits to stores have increased by more than 50 percent.[3]

Implementing a Customer Relationship Management System

Our discussion of a CRM system has assumed two key points. First, customers take center stage in any organization. Second, the business must manage the customer relationship across all points of customer contact throughout the entire organization. In the next sections, we examine how a CRM system is implemented and follow the progression depicted in Exhibit 21.1 as we explain each step in greater detail.

LO2 Identify Customer Relationships

Companies that have a CRM system follow a customer-centric focus or model. **Customer-centric** is an internal management philosophy similar to the marketing concept discussed in Chapter 1. Under this philosophy, the company customizes its product and service offering based on data generated through interactions between the customer and the company. This philosophy transcends all functional areas of the business, producing an internal system where all of the company's decisions and actions are a direct result of customer information.

A customer-centric company builds long-lasting relationships by focusing on what satisfies and retains valuable customers. For example, Sony's Web site (www.playstation.com) focuses on learning, customer knowledge management, and empowerment to market its PlayStation gaming computer entertainment system. The Web site offers online shopping, opportunities to try new games, customer support, and information on news, events, and promotions. The interactive features include online gaming and message boards.

The PlayStation is designed to support Sony's CRM system. When PlayStation users want to access amenities on the site, they are required to log in and supply information such as their name, e-mail address, and birth date. Users can opt to fill out a survey that

customer-centric
a philosophy under which the company customizes its product and service offering based on data generated through interactions between the customer and the company

learning an informal process of collecting customer data through customer comments and feedback on product or service performance

knowledge management the process by which learned information from customers is centralized and shared in order to enhance the relationship between customers and the organization

empowerment delegation of authority to solve customers' problems quickly—usually by the first person that the customer notifies regarding the problem

interaction the point at which a customer and a company representative exchange information and develop learning relationships

asks questions about the types of computer entertainment systems they own, how many games are owned for each console, expected future game purchases, time spent playing games, types of games played, and level of Internet connectivity. Armed with this information, Sony marketers are then able to tailor the site, new games, and PlayStation hardware based on players' replies to the survey and use of the Web site.[4]

Customer-centric companies continually learn ways to enhance their product and service offerings. **Learning** in a CRM environment involves collecting customer information through comments and feedback on product and service performance.

Each unit of a business typically has its own way of recording what it learns and perhaps even its own customer information system. The departments' different interests make it difficult to pull all of the customer information together in one place using a common format. To overcome this problem, companies using CRM rely on knowledge management. **Knowledge management** is a process by which customer information is centralized and shared in order to enhance the relationship between customers and the organization. Information collected includes experiential observations, comments, customer actions, and qualitative facts about the customer.

As Chapter 1 explained, empowerment involves delegating authority to solve customers' problems. In other words, **empowerment** is the latitude organizations give their representatives to negotiate mutually satisfying commitments with customers. Usually, organizational representatives are able to make changes during interactions with customers through phone, fax, e-mail, Web communication, or face to face.

An **interaction** occurs when a customer and a company representative exchange information and develop learning relationships. With CRM the customer, and not the organization, defines the terms of the interaction, often by stating his or her preferences. The organization responds by designing products and services around customers' desired experiences. For example, students can purchase the Student Advantage Discount Card for a nominal fee and use it to obtain discounts from affiliated retailers, such as Dell, Foot Locker, Target, Timberland, and Barnes & Noble. Student Advantage tracks the cardholders' spending patterns and behaviors to gain a better understanding of what the college customer wants. Student Advantage then communicates this information to the affiliated retailers, who can tailor their discounts to meet college students' needs.[5]

The success of CRM—building lasting and profitable relationships—can be directly measured by the effectiveness of the interaction between the customer and the organization. In fact, what further differentiates CRM from other strategic initiatives is the organization's ability to establish and manage interactions with its current customer base. The more latitude (empowerment) a company gives its representatives, the more likely the interaction will conclude in a way that satisfies the customer.

LO 3 Understand Interactions of the Current Customer Base

The *interaction* between the customer and the organization is the foundation on which a CRM system is built. Only through effective interactions can organizations learn about the expectations of their customers, generate and manage knowledge about them, negotiate mutually satisfying commitments, and build long-term relationships.

Exhibit 21.2 illustrates the customer-centric approach for managing customer interactions. Following a customer-centric approach, an interaction can occur through a formal or direct communication channel, such as a phone, the Internet, or a salesperson. Any activity or touch point a customer has with an organization, either directly or indirectly, constitutes an interaction.

EXHIBIT 21.2
Customer-Centric Approach for Managing Customer Interactions

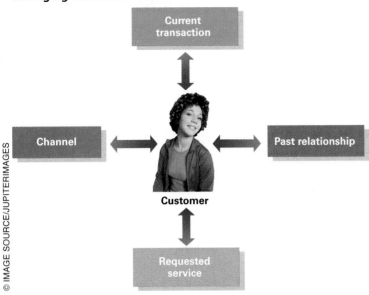

© IMAGE SOURCE/JUPITERIMAGES

Companies that effectively manage customer interactions recognize that customers provide data to the organization that affect a wide variety of **touch points**. In a CRM system, touch points are all areas of a business where customers have contact with the company and data might be gathered. Touch points might include a customer registering for a particular service, a customer communicating with customer service for product information, a customer completing and returning the warranty information card for a product, or a customer talking with salespeople, delivery personnel, and product installers. Data gathered at these touch points, once interpreted, provide information that affects touch points inside the company. Interpreted information may be redirected to marketing research, to develop profiles of extended warranty purchasers; to production, to analyze recurring problems and repair components; and to accounting, to establish cost-control models for repair service calls.

© THINKSTOCK IMAGES/JUPITERIMAGES

Web-based interactions are an increasingly popular touch point for customers to communicate with companies on their own terms. Web users can evaluate and purchase products, make reservations, input preferential data, and provide customer feedback on services and products. Data from these Web-based interactions are then captured, compiled, and used to segment customers, refine marketing efforts, develop new products, and deliver a degree of individual customization to improve customer relationships.

Another touch point is through **point-of-sale interactions** in stores or at information kiosks. Many point-of-sale software programs enable customers to easily provide information about themselves without feeling violated. The information is then used for marketing and merchandising activities, and to accurately identify the store's best customers and the types of products they buy. Data collected at point-of-sale interactions is also used to increase customer satisfaction through the development of in-store services and customer recognition promotions.

touch points all possible areas of a business where customers communicate with that business

point-of-sale interactions communications between customers and organizations that occur at the point of sale, normally in a store

LO4 Capture Customer Data

Vast amounts of data can be obtained from the interactions between an organization and its customers. Therefore, in a CRM system, the issue is not how much data can be obtained, but rather what types of data should be acquired and how the data can effectively be used for relationship enhancement.

The traditional approach for acquiring data from customers is through channel interactions. Channel interactions include store visits, conversations with salespeople, interactions via the Web, traditional phone conversations, and wireless communications. In a CRM system, channel interactions are viewed as prime information sources based on the channel selected to initiate the interaction rather than on the data acquired. For example, if a consumer logs on to the Sony Web site to find out why a Sony device is not functioning properly and the answer is not available online, the consumer is then referred to a page where he or she can describe the problem. The Web site then e-mails the problem description to a company representative, who will research the problem and reply via e-mail. Sony continues to use the e-mail mode of communication because the customer has established this as the preferred method of contact.[6]

Interactions between the company and the customer facilitate collection of large amounts of data. Companies can obtain not only simple contact information (name, address, phone number), but also data pertaining to the customer's current relationship with the organization—past purchase history, quantity and frequency of purchases, average amount spent on purchases, sensitivity to promotional activities, and so forth.

In this manner, a lot of information can be captured from one individual customer across several touch points. Multiply this by the thousands of customers across all of the touch points with an organization, and the volume of data can rapidly become unmanageable for company personnel. The large volumes of data resulting from a CRM initiative can be managed effectively only through technology. Once customer data are collected, the question of who owns those data becomes extremely salient. In its privacy statement, Toysmart.com declared that it would never sell information registered at its Web site, including children's names and birth dates, to a third party. When the company filed for bankruptcy protection, it said the information collected constituted a company asset that needed to be sold off to pay creditors. Despite the outrage at this announcement, many dot-com companies closing their doors found they had little in the way of assets and followed Toysmart's lead.

LO 5 Store and Integrate Customer Data

Customer data are only as valuable as the system in which the data are stored and the consistency and accuracy of the data captured. Gathering data is further complicated by the fact that data needed by one unit of the organization, such as sales and marketing, are often generated by another area of the business or even a third-party supplier, such as an independent marketing research firm. Thus, companies must use information technology to capture, store, and integrate strategically important customer information. This process of centralizing data in a CRM system is referred to as data warehousing.

A **data warehouse** is a central repository (*database*) of customer data collected by an organization. Essentially, it is a large computerized file of all information collected in the previous phase of the CRM process, for example, information collected in channel, transaction, and product/service touch points. The core of the data warehouse is the **database**, "a collection of data, especially one that can be accessed and manipulated by computer software."[7] The CRM database focuses on collecting vital statistics on consumers, their purchasing habits, transactions methods, and product usage in a centralized repository that is accessible by all functional areas of a company. By utilizing a data warehouse, marketing managers can quickly access vast amounts of information required to make decisions.

© ISTOCKPHOTO.COM/SURELY

E-Support at Your Service!

When a company builds its database, usually the first step is to develop a list. A **response list** is based on customers who have indicated interest in a product or service, or a compiled list, created by an outside company that has collected names and contact information for potential consumers. Response lists tend to be especially valuable because past behavior is a strong predictor of future behavior and because consumers who have indicated interest in the product or service are more prone to purchase. Companies may find it valuable to enhance their customer records with information about the customers' or prospective customers' demographics and lifestyle characteristics. They can often accomplish this by augmenting with compiled lists. **Compiled lists** are created by an outside company that has collected names and contact information for potential consumers. This information is usually obtained from telephone directories and membership rosters of various groups. Lists range from those owned by large list companies, such as Dun & Bradstreet for business-to-business data and Donnelley and R. L. Polk for consumer lists, to small groups or associations that are willing to sell their membership lists. Indeed, many lists are compiled from people who have opted in to the list after they have purchased a related product. Data compiled by large data-gathering companies usually are very accurate.

In this phase companies are usually collecting channel, transaction, and product/service information such as store, salesperson, communication channel, contact information, relationship, and brands.

A customer database becomes even more useful to marketing managers when it is enhanced to include more than simply a customer's or prospect's name, address, telephone number, and transaction history. Database enhancement involves purchasing information on customers or prospects to better describe their needs or determine how responsive they might be to marketing programs. Types of enhancement data typically include demographic, lifestyle, or behavioral information.

Database enhancement can increase the effectiveness of marketing programs. By learning more about their best and most profitable customers, marketers can maximize the effectiveness of marketing communications and cross-selling. Database enhancement also helps a company find new prospects.

Multinational companies building worldwide databases often face difficult problems when pulling together internal data about their customers. Differences in language, computer systems, and data-collection methods can be huge obstacles to overcome. In spite of the challenges, many global companies are committed to building databases.

LO 6 Identify the Best Customers

CRM manages interactions between a company and its customers. To be successful, companies must identify customers who yield high profits or potential profits. To do so, significant amounts of data must be gathered from customers, stored and integrated in the data warehouse, and then analyzed and interpreted for common patterns that can identify homogeneous customers who are different from other customer segments. Because not all customers are the same, organizations need to develop interactions that target *individual* customer needs and wants. Recall, from Chapter 8, the 80/20 principle—80 percent of a company's revenue is generated by 20 percent of its customers. Therefore, the question becomes, how do we identify the 20 percent of our customer base that contributes 80 percent of our revenue? In a CRM system, the answer is data mining.

response list a customer list that includes the names and addresses of individuals who have responded to an offer of some kind, such as by mail, telephone, direct-response television, product rebates, contests or sweepstakes, or billing inserts

compiled list a customer list developed by gathering names and addresses from telephone directories and membership rosters, usually enhanced with information from public records, such as census data, auto registrations, birth announcements, business start-ups, or bankruptcies

Data Mining

Data mining is used to find hidden patterns and relationships in the customer data stored in the data warehouse. It is a data analysis approach that identifies patterns of characteristics that relate to particular customers or customer groups. Although businesses have been conducting such analyses for many years, the procedures typically were performed on small data sets containing as few as 300 to 400 customers. Today, with the development of sophisticated data warehouses, millions of customers' shopping patterns can be analyzed.

Using data mining, marketers can search the data warehouse, capture relevant data, categorize significant characteristics, and develop customer profiles. When using data mining, it is important to remember that the real value is in the company's ability to transform its data from operational bits and bytes into information marketers need for successful marketing strategies. Companies must analyze the data to identify and profile the best customers, calculate their lifetime value, and ultimately predict purchasing behavior through statistical modeling. Albertsons supermarkets use data mining to identify commonly purchased items that should be placed together on shelves and to learn what soft drinks sell best in different parts of the country.

Before the information is leveraged, several types of analysis are often run on the data. These analyses include customer segmentation, recency-frequency-monetary analysis (RFM), lifetime value analysis (LTV), and predictive modeling.

Customer Segmentation

Recall that *customer segmentation* is the process of breaking large groups of customers into smaller, more homogeneous groups. This type of analysis generates a "profile" or picture of the customers' similar demographic, geographic, and psychographic traits as well as their previous purchase behavior; it focuses particularly on the best customers. Profiles of the best customers can be compared and contrasted with other customer segments. For example, a bank could segment consumers on frequency of usage, credit, age, and turnover.

Once a profile of the best customer is developed using these criteria, it can be used to screen other potential consumers. Similarly, customer profiles can be used to introduce customers selectively to specific

Wal-Mart currently has over 4,000 terabytes (trillions of characters) of customer transaction data—that's roughly twice the amount of data contained in the entire Internet. Wal-Mart uses its huge data warehouse to help each of its stores adapt its merchandising mix to local neighborhood preferences.[8]

marketing actions. For example, young customers with an open mind can be introduced to home banking. See Chapter 8 for a detailed discussion of segmentation.

Recency-Frequency-Monetary Analysis (RFM) Customers who have purchased recently and often and have spent considerable money are more likely to purchase again. Recency-frequency-monetary analysis (RFM) identifies those customers most likely to purchase again because they have bought recently, bought frequently, or spent a specified amount of money with the firm. Firms develop equations to identify the "best customers" (often the top 20 percent of the customer base) by assigning a score to customer records in the database on how often, how recently, and how much they have spent. Customers are then ranked to determine which ones move to the top of the list and which ones fall to the bottom. The ranking provides the basis for maximizing profits because it enables the firm to use the information in its customer database to select those persons who have proved to be good sources of revenue.

Lifetime Value Analysis (LTV) Recency, frequency, and monetary data can also be used to create a lifetime value model on customers in the database. Whereas RFM looks at how valuable a customer currently is to a company, **lifetime value analysis (LTV)** projects the future value of the customer over a period of years.

One of the basic assumptions in any lifetime value calculation is that marketing to repeat customers is more profitable than marketing to first-time buyers. That is, it costs more to find a new customer in terms of promotion and gaining trust than to sell more to a customer who is already loyal.

Customer lifetime value has a number of benefits. It shows marketers how much they can spend to *acquire* new customers, it tells them the level of spending to *retain* customers, and it facilitates targeting new customers who look as though they will be profitable customers. Some marketers have taken CRM's lifetime value analysis one step further by implementing Customer Value Management (or CVM) strategies. The goal is to determine which individual customers are most valuable so that their total lifetime purchasing can be maximized. CVM requires a series of "value exchanges" that reward customers for providing personal information and use the information to encourage customers to make additional purchases or renew ongoing services. For example, T-Mobile analyzes transactional data to identify high-value customers who seem likely to switch service providers and takes special care to offer these customers great deals for keeping and upgrading their service.[9]

I WONDER WHAT MY CUSTOMER LIFETIME VALUE IS.

Predictive Modeling The ability to reasonably predict future customer behavior gives marketers a significant competitive advantage. Through **predictive modeling**, marketers try to determine, based on some past set of occurrences, what the odds are that some other occurrence, such as an Internet inquiry or purchase, will take place in the future. SPSS Predictive Marketing is one tool marketers can use to answer questions about their consumers. The software requires minimal knowledge of statistical analysis. Users operate from a prebuilt model, which generates profiles in three to four days. SPSS also has an online product that predicts Web site users' behavior.

predictive modeling a data manipulation technique in which marketers try to determine, based on some past set of occurrences, what the odds are that some other occurrence, such as a response or purchase, will take place in the future

campaign management developing product or service offerings customized for the appropriate customer segment and then pricing and communicating these offerings for the purpose of enhancing customer relationships

LO 7 Leverage Customer Information

Data mining identifies the most profitable customers and prospects. Managers can then design tailored marketing strategies to best appeal to the identified segments. In CRM this is commonly referred to as leveraging customer information to facilitate enhanced relationships with customers. Exhibit 21.3 shows some common CRM marketing database applications.

Campaign Management

Through campaign management, all areas of the company participate in the development of programs targeted to customers. **Campaign management** involves monitoring and leveraging customer interactions to sell a company's products and to increase customer service. Campaigns are based directly on data obtained from customers through various interactions. Campaign management includes monitoring the success of the communications based on customer reactions through sales, orders, callbacks to the company, and the like. If a campaign appears unsuccessful, it is evaluated and changed to better achieve the company's desired objective.

Campaign management involves developing customized product and service offerings for the appropriate customer segment, pricing these offerings attractively, and communicating these offers

EXHIBIT 21.3
Common CRM Marketing Database Applications

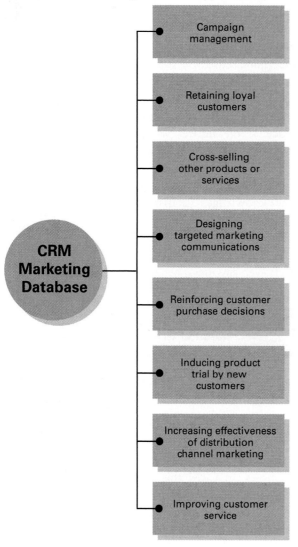

CRM Marketing Database

- Campaign management
- Retaining loyal customers
- Cross-selling other products or services
- Designing targeted marketing communications
- Reinforcing customer purchase decisions
- Inducing product trial by new customers
- Increasing effectiveness of distribution channel marketing
- Improving customer service

in a manner that enhances customer relationships. Customizing product and service offerings requires managing multiple interactions with customers, as well as giving priority to those products and services that are viewed as most desirable for a specifically designated customer. Even within a highly defined market segment, individual customer differences will emerge. Therefore, interactions among customers must focus on individual experiences, expectations, and desires.

Retaining Loyal Customers

If a company has identified its best customers, then it should make every effort to maintain and increase their loyalty. When a company retains an additional 5 percent of its customers each year, profits will increase by as much as 25 percent. What's more, improving customer retention by a mere 2 percent can decrease costs by as much as 10 percent.[10]

Loyalty programs reward loyal customers for making multiple purchases. The objective is to build long-term mutually beneficial relationships between a company and its key customers. Marriott, Hilton, and Starwood Hotels, for instance, reward their best customers with special perks not available to customers who stay less frequently. Travelers who spend a specified number of nights per year receive reservation guarantees, welcome gifts like fruit baskets and wine in their rooms, and access to concierge lounges. In addition to rewarding good customers, loyalty programs provide businesses with a wealth of information about their customers and shopping trends that can be used to make future business decisions.

Cross-Selling Other Products and Services

CRM provides many opportunities to cross-sell related products. Marketers can use the database to match product profiles and consumer profiles so that they can cross-sell customers products that match their demographic, lifestyle, or behavioral characteristics. For instance, outdoor gear retailer REI uses the extensive customer data it collects through its Web site, direct mailings, and retail stores to tailor its stores' product mixes to local market preferences and to uncover patterns that suggest future purchases. Through data mining, analysts at REI know that their customers are involved in lots of different activities, even though they might not have bought all the gear at their store. Marketers at REI can confidently send a bicycling catalog to a customer who bought camping gear, for example, because their data has shown a positive correlation between camping and cycling.[11]

Internet companies use product and customer profiling to reveal cross-selling opportunities while a customer is surfing their site. Past purchases on a particular Web site and the site a surfer comes from give online marketers clues about the surfer's interests and what items to cross-sell.

ONLINE CHARITIES USE CRM TOOLS

Organizations such as Globalgiving.org are enabling people to make extraordinary differences in the lives of people across the globe using CRM tools. Globalgiving.org has a database of small international projects in which donors can participate by donating directly to the project. One of the most popular gifts is to send a child in India to school for a year by donating $40. The organization uses database technology and the Internet to enable people to choose a project and make a direct donation that has an immediate effect. Their Web site connects people with causes around the world and the donor gets regular updates about the progress of the project.[12]

Designing Targeted Marketing Communications

Using transaction and purchase data, a database allows marketers to track customers' relationships to the company's products and services and modify the marketing message accordingly. Kraft Foods teamed with Wegmans supermarkets to determine which advertising campaigns were most effective for frequent buyers of Kraft Macaroni & Cheese.[13]

Customers can also be segmented into infrequent users, moderate users, and heavy users. A segmented communications strategy can then be developed based on which group the customer falls into. Communications to infrequent users might encourage repeat purchases through a direct incentive such as a limited-time price discount for ordering again. Communications to moderate users may use fewer incentives and more reinforcement of past purchase decisions. Communications to heavy users would be designed around loyalty and reinforcement of the purchase rather than price promotions.

Reinforcing Customer Purchase Decisions

As you learned in the consumer behavior chapter, cognitive dissonance is the feeling consumers get when they recognize an inconsistency between their values and opinions and their purchase behavior. In other words, they doubt the soundness of their purchase decision and often feel anxious. CRM offers marketers an excellent opportunity to reach out to customers to reinforce the purchase decision. By thanking customers for their purchases and telling them they are important, marketers can help cement a long-term, profitable relationship.

Updating customers periodically about the status of their order reinforces purchase decisions. Postsale e-mails also afford the chance to provide more customer service or cross-sell other products.

Sumerset Houseboats builds customized, luxury houseboats priced at about $250,000 each. The company uses its Web site to monitor customer profiles, post company information, and communicate with customers. For example, it posts daily pictures of progress on houseboats being built. By reinforcing customers' decisions, Sumerset is able to offset the feeling of cognitive dissonance.[14]

Inducing Product Trial by New Customers

Although significant time and money are expended on encouraging repeat purchases by the best customers, a marketing database is also used to identify new customers. Because a firm using a marketing database already has a profile of its best customers, it can easily use the results of modeling to profile potential customers. EATEL, a regional telecommunications firm, uses modeling to identify prospective residential and commercial telephone customers and successfully attract their business.

Marketing managers generally use demographic and behavioral data overlaid on existing customer data to develop a detailed customer profile that is a powerful tool for evaluating lists of prospects. For instance, if a firm's best customers are thirty-five to fifty years of age, live in suburban areas, and enjoy mountain climbing, then the company can find prospects already in its database or customers who currently are identified as using a competitor's product that match this profile.

Increasing Effectiveness of Distribution Channel Marketing

In Chapter 13 you learned that a marketing channel is a business structure of interdependent organizations, such as wholesalers and retailers, that move a product from the producer to the ultimate consumer. Most marketers rely on indirect channels to move their products to the end user. Thus, marketers often

In order to cut rising printing and mailing costs, **Williams-Sonoma, Inc.** limits distribution of its mail catalogs to established purchasers and to households in certain zip codes. The company checks several factors, like the number of European cars and the percentage of children under the age of four in an area, before sending out its Pottery Barn and Williams-Sonoma catalogs.[15]

© ISTOCKPHOTO.COM/STEPHANIE CONNELL

lose touch with the customer as an individual since the relationship is really between the retailer and the consumer. Marketers in this predicament often view their customers as aggregate statistics because specific customer information is difficult to gather.

With CRM databases, manufacturers now have a tool to gain insight into who is buying their products. Instead of simply unloading products into the distribution channel and leaving marketing and relationship building to dealers, auto manufacturers today are using Web sites to keep in touch with customers and prospects, learn about their lifestyles and hobbies, understand their vehicle needs, and develop relationships in hopes these consumers will reward them with brand loyalty in the future. BMW and other vehicle manufacturers have databases with names of millions of consumers who have expressed an interest in their products.

With many brick-and-mortar stores setting up shop online, companies are now challenged to monitor purchases of customers who shop both in-store and online. This concept is referred to as multichannel marketing. After Lands' End determined that multichannel customers are the most valuable, the company targeted marketing campaigns toward retaining these customers and increased sales significantly.

Companies are also using radio-frequency identification (RFID) technology to improve distribution. The technology uses a microchip with an antenna that tracks anything from a soda can to a car. A computer can locate the product anywhere. The main implication of this technology is that companies will enjoy a reduction in theft and loss of merchandise shipments and will always know where merchandise is in the distribution channel. Moreover, as this technology is further developed, marketers will be able to gather essential information related to product usage and consumption.[16]

Improving Customer Service

CRM marketing techniques increasingly are being used to improve customer service. Amazon.com uses several Web site tools that get customers to return. For example, customers can build wish lists of items, much like a gift registry, so friends and family can make purchases for birthday and other occasions. Amazon also offers recommendations for products based on past purchase and search behavior. These recommendations are listed when a registered customer logs on to the site. Finally, Amazon stores all customer payment and shipping information so customers can make a purchase with one click and then track the shipment (www.amazon.com). Amazon makes the process of searching for and purchasing books and other products easy and efficient.

Privacy Concerns and CRM

Before rushing out to invest in a CRM system and build a database, marketers should consider consumers' reactions to the growing use of databases. Many Americans and customers abroad are concerned about databases because of the potential for invasion of privacy. The sheer volume of information aggregated in databases makes it vulnerable to unauthorized access and use. A fundamental aspect of marketing using CRM databases is providing valuable services to customers based on knowledge of what customers really value. It is critical, however, that marketers remember that these relationships should be built on trust. Although database technology enables marketers to compile ever-richer information about their customers that can be used to build and manage relationships, if these customers feel their privacy is being violated, then the relationship becomes a liability.

The popularity of the Internet for e-commerce and customer data collection and as a repository for sensitive customer data has alarmed privacy-minded customers. Online users complain loudly about being "spammed," and Web surfers, including children, are routinely asked to divulge personal information to access certain screens or purchase goods or services. Many users are unaware of how personal information is collected, used, and distributed. The government actively sells huge amounts of personal information to list companies. Hospitals sell the names of women who just gave birth on their premises. Consumer credit databases are often used by credit-card marketers to prescreen targets for solicitations. Online and off-line privacy concerns are growing and ultimately will have to be dealt with by businesses and regulators.

In 2007, Privacy International, a human rights research and campaign organization, investigated the privacy practices of key Internet-based companies for six months. The results list the best and the worst performers across search, e-mail, e-commerce, and social networking sites. Amazon.com, AOL, Apple, eBay, Facebook, Google, and Yahoo! rank from notable lapses in privacy protection to being hostile to privacy. Privacy International considers its report an initial consultation and will continue soliciting input over several months before releasing a final report.[17]

Privacy policies for companies in the United States are largely voluntary, and regulations on how personal data are collected and used are being developed. But collecting data on consumers outside the United States is a different matter. For database marketers venturing beyond U.S. borders, success requires careful navigation of foreign privacy laws. For example, under the European Union's European Data Protection Directive, any business that trades with a European organization must comply with the EU's rules for handling information about individuals or risk prosecution. More than fifty nations have, or are developing, privacy legislation. Europe has the strictest legislation regarding the collection and use of customer data, and other countries are looking to that legislation when formulating their policies.

My **TiVo** gets me.

CAUTION CAL

Endnotes

1

1. Announcement to the AMA Academic Council from Patricia K. Goodrich, Senior Director, Professional Development, American Marketing Association, October 25, 2007.

2. George Anderson, "Satisfied Workers Generate Greater Returns," *Retailwire*, online, January 16, 2008.

3. Ann Zimmerman, "Home Depot Chief Renovates," *The Wall Street Journal*, June 5, 2008, B1, B2.

4. Robert Levering and Milton Moskowitz, "The 100 Best Companies to Work For," *Fortune*, January 25, 2005, 73.

5. Philip Kotler and Kevin Lane Keller, *A Framework for Marketing Management*, 3rd ed. (Upper Saddle River, NJ: Prentice–Hall, 2007), 3.

6. Woody Driggs, "Serving Up Customer Delight," *Customer Relationship Management*, April 2008, 14.

7. Ibid.

8. George Anderson, "Customer Service Tops NRF Agenda," *Retailwire*, January 16, 2008, online; "The Bean Delivers," *Marketing News*, February 15, 2008, 5.

9. Jena McGregor, "Customer Service Champs," *BusinessWeek*, March 3, 2008, 37–42.

10. Anya Kamenetz, "Cleaning Solution," *Fast Company*, September 2008, 121–124.

11. Ibid.

12. Todd Wasserman, "P&G's Green Guru Tells Us Why There's No Green Tide," *Brandweek*, May 26, 2008, 15, 17.

13. Elena Malykhina, "Purex Detergent Joins the 'Green' Movement," *Brandweek.Com*, July 15, 2008, online.

14. Becky Ebenkamp, "Study: 'Green' Products Leave Consumers Puzzled," *Brandweek.Com*, July 15, 2008, online.

15. Marc Gunther, "Coca–Cola's Green Crusader," *Fortune*, April 28, 2008, 150.

16. Rachel Tobin Ramos, "UPS, Coke, Home Depot Push Green Strategies," ajc.com, April 23, 2008, online.

17. Ibid; "Wal-Mart Says More Consumers Looking For 'Green' Products," *homeworldbusiness.com*, April 22, 2008, online.

18. Todd Wasserman, "Mintel: 'Green' Products Top 5,933 in 2007," *Brandweek.Com*, May 21, 2008, online.

19. Nora Isaccs, "Crash and Burn," *upsidetoday.com*, online.

20. A. G. Lafley and Rom Charan, "The Consumer is Boss," *Fortune*, March 17, 2008, 121–126.

21. Ibid., used by permission.

22. "The Importance of Great Customer Experiences and the Best Ways to Deliver Them," *Insight*, November 2007, 32.

23. Ibid.

24. Phred Dvorak, "Next in Line for Reinvention: The Art of Selling," *The Wall Street Journal*, January 28, 2008, B3.

25. Christopher Musico, "7 Essential Consumer Service Processes," *destinationcrm.com*, January 16, 2008, online.

26. Brian Hindo, "Satisfaction Not Guaranteed," *BusinessWeek*, June 19, 2006, 32–36.

27. Jena McGregor, "Customer Service Champs," *BusinessWeek*, March 5, 2007, 52–64.

28. Ibid.

29. Jeffrey M. O'Brien, "A Perfect Season," *Fortune*, February 4, 2008, 61–66.

30. Julie Barker, "Power to the People: Reducing Turnover With Empowerment," *Incentive*, February 8, 2008, online.

31. Samuel Fromartz, "Good Enough to Eat," *Fast Company*, September 2008, 29.

32. Lafley and Charan, "The Consumer is Boss," 122.

33. en.wikipedia.org/wiki/demographics_of_the_United_States

2

1. Kate Maddox, "Marketer of the Year: Dan Henson, VP-CMO, General Electric, Co.," *BtoB Magazine*, online at www.btobonline.com/apps/pbcs.dll/article?AID=/20071022/FREE/71022003/1068/best2007, October 22, 2007.

2. Joseph Pereira, "Toys 'R' Us Unwraps Plans for Expansion," *The Wall Street Journal*, May 22, 2008, B1.

3. Melanie Warner, "McDonald's' Push a Boon for Produce," *The Star Telegram*, February 26, 2005, C1.

4. Corporate Web site: www.benjerry.com, December 1, 2008.

5. Mark Gongloff, "Golden Arches Offer Shelter in Storm," *The Wall Street Journal*, July 23, 2008, C1; Suzanne Vranica, "Marketers Find Ways to Exploit Gas Prices," *The Wall Street Journal*, July 7, 2008, B5.

6. Corporate Web site: www.nike.com, December 5, 2007.

7. Sarah Butrymowicz and Jayne O'Donnell, "Malls Get Creative to Draw More Shoppers in Tough Economy," *USA Today*, www.usatoday.com, July 17, 2008; Store Review: Bass Pro Shops, www.flyfishing.about.com, December 1, 2008; Bass Pro Shops, www.wikipedia.com, December 1, 2008.

8. Julie Jargon, "New Leaf for Sara Lee, Kraft: Salads," *The Wall Street Journal*, March 26, 2007, A9.

9. John Brodie, "The Many Faces of Ralph Lauren," www.money.com, September 5, 2007.

10. Niraj Sheth, "India Liquor, Tobacco Firms Shift Tack," *The Wall Street Journal*, May 6, 2008, B8; Kounteya Sinha, "Surrogate Ads Luring Kids to Smoking," December 1, 2008, www.epaper.

timesofindia.com; "Surrogate Ads: I&B Asked to Take Action," December 1, 2008, www.ndtv.com.

3

1. Marianne M. Jennings, *Business Ethics*, 5th Ed. (Mason, Ohio: Thomson Higher Education, 2006), 5–6.

2. Based on Edward Stevens, *Business Ethics* (New York: Paulist Press, 1979). Used with permission of Paulist Press.

3. Anusorn Singhapakdi, Skott Vitell, and Kenneth Kraft, "Moral Intensity and Ethical Decision Making of Marketing Professionals," *Journal of Business Research*, 36, March 1996, 245–255; Ishmael Akaah and Edward Riordan, "Judgments of Marketing Professionals about Ethical Issues in Marketing Research: A Replication and Extension," *Journal of Marketing Research*, February 1989, 112–120. See also Shelby Hunt, Lawrence Chonko, and James Wilcox, "Ethical Problems of Marketing Researchers," *Journal of Marketing Research*, August 1984, 309–324; Kenneth Andrews, "Ethics in Practice," *Harvard Business Review*, September/October 1989, 99–104; Thomas Dunfee, Craig Smith, and William T. Ross, Jr., "Social Contracts and Marketing Ethics," *Journal of Marketing*, July 1999, 14–32; Jay Handleman and Stephen Arnold, "The Role of Marketing Actions with a Social Dimension: Appeals to the Institutional Environment," *Journal of Marketing*, July 1999, 33–48; and David Turnipseed, "Are Good Soldiers Good? Exploring the Link between Organizational Citizenship Behavior and Personal Ethics," *Journal of Business Research*, January 2002, 1–16.

4. "Corporate Employees Complete 11 Million Courses on Ethics and Compliance," *PR Newswire*, June 5, 2006.

5. Marc Gunther, "Will Social Responsibility Harm Business?" *The Wall Street Journal*, May 18, 2005, A2.

6. This section is adapted from Archie B. Carroll, "The Pyramid of Corporate Social Responsibility: Toward the Moral Management of Organizational Stakeholders," *Business Horizons*, July/August 1991, 39–48; see also Kirk Davidson, "Marketers Must Accept Greater Responsibilities," *Marketing News*, February 2, 1998, 6.

7. Remi Trudel and June Cotte, "Does Being Ethical Pay?" *The Wall Street Journal*, May 12, 2008, R4.

8. "Globally, Companies are Giving Back," *HR Magazine*, June 1, 2007, 30.

9. "Americans Seek More Responsibility from Companies," *Daytona Beach News Journal*, May 26, 2007, 3B.

10. www.unglobalcompact.org/participantsand stakeholders/index/htm (October 27, 2008).

11. "Secretary-General Opens Global Compact Leaders Summit as Business, Government, Civil Society Leaders Rally for Corporate Citizenship," UNESCAP Press Release, July 5, 2007, Press Release No. L/38/2007.

12. The AOL Abusive Conduct story is from: Michael Liedtke, "AOL Enters Settlement Over Cancellation Process," *Marketing News*, August 15, 2007, 14.

13. www.marketingpower.com. Accessed October 28, 2008.

14. "Marketing a Green Product," *Business Week Online*, March 5, 2007, 13.

15. Ibid.

16. Joe Nocera, "The Promise and Limits of Good Works," *International Herald Tribune*, August 9–10, 2008, 11–12.

17. "Its Not Easy Being Green," www.usbusiness-review.com (July–August 2008), 14–15.

18. "Easy but Green, Rider," *Marketing Magazine*, July 14, 2008, 29.

4

1. "TJX: Dressed to Kill For the Downturn," *Business Week*, October 27, 2008, 60.

2. J. Walker Smith, "A Single-Minded Marketplace," *Marketing Management*, July/August 2004, 52.

3. J. Walker Smith, "Make Time Worth It," *Marketing Management*, July/August 2005, 56.

4. "Family Structure," Child Trends Databank, accessed online, October 11, 2007, www.childtrendsdatabank.org/indicators/59FamilyStructure.cfm.

5. "WB – Statistics & Data," online at www.dol.gov/wb/stats/main.htm (accessed October 10, 2007); "Center for Women's Business Research: Key Facts About Women-Owned Businesses," online at www.cfwbr.org/facts/index.php (accessed October 10, 2007).

6. "Female Persuasion," *Marketing Management*, July/August 2004, 6.

7. Ibid.

8. "Coming of Age in Consumerdom," *American Demographics*, April 2004, 14.

9. Ibid.

10. Karen Akers, "Generation Y: Marketing to the Young and the Restless," *Successful Promotions*, January/February 2005, 33–38.

11. Ibid.

12. "Young, Rich, and Famous," *USA Today*, January 10, 2007, 6B, 7B.

13. Peter Francese, "The Changing Face of the U.S. Consumer," *Advertising Age*, July 7, 2008, online.

14. Louise Lee, "Love Those Boomers," *Business Week*, October 24, 2005, 94–101.

15. "Boomer Bust," *The Wall Street Journal*, October 21, 2008, A13.

16. Lee, "Love Those Boomers."

17. Robert Lee Hotz, "Cellphone Data Tracking Our Migration Patterns," *The Wall Street Journal*, June 10, 2008, A12.

18. "Manifest Destiny 3.0," *American Demographics*, September 2004, 29–34.

19. Francese, "The Changing Face of the U.S. Consumer."

20. "U.S. Buying Power by Race," *Marketing News*, July 15, 2004, 11.

21. "Minorities getting closer to the majority," CNN, online at www.cnn.com/2006/US/05/10/hispanics/index.html (accessed November 22, 2007).

22. Nick Leiber, "A New Entertainment Destination for Latinos," *Business Week*, November 16, 2007.

23. "A Multicultural Mecca," *American Demographics*, May 2003, S4–S7.

24. "Give Me Your Tired, Your Poor, Your Beloved Products," *Business 2.0*, October 2005, 29–30.

25. "Hispanic Radio Today," Arbitron, online at www.arbitron.com/study/hisprt.asp (accessed October 20, 2008).

26. "To Woo Gen Y, Marketers Push Culture, Not Language," *Brandweek*, January 1, 2007, 5.

27. "BAW: About Us," Tom Joyner Show, online at tomjoyner.com/site.aspx/misc/aboutus (accessed November 22, 2007); ABC Radio Network, online at abcradionetworks.com/press/2006releases/032006.pdf (accessed November 22, 2007; "Time Warner Cable Media Sales: BET Cable TV Advertising," Time Warner, online at www.cablemediasales.com/pages/nets/?cp=nets&sp=info&net=bet (accessed November 22, 2007).

28. "Dynamics of Changing Populations," Mediamark Research, Inc., online at www.magazine.org/Advertising_and_PIB/Ad_Categories_and_Demographics/; "Asian American Market Profile," online at www.magazine.org/content/files/market_profile_asian.pdf (accessed July 5, 2007).

29. U.S. Census Bureau, online at www.census.gov/Press-Release/www/releases/archives/facts_for_features_special_editions/006587.html (accessed November 22, 2007).

30. U.S. Census Bureau data, with projections by the authors.

31. "The Rich Get Richer and That's OK," *Business Week*, August 26, 2002, 90.

32. "The State," *Business Week*, July 18, 2005, 16.

33. Gretchen Morgenson, "Given a Shovel, Americans Dig Deeper Into Debt," *The New York Times*, July 20, 2008, online.

34. "NBER Makes it Official: Recession Started in December 2007," *The Wall Street Journal*, December 1, 2008, accessed online, blogs.wsj.com/economics/2008/12/01/nber-makes-it-official-recession-started-in-december-2007 (accessed September 16, 2009).

35. "At the Supermarket Checkout, Frugality Trumps Brand Loyalty," *The Wall Street Journal*, November 6, 2008, D1.

36. "Why Some Brands Cheer a Sour Economy," *Brandweek*, October 13, 2008, 5.

37. "Safety Agency Takes Action on Baby Gear," *The Wall Street Journal*, March 22, 2005, D1–D4.

38. S. Kovitch, "A Second Look at Regulation's Cost," *Regulation*, Summer 2004, 2–4; W. M. Crain and J. M. Johnson, "Determining Workplace Relations's Cost," *Regulation*, Fall 2004, 2–4.

39. "Home Economics," *Business Week*, March 14, 2005, 12.

5

1. William Wrigley Jr. Company, news release, July 2, 2007.

2. *Trade and American Jobs: The Impact of Trade on U.S. and State-Level Employment* (Washington: Business Roundtable), February 2007.

3. Ibid.

4. "Top U.S. Trade Partners," U.S. Department of Commerce, Census Bureau, Foreign Trade Division, International Trade Administration, October 2008.

5. "Globalization's Gains Come with a Price," *The Wall Street Journal*, May 24, 2007, A1, A12.

6. "Foreign Investors Face New Hurdles Across the Globe," *The Wall Street Journal*, July 6, 2007, A1, A7.

7. Theodore Levitt, "The Globalization of Markets," *Harvard Business Review*, May/June 1983, 92–100.

8. "Levi's Marketers Hope One Size Fits All," *The Wall Street Journal*, July 18, 2008, B7.

9. "Convenience Is a Dirty Word to These Italian Consumers," *Quirk's Marketing Research Review*, October 2006, 6.

10. "Gross national income per capita 2008, Atlas method and PPP," *World Development Indicators Database*, World Bank, October 7, 2009, online at siteresources.worldbank.org/DATASTATISTICS/Resources/GNIPC.pdf; "Gross national income 2008, Atlas method," *World Development Indicators Database*, World Bank, October 7, 2009, online at siteresources.worldbank.org/DATASTATISTICS/Resources/GNI.pdf.

11. "World's Most Expensive Cities," *CNNMoney.com*, June 18, 2007.

12. The China/India story is from: Anil K. Gupta and Haiyan Wang, "How to Get China and India Right," *The Wall Street Journal*, April 28–29, 2007, R9. Reprinted with permission of *The Wall Street Journal* © 2007 Dow Jones & Company, Inc. All Rights Reserved Worldwide.

13. "Doing Business 2008," The World Bank.

14. "The Trade Stimulus," *International Trade Administrator*, October 27, 2008, 1.

15. "Most Canadians, Americans Support NAFTA: Poll," *Xinhua News Agency*, October 1, 2007.

16. "Top U.S. Trading Partners," *Top U.S. Export Markets* (Washington: International Trade Association) Summer 2008, 4.

17. "Refighting NAFTA," *Business Week*, March 31, 2008, 56–59; also see: "Make the World Go Away," *Fortune*, February 4, 2008, 105–107.

18. "U.S. Central America-Dominican Republic Free Trade Agreement (CAFTA-DR) Analysis," (Washington: International Trade Association), Summer 2008, 12.

19. www.eurunion.org, accessed November 5, 2008.

20. "European Union's Kroes Says U.S. Criticism of Microsoft Ruling Is Unacceptable," *Associated Press Newswires*, September 19, 2007.

21. Jonathan Bensky, "World's Biggest Market: European Union Offers Great Opportunities for U.S. Companies, But There Are Also Plenty of Challenges," *Shipping Digest*, July 30, 2007.

22. www.sba.gov, accessed November 4, 2008.

23. www.fanchise.org, accessed December 5, 2005.

24. Kenneth Hein, "Emerging Markets Still Like U.S. Brands," *BrandWeek*, April 16, 2007, 4. Used by permission of Aegis Group, plc.; also see: "Best Global Brands," September 29, 2008, 52–57.

25. Peter Gumbel, "Big Mac's Local Flavor," *Fortune*, May 5, 2008, 115–121.

26. "Fad Marketing's Balancing Act," *Business Week*, August 6, 2007, 42.

27. Jane Lanhee Lee, "China Hurdle: Lack of Refrigeration," *The Wall Street Journal*, August 30, 2007, A7.

28. "100 Best Global Brands," *Business Week*, September 28, 2009, 50.

29. "Vietnam Denies Garment Dumping in U.S. Market," *Thai News Service*, October 1, 2007.

6

1. www.persil.com/persil_products/pfam_home/, February 2006; www.eu.pg.com/ourbrands/ariel. html, February 2006.

2. "Virtually Satisfied," *Marketing News*, October 15, 2008, 26.

3. Allen Weiss, Nicholas Lurie, and Deborah MacInnis, "Listening to Strangers: Whose Responses Are Valuable, How Valuable Are They, and Why?" *Journal of Marketing Research*, August 2008, 450–461.

4. Jonah Berger and Grainne Fitzsimons, "Dogs on the Street, Pumas on Your Feet: How Cues in the Environment Influence Product Evaluation and Choice," *Journal of Marketing Research*, February 2008, 1–14.

5. The section on categorization is adapted from: Roger Blackwell, Paul Miniard, and James Engel, *Consumer Behavior*, 10th Edition (Mason, Ohio: Cengage Learning), 2006, 132–133.

6. Jeffrey Inman and Russell Winer, "Impulse Buys," *The Wall Street Journal*, April 15, 1999, A1; David Silvera, Anne Lavack, and Fredric Kropp, "Impulse Buying: The Role of Affect, Social Influence, and Subjective Well-Being," *Journal of Consumer Research*, Vol. 25, Issue 1 (2008), 23–33.

7. Toyota ad, *Wired*, March, 2007, 72–73.

8. Ira Teinowitz, "Kellogg Move Bodes Ill for Ads to Kids," *Advertising Age*, June 18, 2007.

9. Lorenza Muñoz,"Selling Spanish TV to Ad Buyers," *Los Angeles Times*, May 15, 2007.

10. Bradley Johnson, "Mo' Money, Mo' Buyin'," *Advertising Age*, January 15, 2007, Vol. 78, Issue 3, 29.

11. "TJX: Dressed to Kill for the Downturn," *Business Week*, October 27, 2008, 60.

12. Ulrich Orth and Lynn Kahle, "Intrapersonal Variation in Consumer Susceptibility to Normative Influence: Toward a Better Understanding of Brand Choice Decisions," *Journal of Social Psychology*, August 8, 2008, 423–448.

13. Ibid.

14. Ronald Clark, James Zboja, and Ronald Goldsmith, "Status Consumption and Role-Relaxed Consumption: A Tale of Two Retail Consumers," *Journal of Retailing and Consumer Services*, January 2007, 45–59.

15. Katie Delahaye Paine, "How Do Blogs Measure Up? Forget Reach and Frequency. Success in Today's Marketplace Is Measured Not by How Broad Your Reach Is But by How Deep Your Network Is," *Communication World*, Sept–Oct 2007, Vol. 24, Issue 5, 30.

16. Rachel Dodes, "Bloggers Get Under the Tent," *The Wall Street Journal*, September 12, 2006, B1, B2.

17. Chenting See, Kevin Zheng Zhou, Nan Zhou, and Julie Juan Li, "Harmonizing Conflict in Husband-Wife Purchase Decision-Making: Perceived Fairness and Spousal Influence Dynamics," *Journal of the Academy of Marketing Science* (Fall 2008), 378–394; also see: Michel Laroche, Zhiyong Yang, Kim Chankon, and Marie-Odile Richard, "How Culture Matters in Children's Purchase Influence: A Multi-level Investigation," *Journal of the Academy of Marketing Science* (Spring 2007), 113–116.

18. Ibid.

19. Derek Gale, "Who's the Boss?" *Restaurants & Institutions*, February 1, 2007, Vol. 117, Issue 2, 50.

20. Jeanine Poggi, "Teen Queens; The Age Group's Spending Is on the Rise, Making It a Coveted—Albeit Fickle—Market," *WWD*, June 28, 2007, 86.

21. Karin Ekstrom, "Parental Consumer Learning or 'Keeping Up With Their Children'," *Journal of Consumer Behavior* (July/August 2007), 203–217.

22. Bureau of Labor Statistics, Consumer Expenditures Annual Reports: 2005, Census Bureau, www.bls.gov/ces/.

23. Stephanie Rosenbloom, "My Dad, American Inventor," *The New York Times*, August 16, 2007.

24. Nanette Byrnes, "Secrets of the Male Shopper," *Business Week*, online, www.businessweek.com/magazine/content/06_36/b399900I.htm, accessed August 17, 2007; also see: Xin He, Jeffrey Inman, and Vikas Mittal, "Gender Jeopardy in Financial Risk-Taking," *Journal of Marketing Research*, August 2008, 414–424.

25. Anil Mathur, George Moschis, and Euehun Lee, "A Longitudinal Study of the Effects of Life Style Status Changes on Changes in Consumer Preferences," *Journal of the Academy of Marketing Sciences*, Summer 2008, 234–246.

26. www.ampacet.com, December 28, 2007.

27. Laura Petrecca, "Axe Ads Turn Up the Promise of Sex Appeal," *USA Today*, April 17, 2007.

28. Joshua Rosenbaum, "Guitar Maker Looks for a New Key," *The Wall Street Journal*, February 11, 1998, B1, B6.

29. Elizabeth J. Wilson, "Using the Dollar-metric Scale to Establish the Just Meaningful Difference in Price," in 1987 AMA *Educators' Proceedings*, ed. Susan Douglas et al. (Chicago: American Marketing Association, 1987), 107.

30. Kenneth Hein, "Teens Schizophrenic About Their Brands: Millennials Have Complex Feelings About Brands Unless, of Course, It's Apple," *Brandweek*, June 18, 2007.

31. Press Release: "GE Announces Advancement in Incandescent Technology; New High-Efficiency Lamps Targeted for Market by 2010," February 23, 2007; Lloyd Alter, "GE announces High Efficiency Incandescent Light Bulbs. Why?" *Design & Architecture*, February 24, 2007, accessed online at www.treehugger.com/files/2007/02/ge_announces_hi.php, May 29, 2008.

32. Stephanie Thompson, "Cole Haan Fashions an Effort for Women," *Advertising Age*, August 25, 2003, 6.

33. www.cadillac.com, accessed October 25, 2008.

34. Jyothi Datta, "Aspartame: Bitter Truth in Artificial Sweeteners?" Mumbai, Oct. 3, www.thehindubusinessline.com/2005/10/04/stories/2005100404220300.htm, accessed September 14, 2007.

7

1. "2008 Marketing Priorities and Plans," *BtoB Magazine*, July 15, 2008, 25.

2. Michael D. Hutt and Thomas W. Speh, *Business Marketing Management: B2B*, 9e. (Cincinnati: Thomson, 2007) 4.

3. Patricia Riedman, "BtoB's Best Brands," *BtoB Magazine*, Special Issue, 2008, 21–25.

4. Hutt and Speh, 315.

5. Ibid.

6. Mary E. Morrison, "Industrial Buyers Shopping Online," *BtoB Magazine*, October 13, 2008, 19.

7. Karen J. Bannan, "10 Great Web Sites: Overview," *BtoB Magazine*, online, September 15, 2008.

8. "Survey Says! Recent BtoB Webcast Audience Poll Results," *BtoB Magazine*, November 10, 2008, 8.

9. NetGenesis, E-Metrics: Business Metrics for the New Economy, www.spss.com.

10. Morrison, 19.

11. Cade Metz, "RSS Tools," pcmag.com, December 30, 2003, accessed October 20, 2009.

12. "B2B Marketers Missing Out on Influencing Buyers Online," *Marketing Matters Newsletter*, Chicago: American Marketing Association, online, October 28, 2008.

13. "Disintermediation," marketingterms.com, accessed online at www.marketingterms.com/dictionary/disintermediation/.

14. Kate Maddox, "Marketers Look to Boost Customer Retention," *BtoB Magazine*, online, May 5, 2008.

15. Ibid. Reprinted with permission of Crane Communications.

16. "Office Depot Forms Alliance With Netbizz in Singapore," *BtoB Magazine*, online, August 13, 2008.

17. Steven Reinberg, "The Issue: DHL Turns to Rival UPS," *Business Week*, June 11, 2008, accessed www.businessweek.com/managing/content/Jun2008/ca20080611/101915.htm.

18. Erin White, "A Cheaper Alternative to Outsourcing: Choice Hotels and 1-800-Flowers Swap Call-Center Employees," *The Wall Street Journal*, April 10, 2006, B3.

19. Robert M. Morgan and Shelby D. Hunt, "The Commitment-Trust Theory of Relationship Marketing," *Journal of Marketing*, 58, no. 3 (1994): 23.

20. Ibid.

21. Gordon Fairclough, "GM's Chinese Partner Looms as a New Rival," *The Wall Street Journal*, April 20, 2007, A1.

22. Steve Butler, "B2B Exchanges Transaction Activity," *eMarketer*, online.

23. J. Lynn Lunsford, "Boeing Delays Dreamliner Delivery Again," *The Wall Street Journal*, April 10, 2008, B3.

24. Marshall Lager, "Listen Up," *Customer Relationship Management*, March 2007, 24–27.

25. Setting the Standard: Code of Ethics and Business Conduct. Office of Ethics and Business Conduct, Lockheed Martin Corporation, Bethesda, MD, October 2008.

26. "Right Channeling: Making Sure Your Best Customers Get Your Best Service," Right Now Technologies, online at www.rightnow.com/, June 3, 2008.

8

1. Jena McGregor, "At Best Buy, Marketing Goes Micro," *Business Week*, May 26, 2008, 52, 53.

2. Vanessa O'Connell, "Park Avenue Classic or Soho Trendy?" *The Wall Street Journal*, B1, B2, April 20, 2007.

3. Vanessa O'Connell, "Reversing Field, Macy's Goes Local," *The Wall Street Journal*, April 21, 2008, B1, B8.

4. Evan Bailyn, "Keeping It Simple: Marketing to Tweens on a Shoestring," www.mediapost.com, December 2, 2008.

5. Khanh T. L. Tran, "Retailing's Sweet Spot: Stores Look to Lure Millennial Generation," *wwd.com*, July 2, 2008.

6. Sarah Mahoney, "Study: Gen Y Shoppers Drawn To Greener Marketers," www.mediapost.com, September 21, 2007.

7. Jessica Sebor, "Y me," *Customer Relationship Management*, November 2006, 24–35.

8. Toni Whitt, "Boomers Rewrite Rules for Marketing," *Herald Tribune,* June 25, 2007, online at www.heraldtribune.com.

9. Emily Fromm, "Marketing to Women," *Brandweek*, October 4, 2004, 21–28.

10. Ross Kenneth Urken, "EA Sports' Ads Feature New Stars: John (and Jane) Q. Public," *The Wall Street Journal*, July 25, 2008, online.

11. Jennifer Waters, "Home Depot Woos Women with Concept Store Exuding 'Romance'," *The Wall Street Journal*, October 9, 2007, online.

12. "CoolStuffForDads.com, an Online Store Dedicated to Gifts for Dads, Continues to Add Great Products for Men," biz.yahoo.com, September 22, 2008.

13. Tom Ryan, "Targeting Male Grocery Shoppers," www.retailwire.com, June 4, 2007.

14. Francine Kizner, "Where the Rich Shop," www.entrepreneur.com, February 16, 2007.

15. "Luxury Brands: Marketing the Upscale During a Downturn," knowledge.wharton.upenn.edu/article.cfm?articleid=2091, November 13, 2008.

16. Constantine von Hoffman, "For Some Marketers, Low Income Is Hot," *Brandweek*, September 11, 2006, 6.

17. "The New Mainstream: How the Buying Habits of Ethnic Groups Are Creating a New American Identity," knowledge.wharton.upenn.edu/article.cfm?articleid=1270, November 15, 2005. Accessed June 9, 2008.

18. Laura Klepacki, "Ethnic Products Now Front and Center," www.retailwire.com, June 11, 2007.

19. "What's 'Online Marketing' in Spanish?" *RetailWire,* November 5, 2007.

20. "Baby Boomer Segmentation: Kids/No Kids," www.retailwire.com, February 2, 2007, online.

21. Dianne Hales, "What Your Car Says About You," *Parade*, May 15, 2005, 8.

22. Joseph Pereira, "New Exercise Targets Less-Than-Fit," *The Wall Street Journal*, February 1, 2007, B1, B9.

23. Deborah L. Vence, "Divide and Conquer," *Marketing News*, July 15, 2007, 15, 18.

24. Ann Zimmerman, "Home Depot Learns to Go Local," *The Wall Street Journal*, October 7, 2008, B1.

25. claritas.com, December 15, 2008.

26. George Stalk, Jr., "In Praise of the Heavy Spender," www.reportonbusiness.com, May 21, 2007, online.

27. Ellen Byron, "Aiming to Clean Up, P&G Courts Business Customers," *The Wall Street Journal*, January 26, 2007, B1, B2.

28. Barry Silverstein, "Trader Joe's: Quirky Mart," www.brandchannel.com, December 13, 2008; Christopher Palmeri, "Trader Joe's Recipe for Success," *BusinessWeek* February 21, 2008, online; "A Unique Grocery Store," http://eastontowncenter.com, December 13, 2008.

29. "Targeting Wal-Mart's Core Customer Segments," www.retailwire.com, April 2, 2008.

30. "How Teen Eretailer Tripled Revenue by Allowing Consumers to Select What Email Content They Really Want," www.marketingsherpa.com, June 28, 2007.

31. Dianna Dilworth, "AT&T's New Multichannel Work Targets Young, On-the-Go Crowd," www.dmnews.com, September 18, 2007.

32. Ellen Byron, "Can a Re-Engineered Kleenex Cure a Brand's Sniffles?" *The Wall Street Journal*, January 22, 2007, B1.

33. Sonia Reyes, "Can Frozen Treats Sell Outside the Freezer Aisle?" *Brandweek*, March 26, 2007, 16.

34. Sandra Jones, "Sears Steps Back in Time to Go Forward," *Chicago Tribune*, March 12, 2007.

35. Geoff Colvin, "Selling P&G," *Fortune*, September 17, 2007, 163–169.

36. Jenny McTaggart, "Taking a Bite Out of Baggers," *Brandweek*, June 27, 2005, 42–45.

37. Ibid.

38. Gary McWilliams, "Not Copying Wal-Mart Pays Off for Grocers," *The Wall Street Journal*, June 6, 2007, B1, B5.

9

1. Michael Fielding, "A Clean Slate," *Marketing News*, May 1, 2007, 9–10.

2. "The Science of Desire," *BusinessWeek*, June 5, 2006, 104.

3. Raymond R. Burke, "Virtual Shopping: Breakthrough in Marketing Research," *Harvard Business Review*, March/April 1996, 120–131.

4. Ellen Byron, "A Virtual View of the Store Aisle," *The Wall Street Journal*, October 3, 2007, B1, B12.

5. Kira Signer and Andy Korman, "One Billion and Growing," *Quirk's Marketing Research Review*, July/August 2006, 62–67.

6. Ibid.

7. Conversation with Craig Stevens, Senior VP E-Rewards, based upon company research (November 2, 2007); also see "Market Research," *Marketing News*, September 15, 2007, 16.

8. Ibid.

9. Karl Feld, "Do You Know Where Your Data Came From?" *Quirk's Marketing Research Review*, November 2007, 24–31.

10. Suzanne Vranica, "P&G Plunges into Social Networking," *The Wall Street Journal*, January 8, 2007, B4.

11. Conversation with the author from Jerry Thomas, *CEO Decision Analyst*, September 20, 2005. This firm has one of the largest Internet panels in the world; Carol-Ann Morgan, "Using the Focus Group in Market Research," online at www.b2binternational.com/whitepapers.html; "Online Focus Groups and Discussion Boards," online at www.efocus.com/faq.html, accessed October 22, 2007.

12. Gregory S. Heist, "Beyond Brand Building," *Quirk's Marketing Research Review*, July/August 2007, 62–67.

13. "Intelliseek to Provide AOL with Daily Blog Trend Analysis," *PR Newswire*, October 17, 2005; Justin Martin, "Blogging For Dollars: How Would You Like to Survey 20 Million Consumers in Two Minutes?" *Fortune*, December 12, 2005, 178; "Intelliseek's Enhanced BlogPulse Offers Data-Rich Blog Profiles," *PR Newswire*, July 21, 2005.

14. Carl McDaniel and Roger Gates, *Marketing Research*, 6th ed. (Mason, OH: Thomson South-Western, 2005).

15. Products and Solutions: InfoScan Tracking Service, Information Resources, Inc., online at www.usa.infores.com/ProductsSolutions/AllProducts/AllProductsDetail/tabid/159/productid/83/Default.aspx, accessed December 1, 2008.

16. Stephanie Hughes and Fred Beasley, "An Examination of the Existence and Usage of Competitive Intelligence in Professional Sports," *Journal of Competitive Intelligence and Management*, 2007, 108, online at www.scip.org/jcim/4.hughes.6.101_a_.pdf.

10

1. "Coke, Pepsi to Sell Drinks with Stevia," *The Atlantic Journal-Constitution*, online, December 18, 2008.

2. Julie Jargon, "Campbell's Chief Looks for Splash of Innovation," *The Wall Street Journal*, May 30, 2008, B8.

3. "Kool-Aid Announces New Products and Better-For-You Brand Direction," Yahoo! Finance, May 27, 2008.

4. Vanessa L. Facenda, "Procter Dishes Out 3-Tiered Dawn Attack," *Brandweek*, September 24, 2007, 4.

5. Vanessa L. Facenda, "In Search of More Growth, P&G's Febreze Hits the Road," *Brandweek*, August 6, 2007, 6.

6. Al Ries, "The Pitfalls of Megabranding," *Advertising Age*, August 4, 2008, online.

7. Ellen Byron "To Refurbish Its Image, Tiffany Risks Profits," *The Wall Street Journal*, January 10, 2007, A1.

8. Nirmalya Kumar and Jan-Benedict E. M. Steenkamp, "Premium Store Brands: The Hottest Trend in Retailing," www.marketingprofs.com, March 20, 2007.

9. Elaine Wong, "Retailers Rally Behind Their 'Captive Brands'," *Brandweek.com*, September 29, 2008.

10. Elaine Wong, "Mr. Clean Finds Fresh Smell by Teaming with Febreze," *Brandweek*, August 11, 2008, 14.

11. Deborah L. Vence, "Product Enhancement," *Marketing News*, May 1, 2005, 19.

12. Brenda Cotter, "Maximize the Legal Value of Your Brands," *Brandweek*, August 22, 2005, 27.

13. Ibid.

14. "Apple, Google on trademark protection circuit," *The Online Reporter*, August 19, 2006, Issue 505, 8.

15. Stacy Perman, "Wolfgang Puck vs. Wolfgang Zweiner," *BusinessWeek*, May 30, 2008, online.

16. Jim Edwards, "Brand Defense," *Brandweek*, August 25–September 1, 2008, S1, S2.

17. Deborah Ball, "The Perils of Packaging: Nestlé Aims for Easier Openings" *The Wall Street Journal*, November 17, 2005, B1.

18. "Environmentally Responsible Packaging: Convenience vs. Conscience," www.retailwire.com, April 30, 2007.

19. Alissa Walker, "Spin the Bottle," *Fast Company*, June 2008, 54.

20. Ted Mininni, "Packaging That Works for the Planet," *Brandweek*, April 23, 2007, 20.

21. George Anderson, "Consumers Want More/Different Info on Labels," www.retailwire.com, July 17, 2008.

11

1. Reena Jana, "In Data," *BusinessWeek*, September 22, 2008, 48.

2. Jena McGregor, "The World's Most Innovative Companies," *BusinessWeek*, May 2007, online.

3. Reena Jana, "In Data," *BusinessWeek*, September 22, 2008, 48.

4. Vanessa L. Facenda, "Oh Boy! Disney Sees Market for Pre-Teen Fragrances," *Brandweek*, July 23, 2007, 5.

5. Melanie Warner, "P&G's Chemistry Test," *Fast Company*, July/August 2008, 71.

6. James B. Kelleher, "Harley-Davidson Fights Changing Market with Appeals to Blacks, Hispanics," *Target Market News*, online, March 15, 2006; Clifford Krauss, "Women, Hear Them Roar," *New York Times*, July 25, 2007.

7. Renee Hopkins Callahan, Gwen Ishmael, and Leyla Nomiranian, "The Case for In-The-Box Innovation," Innovation Brochure, Arlington, TX: Decision Analysts, 2005.

8. Melanie Warner, "P&G's Chemistry Test," *Fast Company*, July/August 2008, 71.

9. Geoff Colvin, "Here It Is. Now, You Design It!" *Fortune*, May 26, 2008, 34.

10. Jeff Jarvis, "The Buzz from Starbucks Customers," *Business Week*, April 28, 2008, 42, 44.

11. Ibid.

12. David Kirkpatrick, "Innovation Do's and Don'ts," *Fortune*, September 6, 2004, 240.

13. Salvatore Parise, Patricia J. Guinan, and Bruce Weinberg, "The Secrets of Marketing In a Web 2.0 World," *The Wall Street Journal*, December 15, 2008, R4. Used by permission.

14. Chris Pentilla, "Big Ideas," *Entrepreneur*, March 2007, 62.

15. Allison Enright, "P&G Looks Outside for Innovative Solutions," *Marketing News*, March 1, 2007, 20–21.

16. Tom Ryan, "Finding Sources of Innovation," *RetailWire*, July 18, 2008, online.

17. Ibid.

18. John Karolefski, "CPG Matters: P&G Changes Rules for Product Development," *RetailWire*, February 19, 2008, online.

19. Joseph Weber, Stanley Holmes, and Christopher Palmeri, "'Mosh Pits' of Creativity," *Business Week*, November 7, 2005, 98–100.

20. Andrew Marton, "2006: A Face Odyssey," *Fort Worth Star-Telegram*, February 16, 2006, E1, E8.

21. Pete Engardio, "Scouring the Planet for Brainiacs," *Business Week*, October 11, 2004, 106.

22. Allison Enright, "P&G Looks Outside for Innovative Solutions," *Marketing News*, March 1, 2007, 20–21.

23. Tom Ryan, "Crowdsourcing: Power to the People," *RetailWire*, November 20, 2008, online.

24. Mike Beirne, "The Light Brigade," *Brandweek*, June 20, 2008.

25. Amy Chozick, "For Beverage Industry in Japan, New Drink Is Breath of Fresh Air," *The Wall Street Journal*, December 13, 2006, B1, B3.

26. "PG.com—All P&G Products," Proctor & Gamble, online at pg.com/en_US/products/all_products/index.shtml, accessed October 20, 2008.

27. Jena McGregor, "GE Reinventing Tech for the Emerging World," *Business Week*, April 28, 2008, 68.

28. Jenny Mero, "John Deere's Farm Team," *Fortune*, April 14, 2008, 121, 126. Reprinted with permission.

29. Robert Scoble, "PassionPlay," *Fast Company*, November 2008, 90.

30. Kevin J. Clancy and Peter C. Krieg, "Product Life Cycle: A Dangerous Idea," *Brandweek*, March 1, 2004, 26.

31. "Looking for Ways to Replace CD Sales in a Flash," *Retailing Today*, February 11, 2008, 14.

32. Ronald J. Baker, *Pricing on Purpose: Creating and Capturing Value* (Hoboken, NJ: John Wiley & Sons, Inc., 2006) 338.

12

1. "Employment Projections: 2006–16," U.S. Department of Labor, online at www.bls.gov/news.release/ecopro.toc.htm, accessed October 20, 2008.

2. Peter Sanders, "Takin' Off the Ritz—a Tad," *The Wall Street Journal*, June 23, 2008, B1.

3. Valarie A. Zeithaml, Mary Jo Bitner, and Dwayne Gremler, *Services Marketing* (New York: McGraw-Hill, 2006).

4. Ibid.

5. Much of the material in this section is based on Christopher H. Lovelock and Jochen Wirtz, *Services Marketing*, 5th ed. (Upper Saddle River, NJ: Prentice Hall, 2004); Christian Gronroos, *Service Management and Marketing: Customer Management in Service Competition*, 3rd ed. (Hoboken, NJ: John Wiley & Sons, Inc., 2007).

6. Women's Swimsuits on Lands' End, online at www.landsend.com, accessed November 17, 2008.

7. Lovelock and Wirtz, *Services Marketing*, 5th ed.; Gronroos, *Service Management and Marketing: Customer Management in Service Competition*, 3rd ed. (Hoboken, NJ: John Wiley & Sons, Inc., 2007).

8. Ibid.

9. Much of the material in this section is based on Leonard L. Berry and A. Parasuraman, *Marketing Services* (New York: Free Press, 1991), 132–150.

10. Anne Fisher, "Happy Employees, Loyal Employees," *Money*, online, June 12, 2006.

11. Carmine Gallo, "Bringing Passion to Starbucks, Travelocity," *Business Week*, January 9, 2008, online.

13

1. "Pepsi, Starbucks Teaming Up," *Supermarket News*, October 31, 1994, 31; Starbucks Annual Report, 2006.

2. Betsy McKay, "Smaller Brands Hitch Ride with Coke Distributors," *The Wall Street Journal*, January 29, 2007, B1, B2.

3. Eric Newman, "Red Bull, Meet Black Bunny," *Brandweek*, February 25, 2008, accessed online July 22, 2008.

4. Lynnley Browning, "Do-It-Yourself Logos for Proud Scion Owners," *The New York Times*, March 24, 2008, accessed online March 24, 2008.

14

1. "2006 Ford Mustang Pricing and Information," Edmunds, online at www.edmunds.com/new/2006/ford/mustang/100613439/optionsresults.html?action=2&tid=edmunds.n.options.ntmv.1.1.Ford, accessed January 2006.

2. Much of this section is based on material adapted from *21st Century Logistics: Making Supply Chain Integration a Reality*, by Donald J. Bowersox, David J. Closs, and Theodore P. Stank, Council of Logistics Management, Oak Brook, IL.

3. Much of this and the following sections is based on material adapted from the edited volume, *Supply Chain Management: Processes, Partnerships, Performance*, Douglas M. Lambert (Ed.), 2004, Supply Chain Management Institute, Sarasota, FL.

4. Chaman L. Jain and Mark Covas, "Thinking about Tomorrow," *The Wall Street Journal*, July 7, 2008, R10.

5. Julie Schlosser, "Just Do It," *Fortune*, December 13, 2004, online at www.fortune.com.

6. Carlita Vitzthum, "Just-in-Time Fashion," *The Wall Street Journal*, May 18, 2001, B1; Julie Creswell, "Confessions of a Fashion Victim," *Fortune*, December 10, 2001, 48; www.zara.com, February 2006.

7. Ben Worthen, "Weak Links in the Food (Supply) Chain," *The Wall Street Journal*, June 24, 2008, B5.

8. www.amazon.com, February 2006.

9. Alien Technology, online at www.alientechnology.com/tags/index.php, accessed November 17, 2008.

10. Ibid.

15

1. "Retail Industry Indicators 2007," National Retail Federation, online at www.nrf.com, accessed December 27, 2007.

2. Bureau of Labor Statistics, "Industry at a Glance: NAICS 42–45, Wholesale and Retail Trade," online at www.bls.gov, February 2006.

3. "Retail Industry Indicators 2007."

4. U.S. Census Bureau, *Monthly Retail Trade Report*, 2004; Betty W. Su, "The U.S. Economy to 2012: Signs of Growth," *Monthly Labor Review*, February 2006, 127:2, online at www.bls.gov.

5. "Walmart.com: Save Money. Live Better," Wal-Mart, online at www.walmart.com, accessed October 20, 2008.

6. David Moin, "High-End Opportunity for Outlets," *Women's Wear Daily*, April 12, 2008, 10.

7. "Restaurant Trendmapper," *National Restaurant Association*, online at www.restaurant.org/trendmapper, accessed October 20, 2008.

8. Gene G. Marcial, "Vending Machines Are Learning to Love Plastic," *Business Week*, August 13, 2007, online.

9. Aili McConnon, "The Va Va Vooming of Vending Machines," *Business Week*, January 22, 2008, online.

10. Avon Products, "Meet Mark," online at www.meetmark.com, accessed October 20, 2008.

11. Carol Krol, "DMA Report Predicts Spending Increases," *BtoB*, November 12, 2007, 3.

12. Daniel R. Shiman, "An Economic Approach to the Regulation of Direct Marketing," April 6, 2006, online at www.law.indiana.edu/fclj/pubs/v58/no2/Shiman.pdf, accessed October 30, 2007.

13. Laura Novak, "For-Profit Crusade Against Junk Mail," *The New York Times*, September 6, 2007, online.

14. Jeffrey Ball, "In Digital Era, Marketers Still Prefer a Paper Trail," *The Wall Street Journal*, October 16, 2009, A13.

15. "Dell Solutions for Large Business," Dell, online at www.dell.com/content/default.aspx?c=us&cs=555&l=en&ref=hs&s=biz, accessed October 20, 2008.

16. Walter S. Mossberg and Katherine Boehret, "Where to Find a Famous Look," *The Wall Street Journal*, November 8, 2006, D3.

17. Leigh Buchanan, "Battle of the Network All-Stars," *Inc.*, July 2008, 32.

18. McDonald's Corporation, *Inside the U.S. Franchising Fact Sheet*, www.mcdonalds/corp/franchise/faqs.html, January 2006.

19. "Bluefly—Designer Clothing, Handbags, Shoes & Accessories," Bluefly, online at www.bluefly.com, accessed October 20, 2008.

20. "Chicago Food Pizza Restaurants Gift Certificates at The Best of Chicago.com," The Best of Chicago, online at www.thebestofchicago.com; "Fridgedoor," Fridgedoor, online at www.Fridgedoor.com, accessed October 20, 2008.

21. Janet Adamy, "Why Wendy's Finds Vanilla So Exciting," *The Wall Street Journal*, April 6, 2007, B1, B2.

22. Vanessa O'Connell, "Macy's Plans to Open FAO Schwarz Toy Boutiques in Its Stores," *The Wall Street Journal*, May 16, 2008, B1.

23. Khanh T.L. Tran, "Levi's Pops Up at American Rag," *Women's Wear Daily*, April 22, 2008, 18.

24. Calmetta Y. Coleman, "Kohl's Retail Racetrack," *The Wall Street Journal*, March 13, 2001, B1.

25. "USA Technologies: ePort," *USA Technologies*, online at www.usatech.com/eport/index.php; "VeriSign Enables Coca-Cola Vending Machine Purchases via Mobile Phones," VeriSign, online at press.verisign.com/easyir/custmrel.do?easyirid=AFC0FF0DB5C560D3&version=live&prid=181452&releasejsp=custom_97, accessed October 20, 2008.

26. Cate T. Corcoran. "Fashion's New Frontier: Shopping Via Cell Phone Anywhere and Anytime," *Women's Wear Daily,* July 14, 2009, 1, 8.

16

1. Stuart Elliot, "Subway's New Campaign," *New York Times*, February 22, 2003, online; Tim Smart and James Bock, "What Sticks . . . And What Doesn't," *U.S. News & World Report*, January 29, 2007.

2. Kim Hart, "A Flashy Facebook Page at a Cost to Privacy," *The Washington Post*, June 12, 2008, www.washingtonpost.com, accessed February 2008; www.allfacebook.com/2009/facebook-privacy, accessed February 2009; Ralph Gross and Alessandro Acquisti, "Information Relevation and Privacy in Online Social Networks (The Facebook Case)," *ACM Workshop on Privacy in the Electronic Society*, November 7, 2007.

3. prweek.com/news/news_story.cfm?ID=239635&site=3, and prweek.com/news/news_story.cfm?ID=239635&site=3), accessed January 2006.

4. Simona Covel, "Bag Borrow or Steal Lands the Role of a Lifetime," *The Wall Street Journal*, May 27, 2008, online.

5. Joanna Ramsey, "Sephora Aims to Build On Customer Training Event," *Women's Wear Daily*, May 27, 2008, 11.

6. Ellen Byron, "An Old Dice Game Catches On Again, Pushed by P&G," *The Wall Street Journal*, January 30, 2007, A1, A13.

7. "In An Absolut World," Absolut Vodka, online at www.absolut.com/iaaw, accessed October 20, 2008.

8. Jeremy Mullman, "Breaking with Bottle Fires Up Absolut Sales," *Advertising Age*, February 18, 2008.

9. Stuart Elliott, "In an 'Absolut World,' a Vodka Could Use the Same Ads for More Than 25 Years," *The New York Times*, April 27, 2007.

10. "About," Technorati, online at www.technorati.com/about, accessed October 20, 2008.

11. State of the Blogosphere 2008 Technorati, accessed February 2009.

12. Tania Ralli. "Brand Blogs Capture the Attention of Some Companies," *New York Times*, October 25, 2005, C6.

13. "Blogs Can Offer a Big Advantage to Brands—If They're Honest," *New Media Age*, March 23, 2006, 15.

14. www.philips.com.

15. Ibid.

16. The AIDA concept is based on the classic research of E. K. Strong, Jr., as theorized in *The Psychology of Selling and Advertising* (New York: McGraw-Hill, 1925) and "Theories of Selling," *Journal of Applied Psychology*, 9 (1925): 75–86.

17. Thomas E. Barry and Daniel J. Howard, "A Review and Critique of the Hierarchy of Effects in Advertising," *International Journal of Advertising*, 9 (1990): 121–135.

18. Lauren A. E. Schuker, "'Kung Fu Panda' Shows Sequel Potential," *The Wall Street Journal*, June 9, 2008, B9.

17

1. Bradley Johnson, "Global Marketers," December 2008, Ad Age DataCenter, http://www.adage.com, December 8, 2008.

2. "Ad Industry Jobs," Ad Age DataCenter, http://adage.com, accessed February 2009.

3. "Leading National Advertisers," *Advertising Age,* June 23, 2008, online at http://adage.com, accessed September 2008.

4. Natalie Zmuda, "What Went into the Updated Pepsi Logo" *Advertising Age*, October 27, 2008, http://adage.com, accessed February 2009; Natalie Zmuda, "Pepsi, Coke Try to Outdo Each Other with Rays of Sunshine," *Advertising Age*, January 19, 2009, http://adage.com, accessed February 2009; Jim Edwards, "Pepsi's New $1 Million Logo Looks Like Old Diet Pepsi Logo," *BNET Industries*, October 27, 2008, online at http://industry.bnet.com/advertising/1000270.

5. Michael R. Solomon, *Consumer Behavior*, 6th ed. (Upper Saddle River, NJ: Prentice Hall, 2004), 275.

6. Tom Duncan, *Integrated Marketing Communications* (Burr Ridge, IL: McGraw-Hill, 2002), 257.

7. "Leading National Advertisers."

8. Alex Berenson, "Drug Approved. Is Disease Real?" *The New York Times*, January 14, 2008, A1.

9. "SoBe Lizards Take Manhattan by Storm: Unleashing SoBe Life Water Thrillicious Movement in Times Square," *PR Newswire*, February 27, 2008.

10. Laura Q. Hughes and Wendy Davis, "Revival of the Fittest," *Advertising Age*, March 12, 2001, 18–19.

11. Geoffrey Fowler, "For P&G in China, It's Wash, Rinse, Don't Repeat," *The Wall Street Journal*, April 7, 2006, B.

12. Matthew Futterman and Suzanne Vranica, "NBC Super Bowl Ads to Cost $3 Million," *The Wall Street Journal*, May 6, 2008.

13. Gergana Koleva, "Don't Buy It," *MarketWatch*, January 24, 2008, online at www.yahoo.com/banking-budgeting/article/104293/Don%27t-Buy-It, accessed September 30, 2009; Suzanne Vranica, "TV-Ad Test to Show If Less Is More; NBC Universal's Trial Run Will Measure Effectiveness of Fewer Commercials," *The Wall Street Journal*, April 5, 2006, B3; Maria Aspan, "TiVo Shifts to Help Companies It Once Threatened," *The New York Times*, December 10, 2007.

14. Suzanne Vranica, "Latest Pitch Is a Show Within an Ad," *The Wall Street Journal*, May 30, 2008, online.

15. "New Tide Detergent Tied to 'Project Runway,'" *MSNBC*, August 28, 2008, online at www.msnbc.msn.com/id/26394974/ns/business-media_biz/, accessed September 30, 2009.

16. "TNS Media Intelligence Forecast," TNS Media Intelligence, January 7, 2008, online at www.tns-mi.com/news/01072008.htm.

17. Brian Morrissey, "Web Ad Spend to Diversify," *Advertising Age*, October 11, 2007, online.

18. David Ho, "Advertisers Ditch Pop-Ups for New Tricks," *Atlanta Journal-Constitution*, December 4, 2005, C-3.

19. M2 PRESSWIRE, January 30, 2008.

20. Stuart Elliot, "Science Blogs as a Vehicle for Upscale Ads," *The New York Times*, January 10, 2006, C2.

21. John Gaudiosi, "Mountain Dew Makes MMO More Than Just a Game," *Advertising Age*, January 28, 2008, 21.

22. Andrew LaValle, "Start-Ups Find Revenue Source on Hold," *The Wall Street Journal*, June 11, 2008, B9.

23. Christopher Lawton, "Videogame Ads Attempt Next Level," *The Wall Street Journal*, July 25, 2005, B-6; "Video Game Advertising Gets a Boost," *USA Today*, December 16, 2004, B-1; Derek Sooman, "World's First Video Game Advertising Network," TechSpot.com, October 20, 2004, online; "Massive Incorporated: Video Game Advertising," *Microsoft*, online at www.massiveincorporated.com, accessed January 2006.

24. Paul Korzeniowski, "Technology News: Wireless: Cell Phones Emerge as New Advertising Medium," *ECT News Network*, online at www.technewsworld.com/story/46630.html, accessed October 21, 2008; "Agencias - Media Planning Instala En Barcelona La Primera Lona Con Bluethooth De Europa," online at www.marketingdirecto.com/noticias/noticia.php?idnoticia=16532, accessed January 2006.

25. Emily Steel, "Online TV Ads No Longer an Afterthought," *The Wall Street Journal*, May 20, 2008, B9.

26. Andrew Hampp, "Cross-Platform Ads: What's Working?" *Advertising Age*, June 26, 2008, online.

27. Stephanie Kang, "BMW Ran Risk with Silent Role in Mockumentary," *The Wall Street Journal*, June 20, 2008, online.

28. Geoff Williams, "Top 10 Successful Marketing Stunts" *Entrepreneur*, July 20, 2006, online.

29. Adam Bluestein, "Prime-Time Exposure: How Companies Can Make a Splash in the Big-Money World of TV Product Placement—Without Spending a Dime," *Inc.*, March 2008, 66, online at www.sourcewatch.org/index.php?title=Product_placement, accessed June 23, 2008; Kris Oser, "How a Product Placement Strategy Worked for Yahoo," *Advertising Age*, January 31, 2005, http://adage.com/latestnews; money.howstuffworks.com/ product-placement.htm; "Product Placement Spending in Media 2005," www.pqmedia.com, accessed January 2006.

30. Sponsorship Spending; IEG Sponsorship; www.sponsorship.com, accessed February 2009.

31. "Information on Select Cause Marketing Campaigns," Breast Cancer Action, online at www.thinkbeforeyoupink.org/Pages/InfoMktgCampaigns.html, accessed October 21, 2008; *Business in the Community*, online at www.bitc.org.uk/resources/research/research_publications/corp_survey_3.html, accessed January 2006.

32. "PlayStation.com," Sony Computer Entertainment America, online at www.playstation.com, accessed December 2007.

33. Gavin O'Malley, "CBS Puts CSI Miami Twist Online," *MediaPost*, November 16, 2005, online at http://publications.mediapost.com; "Adverblog: Integrated marketing Archives," *AdverBlog*, online at www.adverblog.com/archives/cat_integrated_marketing.htm, accessed January 2006.

34. "Blogs Can Offer a Big Advantage to Brands—If They're Honest," *New Age Media*, March 23, 2006, 15.

35. David E. Gumpert, "Convincing Consumers Your Food Is Safe," *Business Week,* July 14, 2008, online.

18

1. http://.promomagazine.com, October 2008 report.

2. Brian Steinberg, "Valassis-Advo Fracas Puts a Focus on Cash Cow," *The Wall Street Journal*, September 11, 2006, B5.

3. www.cms.inmar.com/newsandevents; Find/SVP, "Cut It Out: Coupons Are on an Upswing," online at http://www.forbes.com, accessed January 2006.

4. www.kroger.com; Internet Coupons link at www.kroger.upons.com.

5. Bruce Mohl, "Retailers Simplify the Rebate Process," *Boston Globe*, November 7, 2004; FTC Consumer Alert, "Taking the 'Bait' Out of Rebates," online at www.ftc.gov/bcp/conline/pubs/alerts/rebatealrt.shtm, accessed December 3, 2007.

6. "E-Commerce Times: E-Business Means Business," *ECT News Network*, online at www.ecommercetimes.com, accessed January 2008.

7. "The New Starbucks Duetto Visa: Wake Up and Smell the Plastic," CreditCards.com, online at www.creditcards.com/credit-card-news/credit-card-reward-points-starbucks-duetto-visa-1273.php, accessed October 21, 2008; "Which Starbucks CreditCard Should You Get?" www.askmrcreditcard.com, online at www.askmrcreditcard.com/starbucksduettovisa.html, accessed October 21, 2008.

8. Matthew Haeberle, "Loyalty Is Dead: Great Experiences, Not Price, Will Create Loyal Customers," *Chain Store Age*, January 2004, 17.

9. "Grocers' Use of E-Mail Growing," Promo P&I, August 2005, online at http://promomagazine.com, accessed January 2006.

10. Peter Sanders, "Starwood's Web Log Caters to Loyalty," *The Wall Street Journal*, April 12, 2006, B3.

11. Lafayette Jones, "Ethnic Product Sampling: The Hidden Opportunity," *Retail Merchandiser*, August 2001, 45; Tim Parry, "Sampling—Teaching Tools," *PROMO Magazine*, online at http://promomagazine.com, accessed January 2006.

12. "Dunkin' Donuts Targets Health Clubs with Sampling Program," *PROMO Xtra*, December 28, 2005, online at http://promomagazine.com, accessed January 2006.

13. Industry report, October 2008, *PROMO Magazine;* http://promomagazine.com, accessed February 2009.

14. Deborah Ball, "As Vodka Sales Skyrocket, Many Newcomers Pour In," *The Wall Street Journal*, A1, A8.

15. "Point-of-Purchase: $17 Billion," *PROMO Magazine*, October 29, 2001, 3; "In Praise of Promotion," *PROMO Xtra*, online at http://promomagazine.com, accessed January 2006.

16. Anne Hollard, "MarketingSherpa: Search Marketing & At-Work Coupon Campaigns: Redemption Rate Data & 4 Useful Hotlinks," MarketingSherpa, online at www.marketingsherpa.com/article.html?ident=29788, accessed October 21, 2008.

17. "Internet," CMS, online at www.coupon-infonow.com/Couponing/Internet.cfm, accessed August 23, 2007.

18. Rosemary Feitelberg, "Kors Ringing Up Sales On Trunk Show Circuit," *Women's Wear Daily*, May 21, 2008.

19. Michael Beverland, "Contextual Influences and the Adoption and Practice of Relationship Selling in a Business-to-Business Setting: An Exploratory Study," *Journal of Personal Selling & Sales Management*, Summer 2001, 207; Gabriel R. Gonzalez, K. Douglas Hoffman, and Thomas N. Ingram, "Improving Relationship Selling through Failure Analysis and Recovery Efforts: A Framework and Call to Action," *Journal of Personal Selling & Sales Management*, Winter 2005, 57.

20. Catherine Seda, "The Meet Market," *Entrepreneur*, August 2004, 68; Jim Dickie, "Is Social Networking an Overhyped Fad or a Useful Tool?" *Destination CRM*, January 21, 2005; Kristina Dell, "What Are Friends For?" *Time*, September 21, 2004; Media Releases, online at www.linkedin.com, accessed December 3, 2007; "About," www.linkedin.com/static?key=company_info, accessed November 21, 2008.

21. B. Weitz, S. Castleberry, and J. Tanner, *Selling* (Burr Ridge, IL: McGraw-Hill/Irwin, 2004), 198–201.

22. "Effective Business Presentation—Sales Presentation—Effective Presentation Skill," *Nielsen Business Media*, online at www.presentations.com.

23. U.S. Senate, www.senate.gov/reference/reference_index_subjects/lobbying.vrd.htm; Conor McGrath, "Grass Roots Lobbying: Marketing Politics and Policy 'Beyond the Beltway,'" *Elections on the Horizon: Marketing Politics to the Electorate in the USA and UK*, March 15, 2004, accessed February 2009; Robert J. Samuelson, "Lobbying Is Democracy in Action," *Newsweek*, December 22, 2008, online at www.newsweek.com, accessed February 2009.

24. Kathleen Cholewka, "E-Market Stats," *Sales & Marketing Management*, September 2001, 21; Jamie Smith Hopkins, "Corporations Podcast Their Marketing Nets," *Baltimore Sun*, December 11, 2005.

19

1. Franziska Volckner, "The Dual Role of Price: Decomposing Consumers' Reactions to Price," *Journal of the Academy of Marketing Science*, Fall 2008, 359–377.

2. Ibid.

3. Roland Rust, Christine Moorman, and Peter R. Dickson, "Getting Return on Quality: Revenue Expansion, Cost Reduction, or Both?" *Journal of Marketing*, October 2002, 7–24.

4. Tammo H. A. Bijmolt, Harald J. Van Heerde, and Rik G. M. Pieters, "New Empirical Generalizations on the Determinants of Price Elasticity," *Journal of Marketing Research*, May 2005, 141–156; Christian Homburg, Wayne Hoyer, and Nicole Koschate, "Customers' Reactions to Price Increases: Do Customer Satisfaction and Perceived Motive Fairness Matter?" *Journal of the Academy of Marketing Science*, Winter 2005,

35–49; Gadi Fibich, Arieh Gavious, and Oded Lowengart, "The Dynamics of Price Elasticity of Demand in the Presence of Reference Price Effects," *Journal of the Academy of Marketing Science*, Winter 2005, 66–78.

5. "What the Traffic Will Bear," *Forbes*, July 3, 2008, 69.

6. Raymund Flandez, "Voluntary Pricing Lets Small Eateries Give—and Get Back," *The Wall Street Journal*, August 28, 2007, B8.

7. Miguel Bustillo and Jeffrey A. Trachtenberg, "Amazon, Wal-Mart Cut Deeper in Book Duel," *The Wall Street Journal,* October 17, 2009, B1.

8. Joseph Cannon and Christian Homburg, "Buyer-Supplier Relationships and Customer Firm Costs," *Journal of Marketing*, January 2001, 29–43.

9. Marcus P. Zillman, "ShoppingBot Resources on the Internet," online at www.shoppingbots.info.

10. "How Shopping Bots Really Work," MSN MONEY, July 11, 2005, online at moneycentral.msn.com.

11. "Seller Performance Standards," ebay.com, accessed November 9, 2009.

12. "Wal-Mart Puts the Squeeze on Food Costs," *Fortune*, June 9, 2008, 16.

13. R. Chandrashekaran, "The Implications of Individual Differences in Reference to Price Utilization for Designing Effective Price Communications," *Journal of Business Research*, August 2001, 85–92.

14. Katherine Lemon and Stephen Nowlis, "Developing Synergies between Promotions and Brands in Different Price-Quality Tiers," *Journal of Marketing Research*, May 2002, 171–185; also see Valerie Taylor and William Bearden, "The Effects of Price on Brand Extension Evaluations: The Moderating Role of Extension Similarity," *Journal of the Academy of Marketing Science*, Spring 2002, 131–140; and Raj Sethuraman and V. Srinivasan, "The Asymmetric Share Effect: An Empirical Generalization on Cross-Price Effects," *Journal of Marketing Research*, August 2002, 379–386.

15. Volckner, "The Dual Role of Price. . . ."

16. Ibid.

17. Merrie Brucks, Valarie Zeithaml, and Gillian Naylor, "Price and Brand Name as Indicators of Quality Dimensions for Consumer Durables," *Journal of the Academy of Marketing Science*, Summer 2000, 359–374; Wilford Amaldoss and Sanjay Jain, "Pricing of Conspicuous Goods: A Competitive Analysis of Social Effects," *Journal of Marketing Research*, February 2005, 30–42; and also see Margaret Campbell, "Says Who?! How the Source of Price Information and Affect Influence Perceived Price (UN)fairness," *Journal of Marketing Research*, May 2007, 261–271.

18. Christina Passariello, "Beauty Fix: Behind L'Oreal's Makeover in India: Going Upscale . . . When Cheap Shampoo Didn't Sell, Company Tapped the Rising Class," *The Wall Street Journal*, July 13, 2007, A1, A8.

20

1. Keith Chrzan, "An Overview of Pricing Research," *Quirk's Marketing Research Review*, July/August 2006, 24–29.

2. Kent Monroe and Jennifer Cox, "Pricing Practices That Endanger Profits," *Marketing Management*, September/October 2001, 42–46.

3. Ibid.

4. "Out-Discounting the Discounter," *Business Week*, May 10, 2004, 78–79; an interesting article on shoppers who use penetration pricing to their advantage is: Edward J. Fox and Stephen J. Hoch, "Cherry-Picking," *Journal of Marketing*, January 2005, 46–62.

5. "One Store's Old Food Is Other's Bread and Butter," *The Wall Street Journal*, February 22, 2008, B1–B2.

6. "Ex-British Air Manager Sentenced to Jail," *The Wall Street Journal*, October 1, 2008, B2.

7. U.S. Department of Justice, online at www.usdoj.gov/atr/public/criminal/220752.htm, accessed December 2007.

8. "How Driving Prices Lower Can Violate Antitrust Statutes," *The Wall Street Journal*, January 24, 2004, A1, A11.

9. Evan Clark and Kristi Ellis, "Price-Fixing Plays Out in Supreme Court," *Women's Wear Daily*, June 19, 2008.

10. Bruce Alford and Abhijit Biswas, "The Effects of Discount Level, Price Consciousness, and Sale Proneness on Consumers' Price Perception and Behavioral Intention," *Journal of Business Research*, September 2002, 775–778; See also: V. Kumar, Vibhas Madan, and Srinin Srinivasan, "Price Discounts or Coupon Promotions: Does It Matter?" *Journal of Business Research*, September 2004, 933–941.

11. James Areddy, "Chinese Customers Overwhelm Retailers with Team Tactics," *The Wall Street Journal*, February 28, 2006, A1, A14.

12. "Food Marketers Cook Up 'Value' Campaigns," *The Wall Street Journal*, September 29, 2008, B1, B5; "Value Pricing," *Marketing News*, January 15, 2008, 8.

13. Timothy Aeppel, "Seeking Perfect Prices, CEO Tears Up the Rules," *The Wall Street Journal*, March 27, 2007, A1, A16.

14. Ibid.

15. Ethan Smith and Vauhini Vara, "Music Service From Amazon Takes on iTunes," *The Wall Street Journal*, May 17 2007, D1; Yahoo! Music, online at http://music.yahoo.com/ymu/, accessed November 2007.

16. "Yahoo! Music Brings You Rhapsody," Yahoo! Music, online at http://music.yahoo.com/ymu, accessed November 2008.

17. Rui (Juliet) Zhu, Xinlei (Jack) Chen, and Srabana Dasgupta, "Can Trade-Ins Hurt You? Exploring the Effect of a Trade-In On Consumers' Willingness to Pay for a Product," *Journal of Marketing Research*, April 2008, 159–170.

18. Ibid.

19. Ibid.

20. To learn more about pricing fairness, see: Lan Xia, Kent Monroe, and Jennifer Cox, "The Price Is Unfair! A Conceptual Framework of Price Fairness Perceptions," *Journal of Marketing*, October 2004, 1–15.

21. David Bell, Ganesh Iyer, and V. Padmanabhar, "Price Competition under Stockpiling and Flexible Consumption," *Journal of Marketing Research*, August 2002, 292–303.

22. Dilip Soman and John Gourville, "Transaction Decoupling: The Effects of Price Bundling on the Decision to Consume," MSI Report, 2002, 98–131; Stefan Stremersch and Gerard J. Tellis, "Strategic Bundling of Products and Prices: A New Synthesis for Marketing," *Journal of Marketing*, January 2002, 55–71; "Forget Prices and Get People to Use the Stuff," *The Wall Street Journal*, June 3, 2004, A2.

23. "How Much for a Sip of Water?" *The New York Times-Global Edition*, August 16–17, 2008, 1, 14.

24. Rebecca Hamilton and Joydeep Srivastava, "When 2+2 Is Not the Same as 1+3: Variations in Price Sensitivity Across Components of Partitioned Prices," *Journal of Marketing Research*, August 2008, 450–461.

25. Eric Newman "As Inflation Resurfaces, So Does Package Shrink," *Brandweek*, June 9, 2008, 5.

26. "Sony's Newest Display Is a Culture Shift," *The Wall Street Journal*, May 8, 2008, B1.

21

1. Joseph Hair, Robert Bush, and David Ortinau, *Marketing Research: Within a Changing Information Environment*, 3d ed. (Burr Ridge, IL: McGraw-Hill/Irwin, 2006), 114.

2. "OnDemand5.com: Online Auto Repair, Estimating, and Service Information," Mitchell 1, online at www.ondemand5.com.

3. Jeff Sweat, "Keep 'Em Happy," *Internet Week.com*, January 28, 2002.

4. "PlayStation.com," Sony Computer Entertainment America, online at www.playstation.com, accessed December 2007; "SAP Customer Success Story, Playstation.com Chooses mySAP CRM," online at h71028.www7.hp.com/enterprise/downloads/playstation.pdf.

5. Student Advantage, online at www.studentadvantage.com/static/press.shtml, accessed November 25, 2008.

6. SAP Customer Success Story, "Playstation.com Chooses mySAP CRM," online.

7. *Random House Webster's Dictionary*.

8. Evan Schuman, "Wal-Mart Plans for Its 4PB Data Warehouse," Ziff Davis, August 3, 2007, online at www.eweek.com/author_bio/0,1908,a=2962,00.asp.

9. Paul Tullo, "Customer Value Management: The True Value of Customers," *Brand Strategy*, May 8, 2008, online.

10. B. Weitz, S. Castleberry, and J. Tanner, *Selling* (Burr Ridge, IL: McGraw-Hill/Irwin, 2004), 184–185.

11. Stacey Cowley, "Data Mining," online at www.itworld.com/App/110/050805datamining/, accessed December 3, 2007.

12. Ben Gose, "Give and Take: Direct Giving Websites Rely on Fees to Help Cover Costs," *Chronicle of Philanthropy*, August 7, 2008, online at www.philanthropy.com, accessed February 2009; Sue Hoye and Elizabeth Schwinn, "Competition for Donations Is Going Global, Fund Raiser Predicts," *Chronicle of Philanthropy*, August 7, 2008, online at www.philanthropy.com, accessed February 2009; Rachel Emma Silverman, "A New Generation Reinvents Philanthropy," *Wall Street Journal*, August 21, 2007, http://online.wsj.com, accessed February 2009; Kiva, www.kiva.org; Global Giving, www.globalgiving.com; Donors Choose, www.donorschoose.org; Modest Needs, www.modestneeds.org; www.santella.com/frequent/htm, accessed February 2009.

13. Karen Schwartz, "Kraft Data Mining Transforms Marketing and Margins," *Consumer Goods*, September 2000, online at www.consumergoods.com.

14. Christopher Caggiano, "Building Customer Loyalty," *Inc.*, November 2003, online; "Sumerset Houseboats," Sumerset, online at www.sumerset.com/difference.php, accessed October 2007.

15. Jennifer Saranow, "A ZIP-Code Screen for Catalog Customers," *The Wall Street Journal*, June 24, 2008, online.

16. Kit Davis, "Track Star, RFID Is Racing to Market," *Consumer Goods*, June 2003, online at www.consumergoods.com.

17. Privacy International, "A Race to the Bottom—Privacy Ranking of Internet Service Companies," June 9, 2007, online at www.privacyinternational.org/issues/internet/interimrankings.pdf.

Index

Boldface indicates key term.

CHAPTER 1

An Overview of Marketing

KEY TERMS

LO 1

marketing the activity, set of institutions, and processes for creating, communicating, delivering, and exchanging offerings that have value for customers, clients, partners, and society at large

exchange people giving up something to receive something they would rather have

LO 2

production orientation a philosophy that focuses on the internal capabilities rather than on the desires of the marketplace

sales orientation the idea that people will buy more goods and services if aggressive sales techniques are used and that high sales result in high profits

marketing concept the idea that the social and economic justification for an organization's existence is the satisfaction of customer wants and needs while meeting organizational objectives

market orientation a philosophy that assumes that a sale does not depend on an aggressive sales force but rather on a customer's decision to purchase product; it is synonymous with the marketing concept

societal marketing orientation the idea that an organization exists not only to satisfy customer wants and needs and to meet organizational objectives but also to preserve or enhance individuals' and society's long-term best interests

LO 3

customer value the relationship between benefits and the sacrifice necessary to obtain those benefits

KEY CONCEPTS

LO 1

Define the term marketing. Marketing is the activity, set of institutions, and processes for creating, communicating, delivering, and exchanging offerings that have value for customers, clients, partners, and society at large.

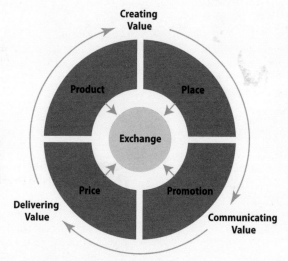

LO 2

Describe four marketing management philosophies. The role of marketing and the character of marketing activities within an organization are strongly influenced by its philosophy and orientation. A production-oriented organization focuses on the internal capabilities of the firm rather than on the desires and needs of the marketplace. A sales orientation is based on the beliefs that people will buy more products if aggressive sales techniques are used and that high sales volumes produce high profits. A market-oriented organization focuses on satisfying customer wants and needs while meeting organizational objectives. A societal marketing orientation goes beyond a market orientation to include the preservation or enhancement of individuals' and society's long-term best interests.

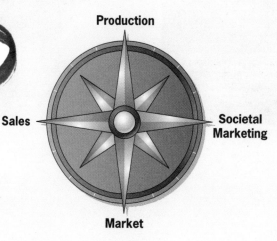

These icons show you at a glance which terms go with which learning objectives.

Chapter Review Cards are printed on perforated card stock so you can study whenever, and wherever you need to.

customer satisfaction customers' evaluation of a good or service in terms of whether it has met their needs and expectations

relationship marketing a strategy that focuses on keeping and improving relationships with current customers

empowerment delegation of authority to solve customers' problems quickly—usually by the first person that the customer notifies regarding a problem

teamwork collaborative efforts of people to accomplish common objectives

LO 3 **Discuss the differences between sales and market orientations.** First, sales-oriented firms focus on their own needs; market-oriented firms focus on customers' needs and preferences. Second, sales-oriented companies consider themselves to be deliverers of goods and services, whereas market-oriented companies view themselves as satisfiers of customers. Third, sales-oriented firms direct their products to everyone; market-oriented firms aim at specific segments of the population. Fourth, although the primary goal of both types of firms is profit, sales-oriented businesses pursue maximum sales volume through intensive promotion, whereas market-oriented businesses pursue customer satisfaction through coordinated activities.

	What is the organization's focus?	What business are you in?	To whom is the product directed?	What is your primary goal?	How do you seek to achieve your goal?
Sales Orientation	Inward, on the organization's needs	Selling goods and services	Everybody	Profit through maximum sales volume	Primarily through intensive promotion
Market Orientation	Outward on the wants and preferences of customers	Satisfying customer wants and needs and delivering superior value	Specific groups of people	Profit through customer satisfaction	Through coordinated marketing and interfunctional activities

LO 4 **Describe several reasons for studying marketing.** First, marketing affects the allocation of goods and services that influence a nation's economy and standard of living. Second, an understanding of marketing is crucial to understanding most businesses. Third, career opportunities in marketing are diverse, profitable, and expected to increase significantly during the coming decade. Fourth, understanding marketing makes consumers more informed.

How To Use This Card

1. Look over the card to preview the new concepts you'll be introduced to in the chapter.

2. Read your chapter to fully understand the material.

3. Go to class (and pay attention).

4. Review the card one more time to make sure you've registered the key concepts.

5. Don't forget, this card is only one of the many MKTG learning tools available to help you succeed in your marketing course.

Important to Society

Good Career Opportunities

Why study marketing?

Important to Business

Marketing affects you every day!

KEY TERMS

 marketing the activity, set of institutions, and processes for creating, communicating, delivering, and exchanging offerings that have value for customers, clients, partners, and society at large

exchange people giving up something to receive something they would rather have

 production orientation a philosophy that focuses on the internal capabilities of the firm rather than on the desires and needs of the marketplace

sales orientation the ideas that people will buy more goods and services if aggressive sales techniques are used and that high sales result in high profits

marketing concept the idea that the social and economic justification for an organization's existence is the satisfaction of customer wants and needs while meeting organizational objectives

market orientation a philosophy that assumes that a sale does not depend on an aggressive sales force but rather on a customer's decision to purchase product; it is synonymous with the marketing concept

societal marketing orientation the idea that an organization exists not only to satisfy customer wants and needs and to meet organizational objectives but also to preserve or enhance individuals' and society's long-term best interests

 customer value the relationship between benefits and the sacrifice necessary to obtain those benefits

KEY CONCEPTS

 Define the term marketing. Marketing is the activity, set of institutions, and processes for creating, communicating, delivering, and exchanging offerings that have value for customers, clients, partners, and society at large.

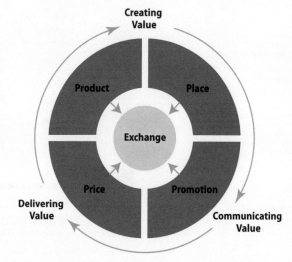

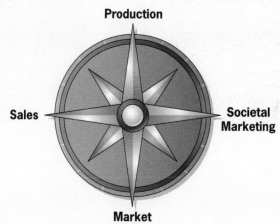 **Describe four marketing management philosophies.** The role of marketing and the character of marketing activities within an organization are strongly influenced by its philosophy and orientation. A production-oriented organization focuses on the internal capabilities of the firm rather than on the desires and needs of the marketplace. A sales orientation is based on the beliefs that people will buy more products if aggressive sales techniques are used and that high sales volumes produce high profits. A market-oriented organization focuses on satisfying customer wants and needs while meeting organizational objectives. A societal marketing orientation goes beyond a market orientation to include the preservation or enhancement of individuals' and society's long-term best interests.

customer satisfaction customers' evaluation of a good or service in terms of whether it has met their needs and expectations

relationship marketing a strategy that focuses on keeping and improving relationships with current customers

empowerment delegation of authority to solve customers' problems quickly—usually by the first person that the customer notifies regarding a problem

teamwork collaborative efforts of people to accomplish common objectives

LO 3 **Discuss the differences between sales and market orientations.** First, sales-oriented firms focus on their own needs; market-oriented firms focus on customers' needs and preferences. Second, sales-oriented companies consider themselves to be deliverers of goods and services, whereas market-oriented companies view themselves as satisfiers of customers. Third, sales-oriented firms direct their products to everyone; market-oriented firms aim at specific segments of the population. Fourth, although the primary goal of both types of firms is profit, sales-oriented businesses pursue maximum sales volume through intensive promotion, whereas market-oriented businesses pursue customer satisfaction through coordinated activities.

	What is the organization's focus?	What business are you in?	To whom is the product directed?	What is your primary goal?	How do you seek to achieve your goal?
Sales Orientation	Inward, on the organization's needs	Selling goods and services	Everybody	Profit through maximum sales volume	Primarily through intensive promotion
Market Orientation	Outward on the wants and preferences of customers	Satisfying customer wants and needs and delivering superior value	Specific groups of people	Profit through customer satisfaction	Through coordinated marketing and interfunctional activities

LO 4 **Describe several reasons for studying marketing.** First, marketing affects the allocation of goods and services that influence a nation's economy and standard of living. Second, an understanding of marketing is crucial to understanding most businesses. Third, career opportunities in marketing are diverse, profitable, and expected to increase significantly during the coming decade. Fourth, understanding marketing makes consumers more informed.

Important to Society

Good Career Opportunities

Why study marketing?

Marketing affects you every day!

Important to Business

KEY TERMS

strategic planning the managerial process of creating and maintaining a fit between the organization's objectives and resources and the evolving market opportunities

planning the process of anticipating future events and determining strategies to achieve organizational objectives in the future

marketing planning designing activities relating to marketing objectives and the changing marketing environment

marketing plan a written document that acts as a guidebook of marketing activities for the marketing manager

mission statement a statement of the firm's business based on a careful analysis of benefits sought by present and potential customers and an analysis of existing and anticipated environmental conditions

marketing myopia defining a business in terms of goods and services rather than in terms of the benefits customers seek

strategic business unit (SBU) a subgroup of a single business or collection of related businesses within the larger organization

SWOT analysis identifying internal strengths (S) and weaknesses (W) and also examining external opportunities (O) and threats (T)

environmental scanning collection and interpretation of information about forces, events, and relationships in the external environment that may affect the future of the organization or the implementation of the marketing plan

marketing objective a statement of what is to be accomplished through marketing activities

KEY CONCEPTS

Understand the importance of strategic marketing and know a basic outline for a marketing plan. Strategic marketing planning is the basis for all marketing strategies and decisions. By specifying objectives and defining the actions required to attain them, a marketing plan provides the basis on which actual and expected performance can be compared.

Although there is no set formula or a single correct outline, a marketing plan should include elements such as stating the business mission, setting objectives, performing a situation analysis of internal and external environmental forces, selecting target market(s), delineating a marketing mix (product, place, promotion, and price), and establishing ways to implement, evaluate, and control the plan.

Develop an appropriate business mission statement. The firm's mission statement establishes boundaries for all subsequent decisions, objectives, and strategies. A mission statement should focus on the market or markets the organization is attempting to serve rather than on the good or service offered.

Describe the components of a situation analysis. In the situation (or SWOT) analysis, the firm should identify its internal strengths (S) and weaknesses (W) and also examine external opportunities (O) and threats (T). When examining external opportunities and threats, marketing managers must analyze aspects of the marketing environment in a process called environmental scanning. The six most-often-studied macroenvironmental forces are social, demographic, economic, technological, political and legal, and competitive.

Explain the criteria for stating good marketing objectives. Objectives should be realistic, measurable, time specific, consistent, and indicate the priorities of the organization. Good marketing objectives: (1) communicate marketing management philosophy; (2) provide management direction; (3) motivate employees; (4) force executives to think clearly; (5) allow for better evaluation of results.

Identify sources of competitive advantage. There are three types of competitive advantages: cost, product/service differentiation, and niche strategies. Sources of cost competitive advantages include experience curves, efficient labor, no-frills goods and services, government subsidies, product design, reengineering, product innovations, and new methods of service delivery. A product/service differentiation competitive advantage exists when a firm provides something unique that is valuable to buyers beyond just low price. Niche competitive advantages come from targeting unique segments with specific needs and wants. The goal of all these sources of competitive advantage is to be sustainable.

Identify strategic alternatives. The strategic opportunity matrix can be used to help management develop strategic alternatives. The four options are market penetration, product development, market development, and diversification. In selecting a strategic alternative, managers may use a portfolio matrix, which classifies strategic business units as stars, cash cows, problem children, and dogs, depending on their present or projected growth and market share.

LO 5 **competitive advantage** a set of unique features of a company and its products that are perceived by the target market as significant and superior to the competition

cost competitive advantage being the low-cost competitor in an industry while maintaining satisfactory profit margins

experience curves curves that show costs declining at a predictable rate as experience with a product increases

product/service differentiation competitive advantage the provision of something that is unique and valuable to buyers beyond simply offering a lower price than the competition's

niche competitive advantage the advantage achieved when a firm seeks to target and effectively serve a small segment of the market

sustainable competitive advantage an advantage that cannot be copied by the competition

LO 6 **market penetration** a marketing strategy that tries to increase market share among existing customers

market development a marketing strategy that entails attracting new customers to existing products

product development a marketing strategy that entails the creation of new products for present markets

diversification a strategy of increasing sales by introducing new products into new markets

portfolio matrix a tool for allocating resources among products or strategic business units on the basis of relative market share and market growth rate

star in the portfolio matrix, a business unit that is a fast-growing market leader

cash cow in the portfolio matrix, a business unit that generates more cash than it needs to maintain its market share

problem child (question mark) in the portfolio matrix, a business unit that shows rapid growth but poor profit margins

dog in the portfolio matrix, a business unit that has low growth potential and a small market share

LO 7 **Discuss target market strategies.** Targeting markets begins with a market opportunity analysis (MOA), which describes and estimates the size and sales potential of market segments that are of interest to the firm. In addition, an assessment of key competitors in these market segments is performed. After the market segments are described, one or more may be targeted by the firm. The three strategies for selecting target markets are appealing to the entire market with one marketing mix, concentrating on one segment, or appealing to multiple market segments using multiple marketing mixes.

LO 8 **Describe the elements of the marketing mix.** The marketing mix (or four Ps) is a blend of product, place, promotion, and pricing strategies designed to produce mutually satisfying exchanges with a target market. The starting point of the marketing mix is the product offering—tangible goods, ideas, or services. Place (distribution) strategies are concerned with making products available when and where customers want them. Promotion includes advertising, public relations, sales promotion, and personal selling. Price is what a buyer must give up to obtain a product and is often the easiest to change of the four marketing mix elements.

LO 9 **Explain why implementation, evaluation, and control of the marketing plan are necessary.** Before a marketing plan can work, it must be implemented; that is, people must perform the actions in the plan. The plan should also be evaluated to see if it has achieved its objectives. Poor implementation can be a major factor in a plan's failure. Control provides the mechanisms for evaluating marketing results in light of the plan's objectives and for correcting actions that do not help the organization reach those objectives within budget guidelines.

LO 10 **Identify several techniques that help make strategic planning effective.** First, management must realize that strategic planning is an ongoing process and not a once-a-year exercise. Second, good strategic planning involves a high level of creativity. The last requirement is top management's support and cooperation.

LO 7 **marketing strategy** the activities of selecting and describing one or more target markets and developing and maintaining a marketing mix that will produce mutually satisfying exchanges with target markets

market opportunity analysis (MOA) the description and estimation of the size and sales potential of market segments that are of interest to the firm and the assessment of key competitors in these market segments

LO 8 **marketing mix** a unique blend of product, place (distribution), promotion, and pricing strategies designed to produce mutually satisfying exchanges with a target market

four Ps product, place, promotion, and price, which together make up the marketing mix

LO 9 **implementation** the process that turns a marketing plan into action assignments and ensures that these assignments are executed in a way that accomplishes the plan's objectives

evaluation gauging the extent to which the marketing objectives have been achieved during the specified time period

control provides the mechanisms for evaluating marketing results in light of the plan's objectives and for correcting actions that do not help the organization reach those objectives within budget guidelines

marketing audit a thorough, systematic, periodic evaluation of the objectives, strategies, structure, and performance of the marketing organization

C3 Ethics and Social Responsibility

KEY TERMS

LO 1 **ethics** the moral principles or values that generally govern the conduct of an individual or a group

LO 2 **morals** the rules people develop as a result of cultural values and norms

code of ethics a guideline to help marketing managers and other employees make better decisions

LO 3 **corporate social responsibility** business's concern for society's welfare

sustainability the idea that socially responsible companies will outperform their peers by focusing on the world's social problems and viewing them as opportunities to build profits and help the world at the same time

pyramid of corporate social responsibility a model that suggests corporate social responsibility is composed of economic, legal, ethical, and philanthropic responsibilities and that the firm's economic performance supports the entire structure

green marketing the development and marketing of products designed to minimize negative effects on the physical environment or to improve the environment

KEY CONCEPTS

LO 1 **Explain the concept of ethical behavior.** Ethical decision making is approached in three basic ways. The first approach examines the consequences of decisions. The second approach relies on rules and laws to guide decision making. The third approach is based on a theory of moral development that places individuals or groups in one of three developmental stages: preconventional morality, conventional morality, or postconventional morality.

> **Ethical Decision Making Processes**
>
> **Examine Consequences**
>
> **Follow Rules and Laws**
>
> **Moral Development**

LO 2 **Describe ethical behavior in business.** Business ethics may be viewed as a subset of the values of society as a whole. The ethical conduct of businesspeople is shaped by societal elements, including family, education, religion, and social movements. As members of society, businesspeople are morally obligated to consider the ethical implications of their decisions.

Many companies develop a code of ethics to help their employees make ethical decisions. A code of ethics can help employees identify acceptable business practices, be an effective internal control on behavior, help employees avoid confusion when determining whether decisions are ethical, and facilitate discussion about what is right and wrong.

Some Factors Attributing to Ethical Conduct

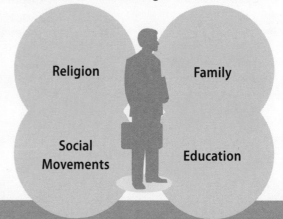

Religion

Family

Social Movements

Education

LO 3 **Discuss corporate social responsibility.** Responsibility in business refers to a firm's concern for the way its decisions affect society. Social responsibility has four components: economic, legal, ethical, and philanthropic. These are intertwined, yet the most fundamental is earning a profit. If a firm does not earn a profit, the other three responsibilities are moot. Most businesspeople believe they should do more than pursue profits. Although a company must consider its economic needs first, it must also operate within the law, do what is ethical and fair, and be a good corporate citizen. The concept of sustainability is that socially responsible companies will outperform their peers by focusing on the world's social problems and viewing them as an opportunity to earn profits and help the world at the same time. Social responsibility is growing, but it can be costly and the benefits are not always immediate. However, ignoring social responsibility can be even more expensive if customers perceive they are being taken advantage of. One branch of social responsibility is green marketing, which aids the environment and often the bottom line of a business.

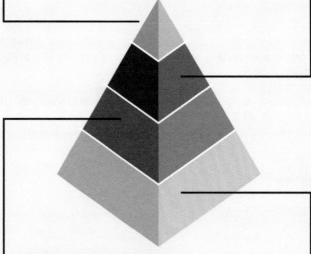

Philanthropic responsibilities
Be a good corporate citizen.
Contribute resources to the community; improve the quality of life.

Ethical responsibilities
Be ethical.
Do what is right, just, and fair. Avoid harm.

Legal responsibilities
Obey the law.
Law is society's codification of right and wrong. Play by the rules of the game.

Economic responsibilities
Be profitable.
Profit is the foundation on which all other responsibilities rest.

4 The Marketing Environment

KEY TERMS

 LO 1 **target market** a defined group most likely to buy a firm's product

environmental management when a company implements strategies that attempt to shape the external environment within which it operates

 LO 2 **component lifestyles** the practice of choosing goods and services that meet one's diverse needs and interests rather than conforming to a single, traditional lifestyle

 LO 3 **demography** the study of people's vital statistics, such as their age, race and ethnicity, and location

Generation Y people born between 1979 and 1994

Generation X people born between 1965 and 1978

baby boomers people born between 1946 and 1964

 LO 4 **multiculturalism** when all major ethnic groups in an area—such as a city, county, or census tract—are roughly equally represented

 LO 5 **purchasing power** a comparison of income versus the relative cost of a set standard of goods and services in different geographic areas

inflation a measure of the decrease in the value of money, expressed as the percentage reduction in value since the previous year

recession a period of economic activity characterized by negative growth, which reduces demand for goods and services

KEY CONCEPTS

 LO 1 **Discuss the external environment of marketing and explain how it affects a firm.** The external marketing environment consists of social, demographic, economic, technological, political and legal, and competitive variables. Marketers generally cannot control the elements of the external environment. Instead, they must understand how the external environment is changing and the impact of that change on the target market. Then marketing managers can create a marketing mix to effectively meet the needs of target customers.

 LO 2 **Describe the social factors that affect marketing.** Within the external environment, social factors are perhaps the most difficult for marketers to anticipate. Several major social trends are currently shaping marketing strategies. First, people of all ages have a broader range of interests, defying traditional consumer profiles. Second, changing gender roles are bringing more women into the workforce and increasing the number of men who shop. Third, a greater number of dual-career families has created demand for time-saving goods and services.

LO 3 **Explain the importance to marketing managers of current demographic trends.** Today, several basic demographic patterns are influencing marketing mixes. Because the U.S. population is growing at a slower rate, marketers can no longer rely on profits from generally expanding markets. Marketers are also faced with increasingly experienced consumers among the younger generations such as tweens and Gen Y. And because the population is also growing older, marketers are offering more products that appeal to middle-aged and elderly consumers.

LO 4 **Explain the importance to marketing managers of multiculturalism and growing ethnic markets.** Multiculturalism occurs when all major ethnic groups in an area are roughly equally represented. Growing multiculturalism makes the marketer's task more challenging. Hispanics are the fastest-growing segment of the population, followed by African Americans. Many companies are now creating departments and product lines to effectively target multicultural market segments. Companies have quickly found that ethnic markets are not homogeneous.

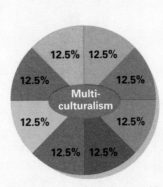

All groups equally represented in given area.

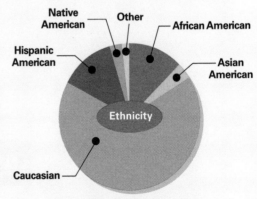

Ethnic markets are not homogeneous.

LO 6 **basic research** pure research that aims to confirm an existing theory or to learn more about a concept or phenomenon

applied research an attempt to develop new or improved products

LO 7 **Food and Drug Administration (FDA)** a federal agency charged with enforcing regulations against selling and distributing adulterated, misbranded, or hazardous food and drug products

Consumer Product Safety Commission (CPSC) a federal agency established to protect the health and safety of consumers in and around their homes

Federal Trade Commission (FTC) a federal agency empowered to prevent persons or corporations from using unfair methods of competition in commerce

LO 5 **Identify consumer and marketer reactions to the state of the economy.** The 2007–2009 recession has drastically reduced the spending power of many people. During a time of inflation, marketers generally attempt to maintain level pricing to avoid losing customer brand loyalty. During times of recession, many marketers maintain or reduce prices to counter the effects of decreased demand; they also concentrate on increasing production efficiency and improving customer service.

LO 6 **Identify the impact of technology on a firm.** Monitoring new technology is essential to keeping up with competitors in today's marketing environment. The United States excels in basic research and, in recent years, has dramatically improved its track record in applied research. Innovation is increasingly becoming a global process. Without innovation, U.S. companies can't compete in global markets.

LO 7 **Discuss the political and legal environment of marketing.** All marketing activities are subject to state and federal laws and the rulings of regulatory agencies. Marketers are responsible for remaining aware of and abiding by such regulations. Some key federal laws that affect marketing are the Sherman Act, Clayton Act, Federal Trade Commission Act, Robinson-Patman Act, Wheeler-Lea Amendments to the FTC Act, Lanham Act, Celler-Kefauver Antimerger Act, and Hart-Scott-Rodino Act. Many laws, including privacy laws, have been passed to protect the consumer as well. The Consumer Product Safety Commission, the Federal Trade Commission, and the Food and Drug Administration are the three federal agencies most involved in regulating marketing activities.

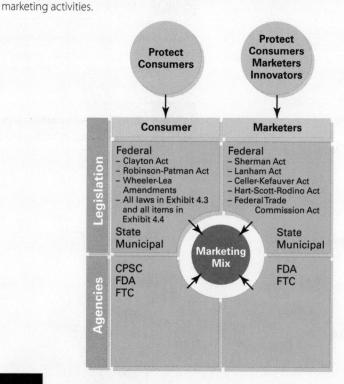

LO 8 **Explain the basics of competition.** The competitive environment encompasses the number of competitors a firm must face, the relative size of the competitors, and the degree of interdependence within the industry.

Developing a Global Vision

KEY TERMS

LO 1 **global marketing** marketing that targets markets throughout the world

global vision recognizing and reacting to international marketing opportunities, using effective global marketing strategies, and being aware of threats from foreign competitors in all markets

job outsourcing sending U.S. jobs abroad

LO 2 **multinational corporation** a company that is heavily engaged in international trade, beyond exporting and importing

capital-intensive using more capital than labor in the production process

global marketing standardization production of uniform products that can be sold the same way all over the world

LO 3 **Mercosur** the largest Latin American trade agreement; includes Argentina, Bolivia, Brazil, Chile, Colombia, Ecuador, Paraguay, Peru, and Uruguay

Uruguay Round an agreement to dramatically lower trade barriers worldwide; created the World Trade Organization

World Trade Organization (WTO) a trade organization that replaced the old General Agreement on Tariffs and Trade (GATT)

General Agreement on Tariffs and Trade (GATT) a trade agreement that contained loopholes that enables countries to avoid trade-barrier reduction agreements

KEY CONCEPTS

LO 1 **Discuss the importance of global marketing.** Businesspeople who adopt a global vision are better able to identify global marketing opportunities, understand the nature of global networks, create effective global marketing strategies, and compete against foreign competition in domestic markets.

LO 2 **Discuss the impact of multinational firms on the world economy.** Multinational corporations are international traders that regularly operate across national borders. Because of their vast size and financial, technological, and material resources, multinational corporations have a great influence on the world economy. They have the ability to overcome trade problems, save on labor costs, and tap new technology.

LO 3 **Describe the external environment facing global marketers.** Global marketers face the same environmental factors as they do domestically: culture, economic and technological development, political structure and actions, demography, and natural resources. Cultural considerations include societal values, attitudes and beliefs, language, and customary business practices. A country's economic and technological status depends on its stage of industrial development, which, in turn, affects average family incomes. The political structure is shaped by political ideology and such policies as tariffs, quotas, boycotts, exchange controls, trade agreements, and market groupings. Demographic variables include the size of a population and its age and geographic distribution.

LO 4 **Identify the various ways of entering the global marketplace.** Firms use the following strategies to enter global markets, in descending order of risk and profit: direct investment, joint venture, contract manufacturing, licensing and franchising, and exporting.

Risk and Profit Increase →

Exporting | Licensing and Franchising | Contract Manufacturing | Joint Venture | Direct Investment

North American Free Trade Agreement (NAFTA) an agreement between Canada, the United States, and Mexico that created the world's largest free trade zone

Central America Free Trade Agreement (CAFTA) a trade agreement, instituted in 2005, that includes Costa Rica, the Dominican Republic, El Salvador, Guatemala, Honduras, Nicaragua, and the United States.

European Union (EU) a free trade zone encompassing 27 European countries

World Bank an international bank that offers low-interest loans, advice, and information to developing nations

International Monetary Fund (IMF) an international organization that acts as a lender of last resort, providing loans to troubled nations, and also works to promote trade through financial cooperation

 LO 4

exporting selling domestically produced products to buyers in another country

buyer for export an intermediary in the global market that assumes all ownership risks and sells globally for its own account

export broker an intermediary that plays the traditional broker's role by bringing buyer and seller together

export agent an intermediary that acts like a manufacturer's agent for the exporter; the export agent lives in the foreign market

licensing the legal process whereby a licensor allows another firm to use its manufacturing process, trademarks, patents, trade secrets, or other proprietary knowledge

contract manufacturing private-label manufacturing by a foreign company

joint venture when a domestic firm buys part of a foreign company or joins with a foreign company to create a new entity

LO 5 **List the basic elements involved in developing a global marketing mix.** A firm's major consideration is how much it will adjust the four Ps—product, promotion, place (distribution), and price—within each country. One strategy is to use one product and one promotion message worldwide. A second strategy is to create new products for global markets. A third strategy is to keep the product basically the same but alter the promotional message. A fourth strategy is to slightly alter the product to meet local conditions.

Global Marketing Mix

Product + Promotion	Place (Distribution)	Price
One Product, One Message	Channel Choice	Dumping
Product Invention	Channel Structure	Countertrade
Product Adaptation	Country Infrastructure	Exchange Rates
Message Adaptation		Purchasing Power

LO 6 **Discover how the Internet is affecting global marketing.** Simply opening an e-commerce site can open the door for international sales. International carriers, such as UPS, can help solve logistics problems. Language translation software can help an e-commerce business become multilingual. Yet cultural differences and old-line rules, regulations, and taxes hinder rapid development of e-commerce in many countries.

Opening an e-commerce site on the Internet . . .

. . . immediately puts a company in the international marketplace.

© ISTOCKPHOTO.COM/BRANDON ALMS / © ISTOCKPHOTO.COM/ANDREA KRAUSE

direct foreign investment active ownership of a foreign company or of overseas manufacturing or marketing facilities

LO 5 **floating exchange rates** prices of different currencies move up and down based on the demand for and the supply of each currency

dumping the sale of an exported product at a price lower than that charged for the same or a like product in the "home" market of the exporter

countertrade a form of trade in which all or part of the payment for goods or services is in the form of other goods or services

KEY TERMS

LO 1 **consumer behavior** processes a consumer uses to make purchase decisions, as well as to use and dispose of purchased goods or services; also includes factors that influence purchase decisions and product use

LO 2 **consumer decision-making process** a five-step process used by consumers when buying goods or services

need recognition result of an imbalance between actual and desired states

want recognition of an unfulfilled need and a product that will satisfy it

stimulus any unit of input affecting one or more of the five senses: sight, smell, taste, touch, hearing

internal information search the process of recalling past information stored in the memory

external information search the process of seeking information in the outside environment

nonmarketing-controlled information source a product information source that is not associated with advertising or promotion

marketing-controlled information source a product information source that originates with marketers promoting the product

evoked set (consideration set) a group of brands, resulting from an information search, from which a buyer can choose

LO 3 **cognitive dissonance** inner tension that a consumer experiences after recognizing an inconsistency between behavior and values or opinions

LO 4 **involvement** the amount of time and effort a buyer invests in the search, evaluation, and decision processes of consumer behavior

KEY CONCEPTS

LO 1 **Explain why marketing managers should understand consumer behavior.** An understanding of consumer behavior reduces marketing managers' uncertainty when they are defining a target market and designing a marketing mix.

LO 2 **Analyze the components of the consumer decision-making process.** The consumer decision-making process begins with need recognition, when stimuli trigger awareness of an unfulfilled want. If additional information is required to make a purchase decision, the consumer may engage in an internal or external information search. The consumer then evaluates the additional information and establishes purchase guidelines. Finally, a purchase decision is made.

LO 3 **Explain the consumer's postpurchase evaluation process.** Consumer postpurchase evaluation is influenced by prepurchase expectations, the prepurchase information search, and the consumer's general level of self-confidence. When a purchase creates cognitive dissonance, consumers tend to react by seeking positive reinforcement for the purchase decision, avoiding negative information about the purchase decision, or revoking the purchase decision by returning the product.

LO 4 **Identify the types of consumer buying decisions and discuss the significance of consumer involvement.** Consumer decision making falls into three broad categories: routine response behavior, limited decision making, and extensive decision making. High-involvement decisions usually include an extensive information search and a thorough evaluation of alternatives. In contrast, low-involvement decisions are characterized by brand loyalty and a lack of personal identification with the product. The main factors affecting the level of consumer involvement are previous experience, interest, perceived risk of negative consequences (financial, social, and psychological), situation, and social visibility.

LO 5 **Identify and understand the cultural factors that affect consumer buying decisions.** Cultural influences on consumer buying decisions include culture and values, subculture, and social class. Culture is the essential character of a society that distinguishes it from other cultural groups. The underlying elements of every culture are the values, language, myths, customs, rituals, laws, and the artifacts, or products, that are transmitted from one generation to the next. The most defining element of a culture is its values. A culture can be divided into subcultures on the basis of demographic characteristics, geographic regions, national and ethnic background, political beliefs, and religious beliefs.

LO 6 **Identify and understand the social factors that affect consumer buying decisions.** Social factors include such external influences as reference groups, opinion leaders, and family. Consumers seek out others' opinions for guidance on new products or services and products with image-related attributes or because attribute information is lacking or uninformative. Consumers may use products or brands to identify with or become a member of a reference group, or to follow an opinion leader. Family members also influence purchase decisions; children tend to shop in similar patterns as their parents.

routine response behavior the type of decision making exhibited by consumers buying frequently purchased, low-cost goods and services; requires little search and decision time

limited decision making the type of decision making that requires a moderate amount of time for gathering information and deliberating about an unfamiliar brand in a familiar product category

extensive decision making the most complex type of consumer decision making, used when buying an unfamiliar, expensive product or an infrequently bought item; requires use of several criteria for evaluating options and much time for seeking information

 culture the set of values, norms, attitudes, and other meaningful symbols that shape human behavior and the artifacts, or products, of that behavior as they are transmitted from one generation to the next

value the enduring belief that a specific mode of conduct is personally or socially preferable to another mode of conduct

subculture a homogeneous group of people who share elements of the overall culture as well as unique elements of their own group

social class a group of people in a society who are considered nearly equal in status or community esteem, who regularly socialize among themselves both formally and informally, and who share behavioral norms

LO 6 **reference group** a group in society that influences an individual's purchasing behavior

primary membership group a reference group with which people interact regularly in an informal, face-to-face manner, such as family, friends, and coworkers

secondary membership group a reference group with which people associate less consistently and more formally than a primary membership group, such as a club, professional group, or religious group

LO 7 **Identify and understand the individual factors that affect consumer buying decisions.** Individual factors that affect consumer buying decisions include gender; age and family life-cycle stage; and personality, self-concept, and lifestyle. Beyond obvious physiological differences, men and women differ in their social and economic roles, and that affects consumer buying decisions. How old a consumer is generally indicates what products he or she may be interested in purchasing. Marketers often define their target markets in terms of consumers' life-cycle stage, following changes in consumers' attitudes and behavioral tendencies as they mature. Finally, certain products and brands reflect consumers' personality, self-concept, and lifestyle.

LO 8 **Identify and understand the psychological factors that affect consumer buying decisions.** Psychological factors include perception, motivation, learning, values, beliefs, and attitudes. These factors allow consumers to interact with the world around them, recognize their feelings, gather and analyze information, formulate thoughts and opinions, and take action. Perception allows consumers to recognize their consumption problems. Motivation is what drives consumers to take action to satisfy specific consumption needs. Almost all consumer behavior results from learning, which is the process that creates changes in behavior through experience. Consumers with similar beliefs and attitudes tend to react alike to marketing-related inducements.

aspirational reference group a group that someone would like to join

norm a value or attitude deemed acceptable by a group

nonaspirational reference group a group with which an individual does not want to associate

opinion leader an individual who influences the opinions of others

socialization process how cultural values and norms are passed down to children

 personality a way of organizing and grouping the consistencies of an individual's reactions to situations

self-concept how consumers perceive themselves in terms of attitudes, perceptions, beliefs, and self-evaluations

ideal self-image the way an individual would like to be

real self-image the way an individual actually perceives himself or herself

 perception the process by which people select, organize, and interpret stimuli into a meaningful and coherent picture

selective exposure the process whereby a consumer notices certain stimuli and ignores others

selective distortion a process whereby a consumer changes or distorts information that conflicts with his or her feelings or beliefs

selective retention a process whereby a consumer remembers only that information that supports personal beliefs

motive a driving force that causes a person to take action to satisfy specific needs

Maslow's hierarchy of needs a method of classifying human needs and motivations into five categories in ascending order of importance: physiological, safety, social, esteem, and self-actualization

learning a process that creates changes in behavior, immediate or expected, through experience and practice

stimulus generalization a form of learning that occurs when one response is extended to a second stimulus similar to the first

stimulus discrimination a learned ability to differentiate among similar products

belief an organized pattern of knowledge that an individual holds as true about his or her world

attitude a learned tendency to respond consistently toward a given object

KEY TERMS

LO 1 **business marketing** the marketing of goods and services to individuals and organizations for purposes other than personal consumption

LO 2 **business-to-business electronic commerce** the use of the Internet to facilitate the exchange of goods, services, and information between organizations

stickiness a measure of a Web site's effectiveness; calculated by multiplying the frequency of visits times the duration of a visit times the number of pages viewed during each visit (site reach)

disintermediation the elimination of intermediaries such as wholesalers or distributers from a marketing channel

reintermediation the reintroduction of an intermediary between producers and users

LO 3 **strategic alliance (strategic partnership)** a cooperative agreement between business firms

relationship commitment a firm's belief that an ongoing relationship with another firm is so important that the relationship warrants maximum efforts at maintaining it indefinitely

trust the condition that exists when one party has confidence in an exchange partner's reliability and integrity

keiretsu a network of interlocking corporate affiliates

LO 4 **original equipment manufacturers (OEMs)** individuals and organizations that buy business goods and incorporate them into the products that they produce for eventual sale to other producers or to consumers

KEY CONCEPTS

LO 1 **Describe business marketing.** Business marketing provides goods and services that are bought for use in business rather than for personal consumption. Intended use, not physical characteristics, distinguishes a business product from a consumer product.

LO 2 **Describe the role of the Internet in business marketing.** The rapid expansion and adoption of the Internet have made business markets more competitive than ever before. The number of business buyers and sellers using the Internet is rapidly increasing. Firms are seeking new and better ways to expand markets and sources of supply, increase sales and decrease costs, and better serve customers. With the Internet, every business in the world is potentially a local competitor.

LO 3 **Discuss the role of relationship marketing and strategic alliances in business marketing.** Relationship marketing entails seeking and establishing long-term alliances or partnerships with customers. A strategic alliance is a cooperative agreement between business firms. Firms form alliances to leverage what they do well by partnering with others that have complementary skills.

LO 4 **Identify the four major categories of business market customers.** Producer markets consist of for-profit organizations and individuals that buy products to use in producing other products, as components of other products, or in facilitating business operations. Reseller markets consist of wholesalers and retailers that buy finished products to resell for profit. Government markets include federal, state, county, and city governments that buy goods and services to support their own operations and serve the needs of citizens. Institutional markets consist of very diverse nonbusiness institutions whose main goals do not include profit.

LO 5 **Explain the North American Industry Classification System.** NAICS provides a way to identify, analyze, segment, and target business and government markets. Organizations can be identified and compared by a numeric code indicating business sector, subsector, industry group, industry, and industry subdivision. NAICS is a valuable tool for analyzing, segmenting, and targeting business markets.

LO 6 **Explain the major differences between business and consumer markets.** In business markets, demand is derived, price-inelastic, joint, and fluctuating. Purchase volume is much larger than in consumer markets, customers are fewer in number and more geographically concentrated, and distribution channels are more direct. Buying is approached more formally using professional purchasing agents, more people are involved in the buying process, negotiation is more complex, and reciprocity and leasing are more common. And, finally, selling strategy in business markets normally focuses on personal contact rather than on advertising.

North American Industry Classification System (NAICS) a detailed numbering system developed by the United States, Canada, and Mexico to classify North American business establishments by their main production processes

 derived demand the demand for business products

joint demand the demand for two or more items used together in a final product

multiplier effect (accelerator principle) phenomenon in which a small increase or decrease in consumer demand can produce a much larger change in demand for the facilities and equipment needed to make the consumer product

business-to-business online exchange an electronic trading floor that provides companies with integrated links to their customers and suppliers

reciprocity a practice where business purchasers choose to buy from their own customers

 major equipment (installations) capital goods such as large or expensive machines, mainframe computers, blast furnaces, generators, airplanes, and buildings

accessory equipment goods, such as portable tools and office equipment, that are less expensive and shorter-lived than major equipment

raw materials unprocessed extractive or agricultural products, such as mineral ore, lumber, wheat, corn, fruits, vegetables, and fish

component parts either finished items ready for assembly or products that need very little processing before becoming part of some other product

processed materials products used directly in manufacturing other products

supplies consumable items that do not become part of the final product

business services expense items that do not become part of a final product

Characteristic	Business Market	Consumer Market
Demand	Organizational	Individual
Purchase volume	Larger	Smaller
Number of customers	Fewer	Many
Location of buyers	Geographically concentrated	Dispersed
Distribution structure	More direct	More indirect
Nature of buying	More professional	More personal
Nature of buying influence	Multiple	Single
Type of negotiations	More complex	Simpler
Use of reciprocity	Yes	No
Use of leasing	Greater	Lesser
Primary promotional method	Personal selling	Advertising

LO 7 **Describe the seven types of business goods and services.** Major equipment includes capital goods, such as heavy machinery. Accessory equipment is typically less expensive and shorter-lived than major equipment. Raw materials are extractive or agricultural products that have not been processed. Component parts are finished or near-finished items to be used as parts of other products. Processed materials are used to manufacture other products. Supplies are consumable and not used as part of a final product. Business services are intangible products that many companies use in their operations.

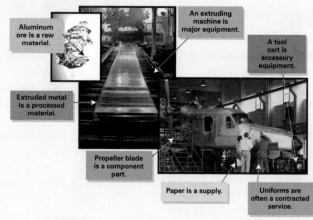

Aluminum ore is a raw material.

An extruding machine is major equipment.

A tool cart is accessory equipment.

Extruded metal is a processed material.

Propeller blade is a component part.

Paper is a supply.

Uniforms are often a contracted service.

LO 8 **Discuss the unique aspects of business buying behavior.** Business buying behavior is distinguished by five fundamental characteristics. First, buying is normally undertaken by a buying center consisting of many people who range widely in authority level. Second, business buyers typically evaluate alternative products and suppliers based on quality, service, and price—in that order. Third, business buying falls into three general categories: new buys, modified rebuys, and straight rebuys. Fourth, the ethics of business buyers and sellers are often scrutinized. Fifth, customer service before, during, and after the sale plays a big role in business purchase decisions.

 buying center all those people in an organization who become involved in the purchase decision

new buy a situation requiring the purchase of a product for the first time

modified rebuy a situation where the purchaser wants some change in the original good or service

straight rebuy a situation in which the purchaser reorders the same goods or services without looking for new information or investigating other suppliers

KEY TERMS

 LO 1

market people or organizations with needs or wants and the ability and willingness to buy

market segment a subgroup of people or organizations sharing one or more characteristics that cause them to have similar product needs

market segmentation the process of dividing a market into meaningful, relatively similar, and identifiable segments or groups

LO 4 **segmentation bases (variables)** characteristics of individuals, groups, or organizations

geographic segmentation segmenting markets by region of a country or the world, market size, market density, or climate

demographic segmentation segmenting markets by age, gender, income, ethnic background, and family life cycle

family life cycle (FLC) a series of stages determined by a combination of age, marital status, and the presence or absence of children

psychographic segmentation market segmentation on the basis of personality, motives, lifestyles, and geodemographics

geodemographic segmentation segmenting potential customers into neighborhood lifestyle categories

benefit segmentation the process of grouping customers into market segments according to the benefits they seek from the product

usage-rate segmentation dividing a market by the amount of product bought or consumed

80/20 principle a principle holding that 20 percent of all customers generate 80 percent of the demand

KEY CONCEPTS

LO 1 **Describe the characteristics of markets and market segments.** A market is composed of individuals or organizations with the ability and willingness to make purchases to fulfill their needs or wants. A market segment is a group of individuals or organizations with similar product needs as a result of one or more common characteristics.

LO 2 **Explain the importance of market segmentation.** Before the 1960s, few businesses targeted specific market segments. Today, segmentation is a crucial marketing strategy for nearly all successful organizations. Market segmentation enables marketers to tailor marketing mixes to meet the needs of particular population segments. Segmentation helps marketers identify consumer needs and preferences, areas of declining demand, and new marketing opportunities.

LO 3 **Discuss criteria for successful market segmentation.** Successful market segmentation depends on four basic criteria: (1) a market segment must be substantial and have enough potential customers to be viable; (2) a market segment must be identifiable and measurable; (3) members of a market segment must be accessible to marketing efforts; and (4) a market segment must respond to particular marketing efforts in a way that distinguishes it from other segments.

LO 4 **Describe the bases commonly used to segment consumer markets.** Five bases are commonly used for segmenting consumer markets. Geographic segmentation is based on region, size, density, and climate characteristics. Demographic segmentation is based on age, gender, income level, ethnicity, and family life-cycle characteristics. Psychographic segmentation includes personality, motives, and lifestyle characteristics. Benefits sought is a type of segmentation that identifies customers according to the benefits they seek in a product. Finally, usage segmentation divides a market by the amount of product purchased or consumed.

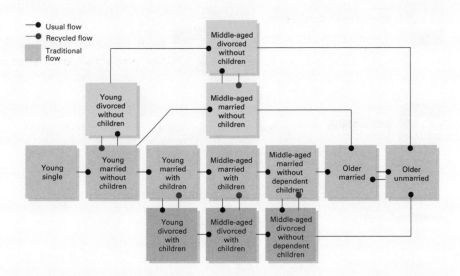

satisficers business customers who place an order with the first familiar supplier to satisfy product and delivery requirements

optimizers business customers who consider numerous suppliers, both familiar and unfamiliar, solicit bids, and study all proposals carefully before selecting one

target market a group of people or organizations for which an organization designs, implements, and maintains a marketing mix intended to meet the needs of that group, resulting in mutually satisfying exchanges

undifferentiated targeting strategy a marketing approach that views the market as one big market with no individual segments and thus uses a single marketing mix

concentrated targeting strategy a strategy used to select one segment of a market for targeting marketing efforts

niche one segment of a market

multisegment targeting strategy a strategy that chooses two or more well-defined market segments and develops a distinct marketing mix for each

cannibalization a situation that occurs when sales of a new product cut into sales of a firm's existing products

one-to-one marketing an individualized marketing method that utilizes customer information to build long-term, personalized, and profitable relationships with each customer

positioning developing a specific marketing mix to influence potential customers' overall perception of a brand, product line, or organization in general

position the place a product, brand, or group of products occupies in consumers' minds relative to competing offerings

LO 5 Describe the bases for segmenting business markets. Business markets can be segmented on two general bases. First, businesses segment markets based on company characteristics, such as customers' geographic location, type of company, company size, and product use. Second, companies may segment customers based on the buying processes those customers use.

LO 6 List the steps involved in segmenting markets. Six steps are involved when segmenting markets: (1) selecting a market or product category for study; (2) choosing a basis or bases for segmenting the market; (3) selecting segmentation descriptors; (4) profiling and evaluating segments; (5) selecting target markets; and (6) designing, implementing, and maintaining appropriate marketing mixes.

LO 7 Discuss alternative strategies for selecting target markets. Marketers select target markets using three different strategies: undifferentiated targeting, concentrated targeting, and multisegment targeting. An undifferentiated targeting strategy assumes that all members of a market have similar needs that can be met with a single marketing mix. A concentrated targeting strategy focuses all marketing efforts on a single market segment. Multisegment targeting is a strategy that uses two or more marketing mixes to target two or more market segments.

Targeting Strategy	Advantages	Disadvantages
Undifferentiated Targeting	• Potential savings on production/marketing costs	• Unimaginative product offerings • Company more susceptible to competition
Concentrated Targeting	• Concentration of resources • Can better meet the needs of a narrowly defined segment • Allows some small firms to better compete with larger firms • Strong positioning	• Segments too small, or changing • Large competitors may more effectively market to niche segment
Multisegment Targeting	• Greater financial success • Economies of scale in producing/marketing	• High costs • Cannibalization

LO 8 Explain one-to-one marketing. One-to-one marketing is an individualized marketing method that utilizes customer information to build long-term, personalized, and profitable relationships with each customer. Successful one-to-one marketing comes from understanding customers and collaborating with them, rather than using them as targets for generic messages. Database technology makes it possible for companies to interact with customers on a personal, one-to-one basis.

LO 9 Explain how and why firms implement positioning strategies and how product differentiation plays a role. Positioning is used to influence consumer perceptions of a particular brand, product line, or organization in relation to competitors. The term *position* refers to the place that the offering occupies in consumers' minds. To establish a unique position, many firms use product differentiation, emphasizing the real or perceived differences between competing offerings. Products may be differentiated on the basis of attribute, price and quality, use or application, product user, product class, or competitor.

product differentiation a positioning strategy that some firms use to distinguish their products from those of competitors

perceptual mapping a means of displaying or graphing, in two or more dimensions, the location of products,

brands, or groups of products in customers' minds

repositioning changing consumers' perceptions of a brand in relation to competing brands

KEY TERMS

marketing information everyday information about developments in the marketing environment that managers use to prepare and adjust marketing plans

decision support system (DSS) an interactive, flexible computerized information system that enables managers to obtain and manipulate information as they are making decisions

database marketing the creation of a large computerized file of customers' and potential customers' profiles and purchase patterns

marketing research the process of planning, collecting, and analyzing data relevant to a marketing decision

marketing research problem determining what information is needed and how that information can be obtained efficiently and effectively

marketing research objective the specific information needed to solve a marketing research problem; the objective should be to provide insightful decision-making information

management decision problem a broad-based problem that uses marketing research in order for managers to take proper actions

secondary data data previously collected for any purpose other than the one at hand

marketing research aggregator a company that acquires, catalogs, reformats, segments, and resells reports already published by marketing research firms

research design specifies which research questions must be answered, how and when the data will be gathered, and how the data will be analyzed

KEY CONCEPTS

LO 1 **Explain the concept and purpose of a marketing decision support system.** A decision support system (DSS) makes data instantly available to marketing managers and allows them to manipulate the data themselves to make marketing decisions. Four characteristics make DSSs especially useful to marketing managers: They are interactive, flexible, discovery oriented, and accessible. Decision support systems give managers access to information immediately and without outside assistance. They allow users to manipulate data in a variety of ways and to answer "what if" questions. And, finally, they are accessible to novice computer users.

LO 2 **Define marketing research and explain its importance to marketing decision making.** Marketing research is a process of collecting and analyzing data for the purpose of solving specific marketing problems. Marketers use marketing research to explore the profitability of marketing strategies. They can examine why particular strategies failed and analyze characteristics of specific market segments. Managers can use research findings to help keep current customers. Moreover, marketing research allows management to behave proactively, rather than reactively, by identifying newly emerging patterns in society and the economy.

LO 3 **Describe the steps involved in conducting a marketing research project.** The marketing research process involves several basic steps. First, the researcher and the decision maker must agree on a problem statement or set of research objectives. The researcher then creates an overall research design to specify how primary data will be gathered and analyzed. Before collecting data, the researcher decides whether the group to be interviewed will be a probability or nonprobability sample. Field service firms are often hired to carry out data collection. Once data have been collected, the researcher analyzes them using statistical analysis. The researcher then prepares and presents oral and written reports, with conclusions and recommendations, to management. As a final step, the researcher determines whether the recommendations were implemented and what could have been done to make the project more successful.

LO 4 **Discuss the profound impact of the Internet on marketing research.** The Internet has simplified the secondary data search process, placing more sources of information in front of researchers than ever before. Internet survey research is surging in popularity. Internet surveys can be created rapidly, reported in real time, are relatively inexpensive and easily personalized. Often researchers use the Internet to contact respondents who are difficult to reach by other means. The Internet can also be used to conduct focus groups, to distribute research proposals and reports, and to facilitate collaboration between the client and the research supplier.

LO 5 **Discuss the growing importance of scanner-based research.** A scanner-based research system enables marketers to monitor a market panel's exposure and reaction to such variables as advertising, coupons, store displays, packaging, and price. By analyzing these variables in relation to the panel's subsequent buying behavior, marketers gain useful insight into sales and marketing strategies.

primary data information that is collected for the first time; used for solving the particular problem under investigation

survey research the most popular technique for gathering primary data, in which a researcher interacts with people to obtain facts, opinions, and attitudes

mall intercept interview a survey research method that involves interviewing people in the common areas of shopping malls

computer-assisted personal interviewing an interviewing method in which the interviewer reads the questions from a computer screen and enters the respondent's data directly into the computer

computer-assisted self-interviewing an interviewing method in which a mall interviewer intercepts and directs willing respondents to nearby computers where the respondent reads questions off a computer screen and directly keys his or her answers into a computer

central-location telephone (CLT) facility a specially designed phone room used to conduct telephone interviewing

executive interview a type of survey that involves interviewing businesspeople at their offices concerning industrial products or services

focus group seven to ten people who participate in a group discussion led by a moderator

open-ended question an interview question that encourages an answer phrased in the respondent's own words

closed-ended question an interview question that asks the respondent to make a selection from a limited list of responses

scaled-response question a closed-ended question designed to measure the intensity of a respondent's answer

observation research a research method that relies on four types of observation: people watching people, people watching an activity, machines watching people, and machines watching an activity

LO 6 **Explain when marketing research should be conducted.** Because acquiring marketing information can be time consuming and costly, deciding to acquire additional decision-making information depends on managers' perceptions of its quality, price, and timing. Research, therefore, should be undertaken only when the expected value of the information is greater than the cost of obtaining it.

LO 7 **Explain the concept of competitive intelligence.** Competitive intelligence (CI) helps managers assess their competition and their vendors in order to become more efficient and effective competitors. Intelligence is analyzed information, and it becomes decision-making intelligence when it has implications for the organization. By helping managers assess their competition and vendors, CI leads to fewer surprises. CI is part of a sound marketing strategy; helps companies respond to competitive threats; and helps reduce unnecessary costs.

mystery shoppers researchers posing as customers who gather observational data about a store

ethnographic research the study of human behavior in its natural context; involves observation of behavior and physical setting

experiment a method a researcher uses to gather primary data

sample a subset from a larger population

universe the population from which a sample will be drawn

probability sample a sample in which every element in the population has a known statistical likelihood of being selected

random sample a sample arranged in such a way that every element of the population has an equal chance of being selected as part of the sample

nonprobability sample any sample in which little or no attempt is made to get a representative cross section of the population

convenience sample a form of nonprobability sample using respondents who are convenient or readily accessible to the researcher—for example, employees, friends, or relatives

measurement error an error that occurs when there is a difference between the information desired by the researcher and the information provided by the measurement process

sampling error an error that occurs when a sample somehow does not represent the target population

frame error an error that occurs when a sample drawn from a population differs from the target population

random error an error that occurs when the selected sample is an imperfect representation of the overall population

field service firm a firm that specializes in interviewing respondents on a subcontracted basis

cross-tabulation a method of analyzing data that lets the analyst look at the responses to one question in relation to the responses to one or more other questions

LO 5 **scanner-based research** a system for gathering information from a single group of respondents by continuously monitoring the advertising, promotion, and pricing they are exposed to and the things they buy

BehaviorScan a scanner-based research program that tracks the purchases of 3,000 households through store scanners in each research market

InfoScan a scanner-based sales-tracking service for the consumer packaged-goods industry

LO 7 **competitive intelligence (CI)** an intelligence system that helps managers assess their competition and vendors in order to become more efficient and effective competitors

10 Product Concepts

CHAPTER REVIEW

KEY TERMS

 LO 1 **product** everything, both favorable and unfavorable, that a person receives in an exchange

 LO 2 **business product (industrial product)** a product used to manufacture other goods or services, to facilitate an organization's operations, or to resell to other customers

consumer product a product bought to satisfy an individual's personal wants

convenience product a relatively inexpensive item that merits little shopping effort

shopping product a product that requires comparison shopping because it is usually more expensive than a convenience product and is found in fewer stores

specialty product a particular item that consumers search extensively for and are very reluctant to accept substitutes

unsought product a product unknown to the potential buyer or a known product that the buyer does not actively seek

 LO 3 **product item** a specific version of a product that can be designated as a distinct offering among an organization's products

product line a group of closely related product items

product mix all products that an organization sells

product mix width the number of product lines an organization offers

product line depth the number of product items in a product line

product modification changing one or more of a product's characteristics

KEY CONCEPTS

LO 1 **Define the term** *product.* A product is anything, desired or not, that a person or organization receives in an exchange. The basic goal of purchasing decisions is to receive the tangible and intangible benefits associated with a product. Tangible aspects include packaging, style, color, size, and features. Intangible qualities include service, the retailer's image, the manufacturer's reputation, and the social status associated with a product. An organization's product offering is the crucial element in any marketing mix.

LO 2 **Classify consumer products.** Consumer products are classified into four categories: convenience products, shopping products, specialty products, and unsought products. Convenience products are relatively inexpensive and require limited shopping effort. Shopping products are of two types: homogeneous and heterogeneous. Because of the similarity of homogeneous products, they are differentiated mainly by price and features. In contrast, heterogeneous products appeal to consumers because of their distinct characteristics. Specialty products possess unique benefits that are highly desirable to certain customers. Finally, unsought products are either new products or products that require aggressive selling because they are generally avoided or overlooked by consumers.

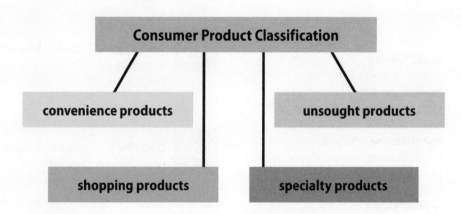

LO 3 **Define the terms** *product item,* **product line,** **and** *product mix.* A product item is a specific version of a product that can be designated as a distinct offering among an organization's products. A product line is a group of closely related products offered by an organization. An organization's product mix includes all the products it sells. Product mix width refers to the number of product lines an organization offers. Product line depth is the number of product items in a product line. Firms modify existing products by changing their quality, functional characteristics, or style. Product line extension occurs when a firm adds new products to existing product lines.

planned obsolescence the practice of modifying products so those that have already been sold become obsolete before they actually need replacement

product line extension adding additional products to an existing product line in order to compete more broadly in the industry

 brand a name, term, symbol, design, or combination thereof that identifies a seller's products and differentiates them from competitors' products

brand name that part of a brand that can be spoken, including letters, words, and numbers

brand mark the elements of a brand that cannot be spoken

brand equity the value of company and brand names

global brand a brand that obtains at least a third of its earnings from outside its home country, is recognizable outside its home base of customers, and has publicly available marketing and financial data

brand loyalty a consistent preference for one brand over all others

generic product a no-frills, no-brand-name, low-cost product that is simply identified by its product category

manufacturer's brand the brand name of a manufacturer

private brand a brand name owned by a wholesaler or a retailer

captive brand a brand manufactured by a third party for an exclusive retailer, without evidence of that retailer's affiliation

individual branding using different brand names for different products

family brand marketing several different products under the same brand name

cobranding placing two or more brand names on a product or its package

trademark the exclusive right to use a brand or part of a brand

service mark a trademark for a service

LO 4 Describe marketing uses of branding. A brand is a name, term, or symbol that identifies and differentiates a firm's products. Established brands encourage customer loyalty and help new products succeed. Branding strategies require decisions about individual, family, manufacturers', and private brands.

Comparing Manufacturers' and Private Brands from the Reseller's Perspective

Key Advantages of Carrying Manufacturers' Brands	Key Advantages of Carrying Private Brands
• Heavy advertising to the consumer by manufacturers such as Procter & Gamble helps develop strong consumer loyalties.	• A wholesaler or retailer can usually earn higher profits on its own brand. In addition, because the private brand is exclusive, there is less pressure to mark down the price to meet competition.
• Well-known manufacturers' brands, such as Kodak and Fisher-Price, can attract new customers and enhance the dealer's (wholesaler's or retailer's) prestige.	• A manufacturer can decide to drop a brand or a reseller at any time or even become a direct competitor to its dealers.
• Many manufacturers offer rapid delivery, enabling the dealer to carry less inventory.	• A private brand ties the customer to the wholesaler or retailer. A person who wants a DieHard battery must go to Sears.
• If a dealer happens to sell a manufacturer's brand of poor quality, the customer may simply switch brands and remain loyal to the dealer.	• Wholesalers and retailers have no control over the intensity of distribution of manufacturers' brands. Wal-Mart store managers don't have to worry about competing with other sellers of Sam's American Choice products or Ol' Roy dog food. They know that these brands are sold only in Wal-Mart and Sam's Club stores.

LO 5 Describe marketing uses of packaging and labeling. Packaging has four functions: containing and protecting products; promoting products; facilitating product storage, use, and convenience; and facilitating recycling and reducing environmental damage. As a tool for promotion, packaging identifies the brand and its features. It also serves the critical function of differentiating a product from competing products and linking it with related products from the same manufacturer. The label is an integral part of the package, with persuasive and informational functions. In essence, the package is the marketer's last chance to influence buyers before they make a purchase decision.

LO 6 Discuss global issues in branding and packaging. In addition to brand piracy, international marketers must address a variety of concerns regarding branding and packaging, including choosing a brand-name policy, translating labels and meeting host-country labeling requirements, making packages aesthetically compatible with host-country cultures, and offering the sizes of packages preferred in host countries.

LO 7 Describe how and why product warranties are important marketing tools. Product warranties are important tools because they offer consumers protection and help them gauge product quality.

Express warranty = written guarantee

Implied warranty = unwritten guarantee

generic product name identifies a product by class or type and cannot be trademarked

 persuasive labeling a type of package labeling that focuses on a promotional theme or logo, and consumer information is secondary

informational labeling a type of package labeling designed to help consumers make proper product selections and lower their cognitive dissonance after the purchase

universal product codes (UPCs) a series of thick and thin vertical lines (bar codes), readable by computerized optical scanners, that represent numbers used to track products

 warranty a confirmation of the quality or performance of a good or service

express warranty a written guarantee

implied warranty an unwritten guarantee that the good or service is fit for the purpose for which it was sold

KEY TERMS

new product a product new to the world, the market, the producer, the seller, or some combination of these

new-product strategy a plan that links the new-product development process with the objectives of the marketing department, the business unit, and the corporation

product development a marketing strategy that entails the creation of marketable new products; the process of converting applications for new technologies into marketable products

brainstorming the process of getting a group to think of unlimited ways to vary a product or solve a problem

screening the first filter in the product development process, which eliminates ideas that are inconsistent with the organization's new-product strategy or are obviously inappropriate for some other reason

concept test a test to evaluate a new-product idea, usually before any prototype has been created

business analysis the second stage of the screening process where preliminary figures for demand, cost, sales, and profitability are calculated

development the stage in the product development process in which a prototype is developed and a marketing strategy is outlined

simultaneous product development a team-oriented approach to new-product development

test marketing the limited introduction of a product and a marketing program to determine the reactions of potential customers in a market situation

KEY CONCEPTS

LO 1 Explain the importance of developing new products and describe the six categories of new products. New products are important to sustain growth and profits and to replace obsolete items. New products can be classified as new-to-the-world products (discontinuous innovations), new product lines, additions to existing product lines, improvements or revisions of existing products, repositioned products, or lower-priced products. To sustain or increase profits, a firm must innovate.

LO 2 Explain the steps in the new-product development process.
First, a firm forms a new-product strategy by outlining the characteristics and roles of future products. Then new-product ideas are generated by customers, employees, distributors, competitors, vendors, and internal R&D personnel. Once a product idea has survived initial screening by an appointed screening group, it undergoes business analysis to determine its potential profitability. If a product concept seems viable, it progresses into the development phase, in which the technical and economic feasibility of the manufacturing process is evaluated. The development phase also includes laboratory and use testing of a product for performance and safety. Following initial testing and refinement, most products are introduced in a test market to evaluate consumer response and marketing strategies. Finally, test market successes are propelled into full commercialization. The commercialization process involves starting up production, building inventories, shipping to distributors, training a sales force, announcing the product to the trade, and advertising to consumers.

1	New-product strategy
2	Idea generation
3	Idea screening
4	Business analysis
5	Development
6	Test marketing
7	Commercialization
	New product

LO 3 Discuss global issues in new-product development. A marketer with global vision seeks to develop products that can easily be adapted to suit local needs. The goal is not simply to develop a standard product that can be sold worldwide. Smart global marketers also look for good product ideas worldwide.

LO 4 Explain the diffusion process through which new products are adopted. The diffusion process is the spread of a new product from its producer to ultimate adopters. Adopters in the diffusion process belong to five categories: innovators, early adopters, the early majority, the late majority, and laggards. Product characteristics that affect the rate of adoption include product complexity, compatibility with existing social values, relative advantage over existing substitutes, visibility, and "trialability." The diffusion process is facilitated by word-of-mouth communication and communication from marketers to consumers.

simulated (laboratory) market testing the presentation of advertising and other promotional materials for several products, including a test product, to members of the product's target market

commercialization the decision to market a product

 innovation a product perceived as new by a potential adopter

diffusion the process by which the adoption of an innovation spreads

 product life cycle (PLC) a concept that provides a way to trace the stages of a product's acceptance, from its introduction (birth) to its decline (death)

product category all brands that satisfy a particular type of need

introductory stage the full-scale launch of a new product into the marketplace

growth stage the second stage of the product life cycle when sales typically grow at an increasing rate, many competitors enter the market, large companies may start acquiring small pioneering firms, and profits are healthy

maturity stage a period during which sales increase at a decreasing rate

decline stage a long-run drop in sales

LO 5 **Explain the concept of product life cycles.** All brands and product categories undergo a life cycle with four stages: introduction, growth, maturity, and decline. The rate at which products move through these stages varies dramatically. Marketing managers use the product life-cycle concept as an analytical tool to forecast a product's future and devise effective marketing strategies.

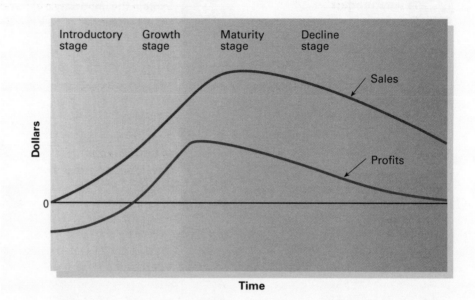

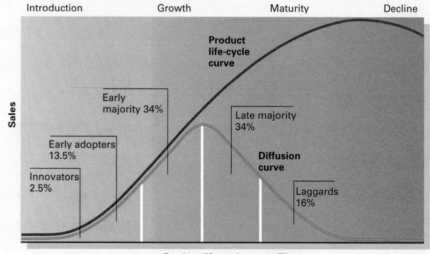

Product life-cycle curve: Time
Diffusion curve: Percentage of total adoptions by category

KEY TERMS

service the result of applying human or mechanical efforts to people or objects

intangibility the inability of services to be touched, seen, tasted, heard, or felt in the same manner that goods can be sensed

search quality a characteristic that can be easily assessed before purchase

experience quality a characteristic that can be assessed only after use

credence quality a characteristic that consumers may have difficulty assessing even after purchase because they do not have the necessary knowledge or experience

inseparability the inability of the production and consumption of a service to be separated; consumers must be present during the production

heterogeneity the variability of the inputs and outputs of services, which causes services to tend to be less standardized and uniform than goods

perishability the inability of services to be stored, warehoused, or inventoried

reliability the ability to perform a service dependably, accurately, and consistently

responsiveness the ability to provide prompt service

assurance the knowledge and courtesy of employees and their ability to convey trust

empathy caring, individualized attention to customers

tangibles the physical evidence of a service, including the physical facilities, tools, and equipment used to provide the service

KEY CONCEPTS

Discuss the importance of services to the economy. The service sector plays a crucial role in the U.S. economy, employing more than 80 percent of the workforce and accounting for a similar percentage of the gross domestic product.

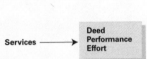
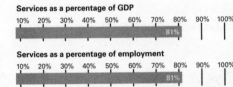

Discuss the differences between services and goods. Services are distinguished by four characteristics. Services are intangible performances in that they lack clearly identifiable physical characteristics, making it difficult for marketers to communicate their specific benefits to potential customers. The production and consumption of services occurs simultaneously. Services are heterogeneous because their quality depends on such elements as the service provider, individual consumer, location, and so on. Finally, services are perishable in the sense that they cannot be stored or saved. As a result, synchronizing supply with demand is particularly challenging in the service industry.

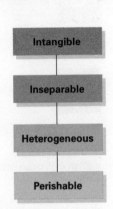

Describe the components of service quality and the gap model of service quality. Service quality has five components: reliability (ability to perform the service dependably, accurately, and consistently), responsiveness (providing prompt service), assurance (knowledge and courtesy of employees and their ability to convey trust), empathy (caring, individualized attention), and tangibles (physical evidence of the service).

The gap model identifies five key discrepancies that can influence customer evaluations of service quality. When the gaps are large, service quality is low. As the gaps shrink, service quality improves. Gap 1 is found between customers' expectations and management's perceptions of those expectations. Gap 2 is found between management's perception of what the customer wants and specifications for service quality. Gap 3 is found between service quality specifications and delivery of the service. Gap 4 is found between service delivery and what the company promises to the customer through external communication. Gap 5 is found between customers' service expectations and their perceptions of service performance.

gap model a model identifying five gaps that can cause problems in service delivery and influence customer evaluations of service quality

 LO 4 core service the most basic benefit the consumer is buying

supplementary services a group of services that support or enhance the core service

mass customization a strategy that uses technology to deliver customized services on a mass basis

LO 6 internal marketing treating employees as customers and developing systems and benefits that satisfy their needs

LO 8 nonprofit organization an organization that exists to achieve some goal other than the usual business goals of profit, market share, or return on investment

nonprofit organization marketing the effort by nonprofit organizations to bring about mutually satisfying exchanges with target markets

public service advertisement (PSA) an announcement that promotes a program of a federal, state, or local government or of a nonprofit organization

LO 4 Develop marketing mixes for services. "Product" (service) strategy issues include what is being processed (people, possessions, mental stimulus, information), core and supplementary services, customization versus standardization, and the service mix. Distribution (place) decisions involve convenience, number of outlets, direct versus indirect distribution, and scheduling. Stressing tangible cues, using personal sources of information, creating strong organizational images, and engaging in postpurchase communication are effective promotion strategies. Pricing objectives for services can be revenue oriented, operations oriented, patronage oriented, or any combination of the three.

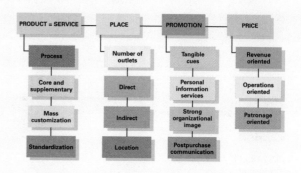

LO 5 Discuss relationship marketing in services. Relationship marketing in services involves attracting, developing, and retaining customer relationships. There are three levels of relationship marketing: level 1 focuses on pricing incentives; level 2 uses pricing incentives and social bonds with customers; and level 3 uses pricing, social bonds, and structural bonds to build long-term relationships.

LO 6 Explain internal marketing in services. Internal marketing means treating employees as customers and developing systems and benefits that satisfy their needs. Employees who like their jobs and are happy with the firm they work for are more likely to deliver good service.

Good service flows from management to customers through employees.

LO 7 Discuss global issues in services marketing. The United States has become the world's largest exporter of services. Although competition is keen, the United States has a competitive advantage because of its vast experience in many service industries. To be successful globally, service firms must adjust their marketing mix for the environment of each target country.

LO 8 Describe nonprofit organization marketing. Nonprofit organizations pursue goals other than profit, market share, and return on investment. Nonprofit organization marketing facilitates mutually satisfying exchanges between nonprofit organizations and their target markets. Several unique characteristics distinguish nonbusiness marketing strategy, including a concern with services and social behaviors rather than manufactured goods and profit; a difficult, undifferentiated, and in some ways marginal target market; a complex product that may have only indirect benefits and elicit very low involvement; distribution that may or may not require special facilities depending on the service provided; a relative lack of resources for promotion; and prices only indirectly related to the exchange between the producer and the consumer of services.

KEY TERMS

LO 1 **marketing channel (channel of distribution)** a set of interdependent organizations that eases the transfer of ownership as products move from producer to business user or consumer

channel members all parties in the marketing channel that negotiate with one another, buy and sell products, and facilitate the change of ownership between buyer and seller in the course of moving the product from the manufacturer into the hands of the final consumer

supply chain the connected chain of all of the business entities, both internal and external to the company, that perform or support the marketing channel functions

discrepancy of quantity the difference between the amount of product produced and the amount an end user wants to buy

discrepancy of assortment the lack of all the items a customer needs to receive full satisfaction from a product or products

temporal discrepancy a situation that occurs when a product is produced but a customer is not ready to buy it

spatial discrepancy the difference between the location of a producer and the location of widely scattered markets

LO 2 **retailer** a channel intermediary that sells mainly to consumers

merchant wholesaler an institution that buys goods from manufacturers and resells them to businesses, government agencies, and other wholesalers or retailers and that receives and takes title to goods, stores them in its own warehouses, and later ships them

KEY CONCEPTS

LO 1 **Explain what a marketing channel is and why intermediaries are needed.** A marketing channel is a business structure of interdependent organizations that reach from the point of product origin to the consumer. Its purpose is to physically move products to their final consumption destination, representing "place" or "distribution" in the marketing mix. A marketing channel gets the right product to the right place at the right time. Members of a marketing channel create a continuous and seamless supply chain that performs or supports the marketing channel functions. Channel members provide economies to the distribution process in the form of specialization and division of labor; overcoming discrepancies in quantity, assortment, time, and space; and providing contact efficiency.

LO 2 **Define the types of channel intermediaries and describe their functions and activities.** The most prominent difference separating intermediaries is whether they take title to the product. Retailers and merchant wholesalers take title, but agents and brokers do not. Retailers are firms that sell mainly to consumers. Merchant wholesalers are those organizations that facilitate the movement of products and services from the manufacturer to producers, resellers, governments, institutions, and retailers. Agents and brokers facilitate the exchange of ownership between sellers and buyers. Channel intermediaries perform three basic types of functions. Transactional functions include contacting and promoting, negotiating, and risk taking. Logistical functions performed by channel members include physical distribution, storing, and sorting functions. Finally, channel members may perform facilitating functions, such as researching and financing.

LO 3 **Describe the channel structures for consumer and business products and discuss alternative channel arrangements.** Marketing channels for consumer and business products vary in degree of complexity.

LO 4 **Discuss the issues that influence channel strategy.** When determining marketing channel strategy, the supply chain manager must determine what market, product, and producer factors will influence the choice of channel. The manager must also determine the appropriate level of distribution intensity. Intensive distribution is distribution aimed at maximum market coverage. Selective distribution is achieved by screening dealers to eliminate all but a few in any single area. The most restrictive form of market coverage is exclusive distribution, which entails only one or a few dealers within a given area.

LO 5 **Describe the different channel relationship types and their unique costs and benefits.** Channel relationships can be plotted on a continuum ranging from arm's length to integrated, with cooperative relationships somewhere in between. Arm's-length relationships generally consist of unique transactions that are intended to occur once or very infrequently, and are pursued when closer relationships are undesirable or impractical. Though arm's-length relationships are low risk, they also provide few benefits in terms of favorable conditions for the agreement, and disputes are often resolved in court. Integrated relationships, on the opposite end of the spectrum, are very close relationships that are backed by formal agreements and can

agents and brokers wholesaling intermediaries who do not take title to a product but facilitate its sale from producer to end user by representing retailers, wholesalers, or manufacturers

logistics the efficient and cost-effective forward and reverse flow as well as storage of goods, services, and related information, into, through, and out of channel member companies

LO 3 **direct channel** a distribution channel in which producers sell directly to consumers

dual distribution (multiple distribution) the use of two or more channels to distribute the same product to target markets

strategic channel alliance a cooperative agreement between business firms to use the other's already established distribution channel

LO 4 **intensive distribution** a form of distribution aimed at having a product available in every outlet where target customers might want to buy it

selective distribution a form of distribution achieved by screening dealers to eliminate all but a few in any single area

exclusive distribution a form of distribution that establishes one or a few dealers within a given area

LO 5 **arm's-length relationship** a relationship between companies that is loose, characterized by low relational investment and trust, and usually taking the form of a series of discrete transactions with no/low expectation of future interaction or service

cooperative relationship a relationship between companies that takes the form of informal partnership with moderate levels of trust and information sharing as needed to further each company's goals

integrated relationship a relationship between companies that is tightly connected, with linked processes across and between firm

result in great efficiency and effectiveness. However, given that integrated relationships tend either to involve high levels of expense (in the case of vertical integration) or require enormous amounts of trust in the partner company (as in the case of supply chains), many companies prefer cooperative relationships in some settings. Cooperative relationships are a hybrid form of relationship that is governed by formal contract, are temporary, and are enforced by the agreement itself.

LO 6 **Explain channel leadership, conflict, and partnering.** Power, control, leadership, conflict, and partnering are the main social dimensions of marketing channel relationships. Channel power refers to the capacity of one channel member to control or influence other channel members. Channel control occurs when one channel member intentionally affects another member's behavior. Channel leadership is the exercise of authority and power. Channel conflict occurs when there is a clash of goals and methods among the members of a distribution channel. Channel conflict can be either horizontal, between channel members at the same level, or vertical, between channel members at different levels of the channel. Channel partnering is the joint effort of all channel members to create a supply chain that serves customers and creates a competitive advantage. Collaborating channel partners meet the needs of consumers more effectively by ensuring that the right products reach shelves at the right time and at a lower cost, boosting sales and profits.

LO 7 **Discuss channels and distribution decisions in global markets.** Global marketing channels are becoming more important to U.S. companies seeking growth abroad. Manufacturers introducing products in foreign countries must decide what type of channel structure to use—in particular, whether the product should be marketed through direct channels or through foreign intermediaries. Marketers should be aware that channel structures in foreign markets may be very different from those they are accustomed to in the United States. Global distribution expertise is also emerging as an important skill for channel managers as many countries are removing trade barriers.

LO 8 **Identify the special problems and opportunities associated with distribution in service organizations.** Managers in service industries use the same skills, techniques, and strategies to manage logistics functions as managers in goods-producing industries. The distribution of services focuses on three main areas: minimizing wait times, managing service capacity, and improving service delivery.

boundaries, and high levels of trust and interfirm commitment

LO 6 **channel power** the capacity of a particular marketing channel member to control or influence the behavior of other channel members

channel control a situation that occurs when one marketing channel member intentionally affects another member's behavior

channel leader (channel captain) a member of a marketing channel that exercises authority and power over the activities of other channel members

channel conflict a clash of goals and methods between distribution channel members

horizontal conflict a channel conflict that occurs among channel members on the same level

vertical conflict a channel conflict that occurs between different levels in a marketing channel, most typically between the manufacturer and wholesaler or between the manufacturer and retailer

channel partnering (channel cooperation) the joint effort of all channel members to create a supply chain that serves customers and creates a competitive advantage

KEY TERMS

LO 1 **supply chain** the connected chain of all of the business entities, both internal and external to the company, that perform or support the logistics function

supply chain management a management system that coordinates and integrates all of the activities performed by supply chain members into a seamless process, from the source to the point of consumption, resulting in enhanced customer and economic value

LO 3 **business processes** bundles of interconnected activities that stretch across firms in the supply chain

customer relationship management process allows companies to prioritize their marketing focus on different customer groups according to each group's long-term value to the company or supply chain

customer service management process presents a multi-company, unified response system to the customer whenever complaints, concerns, questions, or comments are voiced

demand management process seeks to align supply and demand throughout the supply chain by anticipating customer requirements at each level and creating demand-related plans of action prior to actual customer purchasing behavior

order fulfillment process a highly integrated process, often requiring persons from multiple companies and multiple functions to come together and coordinate to create customer satisfaction at a given place and time

KEY CONCEPTS

LO 1 **Define the terms *supply chain*, *supply chain management*, and *supply chain orientation*, and discuss the benefits of supply chain management.** Management coordinates and integrates all of the activities performed by supply chain members into a seamless process from the source to the point of consumption. The responsibilities of a supply chain manager include developing channel design strategies, managing the relationships of supply chain members, sourcing and procurement of raw materials, scheduling production, processing orders, managing inventory and storing product, and selecting transportation modes. The supply chain manager is also responsible for managing customer service and the information that flows through the supply chain. The benefits of supply chain management include reduced costs in inventory management, transportation, warehousing, and packaging; improved service through techniques like time-based delivery and make-to-order; and enhanced revenues, which result from supply chain–related achievements such as higher product availability and more customized products.

LO 2 **Discuss the concept of supply chain integration, and explain why each of the six types of integration is important.** Supply chain integration occurs when multiple firms in a supply chain coordinate their activities and processes so that they are seamlessly linked to one another in the attempt to satisfy customers. The six types of integration are as follows. (1) Relationship integration is the ability of two or more firms to develop tight social connections among their employees, resulting in smoother personal interactions. (2) Measurement integration is the idea that performance assessments should be transparent and similar across all of the supply chain members. (3) Technology and planning integration refers to the creation and maintenance of supply chain technology systems that connect managers throughout the supply chain. (4) Material and service supplier integration reflects a focus on integrating processes and functions with those who provide the company with the things they need in order to execute their core functions. (5) Internal operations integration is the development of capabilities for the firm's internal functional areas to communicate and work together on processes and projects. (6) Customer integration implies that firms evaluate their own capabilities and use them to offer long-lasting, distinctive, value-added offerings in ways that best serve their customers.

LO 3 **Identify the eight key processes of excellent supply chain management, and discuss how each of these processes impacts the end customer.** The key processes that leading supply chain companies focus on are (1) customer relationship management, (2) customer service management, (3) order fulfillment, (4) manufacturing flow management, (5) supplier relationship management, (6) product development and commercialization, (7) returns management, and (8) demand management. When firms practice excellent supply chain management, each of these processes is integrated from end to end in the supply chain. These processes are made up of bundles of interconnected activities that supply chain partners are constantly focused on when delivering value to the customer.

manufacturing flow management process concerned with ensuring that firms in the supply chain have the needed resources to manufacture with flexibility and to move products through a multi-stage production process

supplier relationship management process closely related to the manufacturing flow management process and contains several characteristics that parallel the customer relationship management process

product development and commercialization process includes the group of activities that facilitates the joint development and marketing of new offerings among a group of supply chain partner firms

returns management process enables firms to manage volumes of returned product efficiently, while minimizing returns-related costs and maximizing the value of the returned assets to the firms in the supply chain

LO 4 **logistics** the process of strategically managing the efficient flow and storage of raw materials, in-process inventory, and finished goods from point of origin to point of consumption

logistics information system the link that connects all of the logistics functions of the supply chain

supply chain team an entire group of individuals who orchestrate the movement of goods, services, and information from the source to the consumer

mass customization (build-to-order) a production method whereby products are not made until an order is placed by the customer; products are made according to customer specifications

just-in-time production (JIT) a process that redefines and simplifies manufacturing by reducing inventory levels and delivering raw materials at the precise time they are needed on the production line

LO 4 **Discuss the key strategic decisions supply chain managers must make when designing their companies' supply chains.** The logistics supply chain consists of several interrelated and integrated logistical components: (1) sourcing and procurement of raw materials and supplies, (2) production scheduling, (3) order processing, (4) inventory control, (5) warehousing and materials-handling, and (6) transportation. Integrating and linking all of the logistics functions of the supply chain is the logistics information system. Information technology connects the various components and partners of the supply chain into an integrated whole. The supply chain team, in concert with the logistics information system, orchestrates the movement of goods, services, and information from the source to the consumer. Supply chain teams typically cut across organizational boundaries, embracing all parties who participate in moving product to market. Procurement deals with the purchase of raw materials, supplies, and components according to production scheduling. Order processing monitors the flow of goods and information (order entry and order handling). Inventory control systems regulate when and how much to buy (order timing and order quantity). Warehousing provides storage of goods until needed by the customer while the materials-handling system moves inventory into, within, and out of the warehouse. Finally, the major modes of transportation include railroads, motor carriers, pipelines, waterways, and airways.

LO 5 **Discuss new technology and emerging trends in supply chain management.** Several emerging trends are changing the job of today's supply chain manager. Technology and automation are bringing up-to-date distribution information to the decision maker's desk. Technology is also linking suppliers, buyers, and carriers for joint decision making, and it has created a new electronic distribution channel. Many companies are saving money and time by outsourcing to third-party carriers to handle some or all aspects of the distribution process.

order processing system a system whereby orders are entered into the supply chain and filled

electronic data interchange (EDI) information technology that replaces the paper documents that usually accompany business transactions, such as purchase orders and invoices, with electronic transmission of the needed information to reduce inventory levels, improve cash flow, streamline operations, and increase the speed and accuracy of information transmission

inventory control system a method of developing and maintaining an adequate assortment of materials or products to meet a manufacturer's or a customer's demand

materials requirement planning (MRP) (materials management) an inventory control system that manages the replenishment of raw materials, supplies, and components from the supplier to the manufacturer

distribution resource planning (DRP) an inventory control system that manages the replenishment of goods from the manufacturer to the final consumer

materials-handling system a method of moving inventory into, within, and out of the warehouse

LO 5 **outsourcing (contract logistics)** a manufacturer's or supplier's use of an independent third party to manage an entire function of the logistics system, such as transportation, warehousing, or order processing

electronic distribution a distribution technique that includes any kind of product or service that can be distributed electronically, whether over traditional forms such as fiber-optic cable or through satellite transmission of electronic signals

KEY TERMS

LO 1 **retailing** all the activities directly related to the sale of goods and services to the ultimate consumer for personal, nonbusiness use

LO 2 **independent retailers** retailers owned by a single person or partnership and not operated as part of a larger retail institution

chain stores stores owned and operated as a group by a single organization

franchise the right to operate a business or to sell a product

gross margin the amount of money the retailer makes as a percentage of sales after the cost of goods sold is subtracted

LO 3 **department store** a store housing several departments under one roof

buyer a department head who selects the merchandise for his or her department and may also be responsible for promotion and personnel

specialty store a retail store specializing in a given type of merchandise

supermarket a large, departmentalized, self-service retailer that specializes in food and some nonfood items

scrambled merchandising the tendency to offer a wide variety of nontraditional goods and services under one roof

drugstore a retail store that stocks pharmacy-related products and services as its main draw

convenience store a miniature supermarket, carrying only a limited line of high-turnover convenience goods

KEY CONCEPTS

LO 1 **Discuss the importance of retailing in the U.S. economy.** Retailing plays a vital role in the U.S. economy for two main reasons. First, retail businesses

Retailing as a % of U.S. employment — 11.6%

Retailing as a % of U.S. businesses — 13%

Retailing as a % of GDP — 40%

contribute to our high standard of living by providing a vast and diverse number of goods and services. Second, retailing employs a large part of the U.S. working population—more than 15 million people.

LO 2 **Explain the dimensions by which retailers can be classified.** Many different kinds of retailers exist. A retail establishment can be classified according to its ownership, level of

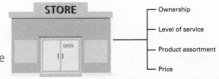

STORE
— Ownership
— Level of service
— Product assortment
— Price

service, product assortment, and price. On the basis of ownership, retailers can be broadly differentiated as independent retailers, chain stores, or franchise outlets. The level of service retailers provide can be classified along a continuum of high to low. Retailers also classify themselves by the breadth and depth of their product assortments; some retailers have concentrated product assortments, whereas others have extensive product assortments. Finally, general price levels also classify a store, from discounters offering low prices to exclusive specialty stores where high prices are the norm. Retailers use these latter three variables to position themselves in the marketplace.

LO 3 **Describe the major types of retail operations.** The major types of retail stores are department stores, specialty retailers, supermarkets, drugstores, convenience stores, discount stores, and restaurants. Department stores carry a wide assortment of shopping and specialty goods, are organized into relatively independent departments, and offset higher prices by emphasizing customer service and decor. Specialty retailers typically carry a narrower but deeper assortment of merchandise, emphasizing distinctive products and a high level of customer service. Supermarkets are large self-service retailers that offer a wide variety of food products and some nonfood items. Drugstores are retail formats that sell mostly prescription and over-the-counter medications, health and beauty aids, cosmetics, and specialty items. Convenience stores carry a limited line of high-turnover convenience goods. Discount stores offer low-priced general merchandise and consist of four types: full-line discounters, specialty discount retailers, warehouse clubs, and off-price retailers. Finally, restaurants straddle the line between the retailing and services industries; although restaurants sell a product, food and drink, to final consumers, they can also be considered service marketers because they provide consumers with the service of preparing food and providing table service.

discount store a retailer that competes on the basis of low prices, high turnover, and high volume

full-line discount store a retailer that offers consumers very limited service and carries a broad assortment of well-known, nationally branded "hard goods"

mass merchandising a retailing strategy using moderate to low prices on large quantities of merchandise and lower levels of service to stimulate high turnover of products

supercenter a retail store that combines groceries and general merchandise goods with a wide range of services

specialty discount store a retail store that offers a nearly complete selection of single-line merchandise and uses self-service, discount prices, high volume, and high turnover

category killers specialty discount stores that heavily dominate their narrow merchandise segment

warehouse membership clubs limited-service merchant wholesalers that sell a limited selection of brand-name appliances, household items, and groceries on a cash-and-carry basis to members, usually small businesses and groups

off-price retailer a retailer that sells at prices 25 percent or more below traditional department store prices because it pays cash for its stock and usually doesn't ask for return privileges

factory outlet an off-price retailer that is owned and operated by a manufacturer

LO 4 **nonstore retailing** shopping without visiting a store

automatic vending the use of machines to offer goods for sale

direct retailing the selling of products by representatives who work door-to-door, office-to-office, or at home sales parties

direct marketing (direct-response marketing) techniques used to get consumers to make a purchase from their home, office, or another nonretail setting

LO 4 **Discuss nonstore retailing techniques.** Nonstore retailing, which is shopping outside a store setting, has three major categories. Automatic vending uses machines to offer products for sale. In direct retailing, the sales transaction occurs in a home setting, typically through door-to-door sales or party plan selling. Direct marketing refers to the techniques used to get consumers to buy from their homes or place of business. Those techniques include direct mail, catalogs and mail order, telemarketing, and electronic retailing, such as home shopping channels and online retailing using the Internet.

LO 5 **Define *franchising* and describe its two basic forms.** Franchising is a continuing relationship in which a franchiser grants to a franchisee the business rights to operate or to sell a product. Modern franchising takes two basic forms. In product and trade name franchising, a dealer agrees to buy or sell certain products or product lines from a particular manufacturer or wholesaler. Business format franchising is an ongoing business relationship in which a franchisee uses a franchiser's name, format, or method of business in return for several types of fees.

LO 6 **List the major tasks involved in developing a retail marketing strategy.** Retail management begins with defining the target market, typically on the basis of demographic, geographic, or psychographic characteristics. After determining the target market, retail managers must develop the six variables of the retailing mix: product, place, promotion, price, presentation, and personnel.

LO 7 **Describe new developments in retailing.** Two major trends are evident in retailing today. First, adding interactivity to the retail environment is one of the most popular strategies in retailing in recent years. Small retailers as well as national chains are using interactivity to involve customers and set themselves apart from the competition. Second, m-commerce (mobile e-commerce) is gaining in popularity. M-commerce enables consumers to purchase goods and services using wireless mobile devices, such as mobile telephones, pagers, PDAs, and handheld computers.

PRODUCT
Width and depth of product assortment

PLACE
Location and hours

PROMOTION
Advertising, publicity, public relations

PRICE

PRESENTATION
Layout and atmosphere

PERSONNEL
Customer service and personal selling

TARGET

telemarketing the use of the telephone to sell directly to consumers

online retailing a type of shopping available to consumers with personal computers and access to the Internet

LO 5 **franchisor** the originator of a trade name, product, methods of operation, and so on that grants operating rights to another party to sell its product

franchisee an individual or business that is granted the right to sell another party's product

LO 6 **retailing mix** a combination of the six Ps—product, place, promotion, price, presentation, and personnel—to sell goods and services to the ultimate consumer

product offering the mix of products offered to the consumer by the retailer; also called the *product assortment* or *merchandise mix*

destination stores stores that consumers purposely plan to visit

atmosphere the overall impression conveyed by a store's physical layout, decor, and surroundings

KEY TERMS

LO 1 **promotion** communication by marketers that informs, persuades, and reminds potential buyers of a product in order to influence an opinion or elicit a response

promotional strategy a plan for the optimal use of the elements of promotion: advertising, public relations, personal selling, and sales promotion

competitive advantage the unique set of features of a company and its products that are perceived by the target market as significant and superior to the competition

LO 2 **promotional mix** the combination of promotional tools—including advertising, public relations, personal selling, and sales promotion—used to reach the target market and fulfill the organization's overall goals

advertising impersonal, one-way mass communication about a product or organization that is paid for by a marketer

public relations the marketing function that evaluates public attitudes, identifies areas within the organization the public may be interested in, and executes a program of action to earn public understanding and acceptance

publicity public information about a company, product, service, or issue appearing in the mass media as a news item

sales promotion marketing activities—other than personal selling, advertising, and public relations—that stimulate consumer buying and dealer effectiveness

personal selling a purchase situation involving a personal, paid-for communication between two people in an attempt to influence each other

KEY CONCEPTS

LO 1 **Discuss the role of promotion in the marketing mix.** Promotional strategy is the plan for using the elements of promotion—advertising, public relations, sales promotion, and personal selling—to meet the firm's overall objectives and marketing goals. Based on these objectives, the elements of the promotional strategy become a coordinated promotion plan. The promotion plan then becomes an integral part of the total marketing strategy for reaching the target market along with product, distribution, and price.

LO 2 **Discuss the elements of the promotional mix.** The elements of the promotional mix include advertising, public relations, sales promotion, and personal selling. Advertising is a form of impersonal, one-way mass communication paid for by the source. Public relations is the function of promotion concerned with a firm's public image. Firms can't buy good publicity, but they can take steps to create a positive company image. Sales promotion is typically used to back up other components of the promotional mix by stimulating immediate demand. Finally, personal selling typically involves direct communication, in person or by telephone; the seller tries to initiate a purchase by informing and persuading one or more potential buyers.

LO 3 **Describe the communication process.** The communication process has several steps. When an individual or organization has a message it wishes to convey to a target audience, it encodes that message using language and symbols familiar to the intended receiver and sends the message through a channel of communication. Noise in the transmission channel distorts the source's intended message. Reception occurs if the message falls within the receiver's frame of reference. The receiver decodes the message and usually provides feedback to the source. Normally, feedback is direct for interpersonal communication and indirect for mass communication.

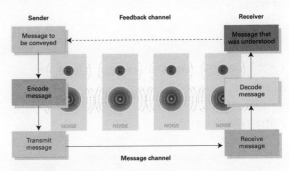

LO 4 **Explain the goals and tasks of promotion.** The fundamental goals of promotion are to induce, modify, or reinforce behavior by informing, persuading, and reminding. Informative promotion explains the purpose and benefits of a good or service. Promotion that informs the consumer is typically used to increase demand for a general product category or to introduce a new good or service. Persuasive promotion is designed to stimulate a purchase or an action. Promotion that persuades the consumer to buy is essential during the growth stage of the product life cycle, when competition becomes fierce. Reminder promotion is used to keep the product and brand name in the public's mind. Promotions that remind are generally used during the maturity stage of the product life cycle.

communication the process by which meanings are exchanged or shared through a common set of symbols

interpersonal communication direct, face-to-face communication between two or more people

mass communication the communication of a concept or message to large audiences

sender the originator of the message in the communication process

encoding the conversion of a sender's ideas and thoughts into a message, usually in the form of words or signs

channel a medium of communication—such as a voice, radio, or newspaper—for transmitting a message

noise anything that interferes with, distorts, or slows down the transmission of information

receiver the person who decodes a message

decoding interpretation of the language and symbols sent by the source through a channel

feedback the receiver's response to a message

corporate blogs blogs that are sponsored by a company or one of its brands and maintained by one or more of the company's employees

noncorporate blogs independent blogs that are not associated with the marketing efforts of any particular company or brand

 AIDA concept a model that outlines the process for achieving promotional goals in terms of stages of consumer involvement with the message; the acronym stands for *attention, interest, desire,* and *action*

 push strategy a marketing strategy that uses aggressive personal selling and trade advertising to convince a wholesaler or a retailer to carry and sell particular merchandise

 Discuss the AIDA concept and its relationship to the promotional mix. The AIDA model outlines the four basic stages in the purchase decision-making process, which are initiated and propelled by

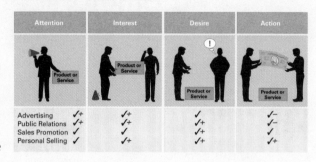

promotional activities: (1) attention, (2) interest, (3) desire, and (4) action. The components of the promotional mix have varying levels of influence at each stage of the AIDA model. Advertising is a good tool for increasing awareness and knowledge of a good or service. Sales promotion is effective when consumers are at the purchase stage of the decision-making process. Personal selling is most effective in developing customer interest and desire.

Describe the factors that affect the promotional mix. Promotion managers consider many factors when creating promotional mixes. These factors include the nature of the product, product life-cycle stage, target market characteristics, type of buying decision involved, availability of funds, and feasibility of push or pull strategies. As products move through different stages of the product life cycle, marketers will choose to use different promotional elements. Characteristics of the target market, such as geographic location of potential buyers and brand loyalty, influence the promotional mix as does whether the buying decision is complex or routine. The amount of funds a firm has to allocate to promotion may also help determine the promotional mix. Finally, if a firm uses a push strategy to promote the product or service, the marketing manager may choose to use aggressive advertising and personal selling to wholesalers and retailers. If a pull strategy is chosen, then the manager often relies on aggressive mass promotion to stimulate consumer demand.

Discuss the concept of integrated marketing communications. Integrated marketing communications is the careful coordination of all promotional messages for a product or service to assure the consistency of messages at every contact point where a company meets the consumer—advertising, sales promotion, personal selling, public relations, as well as direct marketing, packaging, and other forms of communication. Marketing managers carefully coordinate all promotional activities to ensure that consumers see and hear one message. Integrated marketing communications has received more attention in recent years due to the proliferation of media choices, the fragmentation of mass markets into more segmented niches, and the decrease in advertising spending in favor of promotional techniques that generate an immediate sales response.

pull strategy a marketing strategy that stimulates consumer demand to obtain product distribution

 integrated marketing communications (IMC) the careful coordination of all promotional messages for a product or a service to assure the consistency of messages at every contact point where a company meets the consumer

Advertising and Public Relations

KEY TERMS

LO 1 **advertising response function** a phenomenon in which spending for advertising and sales promotion increases sales or market share up to a certain level but then produces diminishing returns

LO 2 **institutional advertising** a form of advertising designed to enhance a company's image rather than promote a particular product

product advertising a form of advertising that touts the benefits of a specific good or service

advocacy advertising a form of advertising in which an organization expresses its views on controversial issues or responds to media attacks

pioneering advertising a form of advertising designed to stimulate primary demand for a new product or product category

competitive advertising a form of advertising designed to influence demand for a specific brand

comparative advertising a form of advertising that compares two or more specifically named or shown competing brands on one or more specific attributes

LO 3 **advertising campaign** a series of related advertisements focusing on a common theme, slogan, and set of advertising appeals

advertising objective a specific communication task that a campaign should accomplish for a specified target audience during a specified period

advertising appeal a reason for a person to buy a product

unique selling proposition a desirable, exclusive, and believable advertising appeal selected as the theme for a campaign

KEY CONCEPTS

LO 1 **Discuss the effects of advertising on market share and consumers.** Advertising helps marketers increase or maintain brand awareness and, subsequently, market share. Typically, more is spent to advertise new brands with a small market share than to advertise older brands. Brands with a large market share use advertising mainly to maintain their share of the market. Advertising affects consumers' daily lives as well as their purchases. Although advertising can seldom change strongly held consumer attitudes and values, it may transform a consumer's negative attitude toward a product into a positive one. Additionally, when consumers are highly loyal to a brand, they may buy more of that brand when advertising is increased. Finally, advertising can also change the importance of a brand's attributes to consumers. By emphasizing different brand attributes, advertisers can change their appeal in response to consumers' changing needs or try to achieve an advantage over competing brands.

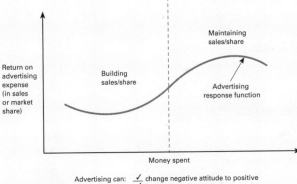

Advertising can: ✓ change negative attitude to positive ✓ reinforce positive attitude ✓ affect how consumers rank brand attributes

LO 2 **Identify the major types of advertising.** Advertising is any form of nonpersonal, paid communication in which the sponsor or company is identified. The two major types of advertising are institutional advertising and product advertising. Institutional advertising is not product oriented; rather, its purpose is to foster a positive company image among the general public, investment community, customers, and employees. Product advertising is designed mainly to promote goods and services, and it is classified into three main categories: pioneering, competitive, and comparative. A product's place in the product life cycle is a major determinant of the type of advertising used to promote it.

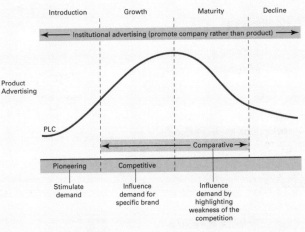

LO 4

medium the channel used to convey a message to a target market

media planning the series of decisions advertisers make regarding the selection and use of media, allowing the marketer to optimally and cost-effectively communicate the message to the target audience

cooperative advertising an arrangement in which the manufacturer and the retailer split the costs of advertising the manufacturer's brand

infomercial a thirty-minute or longer advertisement that looks more like a television talk show than a sales pitch

advergaming placing advertising messages in Web-based or video games to advertise or promote a product, service, organization, or issue

media mix the combination of media to be used for a promotional campaign

cost per contact the cost of reaching one member of the target market

reach the number of target consumers exposed to a commercial at least once during a specific period, usually four weeks

frequency the number of times an individual is exposed to a given message during a specific period

audience selectivity the ability of an advertising medium to reach a precisely defined market

media schedule designation of the media, the specific publications or programs, and the insertion dates of advertising

continuous media schedule a media scheduling strategy in which advertising is run steadily throughout the advertising period; used for products in the later stages of the product life cycle

flighted media schedule a media scheduling strategy in which ads are run heavily every other month or every two weeks, to achieve a greater impact with an increased frequency and reach at those times

pulsing media schedule a media scheduling strategy that uses continuous scheduling throughout the year coupled with a flighted schedule during the best sales periods

LO 3 Discuss the creative decisions in developing an advertising campaign. Before any creative work can begin on an advertising campaign, it is important to determine what goals or objectives the advertising should achieve. The objectives of a specific advertising campaign often depend on the overall corporate objectives and the product being advertised. Once objectives are defined, creative work can begin (e.g., identifying the product's benefits, developing possible advertising appeals, evaluating and selecting the advertising appeals, executing the advertising message, and evaluating the effectiveness of the campaign).

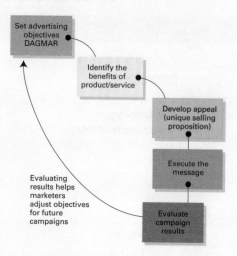

LO 4 Describe media evaluation and selection techniques. Media evaluation and selection make up a crucial step in the advertising campaign process. Major types of advertising media include newspapers, magazines, radio, television, outdoor advertising such as billboards and bus panels, and the Internet. Recent trends in advertising media include fax, video games, shopping carts, computer screen savers, and cinema and video advertising. Promotion managers choose the advertising campaign's media mix on the basis of the following variables: cost per contact, reach, frequency, characteristics of the target audience, flexibility of the medium, noise level, and the life span of the medium. After choosing the media mix, a media schedule designates when the advertisement will appear and the specific vehicles in which it will appear.

LO 5 Discuss the role of public relations in the promotional mix. Public relations is a vital part of a firm's promotional mix. A company fosters good publicity to enhance its image and promote its products. Popular public relations tools include new-product publicity, product placement, consumer education, event sponsorship, issue sponsorship, and Internet Web sites. An equally important aspect of public relations is managing unfavorable publicity in a way that is least damaging to a firm's image.

seasonal media schedule a media scheduling strategy that runs advertising only during times of the year when the product is most likely to be used

LO 5

product placement a public relations strategy that involves getting a product, service, or company name to appear in a movie, television show, radio program, magazine, newspaper, video game, video or audio clip, book, or commercial for another product; on the Internet; or at special events

sponsorship a public relations strategy in which a company spends money to support an issue, cause, or event that is consistent with corporate objectives, such as improving brand awareness or enhancing corporate image

cause-related marketing a type of sponsorship involving the association of a for-profit company and a nonprofit organization; through the sponsorship, the company's product or service is promoted, and money is raised for the nonprofit

crisis management a coordinated effort to handle all the effects of unfavorable publicity or of another unexpected unfavorable event

KEY TERMS

LO 1 **consumer sales promotion** sales promotion activities targeting the ultimate consumer

trade sales promotion sales promotion activities targeting a marketing channel member, such as a wholesaler or retailer

LO 2 **coupon** a certificate that entitles consumers to an immediate price reduction when they buy the product

rebate a cash refund given for the purchase of a product during a specific period

premium an extra item offered to the consumer, usually in exchange for some proof of purchase of the promoted product

loyalty marketing program a promotional program designed to build long-term, mutually beneficial relationships between a company and its key customers

frequent buyer program a loyalty program in which loyal consumers are rewarded for making multiple purchases of a particular good or service

sampling a promotional program that allows the consumer the opportunity to try a product or service for free

point-of-purchase (P-O-P) display a promotional display set up at the retailer's location to build traffic, advertise the product, or induce impulse buying

LO 3 **trade allowance** a price reduction offered by manufacturers to intermediaries, such as wholesalers and retailers

push money money offered to channel intermediaries to encourage them to "push" products—that is, to encourage other members of the channel to sell the products

KEY CONCEPTS

LO 1 **Define and state the objectives of sales promotion.**
Sales promotion consists of those marketing communication activities, other than advertising, personal selling, and public relations, in which a short-term incentive motivates consumers or members of the distribution channel to purchase a good or service immediately, either by lowering the price or by adding value. The main objectives of sales promotion are to increase trial purchases, consumer inventories, and repeat purchases. Sales promotion is also used to encourage brand switching and to build brand loyalty. Sales promotion supports advertising activities.

LO 2 **Discuss the most common forms of consumer sales promotion.** Consumer forms of sales promotion include coupons and rebates, premiums, loyalty marketing programs, contests and sweepstakes, sampling, and point-of-purchase displays. Coupons are certificates entitling consumers to an immediate price reduction when they purchase a product or service. Coupons are a particularly good way to encourage product trial and brand switching. Similar to coupons, rebates provide purchasers with a price reduction, although it is not immediate. To receive a rebate, consumers generally must mail in a rebate form with a proof of purchase. Premiums offer an extra item or incentive to the consumer for buying a product or service. Premiums reinforce the consumer's purchase decision, increase consumption, and persuade nonusers to switch brands. Rewarding loyal customers is the basis of loyalty marketing programs. Loyalty programs are extremely effective at building long-term, mutually beneficial relationships between a company and its key customers. Contests and sweepstakes are generally designed to create interest, often to encourage brand switching. Because consumers perceive risk in trying new products, sampling is an effective method for gaining new customers. Finally, point-of-purchase displays set up at the retailer's location build traffic, advertise the product, and induce impulse buying.

CONSUMER SALES PROMOTION

Coupons and rebates

Premiums

Loyalty marketing program

Contests and sweepstakes

Sampling

P-O-P

Online

LO 5 **relationship selling (consultative selling)** a sales practice that involves building, maintaining, and enhancing interactions with customers in order to develop long-term satisfaction through mutually beneficial partnerships

LO 6 **sales process (sales cycle)** the set of steps a salesperson goes through in a particular organization to sell a particular product or service

lead generation (prospecting) identification of those firms and people most likely to buy the seller's offerings

referral a recommendation to a salesperson from a customer or business associate

networking a process of finding out about potential clients from friends, business contacts, coworkers, acquaintances, and fellow members in professional and civic organizations

cold calling a form of lead generation in which the salesperson approaches potential buyers without any prior knowledge of the prospects' needs or financial status

lead qualification determination of a sales prospect's (1) recognized need, (2) buying power, and (3) receptivity and accessibility

preapproach a process that describes the "homework" that must be done by a salesperson before he or she contacts a prospect

needs assessment a determination of the customer's specific needs and wants and the range of options the customer has for satisfying them

sales proposal a formal written document or professional presentation that outlines how the salesperson's product or service will meet or exceed the prospect's needs

sales presentation a formal meeting in which the salesperson presents a sales proposal to a prospective buyer

negotiation the process during which both the salesperson and the prospect offer special concessions in an attempt to arrive at a sales agreement

follow-up the final step of the selling process, in which the salesperson ensures that delivery schedules are met, that the goods or services perform as promised, and that the buyers' employees are properly trained to use the products

LO 3 **List the most common forms of trade sales promotion.** Manufacturers use many of the same sales promotion tools used in consumer promotions, such as sales contests, premiums, and point-of-purchase displays. In addition, manufacturers and channel intermediaries use several unique promotional strategies: trade allowances, push money, training programs, free merchandise, store demonstrations, and meetings, conventions, and trade shows.

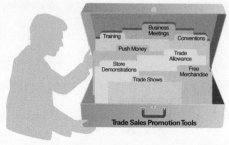

LO 4 **Describe personal selling.** Personal selling is direct communication between a sales representative and one or more prospective buyers in an attempt to influence each other in a purchase situation. Broadly speaking, all businesspeople use personal selling to promote themselves and their ideas. Personal selling offers several advantages over other forms of promotion. Personal selling allows salespeople to thoroughly explain and demonstrate a product. Salespeople have the flexibility to tailor a sales proposal to the needs and preferences of individual customers. Personal selling is more efficient than other forms of promotion because salespeople target qualified prospects and avoid wasting efforts on unlikely buyers. Personal selling affords greater managerial control over promotion costs. Finally, personal selling is the most effective method of closing a sale and producing satisfied customers.

LO 5 **Discuss the key differences between relationship selling and traditional selling.** Relationship selling is the practice of building, maintaining, and enhancing interactions with customers in order to develop long-term satisfaction through mutually beneficial partnerships. Traditional selling, on the other hand, is transaction focused. That is, the salesperson is most concerned with making one-time sales and moving on to the next prospect. Salespeople practicing relationship selling spend more time understanding a prospect's needs and developing solutions to meet those needs.

LO 6 **List the steps in the selling process.** The selling process is composed of seven basic steps: (1) generating leads, (2) qualifying leads, (3) approaching the customer and probing needs, (4) developing and proposing solutions, (5) handling objections, (6) closing the sale, and (7) following up.

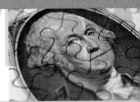

KEY TERMS

LO 1

price that which is given up in an exchange to acquire a good or service

revenue the price charged to customers multiplied by the number of units sold

profit revenue minus expenses

LO 2

return on investment (ROI) net profit after taxes divided by total assets

market share a company's product sales as a percentage of total sales for that industry

status quo pricing a pricing objective that maintains existing prices or meets the competition's prices

LO 3

demand the quantity of a product that will be sold in the market at various prices for a specified period

supply the quantity of a product that will be offered to the market by a supplier at various prices for a specified period

price equilibrium the price at which demand and supply are equal

elasticity of demand consumers' responsiveness or sensitivity to changes in price

elastic demand a situation in which consumer demand is sensitive to changes in price

inelastic demand a situation in which an increase or a decrease in price will not significantly affect demand for the product

unitary elasticity a situation in which total revenue remains the same when prices change

KEY CONCEPTS

LO 1

Discuss the importance of pricing decisions to the economy and to the individual firm. Pricing plays an integral role in the U.S. economy by allocating goods and services among consumers, governments, and businesses. Pricing is essential in business because it creates revenue, which is the basis of all business activity. In setting prices, marketing managers strive to find a level high enough to produce a satisfactory profit.

$$PRICE \times SALES\ UNIT = REVENUE$$
$$REVENUE - COSTS = PROFIT$$
PROFIT DRIVES GROWTH, SALARY INCREASES, AND CORPORATE INVESTMENT.

LO 2

List and explain a variety of pricing objectives. Establishing realistic and measurable pricing objectives is a critical part of any firm's marketing strategy. Pricing objectives are commonly classified into three categories: profit oriented, sales oriented, and status quo. Profit-oriented pricing is based on profit maximization, a satisfactory level of profit, or a target return on investment. The goal of profit maximization is to generate as much revenue as possible in relation to cost. Often, a more practical approach than profit maximization is setting prices to produce profits that will satisfy management and stockholders. The most common profit-oriented strategy is pricing for a specific return on investment relative to a firm's assets. The second type of pricing objective is sales oriented, and it focuses on either maintaining a percentage share of the market or maximizing dollar or unit sales. The third type of pricing objective aims to maintain the status quo by matching competitors' prices.

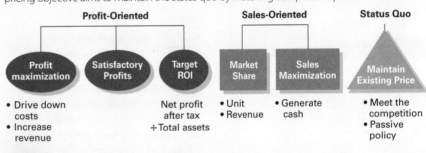

LO 3

Explain the role of demand in price determination. Demand is a key determinant of price. When establishing prices, a firm must first determine demand for its product. A typical demand schedule shows an inverse relationship between quantity

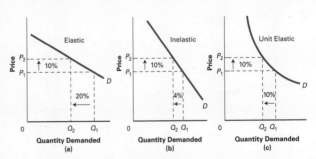

What affects elasticity?
• Availability of substitutes
• Price relative to purchasing power
• Product durability
• Product's other uses
• Inflation rate

demanded and price: When price is lowered, sales increase; and when price is increased, the quantity demanded falls. For prestige products, however, there may be a direct relationship between demand and price: the quantity demanded will increase as price increases.

yield management systems (YMS) a technique for adjusting prices that uses complex mathematical software to profitably fill unused capacity by discounting early purchases, limiting early sales at these discounted prices, and overbooking capacity

variable cost a cost that varies with changes in the level of output

fixed cost a cost that does not change as output is increased or decreased

average variable cost (AVC) total variable costs divided by quantity of output

average total cost (ATC) total costs divided by quantity of output

marginal cost (MC) the change in total costs associated with a one-unit change in output

markup pricing the cost of buying the product from the producer, plus amounts for profit and for expenses not otherwise accounted for

keystoning the practice of marking up prices by 100 percent, or doubling the cost

profit maximization a method of setting prices that occurs when marginal revenue equals marginal cost

marginal revenue (MR) the extra revenue associated with selling an extra unit of output or the change in total revenue with a one-unit change in output

break-even analysis a method of determining what sales volume must be reached before total revenue equals total costs

selling against the brand stocking well-known branded items at high prices in order to sell store brands at discounted prices

extranet a private electronic network that links a company with its suppliers and customers

prestige pricing charging a high price to help promote a high-quality image

---

Marketing managers must also consider demand elasticity when setting prices. Elasticity of demand is the degree to which the quantity demanded fluctuates with changes in price. If consumers are sensitive to changes in price, demand is elastic; if they are insensitive to price changes, demand is inelastic. Thus, an increase in price will result in lower sales for an elastic product and little or no loss in sales for an inelastic product.

LO 4 Understand the concept of yield management systems. Yield management systems use complex mathematical software to profitably fill unused capacity. The software uses techniques such as discounting early purchases, limiting early sales at these discounted prices, and overbooking capacity. These systems are used in service and retail businesses and are substantially raising revenues.

LO 5 Describe cost-oriented pricing strategies. The other major determinant of price is cost. Marketers use several cost-oriented pricing strategies. To cover their own expenses and obtain a profit, wholesalers and retailers commonly use markup pricing: They tack an extra amount onto the manufacturer's original price. Another pricing technique is to maximize profits by setting the price where marginal revenue equals marginal cost. Still another pricing strategy determines how much a firm must sell to break even and uses this amount as a reference point for adjusting price.

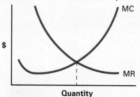

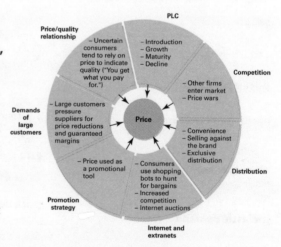

LO 6 Demonstrate how the product life cycle, competition, distribution and promotion strategies, customer demands, the Internet and extranets, and perceptions of quality can affect price. The price of a product normally changes as it moves through the life cycle and as demand for the product and competitive conditions change. Management often sets a high price at the introductory stage, and the high price tends to attract competition. The competition usually drives prices down because individual competitors lower prices to gain market share. Adequate distribution for a new product can sometimes be obtained by offering a larger-than-usual profit margin to wholesalers and retailers. The Internet enables consumers to compare products and prices quickly and efficiently. Price is also used as a promotional tool to attract customers. Special low prices often attract new customers and entice existing customers to buy more. Large buyers can extract price concessions from vendors. Such demands can squeeze the profit margins of suppliers. Perceptions of quality can also influence pricing strategies. A firm trying to project a prestigious image often charges a premium price for a product. Consumers tend to equate high prices with high quality.

KEY TERMS

price strategy a basic, long-term pricing framework that establishes the initial price for a product and the intended direction for price movements over the product life cycle

price skimming a pricing policy whereby a firm charges a high introductory price, often coupled with heavy promotion

penetration pricing a pricing policy whereby a firm charges a relatively low price for a product initially as a way to reach the mass market

status quo pricing charging a price identical to or very close to the competition's price.

unfair trade practice acts laws that prohibit wholesalers and retailers from selling below cost

price fixing an agreement between two or more firms on the price they will charge for a product

predatory pricing the practice of charging a very low price for a product with the intent of driving competitors out of business or out of a market

base price the general price level at which the company expects to sell the good or service

quantity discount a price reduction offered to buyers buying in multiple units or above a specified dollar amount

cumulative quantity discount a deduction from list price that applies to the buyer's total purchases made during a specific period

KEY CONCEPTS

Describe the procedure for setting the right price. The process of setting the right price on a product involves four major steps: (1) establishing pricing goals; (2) estimating demand, costs, and profits; (3) choosing a price policy to help determine a base price; and (4) fine-tuning the base price with pricing tactics. A price strategy establishes a long-term pricing framework for a good or service. The three main types of price policies are price skimming, penetration pricing, and status quo pricing.

Identify the legal and ethical constraints on pricing decisions. Government regulation helps monitor four major areas of pricing: unfair trade practices, price fixing, predatory pricing, and price discrimination. Many states have enacted unfair trade practice acts that protect small businesses from large firms that operate efficiently on extremely thin profit margins; the acts prohibit charging below-cost prices. The Sherman Act and the Federal Trade Commission Act prohibit both price fixing, which is an agreement between two or more firms on a particular price, and predatory pricing, in which a firm undercuts its competitors with extremely low prices to drive them out of business. Finally, the Robinson-Patman Act makes it illegal for firms to discriminate between two or more buyers in terms of price.

Explain how discounts, geographic pricing, and other pricing tactics can be used to fine-tune the base price. Several techniques enable marketing managers to adjust prices within a general range in response to changes in competition, government regulation, consumer demand, and promotional and positioning goals. Techniques for fine-tuning a price can be divided into three main categories: discounts, allowances, rebates, and value-based pricing; geographic pricing; and other pricing tactics.

The first type of tactic gives lower prices to those who pay promptly, order a large quantity, or perform some function for the manufacturer. Additional tactics in this category include seasonal discounts, promotion allowances, and rebates (cash refunds).

Geographic pricing tactics—such as FOB origin pricing, uniform delivered pricing, zone pricing, freight absorption pricing, and basing-point pricing—are ways of moderating the impact of shipping costs on distant customers.

A variety of "other" pricing tactics stimulate demand for certain products, increase store patronage, and offer more merchandise at specific prices.

More and more customers are paying price penalties, which are extra fees for violating the terms of a purchase contract. The perceived fairness or unfairness of a penalty may affect some consumers' willingness to patronize a business in the future.

Discuss product line pricing. Product line pricing maximizes profits for an entire product line. When setting product line prices, marketing managers determine what type of relationship exists among the products in the line: complementary, substitute, or neutral. Managers also consider joint (shared) costs among products in the same line.

noncumulative quantity discount a deduction from list price that applies to a single order rather than to the total volume of orders placed during a certain period

cash discount a price reduction offered to a consumer, an industrial user, or a marketing intermediary in return for prompt payment of a bill

functional discount (trade discount) a discount to wholesalers and retailers for performing channel functions

seasonal discount a price reduction for buying merchandise out of season

promotional allowance (trade allowance) a payment to a dealer for promoting the manufacturer's products

rebate a cash refund given for the purchase of a product during a specific period

value-based pricing setting the price at a level that seems to the customer to be a good price compared to the price of other options

FOB origin pricing a price tactic that requires the buyer to absorb the freight costs from the shipping point ("free on board")

uniform delivered pricing a price tactic in which the seller pays the actual freight charges and bills every purchaser an identical, flat freight charge

zone pricing a modification of uniform delivered pricing that divides the United States (or the total market) into segments or zones and charges a flat freight rate to all customers in a given zone

freight absorption pricing a price tactic in which the seller pays all or part of the actual freight charges and does not pass them on to the buyer

basing-point pricing a price tactic that charges freight from a given (basing) point, regardless of the city from which the goods are shipped

single-price tactic a price tactic that offers all goods and services at the same price (or perhaps two or three prices)

LO 5 **Describe the role of pricing during periods of inflation and recession.** Marketing managers employ cost-oriented and demand-oriented tactics during periods of economic inflation. Cost-oriented tactics include dropping products with a low profit margin, using delayed-quotation pricing and escalator pricing, and adding fees. Demand-oriented pricing methods include price shading and increasing demand through cultivating selected customers, creating unique offerings, changing the package size, and heightening buyer dependence.

To stimulate demand during a recession, marketers use value-based pricing, bundling, and unbundling. Recessions are also a good time to prune unprofitable items from product lines. Managers strive to cut costs during recessions in order to maintain profits as revenues decline. Implementing new technology, cutting payrolls, and pressuring suppliers for reduced prices are common techniques used to cut costs.

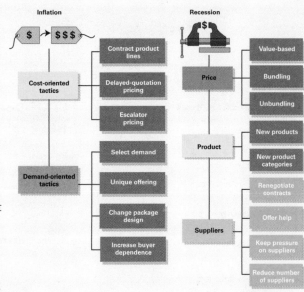

flexible pricing (variable pricing) a price tactic in which different customers pay different prices for essentially the same merchandise bought in equal quantities

price lining the practice of offering a product line with several items at specific price points

leader pricing (loss-leader pricing) a price tactic in which a product is sold near or even below cost in the hope that shoppers will buy other items once they are in the store

bait pricing a price tactic that tries to get consumers into a store through false or misleading price advertising and then uses high-pressure selling to persuade consumers to buy more expensive merchandise

odd–even pricing (psychological pricing) a price tactic that uses odd-numbered prices to connote bargains and even-numbered prices to imply quality

price bundling marketing two or more products in a single package for a special price

unbundling reducing the bundle of services that comes with the basic product

two-part pricing a price tactic that charges two separate amounts to consume a single good or service

consumer penalty an extra fee paid by the consumer for violating the terms of the purchase agreement

LO 4 **product line pricing** setting prices for an entire line of products

joint costs costs that are shared in the manufacturing and marketing of several products in a product line

LO 5 **delayed-quotation pricing** a price tactic used for industrial installations and many accessory items in which a firm price is not set until the item is either finished or delivered

escalator pricing a price tactic in which the final selling price reflects cost increases incurred between the time the order is placed and the time delivery is made

price shading the use of discounts by salespeople to increase demand for one or more products in a line

Customer Relationship Management (CRM)

KEY TERMS

LO 1 **customer relationship management (CRM)** a company wide business strategy designed to optimize profitability, revenue, and customer satisfaction by focusing on highly defined and precise customer groups

LO 2 **customer-centric** a philosophy under which the company customizes its product and service offering based on data generated through interactions between the customer and the company

learning an informal process of collecting customer data through customer comments and feedback on product or service performance

knowledge management the process by which learned information from customers is centralized and shared in order to enhance the relationship between customers and the organization

empowerment delegation of authority to solve customers' problems quickly—usually by the first person that the customer notifies regarding the problem

interaction the point at which a customer and a company representative exchange information and develop learning relationships

LO 3 **touch points** all possible areas of a business where customers communicate with that business

point-of-sale interactions communications between customers and organizations that occur at the point of sale, normally in a store

KEY CONCEPTS

LO 1 **Define customer relationship management.** Customer relationship management (CRM) is a company wide business strategy designed to optimize profitability, revenue, and customer satisfaction by focusing on highly defined and precise customer groups. This is accomplished by organizing the company around customer segments, encouraging and tracking customer interaction with the company, fostering customer-satisfying behaviors, and linking all processes of a company from its customers through its suppliers.

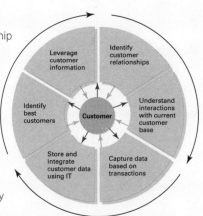

LO 2 **Explain how to identify customer relationships with the organization.** Companies that implement a CRM system adhere to a customer-centric focus or model. A customer-centric company focuses on learning the factors that build long-lasting relationships with valuable customers and then builds its system on what satisfies and retains those customers. Building relationships through CRM is a strategic process that focuses on learning, managing customer knowledge, and empowerment.

LO 3 **Understand interactions with the current customer base.** The interaction between the customer and the organization is considered to be the foundation on which a CRM system is built. Only through effective interactions can organizations learn about the expectations of their customers, generate and manage knowledge about them, negotiate mutually satisfying commitments, and build long-term relationships. Because customers provide information to organizations across a wide variety of touch points, consumer-centric organizations are implementing new and unique approaches for establishing interactions specifically for this purpose. They include Web-based interactions, point-of-sale interactions, and transaction-based interactions.

LO 4 **Outline the process of capturing customer data.** Based on the interaction between the organization and its customers, vast amounts of information can be obtained. Effective use of a CRM system depends on what type of data is acquired and how those data can be used effectively for relationship enhancement. The channel, transaction, and product or service consumed all constitute touch points between a customer and the organization. These touch points represent possible areas within a business where customer interactions can take place and, hence, the opportunity for acquiring data from the customer.

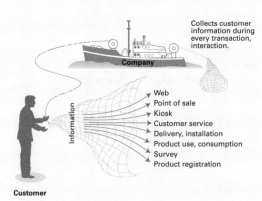

Collects customer information during every transaction, interaction.

Company

Information

Customer

- Web
- Point of sale
- Kiosk
- Customer service
- Delivery, installation
- Product use, consumption
- Survey
- Product registration

data warehouse a central repository for data from various functional areas of the organization that are stored and inventoried on a centralized computer system so that the information can be shared across all functional departments of the business

database a collection of data, especially one that can be accessed and manipulated by computer software

response list a customer list that includes the names and addresses of individuals who have responded to an offer of some kind, such as by mail, telephone, direct-response television, product rebates, contests or sweepstakes, or billing inserts

compiled list a customer list developed by gathering names and addresses from telephone directories and membership rosters, usually enhanced with information from public records, such as census data, auto registrations, birth announcements, business start-ups, or bankruptcies

 lifetime value analysis (LTV) a data manipulation technique that projects the future value of the customer over a period of years using the assumption that marketing to repeat customers is more profitable than marketing to first-time buyers

predictive modeling a data manipulation technique in which marketers try to determine, based on some past set of occurrences, what the odds are that some other occurrence, such as a response or purchase, will take place in the future

campaign management developing product or service offerings customized for the appropriate customer segment and then pricing and communicating these offerings for the purpose of enhancing customer relationships

 Describe the use of technology to store and integrate customer data. Customer data gathering is complicated because information needed by one unit of the organization (e.g., sales and marketing) is often generated by another area of the business or even a third-party supplier (e.g., an independent marketing research firm). Because of the lack of standard structure and interface, organizations rely on technology to capture, store, and integrate strategically important customer information. The process of centralizing data in a CRM system is referred to as data warehousing. A data warehouse is a central repository of customer information collected by an organization.

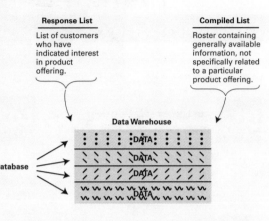

Response List List of customers who have indicated interest in product offering.

Compiled List Roster containing generally available information, not specifically related to a particular product offering.

Describe how to identify the best customers. Customer relationship management, as a process strategy, attempts to manage the interactions between a company and its customers. To be successful, organizations must identify customers who yield high profitability or high potential profitability. To accomplish this task, significant amounts of information must be gathered from customers, stored and integrated in the data warehouse, and then analyzed for commonalities that can produce segments that are highly similar, yet different from other customer segments. A useful approach to identifying the best customers is recency-frequency-monetary (RFM) analysis. Data mining uses RFM, predictive modeling, and other approaches to identify significant relationships among several customer dimensions within vast data warehouses. These significant relationships enable marketers to better define the most profitable customers and prospects.

 Explain the process of leveraging customer information throughout the organization. One of the benefits of a CRM system is the capacity to share information throughout the organization. This allows an organization to interact with all functional areas to develop programs targeted to its customers. This process is commonly referred to as campaign management. Campaign management involves developing customized product/service offerings for the appropriate customer segment and pricing and communicating these offerings for the purpose of enhancing customer relationships.

Marketing Information

CRM Database

Applications

✓ Campaign management
✓ Retaining loyal customers
✓ Cross-selling other products and services
✓ Designing targeted marketing communications
✓ Reinforcing customer purchase decisions
✓ Inducing product trial by new customers
✓ Increasing effectiveness of distribution channel marketing
✓ Improving customer service

FEATURES, ADVANTAGES, BENEFITS

One of the most important decisions in your life is choosing a career. Not only will your career choice affect your income and lifestyle, but it also will have a major impact on your happiness and self-fulfillment.

You can use many of the basic concepts of marketing introduced in this book to get the career you want by marketing yourself. The purpose of marketing is to create exchanges that satisfy individual as well as organizational objectives, and a career is certainly an exchange situation for both you and an organization. The purpose of this appendix is to help you market yourself to prospective employers by providing some helpful tools and information.

It is important to understand what type of job will be beneficial to you in the long run. One way to look objectively at what type of job to undertake is to perform a self-analysis. These two cards contain some exercises, resources, and other guidance to performing self-analysis, and there are many other resources available to professionals.

One way to begin looking objectively at career decisions is to develop a Feature-Advantage-Benefit matrix, such as the one below.

Need of Employer	Feature of Job Applicant	Advantage of Feature	Benefit to Employer
This job requires:	I have:	This feature means that:	You will:
• Frequent sales presentations to individuals and groups.	• Taken 10 classes that required presentations.	• I require limited or no training in making presentations.	• Save on the cost of training and have an employee with the ability and confidence to be productive early.
• Knowledge of personal computers, software, and applications.	• Taken a personal computer course and used Lotus in most upper-level classes.	• I can already use Word, Excel, dBase, SAS, SPSS, and other software.	• Save time and money on training.
• A person with management potential.	• Been president of a student marketing group and social fraternity president for two years.	• I have experience leading people.	• Save time because I am capable of stepping into a leadership position as needed.

INTERVIEW SELF-ASSESSMENT

How assertive are you (or will you be) as you interview for a position? The questions in the assessment below will help you to evaluate your assertiveness.

Answer yes or no to the questions, being honest with yourself. If you have five or fewer yes answers, you still have some work to do. A good score is seven or more yes answers.

Yes	No	
___	___	Have you made an effort to research the company before the interview?
___	___	Have you prepared several questions that you want to ask?
___	___	If an interviewer asks a personal question unrelated to the job, will you be able to tactfully call this to his attention?
___	___	If an interviewer gives you a hypothetical job-related problem, do you have confidence in your ability to respond in a timely and succinct manner?
___	___	If the interviewer seems distracted or uninterested during your interview, will you be able to steer the interview back on track and gain her attention?
___	___	When you meet the interviewer, will you be the first to introduce yourself and begin the conversation?
___	___	If the interviewer continually interrupts when you are responding to questions or giving information about yourself, can you politely handle this?
___	___	If the interviewer never gives you the opportunity to talk about yourself and you have only five minutes remaining in the interview, have you thought about phrases or ways to redirect the interview and regain control of the process?
___	___	When the interviewer is beginning to close the interview, are you prepared to ask questions about how you stand, what the determining factors are for candidate selection, and by what date you will have an answer?

(continued)

SAMPLE INTERVIEW QUESTIONS

At an interview, potential employers appreciate candidates who have taken the time to consider what they would like in a position, or what they need to know about jobs that may not come up without a question. Some questions that are appropriate for job candidates to ask at an interview are:

- Where is the organization going?
- What plans or projects are being developed to maintain or increase its market share?
- Have many new product lines been decided upon recently?
- Is the sales growth in the new product line sustainable?
- Who are the people with whom I will be working? May I speak with some of them?
- May I have a copy of the job description?
- What might be a typical first assignment?
- Do you have a performance appraisal system? How is it structured?
- How frequently will I be evaluated?
- What is the potential for promotion in the organization?
- In promotions, are employees ever transferred between functional fields?
- What is the average time to get to _____ level in the career path?
- Is your policy to promote from within, or are many senior jobs filled by experienced people from outside? Do you have a job posting system?
- What type of training will I receive? When does the training program begin? Is it possible to move through your program faster?
- About how many individuals go through your internship program?
- What is the normal routine of a (an) _____ like? Can I progress at my own pace, or is it structured?
- Do employees normally work overtime?
- How much travel is normally expected? Is a car provided to traveling personnel?
- How much freedom is given to new people? How much discipline is required?
- How much input does a new person have?
- How much decision-making authority is given to new personnel?
- How frequently do you relocate employees? Is it possible to transfer from one division to another?
- What is the housing market for a single person in _____ (city)? Is public transportation adequate?
- How much contact with and exposure to management is there?
- How soon should I expect to report to work?

SOME AVAILABLE MARKETING CAREERS

- Sales
- Public Relations
- Retailing
- Advertising
- Marketing Management
- Marketing Research
- Product Management
- Product Development
- Brand Management
- Event Planning
- Customer Service
- Social Media Marketing

HELPFUL WEB SITES FOR JOB SEARCHES AND RÉSUMÉ WRITING

- www.monster.com
- www.jobweb.org
- www.careermosaic.com
- www.provenresumes.com
- www.careerjournal.com

FREQUENTLY ASKED INTERVIEW QUESTIONS

Thinking of the questions a potential employer may ask at an interview is a great way to prepare. By evaluating questions based on skills, your mind will be able to easily recall and adjust to questions in an interview. Showing a potential employer the ability to quickly respond to questions demonstrates calm under pressure and the time taken to prepare. This card has an extensive list of frequently asked questions at interviews.

- Of the jobs you've had to date, which one did you like best? Why?
- Why do you want to work for our company?
- Tell me what you know about our company.
- Do any of your relatives or friends work for our company? If so, in what jobs?
- Tell me about yourself, your strengths, weaknesses, career goals, and so forth.
- Is any member of your family a professional marketer? If so, what area of marketing?
- Why do you want to start your career in marketing?
- Persuade me that we should hire you.
- In what extracurricular activities did you participate in at college? What leadership positions did you have in any of these activities?
- What benefits have you derived from participation in extracurricular activities that will help you in your career?
- Where do you see yourself within our company in five years? In ten years? Twenty years?
- What is your ultimate career goal?
- What do you consider your greatest achievement to date?
- What is your biggest failure to date?
- What is (was) your favorite subject in school? Why?
- Are you willing to travel and possibly relocate?
- How would the people who know you describe you?
- How would you describe yourself?
- What do you like most about marketing?
- What do you like least about marketing?
- If we hire you, how soon could you start work?
- What is the minimum we would have to offer you to work with us?
- What goals have you set for yourself? How are you planning to achieve them?
- Who or what has had the greatest influence on the development of your career interests?
- What factors did you consider in choosing your major?
- Why are you interested in our organization?
- What can you tell me about yourself?
- What two or three things are most important to you in a position?
- What kind of work do you want to do?
- What can you tell me about a project you initiated?
- What are your expectations of your future employer?
- What is your GPA? How do you feel about it? Does it reflect your ability?
- How do you resolve conflicts?

- What do you feel are your strengths? Your weaknesses? How do you evaluate yourself?
- What work experience has been the most valuable to you and why?
- What was the most useful criticism you ever received, and who was it from?
- Can you give an example of a problem you have solved and the process you used?
- Can you describe the project or situation that best demonstrates your analytical skills?
- What has been your greatest challenge?
- Can you describe a situation where you had a conflict with another individual and explain how you dealt with it?
- What are the biggest problems you encountered in college? How did you handle them? What did you learn from them?
- What are your team-player qualities? Give examples.
- Can you describe your leadership style?
- What interests or concerns you about the position or the company?
- In a particular leadership role you had, what was the greatest challenge?
- What idea have you developed and implemented that was particularly creative or innovative?
- What characteristics do you think are important for this position?
- How have your educational and work experiences prepared you for this position?
- Can you take me through a project where you demonstrated skills?
- How do you think you have changed personally since you started college?
- Can you tell me about a team project that you are particularly proud of and discuss your contribution?
- How do you motivate people?
- Why did you choose the extracurricular activities you did? What did you gain? What did you contribute?
- What types of situations put you under pressure, and how do you deal with the pressure?
- Can you tell me about a difficult decision you have made?
- Can you give an example of a situation in which you failed and explain how you handled it?
- Can you tell me about a situation when you had to persuade another person of your point of view?
- What frustrates you the most?
- Knowing what you know now about your college experience, would you make the same decisions?
- What can you contribute to this company?
- How would you react to having your credibility questioned?
- What characteristics are important in a good manager? How have you displayed one of these characteristics?
- What challenges are you looking for in a position?
- What two or three accomplishments have given you the most satisfaction?
- Can you describe a leadership role of yours and tell why you committed your time to it?
- How are you conducting your job search, and how will you make your decision?
- What is the most important lesson you have learned in or out of school?
- Can you describe a situation where you had to work with someone who was difficult? How was the person difficult, and how did you handle it?

(continued)

- We are looking at a lot of great candidates; why are you the best person for this position?
- How would your friends describe you? Your professors?
- What else should I know about you?

HOW TO ACT DURING AN INTERVIEW

- Think positive. Be enthusiastic, interested, knowledgeable, and confident.
- Take few notes. It is acceptable to take notes during the interview, but limit them to things that are essential to remember. You want to focus more on listening and observing rather than writing.
- Relate to the interviewer. Build positive rapport with the interviewer. Listen and observe; relate yourself to the employer or position.
- Watch your body language. Be aware of nervousness (fidgeting, shaking leg, tapping, etc.). Project confidence (eye contact, firm handshake, upright posture).
- Be aware of the questions the employer asks. Answer with information relevant to the position. Provide a direct answer; avoid being long-winded.
- Think about the questions you ask. They should indicate that you know something about the job. Avoid questions that could easily be answered elsewhere through research. Obtain information you need to know to be satisfied with the job (interviewing is a two-way process). Salary and benefit questions should be asked after the job is offered.
- Achieve effective closure. Ask when the employer expects to make a decision. Restate your interest and ability to perform the job. Show confidence and enthusiasm (smile, end with a firm handshake). Obtain the employer's business card, if possible (it may be useful when writing a thank-you letter).

RECAP: Preparing for an Interview

- PRACTICE
  - Questions you may be asked
  - Questions you want to ask about the position and organization
  - Role-playing an interview
- SELF-ASSESSMENT
  - Goals
  - Skills, abilities, accomplishments
  - Work values (important factors you look for in a job)
  - Experiences
  - Personality
- RESEARCH
  - Obtain company literature
  - Write or visit the organization
  - Talk to people familiar with the organization
- OBTAIN REFERENCES
- PLAN AHEAD
  - Attire to be worn to the interview
  - Directions to the interview site
  - Time of arrival (get there with at least 5–10 minutes to spare)